4

COLLECTED PAPERS ON BUDDHIST STUDIES

OTHER PUBLICATIONS

by PADMANABH S. JAINI

1. *Silonmāṃ be Varsh,* Gujarat Vidyasabha, Ahmedabad, 1952 (in Gujarati).
2. *Abhidharmadīpa with Vibhāṣāprabhā-vṛtti,* K.P. Jayaswal Research Institute, Patna, 1959; reprinted 1977.
3. *Milinda-ṭīkā,* Pali Text Society, London, 1961.
4. *Laghutattvasphoṭa* by Amṛtacandra, Sanskrit text with English translation, L.D. Institute of Indology Series, No. 62, Ahmedabad, 1978.
5. *Sāratamā : A Pañjikā on the Aṣṭasāhasrikā-Prajñāpāramitā* by Ratnākaraśānti, K.P. Jayaswal Research Institute, Patna, 1979.
6. *The Jaina Path of Purification,* University of California Press, Berkeley, 1979. Reprinted by Motilal Banarsidass, Delhi, 1997.
7. *Paññāsa-Jātaka or Zimme Paṇṇāsa* (in Burmese Recension), vol. I (Jātakas 1-25), Pali Text Society, London, 1981.
8. *Jain sampradāy meṃ mokṣa, avatār aur punarjanma,* B.J. Institute of Learning and Research, Ahmedabad, 1982 (in Hindi).
9. *Paññāsa-Jātaka or Zimme Paṇṇāsa* (in Burmese Recension), vol. II, (Jātakas 30-50), Pali Text Society, London, 1983.
10. *Apocryphal Birth-stories* (translation of the *Paññāsa-Jātaka*), vol. I, (with I.B. Horner), Pali Text Society, London, 1985.
11. *Apocryphal Birth-stories* (translation of the *Paññāsa-Jātaka*), vol. II, Pali Text Society, London, 1986.
12. *Lokaneyyappakaraṇaṃ,* Pali Text Society, London, 1986.
13. *Gender and Salvation: Jaina debates on the spiritual liberation of women,* University of California Press, Berkeley, 1991.
14. *Subodhālaṅkāra* with *Mahāsāmi-Ṭīkā* by Saṅgharakkhita Mahāsāmi (critical edition), Pali Text Society, Oxford, 2000.

Collected Papers on Buddhist Studies

Edited by
PADMANABH S. JAINI

With a Foreword by
PAUL DUNDAS

MOTILAL BANARSIDASS PUBLISHERS
PRIVATE LIMITED • DELHI

First Edition: Delhi, 2001

ISBN: 81-208-1776-1

Also available at:
MOTILAL BANARSIDASS
236, 9th Main III Block, Jayanagar, Bangalore 560 001
41 U.A. Bungalow Road, Jawahar Nagar, Delhi 110 007
8, Mahalaxmi Chamber, Warden Road, Mumbai 400 026
120 Royapettah High Road, Mylapore, Chennai 600 004
Sanas Plaza, Subhash Nagar, Pune 411 002
8 Camac Street, Calcutta 700 017
Ashok Rajpath, Patna 800 004
Chowk, Varanasi 221 001

Printed in India
BY JAINENDRA PRAKASH JAIN AT SHRI JAINENDRA PRESS,
A-45 NARAINA, PHASE I, NEW DELHI 110 028
AND PUBLISHED BY NARENDRA PRAKASH JAIN FOR
MOTILAL BANARSIDASS PUBLISHERS PRIVATE LIMITED,
BUNGALOW ROAD, DELHI 110 007

Foreword

P.S. Jaini's career represents a fascinating scholarly journey. In introducing his *Collected Papers on Jaina and Buddhist Studies* to the interested academic and lay world, some words about his intellectual background might be felt to be of some value.[1]

Padmanabh Shrivarma Jaini was born into a devout Digambara Jain family residing in Nellikar, a small town near the famous Jain centre at Mudbidre in Tulunadu, that magical and culturally distinctive area in the southwest of the state of Karnataka. In similar manner to many Jains at the beginning of this century who were influenced by calls within the community to change their names in order to foster a greater sense of identity, Padmanabh's father had abandoned his caste name of Shetty and taken the surname of Jaini, in this case in imitation of J.L. Jaini, a noted translator of the *Tattvārthasūtra*. Although the local languages of Nellikar were Tulu and Kannada, Jaini's highly literate parents also encouraged the study of Hindi, and the household contained a large number of regularly consulted books from North India on Jain and other subjects.

When he was ten and had completed his elementary education, Padmanabh Jaini's parents sent him far from home to the north to board at a Digambara Jain *gurukul* at Karanja in Vidarbha (Maharashtra) in order to continue his schooling at secondary level. This establishment, Mahāvīra Brahmacharyāśrama Jaina Gurukula, had been founded by Brahmachari Devchand, who was later to become the celebrated monk Ācārya Samantabhadra. While the curriculum contained "modern" subjects such as English and the sciences, the school was run firmly on traditional Jain principles and carried out regular daily rituals in accordance with

Digambara practice. It was here during a period of eight years that the young Jaini gained his first familiarity with many basic Jain texts and encountered some of the great Digambara lay scholars of the period, such as Devakinandan Siddhantashastri, Kailashchandra Siddhantashastri, Hiralal Jain, Nathuram Premi and A.N. Upadhye.

After completing his secondary education, Jaini entered the Arts College at Nasik, which was affiliated to the University of Bombay, to take a B.A. Hons. degree in Sanskrit with subsidiary Prakrit. During this time he supported himself by superintending a boarding house for Śvetāmbara Jain students who belonged to the Oswal caste. The duties of this post obliged Jaini to travel to various Śvetāmbara centres to collect donations, as a result of which he became aware for the first time of the social diversity of Jainism and the fact that there were other Jain sectarian groups, such as the Sthānakvāsis, virtually unknown to the Digambaras of Tulunadu. For, while it is true that Jainism is in broad terms doctrinally unified, interaction between members of the two sects, the Śvetāmbaras and Digambaras, was, and to a large extent still is, comparatively rare, apart from occasional ecumenical occasions.

This familiarity with Śvetāmbara Jainism was to stand in good stead when, on graduation in 1947, he was invited by the great Sthānakavāsī scholar Pandit Sukhlal Sanghavi to study with him in Ahmedabad. Although he died as recently as 1978, Sanghavi (born 1880) represents what now seems to be a virtually lost scholarly and intellectual world. Towards the end of the nineteenth century, leading members of the Śvetāmbara Jain community undertook to set up schools to train and develop academically promising youngsters as pandits who, as with the much stronger tradition of lay scholarship amongst the Digambaras, would master and edit Sanskrit and Prakrit scriptural and philosophical literature and thus serve the community's requirements for a learned understanding of the Jain religion. Sanghavi himself had been blind from the age of eleven (a victim of smallpox) but nonetheless became profoundly versed in Jain logic at such an institution, rising to be professor at Banaras Hindu University. Jaini's near-daily meetings with this scholar over this period involved not just formal instruction in *nyāya,* carried out in rigorous fashion through the medium of a close analysis of a portion of Hemacandra's *Pramāṇamīmāṃsā,* but also exposed the young Digambara to Sanghavi's views about the many controversies that had arisen in the Jain community at this time.

Jaini's intellectual formation within this traditional brand of Jain learning was a crucial factor in his scholarly development. It must also be regarded as virtually unique up to this time, because no one of Jaini's generation (nor, one suspects, anyone before it) could claim to have his familiarity with the culture and practice of the two main sects of Jainism. However, his interests were by no means confined to Jainism. Sanghavi had always insisted on the importance of the Pali canon for understanding the Jain scriptures, and Jaini was encouraged by him to utilise the library, housed at the Gujarat Vidyapith, of Dharmananda Kosambi, India's most distinguished scholar of Theravāda Buddhism. Eventually, Jaini resolved to continue his postgraduate work in Sri Lanka and, with the help of Muni Jinavijaya, the director of the Bharatiya Vidya Bhavan in Bombay, to which he had briefly moved from Ahmedabad, became in 1949 the first Dharmananda Kosambi Memorial scholar, studying as a layman in Colombo at the Vidyodaya Pirivena, a monastic training centre headed by the Venerable Baddegama Piyaratana Mahathero, a one-time fellow student of Kosambi.

During his two years there, Jaini thoroughly familiarised himself with the Abhidharma Piṭaka, later to become one of his main areas of scholarly expertise, and also studied widely in the commentary literature on the Sūtra and Vinaya Piṭakas of the Pali canon. Unwilling to restrict himself to the confines of libraries, he was able to witness the richness of Sinhalese Buddhist ritual and devotional life as he accompanied Mahathero on his travels round the island and also memorably met Dr. B.R. Ambedkar, who visited Sri Lanka prior to his momentous decision to convert to Buddhism along with vast numbers of his followers. This period was to provide the basis for Jaini's first publication, *Silonmāṃ Be Varṣa* ("Two Years in Ceylon"), which provides in Gujarati much information about the practicalities of Theravāda Buddhism and a discussion of the potential for a genuine Buddhist revival in India.

After being awarded the degree of Tripiṭakācārya in 1951 at a special ceremony held at Prime Minister Senanayake's residence, Jaini returned to Ahmedabad to take up a lecturer's position. However, he was soon to be on the move again, being appointed in 1952 to a newly created lectureship in Pali at Banaras Hindu University. Paradoxically, there could have hardly been a course of action more likely to ensure that Jaini's academic interests in the religion of his birth remained undiminished, for during the 1950s Banaras and its many educational institutions were home to a large number of distinguished Jain scholars who carried on a lively intercourse on various aspects of Buddhism and Jainism.

However, Jaini's main research at this time remained firmly in Buddhist sphere. Professor A. S. Altekar, Director of the K. P. Jayaswal Institute in Patna, which housed the famous collection of manuscripts brought from Tibet in the 1930s by Rahula Sankrityayana, had succeeded in identifying one particular manuscript as the *Abhidharmadīpa* (along with its commentary, the *Vibhāṣāprabhāvṛtti*), a hitherto unknown work written on the model of Vasubandhu's Sautrāntika-leaning *Abhidharmakośa* and *Bhāṣya* but defending the position of the Vaibhāṣika sect. The editing of this manifestly important text, the only Vaibhāṣika work directed against the great Vasubandhu to have survived in Sanskrit, was entrusted to Jaini. While engaged in this task, he was visited in 1956 by John Brough, then Professor of Sanskrit at the School of Oriental and African Studies at the University of London, who was en route to Nepal. Brough was unquestionably impressed by Jaini's philological acumen, for the meeting quickly led to the offer and the subsequent acceptance of a lectureship at SOAS.

Jaini remained at SOAS from 1956 until 1967 as Lecturer in Pali and, subsequently, Reader in Pali and Buddhist Sanskrit. Under Brough's supervision, Jaini quickly finished his edition of the *Abhidharmadīpa,* for which he was awarded the degree of Ph.D. by the University of London, and then began to broaden his studies in Theravāda Buddhism by travelling in Burma, Thailand, Cambodia and Indonesia in order to collect manuscripts relating to the apocryphal Pali birth stories (*Jātaka*) of the Buddha, which he later was to edit and translate for the Pali Text Society. Eventually, to British Indology's great loss, Jaini moved to the University of Michigan, Ann Arbor as Professor of Indic Languages and Literature and finally in 1972, the culmination of a long journey for the small-town Jain boy from Tulunadu, to California where he served until 1994 as Professor of Buddhist Studies in the Department of South and Southeast Asian Studies at the University of California, Berkeley and afterwards as Professor in the Graduate School at the same institution.

Commentators on the work of any significant scholar generally seek to draw attention to the unity and overall coherence, whether real or imaginary. In P.S. Jaini's case, the structuring feature of his writings can be easily defined. All his energies throughout his career have been devoted to the elucidation of the manifold facets of what Indian scholars call *śramaṇasaṃskṛti*, "the culture of the strivers", that is to say, the religious, philosophical and literary achievements of the Buddhists and the Jains. Jaini's intellectual control over this area has meant that he has been able to adopt various styles of investigation. Sometimes Buddhism and Jainism are approached by him as independent phenomena, or, as with the case of the Jain Purāṇas, with reference to their engagement with the encircling Hindu world. More often, however, Jaini has been preoccupied with the interaction and overlapping of the two great renouncer religions, with evidence from the one tradition being deployed so as to throw light on the other.

To exemplify briefly the fruitfulness of this latter methodology. It is difficult to read far in Jain literature without encountering the terms *bhavya* and *abhavya,* expressions designating respectively those innately capable of advancing along the path of spiritual release and those innately destined to make no progress at all in this respect. This dichotomy, which implies acceptance of something akin to predestination, is highly problematic for a religion which argues for the supposedly essential equality of souls and their common ability to transform their status through effort, although Jaini seems to have been the first to draw serious attention to this. Jaini's explanation in his paper *"Bhavyatva* and *Abhavyatva*: A Jaina Doctrine of 'Predestination'" of the two categories by reference to the Buddhist Vasubandhu's *Abhidharmakośabhāṣya* and what can be reconstructed of the teachings of the Ājīvika leader Makkhali Gosāla is a masterly demonstration of the sectarian modifications of an old *śramaṇa* doctrine of predestination. In similar fashion, Jaini's ability evinced in the paper "Jaina monks from Mathurā: literary evidence for their identification on Kuṣāṇa sculptures" to draw upon Pali sources, as well as a wide range of Jain literary evidence, enables him to confirm and amplify the validity of U.P. Shah's identification of Mathurā images of naked monks holding pieces of cloth as *ardhaphālakas,* possible forerunners of the influential medieval sect of the Yāpanīyas.

In the specifically Buddhist area, Jaini's earliest articles emerged from his work on the *Abhidharmadīpa,* being originally components of the voluminous introduction to his doctoral dissertation. They display at the outset two of the main virtues which have consistently characterised Jaini's work: close familiarity with the primary sources, which are carefully documented, and, above all, clarity. Jaini's travels in Southeast Asia led to the publication of a further body of work on the apocryphal Pali Jātakas. Only recently have scholars begun to approach Theravāda Buddhism as a transnational phenomenon and it is likely that Jaini's publications in this area will prove an important point of reference in shifting the philological and ethnographic emphasis away from the canonical Pali literature of Sri Lanka.

Many scholars in this time of enforced specialisation would have been content to rest on their laurels purely on the basis of these Buddhological publications. Jain studies, however, had never been far from Jaini's thoughts even at the beginning of his career. During his stay in London, for example, he prevailed upon the leaders of the Mahavira Jain Vidyalaya in Bombay to produce editions of the Śvetāmbara Jain scriptures in the (still continuing) Jain Āgama Series on the critical model employed by the Pali Text Society. Having begun productive research on Jainism during the 1970s, most notably with his edition and translation of a unique Digambara philosophical stotra, the *Laghutattvasphoṭa* of Amṛtacandrasūri, for which he used photographs and a handwritten copy of the only manuscript given to him by Muni Puṇyavijaya, Jaini eventually came to realise that Jain studies had to be given a higher profile within undergraduate teaching of Indian religions and, specifically, to be more fully integrated into the South Asian Studies programme at Berkeley. Not finding any suitable textbook with which to effect this, he resolved to write one himself and so produced in 1979 the work for which he is probably best known, *The Jaina Path of Purification*. This book can be regarded, with only slight exaggeration, as having attained the authority of virtual primary source and its value in promoting and providing an entrée to its subject in the English-speaking world in recent years is inestimable, to the extent that the late Kendall Folkert felt able to talk of pre- and post-Jaini eras in recent Jain studies.[2]

It may be the case, as some friendly critics have suggested, that *The Jaina Path of Purification*, and some of Jaini's articles, do occasionally present the Digambara idiom of Jainism at the expense of the various Śvetāmbara sectarian traditions, although this increasingly strikes the present writer as a strength rather than a defect, since Digambara Jainism remains a woefully neglected subject. However, possible bias is certainly not a criticism that can be levelled at Jaini's most recent book, *Gender and Salvation: Jaina Debates on the Spiritual Liberation of Women,* whose Introduction is reprinted in Jaina Studies. In this remarkable and trailblazing work Jaini translates and analyses a range of Śvetāmbara, Digambara and Yāpanīya sources to provide a broad and yet detailed conspectus on what is, for South Asia, a unique debate on female religiosity, a subject growing in importance in Indian studies. As with Jaini's work on the apocryphal Pali *jātakas,* one feels that the full significance of *Gender and Salvation* will continue to emerge on further acquaintance.

If this were the foreword to a festschrift dedicated to Professor Jaini, then no doubt its writer would extol the honorand's many personal attributes, such as his affability, reconteurship and generosity with his copious knowledge. Such productions do, of course, have their place in academic life, but I would suggest that the publication of these two volumes represents something better. They will enable seasoned aficionados to refresh their familiarity with and appreciation of Jaini's work, provide those working exclusively in either Buddhism or Jainism with a sense of the mutual illumination these two traditions can cast upon each other, and, lastly reveal to a younger generation of scholars a corpus of writing at once inspiring, informative and provocative.

May Professor P. S. Jaini's Collected Papers be consulted and profited from for many years to come.

University of Edinburgh PAUL DUNDAS

NOTES

1. I would like to acknowledge the assistance of Professor P. S. Jaini and Ms. Kristi Wiley in the preparation of this Foreword.
2. Kendall W. Folkert, *Scripture and Community: Collected Essays on the Jains* (edited by John E. Cort), Atlanta: Scholars Press 1993, p. xv.

Preface

Papers are written, for the most part, on a wide variety of topics for panels at conferences and for felicitation volumes to honor distinguished colleagues in one's area of research. It never occurred to me when I was writing these papers that one day they would be brought together in some coherent form. Several of my colleagues suggested to me that a collection of them would be useful in focusing attention on two of the heterodox traditions of ancient India, namely Buddhism and Jainism. Notable among these is John Cort, a leading Jainologist at Denison University, who recommended the format of the volumes. It was also his suggestion that a senior scholar well acquainted with both of these areas should write a Foreword, and he invited Paul Dundas, the celebrated author of *The Jains* (Routledge, 1992), to undertake this task. I am grateful to my esteemed friend Paul Dundas for his very generous Foreword, in which he reviews my career and evaluates my research.

Of the fifty papers collected together here and in the volume on Jaina Studies (also published by Motilal Banarsidass), eleven were written as contributions to Festschrifts (Jaina Studies: 4, 5, 10, 14, and 16 and Buddhist Studies: 4, 5, 8, 16, 20, and 22) and fifteen were invited papers at conferences (Jaina Studies: 1, 5, 7, 12, 15, 17 and 21; Buddhist Studies: 1, 7, 9, 10, 17, 21, 24 and 26). There are a few texts and translations of small Sanskrit and Pali works, some in fragmentary form. A total of twelve papers, nine related to Buddhism (10, 11, 12, 13, 14, 18, 24, 25, 27) and three to Jainism (17, 18, 19) were published in the *Bulletin of the School of Oriental and African Studies,* University of London, while others were published in India and elsewhere. This accounts for the variety of stylistic conventions for diacritical marks, spellings of words (Jaina/Jain) as well as bibliographical references, and so forth. Although the papers have not been revised, I have taken the opportunity where appropriate to recommend important works that have appeared since their initial publication.

The first paper of each volume ("Ahiṃsā: A Jaina Way of Spiritual Life" and "States of Happiness in Buddhist Heterodoxy") is presented as an introduction to the Jaina and Buddhist faiths, respectively. These are followed by articles on the state of Jaina Studies and Buddhist Studies at the time of their publication, 1976 for Jainism and 1956 for Buddhism. Seven papers in the Buddhist Studies volume appear under a sectional heading of Buddhism and Jainism. These are primarily based on Buddhist material but include also a number of Jaina sources. Seven papers in the volume on Jaina Studies are also relevant to Buddhist studies. They demonstrate the interdependent nature of these two traditions and stress the need for exploring them together. Their titles are as follows: *Bhavyatva and Abhavyatva*: A Jaina Doctrine of 'Predestination' (1977); Tīrthaṅkara-prakṛti and the Bodhisattva Path (1980); Karma and the Problem of Rebirth in Jainism (1980); Indian Perspectives on the Spirituality of Animals (1987); Jaina Debates on the Spiritual Liberation of Women (1991); Fear of Food: Jaina Attitutdes Toward Eating (1993); and Jaina Monks from Mathurā; Literary Evidence for Their Identification on Kuṣāṇa Sculputres (1995).

I am deeply indebted to the original publishers of these papers for permission to reproduce them here. Special thanks are due to Kristi Wiley, a doctoral student in our program, for efficiently organizing the material and preparing the copy for the Press. I also would like to commend Mr. N. P. Jain for his enthusiasm in publishing these volumes and thus promoting the study of Jainism and Buddhism.

University of California,
Berkeley PADMANABH S. JAINI

Contents

SECTION IV
ABHIDHARMA LITERATURE

SECTION V
JĀTAKA AND AVADĀNA LITERATURE

SECTION VI
MAHĀYĀNA

SECTION VII
RITUAL TEXTS

I

INTRODUCTION TO BUDDHIST FAITH

CHAPTER 1

States of Happiness in Buddhist Heterodoxy*

Among the numerous non-Vedic mendicant sects (*Śramaṇa-s*)[1] in ancient India, the Buddhists truly deserve the title "Heterodox," as they have displayed a most pronounced antagonism toward Brahmanical tradition. They have consistently rejected the scriptural authority of the *Veda-s,* the efficacy of sacrificial rituals, Brahmanical theories of creation, and the purity of the priestly caste. They have repudiated the Upaniṣadic doctrine of the absolute Brahman, as well as the manifold "theologies" based on the theory of divine incarnations (*avatāra-s*). They have, instead, vigorously upheld the sanctity of human teachers, called Tathāgatas, knowers of truth who attain enlightenment (*bodhi*) on their own without any divine assistance. But both the "orthodox" (i.e., the Vedic) and the "heterodox" (i.e., the Buddhist) schools agree that salvation consists of attaining liberation from the beginningless cycle of birth and death (*saṃsāra*), characterized by such expressions as "emancipation" (*mokṣa*) and *nirvāṇa.*

These major differences between the orthodox and the heterodox religious traditions are also reflected in concepts of happiness and attitudes toward the pursuit of it. A close examination of their canonical texts shows that while there is no dispute about the state of unhappiness, called *"duḥkha,"* suffering, there is little agreement on what constitutes its opposite, *"sukha,"* the state of happiness. This is because suffering (*duḥkha*) must, by its very nature,

*This paper was presented at the Fourth Annual Conference of the U.K. Association for Buddhist Studies, London, June 28, 1999.

be confined to *saṃsāra,* while its opposite, i.e., happiness (*sukha*), need not be so restricted. Apparently, like an amphibious being, *sukha* seems to abide and even thrive in the contrary conditions of bondage and salvation. This calls for a comparison of the varieties of feelings loosely described as "happy" in the state of bondage with the experience of "happiness" that is said to be invariably associated with freedom from that bondage.

The Nārada-Sanatkumāra dialogue in the *Chāndogya Upaniṣat* provides an appropriate starting point for our study of the state of happiness in the Vedic tradition. Nārada, a reputed elderly Vedic scholar, once approached the young celibate Sanatkumāra and said:

> Sir, I am conversant with the four Vedas...but I do not know the self. But I have heard...that any man who knows the self transcends unhappiness (*tarati śokam ātmavit iti*); and I am unhappy (*śocāmi*). Please, sir, enable me to transcend unhappiness (*śokasya pāraṃ tārayatv iti*).[2]

Sanatkumāra declared to Nārada that everything he had been studying was no more than a "name" (*nāma*). He should certainly revere the "name" as Brahman, but in order to know the self and transcend unhappiness he must first understand the nature of happiness (*sukha*). Elaborating on this, he then said:

> Happiness (*sukha*) is nothing less than the infinite (*bhūman*): there is no happiness in what is small (*alpa* = finite). Only the infinite is happiness. So [you] should really want to understand the infinite.
>
> Where one sees nothing else, hears nothing else, knows (*vijñā-*) nothing else, that is the infinite...The infinite is the same as the immortal (*amṛta*)...the finite is the same as what is mortal.
>
> A man who sees and thinks and understands in this way has pleasure in the self, ...and has his joy in the self: he becomes an independent sovereign.[3]

The use here of the rather commonplace word *sukha* (happiness) to describe the infinite and the immortal self is certainly unusual. It was probably chosen to counter the term *śoka,* employed by Nārada, which is synonymous with *duḥkha*. The preferred Upaniṣadic term for "happiness" would appear to be *ānanda*, a word for which no opposite is known, and hence is rendered quite often as "bliss." The *Taittarīya Upaniṣat*, for example, gives a catalogue of bliss beginning with a single measure of bliss on the human scale (*mānuṣa ānandaḥ*). A hundred measures of bliss make one measure of bliss of the man well versed in scripture who is not smitten by desire. A hundred measures...of a human *gandharva* (genii), ...of a divine *gandharva*, ...of the ancestors, ...of gods ...of Indra...of Bṛhaspati...of Prajāpati... . A hundred [measures of] bliss on Prajāpati's scale make one [measure of] bliss on the scale of Brahman. As if it were concluding Sanatkumāra's instructions to Nārada, the *Taittarīya* declares:

> That from which [all] words recoil together with the mind,
> Unable to attain it,—That is the bliss of Brahman; knowing it,
> A man has naught to fear from anywhere.[4]

Although occasionally spoken of as an attribute of the self similar to the other attributes like existence (*sat*) and consciousness (*cit*), once realized, this bliss or *ānanda* is verily declared to be as the self itself (*ānanda ātmā*). It forms the essential ground of the self to such an extent that it is called *rasa* (variously translated in differing contexts as the essential savour, the object of taste, love, pleasure, charm, delight, aesthetic disposition, religious sentiment, and so forth) which permeates all beings. This transcendent savour is also immanent in all other forms of happiness:

> Once a man has tasted this savour (*rasa*), he tastes bliss (*ānanda*). For who could breathe, who could live, were this bliss not [diffused] throughout space? For this savour alone brings bliss.[5]

Judging by the testimony of these Upaniṣadic texts, it becomes clear that in the Brahmanical tradition the distinction one perceives in the varieties of happiness is not one of kind but one of degree. All experiences are manifestations of the same "savour" (*rasa*) that constitutes the essence of the cosmic self. All pursuit of happiness, whether sensual or aesthetic, religious or spiritual, is in some measure, therefore, the pursuit of Brahman. Even suffering is but another experience of Brahman, albeit in a finite form. Emancipation from bondage thus equals the realization of infinite bliss.

Transition from this orthodox understanding of "happiness" to that of the heterodox is marked by the conspicuous absence of the term *ānanda* in the Buddhist canonical texts. Except for the proper name Ānanda, the chief mendicant disciple of Gautama the Buddha, the word occurs only twice in the *Suttanipāta*[6] where it means joy, and once in the *Dhammapada*[7] where, appearing together with laughter, it means carefree fun. But this is the extent of the occurrence of the word *ānanda,* probably the result of a deliberate attempt to shun a term that had gained currency as a synonym for the Upaniṣadic Brahman, an anathema to the heterodox tradition.

How do the Buddhists characterize the state of enlightenment attained by the Buddha? Does that supreme state allow for the presence of what we understand as "happiness" in our mundane existence, and if so, how would it be distinguished from the latter? Some answers to these questions can be found in the Theravada *Vinaya Piṭaka* in an account of Gautama's first few weeks immediately following his enlightenment, culminating in his first sermon known as The Turning of the Wheel of Law (*dharma-cakra-pravartana*). This account states:

> At that time the Lord, being recently fully awakened, ...sat cross-legged in one posture for seven days at the foot of the tree of awakening experiencing the bliss of freedom (*vimutti-sukha*).[8]

It must be remembered that this text is not describing Gautama's *bodhi* or enlightenment itself, but events subsequent to it, over a period of several weeks. *Bodhi* is certainly identical with the initial *nirvāṇa*—termed variously as the *sopadhiśeṣa-nirvāṇa* or the *pratisaṃkhyā-nirodha* in Abhidharma literature. The question of whether the "bliss" experienced subsequently was also an invariable concomitant of this *nirvāṇa* is therefore a moot one. It should be noted, however, that the term employed for "bliss" experienced even in so exalted a state is not *ānanda* but *sukha,* the latter distinguished further by the significant term *vimutti* or emancipation, synonymous with *nirvāṇa.* The *Vinaya Aṭṭhakathā* has but a brief comment on *vimutti-sukha,* a compound rare but attested elsewhere in the *Piṭaka.* It paraphrases it simply as *phala-samāpatti-sukha,* that is to say, *sukha* experienced by the Buddha as an immediate fruit (*phala*) of attaining the path [of Arhatship] ([*arahatta-*] *magga-samāpatti*).[9] The latter is known in the Abhidharma as the terminal stage of the supermundane path of meditation (*lokottara-bhāvanā-mārga*), consisting of a single, unique moment in which the mind is emancipated forever from *avidyā* and other passions. The terms *bodhi, nirvāṇa,* and *arhatship* are all designations of this state resulting from the extinction of passions through a process of absorption (*samāpatti*). The two experiences, that of the destruction of passions and that of the consequence of that destruction, cannot take place simultaneously. It is therefore held that the unique moment of the path is followed by several moments of "fruit," during which the Arhat savours the resultant "bliss" in a state of meditational absorption (*dhyāna/samāpatti*).

Meditation (*dhyāna*), whether mundane or supermundane, has but a short duration, usually no more than a few moments. At the end of the "fruit" meditation, therefore, an Arhat will necessarily return to the realm of mundane human existence, leading a new life totally freed from the passions that had dominated him earlier. This moment of the "path" cannot be repeated again as there are no more passions left to be destroyed, but an Arhat may recall at will the "bliss" of the "fruit" moments and may occasionally abide in them. The Buddha of course is no ordinary Arhat; it is believed that he is able to prolong these moments of "fruit" for long durations of time, even as long as a week at a time—sitting in a single posture and without any food—as asserted by the text quoted above.

Unfortunately the *Vinaya* commentary is silent about the precise nature of this *sukha* resulting from emancipation. Being an emotional experience, it must be subsumed under the aggregate known as *vedanā* or feeling. Would it be correct to identify this *sukha* with what is called *sukhā-vedanā,* pleasant feeling experienced in ordinary life? It is well known that the Buddha arrived at the "path" moment of Arhatship in conjunction with the fourth rung of the *rūpa-dhyāna* ladder.[10] This level of meditation anticipates transcendence of all forms of "happy" feelings, whether physical pleasure (*kāyika-sukha*) and mental ease (*saumanasya*) of the lower states, or the refined feelings of meditational rapture (*prīti*) enjoyed at the level of the third *dhyāna.* The only feeling (*vedanā*) available at the fourth *dhyāna* (and above in the *arūpa-dhyāna* level) is *upekṣā*[11], ordinarily translated as "neither happy nor unhappy feeling" or "indifference," but as demonstrated by Gadjin M. Nagao, best interpreted as "tranquil flow of the mind.[12]" It is evident therefore that the state of so-called "happiness" experienced by the Buddha, indicated by the *Vinaya* term *vimutti-sukha* (the "bliss" of freedom), is truly a state of supreme tranquillity, resulting both from the *dhyāna* factor of that stage and, more importantly, from the destruction of the passions by the Arhat path.

The use of the term "*sukha*" whether applied to this supermundane consciousness, or occasionally to *nirvāṇa* itself as in passages like "*nibbānaṃ paramaṃ sukhaṃ*" (*Dhammapada* 203), is purely conventional. "*Sukha*" being a variety of the feeling (*vedanā*) aggregate cannot be a qualifier of the *asaṃskṛta* (uncompounded) *nirvāṇa*; or the Buddha would have declared the third noble truth as "*sukha*"! It is best understood therefore as the state of "destruction of suffering," (*duḥkha-nirodha*), or "tranquillizing" of the compounded elements as in:

> "All compounded elements are transient, subject to growth and decay;
> they are produced, they are dissolved again, their pacification—that is bliss."[13]

How does this freedom from passions and the resultant tranquillity translate into ordinary life? Would an Arhat find happiness (*sukha*) returning from the realm of meditation to *kāmāvacara,* the realm of sense pleasures, and how would his transformation affect the lives of beings who are still immersed in it? The *Vinaya* account quoted above contains a telling example that in addition to answering such questions, provides a comprehensive definition of the term *sukha* given by the Buddha himself. I refer here to the famous scene of Mucalinda's encirclement of the Buddha to protect him from a great storm in which Mucalinda says: "Let not ...the touch of flies, mosquitoes, wind and heat, or creeping things annoy the Lord." It would be fair to say that such a fable would not ordinarily be introduced in the life of the Buddha so close to the great event of his enlightenment. Apparently, its real purpose is to show that Gautama—unlike ordinary mortals—had now become free from all forms of fear and hostility, but additionally to demonstrate that even that serpent, albeit mythical, an ignorant creature which must constantly live in fear for its life, had been so touched by Gautama's "tranquillity" that it too had ceased to fear him. The story thus provides a context for illustrating a new relationship based on trust and friendship that can develop between an emancipated person and a being in bondage. This is evident from the following utterance of the Buddha in response to Mucalinda's act of benevolence, which sums up the Buddhist view of "happiness":

> Happy (*sukho*) his solitude (*viveka*) who glad at heart
> Hath *dhamma* learnt and doth the vision see!
> Happy is that benignity (*abyāpajja*) towards
> The world (*loka*) which on no creature worketh harm.
> Happy the absence of all lust (*virāgatā*), th' ascent
> Past beyond the needs of sense-desires,
> He who doth crush the great 'I am' conceit (*asmimāna*)—
> This, truly this, is happiness supreme (*paramaṃ sukhaṃ*).[14]

The new term, *viveka* (lit., isolation) introduced here is understood by the *Aṭṭhakathā* as *upadhi-viveka*, i.e., separation from passions, a synonym for *nirvāṇa* (*nibbāṇasaṅkhāto upadhiviveko sukho*). *Nirvāṇa* is happiness because it equals freedom from aversion (*avyāpāda*), attachment (*virāgatā*), and egotism (*asmimāna-vinaya*). Buddhists consider these virtues the three roots of all that is good and wholesome (*kuśalamūla*). Their cultivation respectively through friendliness (*maitrī*), compassion (*karuṇā*), and rejoicing in the happiness of others (*muditā*) ensures the transient happiness of this world of suffering, which in turn paves the way for attainment of the "bliss" of *nirvāṇa*.

The entire ministry of the Buddha may be said to have consisted in bringing this happiness of *nirvāṇa* to the rest of the world. At the end of his famous sermon, The Turning of the Wheel of Law, he urged the first group of sixty Arhats "to walk on tour," specifically "for the welfare (*hita*) of many people (*bahu-jana*), for the happiness (*sukha*) of many people ... out of compassion for the world ...of gods and men."[15] The juxtaposition of the words welfare (*hita*) and happiness (*sukha*) in this passage may not be without a purpose. The Buddha, aware of the nature of the ordinary man's cravings, had, in his discourse on the middle path, declared indulgence in sensual pleasures (*kāma-sukha*) as low, ignoble, and unprofitable. Nor did he favour the other extreme of addiction to self-torment, ardently pursued by some of his contemporary ascetics under the misguided belief that happiness could be obtained only through painful means.[16] The middle path was distinguished by the fact that it could accomplish both welfare and happiness through happy means alone. Seen in this light, the Buddha's further instruction to his Arhat disciples that they should "teach ...*dhamma* which is lovely (*kalyāṇa*) at the beginning, lovely in the middle, and lovely at the ending," gains great significance.

The word *kalyāṇa* in popular usage refers to auspicious events such as marriage or the birth of a child, and to objects that are lovely, beautiful, or charming, and thus add to one's physical pleasure or mental repose. In religious and ritual contexts this word often indicates rare and precious articles, such as certain flowers, fruits, grains, trees, conches, metals, or stones revered as "auspicious" (*maṅgala*) "jems" (*ratna-s*), capable of bestowing wealth and prosperity. To these the Buddhists added three new "jems," the Buddha, the dharma, and the saṃgha, and asserted that even a formal act of taking refuge (*śaraṇa-gamana*) in them could produce an enduring karmic force known as "merit" (*puṇya*) capable of yielding happiness at some future time both in this world and the next.[17]

The Buddhists accepted certain Vedic rituals with considerable modification. A good example of this is *śrāddha* in which food—mostly balls of rice with meat—was magically transferred to the spirit of a deceased family member by ritual feeding of a group of Brahmin priests. The Buddhists did not discard this practice altogether, but invented a different way for helping the dead. This was a device called *anumodanā* or "rejoicing" in the "merit" earned by a living member of a family through a variety of charitable acts in the service of the three jewels. In this ceremony the dead are invited to participate in meritorious acts—e.g., the offering of food and robes to monks, the installation of an image of the Buddha, or the construction of a *stūpa*—merely by rejoicing in the good deeds done, an act of appreciation capable of bringing comfort to both the living and the dead. There was no actual transference of any of these objects or of the earned "merit" from the living to the departed, but simply an affirmation of the fact that happiness shared is multiplied.

So strong was this equation of merit with happiness (*sukha*) and of happiness with sharing that the latter became a cardinal Buddhist virtue. Sharing one's food and shelter with one's kinsmen and providing alms for the sick and the needy became the simplest means of cultivating such socio-spiritual virtues as liberality (*dāna*) and the feeling of common good (*samāna-sukha-duḥkhatā*).[18] Bestowing the same to virtuous renunciants enabled the laity to rejoice (*muditā*) in their spiritual progress, thereby acquiring merit leading to rebirth in heavens, the supreme abodes of happiness. Births in heavens (*svarga*), situated within the realm of the sensuous sphere (*kāma-dhātu*) and affording the most sublime forms of sense pleasures, were not frowned upon by the Buddhists. Indeed, the Buddha's initial preaching to laymen was called a "gradual sermon" because it contained discourses on giving and heaven before it introduced the exalted teachings of the four noble truths.[19]

Innovative ideas regarding heaven or the beings inhabiting these celestial realms can hardly be credited to the Buddhists. Long before the advent of the heterodoxies, Brahmanical tradition had promulgated such injunctions as "*svargakāmo yajeta*" (A person desirous of heaven should perform a sacrifice [*yajña*]), and had laid out the most elaborate Vedic sacrifices—some even entailing the killing of many animals—for the attainment of heaven. By the time of the Buddha these had become a monopoly of only the most ambitious kings who could, through warfare and taxation, raise enough wealth to commission them. One cannot deny certain socio-political benefits of such costly enterprises, such as the enrichment of the royal family and a few learned Brahmans; but the populace at large must have borne the burden of pillage, forced labour, and heavy taxation. Several Buddhist texts bear witness to this suffering of the common people, victims of exploitation in the name of sacrifices supposedly leading their patrons to heaven. The Buddha's concern for the "welfare and happiness of the many folk" (*bahujana-hitāya, bahujana-sukhāya*) finds expression in his reorientation of the institution of sacrifice. A good illustration of this is found in the Kūṭadanta-sutta of the *Dīghanikāya*. Here the Buddha narrates to the Brahman Kūṭadanta a story of his own past when as a Bodhisattva he served as royal chaplain of the legendary king Mahāvijita. Ordered by the king to prepare for a grand sacrifice (*mahāyajña*), the Bodhisattva admonished him in the following manner:

> The king's country, Sire, is harassed and harried. There are decoits abroad who pillage the villages and townships, and who make the roads unsafe. Were the king, so long as that is so, to levy a fresh tax, verily his majesty would be acting wrongly. But perchance his majesty might think: 'I will soon put a stop to these scoundrels' game by degradation and banishment, and fines and bonds and death!' But their licence cannot be satisfactorily put a stop to so. The remnant left unpunished would still go on harassing the realm. Now there is one method to adopt to put a thorough end to this disorder. Whosoever there be in the king's realm who devote themselves to keeping cattle and the farm, to them let his majesty the king give food and seed-corn. Whosoever there be in the king's realm who devote themselves to trade, to them let his majesty the king give capital. Whosoever there be in the king's realm who devote themselves to government service, to them let his majesty the king give wages and food. Then those men, following each his own business, will no longer harass the realm; the king's revenue will go up; the country will be quiet and at peace; and the populace, pleased one with another and happy, dancing their children in their arms, will dwell with open doors.[20]

The sermon tells us that the king did accordingly and a great amount of wealth was thereby accumulated and that the sacrifice was carried out as planned. The "Buddhist" sacrifice was distinguished from the Vedic *yajña* by the following notable features:

> And further, at that sacrifice neither were any oxen slain, neither goats, nor fowls, nor fatted pigs, nor were any kinds of living creatures put to death. No trees were cut down to be used as posts... . And the slaves and messengers and workmen there employed were driven neither by rods nor by fear, nor carried on their work weeping with tears upon their faces. Whoso chose to help, he worked; whoso chose not to help, worked not. What each chose to do, he did; what they chose not to do,

that was left undone. With ghee, and oil, and butter, and milk, and honey, and sugar only was that sacrifice accomplished.[21]

In contrast to the elaborate law books (the *Vinaya*) for mendicant community, the Buddhists have produced little that can be considered a "Buddhist" manual on polity, taxation, or government. The above discourse is therefore notable for its views on capital sharing, gainful employment, and "open door" living, goals relevant even today for achieving a happy and prosperous society.

What we have here is a legendary account of an imaginary sacrifice; even so, we should credit the Buddhists for suggesting that slaves and workers in an ideal state could choose to participate or not to participate in a given state project. It is of course no more than wishful thinking that a society governed by rigid Brahmanical caste rules could ever permit such a degree of freedom. This discourse, however, demonstrates the importance that Buddhists attached to freedom of choice as a condition for happiness in the life of an individual. Happiness was not a gift of a divine agent (*īśvara*) or predetermined by a blind force like fate (*niyati*) in the Ājīvika system, but a necessary consequence of one's volitions (*cetanā*), the motivational force behind all actions, especially voluntary ones. Transformation of the Vedic sacrifice into a simple Buddhist ritual of sharing food was only a prelude to the repudiation of the need for any kind of elaborate ritualistic action for rebirth in heaven. This is illustrated by the Buddhist version of the story of Maghavā or Indra, evidently the Vedic divinity of that name. As narrated in the *Dhammapada Commentary*, in his former life Maghavā was a young man named Magha who undertook a voluntary task of making the road in his village smooth and even. How did Magha know that this would be a meritorious act? The narrator makes an astute observation that an act that brings happiness to others must be meritorious. As his work progressed, Magha began to realize: "All these men appear to be pleased. Since this work of mine conduces to the happiness of men, it must be meritorious work," and devoted himself entirely to it.[22] Thirty-two young men from that village also joined him in this task when they learned that "he was treading the path that leads to Heaven (*saggamaggaṃ*)." They were all reborn in the heaven of the thirty-three Gods (Tāvatiṃsa or Trāyastriṃśa *devaloka*), with Magha, now called Maghavā, as the king of that heaven! It may be noted that Trāyastriṃśa is only second below the famous Tuṣita (lit., Joyous) heaven, the present abode of the Bodhisattva Maitreya, who is awaiting his descent on earth as the next Buddha.

The simple rule of accumulating merit by bringing happiness to others was equally applicable to one's duties in the household. The acts of filial piety, hospitality, and thriftiness to which Indian householders were duty bound were seen as meritorious, capable of leading to heaven. The burden of a great many inscriptions of emperor Aśoka (ruled 274-232 B.C.) is to convey this basic Buddhist message:

> Meritorious is obedience to father and mother. Meritorious is generosity to friends, acquaintances, relatives, Brāhmaṇas and Śramaṇas. Meritorious is abstention from slaughter of animals. Meritorious is the minimizing of expenditure and possessions accumulated.[23]

It is clear that the Buddha's message to his mendicant disciples to work for "the welfare of many and happiness of many" had, within a few centuries of his *nirvāṇa,* reached the royal court of the Mauryan kings. Aśoka clearly saw his royal duties as meritorious, bringing happiness to his subjects here, and aiding their rebirth in heaven hereafter, as he states in one of his inscriptions:

> I have ordered thus: I am never completely satisfied with my work of wakefulness or dispatch of business. I consider that I must work for the welfare of all people (*sava-loka-hite*).... There is no other work for me (more important) than doing what is good for the well-being of all people. And why do I work as aforesaid? It is to see that I may discharge my debt of beings and that I may make some happy here (in this world) and they may hereafter gain heaven.[24]

There are few thoughtful villagers like Magha or wise emperors like Aśoka who are happy with their mundane activities and consider them as bearing merit. For ordinary people merit appeared to be as rare as wealth: one needed a certain amount of capital to produce more of both. The majority of the population consisted of lower castes of wage earners who lived on the fringes of a small affluent society of upper castes. They must have found their household life drudgery, a testimony to their own perception that they were lacking in merit. This is articulated by the Buddha himself in illustrating a hypothetical case of a slave who contemplates renunciation (*pravrajyā*) of his household life as a sure way of earning merit:

> Strange is it and wonderful, this issue of meritorious deeds, this result of merit! Here is this king of Magadha, ...—he is a man, and so am I. But the king lives in the full enjoyment and possession of the five pleasures of sense—a very god, methinks—and here am I a slave, working for him, ...keen to carry out his pleasure...
>
> Would that I were like him, that I too might earn merit. Why should not I have my hair and beard shaved off, and don the yellow robes, and going forth from the household state, renounce the world?[25]

The Brahmanical society, as documented by Yājñavalkya's dialogue—with his wife Maitreyī on the eve of his renunciation—in the *Bṛhadāraṇyaka Upaniṣat,* did provide for the stage of renunciation (*sannyāsa-āśrama*) for those few twice-born (*dvija*) men of advanced age who had sought freedom from *gṛhastha-āśrama,* the household life.[26] But it resolutely denied that privilege to women regardless of their castes, and also to members of the lower castes. It is to the credit of the Buddhists that they threw open the doors of mendicancy to even these segments of society, making it possible for them to escape the oppressions of domestic life and to pursue a life of solitude.

Even more radical was the Buddhist willingness to transgress the time-honoured rule that the young were duty bound to marry, raise families, and look after their parents before embarking on the course of renunciation. Young Gautama's sudden and secretive abandonment of his young wife with a year-old child and his aged father in order to embrace the life of a recluse—in stark contrast to the old Yājñavalkya's friendly act of bidding goodbye to his wife—must have seemed totally heartless to his friends and relatives. But his subsequent defiant act of encouraging hundreds like him to follow in his footsteps produced a complete alienation between the old and the new, the orthodox and the heterodox. We learn from a *Vinaya* account that as his movement grew in magnitude and a great many sons of affluent households deserted their families, a loud protest was heard from people crying:

> The ascetic Gautama is intent on childlessness, he is intent on widowhood, he is intent on the destruction of family.[27]

We will never know the unhappy events in their lives that might have induced these young men—in such large numbers—to take this bold step. We can be sure, however, that they were not seeking to gain merit (*puṇya*) or to improve their status in this world, as one could charitably say about the slave of the Magadhan king mentioned above. The idea of merit was founded on the belief in the inherent goodness of the stage of the householder (*gṛhastha-āśrama*), conducive to happiness here and to rebirth in heaven. In abandoning their homes in the manner of Gautama, these young Buddhists had repudiated the popular notions of the desirability of marital happiness or the pleasures of heaven. The following stereotyped passage superbly conveys their sense of deep disenchantment with the pleasures of the household and their grim determination to immediately lead the "higher" life of a recluse:

> Full of hindrance is household life, a path for the dust of passion. Free as the air is the life of him who has renounced all worldly things. How difficult is it for the man who dwells at home to live the higher life (*brahmacariya*) in all its fullness, in all its purity, in all its bright perfection! Let me then cut off my hair and beard, let me clothe myself in the orange-coloured robes, and let me go forth from the household life into the homeless (*anagāriyaṃ*) state.[28]

What kind of happiness could these young celibate men have found in forests away from the comforts of their home? What could have kept them cheerful under the Buddha's relentless message of suffering, impermanence, and non-self? What could have sustained them in their resolve to adhere to the precepts of mendicancy constantly watching their conduct? The *Vinaya Piṭaka* abounds in accounts of weak and renegade monks and nuns, but it also reveals a great many happy individuals, participating freely in the affairs of their new family called the holy community (*saṃgha*). For all its talk about universal suffering (*sabbaṃ duḥkhaṃ*), the Pali *Sutta Piṭaka* is not wanting in discourses on "happiness," (*sukha*), especially for the mendicants. The Sukhavagga of the *Dhammapada,* for example, contains a glowing picture of happy and healthy mendicants savouring the joys of their liberation from the strifes of household life, the arena of victory and defeat, longing and hatred:

> Victory produces hatred:
> He who is defeated is afflicted with suffering;
> He who has renounced both victory and defeat
> lives in tranquillity (*upasanto*) and happiness (*sukhaṃ*).
>
> Oh, happily (*susukhaṃ*) let us live! free from hatred among those who hate;
> Among men who hate, let us live free from hatred.[29]

This happiness moreover was so transparent that it reflected on their faces and brought colour to their skin. In the Sagāthavagga of the *Saṃyuttanikāya* a fairy (*devatā*) asks the Buddha:

> Living in the forests, peaceful holy men:
> Eat only a single meal,
> How does their skin shine bright?[30]

The following answer probably contains the essence of the Buddha's path as well as his idea of happiness as complete health:

> They mourn not the past; nor crave for the future;
> They abide in the present; thus is their skin bright.[31]

The path to Arhatship can be short and may be trod without formally abandoning the household, as was proven by the seemingly exceptional case of the young Yaśa of Varanasi.[32] For the majority, however, that path entailed formal initiation into the mendicant order as well as meditational practices, generically called *dhyāna,* a term translated in varying contexts as absorption, concentration, ecstasy, rapture, trance, and so forth. Well beyond the realms of sensuous heavens (*kāmāvacara-devaloka*)—which a true renunciant would not crave for—there still exist several sublime abodes, free from sexual desire (*kāmarāga*) and repulsion (*pratigha*).

These are the four heavens of refined matter known as the *rūpaloka,* and the four heavens without a trace of matter called the *arūpaloka.* A craving for rebirth (*bhava-rāga*) in these higher heavens could now drive an aspirant to engage in a more exalted variety of meritorious acts (*puṇya-kriyā*), namely, the meditational acts known respectively as *rūpa-dhyāna-s* and *arūpa-dhyāna-s.*

The origins of *dhyāna,* an integral part of the pan-Indian spiritual practice known as *yoga,* certainly go back to a pre-Buddhist period. Certain features of the *rūpa* and *arūpa* meditations, so elaborately described in the Buddhist scriptures, can also be traced to such non-Buddhist sources as the *Yogasūtra-s* of Patañjali.[33] Even so, the ecstasy of the *dhyāna* practice so captivated the ancient Buddhists that they even attributed its discovery to the infant Siddhārtha Gautama! In a rare autobiographical account, the Buddha once recalled his childhood memory of a rapturous "meditational" experience. This memory, he admits, had rescued him from the brink of death—brought about by severe fasting during the long years of striving for *nirvāṇa*—and thus had paved the way for his enlightenment:

> Thought I to myself: Of all the spasms of acute and severe pain that have been undergone through the ages . . . by recluses or brahmins, mine are preeminent; nor is there aught worse beyond. Yet, with all these severe austerities, I fail to transcend ordinary human limits and to rise to the heights of noblest understanding and vision. Could there be another path to Enlightenment?
>
> A memory came to me of how once, seated in the cool shade of a rose-apple tree on the lands of my father the Sakyan, I, divested of pleasures of sense and of wrong states of mind, entered upon, and abode in the First ecstasy (*rūpadhyāna*), with all its zest and satisfaction,—a state bred of inward aloofness but not divorced from observation and reflection. Could this be the path to Enlightenment? In prompt response to this memory, my consciousness told me that here lay the true path to Enlightement.[34]

But Gautama hesitated, for it would have been extremely hazardous for a physically weak person to undergo so strong an ecstatic experience:

> Thought I to myself: Am I afraid of a bliss that eschews pleasures of sense and wrong states of mind?—And my heart told me that I was not afraid.
> Thought I to myself: It is no easy matter to attain that bliss with a body so emaciated. Come, let me take some solid food, rice and junket; and thus I ate accordingly.[35]

This is also a testimony to the fact that Gautama's experience of meditational ecstasy in a strong and healthy body was responsible for the eventual formulation of the middle path, his celebrated course of avoiding the extremes of the pleasures of senses and the pains of self-mortification. The autobiographical account given above concludes with a long and stereotyped description of Gautama's moving with ease through the series of meditations. He transcended the lower ecstatic states and arrived at the fourth *rūpadhyāna,* distinguished by its "tranquil flow of mind" (*upekṣā*). Ordinarily, these meditational acts would automatically entail a rebirth in one of the Rūpaloka heavens. The karmic consequences are nullified by total destruction of *avidyā* and other remaining passions, e.g., *rūpa-rāga,* desire for the pleasures of meditational heavens. This can be accomplished only by the supermundane (*lokottara*) trances of the noble path. As we noted earlier, Gautama, having established his mind firmly in the serene state of the fourth *rūpadhyāna,* entered the path of Arhatship, experienced its fruit, the supreme bliss (*vimutti-sukha*) of enlightenment, and thus became a Buddha.

We may now examine the state of happiness of the Arhats, the earliest disciples of the Buddha. Tradition recognizes a group of some eighty eminent "Great Elders" (*mahāśrāvaka-s*) led by such Arhats as Śāriputra and Mahākāśyapa—who, it is claimed, had attained the goal of *nirvāṇa.* Would it be correct to equate their *nirvāṇa* and subsequent state of happiness with that of the Buddha himself? From the moment of attaining enlightenment under the Bodhi tree until his death in Kusinārā, the Buddha had engaged unceasingly in the task of sharing his sublime vision with others. The Arhats in comparison appeared selfishly content with their personal liberations, lacking in both the heroic aspiration to save others and in the skills requisite for such a noble task. The spectacular rise of the Mahāyāna-Bodhisattva ideal within the school of elders can in some measure be attributed to a legitimate suspicion that the Arhats' "pure" happiness might be tainted with selfishness, and hence incompatible with the attainment of *nirvāṇa.* The aspirant in the *Bodhicaryāvatāra* (*Entering the Path of Enlightenment* by Śāntideva), embarking on the heroic Bodhisattva path, asks himself a very pertinent question that could legitimately be asked of any Arhat:

> Since I and my fellowmen abhor pain (*duḥkha*) and fear (*bhaya*) alike, what distinction can I rightly make for myself, that I should preserve myself and not another?[36]

> All those who suffer in this world suffer because they desire their own happiness.
> All those who are happy in this world are happy because they seek happiness for others.[37]

> Not even worldly happiness is possible without exchanging (*parivarta*) one's happiness with other's suffering; how difficult then the attainment of [the happiness of] being a Buddha![38]

The initial goal of an Arhat's personal salvation was soon superseded by the ultimate goal of universal salvation attained by a Bodhisattva through an extraordinary "exchange" (*parivarta*) in which happiness was freely and unconditionally bestowed on the world. Rightly called a *mahāsattva,* or a magnanimous being, the Bodhisattva—as observed by Śāntideva—had no attraction even for *nirvāṇa,* for he found complete satisfaction in the salvation of others.

> Enough for me these oceans of joy (*prāmodya-sāgarāḥ*) experienced at the deliverance of creatures,
> Indeed, what need for me of the flavourless (*arasika*) emancipation (*mokṣa*)?[39]

These words, spoken in a rhetorical manner no doubt, show the irreversible course that Buddhism had taken within a few centuries after the advent of Gautama the Buddha. The isolationistic asceticism founded on the historical Buddha's theory of the five aggregates (*skandha-s*) was discarded as a "provisional" teaching, in favour of active altruism inspired by the doctrine of an absolute Buddha body (*Dharma-kāya*) manifesting itself in countless resplendent bodies (*sambhoga-kāya-s*) and human bodies (*nirmāṇa-kāya-s*) for the salvation of all mankind. Parallel developments within the Brahmanical schools, notably the teaching of *karma-yoga*—action with critical detachment as the most preferred means of salvation—in the *Bhagavad Gītā*, also helped to soften the sharp differences between orthodoxy and heterodoxy. Eventually, a partial accommodation of the two traditions was achieved as is demonstrated by the curious phenomenon of the induction of Śākyamuni as the most recent *avatāra* of the Brahmanical god Viṣṇu.[40]

There are thus three distinct states of happiness recognized by Buddhist texts. The lowest one is that of the householder whose pursuit is normally confined to accumulating merit by doing good deeds with the aim of attaining health, wealth, and heaven. For renunciants, there is the ecstasy of a more exalted nature, the relishing of which can lead to rebirths in meditational heavens. Finally there is the supreme state of happiness—tranquillity rising from the destruction of passions—attained by the Buddha himself. These three are brought together in the glorious career of the Bodhisattva, who skillfully strives for the welfare of one and all and thus truly carries out the historical Buddha's mission for the good of many, for the happiness of many (*bahujana-hitāya, bahujana-sukhāya*).[41]

NOTES

1. For more detailed information on the Jaina, Ājīvika, and other Śramaṇa traditions, see Padmanabh S. Jaini, "Śramaṇas: Their Conflict with Brahmanical Society," in J. W. Elder, ed., *Chapters in Indian Civilization,* I, pp. 39-81. Dubuque, Iowa (Kendall Hunt), 1970; Padmanabh S. Jaini, *The Jaina Path of Purification,* pp. 1-30. University of California Press, 1979.
2. *so 'haṃ bhagavo mantravid evāsmi nātmavit, śrutaṃ hy eva me bhagavaddṛśebhyas tarati śokam ātmavid iti, so 'haṃ bhagavaḥ śocāmi, taṃ mā bhagavañ śokasya pāraṃ tārayatv iti. taṃ hovāca yad vai kiñcaitad adhyagīṣṭhā nāmaivaitat.* Dvarikadas Shastri, ed. *Aṣṭāviṃśatyupaniṣadaḥ,* p. 137 (=*Chāndogyopaniṣat,* vii, 3). Varanasi, 1965.
3. *yo vai bhūmā tat sukhaṃ, nālpe sukham asti. bhūmaiva sukhaṃ bhūmā tv eva vijijñāsitavya iti. ...yatra nānyat paśyati nānyac chṛṇoti nānyad vijānāti sa bhūmā ... yo vai bhūmā tad amṛtam atha yad alpaṃ tan martyaṃ...sa vā eṣa evaṃ paśyann evaṃ manvāna evaṃ vijānann ātmaratir ātmakrīḍa ātmamithuna ātmānandaḥ sa svarāḍ bhavati...* Ibid. p. 146 (=*Chāndogyopaniṣat,* vii, 21-25).

4. *saiṣā "nandasya mīmāṃsā bhavati....*
yato vāco nivartante aprāpya manasā saha,
ānandaṃ brahmaṇo vidvān na bibheti kutaścana. Ibid. pp. 53-55 (=*Taittarīyopaniṣat,* II. 7-8).
5. *raso vai saḥ. rasaṃ hy evāyaṃ labdhvā "nandī bhavati. ko hy evānyāt kaḥ prāṇyāt, yadi hy evaiṣa ākāśa ānando no syāt? eṣa hy evānandayāti.* Ibid. pp. 53-55 (=*Taittarīyopaniṣat,* II. 7).
6. *ānandajāte tidasagaṇe patīte, Suttanipāta* 679; *ānandajāto vipulam alattha pītiṃ, Suttanipāta* 687. Pali Text Society, London, 1948.
7. *ko nu hāso kim ānando niccaṃ pajjalite sati,*
andhakārena onaddhā dīpaṃ kiṃ na gavesatha? Dhammapada 146. Pali Text Society, London, 1914.
8. *tena samayena Buddho bhagavā ...paṭhamābhisambuddho... bodhirukkhamūle sattāhaṃ ekapallaṅkena nisīdi vimuttisukhapaṭisaṃvedī, Vinaya Piṭaka, Mahāvagga,* p. 1. Pali Text Society, London, 1879-1883.
9. *vimuttisukhapaṭisaṃvedī ti vimuttisukhaṃ phalasamāpattisukhaṃ paṭisaṃvediyamāno. Vinaya-Aṭṭhakathā* (*Samantapāsādikā,* part iii), p. 714. Simon Hewavitarane Bequest, vol. XLVI, Colombo, 1946. (see also note 41.)
10. For a detailed discussion on this problem see Karel Werner, "Bodhi and Arahattaphala: From Early Buddhism to Early Mahayana," in Philip Denwood and Alexander Piatigorsky, eds., *Buddhist Studies: Ancient and Modern,* pp. 167–181. Curzon Press Ltd., London, 1983.
11. On the varieties of *upekṣā* see Harvey B. Aronson, "Equanimity (*upekkhā*) in Theravada Buddhism," in A.K. Narain, ed., *Studies in Pali and Buddhism* (A Memorial Volume in Honour of Bikkhu Jagdish Kashyap), pp. 1-18. B.R. Publishing Corporation, Delhi, 1979.
12. Gadjin M. Nagao: "Tranquil Flow of Mind: An Interpretation of Upekṣā," in *Indianisme et Bouddhisme,* pp. 244-258. Institut Orientaliste Louvain-la-Neuve, 1980.
13. *aniccā vata saṃkhārā uppādavayadhammino,*
uppajjitvā nirujjhante tesaṃ vūpasamo sukho. Dīghanikāya, ii. p. 157. Pali Text Society, London, 1917.
We may note here Vasubandhu's use of the term *sukha* to describe *anāsravadhātu,* the *nirvāṇa* of the Vijñānavāda school. Sthiramati's comment shows that there is no assertion of a positive quality of "bliss." It is *sukha* because it is not perishable, since all that is perishable is of the nature of suffering:
sa evānāsravo dhātur acintyo kuśalo dhruvaḥ,
sukho vimuktikāyo 'sau dharmākhyo 'yaṃ mahāmuneḥ. Triṃśikā 30.
"sa evānāsravo dhātur" iti .... "sukho" nityatvād eva yad anityaṃ tad duḥkham, ayañ ca nitya iti, tasmāt sukhaḥ. sa eva...mahāmuner dharmakāya ity ucyate. Sylvain Levi, ed. *Vijñaptimātratāsiddhi Deux traies de Vasuhandhu:*
Viṃśatikā et Triṃśikā, p. 44. Librairie Ancienne Honore Champion, Paris, 1925.
14. *sukho viveko tuṭṭhassa sutadhammassa passato,*
abyāpajjaṃ sukhaṃ loke pāṇabhūtesu saṃyamo;
sukhā virāgatā loke kāmānaṃ samatikkamo,
asmimānassa yo vinayo etaṃ ve paramaṃ sukhaṃ.
Vinaya Piṭaka (*Mahāvagga*) I, p. 3. Pali Text Society, London, 1879-1883. Tr. by I.B. Horner, *The Book of the Discipline,* I, p. 5. Pali Text Society, London, 1938-66.

15. *caratha, bhikkhave, cārikaṃ bahujanahitāya bahujanasukhāya lokānukampāya atthāya hitāya sukhāya devamanussānaṃ. ...desetha, bhikhhave, dhammaṃ ādikalyāṇaṃ majjhekalyāṇaṃ pariyosānakalyāṇaṃ...brahmacariyaṃ pakāsetha... Vinaya Piṭaka* (*Mahāvagga*) I, p. 21.
16. *dve 'me, bhikkhave, antā pabbajitena na sevitabbā. katame dve? yo cāyaṃ kāmesu kāmasukhallikānuyogo hīno gammo anariyo anatthasaṃhito, yo cāyaṃ attakilamathānuyogo dukkho anariyo anatthasaṃhito.* Ibid. p. 10.
17. According to the Buddhist doctrine of karma, all actions, whether wholesome or unwholesome, carry karmic residues or impressions (*abhisaṃskāra*). These are respectively called "merit" and "demerit," and are preserved in the stream of consciousness. Like seeds sown in fertile ground, they mature and bear fruit in time, usually in the order of their accumulation. Their fruition (*vipāka*) results in the forging of a new material body at rebirth—hellish, animal, human, or celestial—which houses an appropriate aggregate (*skandha*) of four mental constituents, namely, perceptions (*saṃjñā*), feelings (*vedanā*), volition (*cetanā*), and awareness (*vijñāna*). Each new existence is thus a fruition (*vipāka*) of past actions; but the karmic consequence of good and evil actions, namely, pleasure and pain—seen by the ignorant as reward and punishment—is experienced only through the aggregate called *vedanā*. Therefore, happiness or unhappiness is not something that is perceived or willed, but is felt and hence subsumed under *vedanā*. These experiences in turn give rise to new attachments and aversions ensuring an endless series of new actions and rebirths.
18. E. Senart, ed. *Mahāvastu*, I, 3, pp. 11-12. Paris, 1882-1897.
19. *ekam antaṃ nisinnassa kho Yasassa kulaputtassa Bhagavā anupubbiṃ kathaṃ kathesi, seyyathīdaṃ—dānakathaṃ sīlakathaṃ saggakathaṃ, kāmānaṃ ādīnavaṃ okāraṃ saṃkilesaṃ, nekkhamme ānisaṃsaṃ pakāsesi. yadā Bhagavā aññāsi Yasaṃ kulaputtaṃ kallacittaṃ, muducittaṃ, udaggacittaṃ, pasannacittaṃ, atha yā Buddhānaṃ sāmukkaṃsikā dhammadesanā taṃ pakāsesi—dukkhaṃ samudayam, nirodhaṃ, maggaṃ. Vinaya Piṭaka* (*Mahāvagga*), I, pp. 15-16.
20. *bhoto kho rañño janapado sakaṇṭako sauppīḷo. gāmaghātā pi dissanti ...bhavaṃ ce kho pana rājā evaṃ sakaṇṭake janapade sauppīḷe balim uddhareyya, akiccakārī assa tena bhavaṃ rājā. ... tena hi bhavaṃ rājā ye bhoto rañño janapade ussahanti kasigorakkhe tesaṃ bhavaṃ rājā bījabhattaṃ anuppadetu. ye bhoto rañño janapade ussahanti vāṇijjāya tesaṃ bhavaṃ rājā pābhataṃ anuppadetu. ye bhoto rañño janapade ussahanti rājaporise tesaṃ bhavaṃ rājā bhattavetanaṃ pakappetu. te ca manussā sakammapasutā rañño janapadaṃ na viheṭhessanti; mahā ca rañño rāsiko bhavissati. khemaṭṭhitā janapadā anuppīḷā. manussā mudā modamānā ure putte naccentā apārutagharā maññe viharissantī ti. Dīghanikāya.* I, p. 135. Pali Text Society London, 1917. Tr. by T.W. Rhys Davids, *Dialogues of the Buddha,* I, p. 175-176. Sacred Books of the Buddhists, London, 1899.
21. *tasmiṃ kho, brāhmaṇa, yaññe n' eva gāvo haññiṃsu, na ajeḷakā haññiṃsu, na kukkuṭasūkarā haññiṃsu, na vividhā pāṇā saṅghātaṃ āpajjiṃsu, na rukkhā chijjiṃsu yūpatthāya, na dabbhā lūyiṃsu barihisatthāya. ye pi 'ssa dāsā ti vā pessā ti vā kammakarā ti vā te pi na daṇḍatajjitā na bhayatajjitā na assumukhā rudamānā parikammāni akaṃsu; ye na icchiṃsu na te akaṃsu; yaṃ icchiṃsu taṃ akaṃsu, yaṃ na icchiṃsu na taṃ akaṃsu. sappitelanavanītadadhimadhuphāṇitena c' eva so yañño niṭṭhānaṃ agamāsi. Dīghanikāya,* I, p. 136; Tr. by T.W. Rhys Davids, *Dialogues of the Buddha,* I, p. 180.

22. ...*sabbe pi te sukhitā jātā; iminā kammena mayhaṃ sukhadāyakena puññakammena bhavitabban ti... Dhammapada-Aṭṭhakathā*, I, p. 266. Pali Text Society, 1914. Tr. by E.W. Burlingame, *Buddhist Legends*, Part I, p. 313-324. Harvard Oriental Series No. 28, 1921.

23. *sādhu mātāpitusa susūsā. mita-saṃthuta-nātikyānaṃ cā baṃbhana-samanānaṃ ca sādhu dāne. pānānaṃ anālaṃbhe sādhu. apavayatā apabhaṃḍatā sādhu.* G.S. Murti and A. N. K. Iayangar, ed. and tr., *Edicts of Asoka* (Rock Edict III). The Adyar Library, 1951.

24. *hevaṃ ānapayite mamayā. ...nathi hi me tose vā uṭhānasā aṭhasaṃtilanāye cā. kaṭaviya mute hi me savalokahite..., nathi hi kaṃmatalā savalokahitenā. yoṃ ca kiṃ ci palakamāmi hakaṃ kiti? bhūtānaṃ ananiyaṃ yehaṃ hida ca kāni sukhāyāmi palata cā svagaṃ ālādhayitu* ...Rock Edict VII, Ibid.

25. *acchariyaṃ vata bho, abbhutaṃ vata bho, puññānaṃ gati, puññānaṃ vipāko. ayaṃ hi rājā Māgadho Ajātasattu ...manusso, ahaṃ pi manusso. ayaṃ hi rājā...pañcahi kāmaguṇehi samappito samaṅgībhūto paricāreti, devo maññe. ahaṃ pan' amhi 'ssa dāso kammakaro ...so vata 'ssāhaṃ puññāni kareyyaṃ. yannūnāhaṃ kesamassuṃ ohāretvā kāsāyāni vatthāni acchādetvā agārasmā anagāriyaṃ pabbajeyyan ti. Dīghanikāya* (*Sāmaññaphalasutta*), I, p. 60. Tr. by Rhys Davids, Ibid. p. 76.

26. *atha Yājñavalkyasya dve bhārye badhūvatur Maitreyī ca Kātyāyanī ca. ...Maitreyīti hovāca Yājñavalkyaḥ pravrajiṣyan vā are ayam asmāt sthānād asmi hanta te 'nayā Kātyāyanyāntaṃ karavāṇīti. ...iti hoktvā Yājñavalkyo vijahāra. Aṣṭāviṃśatyupaniṣadaḥ*, pp. 224-228 (=*Bṛhadāraṇyakopaniṣat, iv*, 5).

27. *tena kho pana samayena abhiññātā abhiññātā Māgadhikā kulaputtā bhagavati brahmacariyaṃ caranti. manussā ujjhāyanti khiyyanti vipācenti aputtikatāya paṭipanno samaṇo Gotamo, vedhavyāya paṭipanno samaṇo Gotamo, kulupacchedāya paṭipanno samaṇo Gotamo... Vinaya Piṭaka* (*Mahāvagga*), I, p. 43.

28. *sambādho gharāvāso rajopatho, abbhokāso pabbajjā. na-y-idaṃ sukaraṃ agāraṃ ajjhāvasatā ekantaparipuṇṇaṃ ekantaparisuddhaṃ saṅkhalikhitaṃ brahmacariyaṃ carituṃ. yannūnāhaṃ kesamassuṃ ohāretvā kāsāyāni vatthāni acchādetvā agārasmā anagāriyaṃ pabbajeyyaṃ ti. Dīghanikāya*, I, 63.

29. *jayaṃ veraṃ pasavati dukkho seti parājito,*
upasanto sukhaṃ seti hitvā jayaparājayaṃ. Dhammapada 201.
susukhaṃ vata jīvāma verinesu averino;
verinesu manussesu viharāma averino. Ibid. 197.

30. *araññe viharantānaṃ santānaṃ brahmacārinaṃ,*
ekabhattaṃ bhuñjamānānaṃ kena vaṇṇo pasīdati? Saṃyuttanikāya, I, p. 5. Pali Text Society, 1888.

31. *atītaṃ nānusocanti nappajappanti nāgataṃ,*
paccuppannena yāpenti tena vaṇṇo pasīdati. Ibid.

32. See *Vinaya Piṭaka* (*Mahāvagga*), I, pp. 15-18. See note 19 above.

33. See Vyāsa's *Bhāṣya* on Patañjali's *Yogasūtra-s* iii, 25-26 in Ramashankara Bhattacharya, ed., *Pātañjala-Yogadarśanam* (pp. 130-134). Bharatiya Vidya Prakashan, Varanasi, 1963.

34. *tassa mayhaṃ, Aggivessana, etad ahosi: ye kho koci atītam addhānaṃ samaṇā vā brāhmaṇā vā opakammikā dukkhā tibbā kharā kaṭukā vedanā vedayiṃsu, etāvaparamaṃ, na-y-ito bhiyyo. ...na kho panāhaṃ imāya kaṭukāya dukkarakārikāya adhigacchāmi uttarimanussā dhammā alamariyañāṇadassanavisesaṃ. siyā nu kho añño maggo bodhāyā ti?*
tassa mayhaṃ, Aggivessana, etad ahosi: abhijānāmi kho panāhaṃ pitu Sakkassa kammante sītāya jambucchāyāya nisinno vivicc' eva kāmehi vivicca akusalehi dhammehi

savitakkaṃ savicāraṃ vivekajaṃ pītisukhaṃ paṭhamaṃ jhānaṃ upasampajja viharitā. siyā nu kho eso maggo bodhāyā ti? tassa mayhaṃ, Aggivessana, satānusāri viññāṇaṃ ahosi: es' eva maggo bodhāyā ti. Majjhimanikāya, I, p. 246. Pali Text Society, 1887-1902.

35. *tassa mayhaṃ, Aggivessana, etad ahosi: kiṃ nu ahaṃ tassa sukhassa bhāyāmi, yaṃ taṃ sukhaṃ aññatreva kāmehi aññatra akusalehi dhammehī ti? tassa mayhaṃ etad ahosi: na kho ahaṃ tassa sukhassa bhāyāmi...*
tassa mayhaṃ, Aggivessana, etad ahosi: no kho taṃ sukaraṃ sukhaṃ adhigantuṃ evaṃ adhimattakasimānaṃ pattakāyena, yannūnāhaṃ oḷārikaṃ āhāraṃ āhāreyyaṃ odanakummāsaṃ. Ibid. I, p. 247.

36. *yadā mama pareṣāṃ ca bhayaṃ duḥkhaṃ ca no priyaṃ,*
tadātmanaḥ ko viśeṣo yat taṃ rakṣāmi netaram.
P.L. Vaidya, ed. *Bodhicaryāvatāra of Śāntideva,* viii, 96. The Mithila Institute of Darbhanga, 1960.

37. *ye kecid duḥkhitā loke sarve te svasukhecchayā,*
ye kecit sukhitā loke sarve te 'nyasukhecchayā. Ibid. viii, 129.

38. *na nāma sādhyaṃ buddhatvaṃ saṃsāre 'pi kutaḥ sukham,*
svasukhasyānyaduḥkhena parivartam akurvataḥ. Ibid. viii, 131.

39. *mucyamāneṣu sattveṣu ye te prāmodyasāgarāḥ,*
tair eva nanu paryāptaṃ mokṣeṇārasikena kim? Ibid. viii, 108.

40. On the Buddha as an *avatāra* of Viṣṇu, see Padmanabh S. Jaini, "Disappearance of Buddhism and the Survival of Jainism: A Study in Contrast," in A.K. Narain, ed., *Studies in History of Buddhism,* pp. 81-91. B.R. Publishing Corporation, Delhi, 1980.

41. The *Vinaya Piṭaka* passage is repeated in the *Udāna* (pp.1-3). In the Sutta Piṭaka, arhats Aṅgulimāla (*Majjhima Nikāya* II, p. 104) and Vaṅgīsa (*Saṃyutta Nikāya* I, p. 196) are said to experience *vimuttisukha,* as are a large group of arhats in the time of Kassapa Buddha (*Aṅguttara Nikāya* II, p. 218). (All references are to the Pali Text Society edition.) In the *Avadāna Śataka* (no. 40), Subhadra, the last disciple of the Buddha, is said to have experienced the same bliss soon after attaining arhatship: *athāyuṣmataḥ Subhadrasyārhatvaprāptasya vimuktisukhaṃ pratisaṃvedayataḥ etad abhavat* (p. 102, ed. P.L. Vaidya, Darbhanga 1958).

II

BUDDHIST STUDIES

CHAPTER 2

Buddhist Studies in Recent Times: Some Eminent Buddhist Scholars in India and Europe*

According to a Buddhist tradition, the *dharmacakra-pravartana*—the turning of the Wheel of Law—is said to have taken place three times.[1] Historically, the reference is first to the one which took place at Sarnath, the second to the resurgence of Mahāyāna and the third to the rise of the Yogācāra school of Vijñānavāda. To this can be added a fourth awakening, which may be reckoned as co-existent with the period of intensive research on Buddhism in the east and west in the past hundred years. The awakening was sudden and inspired, and it brought about a renaissance in Buddhist studies. This new wave spread through the three continents of Europe, Asia and America, touching almost all branches of the arts and humanities thereby leading to a revival of cultural life in Asian countries and making the world Buddha-saṃjñī, or Buddha-conscious.

One has only to look into the stupendous eight volumes of *Bibliographie Bouddhique* or into *History of Indian Literature*, vol. II, by Winternitz to realize the enormous amount of work done in the field of Buddhist studies. The names of E. Burnouf, Fausböll, Prinsep, Kern, Csoma de Körös, Oldenberg, Poussin, Lévi, Stcherbatsky and the illustrious couple, Mr. and Mrs. Rhys Davids, stand out in glory in the west and one remembers with reverence

*This article was published originally in *2500 Years of Buddhism*, ed. P. V. Bapat, (The Publications Division, Ministry of Information and Broadcasting, Government of India, 1956), pp. 382-397.

such veterans in the east as S.C. Das, S.C. Vidyabhusan, Bunyiu Nanjio, J. Takakusu, D. Kosambi and B.M. Barua. There are also innumerable other scholars in our times who have kept the torch burning and deserve our grateful homage.

Until a century ago the word Pali or even such words as Hīnayāna and Mahāyāna were little known outside Ceylon, Burma and Japan. The discovery of Pali literature, with which Aśoka is closely associated, is an interesting story. In the first quarter of the last century, archaeologists like James Prinsep and others were engaged in deciphering Aśokan edicts. It was the occurrence of the word Piyadassī in the Mahāvaṃsa, a Pali Chronicle of Ceylon, that helped them to identify King Piyadassī of the edicts with King Aśoka. No wonder that a Pali book from Ceylon should have brought to light the name of a king who was so greatly instrumental in carrying the Buddha's message of enlightenment to the island. The credit for this discovery goes to George Turnour who realized the value of the hidden treasures in Pali literature and published a critical edition and translation of the Mahāvaṃsa in 1837.

These developments were received with great interest by western indologists and an eminent scholar, Prof. Vincent Fausböll of Copenhagen, came forward with an edition and a Latin translation of the Dhammapada in 1855. Scholars like E. Burnouf, B. Clough and J. Lewis had already published works on the Pali language based on the few texts that were available. New branches in Buddhist studies were opened. These can roughly be summarized as follows:

(1) Sanskrit studies through the collection of Buddhist Sanskrit manuscripts from Nepal (1821-41), and their distribution in various libraries of India and Europe by B. H. Hodgson;
(2) Tibetan studies through the publication of *Tibetan-English Dictionary* (1834) by Csoma de Körös;
(3) Pali studies through the publication of R.C. Childers' *Pali-English Dictionary* (1875) and the foundation of the Pali Text Society (1881); and
(4) Chinese studies through the publication of Bunyiu Nanjio's *Catalogue of the Chinese Tripiṭaka* (1883).

Hodgson's distinct service in procuring Nepalese manuscripts and the subsequent discoveries of Tibetan and Pali literature helped Eugene Burnouf to write the first history of Buddhism. His famous work, *Introduction a l'Historie du Bouddhisme Indien,* published in 1844, contained an excellent survey of Buddhist literature and threw light on the relations between the Pali and Sanskrit traditions. He translated long passages of the Divyāvadāna, the Kāraṇḍavyūha, the Vajrasūcī and wrote the first notes on the Prajñāpāramitās, the Laṅkāvatāra-sūtra and other extant literature. His second work, *Lotus de la bonne Loi,* was a French translation of the Saddharma-puṇḍarīka, which appeared in 1852.

While Burnouf concentrated on Sanskrit Buddhism, Fausböll made progress with his edition of the Pali texts. His edition of the Dhammapada with a Latin translation (1855) heralded the studies in Buddhist religion and thought. His English translation of another major work, the Suttanipāta, was published in the Sacred Books of the East Series in 1881, while the Pali Text Society published his critical edition of the same text in 1885.

His greatest work, however, was the edition of the Jātakas. This monumental work, which was his first love, will forever remain a standing monument of his astonishing mind and industry. This was a substantial contribution to the studies of popular Buddhism and Indian folklore. Fausböll published this standard edition in six volumes between 1877 and 1897, thus contributing very largely to the study of cultural material in Buddhist literature.

Even before the Pali Text Society was begun, many eminent scholars had devoted themselves to editing Pali texts. The credit for editing the entire Vinaya-piṭaka, for instance, goes to Hermann Oldenberg, a giant among the Indologists in the last century. He was a great Vedic scholar and had set the standard for the critical editions and interpretations of the Ṛgveda. His learned introduction to the Vinaya-piṭaka brought the discipline of the Buddhist order to the forefront and a new field was opened for Buddhist ecclesiastical studies. The Vinaya-piṭaka was published during the period from 1879 to 1883 and his English translations of the Pātimokkha, the Mahāvagga and the Cullavagga, in collaboration with Rhys Davids, appeared in volumes XIII, XVII and XX of the Sacred Books of the East (1881-85). His other celebrated work, *The Buddha,* was translated into English by Hoey in the year 1882. This was the first text-book in Europe based wholly on first-hand

Pali sources. His other major works were the editions of the Thera-Therī-gāthā (P.T.S., 1883) the Dīpavaṃsa (Text and English translation, 1897), and *Literature des alten Indien.*

Apart from these solid works, Oldenberg has many learned articles to his credit. His erudition in Vedic literature helped him to establish the relation between Pali literature and the Vedas. His original suggestion that the introduction to the Sāmaññaphala-sutta is an imitation of the Yājñavalkya-Janaka dialogue in the Bṛhadāraṇyaka Upaniṣad (IV, I), or his contention that the Pali Jātakas are akin to the Ākhyāna hymns of the Ṛgveda is an illustration in point.

Another great scholar of this period was Prof. H. Kern of Leyden. Kern's first work was an edition of the Jātakamālā of Āryaśūra (vol. I., H.O.S., 1891), a Sanskrit counterpart of the Pali Jātakas. His edition of the Saddharma-puṇḍarīka (*Bibl. Buddhica,* 1908) and its translation (S.B.E., vol. XXI, 1884) threw abundant light on the Mahāyāna, and made the study of the religious aspects of Mahāyāna Buddhism easier. In 1896 his famous *Manual of Indian Buddhism* was published in Grundriss der Indo-Arischen Philologie und Altertumskunde, or the Encyclopaedia for Indo-Aryan Research. It gave for the first time a complete, systematic and concise survey of the long history of Buddhism. Even to this day, it remains a valuable book of reference for students of Buddhism. His other monumental work, *Histoire du Bouddhisme dans l'Inde* in two volumes (1901-1903), gives a detailed account of the life of the Buddha, the Dharma and the Saṅgha. It also contains a valuable history of the Buddhist Councils and later developments of various schools and sects.

These works, however, were essentially of a preliminary character. The historical importance of the newly discovered Pali literature was soon recognized by many younger oriental scholars, the foremost of them being Prof. Rhys Davids. In 1864 he entered the Ceylon Civil Service, where he showed a keen interest in his Buddhist surroundings and learnt Pali with Y. Unnase and the Ven. Sumangala of the Vidyodaya College, Colombo. He returned to England in 1872 and associated himself with the works of Childers, Fausböll and Oldenberg. Childers' articles on Nibbāṇa had aroused much controversy and Rhys Davids gave his mature judgment on this topic in his book, *Buddhism* (1878). In 1879 he published his English translation of the Nidānakathā (Buddhist

Birth Stories) with a critical introduction on the transmigration of folklore. With Oldenberg he translated into English the volumes of the Vinaya-piṭaka referred to above. This was his first contribution to the Sacred Books of the East Series (1881-85).

In 1881 Prof. Rhys Davids was invited to give the Hibbert Lectures in America. Here he announced the birth of the famous Pali Text Society. In stately language he described his new outlook towards the field of Buddhist studies and declared, "The Sacred Books of the early Buddhists have preserved to us the sole record of the only religious movement in the world's history which bears any close resemblance to Christianity; and it is not too much to say that the publication of this unique literature will be no less important for the study of history and especially of religious history than the publication of the Vedas has already been." This new project was welcomed both in the east and the west, and many distinguished scholars came forward to help him in the noble cause. The rest of his life is indeed the life of the Pali Text Society. His sympathetic outlook for the east and his missionary zeal for Buddhist studies made him a champion in this sphere; and, until he died in 1922, he served the society for a period of forty-one years with love and devotion and helped to publish almost the whole of the Pali canonical texts, a large number of Pali commentaries, about a dozen translations and some twenty issues of a journal containing learned articles on Buddhism, and on the Pali language and literature. During this period of manifold activities, Prof. Rhys Davids himself edited a number of texts like the Dīghanikāya (1889, 1903, 1910), the Abhidhammattha-saṅgaha (1884), the Dāṭhāvaṃsa (1884) and a manual of Yogāvacara (1896). He also brought out his English translations of the Milinda-pañha (S.B.E. 1890-94) and of the Dīgha-nikāya in 1889, 1910 and 1921 (S.B.B.). His critical introductions to the individual suttas of the Dīgha-nikāya and the learned notes on them are indispensable for the study of this text. Even today this work remains a model for the translation of similar texts. His other works of general interest are many; but two, namely, *Buddhism* (1896) and *Buddhist India* (1903) won great popularity through their novelty and original research.

However, the most important of his works, his *Pali-English Dictionary,* compiled in collaboration with Dr. William Stede, is a monumental work worthy of a great scholar. With the increase of

Hermann Oldenberg
(1854-1920)

T.W. Rhys Davids
(1843-1922)

Mrs. C. A. F. Rhys Davids
(1858-1942)

new publications by the Pali Text Society, the old dictionary by Childers was found inadequate and, in 1902, Prof. Rhys Davids conceived the idea of compiling a dictionary on an international basis. The First World War, however, interrupted his scheme. Therefore, it was not until 1916 that he set to work on this dictionary with the assistance of Dr. William Stede under the auspices of the Pali Text Society. He lived to see the publication of the first three parts of this magnificent work. His eminent colleague, Dr. Stede, completed the work in 1925. Indeed, the services of Prof. Rhys Davids to the cause of Pali studies were singular and original. He was, in the words of his wife, the Max Müller of Buddhism.

Prof. Rhys Davids was perhaps excelled only by his wife, Mrs. C.A.F. Rhys Davids, who brought her mighty contributions to Pali studies as a crowning glory to her husband's work. As a life-long companion and a co-worker of her husband, she took active part in the publications of the Pali Text Society and, after the death of the founder, conducted the affairs of the society admirably in spite of adverse circumstances. Even as early as 1909, she had translated into English the Therī-gāthā (*Psalms of the Sisters*), which, for lyrical beauty, is next only to Sir Edwin Arnold's *Light of Asia* (1885). This book was soon followed by an English translation of the Thera-gāthā (*Psalms of the Brethren,* 1913). In 1917 she gave another fine English translation of the Sagāthāvagga of the Saṃyutta-nikāya. The credit for bringing the abstruse Abhidhamma-piṭaka to light also goes to her. In addition, she gave readable editions of otherwise difficult texts, such as the Vibhaṅga (1904), the Paṭṭhāna (1921), the Yamaka (1912) and the Visuddhimagga (1920). She also translated into English the Dhammasaṅgaṇi (*Buddhist Manual of Psychological Ethics,* 1923), the Abhidhammattha-saṅgaha (*Compendium of Philosophy,* 1910) and the Kathā-vatthu (*Points of Controversy,* 1915), the last two in collaboration with Z. Aung.

Apart from these editions and translations, Mrs. Rhys Davids wrote a number of original books dealing with the history of early Buddhist thought. The impact of the researches in Mahāyāna Buddhism on the one hand, and the repulsion caused by the dogmatic Anātmavāda of the southern Buddhists on the other, inspired Mrs. Rhys Davids to look for the original teachings of the Buddha, and she brought out her thought-provoking *Śākya* or *Buddhist Origins* in 1931. She was a lady of astonishing energy and wrote a number of articles. These have been collected in *Wayfarer's Words* in three volumes which were published posthumously in 1942. Whatever she wrote, she wrote with conviction and every word of her writing bears the stamp of her unique personality.

The Pali Text Society brought into prominence many illustrious scholars of the west like V. Trenckner, R. Chalmers, K.E. Neumann, Léon Feer, F.L. Woodward, R. Morris and E. Hardy. To these we can add the magnificent works of American scholars. *Buddhism in Translations* by Warren and *Buddhist Legends* by E.W. Burlingame (Harvard Oriental Series) contributed considerably to the popularization of Buddhist studies.

The labours of western scholars could not but bring about an awakening among the scholars of India. This led to the foundation of the Buddhist Text Society in Calcutta in 1892. The President of this society expressed the feeling of the whole country, when he observed at the first general meeting, "It certainly does not redound much to our honour that Buddhist literature should be more explored in the west than in the east; but I trust that this society will be the means of wiping off this standing reproach to us." The large number of valuable manuscripts scattered in various libraries in Nepal and outside were catalogued by Rajendra Lal Mitra and Hara Prasad Shastri. They also brought out *Nepalese Buddhist Literature* in 1882. In the same year, the great Indian explorer, Sarat Chandra Das, returned from his travels into the interior of Tibet, where he had collected an immense amount of material from the ancient libraries of the Sakya and Sam-ye monasteries of Lhasa. The thrilling accounts of his journey have been published in *The Journal of the Buddhist Text Society*. He gave a series of lectures on the Indian pandits in Tibet, in which he brought to light the works of Śāntarakṣita, Kamalaśīla, and Dīpaṅkara Śrījñāna or Atiśa. These lectures were later published in his *Indian Pandits in the Land of Snow*. His editions of the Avadāna-kalpalatā of Kṣemendra in 1888 (*Bibl. Indica Series*) and the Suvarṇa-prabhāsa in 1898 were substantial contributions to the study of Buddhist Sanskrit literature. He also prepared a Tibetan-English dictionary.

Sarat Chandra Das was indeed a pioneer in Tibetan studies, and was, thus, the Csoma de Körös of India. The Buddhist Text Society, which he served for many years, published many unknown texts such as the Bodhicaryāvatāra (1894) and the first few chapters of the Visuddhimagga (1893). It is notable that the society had embarked upon a novel and ingenious scheme of publishing a Sanskrit version of the Pali Visuddhimagga. It also published the Svayambhū-purāṇa and a translation of the Aṣṭa-sāhasrikā-prajñā-pāramitā by Hara Prasad Shastri. Harimohan Vidyabhusan's translation of some portions of Candrakīrti's Mādhyamika-vṛtti was also published. Moreover, the society arranged for the teaching of Buddhists from abroad in the Sanskrit college of Calcutta and thus opened a new department of Buddhist studies in India.

Another eminent Indian in this field was Satish Chandra Vidyabhusan, a pupil and colleague of S.C. Das. Dr. Vidyabhusan was a great Sanskritist and had specialized in Indian logic. In 1893 his services were lent by the Government of Bengal to the Buddhist Text Society, under whose auspices he edited a number of Buddhist Sanskrit texts. He came into contact with S.C. Das and assisted him in the preparation of a Tibetan-English dictionary (1879-1900). He was the first Indian to obtain an M.A. degree in Pali at Calcutta University (1901). In 1910 he went to Ceylon and studied for six months with the Ven. High Priest Sumangala, the Principal of the Vidyodaya College, Colombo. On his return he was appointed Principal of the famous Government Sanskrit College at Calcutta, where he carried on intensive research in Indian—particularly Buddhist—logic and philosophy.

His earlier works include editions of the Avadāna-kalpalatā (in co-operation with S.C. Das), parts of the Laṅkāvatāra-sūtra, Kaccāyana's Pali grammar with an English translation (1907), the Buddha-stotra-saṅgraha (1908) and the Nyāyabindu (1917). His greatest contributions were in the field of logic. He wrote several learned articles dealing with the works of Dignāga and Nāgārjuna. His editions of the Mādhyamika aphorisms, about 150 essays on various aspects of Buddhist philosophy, and the monumental *History of Indian Logic* (1922) are an eloquent tribute to a worthy son of India. It will not be an exaggeration to say that he revolutionized research in Buddhism by laying proper emphasis on Mahāyāna logic and philosophy.

Dr. Vidyabhusan's western contemporaries in this field were Max Müller, Bendall, Minayeff, Max Wallesser and Sylvain Lévi. Max Müller, the father of Indian studies in the west, contributed greatly to the progress of studies in Buddhism. His translations of the Dhammapada, the Sukhāvatī-vyūha and the Vajracchedikā-prajñā-pāramitā made more valuable his great work of editing the

Friedrich Max Muller
(1823-1900)

Louis de Ia Vallee Poussin
(1869-1939)

Emile senart
(1847-1928)

translations of the Pali Piṭaka. In 1889, I.P. Minayeff brought out his edition of the Bodhicaryāvatāra. This was followed by the edition (1902) and translation (1922) of the Śikṣā-samuccaya by C. Bendall. These two works helped considerably in the popularization of the excellent works of Śāntideva. Max Wallesser discovered many Tibetan works. Of his important editions reference may be made here to the commentary of Buddhapālita on the Mādhyamika-kārikā (*Bibl. Bud.*, XVI), the Aparimitāyurjñāna-sūtra (1916), and the Manorathapūraṇī (Part I, Pali Text Society, 1924). His German translation of extracts from the Aṣṭasāhasrikā appeared in 1914. He was the author of many valuable books in German, of which the following may be mentioned: *Die Buddhistische Philosophie* (1904), *Die Streitlosigkeit des Subhuti* (1917), *Die Sekten des alten Buddhismus* (1927) and *Sprache und Heimat des Pali Kanons* (1926).

The greatest indologist of this period, however, was Sylvain Lévi who rendered unique service to studies in Sanskrit Buddhism. He was endowed with a profound knowledge of the Chinese, Tibetan and Kuchean languages, which enabled him to give the first critical editions of a number of Mahāyāna texts. In 1892 he published, for the first time, the first chapter of the Buddhacarita and in the same year discovered two Chinese translations of the Milinda-pañha. In 1905 he came to Nepal, explored its libraries anew and wrote his famous *Le Nepal.* In 1907 he wrote a critical study of the Divyāvadāna and, in 1911, published fragments of Buddhist texts in the Kuchean language. In 1912 he wrote an important work on the Dhammapada recensions. During the same period he published the Śatapañcāśatika-stotra and in 1912 discovered a legend of the Karuṇā-puṇḍarīka in the Tokharian language. In 1918 he brought out with Th. Stcherbatsky the first Kośasthāna of Yaśomitra's Sphuṭārthā and in the following year he discovered the Nairātmya-paripṛcchā. He also discovered the Mahākarma-vibhaṅga, a Sanskrit version of the Cūla-kamma-vibhaṅga-sutta of the Majjhima-nikāya, and published it with its Chinese versions in 1932. During 1929-31 he published with Prof. J. Takakusu three fascicules of Hobogirin, and an encyclopaedic dictionary of Chinese Buddhist terms, which unfortunately remained incomplete on account of the Second World War.

Sylvain Lévi's greatest discovery was the Sanskrit texts of the Vijñānavāda school of Buddhism while that of the Mahāyāna-sūtrālaṅkāra was a milestone in Mahāyāna studies. His edition of this text with a French translation and an exposition of Vijñānavāda appeared in 1907. His other major discovery was the twin texts, the Viṃśatikā and the Triṃśikā with their commentaries, which he published in 1925. In 1934 he edited with S. Yamaguchi the Madhyānta-vibhāga-ṭīkā, a systematic exposition of the Yogācāra-Vijñaptivāda as contained in Vasubandhu's Bhāṣya on the Madhyānta-vibhāga-sūtra of Maitreya. These works illuminated a dark period in Buddhist history and many eminent scholars like Poussin, Stcherbatsky and others became interested in the study of Yogācāra which was the final phase of Buddhist philosophy in India.

Another great luminary of this period was Prof. Louis de la Vallée Poussin[2], a pupil of Sylvain Lévi and H. Kern. After completing his studies in linguistics at Louvain, he began his studies in oriental subjects at the Sorbonne as a pupil of S. Lévi in 1891, and in the following years went to Leyden to study the Gāthā dialect with Prof. H. Kern. Here he studied Tibetan and Chinese, which opened for him a vast field of research. In 1893 he became a Professor at the University of Ghent, where he worked for about 35 years and carried on his studies in Buddhism, particularly in Sarvāstivāda Buddhism. In 1921 he organized the Sociéte belge d'Etudes orientales. Under the title *Bouddhisme: Notes et Bibliographie,* he published learned reviews of new books on oriental subjects. He also directed the editing of *Mélanges chinois et bouddhiques,* to which he contributed several valuable articles on the Abhidharma. He contributed about thirty articles on different Buddhist topics to the *Encyclopaedia of Religion and Ethics.* Together with Ph. Colinet he edited and published *Le Museon* in which appeared some of his valuable editions like the Bodhicaryāvatāra, the Bodhisattvabhūmi, the Mādhyamakāvatāra, and the Viṃśikā-kārikā-prakaraṇa of Vasubandhu. His other notable editions are the Pañcakrama (1896), the Bodhicaryāvatāra-pañjikā (1901-1905), the Prasannapadā of Candrakīrti (1903-1913) and the Mahā-niddesa (1916-1917).

His greatest works, however, are his translations into French of the Abhidharma-kośa of Vasubandhu (1923-31) and the Vijñaptimātratāsiddhi of Yuan Chwang (1930). He was a pioneer in the study of the Sarvāstivāda school of Buddhism. Very little was known about the teachings of this school until Poussin published his epoch-making translation of the Abhidharma-kośa with

Vasubandhu's bhāṣya in seven parts. He very successfully reconstructed, on the basis of Chinese and Tibetan material, almost the whole of the text of the kārikās of the Abhidharma-kośa. The valuable and exhaustive notes with which the work is provided show that in this great scholar there was a unique combination of the linguist, the philosopher and the critic. Poussin opened the vast stores of thought that lay buried in a sealed chamber and filled a huge gap between the studies of early Pali works and the late Śūnyavāda doctrines. The publication of this work revolutionized Buddhist studies and gave rise to many controversial topics which engaged the attention of some eminent contemporaries like Mrs. Rhys Davids, Jean Przyluski and Th. Stcherbatsky. His thought-provoking *Nirvāṇa* (1925) propounded a novel view and brought severe criticism from Th. Stcherbatsky, an eminent orientalist of Russia.

Th. Stcherbatsky, like Poussin, had worked for many years in the field of Sarvāstivāda and Mahāyāna. He was a close associate of Sylvain Lévi and had in 1917 edited the Tibetan text of the Kośa and its bhāṣya with the assistance of E. Obermiller, the editor of the Abhisamayālaṅkāra-prajñā-pāramitā-upadeśa-śāstra (1929) and the Uttara-tantra (1931). In 1920 he published *Soul Theory of the Buddhists,* an English translation of chapter IX of the Kośa. In 1923 he published a learned treatise, *Central Conception of Buddhism and the Meaning of the Word Dharma.* In this masterly work he established the fact that the theory of skandha was an element of ancient Buddhism and the pivot of the whole doctrine. In criticism of Poussin's *Nirvāṇa,* he brought out his famous work, *The Central Conception of Buddhist Nirvāṇa,* which was perhaps the last word on this most debated topic. His profound study of the Kośa, the Mādhyamika-kārikā and the later works on Buddhist logic are clearly reflected in this work, which gave for the first time a complete and constructive survey of the entire Buddhist philosophy. These preliminary treatises were followed by his monumental work, *Buddhist Logic,* in two volumes in 1932. It was the first of its kind, exclusively based on the original works of such master minds as Dignāga, Dharmakīrti and Dharmottara.

In the preface to his first volume of *Buddhist Logic* he observes: "There is a widely spread prejudice that positive philosophy is to be found only in Europe. It is also a prejudice that Aristotle's treatment was final, that having had in this field no predecessor, he also had no need of a continuator." The publication of these two volumes not only removed this prejudice against Indian logic, but also crowned the vast and extensive Buddhist studies of the whole century.

Since the Pali Text Society had been publishing the Pali texts, it was not considered necessary to publish them in India, too. However, readers in India did not feel quite at home with the Roman characters in which these editions were published. There was need of a scholar with insight and inspiration who could make the Pali treasures accessible to the masses. This prime need was largely fulfilled by the late Dharmananda Kosambi, who, true to the Indian tradition, left his hearth and home in search of truth and a teacher and built up a tradition of Buddhist studies in his motherland.

His passionate zeal for knowledge and the teachings of the Buddha took him several times to Ceylon, Burma and distant parts of India. For a while he became a Śrāmaṇera in Ceylon (1902) and learnt Pali with the Rev. Sumangala of Vidyodaya College. He spent many years in Burma meditating like a true yogin. He was first discovered by Calcutta University where he served for a while in 1906, but his desire to teach Buddhism among his own people brought him to Maharashtra, where a chance meeting with Prof. J. H. Woods of Harvard University took him to America to edit the Visuddhimagga, a work which was left incomplete by the famous Warren, the author of *Buddhism in Translations.* This work he completed very successfully in 1932, although the volume was not published until 1950, long after the publication of his Devanāgarī edition of the work. For some years (1912-1918) he was Professor of Pali at Fergusson College in Poona, where certain eminent scholars of our day had the privilege of studying with him. It is through these scholars that the Pali language found a place in the schools and colleges of the Deccan, and many Pali texts were published in Devanāgarī editions.

Dharmananda Kosambi was a sincere nationalist. For some years he served the National University of Gujarat started by Mahatma Gandhi, where he wrote several works on Buddhism in Marathi and Gujarati. Some of these are *Buddhacarita, Buddha-līlā-sāra-saṅgraha, Buddha Dharma āṇi Saṅgha, Samādhi-mārga, Jātaka-kathā, Buddha-Saṅgha-paricaya, Hindi Sanskṛti āṇi Ahiṃsā* and *Bodhicaryāvatāra.* Together with a Marathi translation of the

Suttanipāta and several other works, these were all written with a view to popularizing Pali studies and enlightening the masses about the Buddha. He also made valuable contributions in the field of Abhidharma. His *Navanīta-ṭīkā* on the Abhidhammattha-saṅgaha and *Dīpikā* on the Visuddhimagga are of great help to students of Abhidharma. But the greatest contribution of this great scholar of Pali and lover of Buddhism is the Devanāgarī edition of the Visuddhimagga (1940) which was his life work.

Another scholar, the late Prof. C. V. Rajvade, who died very young at the age of 30, may also be mentioned. He was a worthy pupil of Dharmananda Kosambi. He edited, for the first time, in Devanāgarī characters the first fifty suttas of the Majjhima-nikāya, and the Hatthavanagalla-vihāravaṃsa, a small Pali text of the 13th century A.D. His Marathi translation of the Dīgha-nikāya, particularly of the first volume, shows his scholarship and critical acumen.

Professor Kosambi's contemporary, B.M. Barua, was another Indian who continued the Buddhist philosophical studies started by Dr. S.C. Vidyabhusan. Dr. Barua's first work, *The History of Pre-Buddhist Indian Philosophy,* was an epoch-making publication. Through this work he placed early Buddhism in its real perspective and countered the tendency of studying Buddhism in isolation, independently of pre-Buddhist thought. His second work, *Ājīvikas,* brought to light a powerful ancient religious movement, now extinct in its motherland. His Prakrit Dhammapada was the fruit of great literary industry. Dr. Barua also wrote many valuable works on Buddhist inscriptions and history. His *Old Brāhmī Inscriptions in the Udayagiri and Khaṇḍagiri Caves, Bhārhut Inscriptions, Aśoka and his Inscriptions and Ceylon Lectures* considerably advanced the study of the history of Buddhism.

The brilliant contributions of these eminent scholars bear testimony to the growing popularity of Buddhist literature and thought. They also point to the vitality of a culture which could command the wholehearted service of so many scholars of the east and the west.

NOTES

1. See T. R. V. Murti, *The Central Philosophy of Buddhism.*
2. See *Indian Historical Quarterly,* 1940, vol. XVI, no. 2.

Hara Prasad Shastri
(1853-1931)

Rajendralal Mitra
(1824-1991)

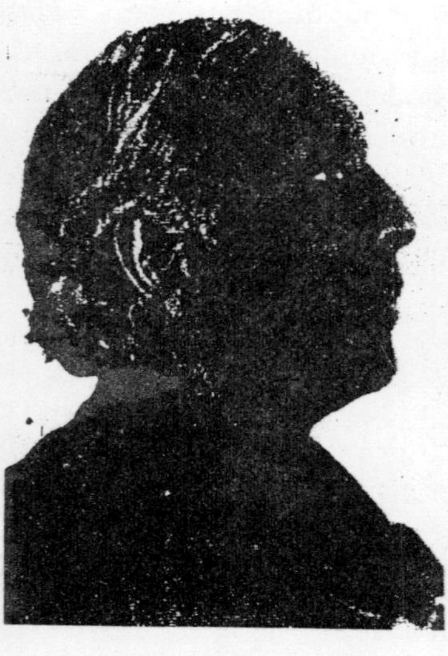

Anagarika Dharmapala
(1864-1933)

Dharmananda Kosambi
(1871-1947)

III

BUDDHISM AND JAINISM

CHAPTER 3

Śramaṇas: Their Conflict with Brāhmaṇical Society*

Background to the Conflict

The unquestioned authority of the Vedas;
the belief in a world-creator;
the quest for purification through ritual bathings;
the arrogant division into castes;
the practice of mortification to atone for sin;
—these five are the marks
of the crass stupidity of witless men.[1]

[vedaprāmāṇyaṃ kasyacit kartṛvādaḥ/
snāne dharmecchā jātivādāvalepaḥ//
santāpārambhaḥ pāpahānāya ceti/
dhvastaprajñānāṃ pañcaliṅgāni jāḍye//]

This bold diagnosis of the malady of Indian society was not pronounced by a modern rationalist but by Dharmakīrti, an eminent seventh-century Buddhist logician of Nālandā. Notwithstanding the strictures of Dharmakīrti, his five 'marks' neatly sum up the basic beliefs that characterize Hindu civilization both as it was at the time of the Buddha and as it is today, after a lapse of more than 2500 years. The first four 'marks', viz., the authority of the Vedas, the belief in a creator, the path of ritualism, and a social structure based on a system of hereditary ranks, constitute the

---

*This article was published originally in *Chapters in Indian Civilization*. vol. I, ed. J.W. Elder (Dubuque, Iowa: Kendall/Hunt Publishing Company, 1970), pp. 40-81. Reprinted with kind permission of Joseph W. Elder, editor.

four cornerstones of the brāhmaṇical schools, whereas the last, *viz.*, the path of asceticism, stands out as the chief characteristic of all the heterodox schools collectively called the *śramaṇas.* Despite their common origin, these two dominant traditions, the orthodox and the heterodox, gave rise to innumerable crosscurrents, sometimes completely losing their identity, and at other times merging in a confluence, only to re-emerge again in a new form and flow in opposite directions. The history of Indian civilization is truly the history of the mutual influence of these two traditions that resulted in the transformation of the Vedic religion of the Indo-Āryans into modern Hinduism.

It is not easy to trace the entire course of this transformation with any great certainty. But it is possible to observe the moments of their mutual impact and consequent adjustment to each other's position as reflected in the vast Indian literature beginning from the Vedas and continuing up to the writings of Mahātmā Gāndhī, who is claimed as a saint by the upholders of both the brāhmaṇical and the *śramaṇa* ideals of modern India.

Of the only two references to the word *śramaṇa* (practicer of religious exertions—from, *śram* 'to exert') in the Vedic literature, one is found in the *Bṛhadāraṇyaka Upaniṣad*[2] where it is placed side by side with *tāpasa* (practicer of religious austerities—from *tap,* 'to warm') indicating that a *śramaṇa,* like *tāpasa,* belonged to a class of mendicants. It is not clear if this word *śramaṇa* at this stage referred exclusively to a member of the heterodox orders of monks whom we meet frequently in the Pali scriptures of the *Theravāda* school of Buddhism. In the latter the compound word *śramaṇa-brāhmaṇa* is of common occurrence and definitely refers to two distinct groups of holy men, the former denoting all kinds of mendicants including the Buddhists, and the latter solely reserved for the brāhmaṇs, the lay upholders of the Vedic tradition. The brāhmaṇ mendicants are here designated by the term *tāpasa* but never by the word *śramaṇa.* In contrast, the Buddha is called a great (mahā) *śramaṇa,* and the members of his order (*saṅgha*) are referred to by the non-Buddhists as the *śramaṇas,* the sons of *Śākya.* In the Jain texts also, Mahāvīra the Jain teacher, a contemporary of the Buddha, is called a *śramaṇa,* a title by which later Hindu writers identified the ascetics of the Jain and Buddhist faith.

The Pali scriptures occasionally betray a certain animosity between the *śramaṇas,* particularly the Buddhists, and the brāhmaṇs.

But on the whole their attitude to each other was one of cordiality. In subsequent periods, however, the successes of Buddhists in converting the great emperor Aśoka and in winning for their order the support of a large number of rich merchants, traditionally the patrons of the brāhmaṇs, must have produced great hostility between them; so much so, that Patañjali (*c.* 150 B.C.) in his *Mahābhāṣya*[3] cites '*śramaṇa*-brāhmaṇa', together with 'cat and mouse', 'dog and fox' and 'snake and mongoose', as illustrations of such hostility. Centuries later, Hemacandra (12th century A.D.) himself a *śramaṇa* (a Jain monk), cites the same example in an identical context in his grammar',[4] thus emphasizing the traditional hostility between the *śramaṇas* and the brāhmaṇs that permeated medieval Indian society.

The rise of the *śramaṇas* as a dominant force in Indian life is seen in the emergence of Jainism and Buddhism as the great salvation religions in the sixth century B.C. The people who witnessed their emergence had moved a long way from their ancestors the Indo-Āryans, who had settled at least a thousand years earlier in the northwest after conquering the indigenous people of the Indus valley civilization.

The Vedas, the sacred texts of the early Āryans, had already attained the status of 'revealed' texts, and their authors had long since become 'the ancient seers'. The anthropomorphism of the Vedas, after passing through the successive stages of henotheism and pantheism, had now entered a new and possibly final stage of its development, the monotheism of the Upaniṣads. The old Vedic god Varuṇa, the mighty upholder of the moral law, had long been relegated to the position of a minor deity. Even his flamboyant successor, the warlike Indra, had been replaced by Prajāpati, the creator God, the God preeminent in the Brāhmaṇa literature, the main source of Hindu theism. The primeval self-sacrifice of Prajāpati, as narrated in the epochmaking *Puruṣasūkta*,[5] having for centuries remained a source of interminable speculation on the nature of the sacrifice and its relation to gods and men, had resulted simultaneously in uniting the gods in the concept of an impersonal *Brahman* and dividing men permanently into the division of four *varṇas* (ranks), leaving both gods and men in the hands of a sacerdotal class of priests who alone knew the magic of that cosmogonic sacrifice.

It is at this juncture in the history of India, which marks the end of the classical Vedic period and the beginning of the Upaniṣadic period, that we have the first glimpse of certain new theories, clearly identifiable with those of the later *śramaṇas,* coming into direct contact with the brāhmaṇical ideals. The heterogeneous nature of the Upaniṣadic speculations, when compared with that of the Vedas and the Brāhmaṇas, shows infusions of further elements, both social and philosophical, to an unprecedented degree. The participation of kṣatriyas like Aśvapati Kaikeya, Ajātaśatru of Kāśi, Janaka of Videha, Pravāhaṇa Jaivali, and Sanatkumāra, not as disciples but as authorities, and sometimes even as teachers of the brāhmaṇs, points to the evolution of new doctrines originating from non-brāhmaṇical sources. The Upaniṣadic doctrines of *Brahman* and *Ātman* can be consistently traced back to their original sources, viz., the Vedas and the Brāhmaṇas. But the doctrines of transmigration (*punarjanma*), action (*karma*), and emancipation (*mokṣa*), doctrines fundamental to the *śramaṇa* religions and at a later stage to all Indian religions, do not follow with equal consistency from the Vedic tradition. These were probably introduced into the main tradition by the kṣatriyas, the new teachers of the Upaniṣadic period.

One of the major Upaniṣadic passages dealing with the earliest notion of the transmigration of the soul is attributed to a prince called Pravāhaṇa Jaivali. The latter, when approached by a learned brāhmaṇ, Gautama Āruṇi, seeking instruction in this knowledge, says:

> As truly as this knowledge has never heretofore dwelt with any brāhmaṇ whatsoever, so truly may not you and your grandfathers injure us. But I will tell it to you, for who is able to refuse you when you speak thus [i.e., 'I come to you, sir, as a pupil']![6]

The doctrine of *karma* is not explicitly attributed to the kṣatriyas. Its exponent in the Upaniṣads is Yājñavalkya, the great *brahmavādin.* But his manner of expounding this doctrine in the assembly of Janaka betrays its non-brāhmaṇical origin. We quote here the relevant portion:

> 'Yājñavalkya,' said Ārtabhāga, 'when the voice of a dead man goes into fire, his breath into wind, his eye into the sun, his mind into the moon, his hearing into the quarters of heaven,

> his body into the earth, his soul (*ātman*) into space, the hairs of his body into trees, and his blood and semen are placed in water, what then becomes of this person (*puruṣa*)?'
> 'Ārtabhāga, my dear, take, my hand. We two only will know of this. This is not for us two [to speak of] in public.'
> The two went away and deliberated. What they said was *karma* (action). What they praised was *karma*. Verily, one becomes good by good action, bad by bad action.

Yājñavalkyā's reluctance to discuss the doctrine of *karma* in public (a reluctance not shown on any other occasion) can perhaps be explained by the assumption that it was, like that of the transmigration of the soul, of non-brāhmaṇical origin. In view of the fact that this doctrine is emblazoned on almost every page of the *śramaṇa* scriptures, it is highly probable that it was derived from them.

A major effect of the ascendency of the kṣatriyas and of the doctrines of *saṃsāra* (the transmigration cycle) and *karma* (action) was the decline in importance of sacrifice (*yajña*) and its replacement by asceticism (*tapas*) as a means of achieving the new aim of life, salvation (*mokṣa*) from *saṃsāra*. The ancient institution of *yajña*, the centre of the Indo-Āryan culture, around which moved the entire social and religious life of the Āryans, and which promised them abundance on earth and the worlds of fathers and gods after death, was now looked upon as a snare binding its performer ever more to the ignoble desires of life and perpetuating the cycle of endless births and deaths here as well as in heaven. Quite contrary to the spirit of the Vedas and the Brāhmaṇas, the Upaniṣads read:

> What shall we do with offspring, we whose is this soul, this world? They, verily, rising above the desire for wealth and the desire for the worlds, lived the life of a mendicant.[8]

By renouncing his abundant wealth and two dear wives, Yājñavalkya, the greatest exponent of the *Brahma-vidyā*, had, like his illustrious *śramaṇa* successor the Buddha, renounced the sacrifice, and by implication all hereditary social duties and ritualism enjoined by the Vedas.

Scores of references to ascetics variously called *muni*, *yati* and *parivrāṭ* and to their asceticism or the practice of *tapas* are to be found in the Vedic literature. The Brāhmaṇas speak of Prajāpati's *tapas* prior to the act of creation. The name Āraṇyaka (forest dweller) itself indicates a shift from sacrifice to renunciation leading towards asceticism. One of the principal Upaniṣads, the *Muṇḍaka,* while recommending the sacrifices enjoined by the Vedas, clearly warns that they are 'unsafe boats' leading to repeated births and deaths, and declares that 'by austerity (*tapas*) *Brahma* becomes built up.'[9] The brāhmaṇical theory of the four *āśramas* (stages of life) accords supreme place to asceticism in the life of a *dvija* (twice-born). The *Vaikhānasasūtras,* a post-Upaniṣadic law-book for the ascetics of the brāhmaṇical traditions, lists various kinds of ascetics and their manifold practices. It would thus appear that asceticism had become an acceptable way of life for the brāhmaṇs even before the rise of the *śramaṇas* in the sixth century B.C. It must however, be remembered that it was never accepted by the brāhmaṇs as a norm but as a concession to certain elements of the Āryan community who did not recognize the Vedic tradition. The *Atharva Veda* contains a story of Indra's killing the *yatis* (ascetics). Commenting on the word *yati,* Sāyaṇa says these are to be identified with mendicants 'devoid of the thoughts of the *Vedānta',* or 'a people belonging to the *asuras'.*[10] In the *Aitareya* and the *Pañcaviṃśa Brāhmaṇas* the same story is repeated. Here Sāyaṇa explains the term *yati* as 'people opposed to the sacrifices (*yajñavirodhijanān*), and 'endowed with rules contrary to the Vedas (*vedaviruddhaniyamopetān*).'[11] The *Dharma Śāstras*, the epics and even the Purāṇas, as will be seen below, reflect the tensions produced in the Indian society by the impact of these *yatis,* whose tradition was carried on by the *śramaṇas* in the post-Upaniṣadic period.

The concept of asceticism in India appears to go back to the prehistoric Indus valley civilization. Several seals from Harappā depict a horned god seated in the cross-legged posture of the later Indian *yogins,* surrounded by animals, which is identified by Marshall with Paśupati, Śiva of later Hinduism.[12] There are also found a few figures in terracotta of nude men with coiled hair; their posture, rigidly upright, resembles that of the latter day Jain images in *kāyotsarga* meditation.[13] The *Ṛg Veda* contains a solitary hymn that describes a *muni* (a silent one). In the words of Keith,

> He differs entirely from the Brahman student or the man undergoing consecration, for his ecstacy is not connected either with the sacrifice or with any of the rites ancillary to it or the entry of the youth into the full life of the community.[14]

He is described as girdled with the wind, his hair is long, and his soiled garments are of yellow hue. Men see only his mortal body but he

> looking upon all varied forms flies through the region of the air, treading the path of sylvan beasts, Gandharvas and Apsarasas.[15]

He knows secret desires, is a most delightful friend; he is the heaven and the light, and he drinks with Rudra a draught from the same cup. This hymn strongly suggests a close connection between these *munis* and Rudra/Śiva, the only ascetic god of the later Hindu pantheon.

Another enigmatic figure connected with asceticism is that of the *vrātya*. The *Atharva Veda*[16] refers to his standing motionless for a whole year and similar ascetic practices, and even elevates him to a cosmic power. He wanders in different directions accompanied by a harlot and a *māgadha* (a bard from Magadha, the cradle of *śramaṇa* culture) and arrives in the courts of kings as a guest. He is called a *vidvān* (a learned one), and his hosts are expressly asked not to revile him. If the host is preparing a fire-offering when a *vrātya* arrives as an *atithi* (a guest), the former should ask his permission to make an oblation. References are also made to non-*vrātyas* calling themselves *vrātyas* but bearing the name only. According to tradition the *vratyas* are Āryans living outside that community and hence fallen from pure Āryanhood. There are special rites called *vrātyastomas* which were intended for their readmission into the brāhmaṇical community. These *vrātyas*, the dissident or the renegade Āryans, with their non-Vedic practices and close connection with kṣatriyas and the people of Magadha, together with the *yatis* mentioned above, appear to be the forerunners of the later *śramaṇa* saints who also called themselves Āryans but persistently refused to conform to the Vedic scriptures and the brāhmaṇical institutions of rank (*varṇa*) and *āśrama*.

The purpose of asceticism and the austerities connected with it may have been the acquisition of magic powers similar to those that were promised by the Vedic sacrifices; but by the time of the Upaniṣads these were definitely geared towards the realization of *mokṣa*, i.e., the emancipation of the individual from the cycle of transmigration (*saṃsāra*). As the latter was the result of actions (*karma*), whether undertaken out of ignorance and thus yielding evil births, or according to the Vedic injunctions assuring heavenly states, all actions were to be renounced by a true aspirant. Since this is impossible, a search for actions or the modes of their accomplishments that did not bind one to *saṃsāra* became necessary. The birth of the Indian *darśanas* (systems of philosophy) can be traced to this single problem, the chief preoccupation of all Indian thinkers whether of the orthodox or of the heterodox persuasion.

One of the earliest attempts to resolve this problem, as is seen in the earliest Upaniṣads, was to interpret the major animal-sacrifices as of cosmic significance. The sacrificial horse in the *aśvamedha*, for instance, was not merely an animal, but represented the whole universe, the various parts of its body being identified with the diverse members of the cosmic person.[17] During subsequent periods, this led brāhmaṇical law-givers as well as exponents of the *Mīmāṃsā* school to exempt sacrificial violence from the purview of *hiṃsā*, the first of the forbidden acts for all claiming the status of an Āryan. But sacrifice was not the only act that was enjoined by the Vedas. There were other duties, flowing from the authority of the Vedic scriptures, such as the duties of *varna* (rank) and *āśrama* (stages of life), the duties devolving upon a person in paying the debts to the gods, the fathers and the teachers, which would involve manifold acts and thus perpetuate the *saṃsāra*. The Upaniṣadic seers resolved this problem by advocating the overriding nature of the knowledge of the *Ātman* (the cosmic self) over all deeds. Endowed with this knowledge, a person might engage in any and all deeds and yet may not be bound by their results. Indra, the warrior god of the Vedas, who becomes the embodiment of the *Ātman* in the Upaniṣads, while addressing Pratardana, who arrived at his abode (the heavens) by fighting, says:

> Understand me, myself. This indeed I deem most beneficient to man—namely, that one should understand me. I slew the

three-headed son of Tvashṭṛi. I delivered the Arunmukhas, ascetics, to the wild dogs. Transgressing many compacts, I transfixed the people of Prahlāda in the sky, the Paulomas in the atmosphere, the Kālañjakas on earth. Of me, such a one as I was then, not a single hair was injured. So he who understands me—by no deed whatsoever of his is his world injured, not by stealing, not by killing an embryo, not by the murder of his mother, not by the murder of his father; if he does any evil (*pāpa*), the dark colour departs not from his face (i.e., he does not become pale).[18]

Although Indra's claim to these acts is substantiated by the Vedic scriptures, it is nevertheless not the case that the Upaniṣads allow anyone with the knowledge of the *Ātman* to commit the cardinal sins with impunity. The purport of the statement, in the light of the spirit of the Upaniṣads, is that such a person endowed with the knowledge has already attained the unity with the *Brahman*, has ceased to be an individual. His actions are real only in an empirical sense; but from a transcendental point of view they are either illusions or (even if real) do not belong to him.

The illusionists, for whom all multiplicity, the operative field of all actions (*karma*), was a mere name, found their support in the innumerable passages that described the sole reality of the *Brahman,* the one, eternal and irreducible principle of the Upaniṣads. But the scriptures also spoke of the *Brahman* 'creating the universe and then entering into it as soul', thus confirming the immanent nature of this transcendent spirit. The distinction drawn here between the creator and the creation, i.e., 'between the supreme and the individual soul' led to the theism of the *Śvetāśvatara Upaniṣad,* the main source of Indian theism. Discussing the genesis of *saṃsāra* and the role human beings played in their own emancipation, the *Śvetāśvatara Upaniṣad* emphatically declares that neither time, nor inherent nature (*svabhāva*), nor necessity (*niyati*), nor chance (*yadṛcchā*), nor the elements (*bhūta*), nor heredity, nor a combination of all these are to be considered as the cause of *saṃsāra* (transmigration), and that 'the soul certainly is impotent over the cause of pleasure and pain', for 'He is the one who rules over all these causes, from 'time' to the 'soul'.[19] The Upaniṣads thus sought to resolve the problem of *karma* either by a denial of its reality or by the imposition of a supreme will that deprived the human being of any responsibility in its operation.

Even the 'Realist' Sāṅkhya, who shows a remarkable affinity with the *śramaṇas* in his unqualified rejection of both the *Brahman* (of the idealists) and the Iśvara (of the theists), failed to offer a new solution to the problem of *karma*. The *Sāṅkhya*, quite contrary to the spirit of the Upaniṣads, accepted the reality of the multiple universe (*prakṛti*) and of the multiplicity of the individual souls (*puruṣas*). Nevertheless, the school retained the basic doctrine of the Upaniṣads by transferring all actions (*karma*) to the material *prakṛti*, thus preserving the eternal and incorruptible nature of the *puruṣa*. Indeed it may be said that in subsequent periods the adherence to this one single doctrine, viz., the eternal and unchanging nature of the soul, to the exclusion of many other cherished notions of the Vedas and the Upaniṣads already rejected by the *Sāṅkhya*, became the hallmark of all brāhmaṇical schools. The *śramaṇas*, while assimilating several brāhmaṇical theories regarding matter and spirit, and a large number of practices current in the schools of *Yoga*, remained uncompromisingly opposed to this cardinal doctrine of the Vedic Āryans. It is not surprising, therefore, that at the time of their first emergence in a period immediately following the rise of *Sāṅkhya* doctrines, the *śramaṇas* appear as leaders of heterodox religions proclaiming novel theories of *karma* and *mokṣa* and above all, of the soul (*ātman*).

One of the outstanding distinctions between the brāhmaṇical and the *śramaṇa* doctrines is that whereas the former can be traced only to a body of literature of varying antiquity, the latter can be attributed to definite historical persons who flourished around the 6th century B.C. in the ancient kingdoms of Videha and Magadha. Our main sources for the history of the *śramaṇas* are not the epics like the *Rāmāyaṇa* and the *Mahābhārata*, nor the Hindu Purāṇas, the traditional sources of Indian history, but the scriptural literature of the Jains and the Buddhists, written not in Sanskrit, the language of the brāhmaṇs, but in the vernacular popular languages of Magadha, called respectively Ardhamāgadhī and Pali. Although the date of their final redaction is fairly late, the 1st century B.C. (in Ceylon) in the case of the Buddhists, and the 5th century A.D. (at Valabhi in India) in the case of the Jains, certain historical data provided by them are corroborated by the edicts of Aśoka (269 B.C. - 232 B.C.) and a large number of inscriptions of the subsequent period. These are supplemented by the traditions preserved in a large number of commentaries (*Aṭṭhakathās* and *Ṭīkās*) and chronicles like the *Mahāvaṃsa* (5th century A.D.) and the eye-witness accounts of Chinese travellers like Fa-hsien (399-414 A.D.), Hsüan Tsang (629-645 A.D.) and I-Tsing (671-695 A.D.).

Śramaṇas of Pre-Buddhist India

Traditions vary on the exact date of the Buddha's death, but it is now generally accepted that he died at the age of eighty in or around 483 B.C. A famous Buddhist text called the *Sāmaññaphala-sutta* ('Fruits of the life of a *śramaṇa*'),[20] alluding to an incident that took place towards the end of the Buddha's life, gives a fairly long account of six 'heretical' *śramaṇa* leaders, contemporaries of the Buddha himself. The dialogue takes place between the Buddha and Ajātasattu, a patricide king of Magadha, who had usurped the throne only some seven years before the Buddha's death. Ajātasattu, after pointing out the advantages derived by the ordinary house-holders from pursuing their manifold activities, asked the Buddha whether the members of his order derived any corresponding advantages, visible in this life, by following the life of a recluse (*śramaṇa*). The Buddha asked the king if he had ever approached other *śramaṇas* and brāhmaṇs with that question and wanted to know their replies. The king's answer, describing the six philosophical systems, as it follows here,[21] is our earliest and main source for the history of the *śramaṇas* of pre-Buddhist India.

1. Antinomian ethics of Pūraṇa Kassapa:
   To him who acts or causes another to act, mutilates, ...punishes, ...causes grief or torment, ...to him who kills a living creature, who takes away what is not given, who breaks into houses, who commits robbery, ...or adultery, or who speaks lies, to him thus acting there is no guilt. If with a discus with an edge sharp as a razor he should make all the living creatures on the earth one heap, one mass, of flesh, there would be no guilt thence arising, no increase of guilt would ensue. Were he to go along the south bank of the Ganges striking and slaying, ...no increase of guilt would ensue. Were he to go along the north bank of the Ganges giving alms, offering sacrifices..., there would be no merit thence resulting, no increase of merit. In generosity, in self-mas-

tery, in control of the senses, in speaking truth there is neither merit, nor increase of merit.

2. Fatalism or determinism of Makkhali Gosāla:
There is no cause, either ultimate or remote, for the depravity of beings..., or for the rectitude of beings. The attainment of any given condition, of any character, does not depend either on one's own acts, or on the acts of another, or on human effort. There is no such thing as power or energy, or human strength or human vigour. All beings are without force and power and energy of their own. They are bent this way and that by their fate (*niyati*), by the necessary conditions of the class to which they belong, by their individual nature: and it is according to their position in one or the other of the six classes (*abhijāti*) that they experience ease or pain.... There are eighty-four hundred thousand periods during which both fools and wise alike, wandering in transmigration, shall at last make an end of pain. Though the wise should hope: 'By this virtue or this performance of duty, or this penance, or this righteousness will I make the *karma* [I have inherited], that is not yet mature, mature' —though the fool should hope, by the same means, to get gradually rid of *karma* that has matured—neither of them can do it. The ease and pain, measured out as it were, with a measure, cannot be altered in the course of transmigration; there can be neither increase nor decrease thereof, neither excess nor deficiency. Just as when a ball of string is cast forth it will spread out just so far, and no further, than it can unwind, just so both fools and wise alike, wandering in transmigration exactly for the allotted term, shall then, and only then, make an end of pain.

3. Materialism of Ajita Kesakambali:
There is no such thing as alms or sacrifice or offering. There is neither fruit nor result of good and evil deeds. There is no such thing as this world or the next. There is no [benefit accruing from the service of] father or mother, nor beings springing into life without them [as in heaven and hell]. There are in the world no recluses or brāhmaṇs

who have reached the highest point, who walk perfectly, and who having understood and realized, by themselves alone, both this world and the next, make their wisdom known to others. A human being is built up of the four elements. When he dies the earthy in him returns and relapses to the earth, the fluid to the water, the heat to the fire, the windy to the air, and his faculties (the five senses and the mind) pass into space. The four bearers, on the bier as a fifth, take his dead body away; till they reach the burning ground men utter forth eulogies, but there his bones are bleached, and his offerings end in ashes. It is a doctrine of fools, this talk of gifts....Fools and wise alike, on the dissolution of the body, are cut off, annihilated, and after death they are not.

4. Atomism of Pakudha Kaccāyana:
The following seven things are neither made nor commanded to be made, neither created nor caused to be created, they are barren (so that nothing is produced out of them), steadfast as a mountain peak, as a pillar firmly fixed. They move not, neither do they vary, they trench not one upon another, nor avail as to ease or pain or both. And what are seven? The four elements—earth, water, fire and air—ease, and pain, and the soul as a seventh. So there is neither slayer nor causer of slaying, hearer or speaker, knower or explainer. When one with a sharp sword cleaves a head in twain, no one thereby deprives any one of life, a sword has only penetrated into the interval between seven elementary substances.

5. Fourfold restraint of Nigaṇṭha Nātaputta:
A Nigaṇṭha (a man free from bonds) is restrained with a fourfold self-restraint (*cātu-yāma-saṃvara-saṃvuto*). He lives restrained as regards all evil; all evil he has washed away; and he lives suffused with the sense of evil held at bay. Such is his fourfold self-restraint.

6. Agnosticism of Sañjaya Belaṭṭhiputta:
If you ask me whether there is another world—well, if I thought there were, I would say so. But I don't think it is

> thus or thus. And I don't think it is otherwise. And I don't deny it. And I don't say there neither is, nor is not, another world. [The same formula is repeated after various questions arising from Ajita's doctrine of Materialism]... to each or any of these questions do I give the same reply.

With the exception of Nigaṇṭha Nātaputta who alone speaks of 'restraint', the remaining five *śramaṇas* are adherents of doctrines which, in varying degrees, deny the moral basis of *karma* and consequently of salvation, the chief aim of asceticism. This apparent discrepancy can partly be explained by the fact that the Buddhist account is a biased one and does not give us a true picture of their rival schools. Yet the same text describes each one of them in a stereotyped manner as being:

> the head of an order (*saṃghī*); of a following (*gaṇī*), the teacher of a school (*gaṇācariyo*), well known (*ñāto*) and of repute (*yasassī*), as a ford-maker (*titthakaro*), revered by the people, a man of experience, who has long been a recluse (*cira-pabbajito*) and (*addhagato*) and well stricken in years (*vayo anuppatto*).

This is an indication of the fact that the six *śramaṇa* teachers are historical persons who had well established their position as ascetic leaders long before the advent of Buddhism. Of these, Ajita, the protagonist of materialism, might have been the forerunner of the later Cārvākas. Sañjaya, the agnostic, seems to be identical with an ascetic of that name, the original teacher of Sāriputta and Moggallāna, the two chief disciples of the Buddha. Pakudha Kaccāyana and Pūraṇa Kassapa still remain unidentified, but are often found associated with Makkhali Gosāla, the Ājīvika leader.[22] Finally, the Nigaṇṭha Nātaputta is now accepted as being identical with Mahāvīra, the last Tīrthaṅkara of the Jains.

Considerable interest attaches to the Jain term Tīrthaṅkara, for it is still used by the Jains to designate their teacher Mahāvīra (the great hero), as it was used by the Buddhists in the days of the Buddha to describe all 'heretic' *śramaṇas.* According to the Jains, a Tīrthaṅkara (literally one who makes a ford, as it were, to cross the flood of *saṃsāra)* is a person who having completely eradicated all passions (*vītarāga*) and all possessions (*nirgrantha*), and consequently having attained omniscience (*sarvajña*) preaches the norm until he enters *nirvāṇa* or emancipation from the cycle of transmigration. Such was, according to the Jains, Mahāvīra, whose claim to omniscience is also attested by the Buddhist texts. A similar claim was made, according to the Jain texts, by Makkhali Gosāla, leader of the Ājīvikas. Unfortunately, no literature of the Ājīvikas has survived, and the school itself became extinct around the 12th century A.D., leaving only a few traces of its existence in the form of short inscriptions and stray references in the literature of its rivals. By contrast, the followers of Mahāvīra called the Jains (after *jina,* a victor) have not only preserved a large body of religious and secular literature but even managed, where others failed, to survive in India, albeit as a very small minority, as the sole representatives of the ancient *śramaṇa* tradition.

The Ājīvikas

The Jain tradition depicts Makkhali Gosāla as a person of low parentage (mendicant parents) born in a cow-shed (hence *Go-Śāla*). He maintained himself by the profession of a *maṅkha,* displayer of picture-boards. Early in life he approached Mahāvīra, in the third year of the latter's asceticism, at Nalandā. Mahāvīra refused to accept him as his disciple, but the two lived together for a period of some six years. During this period, Gosāla, in imitation of Mahāvīra, became a naked mendicant and developed magic powers of great potency. He was strongly influenced by Mahāvīra's gift of prophesying and was thus confirmed in his doctrine of predetermination. The two disagreed about this doctrine, and Gosāla, humiliated by the spectacular successes of his rival, separated from Mahāvīra, and declared himself to be a Jina (a victor), a Tīrthaṅkara, and a Kevalin (possessor of omniscience). He seems to have spent some sixteen years after this event wandering in the region of the Ganges valley, proclaiming himself to be the leader of the already existing community of the Ājīvika mendicants and laymen. Towards the end of this period he settled down in Sāvatthī, a stronghold of the followers of Mahāvīra, in the workshop of a potter-woman called Hālāhalā. Here he was visited by six *disācaras* ('wandering evangelists') of the Ājīvika community, and Gosāla in consultation with them codified the Ājīvika scriptures and declared the six inevitable and predestined factors of life, viz., gain and loss, joy and sorrow, life and death. The visit of the *disācaras* and the codification of the new scriptures seems to have aroused the Jain opposition. Mahāvīra is said to have then exposed the true nature of this 'pseudo-*jina*'. This led to great disputes between the two leaders, Gosāla trying his deadly magic powers against Mahāvīra. The latter escaped unhurt, and Gosāla died shortly afterwards in the potter-woman's house repenting his evil deeds and declaring that 'he was not a jina but a cheat, and that Mahāvīra was the only true jina.'[23]

There is no means of verifying this evidently biased Jain account of Gosāla. Even the Buddhists considered the Ājīvikas as their chief rivals, given to extreme forms of self-mortification, and they ridiculed their cult of nudity and unclean habits. The purpose of such a penance to an absolute fatalist like Gosāla will always remain a riddle. It is impossible to solve it until we know his doctrine of karma.

In the teachings of Mahāvīra, the doctrine of karma is closely linked together, as in no other Indian system, with penance (*tapas*), and this must have had some bearing on his denial of Jinahood to Gosāla. In outward behaviour, such as the observance of nudity and of begging and dietary practices, the Ājīvikas and the followers of Mahāvīra show no great difference; indeed at a later time the Ājīvika mendicants appear to have been absorbed into the Jain order of monks in the south. The Ājīvika doctrine of abhijāti (six classes of mankind) shows close resemblance to the Jain doctrine of *leśyā* (psychic colour of all beings). The latter is also closely linked with the doctrine of karma, and the same may have been true of the theory of abhijāti. Finally, fatalism in a modified form is also to be found in the Jain division of living beings into two basic categories, viz., *bhavya* and *abhavya*, the former destined to attain liberation and the latter eternally subjected to the cycle of *saṃsāra*. The main difference between Gosāla and Mahāvīra would appear to be not so much in their adherence to the doctrine of fatalism and free-will, but in their advocacy of an absolutist (*ekānta*) or non-absolutist (*anekānta*) position regarding the self, karma and salvation.

The Jains

Mahāvīra, as noted above, is identical with Nātaputta (son of the Ñātṛ clan) the Nigaṇṭha (free from bonds) of the Pali canon. The Nigaṇṭhas, the present day Jains, fix the date of his death as 527 B.C., and consider him to be the last of the twenty-four Tīrthaṅkaras of the present age, his immediate predecessor being Pārśva, who is believed to have attained Nirvāṇa some 250 years earlier at the famous Pārasnath hills, in Bihar. They also maintain that the cātuyāma-saṃvara (the fourfold restraint) attributed to Nātaputta by the Pali canon was actually the teaching of Pārśva, in whose tradition Mahāvīra was born and which he reformed by adding one more saṃvara (restraint) and also by instituting a well-organized community of monks and nuns, laymen and laywomen. In view of the fact that the Pali scriptures testify to the presence of a large number of Nigaṇṭha laymen, including Vappa, an uncle of the Buddha,[24] the Jain tradition of Pārśva is now generally accepted. Scholars do not accept the traditional date for Mahāvīra's nirvāṇa, locating it instead in 467 B.C., some sixteen years after the Buddha's death.

Little is known of Mahāvīra's personal life, and the traditional biographies[25] read very much like those of the Buddha. Mahāvīra, who is also called Vardhamāna, was the son of Siddhārtha, a kṣatriya chieftain of the Licchavis, and of Triśalā, a sister of king Ceṭaka of Vaiśāli. He was born at a place called Kuṇḍagrāma, near modern Patna, in Bihar. Through his mother he was related to the major royal families of that time, particularly of Videha, Magadha, and Campā. He was, according to one tradition, married to Yaśodā, who bore him a daughter called Anojā. Mahāvīra, it is said, wanted to renounce the household stage in life early in his youth, but in deference to the wishes of his parents waited until their death; then at the age of twenty-eight he became a Jain mendicant in the tradition of Pārśva.

For twelve years Mahāvīra led a life of severe austerities, discarding even his loincloth in the second year. Henceforth he went about naked, wandering in the Ganges valley, suffering extreme privation, and practising the virtues of a great saint. In his third year he was joined by Makkhali Gosāla, who witnessed a great many miracles performed by Mahāvīra and left the latter after six years of wandering together in distant parts and among the wild tribes of Bengal and Bihar. In the thirteenth year, after a prolonged fast lasting for several weeks, Mahāvīra,

> outside the town Jṛmbhikagrāma, on the northern bank of the river Ṛjupalika, in the field of the householder Samaga, under

> a Sāla tree, in deep meditation, reached complete and full, the unobstructed, unimpeded, infinite and supreme, best knowledge and intuition, called *kevala*.[26]

He now became an omniscient:

> He knew and saw all conditions of the worlds of gods, men and demons; whence they came, whether they are born as men or animals or became gods or hellish beings, the ideas, the thoughts of their mind, the food, doings, desires, the open and secret deeds of all living beings in the whole world; the Arhat (holy), for whom there is no secret, knew and saw all conditions of all living beings in the world, what they thought, spoke, or did at any time.[27]

He was now recognized as a Jina (the victor), Sarvajña (the omniscient) and above all, a Tīrthaṅkara.

Immediately after this event, Mahāvīra, it is said, proceeded to a place in the neighbourhood where a big *yajña* was being organized by a brāhmaṇ, Somilācārya, and preached his first sermon, denouncing the sacrifice and converting eleven learned brāhmaṇs assembled there who became his chief disciples called *gaṇadharas*. Chief of them was Indrabhūti Gautama who received the master's words that were compiled at a later stage in the canons of the Jains, called the Aṅgas.

Mahāvīra spent thirty years of his life as a Tīrthaṅkara and entered *nirvāṇa* at the age of seventy-two, leaving behind him a well-organized community of Jains consisting of 'fourteen thousand monks, thirty-six thousand nuns, one hundred and fifty thousand laymen and three hundred and fifty-eight thousand laywomen'.[28]

This vast community of the *nigaṇṭhas* (Jain monks) and their *upāsakas* (lay devotees) must have included a large number of the followers of the ancient order of Pārśva. Modern Jain scholars maintain that Pārśva's community of monks observed only four vows, viz., *ahiṃsā* (non-violence), *satya* (refraining from untruthfulness), *asteya* (refraining from stealing) and *aparigraha* (renouncing all worldly possessions), included in the *cātu-yāma-saṃvara* of the Pali canon. It is held on the evidence of a late Jain text called *Uttarajjhayaṇa-sutta*[29] that the monks of Pārśva's order were not given to the practice of nudity but considered it purely optional for a Jain ascetic. Mahāvīra, it is said, introduced several major changes in the reorganization of this community. He is said not only to have introduced a fifth vow consisting of *brahmacarya* (complete celibacy), but also to have made nudity, a mark of total renunciation, a binding condition on all monks. He also instituted a special class of laymen and laywomen called *śramaṇopāsakas* ('devotees of the *śramaṇa*') who, unlike the multitude of the ordinary lay members comparable to the Buddhist *upāsakas,* undertook to observe a series of twelve vows[30] restricting their mundane activities and worldly possessions, and strove to lead a life of complete renunciation in the footsteps of the master. These *śramaṇopāsakas* were the true Jains, the dedicated supporters of Mahāvīra, who patronized only the *nigaṇṭhas* to the exclusion of all other *śramaṇas.* Ānanda, a lay disciple of Mahāvīra declares:

> Truly, Reverend sir, it does not befit me from this day forward to praise and worship any man of a heretic community or any of the devas or objects of reverence of a heretic community; or without being first addressed by them to address them or converse with them; or to give them or supply them with food and drink or delicacies or dainties except it be by the command of the king or the community or any powerful man or a deva or by the orders of one's elders or by the exigencies of living.[31]

The *śramaṇopāsakas,* with their exclusive dedication, not only maintained a large number of *nigaṇṭha* monks and nuns, but also provided the lay Jains with the necessary leadership, both in secular and spiritual matters. Even when communities of Jains were without monks, as for instance in south India in medieval times, the presence of the *śramaṇopāsakas* prevented the gradual absorption of the community into brāhmaṇical Hinduism. It was the absence of such leadership that mainly brought about the gradual extinction of Buddhist communities in India.

Despite this organization, about a century and a half after the *nirvāṇa* of Mahāvīra, the community of Jains divided into two sects on the controversial point of total renunciation. Those monks who took Mahāvīra's nakedness as purely optional maintained the practice of wearing robes made of white cloths and hence were called *Śvetāmbaras* ('white-clad'). Those who declared the master's nakedness to be not only exemplary but obligatory for the attainment of the state of a *vīta-rāga* ('the passionless'), adhered to that practice and were called *Digambaras* ('sky-clad'). According to tradition the schism took place during the reign of the Mauryan emperor Candragupta (*c.* 317-293 B.C.), who is believed to have abdicated the throne and to have accepted the vows of a *Digambara* monk. The *Digambaras* led by their pontiff Bhadrabāhu declared the *Śvetāmbaras* as apostate and condemned the scriptures compiled by them under the guidance of Sthūlabhadra as spurious.

Since then the two sects have remained indifferent to each other, the *Digambaras* insisting that the *Śvetāmbara* monks are no better than their own more ascetic householders and refusing to worship at the *Śvetāmbara* shrines with their highly decorated images of the Jinas. The *Digambara* shrines still depict their Tīrthaṅkaras as naked, but the sect has all but lost the order of monks, their place being taken by the *śramaṇopāsakas* of varying grades. By contrast, the *Śvetāmbaras* still have a large group of mendicants comparable in size to the order of monks in Buddhist countries like Ceylon or Burma. These two sects are also separated from each other geographically. The *Digambaras* are found mostly in the south of Deccan and the *Śvetāmbaras* are concentrated in the West, mostly in Rajasthan and Gujarat.

But for the sole controversy on the definition of total renunciation, the two sects remain in full agreement on all other teachings of Mahāvīra. These can be summed up in three basic terms, viz., *anekāntavāda* (non-absolutism), *karmavāda* (the doctrine of *karma*) and *ahiṃsā* (non-violence), dealing respectively with the nature of reality, the relation between matter and spirit, and the path of salvation.

The doctrine of non-absolutism follows from a basic Jain theory that a thing, i.e., an object of knowledge, consists of three things, viz., a substance (*dravya*), innumerable qualities (*guṇa*), and an infinite number of forms or modifications (*paryāya*) through which the substance passes in the infinity of time and space. In this process of constant flux, the substance is characterized by the simultaneous operation of origination (of new forms), destruction (of old forms) and permanence (of the substance itself). An object like the soul (*jīva*), for instance, is eternal since consciousness, which is its essential nature, never abandons it. But the same soul is also impermanent, since at any given moment, it must relinquish an old form while it acquires a new one. To declare, as the *Vedāntin* or the *Sāṅkhya* does, that the soul is only eternal, not subject to any change whatsoever, is an absolutist point of view (*ekānta*) that totally denies the reality of change. To declare, on the other hand, as the Buddhists did, that nothing is eternal, and that things are only series of momentary flashes, is another extreme (*ekānta*). The former denies the reality of *saṃsāra* (the cycle of transmigration), the latter fails to explain *nirvāṇa* (the state of final bliss). The Jain position takes into consideration both the substance and its modifications, and maintains that the soul is eternal from the point of view of substance and non-eternal from the point of view of modifications. It thus abandons the extremes (*ekānta*) of other schools and holds that the soul is bound as well as free when looked at from these two different viewpoints (*anekānta*).

From this unique position of non-absolutism follows the equally original Jain doctrine of *karma*. According to the Jains, a soul (*jīva*, a living being, *ātman*) is omniscient when it abides in its natural state (*svabhāva*). This is the state of freedom (*mokṣa*) in which the soul is endowed with infinite knowledge and infinite bliss.

In its unnatural state, called *saṃsāra*, the soul is also material, as it is capable of contraction and expansion, and is co-extensive with the body which it inhabits. This unnatural state of the soul has no beginning in time, nor is it the result of any outside agency like the creator of the theists, or the *Niyati* of the Ājīvikas. During this state the soul moves in the cycle of transmigration bound not only by its gross body which is visible to the eyes, but also enmeshed by a special kind of matter consisting of extremely subtle atoms. This matter, when bound with the soul, is capable of obstructing the latter's innate nature of omniscience, and is technically called *karma*. Molecules composing the organ of mind, the organ of speech and the body when activated produce vibrations in the soul. Such vibrations are technically called *yoga*. The *karmic* matter flows into the soul through the channels of activity, and this process is called *āsrava* (influx). The influx of the *karmic* matter, however, does not automatically result in a new bondage of the soul. That happens only when the soul is actuated by passions and indulges in such evil things as wrong belief, non-abstinence (from evil deeds), or negligence. Then, as a wet surface absorbs dust, there takes place the involution of the *karmic* matter with the space-points of the soul. This is technically called bondage or *bandha.* The *karmic* matter thus absorbed and united with the soul remains with it for a certain duration of time, sometimes lasting as long as millions of years and sometimes as short as a moment, at the end of which it matures and yields fruits corresponding to the passions and deeds that caused the *bandha.* The Jains divide these *karmas* into eight kinds: the knowledge-obscuring *karmas* produce non-comprehension of objects. The perception-covering *karmas* produce non-perception of objects. The feeling-producing *karmas* cause pleasant and unpleasant feelings. The faith-deluding *karmas* cause disbelief in the true nature of reality. The conduct-deluding *karmas* cause non-abstinence (want of restraint). The life-determining *karma* determines the span of life in a particular existence. The name-*karmas* decide the 'names' of such as infernal beings, human beings, celestial beings, and animals. The status determining *karmas* determine high and low status. And obstructive *karmas* stand in the way of giving, gaining and enjoyment. Thus the *karmas,* like a giant computer, take note of each and every passion and action and work out their consequences for each individual in strict accordance with the law of moral retribution without the aid or the supervision of a conscious being like a God. And when the *karmas* have yielded their respective results, the *karmic* matter disassociates (*nirjarā*) of its own accord from the soul, only to be re-absorbed by a new series of actions and passions keeping the wheel of *saṃsāra* in constant movement:

> Each soul indeed has taken in (enjoyed) successively all the molecules of matter in the entire universe and has cast them off. And each soul has been revolving innumerable times in the cycle of matter. There is no point in the entire space of the universe, which has not been the seat of birth of a soul. In this way each soul has been many times roaming, occupying all points in the cycle of space.[32]

The number of souls thus undergoing the sufferings of transmigration is infinite. Beings are led into different states, becoming celestial or human beings according to their good deeds, and infernal or animal beings through bad *karma.* But the largest number consists of beings with little or no intelligence, such as insects, moths and worms, with only four, three or even two sense-faculties, and the vast vegetable kingdom that has but one faculty, viz., that of touch. Vegetable bodies are extremely complex; some plants may be inhabited by only one individual soul; others may serve as a collective body for innumerable souls who are born together and die a common death, as also is the case with the four elements, earth, water, air and fire. The Jains, unlike people of any other religion, consider that there are countless souls that have these elements as their bodies, so that, for instance, when a match is struck, innumerable souls simultaneously spring into existence, having the flame itself as their common body, only to meet a collective death the moment the flame is extinguished.

The process of this transmigration of the soul may be without beginning, but it is not endless. For omniscience is the true nature of all these beings, including even animals, and those imprisoned in sticks and stones. Even in these states, the characteristic of the soul, viz., consciousness, is not totally lost. But the way to freedom from *karma* is not automatic as in the system of Makkhali Gosāla, in which beings are neither bound to their states by their own actions, nor will they be freed by their own will. In the teachings of Mahāvīra, there is no room for this fatalism. *Karma* is caused by passion; the removal of the latter will also remove the *karma.* Freedom from *saṁsāra* and consequently the attainment of omniscience is possible by exertion, and by one's own exertion only. This is because Jainism does not recognize a creator or an Almighty God who might intervene and save a being from the laws of *karma.* But it recognizes the existence of a number of teachers or Tīrthaṅkaras who by dint of their exertion develop their innate wisdom and realize the true nature of the self and that of the *karma.* With that saving knowledge they are able to arrest (*saṃvara*) the rise of new passions and consequently of new *karma.* With boundless energy and diligence they then apply themselves to severe penances and *yogic* practices and thus gradually succeed in loosening the grip of the accumulated *karma.* When they are entirely free from passions and from the shackles of *karma,* their innate quality of consciousness reaches the state of omniscience. Henceforth, until their life-span is completed, the Tīrthaṅkaras teach the law to the suffering world and finally pass away into the state of a pure spirit. Mahāvīra was only one of many such Tīrthaṅkaras who have appeared from beginningless time and who will also appear for all eternity. Only a few can aspire to be a Tīrthaṅkara, as the attainment of this calls for special discipline, but those who follow the path are also assured of the same state of complete liberation with the full glory of omniscience, as that of Mahāvīra.

Right faith (*samyak-darśana*), right knowledge (*samyak-jñāna*), and right conduct (*samyak-cāritra*) constitute the path to liberation. Through right faith man believes in the true nature of the soul (*jīva*), the non-soul (*ajīva*), the influx and bondage of *karma*, the stoppage and dissociation from *karma*, and liberation. Right faith is gained not only by the innate disposition of the soul that is never completely stifled by any *karma*, but also by the acquisition of knowledge from those who have fully realized it. This cannot be had from the false gods (*devas*) like Indra, Varuṇa, Agni, etc., who are clearly subject to passions and are not themselves free from the cycle of transmigration. Nor can it be had from the false scriptures (*śāstras*) like the Vedas, or the Brāhmaṇas and similar texts, that not only propound absolutist views (*ekānta*) but also enjoin such grossly irreligious acts as sacrifices involving violence that can lead only to hell. Nor can it be gained from such false teachers (*gurus*) as the brāhmaṇs who worship false gods and perform sacrifices, or from those *śramaṇas* who adhere to false doctrines and indulge in penances that are not conducive to the complete cessation of passions. A true aspirant therefore abandons all these and takes refuge in a god (i.e., a teacher) who is passionless and omniscient, in a scripture that contains his teachings, and in a preceptor (*guru*) who actively leads a life according to those teachings. All Jains worship Mahāvīra and the other Tīrthaṅkaras, but the relation between the disciple and the teacher is strictly impersonal. The famous Jain litany (*namaskāra-mantra*) has no place for an historical person, but refers only to an *arhant* (the holy), a *siddha* (the perfect), an *ācārya* (a teacher), an *upādhyāya* (a preceptor) and a *sādhu* (an aspirant). The first two have achieved omniscience and the last three are designations of Jain ascetics.

The moral basis of 'right conduct' is *ahiṃsā* (non-violence). This is achieved by the renunciation of all activities that proceed from passions such as anger, pride, deceit, and greed, and which eventually or instantly involve violence within oneself as well as towards others. All life is sacred and should not be wilfully violated; least of all those of the animals who cannot help being what they are and are but suffering the fruits of their own *karma*. Violence against the infinite number of souls with only one sense-faculty cannot be avoided; but it can be limited to the absolute minimum for a monk who has renounced all worldly activities, and it can be permitted to a householder with discretion. The Jain scriptures therefore give considerable prominence to the dietary rules for a Jain. He must not only not eat meat in any circumstances, but must also refrain from alcohol and honey. Even in his vegetarian food he must exercise further care not to eat a large variety of uneatables (*abhakṣya*)[33] which include such things as the fruits of trees of the genus ficus (Udumbara) and fruits with many seeds, to avoid a kind of 'mass slaughter', and should confine his needs to fruits, grains, and vegetables that are dry and to milk products that will not ferment.

The Vedic ancestors of the present day Hindus were evidently not vegetarians. The Upaniṣads and the *Dharma Śāstras* openly support animal sacrifices and even prescribe meat dishes as a special treat to an honoured guest, particularly a brāhmaṇ. The Buddhists had monastic rules preventing the monks only from killing the animals but not from eating meat freely offered by their lay devotees. It seems safe to conclude that the widespread vegetarianism of the present day Hindus, even in times of a crippling famine, is very much due to the influence of the Jains who not only made vegetarianism binding on their followers but even raised it to the hallmark of true Āryanhood. This preoccupation with *ahiṃsā* is again evident in the long lists of trades and professions forbidden to a Jain householder. He may not earn his livelihood from charcoal, from destroying plants, from hewing and digging, nor may he engage in trades involving milling and mutilation, the use of fire, water, alcohol or forbidden foodstuffs and slavery and animal husbandry. Under a special vow peculiar to the Jains, called *aparigraha* (non-possession) there appeared an elaborate list of possessions (such as movable and immovable properties) that a householder had gradually to renounce until he was ready to take the advanced vows of a monk entailing total renunciation of all possessions.

The limitations thus imposed on the activities of a Jain layman must have restricted the spread of Jainism to the upper and lower middle classes of the vaiśya rank. The Buddhist texts attest to the presence of a large number of kṣatriyas among the followers of Mahāvīra, himself a kṣatriya, and even boast about the conversion to Buddhism of such eminent Jain laymen as Sīha, a general of the Licchavis, and princes like Abhayarājakumāra and Asibandhakaputta. The number of such people must have been relatively small, and like many other kṣatriyas in the history of ancient India they might have been patrons of other *śramaṇas* as well as the brāhmaṇs. The latter, with a few exceptions, could hardly have embraced Jainism which not only denied the authority of the Vedas and the divinity of the Vedic gods, but also deprived the brāhmaṇs of their chief means of livelihood by condemning the sacrifices and other rituals connected with domestic sacraments. The śūdras, given as they were to professions expressly disfavoured by the Jain monks, could not have been admitted as full members of the Jain community. The class that came closest to living in accord with Jain ethics were the vaiśyas (of the merchant rank), who were the main supporters of Jainism in the days of Mahāvīra, and have remained so even to this day. The Jains did not recognize the theological basis provided by the Puruṣasūkta for the institution of the four ranks (*varṇas*), and to that extent may be said to have opposed the caste system. But the opposition, if it ever existed, was purely a theoretical one, and was in all probability restricted to a denial of the supremacy of the brāhmaṇical caste. In actual practice the Jains remained indifferent to the general social structure, and in medieval times, as will be seen below, even claimed to be the originators of the system of hereditary ranks.

As for a Jain monk, he owned nothing and, in the case of the *Digambaras,* possessed not even a loincloth. He spent his wandering life actively engaged in the exercise of severe penances conducive to the loosening of the bonds of *karma.* Prominent among these was the act of fasting which might last for days and sometimes even for weeks, a practice that survives to this day among the Jains. He must not accept an invitation to a meal nor partake of food that has been specially prepared for him. The strict dietary rules limited the houses he could approach for begging, and must have led him to emigrate from place to place in search of new patrons. He was not allowed the use of any means of conveyance nor an umbrella nor a pair of sandals to protect himself from the scorching heat. He must not bathe, nor may he use a brush to clean his teeth. Services of a barber to shave his head were forbidden: he must pluck his hair in five handfuls. Thus living a life of great hardship voluntarily undertaken, he should near the end of his days court death by fasting, and so die the death of a saint.

The Buddhists

Siddhārtha Gautama, the historical founder of Buddhism, was also born a kṣatriya, like his contemporary Mahāvīra, and was surrounded by the *śramaṇas* of his time. He also renounced the worldly life in the prime of his youth and wandered for some six years practicsing the most severe penances. But whereas Mahāvīra is said to have attained the desired goal of omniscience after twelve years of such penance, Gautama turned completely away from his austere life as is described in a famous discourse called 'The Lion's Roar':

> Because I ate so little, all my limbs became like the knotted joints of withered creepers; because I ate so little, my buttocks became like a bullock's hoof; because I ate so little, my protruding backbone became like a string of balls; because I ate so little, my gaunt ribs became like the crazy rafters of a tumble-down shed; because I ate so little, the pupils of my eyes appeared lying low and deep in their sockets as sparkles of water in a deep well appear lying low and deep;... But I, even by this procedure, by this course, by this mortification, did not reach states of further-men or the excellent knowledge and insight befitting the Āryans. What was the cause of this? It was that by these there is no reaching the Āryan intuitive wisdom which, when reached, is Āryan, leading onwards, and which leads onwards the doer of it to the complete destruction of anguish.[34]

Gautama's bold condemnation of the revered ideal of the *tapas* as non-Āryan and his subsequent return to moderation marks a great departure from the ancient *śramaṇa* tradition. From now on he was not following any but his own path, this 'Āryan middle path' through which he attained the 'supreme enlightenment'. He now not only claimed to be a 'Jina' and an 'omniscient' in the manner of Gosāla and Mahāvīra, but even claimed to be a 'master of the

Vedas', and a 'Brahmavādin'.[35] He was thus a true *śramaṇa* as well as being a 'true brāhmaṇ'.

This middle path of the Buddha is set forth in his first sermon entitled 'The Rolling of the Wheel of the Law':

> These two extremes, monks, should not be followed by one who has gone forth (from the life of a householder to the life of a mendicant). Which two? That which is, among sense pleasures, addiction to attractive sense-pleasures, low, of the common, of the average man, un-Āryan, not connected with the goal; and that which is addiction to self-torment, ill, un-Āryan, not connected with the goal. Now, monks, without adopting either of these two extremes, there is a middle course, fully awakened to by the truthfinder, making for a vision, making for knowledge, which conduces to calming (of passion), to super-knowledge (of the four truths), to awakening, to *nirvāṇa* ... And what, monks, is this middle course? It is this Āryan eightfold way itself, that is to say: right view, right thought, right speech, right action, right mode of living, right endeavour, right mindfulness, right concentration.[36]

But the middle path of the Buddha was not merely a return to a life of moderation. It was also a turning away from the interminable speculations regarding problems of the self, problems that were central to all mendicants, whether of the *śramaṇa* or of the brāhmaṇical persuasion. These speculations ranged from the absolute idealism of the Upaniṣads that affirmed a theory of an eternal self to the uncompromising materialism of Ajita propounding total annihilation of the soul after death. Between the two poles lay a large number of doctrines such as the Anekāntavāda of the Nigaṇṭhas and the Niyativāda of the Ājīvikas. These holy men, the Buddha said, proclaimed themselves to be free from all possessions, but were possessed by their dogmas; they professed to be free from attachments, but were actually addicted to the intellectual luxury of speculation. The Buddha, having climbed 'the peak of wisdom' had seen these people caught in their self-woven 'net of *Brahma*' (*brahmajāla*), lost in what he boldly called a thicket, a wilderness, a puppet-show, coils and fetters of speculations.[37] He did not subscribe to any of these dogmas and, as he explained to his desciple Māluṅkyaputta, did not care to pronounce an answer on any of the questions raised:

> The religious life, Māluṅkyaputta, does not depend on the dogma that the world is eternal; or that the world is not eternal; it does not depend on the dogma that the world is finite or that the world is infinite; it does not depend on the dogma that the soul and body are identical, or that they are non-identical; it does not depend on the dogma that the Buddha (since he has brought an end to *saṃsāra*) exists after death or does not exist after death. Whether this dogma obtains or that, there still remain birth, old age, death, sorrow, lamentation, misery, grief and despair, for the extinction of which in the present life I am prescribing.[38]

He might well have pronounced a dogma or elucidated a metaphysical point like the other 'saints', had this been conducive to the extinction of the *saṃsāra.* But such was not the case:

> I have not elucidated, Māluṅkyaputta, that the world is eternal... or that the saint does not exist after death, because Māluṅkyaputta, this profits not, nor has it to do with the fundamentals of religion, nor does it tend to aversion, absence of passion, cessation, quiescence, supreme wisdom and *nirvāṇa,* therefore have I not elucidated it.[39]

This was a most radical departure from all existing notions of a teacher and of a 'Supremely Enlightened Person'. One of the few non-Buddhists who were able to perceive this extraordinary difference between the Buddha and the other teachers was Aggika Vacchagotta, evidently an ascetic of a brāhmaṇical order, who asked a pointed question: 'But has Gautama any theory of his own?' The answer Vacchagotta received was short and emphatic: 'The tathāgata (truthfinder), O Vaccha, is free from all theories.'[40]

If the Buddha did not subscribe to any dogmas and condemned them all as being irrelevant to the leading of a holy life, how did he account for the 'right view' (*sammā diṭṭhi*), the first and foremost of the eight constituents of the Āryan middle path? The middle path of the Buddha was not one more path, nor was the right view one more view; it was the very cessation of all views:

> The world, Kaccāyana, is for the most part attached to two

> (propositions)—existence as well as non-existence. 'That everything exists (substantialism)' is, Kaccāyana, one extreme; 'That everything does not exist (nihilism)' is another. Not accepting either of these two extremes, the Tathāgata proclaims the truth (*dharma*) from the middle position: conditioned by the ignorance (*avidyā*) are the constructions (*saṃskāra*); the stopping of the constructions is from the utter fading away and stopping of the ignorance...[41].

All things in the realm of subject and object (matter, sensations, perceptions, predispositions and consciousness) are conditioned and consequently are impermanent (*anitya*), ill (*duḥkha*) and devoid of self (*anātma*—devoid of an abiding principle such as the *Ātman*). Ignorance (*avidyā*) of the true nature of things leads beings to seek permanence in what is momentary, ease in what is essentially associated with suffering, and identity in what is devoid of a 'self'. These perverted views lead one to the formulation of one or another of the theories, either of substantialism or nihilism, driving them to undertake different kinds of rites and rituals ending in self-indulgence or in self-mortification. This can only result in frustration and further vain searches after new dogmas and new practices, binding the person to an endless cycle of births and deaths:

> Monks, it is by not awakening to, not penetrating the four Āryan truths that there is thus this long faring-on and running-on both for me and for you...[42]
> Incalculable, monks, is the beginning of this faring-on. The earliest point is not revealed of the running-on, the faring-on, of being hindered by ignorance, fettered by craving...[43]

However, one can discard the perverted views by the understanding of the true nature of things; then all constructions are ended and the mind is released from the 'entire mass of suffering' (*dukkhakkhandha*).

A belief in the efficacy of *karma* and the cycle of *saṃsāra* is necessary for the undertaking of a holy life, but freedom of mind from all other preconceived ideas of the self and the *Brahman* was the prerequisite of one who wished to follow the path of the Buddha. The Buddha replaced all elaborate rites and painful penances by a simple and straightforward method and exalted it as

> the one and only path leading to the purification of beings, to passing beyond grief and lamentation, to the dying out of all ill and misery, to the attainment of right method, and to the realization of *nirvāna*.[44]

This path consisted of 'a steady alertness of inward vision' (*satipaṭṭhāna*) directed to the contemplation of the true characteristics (*anitya, duḥkha, anātma*) of the body, of the feelings, of the mind, and of the content of consciousness. Endowed with this mindfulness,

> the instructed disciple disregards material shapes, disregards feeling, disregards perceptions, disregards constructions, disregards consciousness; by disregarding he is passionless; through passionlessness he is freed; in freedom, the knowledge comes to be: I am freed, and he has fore-knowledge: destroyed is birth, lived is the holy-life, done is what is to be done, there is no more of being such and such.[45]

Śramaṇa and Brāhmaṇical Conflicts

Although the middle path was condemned by the Nigaṇṭhas and the Ājīvikas as a life of 'abundance', it soon found acceptance from the traditionally moderate ascetics of the brāhmaṇical Order. Foremost among these were a group of a thousand *jaṭilas* (matted hair ascetics) of Gayā practising penances in a fire-hall (*aggi-śālā*).[46] According to the Pali canons these were won over by the Buddha by a display of superior psychic powers. The abandoning of the 'sacred fire' by these revered *jaṭilas* and their public acknowledgement of the Buddha as their new teacher in the presence of the king of Magadha must have had a profound effect on the populace in general and on the rich and well-to-do merchant class, the mainstay of all ascetics. The state of unfailing mindfulness of which the Buddha spoke was not easy for a man of the household given to the pleasures of the senses, to ill-will, to sloth and torpor, to flurry and worry, and above all to the endless series of rites and rituals. The Buddha's path was essentially for a recluse who had, like the Buddha, rid himself of all possessions and had voluntarily accepted a life free from all wordly responsibilities, a life of a 'homeless wanderer'.

> Full of hindrance is household life, a path for the dust of passion. Free as the air is the life of him who has renounced all worldly things.[47]

Many hundreds of young men in the prime of their youth abandoned their professions and homes to assume the yellow robes of a monk. The sight of these new and young ascetics must have caused a great commotion in a society dedicated to the service of parents, stability of family life, and above all to the preservation of the ancient traditions of *varṇa* and *āśrama*. The Pali scriptures themselves have preserved for us the immediate reaction of a society so ruthlessly shaken by the new movement:

> Now at that time very distinguished young men belonging to respectable families of Magadha were leading holy lives under the Lord.
> People looked down upon them, criticised and disparaged them saying: 'The recluse Gotama [Gautama] wants to make (us) childless, the recluse Gotama is bent on making (us) widows, the recluse Gotama gets along by breaking up families.'[48]

The Buddha's reply to this accusation was one of calm indifference:

> Verily great heroes, truthfinders,
> lead by what is true *dhamma* [*dharma*].
> Who would be jealous of the wise
> led by *dhamma*?[49]

Asceticism was not unknown to the Indians: nor was the sight of a mendicant a novelty. The *āśrama* (stage of life) of the *sannyāsin* (a wandering ascetic) was long accepted as a natural aim of life and was resorted to by the pious towards the end of a fruitful household life (*gṛhasthāśrama*). During the state of householder, a person, at least of the higher ranks, discharged his duties towards his parents, saw his sons well established in their professions, performed the required sacraments enjoined by the scriptures and tradition, and prepared himself for the final stages of retirement and renunciation. The break from normal life was gradual, since, in the stage of retirement to the forest (*vānaprastha*) he would still be accompanied by his wife and they would lead together a life of chastity and poverty subsisting on the fruits gathered freely or on the gifts gratefully provided by their kith and kin. Complete renunciation (*sannyāsa*) came only at the end of this long active life, when a man was fairly advanced in age, and was then considered to have earned the privilege of leading a solitary life free from all family duties and subsisting entirely on the 'country's alms-food' (*raṭṭha-piṇḍa*).

It is not possible to determine the period at which this graduated system of the *āśramas* came to be accepted as an ideal for the upper strata of Indian society. It appears to have evolved by the time of the Āraṇyakas as a result of an integration of the brāhmaṇical institution of *yajña* with the *śramaṇa* tendencies of renunciation and asceticism. A proper execution of the duties of one's position and the performance of sacrifices and sacraments were dependent on a stable family life. A person who after completing his student life (*brahmacaryāśrama*) either refused to marry or who prematurely abandoned his household was anti-social and was treated as a vagabond or at best a beggar, deserving only food given as charity. Now and then, no doubt, there would appear among these a person of rare spiritual awakening who, like Gautama the Buddha, might be treated as an exception to the rule and be given the honours due to a person of the *sannyāsin* stage. The Buddhist scriptures are fully aware of this:

> While he was still a young man, without a grey hair on his head, in the beauty of his early manhood, he has gone forth from the household life into the homeless state...though his father and mother were unwilling, and wept, their cheeks being wet with tears, nevertheless he cut off his hair and beard, and donned the yellow robes, and went out from the household life into the homeless state....[50]

But Gautama was not seeking only his own emancipation: he was a 'Buddha'; he was determined to show the way to thousands of others and was not to be stopped by worldly considerations of a stable society or by the tears of the wailing wives who rightly accused him of driving them into a forced widowhood and involuntary childlessness. For them also the Buddha, after great hesitation, opened the gates of freedom by founding an order of nuns. This new order was admittedly subordinated within the order of monks, but the sisters were declared to be equals in the spiritual progress towards *nirvāṇa*.

In advocating a life of homelessness not only for a handful of extraordinary individuals, but almost as a norm for all men and women so inclined, the Buddha had shaken the very foundations of a society built on the concept of the four *āśramas*. In repudiating the Vedas and the wisdom of their metaphysical speculations, the divinity of the Vedic gods and the efficacy of the sacrifices offered to them, the Buddha had already challenged the sources of orthodox brāhmaṇism. With his new band of young and ardent followers, drawn mostly from a stratum of society that not only enjoyed but even conferred social status, he now questioned the claims of the brāhmaṇs to a position of superiority over the other three ranks. To those who claimed that 'only brāhmaṇs are pure, not non-brāhmaṇs,'[51] the Buddha pointed out that 'the brāhmaṇ women have their periods, conceive, give birth, and suck,'[52] thus emphasizing that the brāhmaṇs too belong to the species of human beings. To those who relied on the scriptural authority (of the *Puruṣasūkta*) for their superior origins and maintained that 'only brāhmaṇs are sons of Brahmā, born of his mouth, born of Brahmā, heirs of Brahmā...', the Buddha pointed out that 'in some of the adjacent districts there were only two castes—masters and slaves, and that a member of the one can become a member of the other,'[53] suggesting thereby that the distinctions of rank were man-made and were not of a divine origin. Even supposing that the Brahmā of the scriptures did exist, the Buddha questioned whether brāhmaṇs, blinded by passion and pride in their own birth, and shackled with wives and possessions, would ever achieve union with Brahmā. He suggested rather that such union was more likely to be granted to Buddhist monks of humble birth, perhaps even of low rank, who had managed to clear the obstacles of anger and malice, and had attained self-control and purity of mind.[54] The Buddha was indifferent towards the social implications of rank but was emphatic in repudiating its spiritual implications; for he insisted that a man's spiritual status and destiny were determined not by family and birth but by his own character and actions (*karma*).

The Pali scriptures emphasize that individual brāhmaṇs, thus confronted by the Buddha's invincible logic, were converted to Buddhism and even became zealous supporters of his cause. But the brāhmaṇical society at large, led by the learned lawgivers, the upholders of the ancient Vedic tradition, appear to have been alarmed by his bold views and still bolder utterances addressed primarily to the young and resourceful members of the kṣatriya and vaiśya ranks. A sudden defection from orthodoxy of thousands of young and able members of a stable society—according to the Pali chronicles[55] the number of monks expelled by Aśoka in purifying the order alone amounted to 60,000—whether under the pressures of unstable political conditions or of controls exercised by an outdated priestly class, would not be overlooked even by those who held the most liberal attitudes towards the reorganization of that society. The defection here was not from one rank or one profession to another; it was to a new class of organized monkhood which, while it was contemptuous of the orthodox disciplines of *āśrama* and *varṇa,* could not offer a feasible alternative, its preoccupation being exclusively with the ideal of individual salvation. A new balance had to be struck between the interests of society and individual, between the ideals of social stability and of individual salvation, between action and renunciation. The *Dharma Śāstras* (like the codes of law enunciated by Viṣṇu, Yājñavalkya and Manu), and the great epics, the *Rāmāyaṇa* and especially the *Mahābhārata,* show unmistakable signs of this awareness and a new motivation behind their vigorous attempts to fortify the battered foundations of the old society.

The main point of the Buddha's criticism that the brāhmaṇs themselves had fallen from the ancient disciplines of austerity and restraint was not, it seems, lost on the compilers of the *Dharma Śāstras.* In defining the duties and the privileges of the different ranks, the lawgivers henceforth set very high standards for brāhmaṇs, admonishing them all to lead a life of voluntary poverty, dedicated to the study of the Vedas and the performance of sacrifices. While the lawgivers recommended to them the third and the fourth *āśramas* (of retirement and renunciation), they also reminded them that 'a twice-born man who seeks final liberation, without having studied the Vedas, without having begotten sons, and without having offered sacrifices, sinks downwards.'[56] Although addressed to the brāhmaṇs, the warning was equally or even more pertinent to the two lower ranks, especially the kṣatriyas, to which the Buddha had belonged and from which had come a large number of his 'young ascetics', the rebels against the *āśrama* discipline. Under the heading of *rāja-dharma* (duties of a king) the lawbooks dwell at length on the sacred duties of a kṣatriya to his kingdom, to his subjects, to the Gods and the brāhmaṇs, and above all to the proper maintenance of the orders of *varṇa* (rank) and *āśrama*. Chapter after chapter of the *Mahābhārata* are filled with spirited admonitions to Yudhiṣṭhira (the eldest of the five Pāṇḍavas) not to yield to an unmanly and premature desire of 'renunciation' after winning a bloody war in the cause of justice. The author for the *Mahābhārata* in this connection reminds him of a famous discourse that took place between King Janaka of Videha (the *brahmavādin* of the Upaniṣads) and his queen when her Lord too was resolved to abandon his kingdom in order to lead a life of mendicancy. Reading between the lines, the discourse is an impassioned plea by the lawgivers to desist from the Buddha's path and a call for the restoration of the duties of *varṇa* and *āśrama*:

> Casting off wealth and children and wives and precious possessions of various kinds and the established path for acquiring religious merit and fire (sacrifice) itself, King Janaka shaved his head (and assumed the garb of a mendicant). His dear spouse beheld him deprived of wealth, installed in the observance of the vow of mendicancy,...and prepared to subsist upon a handful of barley fallen off from the stalk. Approaching her lord, at a time when no one was with him, the queen, endowed with great strength of mind, fearlessly and in wrath, told him these words fraught with reason: Why hast thou adopted a life of mendicancy, abandoning the kingdom full of wealth and corn? A handful of fallen off barley cannot be proper for thee!...With this handful of barley, O king, shalt thou succeed in gratifying the guests, gods, *ṛṣis* and *pitṛs*? Alas, abandoned by all these, viz., gods, guests, and *pitṛs*, thou leadest a life of wandering mendicancy, O king, having cast off all action! Thou wert, before this, the supporter of thousands of brāhmaṇs versed in the three Vedas and of many more besides! How canst thou desire to beg of them thine own food today? Abandoning thy blazing prosperity, thou castest thine eyes around like a dog (for his

food)! Thy mother hath today been made sonless by thee, and thy spouse, the princess of Kośala, a widow! These helpless kṣatriyas, expectant of fruit and religious merit, wait upon thee, placing all their hopes on thee! By killing those hopes of theirs, to what regions shalt thou go, O king, especially when salvation (*mokṣa*) is doubtful and creatures are dependent on actions? Sinful as thou art, thou hast neither this world nor the other, since thou wishest to live, having cast off thy wedded wife?...How couldst thy heart be set on that mode of life which recommends an earthen pot, and a staff, and which forces one to abandon his very clothes and which permits the acceptance of only a handful of barley after abandonment of everything? If, again, thou sayest that kingdom and a handful of barley are the same to thee,...then why dost thou abandon the former! If, again, a handful of barley becomes an object of attachment with thee,...then who am I to thee, who art thou to me, and what can be thy grace to me? If thou beest inclined to grace, rule then this earth! They that are desirous of happiness but are very poor and indigent and abandoned by friends may adopt renunciation. But he who imitates those men by abandoning palatial mansions, acts improperly, indeed.... In this world, the food that is given by a charitable person is the sure support of the pious. If, therefore, the king does not give (food), where will the pious that are desirous of salvation go? They that have food (in their houses) are householders. Mendicants are supported by them. Life flows from food. Therefore, the giver of food is the giver of life. Coming out from among those that lead a domestic mode of life (*gṛhasthāśrama*), mendicants depend upon those very persons from whom they come. Those self-restrained men (of family), by doing this, acquire and enjoy fame and power.... They who, casting off the three Vedas, their usual occupations, and children, adopt a life of mendicancy by taking up the triple-headed crutch and the brown robe, are really persons of little understanding.... Therefore, O king, keeping thy passions under control, do thou win regions of bliss hereafter by supporting them that are truly pious amongst men of matted locks or clean-shaven heads, naked or clad in rags, or skins or brown robes! Who is there that is more virtuous than he who maintains his sacred fire, who performs sacrifices with presents of animals and *dakṣiṇā* (sacrificial fee), and who practices charity day and night?[57]

These words of the wife of Janaka might as well have been uttered by Yaśodharā, the deserted wife of Gautama, to her Lord. They are reminiscent of the outbursts recorded in the Pali scriptures of an enraged society whose youth had set its face against the established order. They also echo the words of the *Bhagavad Gītā,* addressed by Lord Kṛṣṇa to Arjuna, the hero of the *Mahābhārata,* not to relinquish the duties of his martial rank, nor to find an escape in a life of renunciation, but to engage manfully in the task of fighting a righteous war. But the call upon Arjuna was not made by a commander in a battle field, but by a spiritual counselor, and according to the *Gītā,* by a person divine, who was urging him not to indulge in an act of self-aggrandizement, but to participate in that cosmic phenomenon with the humility of a saint who had resigned himself to the superior will of a divine principle.

Śramaṇa and Brāhmaṇical Modifications

The *Gītā* sought to resolve the age-old dilemma of action (*karma*) and renunciation (*sannyāsa*), produced by the mutually conflicting philosophies of the brāhmaṇs and the *śramaṇas,* through a new synthesis called the *karma-yoga* (disinterested action), a Hindu 'middle path' as it were, which steered clear of the excesses of both. The *Gītā,* despite its brāhmaṇical origin, comes out rather vehemently against the professional priests, the traditional supporters of action. It calls these mere reciters of the Vedas, men 'who are robbed of insight by that (speech),' the 'undiscerning men [who] utter, who take delight in the words of the Veda...saying that there is nothing else,' men 'whose nature is desire, who are intent on heaven,' and whose actions are 'replete with various (ritual) acts aiming at the goal of enjoyment and power,' yielding rebirth only as its fruit.[58] But the 'salvationist' who followed the other extreme was equally 'deluded':

> Not by not starting actions
> Does a man attain actionlessness,
> And not by renunciation alone
> Does he go to perfection.
>
> For no one even for a moment
> Remains at all without performing actions;

For he is made to perform action willy-nilly,
Every one is, by the strands that spring from material nature.

Restraining the action-senses
Who sits pondering with his thought-organ
On the objects of sense, with deluded soul,
He is called a hypocrite.[59]

Neither 'action' nor 'renunciation', but 'disinterested action' is what the *Gītā* prescribes for salvation:

But whoso the senses with the thought-organ
Controlling, O Arjuna, undertakes
Discipline of action with the action-senses,
Unattached (to the fruits of action), he is superior.
Perform thou action that is (religiously) required;
For action is better than inaction.[60]

In advocating 'disinterested action', the *Gītā* had achieved a major objective of the brāhmaṇical revival, viz., the consolidation of the *āśrama* and *varṇa* discipline. It had categorically rejected the path of mendicancy as practised by the *śramaṇas*, and had at the same time devised a way of achieving salvation through the very duties of one's social position, not through relinquishing these duties. The *śramaṇa* path, the argument ran, was impracticable because a state of complete inactivity was inconceivable, and was also irrelevant, since it was desire (*kāma*) and not action (*karma*—performance of socially-prescribed duties) itself that stood in the way of salvation. As the latter did not depend on any particular mode of action, such as a brāhmaṇ's or a śūdra's, but solely on the elimination of desire, a change in one's actions or profession was completely unwarranted, could even be considered harmful to oneself as well as society.

The new theory that all ranks (*varṇas*) were equal in the path of salvation was certainly a most revolutionary one, and might reasonably be attributed to the impact of the *śramaṇa* movements, particularly of the Buddha. But while it granted this equality, the *Gītā* did not fail to emphasize that the duties of one's *varṇa* were obligatory and were not at the disposal of human will. The duties of each individual were defined by the lawbooks according to his rank (*varṇa*), which was determined on the basis of his inherent nature (*prakṛti*) by the creator Himself.[61] The Lord had set the wheel of creation in motion by apportioning the duties of all men, and also those of the gods, and it was the bounden duty of all to keep the wheel turning.[62] Performance of the duties of one's own rank, when undertaken with disinterestedness, was itself an act of worship, and thus rendered a man worthy of the Lord's grace which alone released him from the cycles of transmigration.

To a society that could neither comprehend the impersonal absolute of the Upaniṣads, nor bear the call of the *śramaṇas* for renunciation, a promise of salvation not only to brāhmaṇs and kṣatriyas, but also to 'women, vaiśyas and śūdras', by a simple method of devotion to a personal deity must have come as a great relief, further stabilizing the duties of rank and *gṛhasthāśrama*. The *śramaṇa* orders had human beings as their founders who claimed omniscience and, being atheists, could become the centre of cults that excluded all other gods and saints. By contrast, brāhmaṇical thought was fundamentally theist, yet the Vedic pantheon had fallen into disuse, and the individuality of the gods was lost in the panoply of ever more elaborate sacrifice and in the abstractions of Upaniṣadic metaphysical thought. The priesthood could scarcely usurp the divine status of the gods they were bound to serve, especially since their hereditary social position was being undermined by the rising *śramaṇas*.

In adopting Kṛṣṇa, the deity of a popular and local cult, orthodox brāhmaṇism was clearly fulfilling a need for a personal God and saviour. Brāhmaṇs declared him to be an incarnation of Viṣṇu (an exalted deity of the Vedic hymns, in the Brāhmaṇa literature the highest personification of the sacrifice) and attributed to him identity with the Upaniṣadic Absolute.[63] The device of assimilation by which, during the Vedic period, all gods were identified with the great god Prajāpati, was once more applied, this time on a far wider scale, to absorb all Vedic and non-Vedic cults and deities, into a single cult of Viṣṇu personified on earth as Kṛṣṇa, the Lord of the *Gītā*. Probably at the same time or even earlier, the other great non-Vedic deity Śiva, together with the cult of *liṅga*-worship associated with him, was identified with the Vedic god Rudra and accepted into brāhmaṇism. In its struggle for survival, orthodox brāhmaṇism had revised old theories, had adapted itself to meet the challenge of the *śramaṇas,* and, in the process of this transformation, had entered a new world, the world of Vaiṣṇava and Śaiva Hinduism.

It was not long before Buddhism too was subjected to a similar transformation. Despite its anti-theistic dogma, shared by many other *śramaṇa* schools, early Buddhism had all the ingredients of a theistic cult. Unlike the Jains who made no distinction between a Tīrthaṅkara and an ordinary Arhant (one who had attained liberation) as far as the attainment of omniscience was concerned, the Buddhists had set different standards of perfection for a Buddha and his Arhant disciples. The Buddha, in addition to being an Arhant, was also omniscient, a distinction denied to an ordinary Arhant. He was believed to have been endowed with marks of divinity, such as the thirty-two marks of a *mahāpuruṣa* (a great being) and was entitled to be called a *bhagavat,* an appellation normally reserved for divinities like Viṣṇu and Kṛṣṇa.

The distinction does not seem to have mattered during the lifetime of the Buddha, but it soon developed a doctrine of two *bodhis* (enlightenments), that of the Buddha, superior and perfect, and that of the Arhants, inferior and limited. In the subsequent period, towards the beginning of the Christian era, it led to the emergence of two rival schools, respectively called *Mahāyāna* (the great vehicle) and *Hīnayāna* (the little vehicle). The latter was a derogatory title given by the *Mahāyānists* to the schools of the arhants (one of these called the *Theravāda*—the school of the elders—survives now in Ceylon, Burma, Thailand, Laos and Cambodia) for their 'egotistic' and 'selfish' search after their own salvation (*nirvāṇa*) devoid of the full glories of the Buddhahood. The protagonists of the *Mahāyāna* even doubted the spiritual status of the *arhants* and challenged their claim to *nirvāna.* The belief of the *arhants* that they had brought an end to the cycle of transmigration was erroneous, since they had yet to attain omniscience, without which the task of an aspirant was incomplete. The *Mahāyānists* did not deny the fact that the path of the arhant was also preached by the Buddha; but they maintained that it was not final, and that the Buddha had preached it as a means (*upāya*) of preparing those of low aspiration for a higher purpose; it must be discarded in favour of *Mahāyāna,* the path of the Buddha.

The path of the Buddha was however a long one, not to be completed within a few years or even within a lifetime. According to this new Buddhology, Gautama, in the distant past, in the presence of Dīpaṅkara, a mythical Buddha of 'incalculable aeons' ago, had resolved to be a saviour and had deliberately chosen the career of a *Bodhisattva* (an aspirant Buddha). With his boundless compassion for the suffering world, he had then spent 'countless' births cultivating such 'perfections' (*pāramitās*) as charity, morality, forbearance, energy, meditation, and above all, the 'perfection of wisdom' (*prajñā-pāramitā*), by virtue of which he had in his last birth, as Gautama, attained to omniscience and had set the 'wheel of law' moving. The *Theravādins* and others of the older school condemned the doubts about arhant's status as a heresy but welcomed wholeheartedly the greatness now accorded to their master. They accepted a large number of mythical Buddhas under whose guidance Gautama pursued his career of a bodhisattva. They even produced a massive literature consisting of hundreds of edifying stories (Jātakas and avadānas) illustrating his heroic and noble deeds. But the orthodox Buddhists were not to succeed in preventing this myth from developing further in a theistic direction. The *Mahāyānists* or their forerunners the *Mahāsaṅghikas* were convinced that the Buddhas belonged to a different order of beings altogether; they were not human beings but were descendents of a spiritual lineage (*Buddha-vaṃśa*), who, although perfect, roamed the earth out of compassion. The *Mahāvastu,* a sacred text of the *Lokottaravādin* (Transcendentalist) Buddhists, declares the Buddha to be a transcendental being voluntarily subjecting himself to repeated births in order to save the suffering world of gods and men:

> The Buddhas conform to the world's condition, but in such a way that they also conform to the traits of transcendentalism.
>
> Although the Buddhas' body is not due to the sexual union of parents, yet the Buddhas can point to their fathers and mothers. This is mere conformity with the world.
>
> From Dīpaṅkara onwards, the Tathāgata is always free from passions. Yet (the Buddha) has a son, Rāhula, to show. This is mere conformity with the world.[64]

The theme was carried to its logical conclusion when *Saddharma-puṇḍarīka,* a fully-fledged *Mahāyāna* text, declared categorically that even the *nirvāṇa* (i.e. the death) of Gautama at the end of his cycle of transmigration was not real but only an enactment staged by him as a means (*upāya*) of preaching the law.[65] Even the multiplicity of the Buddhas was no more than a device, since in reality there was but only one undifferentiated principle, called the *Dharmakāya*, the *Śūnya* (the void) or the ineffable about which Gautama had refused to formulate any theories. This *Dharmakāya* manifested itself from time to time in a spontaneous manner, assuming different names such as a Dīpaṅkara or a Gautama, and it would continue to do so at all times in future. This *Dharmakāya*, the principle corresponding to the Upaniṣadic absolute, was the real nature of the Buddhas, as well as of the *bodhisattvas*, and indeed of all beings.

In treating the various Buddhas as emanations of a transcendental principle, the *Mahāyāṇists* had clearly accepted the doctrine of *avatāra* (human incarnation of the deity) so successfully applied by the Vaiṣṇavites in propagating their new cults. As in the case of Kṛṣṇa, the Buddhists too devised two bodies (apart from the *Dharmakāya*) for the Buddhas, a resplendent one (*sambhogakāya*) which was manifest only to the bodhisattvas, and a human body (*nirmāṇakāya*) which the Buddhas could assume at their will to lead such life as Gautama did 'in conformity with the world'. The Buddhists had been pioneers in the art of temple sculpture even from the time of the Sātavāhanas (1st century B.C. - 3rd century A.D.) in the southeast and the Greco-Bactrian, Śaka, and Kuṣāṇa kings (2nd century B.C. - 3rd century A.D.) of the northwest. Now during the Gupta period (320-550 A.D.) they derived fresh inspiration from the developing theory of the three bodies of the Buddha. The new Buddha in his various aspects as brilliant (*Vairocana*), imperturbable (*Akṣobhya*), boundless light (*Amitābha*) and infallible success (*Amoghasiddhi*) came to be worshipped as the dispenser of grace who would attend to the call of the devotees in the same way as the Kṛṣṇa of the *Gītā*. There was however one basic difference between these two gods. The God of the *Gītā* was a human incarnation of a deity (Viṣṇu) who was the creator, and the dispenser of justice. In the Buddhist dogma, even in *Mahāyāna*, there was no provision for such a deity. The Buddhists relegated the functions of creation to the principle of *karma* and invested the Buddhas with only the power of dispensing grace.

The Hindu revivalists, particularly the Vaiṣṇavites, who could neither ignore the popularity of the new God nor impose upon his followers the traditional disciplines of brāhmaṇism, found a new way of assimilating the Buddha—by declaring him one more incarnation (*avatāra*) of Viṣṇu in addition to Kṛṣṇa. The Buddha's preachings against the Vedic institution of sacrifice and the disciplines of *varṇa* and *āśrama,* they maintained, had a divine purpose: the preaching was intended for evil beings (*asuras*) who would cease to offer the sacrifices and as a consequence would be consigned to hell![66] At a later date, a more generous role was assigned to this new *avatāra* by Jayadeva, the great Vaiṣṇava poet of Bengal, in his *Gīta Govinda*:

> You blame the multitude of Vedic texts of the sacrificial ritual which you showed involved the slaughter of animals, O Keśava (Viṣṇu) of pitying heart, bearing the form of Buddha. Hail Hari, lord of the world.[67]

This new move towards assimilation is unlikely to have had any effect on the informed Buddhists, particularly the monks, but might have helped the Vaiṣṇavites in winning over the Buddhist laity. The Buddhist monks, unlike the Jains, were traditionally indifferent to their laity. They had neither cared to legislate the duties of different ranks, nor to offer alternative ceremonies in the place of the traditional domestic rituals. A Buddhist layman might worship the Buddhas and support the monks with food and shelter, yet he was dependent on the brāhmaṇ priests for ceremonies at birth, marriage, and death, and was guided by them according to the lawbooks of Manu.

Now with the adoption of the Buddha as an *avatāra* of Viṣṇu, a way was open even for introducing the brāhmaṇ priests to officiate at the Buddhist temples. In course of time these temples, often rich and generously endowed, as in the case of the Jagannāth-Puri temple in Orissa,[68] the Kadri *vihāra* in South India, and (until they were handed back to Buddhists from Ceylon by the British Government) even the Buddha-Gayā and the Sārnāth temples passed into the hands of the brāhmaṇ priests and were converted into Vaiṣṇava or Śaiva temples.

The Order of Buddhist monks, weakened by factionalism and interminable doctrinal disputes, had become isolated in the monasteries but continued to wage a relentless war against the orthodox brāhmaṇical systems through its eminent logicians in the

University of Nālandā. They even prevailed upon Śaṅkara, founder of the *Advaita Vedānta* system and also foremost among the revivalist Hindu *ācāryas,* to accept the Buddhist theory of Illusionism (*Māyāvāda*). As a consequence, Śaṅkara was condemned by the later theologians as a crypto-Buddhist. Buddhist influence can also be seen in Śaṅkara's pioneering effort in organizing the brāhmaṇical order of young *sannyāsins* (ascetics), which admitted candidates directly from student life (*brahmacaryāśrama*) without going through the stage of a householder, and in the establishment of several monasteries (*pīṭha*) all over India, presided over by abbots with spiritual powers over large parishes. These were largely instrumental in rehabilitating the orthodox system on the basis of new theistic cults and in holding the society together in medieval times against the onslaught of Islam in the North. But it would be an exaggeration to credit Śaṅkara and his apostles, as is often done by a section of Hindus, with the feat of total extermination of Buddhism in India.

The decline of Buddhism had set in long before with the rise of *Mahāyāna* and the consequent loss of fervour for the monastic system. Even during the time of its founder, Buddhism was not free from heresies, and in subsequent periods it was torn with intersectarian disputes at a time when the theistic cults of Vaiṣṇavism and Śaivism were vigorously moving towards a greater unity. The Buddhist laity—a small minority compared with the Hindu population—had lost its separate identity, and had even seen its own God taken over by a people who had never believed in him and were soon to discard him as an alien. As for the monks, thanks to the Master's call for moderation they had long since abandoned the rigours of asceticism. Patronized by powerful kings and wealthy merchants, their monasteries had amassed large estates where the new *śramaṇas* freely abandoned themselves to the mysticism of *Mahāyāna* and adopted the tantric practices then prevalent among the cults of Nāthas and Siddhas belonging to the Śaiva religion. In Bengal and Bihar Buddhism lingered on in this state of decay and corruption until the twelfth century, when marauding armies of Muslim fanatics sacked the monasteries, burned their libraries, and caused the few monks who survived to flee into Nepal and Tibet.

Jainism would have met with a similar fate had it relaxed its discipline for the monks and laity or allowed any major departure from its basic dogmas of *anekānta* and atheism. Early in their history the Jains had migrated towards the west (Rajasthan and Gujarat) and the south where they had established themselves in the courts of the Cālukya and Rāṣṭrakūṭa kings and were counted among the prosperous communities of the upper middle class. There they concentrated on the propagation of their cherished doctrines of *ahiṃsā*, condemned the animal sacrifices that had by now fallen into disuse, and preached the virtues of a vegetarian diet.

The Jains' opposition to theism was not in the least diminished, but they fought off the mounting opposition of the apostles of the Vaiṣṇava faith by adopting Rāma, one of the *avatāras* of Viṣṇu, as a Jain saint and produced, in the vernaculars of the South, Jain versions of the *Rāmāyaṇa* and the *Mahābhārata*. Although they thus adopted all the heroes of ancient brāhmaṇism, they did not accept their divinity, and in strict accordance with their doctrine of *ahiṃsā* they even had Kṛṣṇa sent to purgatory for having instigated Arjuna to fight the Great War.

But the doctrine of *karma-yoga* had come to stay, the discipline of social rank was in force as never before, and the Jains, especially the Digambaras in the south, could only preach against it at the cost of their survival. It would have been suicidal to accept the brāhmaṇical lawbooks for this purpose or to let the brāhmaṇs dictate to the Jain laymen how they should perform their social duties and observe the rites prescribed for each rank. The Jain monks saw to this need for fresh legislation, and Jinasena (8th century A.D.) among others produced Jain lawbooks in the guise of Purāṇas glorifying the lives of the Jain Tīrthaṅkaras. They declared that the system of *varṇas* (ranks) was not of brāhmaṇical origin but was promulgated by the first of the twenty-four Tīrthaṅkaras, Vṛṣabha, at the beginning of the present *kalpa* (cosmic cycle).[69] Vṛṣabha had also prescribed Jain rites complete with litany appropriate on the occasions of birth, marriage and death. To give full effect to this theory, the Jains even instituted a special hereditary class of lay priests, called Jain-brāhmaṇs, entrusted with the duty of conducting services at the Jain temples and ceremonial rites in the homes of Jain laymen. These neo-brāhmaṇs were of course not to be raised to the status of their equivalents in the brāhmaṇical system. The Jains still adhered to their notion of the supremacy of kṣatriyas and maintained that Tīrthaṅkaras, like

Mahāvīra himself, came only from the ranks of the kṣatriya. But the majority of Jains were merchants and petty landlords by profession and continued to claim for themselves the rank of vaiśya. The menial workers and any who engaged in activities involving *hiṃsā* (tilling, etc.) seem to have qualified for the rank of śūdra, since the name *Caturtha* ('fourth') is applied to a certain section of the Jain farmers in the Deccan today. Thus, in their struggle to achieve ranked status without endangering their survival as a separate group within the community, the Jains had come to accept the outward forms of brāhmaṇical orthodoxy and had as a result produced a society parallel to it.

This, however, was hardly a basis for a lasting peace between the two 'natural enemies'. Rank (*varṇa*) according to the brāhmaṇs was not a matter of choice; rather like sex, one was born with it. The institution of a category of brāhmaṇs was the prerogative of a Vedic God and could not be left to a handful of unrepentant atheists. The struggle between the Jains (*bhavyas*) and the theists (*bhaktas*) continued unabated for several hundred years, until about the twelfth century. Then the *Digambara* Jains, in the South, were overpowered by the Vaiṣṇavas led by Rāmānuja, the great founder of the *Viśiṣṭādvaita* school, and by the Vīraśaivas (Liṅgāyats) under the leadership of Basava, the founder of the reformed Śaiva sect. They were driven from the seats of power, and, in a state of undeclared peace, lived humble lives within their own small communities.

In the west however the *Śvetāmbara* Jains found their great champion in *ācārya* Hemacandra, who was influential in the conversion of Kumārapāla, the Śaivite king of Gujarat, to Jainism. An outstanding and prolific writer, Hemacandra inaugurated a new era in the history of the Jains. With their austere ascetic outlook, they had hitherto, like their fellow *śramaṇas* the Buddhists, confined their literary interests to their scriptures and to works of literature in the fields of logic and philosophy. With the voluntary acceptance of brāhmaṇical institutions and mythology, albeit in a modified form and having already begun to compose their own religious epics and Purāṇas, the Jains were ready to cast off their inhibitions and now enthusiastically invaded the secular fields so far dominated by the brāhmaṇs. Hemacandra not only wrote voluminously on Jain doctrine but was equally at home in the secular sciences of polity, logic, philology, grammar, lexicography and rhetoric and earned for himself the title of polymath of the modern world (*kali-kāla-sarvajña*). The Jain monasteries became veritable storehouses of rare manuscripts not only of Jainism but also of all other religions covering almost all branches of learning. The scope of their libraries and of their scholastic study, in marked contrast to the attitudes of Buddhists and Hindus alike, not only gave them a scholarly advantage but also contributed towards a closer relationship between the *śramaṇa* communities and brāhmaṇical society.

After nearly two millennia of vigorous, and in many ways successful, struggle against the orthodox brāhmaṇical religion and social hierarchy, now, with Jainism held in check and Buddhism neutralised even to the point of complete effacement, the *śramaṇa* tradition had reached a low ebb. The *śramaṇas,* who had sought salvation through atheism with a consistency unique in world history, were henceforth left to pursue a solitary path on the periphery of Indian society. Brāhmaṇism had yielded its position on ritual and, to some extent, on hereditary rank when faced with a vigorous and articulate *śramaṇa* movement. But now, when the forces of Islam threatened the nation, it was the orthodox theism (of the *Gītā*) that seemed to offer a rallying point for the vast majority against the onslaught of an alien culture. It is within the great theistic movements of Hindu poets and mystics, from Kabir to Caitanya, that the last vestiges of an effective and articulate *śramaṇa* tradition are to be sought.

NOTES

1. Rahula Sankrityayana (ed.), *Pramāṇavārtika-svavṛtti-ṭīkā,* Allahabad: Kitab Mahal, pp. 617-618.
2. *Bṛhadāraṇyaka Upaniṣad,* IV, 3, 22.
3. Franz L. Kielhorn, *Vyākarana Mahābhāṣya of Patañjali,* Bombay: Government Central Book Depot, 1892, vol. I, p. 476.
4. *Siddhahema,* III, 1, 141.
5. *Ṛg Veda,* X, 90.
6. Robert E. Hume (tr.), *The Thirteen Principal Upaniṣads,* London: Oxford U. Press, rev. ed., 1962, p. 162.
7. *Ibid.*, p. 110.
8. *Ibid.*, p. 143.
9. *Ibid.*, p. 367.
10. *Atharva Veda,* II, 5, 3. (See W. D. Whitney and C. R. Lanman, *Atharva Veda Samhita,* Cambridge, Mass.: Harvard U. Press, 1905. Harvard Oriental Series, vol. 7, p. 44.)

11. *Pañcaviṃśabrāhmaṇa,* VIII, 1, 4; XIII, 4, 17. (See H. D. Sharma, "History of Brahmanical Asceticism," *Poona Orientalist,* 3-4, 1938-40.)
12. Arthur L. Basham, *The Wonder That Was India,* New York: Grove Press, 1959, p. 23.
13. *Ibid.*
14. A. Berriedale Keith, *Religion and Philosophy of the Veda and Upanishads,* Cambridge, Mass.: Harvard U. Press, 1925. Harvard Oriental Series, vol. 32, p. 402.
15. *Ibid.*
16. *Atharva Veda,* XV.
17. *Bṛhadāraṇyaka Upaniṣad,* I, 1, 1.
18. Robert E. Hume, *op. cit.,* pp. 320-321.
19. *Ibid.,* p. 394.
20. Thomas W. Rhys Davids (tr.), *Dialogues of the Buddha,* London: Luzac, 1956, vol. I, pp. 65-95.
21. *Ibid.,* pp. 69-76.
22. Arthur L. Basham, *History and Doctrines of the Ājīvikas,* London: Luzac, 1951, ch. 5.
23. *Ibid.,* p. 64.
24. *Dictionary of Pali Proper Names.*
25. Hermann G. Jacobi (tr.), *Jaina Sūtras,* Oxford: Clarendon Press, 1884. Sacred Books of the East, vol. 22. Bool Chand, *Lord Mahavira,* Benaras: Jain Cultural Research Society, 1948.
26. *Jaina Sūtras,* p. 264.
27. *Ibid.,* p. 264.
28. Bool Chand, *op. cit.,* p. 58.
29. Hermann G. Jacobi (tr.), *Jaina Sūtras,* Oxford: Clarendon Press, 1895. Sacred Books of the East, vol. 45.
30. See R. Williams, *Jaina Yoga, A Survey of the Medieval Śrāvakācāras,* London: Oxford U. Press, 1963, pp. 14ff.
31. Bool Chand, *op. cit.,* p. 54.
32. S. A. Jain (ed.), *Sarvārthasiddhi,* Calcutta: Vira Sasana Sangha, 1960, p. 57.
33. *Jaina Yoga, A Survey of the Medieval Śrāvakācāras,* pp. 110ff.
34. *Majjhimanikāya* I, 80. (*Further Dialogues of the Buddha,* I, p. 56).
35. *Vinaya Piṭakam,* I, pp. 3-8.
36. *Ibid.,* p. 10. *Book of the Discipline,* part 4, p. 15.
37. *Majjhimanikāya,* I, p. 486.
38. *Ibid.,* I, p. 430.
39. *Ibid.*
40. *Ibid.,* I, p. 486.
41. *Saṃyuttanikāya,* II, 17.
42. Ananda K. Coomaraswamy and I. B. Horner, *The Living Thoughts of Gotama the Buddha,* London: Cassell and Co., 1948, p. 166.
43. *Ibid.,* p. 167.
44. *Dialogues of the Buddha,* I, p. 78.
45. Ananda K. Coomaraswamy and I. B. Horner, *op. cit.,* p. 101.
46. *Vinaya Piṭakaṃ,* I, p. 24.
47. *Dialogues of the Buddha,* I, p. 24.
48. *Vinaya Piṭakaṃ,* I, p. 43.
49. *Book of the Discipline,* part 4, p. 56.
50. *Dialogues of the Buddha,* I, p. 148.

51. Ananda K. Coomaraswamy and I. B. Horner, *op. cit.*, p. 125.
52. *Ibid.*
53. *Ibid.*
54. *Dialogues of the Buddha,* I, pp. 300-320 (*Tevijja-sutta*).
55. *Mahāvaṃsa,* V, 270-1.
56. *The Laws of Manu,* VI, 37.
57. Protap C. Ray and K. M. Ganguly (trs.), *The Mahābhārata of Krishna-Dwaipayana,* Calcutta: Oriental Publishing Co., 2nd ed., 1952-1962, *Sāntiparva,* ch. 18.
58. Franklin Edgerton (tr.), *Bhagavad Gītā,* Cambridge, Mass.: Harvard U. Press, 1944, vol. I, II, 42-44.
59. *Ibid.*, III, 5-6.
60. *Ibid.*, III, 7-8.
61. *Ibid.*, IV, 13.
62. *Ibid.*, III, 16.
63. See Franklin Edgerton (tr.), *Bhagavad Gītā,* vol. 2, ch. 4.
64. John J. Jones (tr.), *The Mahāvastu,* London: Luzac, 1949, I, 132-134.
65. *Saddharmapuṇḍarīkasūtra,* XV, 3-14.
66. *Mahābhārata,* XII, 46, 107; *Matsyapurāṇa,* 47, 247.
67. *Gīta Govinda,* I, 1, 9.
68. Sir Rupendra C. Mitter, *The Decline of Buddhism in India,* Viśvabhāratī: Santiniketan, 1954, p. 99.
69. Pannalal Jain (tr.), *Mahāpurāṇa,* Benaras: Bharatiya Jnanapitha, 1951, I, ch. 16.

CHAPTER 4

On the *Sarvajñatva* (Omniscience) of Mahāvīra and the Buddha*

"May we have the vision of the Saint Mahāvīra:
The Saint, whose pure consciousness,
Like a clear mirror,
Reflects simultaneously all objects
—Both sentient and insentient—
Characterized by their infinite modes;
The Teacher, like the sun,
A witness and illuminator of the path of salvation."[1]

Sarvajñatva or omniscience is an attribute which, like omnipotence (*sarva-śaktimatva*) and omnipresence (*sarva-gatatva*), is considered to be a prerogative of god. The Vedic seers were well acquainted with the concept of omniscience, as can be seen from adjectives like *viśva-vit, viśva-vidvān, viśva-cakṣu* and *sarva-vit,* applied to the Vedic deities, and notably to Agni. We do not meet with the term *sarvajña* until the period of the *Muṇḍakopaniṣat,* presumably a pre-Buddhist text, where it comes to be used for the Brahman, the Absolute "from whom this, namely the *saguṇa* Brahman, comes to birth as name, form and food".[2] In the *Māṇḍūkyopaniṣat*[3] and in the literature of the subsequent periods, the term comes to be used exclusively to describe the *Īśvara* of philosophical systems like Yoga,[4] Nyāya and Vaiśeṣika, as well as the Purāṇic trinity of

*This article was originally published in *Buddhist Studies in Honour of I.B. Horner,* eds. L. Cousins et al., (Dordrecht: D. Reidel Publishing Company, 1974), pp. 71-90. Reprinted with kind permission of Kluwer Academic Publishers.

Brahmā, Viṣṇu and Śiva. In all these cases the word is taken in its literal meaning, viz., the knower of ALL, with emphasis not only on the infinite content of this knowledge, but also on the ability of direct perception, independent of the mind and body.

However, the Upaniṣads also employ the term *sarvajña* in a metaphorical sense, where it becomes a synonym for *Brahmajña* or *Ātmajña,* the knower of the eternal self. The Upaniṣadic seers are greatly preoccupied with the search for "that One thing by the knowledge of which all this is known",[5] and in keeping with their predilection for a monistic world-view, proclaim that the knower of Brahman knows all, indeed becomes All. Thus it is declared in the *Praśnopaniṣat,* that an aspirant "who comes to know that pure Imperishable, he knowing all enters the All".[6]

It is evident that the term *sarvajña* in this passage, applied to an aspirant upon reaching the goal, has a different connotation than the one used in describing the Brahman or the Īśvara. The aspirant as well as the Īśvara knows the nature of reality; but the latter is, in addition, an omniscient being, an excellence neither claimed for the aspirant nor presumed to be an invariable consequence of his knowledge of the Brahman. As Śaṅkarācārya in his *Bhāṣya* on the *Praśnopaniṣat* puts it, "the aspirant was previously the knower of the finite on account of his *avidyā,* but with the removal of the latter he now becomes the All."[7]

It is obvious that in any doctrine of theism, monotheistic, pantheistic or even monistic, a human being, however great, may not be designated as a *sarvajña* in its primary sense, since such a designation could put him alongside god himself. As for the word *sarvajña* in its secondary meaning, although it can be theoretically applied to an exalted human being renowned for the knowledge of the Brahman, such as a Yājñavalkya, a Janaka, a Śvetaketu or a Śaṅkarācārya, one looks in vain for even one such reference in the entire Brahmanical literature, including the Upaniṣads.

Paradoxical as it may seem, the claimants to the status of an omniscient being (*sarvajña*) are to be found not in the theistic, but in the professedly atheistic schools, namely, Jainism and Buddhism, the two chief rivals of the Brahmanical tradition of ancient India. Vardhamāna Mahāvīra, the last of the twenty-four Tīrthaṅkaras of the Jains, and Siddhārtha Gautama, the founder of Buddhism, appear to represent the only two recorded cases of human beings who have claimed such a distinction; this claim is certainly a unique phenomenon in the entire history of human civilization. The Jain and the Buddhist scriptures provide indisputable evidence that the followers of these two religious leaders not only accepted their claims to omniscience, but considered omniscience to be the very essence of the enlightenment (*sambodhi*) which enabled the two great Saints to enunciate their respective paths of salvation. Being contemporaries who sojourned in close proximity in the region of Magadha, Mahāvīra and Siddhārtha, the two 'omniscient' beings, each unacceptable to the followers of the other, could not have long escaped critical comparison and a subsequent mutual repudiation of the other's claim for *sarvajñatva*. An attempt will be made in this paper to identify the major differences that exist between the Jains and the early Buddhists concerning the concept of *sarvajñatva*, and to trace the change which that concept undergoes in Mahāyāna Buddhism under the impact of the polemics initiated by the Mīmāṁsakas, who totally rejected the possibility of an omniscient being, whether human or divine.

Our earliest and most authentic source for the account of Mahāvīra's attainment of omniscience is the *Kalpa-sūtra*, the traditional canonical work on the lives of the Jinas. There we learn that soon after the death of his parents, Mahāvīra, aged thirty, renounced the life of a householder and became a mendicant (*muni*) in the order of his predecessor Jina Pārśva, the 23rd Tīrthaṅkara (850 B.C.). He led the life of an ascetic for a period of twelve years, engaged in severe austerities and deep meditation. Then,

> during the thirteenth year, in the second month of summer, in the fourth fortnight, on the day called Suvrata, outside of the town called Jṛmbhikagrāma on the bank of the river Ṛjupālika, not far from an old temple, in the field of the householder Sāmāga, under a Sāl tree, (the Venerable One), in a squatting position with joined heels, exposing himself to the heat of the sun, after fasting two and a half days without drinking water, being engaged in deep meditation, reached the highest knowledge and intuition, called *Kevala*, which is infinite, supreme, unobstructed, unimpeded, complete and full.
>
> When the Venerable Ascetic Mahāvīra had become a Jina and arhat, he was a *Kevalin*, omniscient (*sabbaññū*) and com-

> prehending all objects (*sabba-bhāva-darisī*); he knew and saw (*jāṇamāṇe pāsamāṇe*) all conditions of the world, of gods, men and demons: whence they come, whither they go, whether they are born as men or animals or become gods or hellbeings, the ideas, the thoughts of their minds, the food, doings, desires, the open and secret deeds of all the living beings in the whole world; he the Arhat, for whom there is no secret, knew and saw all conditions of all living beings in the world.[8]

Although words like *sabbaññū* and *sabba-bhāva-darisī* are fully expressive of the state of 'omniscience' claimed for Mahāvīra, the word *kevala,* being a Jain technical term, needs further elaboration. According to the Jains, knowledge (*jñāna* or *upayoga*), like bliss (*sukha*), is a distinctive quality (*guṇa*) of the soul (*jīva*) as opposed to the other five substances (*dravyas*) admitted by them, namely, matter (*pudgala*), the principle of motion (*dharma*) and of rest (*adharma*), space (*ākāśa*) and time (*kāla*). During the state of its bondage (*saṃsāra*), this innate quality of the soul, like the reflecting quality of a mirror covered by dust, is obstructed by the force of *karma.* This force, according to the Jains, consists of a special kind of subtle and invisible 'karmic' matter. When a soul, activated by ignorance of its true nature (*avidyā* or *moha*), pursues actions (through mind, speech, or body) which are tainted by passions (*kaṣāya*) such as attachment (*rāga*) or aversion (*dveṣa*), it begins to draw the karmic matter toward it as a wet cloth might absorb a dye. The accumulated karma acts like dust or wet cement, enmeshing the soul, as it were, and reduces the operation of its innate qualities. This accounts for the infinite variety of the knowledge of beings in bondage depending upon the amount of karma they have accumulated. According to this theory there is a direct relationship between the density (*pradeśa*) of the karmic matter and the organic growth and development of the sense-faculties and the mind. The less developed forms of life, such as plants, have only one sense, namely the tactile, since the souls undergoing that existence carry with them a larger and heavier burden of karma than, for example, those incarnated as elephants, which are endowed with all the five sense-organs and the faculty of mind. At the human level, the density of karma is greatly reduced, and consequently, a human being is even capable of asserting his independence over the senses and the mind. At the lower levels of life the senses and the mind are instruments of knowledge, but at the human level, where these instruments reach their ultimate limit of growth, they are regarded as impediments, in as much as they prevent the soul from directly comprehending objects of knowledge. The knowledge of beings in bondage is necessarily indirect or 'mediate' (*parokṣa*) and hence incomplete (*vikala*); the infinite varieties and gradations of this mediate knowledge are broadly classified into the following four categories:

(1) *Mati-jñāna*[9]: Sensory cognition caused by the senses and the mind. Where appropriate, it also includes remembrance, recognition, induction and deduction.

(2) *Śruta-jñāna*[10]: Sensory knowledge followed by instruction, whether verbal or non-verbal. This also includes scriptural knowledge.

(3) *Avadhi-jñāna*[11]: 'Clairvoyance'. This knowledge can be acquired by human beings through Yogic methods. It is comparable to the Buddhist concept of the 'Heavenly Eye' and the 'Heavenly Ear' (*dibba-cakkhu* and *dibba-sota-ñāṇa*).

(4) *Manaḥ-paryayajñāna*[12]: 'Telepathy'. It is "that knowledge through which the objects thought of by the minds of others are known". It is comparable to the Buddhist *ceto-pariya-ñāṇa.*

Since the *avadhi* ('clairvoyance') and the *manaḥparyaya* ('telepathy') are merely the results of an increased power of mind developed by special yogic methods, they may be considered to be extensions of the first two kinds of knowledge, namely, the *mati* and the *śruta.* These two are present, in varying degrees of course, in all beings in bondage, including the vegetable kingdom. Consequently, the Jains admit an infinite variety of gradations in these two kinds of knowledge. The senses have competence only with regard to their appropriate objects within a certain range of time and space; the mind cannot operate very much beyond the data supplied by the senses. Therefore, even at the highest point of their development, whether achieved by conventional means or by yogic methods, the senses and the mind can cope with only a small fraction of the infinite mass of the knowables (*jñeya*). The latter comprises everything (*sarvaṃ*) that exists, viz., the infinite (*ananta*) number of souls (*jīvas*), the infinitely infinite (*anantānanta*) amount of matter (*pudgalas*), the principles of motion (*dharma*) and of rest (*adharma*), space (*ākāśa*) and time (*kāla*), and the infinite number of transformations (*paryāyas*) through which they all pass. These transformations are subject to a Jain law involving simultaneous origination (*utpāda*) of a new mode, destruction (*vyaya*) of the old mode, and permanence (*dhrauvya*) of the substance (*dravya*).[13]

The Jain maintains that since *jñāna* is the innate nature (*svabhāva*) of the soul, the latter must, under proper conditions, be able to cognise the entire mass of knowables (*sarvaṃ jñeyaṃ*). The amount of *karma* destroyed correlates directly with gain in purity of the soul and increase in the range of knowledge. Therefore, a total destruction of the forces of *karma*, together with the causes of their accumulation, must invariably result in perfect purity, which would automatically usher in the state of 'omniscience'. It would also be an irreversible state as there would be no further contamination of the soul by new forces of *karma*. In such a state, the soul, being totally independent of the senses and the mind, will, without any conscious effort whatsoever, directly and simultaneously mirror the whole range of the knowables. This is called *kevala-jñāna*,[14] attained by the soul once it is totally isolated (*kaivalya*). The Jains maintain that *all* freed souls, whether they are exalted personages like the Tīrthaṅkaras, or are ordinary Arhats content with their own emancipation (*mokṣa*) must necessarily attain omniscience (*kevala-jñāna*). Mahāvīra had, according to the scriptures quoted above, attained to such an absolutely irreversible state of purity and omniscience.

Our task in defining the omniscience of Mahāvīra was fairly easy because of the precise and uniform meaning of the term *kevala-jñāna*, found in all Jain texts, whether applied to a Tīrthaṅkara or to an ordinary Arhat. Defining the 'omniscience' of the Buddha, however, is more difficult, as one meets with a bewildering variety of meanings in different Buddhist schools for such terms as *bodhi, samyak-sambodhi, tevijja, sabbaññuta-ñāṇa, buddha-cakkhu, anāvaraṇa-ñāṇa, sarvajñatā, sarvākārajñatā, prajñā-pāramitā*, etc. The problem is rendered even more complex by the refusal of even the Hīnayāna school to apply these terms to the Arhats, who also were believed to have attained *nirvāṇa*, and were therefore as free from *saṃsāra* as their 'omniscient' Master. Whatever be the precise difference between the status of an arhat and a Buddha even a casual study of the Buddhist scriptures would show that the Buddha's 'omniscience' was of a different kind than that of Mahāvīra, and also that the Buddhists, aware of this difference, altered their interpretations in order to minimize it.

Of the many references to the enlightenment (*sambodhi*) of Siddhārtha Gautama, the one which most graphically describes that event is to be found in the *Jātaka-Nidānakathā*, the traditional Theravāda biography of the Buddha. The account states that the *bodhisattva* spent the night of the full-moon of the month of Vaiśākha, seated under the Bodhi-tree, in deep meditation. In the first watch he gained remembrance of his former existences (*pubbe-nivāsānussati-ñāṇa*); in the middle watch he attained the 'heavenly eye' (*dibba-cakkhu-ñāṇa*); in the last watch he revolved in his mind the Chain of Causation (*paṭicca-samuppāda*). As he mastered this, adds the text, the earth trembled, and, with the dawn, the Great Man attained 'omniscience' (*sabbaññuta-ñāṇa*).[15]

The use of the word *sabbaññuta-ñāṇa* is highly significant as it distinguishes the Buddha's enlightenment from the ordinary yogic perceptions like 'clairvoyance', 'telepathy', etc., and clearly identifies it with nothing less than omniscience. But the Buddhist commentaries are not too helpful in determining the content of this omniscience, the manner of its operation, and the conditions of its survival during the mundane activities following the enlightenment. In the case of Mahāvīra, the word *sarva* (all) stood for the totality of knowables, viz., the six substances (*dravyas*) with their infinite modes (*paryāyas*).[16] Are we to assume that in the case of the Buddha also, the word *sabba*[17] indicated those momentary elements of existence admitted by the Buddhists, namely, the five *skandhas,* the twelve *āyatanas* and the eighteen *dhātus,* which were supposed to be suppressed and destroyed in the *nirvāṇa?* In the case of Mahāvīra there is an emphasis on the knowledge of the infinite number of past and future modes of the eternal substances. The Buddha, being an advocator of the doctrine of momentariness, attached very little importance to the knowledge of past and future, as these were considered merely imaginary extensions of the present, devoid of reality. Would the Buddha, who had already gained knowledge of his previous births by mundane means, make it a function of the enlightenment to yield knowledge of the 'unreal' future? Finally Mahāvīra's own pure self (*śuddhātmā*) was the first and foremost object, and also the subject, of his omniscience. Is it likely that the Buddhists, distinguished by the *anātma* doctrine, would have considered the 'knowledge of one's own pure self' to be an objective of the omniscience of their Master?

The Buddhist scriptures, particularly those of the Theravāda school, indicate that unlike the Jains, who understood the term *sarvajña* in a literal manner, the early Buddhists used that term in a secondary metaphorical sense, namely, the 'knower of truth', equivalent to the exclusively Buddhist term *tathāgata.* The *Mahāvagga* of the *Vinaya-piṭaka,* in which are described the events leading to the first sermon, contains a passage which sums up those things which the recently enlightened Buddha was hesitant to speak about:

> This *dhamma,* won to by me, is deep, difficult to see, difficult to understand, peaceful, excellent, beyond dialectic, subtle, intelligible only to the learned. But this is a creation delighting in sensual pleasure. ...So that for a creation delighting in sensual pleasure, this were a matter difficult to see, that is to say causal uprising by way of cause (*idaṃ-paccayatā paṭicca-samuppādo*). This too were a matter very difficult to see, that is to say the calming of all habitual tendencies, the renunciation of all attachment, the destruction of craving, dispassion, stopping, *nirvāṇa.* And so if I were to teach *dhamma* and others were not to heed me, this would be a weariness to me, this would be a vexation to me.[18]

Three important words, namely, *dhamma, paṭicca-samuppāda* and *nibbāna,* stand out prominently in this passage. It contains a definition, albeit in a succinct form, of the *paṭicca-samuppāda* and *nibbāna,* the former providing an insight into the Buddhist path and the latter describing the fruits of salvation. But the crucial term *dhamma,* which undoubtedly constitutes the very essence of the Buddha's enlightenment, remains unexplained; indeed it is declared as being inaccessible to dialectic. It is not surprising therefore to see the silence maintained by the commentators regarding this term. The word, however, does appear elsewhere in the potent phrase *dhamma-dhātu-paṭivedha,*[19] variously translated as 'discernment of the principle of truth', or 'full penetration of the constitution of *dhamma*'. The Pali Commentary explains the term *dhamma-dhātu* as *dhamma-sabhāva,* and, as Miss Horner rightly observes, the term stands for "the ultimate principle of own-nature, own-being, self-nature".[20] It is precisely in this sense that the Mahāyānists also understood the term *dharmatā* and developed their concept of the *dharma-kāya.* As a matter of fact, the Mahāyānist logicians, notably Dharmakīrti, as we shall see, gave currency to a new term, '*dharmajña*', in preference to the older *sarvajña*, and even maintained that the Buddha was superior to all other teachers on account of his being a 'knower of *Dharma*'. These references confirm our belief that for the early Buddhists also the 'omniscience' of the Buddha consisted in his 'knowledge of *dhamma*'.

We have seen earlier that omniscience was regarded by the Jains as an irreversible state. But they also believed that its acquisition was not coincidental with death, the final mundane event that would emancipate (*mokṣa*) the omniscient soul from the bondage of karma. Mahāvīra, for instance, lived for some thirty years after attaining the *kevala-jñāna* and, being a Tīrthaṅkara, was credited with having founded and guided a fourfold order of monks, nuns, lay-men and lay-women, until he died at the age of seventy-two. How does one explain the obvious inconsistency in admitting the simultaneous operation of omniscience and the mundane activities of teaching and preaching, not to mention the ordinary functions of the body, senses and mind? The Jains solve this dilemma by postulating two kinds of karma. First, there are four karmas called 'obscuring' (*ghātiyā*), which, wholly or partially, obstruct the full manifestation of the four infinite qualities of the soul, viz., knowledge (*jñāna*), intuition (*darśana*), bliss (*sukha*) and energy (*vīrya*). Then there are four 'non-obscuring' (*aghātiyā*)[21] karmas which, respectively, produce feelings of pleasure and pain (*vedanīya-karma*); project different types of bodies—human, animal, etc.,—(*nāma-karma*); define a certain status—for instance the class and caste distinctions—(*gotra-karma*); and determine the longevity in a given existence (*āyu-karma*). The Jains maintain that only the destruction of the four 'obscuring' (*ghātiyā*) karmas is necessary for the manifestation of omniscience (*kevala-jñāna*). The remaining four karmas are by themselves powerless to effect either a diminution or a loss of the innate qualities of the soul. These *aghātiyā karmas* form a secondary bondage, forging the physical and mental apparatus for the soul which is kept in bondage by the *ghātiyā karmas*. The latter produce delusion, ignorance, etc., and thus perpetuate the cycle of new *aghātiyā karmas*. Once the 'obscuring' (*ghātiyā*) karmas are destroyed, the non-obscuring (*aghātiyā*) karmas, which were determined long before the present incarnation of a given soul, will run their normal course and then, when the time limit set by the longevity-determining (*āyu-karma*) karma has run out, the remaining three will also terminate, never to be renewed again. In other words, the Jains admit that even an omniscient being, as long as he lives in this world, must be considered as being subject to the laws that govern his physical existence. He can neither escape the dependence on his sense-faculties, nor dispense with the mind (both products of the *nāma-karma*), as long as he remains engaged in the mundane activities of teaching and preaching. It should be added here that, the major differences with the Jain theories of karma notwithstanding, the Buddhists also admitted that the Buddha was subject to the laws of mortals, that he too suffered injury and decay, and that he was as much dependent on the senses and the mind for his mundane activities as any other human being.

One might argue that the Jain omniscience (*kevala-jñāna*), especially as it was considered eternal and all-comprehensive, would not be compatible with any mundane activity whatsoever, as the latter must depend upon an ever changing advertence of the senses and upon the reflections of the mind on particular objects defined by time and space. The Jains, however, overcome this apparent incompatibility by arguing that mere presence of the sense-organs and of the mind, which are simply mechanisms formed out of special kinds of matter (*indriya-vargaṇā* and *mano-vargaṇā*), does not necessarily imply dependence on them. While it is true that during its impure state the soul is dependent on these instruments for the manifestation of knowledge, once the soul has attained omniscience, it will subsume the functions of the sensory knowledge (*mati-jñāna*) as well, merely giving the appearance of acting through these mediums. In short, the soul is the knower; the mind and the senses become redundant once the omniscience is achieved. As regards the necessity of advertence, etc., the Jains argue that in actual fact the omniscient being does not engage himself in any activity; he nevertheless accomplishes the functions of teaching by an act of will executed prior to his omniscience, when he was pursuing the career of a Tīrthaṅkara, very much similar to that of a Bodhisattva. By virtue of now in his last birth being born as a Tīrthaṅkara, his *nāma-karma* will produce for him such a body and such an organ of speech that he will be able to impart the knowledge of truth without engaging in a volitional act.[22] Accordingly, the Jains maintain that Mahāvīra, although for all intents and purposes he appeared to be a mortal human being even after the attainment of the *kevala-jñāna*, was nevertheless in permanent possession of his omniscience.

Several Pāli suttas bear witness to the fact that such a claim was indeed made by the followers of Mahāvīra. As a matter of fact, the Buddha is reported to have learnt of such a claim not by hearsay, but directly from a group of Jain ascetics; this is shown in the following passage in which he describes this encounter to Mahānāma the Sakyan:

> "At one time I, Mahānāma, was staying near Rājagaha on Mount Vulture Peak. Now at that time several Jains (Nigaṇṭhas) on the Black Rock on the slopes of (Mount) Isigili came to be standing erect and refusing a seat; they were experiencing feelings that were acute, painful, sharp, severe. Then I, Mahānāma, having emerged from solitary meditation towards evening, approached ... those Jains; having approached I spoke thus to those Jains: Why do you, reverend Jains, standing... experience feelings that are severe? When I had thus spoken, Mahāṇāma, those Jains spoke thus to me: 'Your reverence, Nāthaputta the Jain (i.e., Mahāvīra) is all-knowing *(sabbaññu)*, all-seeing *(sabbadassāvi)*; he claims all-embracing knowledge-and-vision *(aparisesaṃ ñāṇa-dassanaṃ paṭijānāti)*, saying: 'Whether I am walking or standing still or asleep or awake *(carato ca me tiṭṭhato ca me suttassa ca jāgarassa ca)*, knowledge-and-vision is permanently and continuously before me *(satataṃ samitaṃ ñāṇadassanaṃ paccupaṭṭhitaṃ ti)*.[23]
>
> He speaks thus: "If there is, Jains, an evil deed that was formerly done by you, wear it away by this severe austerity. That which is non-doing of an evil deed in the future is from control of body... speech... of thought here, now. Thus by burning up, by making an end of former deeds *(purāṇānaṃ kammānaṃ tapasā vyantibhāvā)*, by the non-doing of new deeds *(navānaṃ kammānaṃ akaraṇā)*, there is no flowing in the future *(āyatiṃ anavassavo)*. From there being no flowing in the future is the destruction of deeds *(kammakkhayo)*, from the destruction of deeds destruction of ill *(dukkhakkhayo)*, from the destruction of ill is the destruction of all feelings *(vedanākkhayo)*, from the destruction of feelings all ill will become worn away *(sabbaṃ dukkhaṃ nijjiṇṇaṃ bhavissatīti)*."[24]

We have quoted this sutta rather extensively because it is remarkable on two counts: First, it gives a very accurate summation of the ancient Jain doctrine of *karma* and *mokṣa*. Secondly, it adds greater credibility to the Jain claims of the state of permanent omniscience for Mahāvīra, coming as it does from the scriptures of a contemporary and rival religious movement. Even the words used in describing that alleged status appear to be authentic as they are repeated verbatim in several other suttas of the Pali canon. The Buddhists were no doubt reporting these claims to ridicule the Jains,[25] not so much because they regarded Mahāvīra as unworthy of such a distinction, but because they found the doctrine of permanent omniscience *(kevala-jñāna)* itself unacceptable, and even irrelevant for the pursuit of the Path. In the *Cūla-Sukuludāyi-sutta*, for instance, the wanderer Udāyi reports to the Buddha how he had met Mahāvīra (who had claimed omniscience in the words quoted above), and had asked him a question 'concerning the past' and how Mahāvīra had 'shelved the questions by asking another', etc. The Buddha, of course, as was his wont, did not engage in a refutation of the claim of Mahāvīra, but confidently asserted that 'anyone could ask him a question regarding the past', or 'concerning the future of creatures according to the consequences of their deeds'. Having said this he immediately showed his indifference to these super-knowledges *(abhiññās)* by declaring:

> Wherefore, Udāyin, let the past be, let the future be. I will teach you *dhamma*: If this is, that comes to be; from the arising of this, that arises; if this is not, that does not come to be; from the stopping of this, that is stopped.[26]

The passage clearly brings out the Buddha's annoyance at the idle curiosity of worldly men for the knowledge of the past and the future. It also draws our attention to the supreme importance he attached to the insight into the Dhamma which he had perceived. In the face of the extraordinary claims of the Jains for their Tīrthaṅkaras, however, it is inconceivable that the eager followers of the Buddha could have long refrained from pressing similar claims for their 'enlightened' Master. It is, therefore, not surprising to see the Wanderer Vacchagotta reporting what he heard to the Buddha and asking him to verify its truth. The entire passage of the *Tevijja-Vacchagotta-sutta* merits reproduction here as it appears to be the official Buddhist position put forth to counter the popular notions about the Buddha's omniscience:

> Reverend sir, I have heard: The recluse Gotama is all knowing, all seeing; he claims all-embracing knowledge-and-vision, saying: 'Whether I am walking or standing still or asleep or awake, knowledge-and-vision is permanently and continuously before me'. Reverend sir, those who speak thus ... are speaking of the Lord in accordance with what has been said and are not misrepresenting the Lord, with what is not fact, but are explaining in accordance with *dhamma*, and that no one of his fellow *dhamma*-men, of this way of speaking, gives ground for reproach?

The answer given by the Buddha is, for once at least, categorical and final:

> Vaccha, those who speak thus: (repeated)- these are not speaking in accordance with what has been said, but they are misrepresenting me with what is untrue, not fact.[27]

To the further question by Vacchagotta:

> Expounding in what way, reverend sir, would we be speaking in accordance with what has been said,

The Buddha expounds the Three-fold knowledge *(tevijja)*, the true content of the Buddha's enlightenment:

> Vaccha, expounding: 'The recluse Gotama is a threefold-knowledge man', you would be one who speaks in accordance with what has been said by me ... For I, Vaccha, whenever I please to recollect a variety of former habitations, that is to say one birth, two births... thus, do I recollect diverse former habitations in all their modes and details. And I, Vaccha, whenever I please, with the purified *deva*-vision (*dibba-cakkhu*) ... surpassing that of men ... see beings as they pass hence and come to be ... according to the consequences of deeds, and I, Vaccha, by the destructions of the cankers *(āsavā)*, having realised here and now by my own superknowledge *(abhiññā)* the freedom of mind *(ceto-vimuttiṃ)* and the freedom through wisdom *(paññā-vimuttiṃ)* that are cankerless, entering thereon, abide therein. Vaccha, expounding thus ... no fellow *dhamma*-man of this way speaking could give grounds for reproach.[28]

It should be noticed that the Theravādins regarded the first of these three *vidyās* (viz., the *pubbe-nivāsānussati-ñāṇa*, and the *dibba-cakkhu-ñāṇa)* as mundane powers *(lokiyā abhiññā)* unrelated to the Path, and hence accessible, in varying degrees, to persons adept in yoga. As for the third *vidyā*, viz., the *āsava-kkhaya-ñāṇa*, this was certainly a supermundane power *(lokuttarā abhiññā)*, and was invariably found in those who had realized *nirvāṇa*. In other words, even the Arhats, whose enlightenment was admittedly of an inferior kind to that of the Buddha, could claim the 'threefold-knowledge' as described in the sutta quoted above. It goes without saying that the Buddha was either claiming for himself only that much knowledge which his disciples, the Arhats, were capable of achieving, or he was indirectly telling Vacchagotta that the latter's idea of omniscience (borrowed no doubt from the Jains), was fanciful and unacceptable to him. Unfortunately, Vacchagotta does not press further the point and, we are once more left in doubt about the precise nature of the Buddha's omniscience.

However, the Buddhists could not have long maintained their suspense on so fundamental a topic as the omniscience of their Master. Sooner or later someone acquainted with the Jain claim would have drawn comparisons between Mahāvīra and the Buddha, and confronted the latter, demanding a definite answer. The *Kaṇṇakatthala-sutta* of the *Majjhima-nikāya* provides us with what appears to be the Theravādin resolution on the controversy. The interlocutor in this sutta is not a wanderer ascetic or a Buddhist monk, but significantly a layman, the king Pasenadi of Kosala, who, while known to the Jains as their benefactor, was also a great admirer and devotee of the Buddha. We are told that a Brahman minister of the King had heard from the mouth of the Buddha a certain view pertaining to omniscience, and had reported it to the King. The latter had now approached the Lord in order to verify that speech. The dialogue merits a full reproduction:

> King Pasenadi: I have heard this about you, revered sir: 'The recluse Gotama speaks thus: There is neither a recluse nor a Brahman who, all-knowing, all-seeing, can claim all-embracing knowledge-and-vision — this situation does not exist'. Revered sir, those who speak thus ... I hope that they speak what was spoken by the Lord, that they do not misrepresent the Lord by what is not fact, that they explain *dhamma* according to *dhamma*, and that no reasoned thesis gives occasion for contempt?

The Buddha: Those, sire, who speak thus: (repeated) —these do not speak as I spoke but are misrepresenting me with what is not true, with what is not fact.[29]

King Pasenadi: Could it be, revered sir, that people might have transferred to quite another topic something (originally) said by the Lord in reference to something else? In regard to what, revered sir, does the Lord claim to have spoken the words?

The Buddha: I, sire, claim to have spoken the words thus: There is neither a recluse nor a Brahman who *at one and the same time can know all*, can see all — this situation does not exist.[30]

Apparently the King was satisfied with the answer of the Buddha as he applauds him with the words "Revered sir, the Lord's words are well founded, and it is with good reason that the Lord says this".[31] Whether the King had really grasped it or not, the full implications of the Buddha's statement were not lost on the commentators. They rightly understood the term *sabbaṃ* (all) to mean "the whole past, future and present", and paraphrased the expression *sakid eva* as "with one 'adverting' (of the mind), one thought, one impulsion".[32] It meant that the Buddhists defined 'omniscience' as an ability to know ALL objects but only one object at one time.

It is evident that no mortal could ever exhaust the infinite objects at the rate of knowing them 'one at a time'. It is doubtful if even the Buddha, despite his mighty yogic powers, could have accomplished such an extraordinary feat, or would have admitted its possibility by any other human being! As a matter of fact, the non-Buddhist ascetics of the time were often sceptical about his alleged yogic powers and thought it rather strange, understandably enough, that he should not even know his own future after death! Time and again, the Pāli suttas allude to the unfavourable comments of these 'wanderer ascetics' concerning the Buddha's omniscience. In the *Pāsādika-sutta* of the *Dīgha-nikāya*, a sermon delivered upon hearing of a schism among the Jains following Mahāvīra's death, the Buddha cautions Cunda the novice against being influenced by the doubts of outsiders:

It may happen, Cunda, that Wanderers who hold other views

> than ours may declare: Concerning the past Gotama the Recluse reveals an infinite knowledge and insight, but not so concerning the future, as the what and why of it ... Concerning the past, Cunda, the Tathāgata has cognition reminiscent of existences. He can remember as far back as he desires. And concerning the future there arises in him knowledge born of Enlightenment *(bodhijaṃ)* to this effect: This is the last birth; now is there no more coming to be.[33]

He affirms, moreover, the wide range of his knowledge in terms reminiscent of the Jain claim for Mahāvīra:

> Whatever, O Cunda, in this world with its devas and Māras and Brahmas, is by the folk thereof, gods or men, recluses or Brahmans, seen *(diṭṭha)*, heard *(suta)*, felt *(muta)*, discerned *(viññāta)*, accomplished *(patta)*, striven for *(pariyesita)*, or devised in mind *(anivucaritam manasā)*, — all is understood by the Tathāgata. For this is he called Tathāgata.[34]

Despite such reassuring sermons, doubts seem to have persisted in the Saṅgha about the Buddha's omniscience. The silence of the *Kathāvatthu,* treasure house of the Buddhist controversies, on such a vital point probably suggests that during the Mauryan period it had not yet become a matter of contention among rival Buddhist schools. The problem was not entirely forgotten, however, as it surfaced during the reign of the Indo-Greek king Menander. In the famous *Milinda-pañho,* the King confronts the Venerable Nāgasena with a question of the omniscience of the Buddha. Nāgasena's answer is remarkable since it refutes at the very outset the notion of '*satataṃ samitam*', the root of the whole controversy.

> Yes, O King, the Buddha was omniscient. But the insight of knowledge was not always and continually (consciously) present in him. The omniscience of the Blessed One was dependent on reflection. By reflection he knew whatever he wanted to know.[35]
>
> Then, sir, the Buddha cannot have been omniscient, if his all-embracing knowledge was reached through investigation ... Moreover, sir, reflection is carried on for the purpose of seeking (that which is not clear when the reflection begins). Convince me ...[36]

Nāgasena is, as usual, dogmatic and analogical. He reminds the King of the greatness of the Buddha, of how well endowed he is with the exclusive ten powers *(dasa-balas)*, the four kinds of 'self-confidence' *(catu-vesārajjas)*, the eighteen *buddha-dhammas*, etc. He then compares the Buddha to an Imperial Lord *(cakkavatti)* who

> calling to mind his glorious wheel of victory *(cakkaratana)* wishes it to appear, and no sooner is it thought of than it appears — so does the knowledge of the Tathāgata follow continually on reflection.[37]

A more serious and probably final Theravāda attempt to deal with the problem is found in the *Paramattha-mañjūsā* [38] Dhammapāla's (sixth century A.D.?) commentary on the *Visuddhi-magga* of Buddhaghosa. While explaining the term *sammā-sambuddha*, the commentator points out that this is an exclusive title of the Buddha, indicating realization of the *sabbaññuta-ñāṇa* (omniscience), or *anāvaraṇa-ñāṇa* (knowledge free from all obstructions). Dhammapāla takes this opportunity to initiate a fairly long discussion on the controversies over the omniscience of the Buddha:

> But, surely, the *anāvaraṇa-ñāṇa* is, according to *Paṭisambhidā-magga*, different from the *sabbaññuta-ñāṇa*. Not really. The same knowledge was spoken of in two ways, one with respect to the manner of knowing and one with respect to the objects known. Knowledge, which has its object the entire range of *dharmas* viz., the compounded *(saṃkhata)*, the uncompounded *(asaṃkhata*, i.e. *nibbāna*, etc., and the nominal [*sammuti*, i.e., personality, etc.) *dharmas*], is called *sabbaññuta-ñāṇa*. Because there is no obstruction, and also because of the absence of doubt it is called *anāvaraṇa-ñāṇa*. These two must be identical, for otherwise the *sabbaññutañāṇa* would not be free from obstructions.
>
> Even if we admit that these two are different, in the present context of defining the term *sammā-sambuddha*, they are to be considered identical because of the unimpeded operation of the Buddha's knowledge. By the realization of the *sabbaññuta-ñāṇa* the Lord is called *sabbaññū* (omniscient), *sabba-vidū* (knower of all), etc.; it is not by knowing all dharmas at one

and the same time that he is called thus *(na sakiṃ yeva sabba-dhammāvabodhanato)*. There is the potentiality *(samatthatā)* in the knowledge of the Lord to penetrate the entire range of objects on account of his realization of that knowledge which is able *(samattha)* to know all *dharmas*.

A question may be raised here: Does this knowledge, when it operates, cognise all objects at once, (simultaneously), or in succession? *(sakiṃ eva...udāhu kamena?)*

If it simultaneously comprehends all 'compounded' *(saṃkhata)* objects (divided by distinctions of past, future, present, external, internal, etc.,) as well as all 'uncompounded' *(asaṃkhata)* and 'nominal' *(sammuti)* dharmas, like a person looking from a distance at a painting of mixed colours, there will be no cognition of them individually. If that happens, then there would be a deficiency in the knowledge of the Lord; he would be seeing these things as if they were not fully seen. This is comparable to the vision of a yogin, who when he perceives all objects only from the *anātma* point of view, thinking *sabbe dhammā anattā*, sees only this aspect and nothing else.

Again there are those who say that the Buddhas are called *sabba-vidū* because their cognition always exists having only the present characteristics [birth, decay, death] of all the knowables as its object, and is free from all imaginations. On account of this it is properly said: "The Elephant (i.e., Buddha) is attentive whether walking or standing". *(sabba-ñeyya-dhammānaṃ ṭhita-lakkhaṇa-visayaṃ vikappa-rahitaṃ sabba-kālaṃ buddhānaṃ ñāṇaṃ pavattati.)*

But this view also cannot escape the fault shown above, for having the present characteristics *(ṭhita-lakkhaṇas)* as the focus of one's knowledge must exclude the past and future dhammas as well as the nominal dhammas, all of which are devoid of those characteristics. Consequently the Lord's knowledge will have only a portion of the knowables as its objects, and it therefore cannot be said that the knowledge of the Buddha cognises all objects at once.

But if, on the other hand, it is maintained that he perceives all objects in individual succession *(kamena sabbasmiṃ visaye ñāṇaṃ pavattati)*, that too is not correct. The knowables divided by genus, nature, place and time, etc., are infinite; hence there is no possibility of knowing them all one by one.

Then there are those who say: The Lord is omniscient because he knows a portion of the knowables by direct perception *(ñeyyassa ekadesaṃ paccakkhaṃ katvā)*; since there is consistency between this knowledge and the true nature of the objects known, he determines that the rest of the objects are also like that. Such a knowledge is not based on inference as might be objected, because in the world, knowledge based on inference is accompanied by doubt. This knowledge, however, is absolutely free from doubt.

Such a view is also not correct. Because in the absence of direct perception of all, it is not possible to establish inconsistency with that portion which has not been directly perceived.

Having examined several views prevalent during his time, Dhammapāla proceeds to lay down what must have been the official Theravāda doctrine:

All this is irrelevant *(akāraṇaṃ)*. Why? Because what we have here is speculation about something which is beyond the realm of speculation. Has not the Lord said: O Monks, the range of objects of the Buddha's knowledge transcends all thoughts on the subject; whosoever indulges in thinking on it will only suffer mental aberration and distress.

This therefore is the resolution of the controversy: Whatever the Lord wishes to know, whether the whole or a portion of it, of that the Lord has knowledge by direct perception, for there is no obstruction to the operation [of his mind]. And in the absence of any disturbances *(vikṣepa)*, attentiveness is also ever present in him. If the entire range of *dhammas* were not to become his object when he desired to know them, then that would not conform — and such conformation is absolutely necessary — to the Law: "All dhammas are bound to the 'adverting' *(āvajjana-paṭibaddhā)* of the Buddha, joined to his mental concentration *(manasikāra-paṭibaddhā)*, connected with his expectation *(ākaṇkhā-paṭibaddhā)*, and available as objects to his production of a thought *(cittuppāda-paṭibaddhā)*".

Even his knowing of past and future objects should be considered an act of direct perception, as it is not dependent upon inference, scripture or reasoning.

It may be asked: Even if it is admitted that the Buddha would know the entire range of objects if he so wished, would not this knowledge of his be subject to the same defect, viz., that of cognizing in an indistinct manner due to not having perceived each object separately?

No. This objection has already been ruled out by the [scriptural] declaration: 'The realm of the Buddha's knowledge is beyond all speculation'. Otherwise, how could there by any inconceivability, if his cognition were to be similar in operation *(samavutti)* to the cognition of the many-folk? The inconceivability consists in the fact that although his cognition has all dharmas as its objects, it nevertheless grasps them all as distinctly and as definitely as it would a single dharma.

Finally, in conformity with the Law—

'As far the extent of knowables, so far the range of cognition; as far the limit of
knowledge, so far the limit of knowables',

the Buddha, whether he wishes to know the objects all together, or separately, all at once or one by one, knows them all as he wishes. Therefore is he called *sammā-sambuddha*.[39]

Dhammapāla was only able to defend his inherently weak position by an appeal to the scriptures; this was adequate because he was writing his commentary for the benefit of his fellow Theravādins of the Mahāvihāra in Ceylon, staunch upholders of the ancient tradition. They believed in the pluralistic and realistic world of dharmas, and could not conceive of an omniscience which would not comprehend the 'All'. The Mahāyāna Buddhists, however, notably Dharmakīrti and his followers at the Nālandā University, could hardly ignore the inherent defects in the traditional interpretation of omniscience. The emphasis which that interpretation placed on the knowledge of the 'All', a legacy of the days of Mahāvīra, was especially vulnerable and must have annoyed them greatly. The possibility of simultaneous cognition of the 'All' had already been rejected by the Buddha, and the alternative, cognition in succession (in sequential order), would not stand logical scrutiny.

The need to deal more vigorously with this entire issue received a further impetus with the rise of the neo-Mīmāṃsā school, which claimed that knowledge of *dharma* and *adharma* was not possible through perception *(pratyakṣa)* or inference *(anumāna)* but only through the 'eternal' Vedas, which were held to be *apauruṣeya,* i.e. neither revealed by an omniscient God nor pronounced by a human being claiming similar status. This follows from the Mīmāṃsaka doctrine which rejects both the "eternally omniscient god" concept of the Yoga school and the theistic theories of creation propounded by other orthodox schools. Nor did the Mīmāṃsaka accept the possibility of a super-sensuous perception *(yogi-pratyakṣa)* such as that claimed for Mahāvīra or the Buddha. Kumārila, in his *Śloka-vārttika,*[40] led a vigorous attack on these denouncers of the Veda for what he considered their exaggerated pretensions to omniscience. Moreover, what the Mīmāṃsakas found most offensive was not so much the claim to know 'All' (objects) but rather the supposed knowledge of *Dharma* (the Vedic Law).

At the same time, the Mahāyānists themselves, having moved toward either the Yogācāra Vijñānavāda or the Mādhyamika Śūnyavāda, were deemphasizing the significance of external objects. Consequently, they were unlikely to be impressed by the 'spectacular' feat of knowing the 'All'. This trend, combined with the desire to counter the Mīmāṃsā position, led them to proclaim that what made the Buddha a truly omniscient being was not his 'far-sight' encompassing many things, but rather an *in-sight* into the *Dharma.*

The following words of Dharmakīrti define this new position and throw a challenge to the Jains to take a similar view:

> People, afraid of being deceived by false teachers
> in the matter of directing the ignorant,
> Seek out a man with knowledge,
> for the sake of realizing his teaching.

What is the use of his wide knowledge
pertaining to the number of insects in the whole world?
Rather, enquire into his knowledge of
that which is to be practised by us.

For us, the most desired authority
is not the one who knows everything [indiscriminately];
Rather, we would have a Teacher who knows the Truth
which leads to prosperity in this world,
as well to the insight into things to be forsaken
and things to be cultivated.

Whether he sees far or whether he sees not,
let him but see the desired Truth.
If one becomes an authority
merely because of seeing far and wide,
Let us worship these vultures
who can do it better![41]

A few centuries later, another Mahāyānist, the great Śāntarakṣita, was to repeat this sentiment in his famous *Tattva-saṅgraha,* composed primarily to refute the Mīmāṃsakas:

> If an attempt were made to prove that one has the knowledge of the details of all individuals and components of the whole world—it would be as futile as the investigation of the crow's teeth.
>
> By proving the existence of the person knowing only *dharma* and *adharma,* which the Buddhist postulates—one secures the realiability and acceptibility of the scripture composed by him; and by denying the said person, one secures the unreliability and rejectability of the said scripture.
>
> Thus when people [the Jains for instance] proceed to prove the existence of the person knowing all the little details of the entire world, they put themselves to the unnecessary trouble of writing treatises on the subject and carrying on discussions on the same.[42]

It will be noticed that in the passage quoted above, Śāntarakṣita deliberately sets the words *dharma* and *sarva* in opposition, stating his preference for *dharmajña* (the knower of *dharma*) as against *sarvajña* (the knower of All). *Dharma,* as we have seen earlier, was the very essence of the Buddha's enlightenment, and is a term which one finds on almost every page of the Pāli canon. Nevertheless, while the term *sabbaññū* is encountered ever so often as a designation of the Buddha, the term *dhammaññū* (*dharmajña*) is conspicuous by its absence throughout the Pāli canon, with the possible exceptions of the variants *dhammagū* and *dhammavidū* cited in texts like the Jātaka book. In the light of our previous discussion, it would be reasonable to assume that the word *sabbaññu* (together with its companion *sabba-dassāvī*) was an ancient Śramaṇa technical term, and was in vogue among the Jains, one of the leading Śramaṇa sects, at the time of Mahāvīra. It was probably adopted by the early Buddhists for their Master, as were other Jain terms of distinction, notably *jina* (victor) and *arhat* (the worthy, the holy). Both of these terms became part of the Buddhist vocabulary, but within a short time *jina* was left behind in preference for *buddha,* and *arhat* was 'devalued' to be used only for the disciples (*śrāvakas*). But the term *sarvajña,* being associated with a definite ontological and epistemological doctrine expressed by the Jain term *kevala-jñāna,* was less easily assimilated. Omniscience for the Jains was a permanent manifestation of the inalienable power of the pure soul (*ātman*) to cognise itself as well as all knowables at one and the same time, as expressed in the famous saying: "*je egaṃ jāṇai se sabbaṃ jāṇai*",[43] "knowledge of one (thing) is knowledge of all". For the Buddhists, however, it was merely a potential power of the 'free' mind; although this power could be used at will and could cognise objects of any nature whatsoever, it was nevertheless restricted, as in the mind of an ordinary human being, to only one object at a time. In other words, the Buddhists were, even in regard to the Buddha himself, unable to dispense with the mind or to replace it with anything corresponding to the *ātman* or the *brahman* of the non-Buddhistic schools. This was the consequence of their adherence to the *anātma* doctrine, which forbade the admission of a Knower over and above the psycho-physical complex of the 'five *skandhas*' of existence.[44]

NOTES

1. yadīye caitanye mukura iva bhāvāś cidacitaḥ
samaṃ bhānti dhrauvyavyayajanilasanto 'ntarahitāḥ //
jagatsākṣī mārgaprakaṭanaparo bhānur iva yo /
Mahāvīrasvāmī nayanapathagāmī bhavatu naḥ //
Nitya-naimittike-pāṭhāvali, p. 17, Karanja 1956.
2. yaḥ sarvajñaḥ sarvavid yasya jñānamayaṃ tapaḥ /
tasmād etad brahma nāma rūpam annaṃ ca jāyate // *Muṇḍaka*, I.i,9.
3. eṣa sarveśvara eṣa sarvajña eṣo 'ntaryāmy eṣa yoniḥ // *Māṇḍūkya*, 6.
4. kleśakarmavipākāśayair aparāmṛṣṭaḥ puruṣaviśeṣa īśvaraḥ /
tatra niratiśayaṃ sarvajñabījam / *Pātañjalayogasūtram*, I. 24-5.
5. *Chāndogya*, VI. 1.
6. ... *Sa sarvajñaḥ sarvo bhavati / tad eṣa ślokaḥ:*
"vijñānātmā saha devaiś ca sarvaiḥ
prāṇā bhūtāni sampratiṣṭhanti yatra /
tad akṣaraṃ vedayate yas tu somya
sa sarvajñaḥ sarvam evāviveśa" iti / Praśna, IV. 10.
7. *yas tu sarvatyāgī somya, sa sarvajño na tenāviditaṃ kiñcit sambhavati / pūrvam avidyayā asarvajña āsīt punar vidyayā 'vidyāpanaye sarvo bhavati / Praśnabhāṣya*, IV. 10.
8. *Kalpasūtra*, (120-1), H. Jacobi (tr.): *Jaina Sūtras*, Pt. I, (SBE, Vol. XXII), p. 263.
9. *matiḥ smṛtiḥ saṃjñā -cintā 'bhinibodha ity anarthāntaram / tad indriyānindriyanimittam/ Tattvārthasūtra*, I, 13-4.
10. *śrutaṃ matipūrvaṃ dvyanekadvādaśabhedam / ibid.* I, 20.
11. *rūpiṣv avadheh / ibid. I, 27. bhavapratyayovadhir devanārakāṇām / kṣayopaśamanimittaḥ ṣaḍvikalpaḥ śeṣāṇām / ibid.* I, 21-2.
12. *ṛjuvipulamatī manaḥparyayaḥ / ibid.* I, 23. *vākkāyamanaḥkṛtārthasya parakīyamanogatasya vijñānāt ...Sarvārthasiddhi*, I, 23.
13. *utpādavyayadhrauvyayuktaṃ sat / Tattvārthasūtra*, V, 30.
14. *sarvadravyaparyāyeṣu kevalasya / ibid.*, I, 29. *mohakṣayāj jñānadarśanāvaraṇāntarāyakṣayāc ca kevalam / ibid.*, X, 1.
15. *The Jātaka* (Fausbøll). Vol. I, p. 75.
16. See note 14.
17. *kiñ ca bhikkhave sabbaṃ? cakkhuṃ c'eva rūpā ca ... pe ... ... mano ca dhammā ca / idam vuccati bhikkhave sabbaṃ / Saṃyuttanikāya*, IV, p. 15.
18. *Mahāvagga*, I, 5, 8. [*The Book of the Discipline*, I,5. 8.]
19. *Abhayarājakumārasuttaṃ* (*Majjhima* 58); *Mahāpadānasuttaṃ* (*Dīgha*, 14).
20. *MA*, iii, 113; *MLS*, II, p. 64, n. 1.
21. See Tatia : *Studies in Jaina Philosophy*, p. 239, Benaras 1951.
22. *Tattvārthasūtra* VI, 24; IX, 11.
23. *Cūḷadukkhakkhandasutta, M*, I. 92-3.
24. *The Middle Length Sayings*, II, 228-9.
25. e.g. *the Sandakasutta, M.* I. 519.
26. *The MLS*, II, pp. 228-9. [*M*, II, p. 31-2]
27. *M*, I. 482.
28. *MLS*, II, P. 160.
29. *M*, II, 127.
30. *natthi so samaṇo vā brāhmaṇo vā sakideva sabbaṃ ñassati, sabbaṃ dakkhiti, netaṃ ṭhānaṃ vijjatīti / M*, 11, 127.

31. *Ibid.*
32. *MA*, iii, *MLS*, II, 310, n. 1.
33. *Dīgha*, iii, 134.
34. *Dialogues of the Buddha*, Pṭ 3, p. 126.
35. *bhagavā sabbaññū, na ca bhagavato satataṃ samitaṃ ñāṇadassanaṃ paccupaṭṭhitaṃ, āvajjanapaṭibaddhaṃ bhagavato sabbaññutañāṇaṃ ... āvajjitvā yad eva icchitaṃ jānātīti / Milindapañho*, p. 102.
36. *tena hi buddho asabbaññu, yadi tassa pariyesanāya sabbaññutañaṇaṃ hotīti ... Ibid.*
37. *Ibid.*, p. 107.
38. *Paramatthamañjūsā*, Pt. 1, (ed. by M. Dhammananda Thero), Colombo, 1928, pp. 188-191.
39. *tasmā sakaladhammārammaṇam pi taṃ ekadhammārammaṇaṃ viya suvavatthāpite yeva te dhamme katvā pavattatīti idam ettha acinteyyaṃ / "yāvatakaṃ ñeyyaṃ, tāvatakaṃ ñāṇaṃ; yāvatakaṃ ñāṇaṃ, tāvatakaṃ ñeyyaṃ; ñeyyapariyattikaṃ ñaṇam, ñāṇapariyattikaṃ ñeyyaṃ" ti evam ekajjhaṃ visuṃ visuṃ sakiṃ kamena vā icchānurūpaṃ sammā sāmañca sabbadhammānaṃ buddhattā sammāsambuddho / Ibid.*, p. 191.
40. *Ślokavārttika*, 110-2ff. For details on this controversy between the Mīmāṃsaka, the Buddhist and the Jaina see Sukhalalji Sanghavi: *Pramāṇamīmāṃsā*, notes pp. 27-33 [Singhi Jain Series, No. 9]; A.N. Upadhye: *Pravacanasāra*, Intro. pp. 70-6 (Rājacandra Jain Śāstramālā, 1964).
41. *Pramāṇavārttika*, I, 32-5.
42. *samastāvayavavyaktivistarajñānasādhanam /*
kākadantaparīkṣāvat kriyamāṇam anarthakam //
yathā ca cakṣuṣā sarvān bhāvān vettēti niṣphalam /
sarvapratyakṣadarśitvapratijñāpy aphalā tathā//
svadharmādharmamātrajñasādhanapratiṣedhayoḥ/
tatpraṇītāgamagrāhyaheyatve hi prasiddhyataḥ //
tatra sarvajagatsūkṣmabhedajñatvaprasādhane /
asthāne kliśyate lokaḥ saṃraṃbhād granthavādayoḥ // Tattvasaṅgraha, 3138-3141.
It should be noted that later Buddhists like Kamalaśīla came to accept the Jain position regarding the knowledge of 'All': *mukhyaṃ hi tāvat svargamokṣasamprāpakahetujñatvasādhanaṃ Bhagavato 'smābhiḥ kriyate, yat punar aśeṣārthaparijñatṛtvasādhanam asya tat prāsaṅgikam anyatrāpi Bhagavato jñānapravṛtter bādhakapramāṇābhāvāt sākṣād aśeṣārthaparijñānāt sarvajño bhavan na kenacit bādhyata iti. Tattvasaṅgraha-pañjikā*, 3309.
43. *Āyāraṃga-suttaṃ*, I, 3, 4.
It should be emphasized here that even the Jains considered the knowledge of the external objects as of secondary importance. Kundakunda is emphatic when he declares that the Kevalin is said to know all objects only from the *vyayahāra* point of view:
jāṇadi passadi savvaṃ vavahāraṇayeṇa kevalī bhagavaṃ /
kevalaṇāṇī jāṇadi passadi ṇiyameṇa appāṇaṃ // Niyamasāra, 159.
44. The Pudgalavādins were aware of this difficulty: *yady evaṃ/ tarhi na Buddhaḥ sarvajñaḥ prāpnoti. na hi kiñcic cittam asti caittā vā yat sarvaṃ jānīyāt, kṣaṇikatvāt. pudgalas tu jānīyāt. Abhidharmakośa-Bhāṣya*, X. p. 467 (Pradhan's edition).

Additional reading: "Omniscience in the *Mahāyānasūtrālaṅkāra* and its commentaries" by Paul J. Griffiths, *Indo-Iranian Journal*, Vol. 33, No. 2 (1990), pp. 85-120.

CHAPTER 5

The Jina as a Tathāgata: Amṛtacandra's Critique of Buddhist Doctrine*

One noteworthy feature of the heterodox religions of ancient India is the ability of these schools to absorb technical terms of their rivals and then apply them to their own concepts, seemingly without any inconsistency. The term *brāhmaṇa,* for example, normally indicates a person born in that caste. The Buddhists and the Jains, however, appropriated the term as a designation for their Masters justifying this with strange etymological derivations, e.g. *bāhitapāpo brāhmaṇo* or *mā haṇa* (don't kill) *iti māhaṇo* (pkt for *brāhmaṇa*).[1] The term *jina* (victor) is itself of pre-Buddhist origin. It was extensively used by the Nigaṇṭhas and the Ājīvikas for their teachers, and as suggested by Edgerton, could be applied to the founder of any religious sect; the followers of Ārāḍa Kālāma and those of Udraka Rāmaputra, for example, are referred to as *jina-śrāvaka.*[2] The Buddha claimed to be a *jina*[3] and the term was applied to him in imitation of the founders of other sects. The *Mahāvyutpatti* lists several names beginning with *jina*—Jinakāntāra, Jinacakra, Jinabhāskara, Jinavaruttama, etc.—for previous Buddhas, as well as an epithet like *jinaputra* for the Bodhisattvas.[4] The term must also have been popular among members of the Theravāda tradition since they composed books bearing such titles as *Jinacarita* (of Vanaratana Medhaṅkara), *Jinabodhāvatāra* (of Dhammakitti),

*This article was originally published in *Malalasekera Commemoration Volume,* ed. O.H. De A. Wijesekera, (Colombo, 1976), pp. 148-156.

Jinālaṅkāra (of Buddhadatta?), and *Jinakālamālī* (of Ratanapañña, 1516 A.D.).[5]

The Jains, for their part, made use of epithets for the Hindu gods, e.g. *ādideva, acyuta, purāṇa-puruṣa, trinetra, sahasrākṣa, svayambhū*, etc., in eulogizing their own teachers, particularly the first Tīrthaṅkara Ṛṣabha, who could be favourably compared with Prajāpati (Brahmā) and was often referred to by that name.[6]

As for expressions like *śramaṇa* and *sarvajña,* these were common to both the Buddhists and the Jains, being applied to Buddha and Mahāvīra by their respective followers. The epithets *sugata* and *tathāgata,* however, seem to have been exclusively Buddhist; so far as we know, these terms are not attested in any pre-Buddhist literature or contemporary non-Buddhist sources. The recently discovered manuscript of *Laghutattvasphoṭa,*[7] a tenth-century composition, would appear to be the first Jain work known to address the Jina as '*sugata*' and also as '*tathāgata*'. This work belongs to the genre called *stotra* and ranks in quality with such philosophical 'poems' as the *Svayambhūstotra* of Samantabhadra or the *Anyayogavyavacchedikā* of Hemacandra. The *Laghutattvasphoṭa* was composed by Amṛtacandra, author of *Tattvārthasāra* and *Puruṣārthasiddhyupāya,* and the celebrated commentaries on *Samayasāra* and *Pravacanasāra* of Kundakunda called *Ātmakhyāti* and *Tattva-pradīpikā* respectively.[8]

The *Laghutattvasphoṭa* consists of six hundred twenty-five verses in different metres, equally divided into twenty-five chapters. Each chapter is, as indicated by the title, a brief exposition of reality (*tattva-sphoṭa*) from different points of view called *nayas.* The Jain maintains that reality has infinite aspects (*ananta-dharmātmakaṃ vastu*). It appears to be single and unified when seen as a substance (*dravya*), but many and disparate when seen as modes (*paryāya*), and ultimately comprises both substance and modes.[9] Human speech is capable of giving only a successive description of these infinite aspects; it must indicate one aspect only at a time. If this is done without at the same time suggesting by some device the presence of the non-expressed aspects, then the exposition must be considered incomplete and consequently untrue (*mithyā*). The Jain thus alleges that the classical *darśanas* are partial expositions of reality. The Vedāntic doctrine of monistic absolutism and the Buddhist doctrine of momentary *dharmas* are condemned as examples of the one-sided (*ekānta*) approach; the former apprehends only substance (*dravya*), declaring the modes (*paryāyas*) to be unreal, while the latter concerns itself with the present moment only and totally excludes that 'substance' (*dravya* or *ātman*) which is the underlying unity of past and future states. Both doctrines are mutually exclusive and so must give a false (*mithyā*) description of reality.

The Jain admits that there is an element of truth in both these points of view if they are qualified by an expresssion like 'maybe' (*syāt*), hence asserting one view while suggesting the existence of the remaining aspects of reality. Qualified in this manner, the Vedāntic doctrine can be accepted as a 'synthetic' or *saṅgraha-naya*'[10] and the Buddhist momentariness as a 'straight-thread' or *ṛjusūtranaya*,[11] both valid insofar as they represent reality as it is successively perceived. The Jain claims that he alone, by adherence to the doctrine of qualified expression (*syādvāda*), comprehends all aspects and hence speaks the complete truth (*anekānta*).

By the use of *syādvāda* the Jain can not only transform the false, i.e. the absolutist, doctrines into instruments of valid knowledge, but he can even play 'devil's advocate' with no apparent inconsistency. The XXth chapter of the *Laghutattvasphoṭa* selections from which appear below, is a fine example of a Jain attempt to accord validity to the Buddhist tenet of momentariness by transforming it into the *ṛjusūtranaya*. That tenet can now be accommodated with the rest of Jain doctrine and can even be presented as a teaching of the Omniscient Jina, who thus deserves to be called '*sugata*' or even '*tathāgata*', two time-honoured epithets of Śākyamuni Buddha!

Although *kṣaṇabhaṅgavāda* is the main tenet chosen for 'assimilation', Amṛtacandra makes a broad sweep, bringing almost all shades of Buddhist doctrine under his purview in the brief span of twenty-five verses. The chapter abounds in Buddhist technical terms, e.g. *niraṃśa-tattvāṃśa* (3), *vibhajyamāna, viśīrṇa-sañcaya, bodha-dhātavaḥ* (4), *kṣaṇa-kṣaya, niranvaya, nairātmya* (6, 7), *nirvāṇa, antya-cit-kṣaṇa* (9), *pradīpa-nirvṛti, eka-śūnyatā* (10), *vijñāna-ghana* (11), *bahir-artha-nihnava* (15), *apoha* (16), *sugata, tathāgata* (20), *samasta-śūnyatā* (21), etc.

It hardly needs to be stated that although such an 'assimilation' appears to be theoretically possible, the whole exercise is purely poetic, bereft of deeper insights into the manifold Buddhist doctrines alluded to. Amṛtacandra's handling of the *kṣaṇa-kṣaya* appears reasonably satisfactory, since that position is, with qualifications, acceptable to the Jain. But his 'defence' of the *bahir-artha-nihnava-vāda* is superficial, if not fanciful; lacking a metaphysical basis in the Jain system for the rejection of external objects, he is content with a metaphorical treatment, as given in verse 15. Elsewhere, lacking even a metaphor, he resorts merely to a play on words as in his approach to the concept of *apoha*. He ignores the Buddhist technical meaning of the term and chooses to understand it as simple 'exclusion'. This rendering will serve well to describe the Jain doctrine of 'reciprocal exclusion' (*parasparāpoha*), a doctrine leading to the establishment of the separate existence of one's own nature (*sva-dravya-kṣetra-kāla-bhāva*) and that of others (*para-dravya*, etc.), essential to simultaneous affirmation and negation of one and the same object. In all this, Amṛtacandra is not without precedent; even the Buddha is said to have resorted to a similar device to overcome the criticism of his opponents. When asked by a brahmin if he was an *akiriyavādi*, an *ucchedavādi*, a *jegucchī*, a *venayika* or a *tapassī*, the Buddha is reported to have said that there was indeed a way in which he could be described by all these terms, i.e., by understanding each of them in a sense different from what the questioner had in mind.[12] We should probably look at these verses as a Jain attempt to appreciate the Buddhist doctrines in the spirit of *anekānta*, although hindered in its effort at assimilation by the antipodal position of the two schools. Even if unsuccessful and occasionally superficial, Amṛtacandra's attempt at Jainisation of the Buddhist doctrine is certainly unique and not without a certain irony when we hear him pray to his 'Tathāgata': "*praveśya śūnye kṛtinaṃ kuruṣva mām*" (25).

II

Selections from the *Laghutattvasphoṭa*, Ch. XX.

atattvam eva praṇidhānasauṣṭhavāt
taveśa tattvapratipattaye param/
viṣaṃ vamantyo 'py amṛtaṃ kṣaranti yat
pade pade syātpadasaṃskṛtā giraḥ/1//

O Lord! Even false (i.e. absolutist) doctrines, when profoundly contemplated (in the light of) your teaching, (which is) characterized by the term "maybe" (*syāt*), can lead to attainment of the highest reality; (for when this teaching is applied), its very word causes (these absolutist doctrines) to throw off the poison (of their absolutism), and inundates them with the ambrosia (of truth). (1)

viśuddhyativyāptirasena valgitā—
api skhalantyo 'skhalitā ivocchikhāḥ/
niraṃśatattvāṃśaniveśadāruṇās
tvayīśa mūrcchanty ṛjusūtradṛṣṭayaḥ//3//

O Lord! In you the *ṛju-sūtra dṛṣṭis,* (which perceive the moment to moment transformations of the substance, and thus consider reality mainly with reference to the present mode, ignoring the other modes), come to full manifestation. And these (*dṛṣṭis*) are made active by the extensive spread of the essence of (the soul's) purity. Although (from our mundane, gross point of view), these (*dṛṣṭis*) seem to slip away (from their subtle object, the present moment), they do not (really) slip away, but are like a constantly burning flame; they are sharp in that they focus upon that part of reality which is (itself) partless. (3)

samantataḥ svāvayavais tava prabho
vibhajyamānasya viśīrṇasañcayāḥ/
pradeśamātrā ṛjavaḥ pṛthak pṛthak
sphuranty anantāḥ sphuṭabodhadhātavaḥ//4//

When you are divided on all sides with reference to your space-points, the infinite clear particles of your knowledge shine forth separately (to the limits of these space-points). And these particles of knowledge, (when seen from the *ṛju-sūtra* point of view), having (thus) fallen away from "collection", each appear to occupy only one space-point, having the form of the present mode. (4)

viśīryamāṇaiḥ sahasaiva citkaṇais
tvam eṣa pūrvāparasaṅgamākṣamaḥ/
anādisantānagato 'pi kutracit
parasparaṃ saṅghaṭanāṃ na gāhase//5//

Although endowed with beginningless continuity, you nevertheless appear, (from the *ṛju-sūtra* point of view, as if) unable to join together the prior and later particles of knowledge, which have suddenly (i.e. when seen from this point of view) broken away from "collection"; and thus you nowhere attain to the mutual integration of these (particles). (5)

kṣaṇakṣayotasaṅgitacitkaṇāvalī—
nikṛttasāmānyatayā niranvayam/
bhavantam ālokayatām asikṣatam
vibhāti nairātmyam idaṃ balāt tvayi//6//

(If the particles of knowledge are seen as) devoid of integration (i.e. devoid of substance) because the universal (which resides in them) has been excluded through embracing the viewpoint that there is "destruction at each moment" (i.e. the *ṛju-sūtra* viewpoint, and if this viewpoint is not qualified by knowledge of the *syād-vāda*), there ensues the forceful (establishment) of (a belief in) your substance-less-ness (as among the Buddhists, a belief) which is like a sword (i.e. a destroyer of the self) for those who look at you (in that way, namely without recourse to *saṅgraha-naya*). (6)

gato gatatvān na karoti kiñcana
prabho bhaviṣyann anupasthitatvataḥ/
sa nūnam arthakriyayeśa yujyate
pravartamānakṣaṇagocaro 'sti yaḥ//7//

O Lord! Since the past object has gone out of existence, it does not do anything (i.e. it has no function), and since the future object has not yet come into existence, it (also) does not do anything. But that thing which is seen in the present moment is indeed endowed with useful function. (In this way the relative validity of the *ṛjusūtra-naya,* which takes note of the present moment, is established). (7)

galaty abodhaḥ sakale kṛte balād
uparyupary udyati cākṛte svayam/
anādirāgānalanirvṛtikṣaṇe
tavaiṣa nirvāṇam ito 'ntyacitkṣaṇaḥ//9//

Ignorance disappears with the approach of that moment in which there is the total extinction of the fire of beginning-less attachment. (If that moment does not approach), then (the fire of) ignorance forcefully climbs higher and higher; (since, in your case), the fire has been extinguished, your last moment of consciousness attains to *nirvāṇa.* (9)

tvayīśa vijñānaghanaughaghasmare
sphuṭīkṛtāśeṣaviśeṣasampadi/
sphuraty abhivyāpya samaṃ samantato
balāt pravṛtto bahirarthanihnavaḥ//15//

O Lord! In you who are a mass of knowledge, all the particularities of the entire world of objects are (individually) reflected, and your knowledge, having pervaded everything on all sides, sparkles and forcefully hides, (as it were), the external objects. (i.e. Since everything is in a sense consumed by your knowledge, it seems, from a certain point of view, that there are no external objects). (15)

tad eva rūpaṃ tava sampratīyate
prabho parāpohatayā vibhāsi yat/
parasya rūpaṃ tu tad eva yat paraḥ
svayaṃ tavāpoha iti prakāśate//16//

O Lord! Shining forth by way of the exclusion of others is itself experienced as (your) form (i.e. your own-being consists in the exclusion of others, namely the objects of knowledge). Likewise, the other (objects) have a nature which consists in being separated from you. (In other words, knowledge and its objects are mutually separate things). (16)

abhāva evaiṣa parasparāśrayo
vrajaty avaśyaṃ svaparasvarūpatām/
prabho pareṣāṃ tvam aśeṣataḥ svayaṃ
bhavasy abhāvo 'lpadhiyām agocaraḥ //17//

This reciprocal absence (of the nature of knowledge from the nature of objects, and vice-versa), necessarily leads to the establishment of (the separate existence of) one's own nature and the nature of others. O Lord! you yourself have become total absence from the point of view of others, and so you are not seen by those who lack intelligence (i.e. who cannot understand your dual aspect). (17)

parasparāpohatayā tvayi sthitāḥ
pare na kāñcij janayanti vikriyām/
tvam eka eva kṣapayann upaplavaṃ
vibho 'khilāpohatayā 'vabhāsase//19//

O Omniscient One (*vibhu*)! The other objects, reflected in you under conditions of mutual exclusion, produce no vitiation (of yourself). Thus, destroying the calamity (which could result if there were not separation of self and other), you shine forth alone through the exclusion of the entire range of objects. (19)

gataṃ tavāpohatayā jagattrayaṃ
jagattrayāpohatayā gato bhavān/
ato gatas tvaṃ sugatas tathāgato
jinendra sākṣād agato 'pi bhāsase//20//

By means of mutual exclusion, the three worlds have gone away from you and you have gone away from them. Therefore, O Lord Jina, although in reality you have not gone anywhere, you still shine forth as one who is gone (*gata*), well-gone (*su-gata*), and "thus-gone" (*tathāgata*). (20)

upaplavāyocchalitāḥ samaṃ balāt
kileśa śūnyaṃ parimārṣṭi kalpanāḥ/
kva kiṃ kiyat kena kutaḥ kathaṃ kadā
vibhātu viśve 'stamite samantataḥ//22//

O Lord! (The Śūnyavādins claim that) the doctrine of the void forcefully wipes away at one time all the imaginings that spring upward to afflict consciousness, (because they maintain that) when the universe has been eclipsed on all sides, what shines forth? Where does it shine forth? To what extent and by what means does it shine forth? (In other words, all such speculations become meaningless in the absence of objects.) (22)

na yasya viśvāstamayotsave spṛhā
sa vetti nirṇīktatamaṃ na kiñcana/
asīma viśvastamayapramārjite
praveśya śūnye kṛtinaṃ kuruṣva mām//25//

One who has no desires towards this "festival" of setting all (dharmas? speculations?) to rest does not know anything in a clear manner. (i.e. He still does not develop pure consciousness.) Therefore, O Boundless One, make me content; usher me into void which has been cleansed by the (true) setting to rest of all (speculations). (25)

NOTES

1. For *māhaṇa* see Hemacandra's *Triśaṣṭiśalākā°* I, vi, 190-229.
2. *Buddhist Hybrid Sanskrit Dictionary,* 242-3.
3. *"mādisā ve jinā honti ye pattā āsavakkhayaṃ/ jitā me pāpakā dhammā tasmā 'ham Upakā jino" ti/ Vinayapiṭaka, Mahāvagga,* I, 6, 11.
4. *BHSD.* ibid.
5. Malalasekera: *Dictionary of Pali Proper Names.* (PTS) 1960.
6. Jinasena's *Ādipurāṇa,* xxv, 99-217. Also see my article 'Jina Ṛṣabha as an avatāra of Viṣṇu' to be published in B.S.O.A.S., London, xl, 2, 1977.
7. The MS. of this work was discovered by the late Śrī Muni Puṇyavijayaji. It has been edited and translated by the author of this article and will soon be published by the L.D. Institute of Indology, Ahmedabad, India. (Published in 1978.)
8. For details on the life and works of Amṛtacandra, see A. N. Upadhye's edition of *Pravacanasāra,* Intro. pp. 93-96. (Bombay, 1964).
9. *sad dravyalakṣaṇam/ utpādavyayadhrauvyayuktaṃ sat/ tadbhāvāvyayaṃ nityam/ arpitānarpitasiddheḥ/* and *guṇaparyayavad dravyam//Tattvārthasūtra V,* 29-32 and 38.
10. *svajātyavirodhenaikadhyam upānīya paryāyān ākrāntabhedān aviśeṣeṇa samastagrahaṇāt saṅgrahaḥ; sat, dravyaṃ, ghaṭa ity adi/ Sarvārthasiddhi,* I, 33.
11. *ṛjuṃ praguṇaṃ sūtrayati tantrayatīti ṛjusūtraḥ/ pūrvāparāṃs trikālaviṣayān atiśayya vartamānakālaviṣayān ādatte, atītānāgatayor vinaṣṭānutpannatvena vyavahārābhāvāt/ tac ca vartamānaṃ samayamātram/tadviṣayaparyāyamātragrāhyam ṛjusūtraḥ/ Sarvārthasiddhi,* I, 33.
12. *"arasarūpo... nibbhogo... akiriyavādo ... ucchedavādo ... jegucchi ... venayiko ... tapassī ... apagabbho ... bhavaṃ Gotamo" ti? "atthi khv' 'esa, brāhmaṇa, pariyāyo yena maṃ pariyāyena sammā vadamāno vadeyya'arasarūpo ... apagabbho samaṇo Gotamo' ti ... no ca kho yaṃ tvaṃ sandhāya vadesī"* ... (abridged) *Pārājika,* I, i.

CHAPTER 6

Saṃskāra-Duḥkhatā and the Jaina Concept of Suffering*

In Chapter Six of the *Abhidharmakośa-Bhāṣya* Vasubandhu engages in a lengthy discussion of the meaning of suffering, or *duḥkha,* the first noble truth of Buddhism. This discussion revolves around the following interesting question: if feeling (*vedanā*) is defined as threefold—pleasant (*sukhā*), unpleasant (*duḥkhā*) and neither pleasant nor unpleasant (*aduḥkhāsukhā*), why is it that all *sāsrava,* or defiled, dharmas are held to be *duḥkha?* To answer this question Vasubandhu distinguishes three kinds of *duḥkha:* the suffering of pain (*duḥkha-duḥkhatā*), the suffering of change (*vipariṇāma-duḥkhatā*) and the suffering of conditionedness (*saṃskāra-duḥkhatā*). The suffering of pain is associated with painful feeling (*duḥkhā-vedanā*); the suffering of change, with pleasant feeling (*sukhā-vedanā*), because the loss of what is pleasant is suffering; the suffering of conditionedness is associated specifically with neutral feeling (*aduḥkhāsukhā-vedanā*) but more generally with all *saṃskṛta* dharmas, because they are produced by conditions (*pratyayābhisaṃskāra*) and are impermanent (*anitya*).

It is sometimes maintained that in the first noble truth the Buddhists by emphasizing suffering, take a one-sided view of life and fail to do justice to the pleasant aspects of man's experience. But Vasubandhu argues strongly for the reality of pleasure, despite the fact that on another and more profound level it repre-

*This article was originally published in *Revelation in Indian Thought: A Festschrift in Honour of Professor T.R.V. Murti,* eds. H. Coward and K. Sivaraman, (Emeryville, California: Dharma Publishing, 1977), pp. 152-157. Reprinted with kind permission of Dharma Publishing.

sents a form of suffering. The notion of 'level' here is a critical one; for in effect Vasubandhu is distinguishing between two quite different levels of *duḥkha;* suffering as a conditioned feeling of pain (*duḥkha-d.*), and suffering as the awareness of conditionality itself (*samskāra-d.*). The former might be called mundane, or *a posteriori,* suffering—a psycho-physical state brought about by what is unpleasant (*amanāpa*) and opposed to the feeling of pleasure (*sukha*); the latter represents a transcendental, or *a priori,* a kind of suffering—the metaphysical condition for both pleasure and pain, opposed only to *nirodha,* the unconditioned (*asaṃskṛta*) state free from all feelings. As a painful feeling *duḥkha-d.* is a *vipāka*—that is, an experience brought about by past karma (in this case bad karma). *Saṃskāra-d.,* on the other hand, is not a feeling as we ordinarily understand it, nor is it the product of any specific past action; rather it is an expression of ignorance (*avidyā*) and its attendant craving (*tṛṣṇā*). Thus, the cause of *saṃskāra-d.* lies at the very root of *saṃsāra* itself; and it is for this reason that it is said to be recognized only by the *āryas,* those who have had an insight into the nature of man's existence. It is this kind of suffering in particular which is intended by the first noble truth.

The distinction between mundane and transcendental suffering allows us to understand how Buddhism, and other Indian systems, while proclaiming the unsatisfactoriness of man's basic condition, can yet recognize the validity of his search for pleasure. Good karma will produce the fruit of pleasure; and this fruit is not to be eschewed, for without it we should be condemned to an existence of unrelieved pain in some dark corner of hell. Still, no amount of good karma will free us from the conditioned state in which we are forever striving to gain pleasure and avoid pain; the suffering of this conditionedness can be extinguished only through the elimination of ignorance, which is the very condition for karma. This twofold structure of *duḥkha,* with its distinction between suffering as painful feeling and suffering as the state of conditionedness and ignorance is characteristic, not only of Buddhism, but of other Indian religious systems as well. It is probably nowhere more clearly expressed than in the teachings of the Jainas; and it is these teachings which I should like to discuss here.

The Jaina religion has been referred to by Renou as "Buddhism's darker reflection." Yet for all its austerity and other-worldliness the Jainas, too, recognize that this life is not only suffering but is a mixture of pleasure and pain. In its embodied state the soul (*jīva*) experiences—and, indeed, must experience—both pleasant and unpleasant feelings (*veda*). The former are referred to by the Jainas as *sātā,* and are understood as both the mental and the physical states of ease, happiness, pleasure, etc. Their opposite is *asātā.* Like the *sukha* and *duḥkhā-vedanā* of the Buddhists, both *sātā* and *asātā* are the fruit (*vipāka*) of karma: good karma (*puṇya*) produces *sātā,* bad karma (*pāpa*) produces *asātā.* Unlike the Buddhists, however, the Jainas distinguish different kinds of karma which effect the soul differently. Thus, the karma productive of good (*śubha*) and evil (*aśubha*) bodies (in the human, heavenly, animal and infernal existences) is known as *nāma-karma.* The *nāma* and the *vedanīya* karmas are always present to the *jīva* as long as it is bound to a body; hence, the embodied soul is never free from pleasant and unpleasant feelings. Consequently, the Jainas recognize that in our ordinary life we have no choice but to act in such a way as to bring about the production of *sātā* and avoid the production of *asātā.* Since these two arise in accordance with our own actions (such as compassion, charity, asceticism and their opposites), it is possible for us to follow a moral course which will maximize our happiness and reduce our suffering. Yet it is not possible for us, so long as we remain in this body, to free ourselves entirely from unpleasant feelings.

Like the Buddhists the Jainas believe that an existence characterized by the incessant fluctuation of pleasant and unpleasant feelings is basically unsatisfactory and an expression of man's karmic bondage. The *vedanīya-karma* which binds man to a life of feeling is, like all types of karma, not inherent in the soul. According to the Jainas the *jīva* in its pure isolated state (*kaivalya*) is characterized by the qualities (*guṇa*) of infinite knowledge (*jñāna*), perception (*darśana*), vigour (*vīrya*) and bliss (*sukha*). These qualities are obstructed or defiled by the influx (*āsrava*) of the various kinds of karmic matter, whose association with the soul represents the bondage (*bandha*) from which the Jaina path seeks to free man. Once freed from this bondage, the *jīva* perfectly manifests its inherent qualities.

The discrimination of karma into various types is based on the qualities of the soul: for each *guṇa* there is a corresponding karma which adversely affects it. The four major *guṇas*—knowledge, perception, vigour and bliss—are described by the Jainas as 'positive qualities' (*anu-jīvi-guṇa*)—that is, qualities of which we are partially aware in the state of bondage and which can be brought to perfection when the soul attains isolation from karmic matter. Interestingly enough, the Jainas reserve a special kind of 'negative quality' (*pratijīvi-guṇa*) to describe the *jīva*'s freedom from *vedanīya-karma*. This quality is known as *avyābādha*, the absence of restlessness or hurt; it would appear to be negative, not only in the sense that it is characterized by an absence of feeling, but because it is never experienced during the state of bondage. In the notion of *avyābādha* the Jainas seem to be emphasizing, perhaps even more than the Buddhists, that the restlessness associated with the presence of feeling—even pleasant feeling—is at some level alien and painful to man. Vasubandhu understands both *sukha* and *duḥkha* as suffering because they are conditioned and impermanent; in this respect feelings (*vedanā*) are suffering—in the same sense, and for the same reason that all *saṃskṛta* dharmas are ultimately suffering. Thus he specifically says that *vedanā* is to be seen as *duḥkha* in the same way that the other four *skandhas* are *duḥkha*. The Jainas, however, by positing a special negative quality of the soul specifically representing the absence of feeling (*veda*) would appear to give particular significance to the suffering associated with *vedanīya* karma.

As in Buddhism and other Indian religious systems the root cause of man's bondage is ignorance and the passions, called by the Jainas '*moha*' and '*kaṣāya*' respectively. The influx of *vedanīya* and other forms of karmic matter ultimately depends on the existence of *moha*, which is itself the expression of another kind of karma known as *mohanīya*, or delusion-producing. *Mohanīya* karma is understood as two-fold: *darśana-mohanīya*, or that which deludes one's insight (into the nature of reality); and *cāritra-mohanīya*, or that which deludes one's actions. The former is associated with ignorance proper; the latter, with its attendant passions (*kaṣāya*). As long as *mohanīya-karma* operates the soul remains embodied, and the *vedanīya* and other kinds of karma continue. Once *mohanīya* has been destroyed, the *jīva* will automatically (and within that life-time) be liberated from all karmic matter, return to its proper state of isolation (at the moment of death), perfectly manifest its inherent qualities.

Like other kinds of karma, *mohanīya* affects a specific quality of the soul. Yet surprisingly, the Jainas tell us that the *guṇa* affected by *mohanīya* is bliss (*sukha*). Here the term *sukha* is not to be confused with the Buddhist notion of *sukhā-vedanā,* which we have been translating as 'pleasant feeling' and which corresponds to the Jaina *sātā*. Unlike these latter notions, *sukha* is not a feeling—i.e., it is neither a physical nor a mental event; for the mind (*manas*), it will be remembered, is for the Jainas itself a form of matter, and as such is as alien to the *jīva* as the body. Rather, like the other *guṇas* which qualify the soul, *sukha* emerges precisely when the *jīva,* by attaining omniscient cognition, frees itself from dependence on the senses and the mind. It is, then, an absolute state of bliss which, like knowledge (*jñāna*), is inherent in the soul's very existence.

Sukha differs from knowledge, however, in one important respect. Knowledge in the presence of karma is not itself altered by that karma. The karma which affects knowledge is known as *jñānāvaraṇa,* or knowledge-obstructing. It is so called because it represents an obstruction (*āvaraṇa*) to knowledge much as an object may obstruct a light. In the case of *sukha,* however, the presence of *mohanīya-karma* brings about an actual transformation in the *guṇa* itself. This transformation, known as *vibhāva-pariṇāma,* represents the defilement of *sukha* and constitutes a change of state, much as a liquid may change its state into a solid. The defiled state of *sukha* is *moha.*

The fact that, unlike other types of karma, *mohanīya* brings about a real transformation of the soul—or rather, of its *sukha* quality—suggests its centrality in the system, and allows us to understand in what sense it represents suffering. The Jainas do not specifically describe the state of *moha* as *duḥkha.* Indeed, the term *duḥkha* is conspicuously absent from their technical lexicon. Nevertheless, the function of *moha* in the Jaina system is clearly parallel to the Buddhist notion of *saṃskāra-duḥkhatā.* Like the latter it represents the *a priori* condition for all our ordinary experience, and, hence, for our experience of pleasure and pain. It stands, then, in opposition, not to pleasure as we ordinarily understand it, but to an absolute state of bliss, which is realized precisely in the absence of both pleasure and pain. This state of bliss is, as it were, our birthright, the very nature of our souls. But through the agency of karma it has undergone *vibhāva-pariṇāma,* and has been transformed or perverted into *moha.* In this sense *moha* might be called a metaphysical kind of suffering—the instability and internal contradiction of a being whose actual state is a denial of his true nature. Conversely, *sukha* may be understood as the peace and the completeness of the *jīva* existing in a state of perfect accord with its own being (*svabhāva-sthita*).

If we are correct in identifying *moha* with suffering it is clear that it shares with the Buddhist *saṃskāra-duḥkhatā* a somewhat paradoxical character. For in both Buddhism and Jainism suffering, because it is transcendental, is not recognized by the ordinary man. In a sense we suffer without realizing it. Both systems teach that only one with insight into the basic structure of our existence is really aware that such an existence is unsatisfactory. In Buddhism only one who is free from *avidyā* can clearly recognize the universality of *anitya;* in Jainism only one who is free from *moha* can understand that the true quality of the soul is *sukha.*

CHAPTER 7

The Disappearance of Buddhism and the survival of Jainism in India: A study in Contrast*

One of the most puzzling of the many enigmas that characterize Indian history is the decline and disappearance, between the seventh and thirteenth centuries A.D., of the religion of the Buddha from its native land. Numerous theories have been put forth in the attempt to explain this phenomenon; these are summarized as follows by R.C. Mitra in his excellent work, *The Decline of Buddhism in India*:[1]

1. "Exhaustion"
2. Withdrawal of royal patronage
3. Brahmanical persecution
4. Muslim invasion
5. Internal corruption and decay
6. Divisive effect of sectarianism
7. Insufficient cultivation of the laity.

The first of these suggestions, namely, that Buddhism was simply "exhausted" or "ready to die" in India by 1200 A.D., must be dismissed as adding little or nothing to our understanding; no light is cast by such a statement upon the actual *cause* of the death in question.[2] The remaining six theories, on the other hand, de-

*This article was originally published in *Studies in History of Buddhism*, ed. A. K. Narain, (Delhi, 1980), pp. 81-91. Reprinted with kind permission of A. K. Narain, editor.

serve more serious consideration, for each takes note of a situation or set of events that certainly exerted some influence upon Buddhist fortunes. It is hard to accept, however, that any one of these factors (or even, for that matter, all of them taken together) could have been decisive in precipitating the demise of institutional Buddhism on the sub-continent, for as we shall see, similar and often identical forces were at work on another non-Vedic community and yet failed to bring about its extinction. The community referred to is that of the Jainas, whose own circumstances during the Buddhist "period of decline" have been virtually ignored by scholars. This is most unfortunate, for it is perhaps only by asking the question, "How is it that one Gangetic, non-theistic *Śramaṇa* tradition was able to survive while another closely related one was not?", that we may discover the unique aspects of the Buddhist religion that ultimately led to its downfall. The task of the present essay, then, will be to pursue this long-neglected line of inquiry, and to produce on the basis thereof a new and, it is hoped, more plausible explanation for the strange end of Indian Buddhism.

We should at the outset establish our grounds for asserting that Buddhism and Jainism are in fact "similar" enough to warrant the sort of comparison proposed above. Gautama and Mahāvīra, respective teachers of these two traditions, both seem to have come from princely families, families that were not part of an empire, but rather headed certain small *janapadas* ("republics") of the Gangetic valley. Both are said to have left the household in the prime of life and to have spent several years in great austerities and mortifications, practices common among *Śramaṇas,* the non-Vedic ascetics of ancient India.[3] In addition, Buddha and Mahāvīra are perhaps the only two human beings in history to have claimed for themselves the attainment of "omniscience" (*sarvajñatva*).[4] Following this attainment, each man founded a *saṅgha* (congregation) consisting of both monastic and lay followers, and each attracted large numbers of brahmins and sons of wealthy families to his order. Finally, the two great teachers wandered and preached in the same general area for more than thirty years, passing at last into what was claimed to be their final death (*nirvāṇa*).[5]

The institutional histories of the religions originating from these *kṣatriya* saints also run in a parallel manner. Both movements actively sought and often gained royal patronage, and typically migrated along the trade routes (often one behind the other) in its pursuit; both developed extensive bodies of philosophical literature and were vilified for propounding anti-Vedic doctrines. Most important, both lived in what might be called a constant state of seige, struggling to preserve their integrity amidst a veritable sea of more or less hostile Hindu custom and belief. Thus, while Jainas and Buddhists often engaged in heated polemics against each other, we are nevertheless justified in viewing them as "cousin" traditions occupying an equivalent position relative to the surrounding environment.

Moving now to the theories enumerated by Mitra, let us first consider the issue of royal patronage. While Indian kings were bound by custom to assist all religions, their active support of a given sect almost always brought with it a great increase in the status enjoyed by that sect. This took the form not only of greater prestige among the common people, but also of tangible material gain (a certain percentage of tax revenues, for example, might be turned over to a mendicant community) and of access to the court itself. From the very beginning of their careers, both Buddha and Mahāvīra enjoyed the generous patronage of the Magadhan king Śreṇika and of his patricide son Ajātaśatru. Jainas have traditionally held that the Nanda kings who followed Ajātaśatru were adherents to their faith (a claim supported by inscriptional evidence),[6] and that Candragupta, first emperor of the subsequent Mauryan dynasty, was a Jaina convert who even became a monk late in life. Candragupta's grandson Aśoka, on the other hand, is well-known to have been an ardent supporter of Buddhism; indeed, his missionary zeal caused the spread of that religion to Śri Lanka and laid the foundation for its eventual successes in South and Southeast Asia. The rise of the Brahmanical Śungas, ending the Mauryan dynasty, meant the end of good times for non-Vedic sects in Magadha; thus large numbers of both Jainas and Buddhists moved out of their native region towards Mathura in the west, thence along the mercantile routes into other areas hospitable to their cause.[7] For the Jainas, this initially meant Valabhi and Girnar in Saurashtra, and later the Karnataka region of South India (where eventually arose the great Jaina ruling houses of Ganga and Hoysala).[8] The Buddhists, for their part, obtained a tremendous amount of assistance from the Indo-Scythian king Kaniṣka. Many moved northward, penetrating into

Kashmir, Central Asia, and beyond, while others followed the example of the Jainas and proceeded into the pro-*śramaṇa* regions of the South. The point to be made here is that royal patronage was definitely a significantly positive factor during the formative years of both the Jaina and Buddhist movements. Nevertheless, we cannot blindly extrapolate from this fact and assert that withdrawal of such patronage (especially during the Hindu resurgence of later centuries) meant the total eclipse of these traditions. The continued existence of Jainism, which was every bit as dependent upon royal support as was Buddhism, belies any such claim.

Certain historians have emphasized the effect of Brahmanical persecution upon the non-Vedic traditions. While isolated instances of actual violence by Hindu zealots doubtless did occur, these were probably not sufficient in number or impact to seriously cripple the groups toward which they were directed. It might be argued that Jainas came in for fewer such attacks than did Buddhists, because Mahāvīra's doctrine allowed for existence of the *ātman*, a fundamental Hindu belief which the Buddhists rejected. Even if a relative easing of anti-Jaina hostility did take place on this basis, however, it would have been more than offset by the Jainas' active and vehement condemnation of animal sacrifice in Hindu rituals, about which the Buddhists, as meat-eaters, could make little effective protest. Thus, we have here another negative situation from which both schools probably suffered to an equal extent.

The case pertaining to the Muslim incursions of the twelfth and thirteenth centuries is not so easily written off. Thanks to their geographical position (largely in Western India and the Deccan), Jainas escaped the fury of the early Muslim onslaughts; Buddhist communities, especially the great "university" centres at Nalanda and elsewhere, were not so lucky.[9] It cannot be denied that the sacking of such centres of monastic learning dealt Buddhism a severe blow. Even so, one still must ask how it was that the Buddhists were not able to regroup and rebuild after the initial holocaust had come to an end. We find, for example, that although a great number of Jaina temples in Gujarat and Rajasthan were converted into mosques in later centuries, the Jainas of those areas not only survived but were able to become important leaders in the economic life and government of the Muslim regimes.

Hence, the Islamic invasion, though admittedly the most destructive of the external factors considered thus far, should not have been sufficient to destroy Buddhist society altogether.

Even the earliest Buddhist texts reveal an awareness of tendencies towards laxity and corruption within the *saṅgha,* tendencies that eventually developed to the point where large numbers of monks were performing magical practices, amassing personal or community wealth, and engaging in various other improprieties. Those who have emphasized the significance of this phenomenon are certainly correct in claiming that it represented a serious weakness in the Buddhist community. It should be borne in mind, however, that probably every religious community has gone through periods of decay; those that survived seem to have responded to these situations with spontaneous internal reform, after which the movement often became stronger than ever. The ninth-century Jaina mystic Haribhadra, for example, rallied against the luxurious life style of many monks in his community and was able to arouse popular indignation to the point where such practices were greatly reduced.[10] Similarly, the dissatisfaction of certain Jaina lay people with excessive emphasis on temple ritual and with the grossly expanded power of the temple cleric-administrators led to development of an entire "anti-temple" sect in the fifteenth century. While this group, the Sthānakavāsi, failed to gain many adherents, it did manage to rouse the orthodox from their apathy and thus bring about many important and necessary reforms within the larger Śvetāmbara community.[11] Decay itself, then, need not be fatal; the inability of the Buddhists to generate any meaningful reforms must, like their failure to recover from the loss of their "universities", be ascribed to still deeper causes.

The existence of widespread sectarianism within Buddhism (as many as eighteen doctrinally-distinct schools at one point) has often been construed as indicative of internal weakness. This interpretation, however, is not necessarily valid. In fact, when dealing with the kind of non-centralized movement that Buddhism comprised, the emergence of numerous sects should probably be taken as a sign of both intellectual and spiritual vigour. Even more important, Buddhist sectarianism was confined to *interpretation* of texts; members of all schools more or less accepted the validity of the basic Tripiṭaka, shared an almost identical code of conduct, and moved easily among each other's communities.

Contrast this situation with that of the Jainas, whose major sects, though only two in number, were from almost the earliest times completely estranged.[12] Digambaras rejected the validity of nearly all texts in the Śvetāmbara canon and simply produced their own secondary scriptures. The definition of conduct suitable to a monk, moreover, was an issue of such magnitude that Digambaras viewed Śvetāmbara clerics as nothing more than advanced lay disciples. Members of these two schools have traditionally not set foot in each other's temples, and it is indeed only very recently that even the most tentative Digambara-Śvetāmbara dialogue has been initiated. It is fair to say, then, that the divisiveness associated with sectarianism was much more severe among Jainas than among the Buddhists; such divisiveness cannot, therefore, reasonably be suggested as central to the downfall of Buddhism in India.

We now come to the most important and complex of the issues raised by Mitra, that of the Buddhists' failure to pay sufficient attention to their laity. This tendency seems to have been apparent from an extremely early period, for the very term "Buddhist" itself generally referred only to those who had actually left the household and taken up the yellow robes of the mendicant. While there certainly existed large numbers of lay people who *supported* Buddhism, there seems to have been no clearly defined set of criteria (vows, social codes, modes of worship, etc.) whereby these individuals could be identified as belonging to a separate and unique group within the larger society. Whereas Jaina clerics were, according to canonical evidence, always closely involved with their lay people, their Buddhist counterparts tended to remain aloof from all non-mendicants. The Jainas moreover, eventually produced some fifty texts on conduct proper to a Jaina lay person (*śrāvakācāra*),[13] while the Buddhists, as far as we know, managed only one (and that not until the eleventh century).[14] There can be little doubt, then, that the sense of religious participation or identification felt by the Buddhist lay community was often a weak one at best. This situation probably goes far towards explaining the lack of any "grass-roots" revival once the trappings of the monastic establishment, *viz.*, the great university centres, had been destroyed.

Serious as their neglect of the need for lay involvement was, the Buddhists committed an even greater error by failing to respond meaningfully to the threat posed by the waves of *bhakti* that swept across India from the fourth or fifth century onwards. The popularity of the various Hindu devotional cults, and particularly of those associated with Rāma and Kṛṣṇa, must have engendered a great many lay defections from the Buddhist ranks. This problem was compounded by the depiction of the Buddha himself, in the *Mahābhārata,* certain *Purāṇas,* and Jayadeva's *Gītagovinda,* as nothing more than another *avatāra* of Viṣṇu.[15] Buddhist monks were perhaps unaware of the grave dangers represented by these developments; not a single extant text shows any attempt either to assimilate the popular Hindu deities into Buddhist mythology or to refute the notion of Buddha as *avatāra.* The latter point was perhaps most crucial, for by their very silence Buddhist writers seemed to lend tacit support to the Hinduization of their founder; this process certainly contributed to the undermining of whatever sense of uniqueness the laity may have felt.

The response of the Jainas to similar pressures was markedly different. They attempted to counteract Hindu suggestions (such as those which survive in the *Bhāgavatapurāṇa*)[16] that Ṛṣabha, their first Tīrthaṅkara, had been an incarnation of Viṣṇu by attacking the "divine" status of Viṣṇu himself, particularly through a criticism of the immoral behaviour shown by the *avatāras.*[17] More important, they produced entire alternate versions of the *Rāmāyaṇa*[18] and *Mahābhārata,*[19] wherein Rāma and Kṛṣṇa were depicted as worldly Jaina heroes subject to the laws of Jaina ethics. Rāma, for instance, does not kill Rāvaṇa in the Jaina rendition of the tale; this deed is instead performed by his brother Lakṣmaṇa, and Rāma is reborn in heaven for his strict observance of *ahiṃsā.* Such a transformation was not possible for Kṛṣṇa, whose deeds of violence and treachery were too numerous to cover up; thus, he is depicted as going to hell for a long period after his earthly death. The point here is that the Jainas sought to outflank the *bhakti* movement by taking its main cult-figures as their own, while placing these figures in a uniquely Jaina context.

This effort, together with the careful attention to lay conduct referred to above, makes it clear that Jainas were much more concerned with maintaining the internal cohesion of their lay community than were the Buddhists. It is tempting to assume that in this fact we have found the key distinction between these two traditions, the fundamental element in terms of which the demise of one and survival of the other may be explained. Closer examination of Jaina history, however, calls such an assumption into question, for it seems that even the most extreme measures undertaken to hold the laity together were not in themselves crucial to the ultimate fate of the community.

We have already seen the accommodation of Hindu elements with reference to *bhakti;* this tendency was carried much further by Digambaras of the Karnataka region, who introduced, for example, a set of *saṃskāras* (worldly rituals, *e.g.,* those pertaining to birth, weddings, death, etc.) virtually indistinguishable from those of the surrounding Hindu majority.[20] While this certainly constituted "paying attention to the laity", it failed to prevent a serious decline in the overall strength of Jaina society in the South. Śvetāmbaras and Digambaras of the North, on the other hand, resorted to very few such measures, and yet remained relatively prosperous.

It will be apparent that all of the "explanations" thus far offered for the decline of Buddhism, whether referring to external pressures or to inherent structural weaknesses, reflect a purely socio-historical perspective. Having found each of these theories wanting in some degree, particularly in their ability to explain the divergent fates of Buddhism and Jainism, we should perhaps turn our attention away from strictly social issues and focus instead upon the area of doctrine. Here, one suspects, may be found within Buddhism some element that rendered it uniquely susceptible to certain of the destructive influences discussed above.

The impact of Buddhist-Jaina differences over the existence of a soul, in terms of the greater or lesser degree of Hindu hostility resulting therefrom, has already been considered. Probably, both heterodox traditions were equally subject to direct orthodox aggression. It must, therefore, be asked which of them was more doctrinally open to the force of Hindu *sabotage,* the insidious weaning away of lay support by absorption of heterodox beliefs and cults into the Hindu sphere. In this connection, one is immediately struck by the Mahāyāna Buddhist doctrine of the heavenly *bodhisattvas,* a class of exalted beings having absolutely no counterpart in Jaina belief. The origin of this doctrine, which asserted the existence of numerous figures who had attained the enlightenment of the Buddha and yet chose to remain forever in the *sāṃsāric* realm, is not entirely clear. On the philosophical level, it probably developed out of dissatisfaction with the earlier notion of the *arhats*, individuals whose apparent personal attainment of *nirvāṇa* seemed to conflict with the fundamental tenet of no-self. More to the point of the present discussion, the heavenly *bodhisattvas* may well have represented an attempt to provide some outlet for the devotional needs of the Buddhist laity. These beings, however, were conceived of in such a way that the very fact of their enormous popularity worked for, rather than against, the destruction of Buddhism in India. This took place because the great *bodhisattvas* were described as completely supramundane by nature; rather than providing a human model of struggle and attainment, they became virtual gods, who dispensed worldly boons and even spiritual grace in a manner not unlike that of the Hindu deities. At last, the place of the historical Buddha himself was functionally usurped by these figures; although the Buddha remained nominally the most hallowed of beings, the bulk of popular interest and devotion was centred not upon him but upon the great *bodhisattvas*, especially Mañjuśrī and Avalokiteśvara.[21]

While Jainas also allowed certain non-human figures to play a part in their rituals, these were always limited to mere spirits (*yakṣas*) who were of lower status than Jaina mendicants. The *yakṣas* functioned as "guardians" of the holy shrines of the Tīrthaṅkaras; no great divinities on the Hindu model ever gained legitimacy in either Jaina doctrine or worship. Thus, there was little common ground to support the development of a subversive synthesis with Hindu belief and practice. By embracing the notion of the heavenly *bodhisattvas*, however, Buddhism laid itself open to precisely this sort of synthesis, particularly with the powerful Nātha cult of the tantric Śaivite tradition. It was this fact, we believe, that finally made the essential difference in the respective abilities of Jainism and Buddhism to survive.

That various Buddhist temples fell into the hands of Hindu groups is well known; notable examples are the shrines at Bodhgayā and Sāranāth, returned to Buddhist control only in modern times.[22] What has remained obscure, however, is the exact sequence of developments whereby such Hindu appropriation took place. Certain little-known discoveries by the late Indian historian M. Govinda Pai cast great light upon this question, and also provide material in direct support of our contention that Buddhism was subverted by the cult of the heavenly *bodhisattvas*.[23] In the suburbs of Mangalore, a city in southern Karnataka, stands a Śaivite temple known as Kadri-Mañjunātha; "Mañjunātha" designates the *Śiva-liṅga* enshrined therein. Now, although Śiva is commonly referred to by titles terminating in "*nātha*" (*e.g.*, Somanātha, Oṃkāranātha, Kedāranātha, Viśvanātha), this particular name "Mañjunātha" is *nowhere else* attested as a proper epithet of the god. Intrigued by this strange fact, Pai undertook to work out a chronological history of the temple in question. He found, first of all, that it had once been a Buddhist monastery and temple called Kadarikā-vihāra; within the shrine room stands an image of the Buddha. More important, from our point of view, is the additional presence therein of a beautiful bronze image of the *bodhisattva* Avalokiteśvara, also called Lokeśvara[24]. An inscription at the base of the Lokeśvara image credits its establishment to one king Kundavarmā of the Alūpa dynasty, stating that "Kundavarmā, the Alūpa king, a great devotee of *Bālacandraśikhāmaṇi* ('he who has the crescent moon as his crest-jewel,' *i.e.* Śiva), consecrated the image of Lord Lokeśvara in this pleasant *vihāra* called Kadarikā, four thousand one hundred and sixty-eight years after Kaliyuga" (*i.e.*, 1068 A.D.).[25] The interesting point here is that an image of Lokeśvara should have been erected in a Buddhist temple by a king who was devoted to Śiva. Clearly it was not the Buddha who was being worshipped, but a *bodhisattva* who had in some way been *integrated with Śiva.*

Concerning the identification of Lokeśvara with Avalokiteśvara, see B. Bhattacarya, *The Indian Buddhist Iconography,* Calcutta, 1958, Chapter 4. Also in this connection, compare the antelope skin appearing on the image above with that of the Sanchi Avalokiteśvara (ninth century). (The latter figure is discussed by John Irwin in the *Victoria & Albert Museum Yearbook,* 1973.)

It is interesting to note that the Kadri Lokeśvara image has not been mentioned either by Irwin or by Marie-Therese de Mallman in her book *Introduction a l'étude d'Avalokiteśvara,* Paris, 1948. Pai has shown, further, that Lokeśvara was identified with Matsyendranātha, a Śaivite saint said to have become divine by attaining oneness with Śakti.[26] Numerous caves in the vicinity of Kadri are dedicated to ascetics of the Nātha order which this saint established, and an image of Matsyendranātha himself (identified by the mark of a fish) adorns the outer wall of the "Kadarikā-vihāra" temple. Considering the name "Mañjunātha" in light of all this information, Pai concluded that the *vihāra* was originally a centre of the cult of the *bodhisattva* Mañjuśri. At a later time, when this and other heavenly *bodhisattvas* had become identified with Śaivite deities, Nātha ascetics established a *Śiva-liṅga* in the temple and called it by the present name. Still later, disciples of Matsyendranātha, among whom should be included king Kundavarmā, arranged for the placing of the extant Lokeśvara image, an image representing what they must have regarded as the divine form of their master.

The worship of the *Śiva-liṅga* and its associated *bodhisattva* no doubt continued for several centuries, until what had originally been a Buddhist centre was converted into a purely Śaivite temple.[27] Although the Kadarikā *vihāra* provides the only known example of solid inscriptional evidence for this sort of transformation, it must nevertheless be the case that the process witnessed here was an extremely typical one. The Buddhist doctrine of the heavenly *bodhisattvas* allowed not only the kind of absorption-by-identification that we have seen, but also opened the door to the myriad Śaivite gods, goddesses, *mantras, dhāraṇis,* and mystical tantric practices surrounding such other-worldy figures. Nātha influence on the Jainas, by contrast, was kept to a minimum; although certain tantric elements do appear in conjunction with the *yakṣas,* these are of an extremely superficial sort and cannot in any way be construed as a fundamental aspect of Jaina worship. It is true that the term "-nātha" itself came to be attached to the names of certain Tīrthaṅkaras (*e.g.*, Neminātha, Pārśvanātha), this alteration, however, was purely a nominal one, representing no change whatsoever in the nature of the saints so designated.

It has been the aim of this paper to go beyond the various theories which Mitra has set forth by searching for more basic factors, factors that underlay or made possible whatever set of circumstances each of these theories describes. This same methodology, then, should be applied to our own proposal, *viz.*, that the doctrine of the heavenly *bodhisattvas* made Buddhism uniquely vulnerable to the assimilating tendencies of the surrounding Hindu cults. The development of the heavenly *bodhisattvas* theory, and indeed that of the entire Mahāyāna in Buddhism, can perhaps be ultimately traced back to the celebrated "silence (*avyākṛta*) of the Buddha", his unwillingness to commit himself regarding certain fundamental philosophical issues. The inability of the Buddhists to agree upon the meaning of this silence led to a situation in which various contradictory absolutist doctrines could emerge, each one claiming to be the correct interpretation of the master's teachings. Of particular interest here was the doctrine of *śūnyatā,* which implied, among other things, that there was no real distinction between *saṃsāra* and *nirvāṇa.* In such a context it was a short step to postulate beings on the model of the heavenly *bodhisattvas,* beings who, unlike the Buddha, dwelt in both realms simultaneously.

In Jainism, as is well-known, no counterpart of the Buddhist *Mahāyāna* ever appeared. Again, we can understand this fact on the basis of fundamental doctrine, *viz.,* the Jaina assertion that no absolute philosophical statement could be taken as valid. This view was expressed by the term *anekānta* (non-absolutism), and led to the cardinal Jaina tenet of *syādvāda* ("qualified assertion"). For Jainas, in other words, no synthesis of the human and the supramundane was ever possible; hence the Tīrthaṅkaras remained the highest models of spiritual development, and such Tantric practices as identification of the self with the deity were simply out of the question.

By excluding absolutism in any form, the Jainas limited themselves to a rather unexciting set of theories which probably exerted very little influence on Indian philosophical thoughts as a whole; certainly their texts cannot compare in beauty or interest with the spectacular flights of imagination and brilliant speculations found in the *Prajñāpāramitās.* Nevertheless, the tenacious adherence of Jaina *ācāryas* to the *anekānta* doctrine did have one result worth more to them than any praise for literary or philosophical merit; this was of course the survival of their religious community, an accomplishment which the Buddhists were ultimately unable to match.

NOTES

1. R.C. Mitra, *The Decline of Buddhism in India,* Shantiniketan, 1954.
2. This view has found favour with certain Buddhologists, notably Conze: "...what Buddhism in India died from was just old age, or sheer exhaustion". *A Short History of Buddhism,* 1960, p. 86.
3. Regarding the application of the term *Śramaṇa* exclusively to Buddhists and Jainas, see P.S. Jaini "*Śramaṇas:* Their conflict with Brāhmaṇical society", in *Chapters in Indian Civilization,* Volume I (ed. J.W. Elder), Dubuque, 1970, pp. 39-81.

4. P. S. Jaini "On the *Sarvajñatva* (Omniscience) of Mahāvīra and the Buddha", in *Buddhist Studies in Honour of I. B. Horner,* Dorderecht, 1974, pp. 71-90.
5. For the Jaina account of Mahāvīra's life, see H. Jacobi, *Jaina Sūtras,* Parts 1 and 2, Sacred Books of the East, Volumes XXII and XLV.
6. The Hathigumpha Inscription of King Khāravela of Kaliṅga (*circa* 150 B.C.) is cited in this connection. The following line is most relevant : *nandarājanītaṃ kāliṅgajinam samnivesam...*[*rāja*] *gaharatanaparihāre hi angamagadhabasum ca nagati.* See N.K. Sahu, *Utkal University History of Orissa,* Vol. 1, 1964, pp. 359 ff.
7. For a history of Jaina migration in the north, cf. C. J. Shah, *Jainism in North India,* London, 1932, pp. 187-200.
8. For a political and cultural history of the Jainas in Karnataka, cf. B.A. Saletore, *Mediaeval Jainism,* Bombay, 1938.

9.(a) For an allusion to the Śaivite persecution of the Jainas at Madurai, see *Periyapurāṇaṃ* by Cekkilar (10th century), ed. T.M.K. Pillai, Srivaikuntam, 1964, p. 533; *Tiruvilayātar Purāṇam* by Parañcoti Munivar (16th century), ed. N.M.V. Nattar, Madras, 1965, pp. 441-479.

9.(b) On the destruction of Nālandā, see A.L. Basham, *The Wonder That was India,* New York, 1959, p. 266.

10. For Haribhadra's comments on corrupt Jaina practices, cf. Nathuram Premi, *Jain Sāhitya aur Itihās,* Bombay, 1965, pp. 480 ff.
11. On the history of the Sthānakavāsi, cf. W. Schubring, *The Doctrine of the Jainas,* Delhi, 1962, pp. 65 ff.
12. On the Digambara-Śvetāmbara schism, see *Ibid.,* p. 50 ff.
13. For a complete bibliography, see R. Williams, *Jaina Yoga—A Survey of the Mediaeval Śrāvakācāras,* London, 1963.
14. H. Saddhatissa (editor), *Upāsakajanālaṅkāra* of Ānanda, Pāli Text Society, London, 1965 (a twelfth-century Pāli work written by a Singhalese monk in South India).
15. *dānavāmstu vaśe kṛtvā punarbuddhatvam āgatah/sargasya rakṣaṇārthāya tasmai Buddhātmane namah. Mbh.* XII, 47, 67; *Matsyapurāṇa,* 47, 247; *Gītagovinda,* I, 1, 9.
16. *Bhāgavata Purāṇa,* V, iii-viii. P. S. Jaini, "Jina Ṛṣabha as an *avatāra* of Viṣṇu", *Bulletin of the School of Oriental and African Studies,* Vol. XL, 2, 1977.
17. This criticism appears in the *śrāvakācāras* (see note 13, above) under the description of "false gods, scriptures and *gurus*" whose worship is forbidden to the Jaina laity.
18. Atleast sixteen Jaina *Rāmāyaṇas* are known to exist (ten in Sanskrit, five in Prakrit, one in Apabhraṃśa). For a complete list, see V.M. Kulakarni's Introduction (pp. 1-6) to the *Paumacariu,* Vol. I, Varanasi, 1962. Compare the extent of this collection with the fact that only one such story, *viz.,* the *Dasaratha-jātaka* (*Jātaka* No. 461) exists in the Buddhist tradition. cf. Kamil Bulche, *Rāmakathā : utpatti aur vikās,* Prayag, 1950, p. 56 ff.
19. For the Jaina versions of the life of Kṛṣṇa, see Jinasena's *Harivaṃśa Purāṇa* (ed. Pannalal Jain, Varanasi, 1944) and Hemacandra's *Triṣaṣṭiśalākāpuruṣa-caritra,* Book VIII (translated by Helen M. Johnson, G.O.S. No. 139), Baroda, 1962. No comparable Buddhist texts have come down to us.
20. The *Ādipurāṇa* of Jinasena (9th century) (ed. Pannalal Jain, Varanasi, 1963) would appear to be the earliest text to mention these rituals for the Jaina laity. For further details, see V. A. Sangave, *Jaina Community,* Bombay, 1942.
21. This development is perhaps symbolically shown by the typical iconographic

representation of the Buddha as a small inset in the crown of the *Bodhisattva;* his position is "highest" (in accordance with doctrine) and yet relatively unimportant in the eyes of the worshipper.

22. This was accomplished through litigation initiated by the Mahābodhi Society of Calcutta, an international organization, mainly representing Buddhists of Śri Lanka and Burma. The shrines were awarded to this organization on the basis of its contention that Singhalese and Burmese kings had for many years provided funds for their maintenance.
23. M. Govinda Pai, "Dharmasthalada śiva-liṅgakke Mañjunātha emba hesaru hege bantu?" in *Samarpaṇe* (*Felicitation Volume in Honour of Shri Manjayya Heggade*), Mangalore, 1950, pp. 65-77.
24. Concerning the origin of the Śiva-liṅga, see note 27, below.
25. The inscription reads as follows :
śrī Kundavarmā guṇavān Āḷupendro mahīpatih/
pādāravindabhramaro Bālacandra-Śikhāmaṇeh/6/
Lokeśvarasya devasya pratiṣṭhām akarot prabhuh/
Śrīmat Kadarikānāmni Vihāre sumanohare/9/
Kalau varṣasahasrāṇām atikrānte catuṣṭaye/
punar abdag(ś)ate caivāṣṭaṣaṣṭyā samanvite/10/
Samarpaṇe, p. 70.
26. In this connection Pai quotes the following verse from a Nepalese inscription:
Śrī Lokeśvarāya namah
Matsyendram yogināṃ mukhyāh śāktāh śaktiṃ vadanti yam/
bauddhā Lokeśvaraṃ tasmai namo brahmasvarūpiṇe/1
Pandit Bhagavanlal Indraji and G. Buhler, "Inscriptions from Nepal", *The Indian Antiquary,* June, 1880, p. 192.
27. Local Kannaḍa legend (*Sthaḷa-purāṇa*) concerning this shrine gives its traditional name as Suvarṇa-Kadaḷīvana-Śrī Mañjunātha Devasthāna (Golden-banana-grove, the temple of Mañjunātha). This account (said to be based upon the *Bhāradvāja-samhitā*) can be briefly summarized as follows :

"In ancient times Lord Paraśurāma (one of the *avatāras* of Viṣṇu), having (killed the *kṣatriyas* and) given the entire earth to the *brāhmaṇas,* undertook severe penances. Śiva, pleased with his performance thereof, said, "O Paraśurāma, I have a permanent abode in the Well of Ambrosia (*rasa-kūpa*), located in Suvarṇa-kadalīvana; go there and worship me". At that time, however, Suvarṇa-kadalīvana was temporarily covered by ocean water. Paraśurāma wrested the land back from the sea, and then proceeded to carry out further penances there. At last the members of the divine Trinity, Brahmā, Viṣṇu and Maheśvara, came together and were spontaneously manifested in the form of the mañjunātha (i.e., the *Śiva-liṅga*)". (Does this unusual coalescence of the three deities perhaps reflect a confused reference to the three-faced Lokeśvara image?)

An alternate version, forming the latter part of the *Sthaḷa-purāṇa,* suggests that Matsyendranātha came to this place from the kingdom of Sati (probably Kerala, where matrilineal inheritence prevailed) and, like Paraśurāma, underwent severe penances to please Śiva. The deity thus appeared as the present *Śivaliṅga.* This latter story tends to confirm the association of Matsyendranātha with the temple in question, and even suggests that he may have been personally responsible for the establishment of the *Śiva-liṅga* found there.

Kadri Image of Lokeśvara
For the inscription on the pedestal of this image, see note no. 25.

CHAPTER 8

Values in Comparative Perspective: *Svadharma* versus *Ahiṃsā**

As Louis Dumont's publications on the sociology of India have conclusively established, Hindu society is characterized by a caste hierarchy based upon the opposition between the pure and the impure.[1] The caste system places the brahman, the emblem of purity, at one extreme, and the untouchable, the embodiment of impurity, at the other. In between are found the *kṣatriya* (warrior), *vaiśya* (merchant), and *śūdra* (labourer), who share relatively in both purity and impurity. The occupations of the four castes and the untouchables have been apportioned according to their respective purity as inherited by birth. In principle, no member of these castes is free to exchange his duties and privileges for those of any other caste, and is thus denied all freedom of choice. The loss of such liberty and the incumbent rejection of individuality are thus considered to be the fate of people belonging to the Hindu community. However, the system has a built-in escape, in theory at least, for members of the first three castes, the so-called "twice-born." A male "twice-born" may renounce the world and establish himself outside of the duties, obligations, and privileges of society, and in doing so asserts both his individuality and his freedom from social restraints. Although outside caste society, the renunciate (*sannyāsin*) is considered to have in fact transcended it. Hence, to some extent he replaces the brahman as the apex of

*This article was originally published in *Śramaṇa Vidyā: Studies in Buddhism: Professor Jagannāth Upādhyāya Commemoration Volume*, ed. N.H. Samtani, (Sarnath, Varanasi, 1987), pp. 111-122.

purity. By virtue of this position, he may influence the behaviour of his society in such a way as to remove whatever gross inequalities might occasionally occur.

It is patently clear that the hierarchical structure outlined above is incompatible with Western norms of equality, in which an individual may not be denied the freedom of occupational choice. Hindu law makers have used two terms to explain the coercive nature of caste hierarchy. These are *svadharma* (one's own duty) and *svabhāva* (one's own nature).[2] It is believed that the duties of each individual follow from his *svabhāva*. But how does one know one's own nature? It is discovered by observing the various combinations of the three basic constituents (*guṇas*) of the psychophysical nature, namely *prakṛti*. The *prakṛti*, the source of all material creation, is composed of three guṇas: *sattva* (knowledge, happiness and light), *rajas* (energy, unhappiness and heat) and *tamas* (ignorance, inertia and darkness). The domination of one or another of these three qualities accounts for the variety of all types of life-forms, human as well as non-human. The Hindus have believed that the brahman has a larger share of *sattva* than other human beings and, consequently, partakes of a greater amount of purity and spiritual knowledge. This being his nature (*svabhāva*), he is fit to be a teacher, a reciter of the sacred texts, a priest who can offer sacrifices to the gods, as well as a wise man who is the lawgiver. His means of livelihood is thus restricted to status-bringing professions, even while denying him the splendour of royalty or the wealth of the merchant class. The kṣatriya is said to be dominated by *rajas*. His *sattva* is thus subdued by his ambition for power—the will to destroy and to dominate. For this reason, his *svadharma* is to rule and to administer justice, and to uphold, by force if necessary, the hierarchical order and the social constraints stipulated by the brahman. *Artha* or polity is his realm, and it is believed that he has no inclination whatever to be a priest. The vaiśya is inferior to the kṣatriya, because his *rajas* is tainted to a large degree by *tamas*. His boundless greed forces him to acquire larger markets and generate profits. *Kāma*, the pleasures of the senses, is the guiding principle for this class. Below this class comes the śūdra whose nature is said to be overpowered by stupidity and inertia. One expects him to be lazy, lacking in the will to learn, to fight, or even to gain a surplus of wealth. Hence his *svabhāva* stipulates that his *svadharma* be that of a wage earner, who obediently serves the three upper castes. He may be sufficiently intelligent to master the worldly arts and crafts of the carpenter, barber, or laundryman, but his *sattva* is so debilitated that he cannot be initiated into the spiritual mysteries which are available to the twice-born, through the traditional rites of passage (*saṃskāras*). For the same reason, he is barred from becoming a renunciate, the only escape available even to the three upper castes. As far as the untouchable is concerned, the overpowering *tamas* of his constitution pervades even his shadow, effectively shutting him off from any contact with all the other castes. His *svadharma* is thus to be a scavenger, responsible for the removal of the most impure substance for a Hindu, the dead bodies of animals.

The idea that one should follow a vocation that accords with one's own nature seems reasonable enough. But is there any way a man might know what his *svabhāva* is by analyzing his urges or by reflecting on his conscience? Can he educate himself by self-examination and bring about a change in his *svabhāva,* which would then effect a suitable change in his *svadharma*? In other words, is the *svabhāva* a changeable substance, or must it remain a fixed, unalterable part of one's personality, like one's sex? The answer given in the law-books is emphatic in affirming that the *svabhāva* of an individual is inherited through birth in a given caste. The lineage of the four castes was fixed from the time of the primordial man, the great *Puruṣa* and although each birth in the life of an individual is determined by his own *karma,* the *svabhāva* apportioned to each caste can neither be acquired by that individual by recourse to new acts, nor relinquished at will. One therefore knows one's *svabhāva* by knowing the caste of one's own parents, and this knowledge defines for him, from virtually the moment of his birth, the range of his *svadharma* and his place in the hierarchy.

Given these doctrines of the primordial man, the lineage of castes, the force of *karma* and rebirth, the consequent *svabhāva* and the corresponding *svadharma,* it is clear that there can be no egalitarianism in Hindu society. All men are inherently unequal. Caste identity may confer a certain amount of intrafraternal equality, but even this is subject to the internal hierarchies of the innumerable sub-castes (*jātis*) found within that caste. The denial of equality must therefore deprive the Hindu both of individuality as well as one of the basic rights of modern man: the freedom of choice regarding one's own livelihood.

Evidently the rationale of *svadharma* and *svabhāva* was used by some lawmakers to explain a situation in Indian society which prevailed at some remote time in history. But Hindus themselves appear to have accepted the structure as the foundation of their society, in the same way, for example, the Christians have accepted the Biblical story of Genesis as the beginning of human civilization. Whether only a handful of brahmans knew this Indian "Genesis", or whether it pervaded the consciousness of all Hindus at all levels of society, is unimportant. What is significant, however, is that the great epics (including the *Gītā*), the *Purāṇas,* and the traditional Law Books, have sought to explain the four human goals—*dharma, artha, kāma,* and *mokṣa*—by recourse to these two key concepts. Such an explanation was probably necessary in order to defend the system against protests from those sections of society which felt discriminated against in this world, if not also in the next.

The existing literary documents attest to the fact that all four castes raised their voice in protest, although for obvious reasons only the protests of the upper castes have been heard. One would think that the brahmans had everything to gain by the status quo, as they were placed at the top of the pyramid. Yet it would be naive to think that a brahman might not be tempted to enjoy the privileges of kingship. The mythological story of the brahman Paraśurāma (Rāma with axe)—who slaughtered the entire kṣatriya race seven times over, giving the earth to a brahman king and the widows of the slain kṣatriyas to brahman men—should be understood not only as the reassertion of the brahman's superiority over the kṣatriya, but also as an indication of the enormous jealousy brahmans held towards the innate right of the kṣatriya to rule. Paraśurāma's behaviour betrays the claim made by the brahmans that they embody the highest *sattva.* Despite the high status of the kṣatriya and his privilege of ruling, this has not been immune from protest either. The battlefield protest of Arjuna, the hero of the *Mahābhārata,* has echoed through the centuries and is sure witness to the fact that these warriors, as brave as they might have been, were able to accept their alleged *svadharma* only in defiance of their conscience.[3] It is unlikely that the merchant caste despised its assigned roles, as they involved neither the poverty of the brahman nor the dangers confronting the kṣatriya. Even so, however, the fact that historically this group supported the heterodoxies of Buddhism and Jainism would indicate that they too did not wholeheartedly accept their place in the orthodox hierarchy. As far as the Śūdra and, to an even greater extent, the untouchable are concerned, the documents are understandably silent. One can only speculate about the extraordinary amount of coercion they must have suffered to accept their miserable lot without excessive protest. We should probably also include women of all castes in a similar category with the śūdra. They too were denied all rights of inheritance, and were also not permitted to participate in the *saṃskāras* (in particular, the rite of initiation, or *upanayana*) available to their male counterparts. Like the śūdra also, they were not allowed to renounce the world and thus find freedom from the duties of the household. Thus the *svadharma* of all four castes appears to have been accepted not voluntarily, but under duress, sustained by the belief in the possibility of improving one's lot in the next life or of attaining salvation through the grace of the Lord. It was asserted time and again that the Creator extended his grace to those who patiently abided by the system of *svadharma* and fulfilled their duties as participants in the divine plan. Devotion (*bhakti*) to the Lord thus served to reinforce the system of *svadharma*, legitimizing the built-in inequality and forcing the individual to submit to the dictates of the traditional Law Books.[4]

The only effective protest against the inequities of such a society would come from those who had rejected without reservation the theological claims made in support of this system. The Buddhists and Jainas did not deny the belief in reincarnation, nor did they deny that man's own actions generated the forces which would determine the social circumstances in which a person would find himself at birth. While a certain occupational or hierarchical class was therefore "given" for each individual, the heterodox faiths did not accept the theory that the child inherited from his parents the *svabhāva* or the combination of the *guṇas* discussed above. In the absence of such a theory there was no fixed *svadharma* for any individual. It is understandable that most people would follow in the footsteps of their parents and be trained in their "family" occupations. But it was not considered obligatory to pursue the same course if one lacked either the necessary inclination or the force of conviction to maintain oneself in the parent's tradition. The idea that one should perform one's *svadharma* even against the call of conscience (as Kṛṣṇa had admonished Arjuna) would be unacceptable to Buddhists and Jainas, the two foremost Śramaṇa schools, who resolutely discarded theistic bulwarks of Hindu society: the myth of the Primal Man as the source of the caste geneology; the concept of *prakṛti* and its three *guṇas;* and the claim that evil incurred during the performance of one's *svadharma* could be nullified by the grace of an almighty Being. The rejection of these three dogmas meant that an individual could fashion for himself whatever course of action he might choose to follow. There was no obligation on his part to act against his conscience, since there was no "divine play" in which one must participate. Each individual was ultimately responsible for himself alone, and took the consequence of his actions. There was no agency of divine intervention which could cancel the irrevocable consequences of deeds done, as Kṛṣṇa had promised Arjuna. Of course, the Buddhists and the Jainas did not deny the conventional legitimacy of caste distinctions; at the same time, however, they emphasized that the caste of one's birth was not a permanent feature like one's sex, for example, but rather an accidental if unavoidable, factor like one's given name. One could change one's caste and move upwards or downwards by one's own freely chosen activities. Since they did not believe in divinely ordained differences in caste, they were not frightened by the spectre of *varṇasaṅkara,* or confusion of castes, the deadly enemy of the orthodox social system. As a Jaina author boldly declared, there was a single *jāti,* the *jāti* of human beings (*manuṣyajātir ekaiva*);[5] differences of occupation did not produce different species.

In adopting the doctrine of karma leading to rebirth, the Buddhist and Jainas had accepted basic differences between men at the time of their birth. But this inequality was not derived from the inherited *svabhāvas,* as believed by the orthodox schools. *Karma* was not identical with the *guṇas,* since the former could be overcome by anyone regardless of his position in society at the time of birth. Buddhists and Jainas emphasized that in looking for hierarchy one should examine conduct, not birth (*mā jatiṃ puccha, carṇaṃ puccha*), and one's sex or family affiliation were of no consequence in perfecting conduct. They were able, therefore, to open their monastic orders to large numbers of śūdras and women who were hitherto forbidden to move out of their given '*svadharma*'. Neither did they hesitate to challenge the brahmans about their alleged natal sacredness, nor to urge their kṣatriya and vaiśya lay devotees to forsake warfare and the pursuit of wealth, regardless of the consequences to society at large.

It should not be thought, however, that these two heterodoxies were content merely to expand the membership of already existing institutions of renunciants. The institution of renunciation certainly appears to be pre-Buddhistic as it is expounded in the older Upaniṣads and is known from the example of the great philosopher Yājñavalkya who, after leading a fruitful life, amicably took leave of his two wives to enter the stage of recluseship. Buddhist and Jaina mendicants broke away from the pattern of gradual renunciation either by skipping altogether the stage of the householder, or by abandoning their wives and children and their aged parents in the prime of life as was the case with Siddhārtha Gautama and Vardhamāna Mahāvīra. Since one discharges one's family duties (such as caring for parents, raising children, and offering oblations to one's ancestors) and fulfills one's prescribed dharma—whether as a priest, warrior or merchant—primarily during the householder period, a total renunciation at this stage must be seen as a complete rejection of the values held sacred by the orthodox system. It cannot be said that these were stray individuals, exceptions to the general rule. Both Buddhist and Jaina texts proclaim repeatedly that tens of thousands of young men and women of good family (*kulaputtas* and *kuladuhitās*), their hair still jet black, left their household in search of the goal of salvation. One scene depicts the Buddha returning to his home town with a retinue of 1200 young monks soon after his enlightenment. As they moved along the main street, the people cried in anguish, "This ascetic Gautama is bent on turning women into widows, is intent on forcing them into childlessness." The Buddha is said to have remained calm, assuring his ardent followers that the noise would die down within seven days, "for surely who could blame us for following the dharma?"[6] The dharma Buddha was teaching about was surely not the *svadharma* of the orthodox tradition. It was rather a dharma which rejected the claims of *svadharma* and asserted the right of the individual to break away from social obligations if and when he chose to do so.

It would be wrong to think, however, that Buddhists and Jainas were interested merely in recruiting members for their respective mendicant orders. The dharma which they proclaimed was preeminently associated with *ahiṃsā* : renunciation of the intention to harm any living being. They began their propagation of this holy law by pointing out the *hiṃsā* which was perpetrated by different castes in the name of *svadharma.* Hence, a brahman, undertaking the slaughter of animals during the performance of a Vedic sacrifice, a king engaged in hunting as a part of his royal duties, or a merchant involved in arms trade were all condemned and encouraged to abandon their evil practices. The fact that the Vedic practice of animal sacrifice has totally disappeared and that a large number of upper caste men have become vegetarian attest to the extraordinary success achieved by the heterodox faiths in their attempt to create new values for the society based not on *svadharma* but on *ahiṃsā.* As they gathered strength, they were able to convert a great many royal houses to their religion and through them propagate the holy law of non-violence in the conduct of government as well. Aśoka, the great emperor, is depicted in the Buddhist chronicles as having been a wicked king before his conversion to Buddhism. We know from his inscriptions that he did indeed engage in a bloody war against the Kalingas in which by his own admission "150,000 persons were carried away as captives, 100,000 were slain, and many times that number died." He could probably have justified his actions as legitimate for a *cakravartin,* a world conqueror, in carrying out his *svadharma.* But the Buddhist texts have consistently condemned his violent acts without absolving him from the evil deeds he committed. He was acceptable to them only after he repented from his actions and resolved never to repeat them; from that point on he was known as the righteous king, the king of dharma (*dhammiko, dhammarājā*). We are fortunate that we do not have to depend entirely on the Buddhist chronicles for evidence of the King's renunciation of violence. His own inscription attests to his remorse when he declares, "The conqueror of the Kalingas has remorse now, because of the thought that the conquest is no conquest, for there was killing, death or banishment of the people. This is keenly felt with profound sorrow and regret...This rescript on dharma has been written for the purpose that my sons and grandsons who will hear about my new conquests should not consider that further conquest is to be undertaken. ... They should consider that the only true conquest is conquest by dharma."[7] By any standards, this must be considered an extraordinary confession for an Emperor; few rulers in the history of civilization have thought it fit to admit the wrongs committed against people conquered in war. It is the replacement of the orthodox *svadharma* by this new value of non-violence which probably went a long way towards removing the conflict between caste hierarchy and renunciation, and helped to bring about a unity of purpose for both caste members and renunciants.

Among the Jainas, the espousal of *ahiṃsā* was so total that they could not bring themselves to sanction violence in any form. For them, the very expression 'righteous war' would have been a contradiction. The Jainas have claimed many kings for their faith, including Candragupta Maurya, the founder of the Maurya dynasty and grandfather of Aśoka. One would expect Jaina authors to have left some account of these heroes, but only those kings are remembered in their literature who either became mendicants or attained a holy death by fasting in the prescribed Jaina manner. One name of a non-Jaina ruler stands out, however, in their narrative works: the great Moghul Akbar. He is not remembered for his conquests, but for his decrees prohibiting the slaughter of animals on certain holy days, made at the request of Jaina mendicants.[8] He thus adhered, however marginally, to the creeds of non-violence and vegetarianism. As for Jaina views on warfare, one need only glance at their enormous literature for evidence of their condemnation of violence, even when it appeared legitimate to the ordinary Hindu. In the brahmanical *Rāmāyaṇa*, Rāma slays Rāvaṇa for his unlawful act of abducting Sītā; but rather than incurring guilt from this transgression, he instead is praised, for his mission as an *avatāra* of Viṣṇu was precisely the destruction of this ungodly demon. The Jainas, however, saw the contradiction inherent in killing without incurring the karmic consequence of the deed. Rather than accept this, they modified the story so that Rāma could attain *mokṣa* by attributing the slaying of Rāvaṇa to Rāma's younger brother, Lakṣmaṇa. One can appreciate the ethical awareness of the Jainas in their insistence that the path of *mokṣa* cannot admit acts of violence, however justifiable they might be. But what is truly striking in this new rendition is that Lakṣmaṇa, who commits this heroic act, is born not in heaven, as we might expect, but in the same hell to which the Jainas consign Rāvaṇa.[9]

Compare this story, for example, with the brahmanical story of the *Mahābhārata*, where we are told that the villain, Duryodhana, and the hero, Yudhiṣṭhira, were both reborn in heaven.[10] The former attained this destiny because he perished on the battlefield, thus fulfilling the "*svadharma*" of the kṣatriya; the latter gained this reward because of his celebrated virtues. The contrast between the two attitudes should demonstrate conclusively the difference between the ethics of *svadharma* and *ahiṃsā*, and the extent to which the Jainas would go in refusing to legitimate warfare or reward an act of killing.[11]

The Jainas applied the same principle of *ahiṃsā* to the sphere of the two lower castes also. They drew up long lists of professions which involved the killing of animals or the excessive destruction of vegetable life, and declared them unsuitable for a Jaina of the merchant class. As far as the śūdra and the untouchable were concerned, it must be admitted that the Jainas did not do enough to bring them under their persuasion. However, they held them impure not because of the presence of any alleged substance like *tamas*, but because of the violence inherent in their occupations, such as farming, logging, or butchery. They therefore concentrated on preaching vegetarianism to them and welcomed them to their fold as full members of the Jaina community if they could conform to the vegetarian diet. The Jainas thus sought to make *ahiṃsā* into a universal principle which could serve as a guideline for all members of the community, a dharma undertaken voluntarily and in keeping with one's conscience.

It would not be impertinent to inquire whether the Buddhists and Jainas ever succeeded in establishing a society based on *ahiṃsā*. Hindus have maintained that their civilization survived through the centuries precisely because the members of its caste society scrupulously adhered to their *svadharma*, even to the extent of providing sustenance to the heterodoxies that grew like parasites on the Hindu tree. Some modern Hindus, among whom we should include the militant revivalists known as the R. S. S. (Rāshṭrīya Svayaṃsevaka Sangha) look back on the rule of the minister Kauṭilya Cāṇakya and his king Candragupta Maurya, the contemporary of Alexander the Great, and accuse the Buddhists and Jainas of undermining India's military power by their excessive zeal for *ahiṃsā* during the Aśokan period. The sudden fall of the Aśokan empire and the successive defeats of the Indian dynasties at the hands of the Scythians, Huns, and the forces of Islam, is also said to have resulted from the debilitating message of non-violence. We do not know how Buddhists or Jainas would have responded to these accusations. Buddhists disappeared from the Indian scene centuries ago, and Jainas have been reduced to the status of a minority caste, living on the fringes of the society of the "twice-borns", struggling to maintain their identity in conformity with their ancient teachings. However, Indian history might in fact suggest that Hindus lost their political autonomy not so much because of the high ideals of their "otherworldly" men, but instead because of the brahmanical enforcement of inequitable *svadharmas.* It is small wonder that the Hindu nation was never able to win a single decisive victory over its invaders, since kṣatriyas, who were supposedly responsible for the fighting, vaiśyas who bore the burden of financing the wars, and śūdras (as well as the untouchables) who offered their slave labour for the rest of society, did not willingly and spontaneously participate in fulfilling their alleged *svadharma.* By contrast, one could point to the extraordinary victory achieved by Mahatma Gandhi in our own age, through recourse to the principles of *ahiṃsā* and asceticism. Under his leadership, the entire nation, irrespective of the *svadharmas* of caste or sex, reasserted the universal values of Indian civilization: brotherhood, non-violence, and peace for all.

NOTES

1. Louis Dumont, *Homo Hierarchicus: An Essay on the Caste System,* University of Chicago Press, 1970; "World Renunciation in Indian Religions" in *Contributions to Indian Sociology,* no. iv, 1960.
2. *Manusmṛti,* i, 88-93; viii, 4. Compare *Bhagavad Gītā,* ii, 31; iv, 13.
3. *Bhagavad-Gītā,* i, 32-41.
4. *Bhagavad-Gītā,* iii, 35; xviii, 47.
5. *manuṣyajātir ekaiva jātināmodayodbhavā/*
   vṛttibhedāhitād bhedāc cāturvarṇyam ihāśnute//
   Ādipurāṇa of Jinasena, xxxviii, 45 (Bharatiya Jnanapitha, 1963).
6. See *Vinaya Piṭaka,* I, p. 43 (Pali Text Society, London).
7. *Edicts of Asoka,* Rock Edict xiii (Adyar Library, 1951).
8. Vincent A. Smith. "The Jain Teachers of Akbar", in *Essays Presented to Sir R. G. Bhandarkar,* pp. 265-276, Poona, 1971.
9. See Helen M. Johnson, *The Lives of Sixty-three Illustrious Persons* (trans. of Hemacandra's *Triṣaṣṭiśalākāpuruṣacaritra*), vol. 4 (Gaekwad's Oriental Series, cxxv Baroda, 1954).

10. *svargaṃ triviṣṭapaṃ prāpya dharmarājo Yudhiṣṭhiraḥ/ Duryodhanaṃ śriyā juṣṭaṃ dadarṣāsīnam āsane//* *Mahābhārata,* xviii, i, 4.
11. For a discussion on the Jaina attitude toward the svadharma of a kṣatriya, see P. S. Jaini, *The Jaina Path of Purification* (University of California Press, Berkeley, 1979), p. 311 ff.

CHAPTER 9

On the Ignorance of the Arhat*

In the opening verse of his *Abhidharmakośa,* Vasubandhu (*ca.* 400), while commenting on the words *yaḥ sarvathā sarvahatāndhakāraḥ,* which describe the omniscience of the Buddha, speaks of two kinds of ignorance.[1] The first is called *kliṣṭasammoha* (defiled delusion), which means ignorance of the four noble truths. The pratyekabuddhas (those who attain arhatship without the aid of a buddha) and the śrāvakas (those disciples of the Buddha who attain arhatship) are free from such ignorance, since they have realized the true nature of all (*sarvaṃ*) that exists as being *duḥkha* (suffering), *anitya* (impermanent), and anātma (nonself). However, Vasubandhu claims that they have not overcome the second kind of ignorance, *akliṣṭa-ajñāna,* the "undefiled," ordinary ignorance of the infinite varieties of objects that are distant in space and time. Vasubandhu states in passing that the Buddha has achieved this total freedom from ignorance (*ajñāna*) through cultivating its counterpart, but fails to indicate what that counteragent (*pratipakṣa*) could be.[2]

Yaśomitra (*ca.* 700), in his commentary to the *Kośa,* the *Sphuṭārthā-vyākhyā,* states that *pratipakṣa* means *āryamārga* (the noble path), since it is the opposite of the adversary called *kleśa* (defilement). Yaśomitra does not seem happy with this explanation, because the śrāvakas and the pratyekabuddhas have destroyed the *kleśas* and yet have not overcome all forms of *ajñāna.* He therefore gives an alternative meaning, saying that *pratipakṣa* is

*This article was originally published in *Buddhist Soteriology: The Mārga Approaches to Liberation,* eds. Buswell and Gimello, (Kuroda Institute: University of Hawaii Press, 1992), pp. 135-146. Reprinted with kind permission of University of Hawaii Press.

anāsravaṃ jñānam, knowledge freed from *āsravas* (influxes).[3] Whether this *anāsravajñāna* is merely the understanding achieved by the destruction of the *anuśaya* (disposition or defilement) known as *avidyā* (ignorance), or whether it entails some additional achievement, is not explained by Yaśomitra. He is also silent on the precise difference between the *kleśapratipakṣa* and the *ajñānapratipakṣa,* and about the possible stage on the path (*mārga*) at which the latter may be cultivated. Yet there must be some distinction, since the *akliṣṭa-ajñāna* is defined as a deficiency that the arhats failed to overcome even when they were presumed to have followed the same noble path traversed by the Buddha, which was believed to culminate in the same kind of *nirvāṇa.* Neither Vasubandhu nor Yaśomitra addresses this issue specifically, but an investigation of the Vaibhāṣika rules on the mārga pertaining to the destruction of the *akliṣṭa-ajñāna* may yield a solution.

Yaśomitra is acutely aware of the anomaly of admitting in the arhat a form of ignorance that remains even in the absence of *kleśas*:

> Surely, [a questioner asks,] all that is considered *sāsrava* [affected by influxes] is destroyed by both the *śrāvakas* and the pratyekabuddhas as in the case of the Buddha; so how could you maintain that in their case only the *kliṣṭasammoha* is destroyed? Has it not been said in the sūtra : "I do not say that there is the complete destruction of suffering as long as even a single dharma remains without being known (*aparijñāya*) and abandoned (*aprahāya*)?" Therefore it must be admitted that this *akliṣṭa-ajñāna* was abandoned by the arhats and the pratyekabuddhas as well, analogous to their destruction of eye (*cakṣu*) and other dharmas [i.e., the ten material elements] by the method of overcoming delight (*chandarāga*) toward them. Otherwise there would be no total destruction of suffering in their case?[4]

Yaśomitra accepts this sūtra and concedes that, even in the case of the arhats and pratyekabuddhas, this so-called *akliṣṭa-ajñāna* must be considered destroyed (*prahīṇam*) like the *kliṣṭasammoha,* but nevertheless pleads that there is a difference: whereas the *akliṣṭa-ajñāna,* unlike the *kliṣṭasammoha,* can be destroyed, it is liable to reappear (*samudācarati*) and needs to be dispelled anew on each subsequent occasion. In the case of the Buddha, however, once his *chandarāga* is destroyed, it will not reappear (*buddhasya tu prahīṇaṃ san na samudācarati*) at each instance of a new perception. Yaśomitra adds that, for this very reason, Vasubandhu qualified the Buddha's destruction (*prahāṇa*) as not subject to reemergence (*punar anutpattidharmatvāt hatam*), and hence the Buddha alone is totally free from both kinds of ignorance. It is this excellence which distinguishes him from other arhats.[5]

What we glean from this rather obscure commentary is that there is a form of ignorance that pertains not to the true nature of dharmas (which is dispelled by the knowledge of the four noble truths) but to the worldly nature of things, and that persists even after one has become an arhat. An ordinary person can be consumed by curiosity (a form of desire or *chanda*) and will experience dejection at not knowing—or delight (*chandarāga*) at knowing—the desired object. For the arhat, however, his *kleśas* having been destroyed, ignorance of "things" is unable to obstruct the purity of his mind. When a need arises to know something hitherto unknown (i.e., when he becomes aware of his ignorance), the arhat will be mindful and will dispel any delight that may accompany the act of knowing the new object. In the case of the Buddha there is no such deficiency because he lacks all forms of curiosity and consequent delight, since the objects he wants to know become instantaneously known to him without any effort (*prayoga*) whatsoever.

What is the arhat ignorant of? Vasubandhu mentions three items: (1) the eighteen special (*āveṇika*) dharmas of the Buddha, which are extremely subtle (*paramasūkṣma*); (2) the infinite variety of gross and subtle material aggregates (*paramāṇusañcita*) that are distant in place (*viprakṛṣṭadeśa*), and (3) those that are remote in time (*viprakṛṣṭakāla*). Yaśomitra illustrates these with examples about the arhats Śāriputra and Maudgalyāyana.[6] When questioned by the Buddha, Śāriputra admitted that he had no knowledge of the extent of the Tathāgata's countless aggregates of the practices of *śīla* (moral precepts), samādhi (meditation), prajñā (wisdom), and so on. This is because, as Yaśomitra points out, the special (*āveṇika*) dharmas of the Buddha are extremely subtle and no one but the buddhas can know them.

Nor are the other material objects accessible to the cognition of arhats, even when they are not subtle but are distant--that is, separated (*antarita*) by different world systems (*lokadhātu*). This is illustrated by the Elder Maudgalyāyana's ignorance of the extremely distant world system called Marīci where his mother was reborn; only the Buddha knew her whereabouts. Similarly, remoteness in time can prevent an arhat from knowing a past incident, as happened when a certain person approached Śāriputra seeking renunciation. Śāriputra rejected him because he failed to discern any roots of good (*kuśalamūla*) in him that might lead to nirvāṇa, but the Buddha was able to perceive a subtle seed of salvation (*mokṣabīja*)—the result of a certain wholesome act—which lay hidden like a speck of pure gold in ore, and granted him ordination. As for the countless variety of material objects in their infinite details, only the buddhas, if they cared to, could know them all, for it is said that even the totality of causes that come together to produce the "eye" on a peacock's feather cannot be known by anyone but a buddha, since that is the realm of omniscient cognition. Of course, not all arhats need be equally deficient in all these areas; but all fall far short of that omniscience (*sarvajñabala*) which characterizes a buddha.[7]

The Theravādins shared the Vaibhāṣika belief that omniscience is that mark which distinguishes a buddha from arhats and pratyekabuddhas. We learn from the *Kathāvatthu* and its *Aṭṭhakathā* that the Pubbaseliyas held a view—similar to that of the Vaibhāṣikas— that the arhat may still possess ignorance (*aññāṇa*) and doubt (*kaṃkhā*) because he may be ignorant and doubtful about worldly things, such as names of men, trees, and so forth, and may be excelled in such matters by worldlings (*puthujjana*).[8] The Theravādins admitted this but concluded that since the arhat has eliminated the *anuśayas*, the ignorance of worldly things does not in any way affect his attainment of arhatship. This shows that, unlike the Vaibhāṣikas, the Theravādins did not take the term "*aparijñāya*" quoted above literally (as "without having known") but interpreted it as "without truly having understood [every dharma]." They therefore had no dispute with the Pubbaseliyas as long as it was agreed that the arhat's ordinary ignorance did not imply any residual presence of the *anuśayas* of *vicikitsā* (skeptical doubt) and *avidyā*.

This explains why the expression "*akliṣṭa-ajñāna*" is not attested in the Theravāda Abhidharma, which also fails to provide any explanation (such as those given by Vasubandhu and Yaśomitra) for the absence of this particular form of ignorance in the historical Buddha. Thus we need only examine the Vaibhāṣika texts for a possible solution to the problems of determining (1) the dharmic nature of this *akliṣṭa-ajñāna;* (2) when and how the Buddha destroyed this particular ignorance; and (3) whether its persistence could in any way be detrimental to the status of an arhat.

As seen earlier, *akliṣṭa-ajñāna* is, by definition, ignorance of worldly things—that is, the absence in varying degrees of what is called *saṃvṛti-jñāna* (knowledge of conventional objects).[9] It is therefore not subsumed under *avidyā* (the foremost *kleśa*) or under such lesser ones as skeptical doubt (*vicikitsā*), all of which are annihilated through the process of mārga. Could the *akliṣṭa-ajñāna* be one of the *kleśavāsanās* (impregnations of passions) which, as Étienne Lamotte has so convincingly demonstrated, are destroyed only by the Buddha at the time of attaining perfect enlightenment (*samyaksambodhi*), but which are never destroyed by arhats and which persist to the end of their lives?[10] This does not seem possible because the *akliṣṭa-ajñāna* does not fit the description of an impregnation (*vāsanā*). The *kleśavāsanās* are said to be special potentials of past passions that reside in the mind (hence designated impregnations) and that cause a special distortion in vocal and bodily behaviour in the arhat's present life. For this reason they are said to be morally indeterminate (*avyākṛta*) special thoughts (*cittaviśeṣa*).[11] The *akliṣṭa-ajñāna,* characterized merely as absence of the knowledge of worldly things, whether gross or subtle, can hardly be described as the source of special distortions of behaviour. Nor can this *ajñāna* be a *vāsanā* because, as Yaśomitra states, arhats overcome *ajñāna* (albeit temporarily at the time of attaining arhatship), whereas the *kleśavāsanās* are never destroyed by them. This is further supported by Vasubandhu's statement that the eighteen qualities of the Buddha are called *āveṇika* (special) because he alone has destroyed the *kleśas* together with their *vāsanās.*[12]

If the *akliṣṭa-ajñāna* is neither a *kleśa* nor its *vāsanā,* yet is something that can be destroyed, then what is its dharmic nature? It must surely stand for some obscuration or obstruction (*āvaraṇa*) that is capable of preventing the mind from functioning to its fullest capacity—namely, cognizing, as the Buddha did, even the subtlest objects situated in distant space and time.

This obstruction evidently could not be of the nature of karma (present action), *vipāka* (the fruition of past actions), or *kleśas,* the three kinds of obstructions known to the Vaibhāṣikas.[13] The word that comes immediately to mind is, of course, *jñeyāvaraṇa,* which is often cited as the agent of such obstruction. But strange as it may seem, *jñeyāvaraṇa* is not attested in the works of Vasubandhu and Yaśomitra, although it is not unknown to the *Mahāvibhāṣā.*[14] We do not know the Vaibhāṣika meaning of this term, but they certainly could not have understood it in the manner of the Vijñānavādins, for whom the *jñeya* (the object itself, as separated from the subject, i.e., consciousness) was an *āvaraṇa* (obstruction).[15]

We are thus left with no specific dharma that can be identified with the *akliṣṭa-ajñāna.* Yet how could the Vaibhāṣikas have introduced this whole controversy over the destruction of the *akliṣṭa-ajñāna* without first introducing a separate dharma of that name into their dharma list?! Could it be that the *akliṣṭa-ajñāna* is indeed a kind of a hindrance—like *styāna* (torpor), for example—but a nonmental dharma of the *cittaviprayukta* (neither material nor mental) category, capable of preventing the mind from achieving its full potential of absolute clarity? The *kleśas* certainly contribute to the prevention of this clarity by creating impurities such as wrong views, doubt, lust, hatred, pride, restlessness, and avidyā; but the destruction of these passions alone does not seem to result in total clarity of mind. The *akliṣṭa-ajñāna* must therefore be conceived of as that (undesignated!) dharma that can survive even when the passions are removed, and that can hinder the mind from achieving its full potential of cognizing all that is knowable.

The ignorance that persists after achieving arhatship may rightly be called *akliṣṭa* because there are no defilements (*kleśas*) beyond that stage. But in the case of the Buddha this ignorance is said to be forever eliminated with the destruction of the *kleśas.* Hence it is appropriate to investigate the stage on the *mārga* (path) where this elimination occurs. Also, is the *akliṣṭa-ajñāna* destroyed at one stroke, like *satkāyadṛṣṭi* (personality-belief) at the level of *darśanamārga* (the path of vision), or is it overcome piecemeal, like the afflictions of *rāga* (desire), *māna* (pride), and *avidyā,* through the various stages of the *bhāvanāmārga* (the path of practice)? We know that the destruction of this ignorance cannot occur at the stage of *darśanamārga,* because according to the

Vaibhāṣika Abhidharma anything that is of the nature of the unafflicted (*akliṣṭa*) cannot be destroyed by that path.[16] But it cannot be destroyed on the *bhāvanāmārga* either, because on that path a specific *anuśaya* is eliminated through the cultivation of its counteragent, and we have determined that *ajñāna* is not an *anuśaya*. Since both these supramundane or *lokottara* paths are not relevant here, it seems to follow that in the Vaibhāṣika system, the *akliṣṭa-ajñāna* can be destroyed only by the *laukikabhāvanāmārga*, that is, the mundane path of meditation, which can be practised by any one, at any stage in one's yogic career, with or without the total destruction of the *kleśas*.

The Buddhist texts recognize a variety of meditative techniques, known as *samāpattis*, that can be employed to enlarge progressively the mind's range of cognition. The most important of these are those which confer the six superknowledges (*abhijñās*), five of which pertain to worldly knowledge (*saṃvṛtijñāna*).[17] The absence of this mundane knowledge, together with all the other minor varieties of ignorances, could properly be designated *akliṣṭa-ajñāna*. These knowledges include (1) magical powers (*ṛddhiviṣaya*), (2) the divine eye and ear (*divyacakṣuḥ/śrotra*), (3) penetration of others' minds (*cetaḥparyāya*), (4) remembrance of former existences (*pūrvanivāsānusmṛti*), and (5) knowledge of the births and deaths of others (*cyutyupapādajñāna*). Although they admittedly do not constitute "omniscience," these five do encompass a great many objects described by Vasubandhu as "subtle" and "distant in space and time," knowledge of which is blocked by *akliṣṭa-ajñāna*. If, as Yaśomitra states, an arhat temporarily overcomes *akliṣṭa-ajñāna* prior to attaining arhatship, this probably means that for a time he acquires these five *abhijñās*, together with the sixth *abhijñā*—namely, *āsravakṣayajñāna* (knowledge of the extinction of the influxes), which confirms his status as an arhat. Only this final *abhijñā* has a lasting effect, because it alone is accomplished by *pratisaṃkhyānirodha* (extinction through knowledge of the four noble truths); still, it has no effect on the arhat's ignorance in worldly matters, since the other five *abhijñās* are of only temporary duration. In the case of the Buddha, however, the Vaibhāṣikas claimed that even *akliṣṭa-ajñāna* is annihilated forever, because it is destroyed by the practice of its counteragent (*pratipakṣa*) and, in the words of Yaśomitra, through *anāsravajñāna*. Although the precise meaning of this rather unusual term is not known, Yaśomitra probably uses it as a synonym for *āsravakṣayajñāna,* the sixth *abhijñā* and terminus of the *bhāvanāmārga.*

Would it be correct to postulate, then, that whereas an arhat attains only the last *abhijñā* by the *lokottarabhāvanāmārga,* the Buddha achieves all the *abhijñas* by the same exalted path? The arhat, after all aspires only to attain his own nirvāṇa and needs only sufficient worldly knowledge to help him toward that goal. The five mundane *abhijñās* should be adequate for his purposes—especially the fourth and the fifth, dubbed *vidyās* (knowledges), which remove any perplexity regarding his past and future.[18] In the case of the Buddha, however, who aspires to teach all beings, even his *saṃvṛtijñāna* would be infinitely wider in scope and would need to be achieved in a manner consistent with his role. Thus a Buddha perfects his *abhijñās* to such an extent that he destroys the *kleśavāsanās* as well as the *akliṣṭa-ajñāna* and thus becomes omniscient forever. This explains the Abhidharma claim that in the case of the Buddha nothing is born of effort (*prayogaja*), that all knowledge is immediately present to him, and that he is called one who not only knows everything but also knows everything in its entirety.[19]

Although an apparent deficiency, the persistence of *akliṣṭa-ajñāna* is no more destructive of arhatship than the persistence of the *kleśavāsanās,* and both are automatically terminated when the final *apratisaṅkhyānirodha* (cessation without knowledge of the four noble truths) is attained. Although the Vaibhāṣika accepts the possibility of a fall from arhatship for a certain kind of arhat, the reason given is not the presence of this *ajñāna* or of the *vāsanās* in him, but a sūtra passage cautioning an arhat against "gain and honour," the true meaning of which is hotly disputed by the Sautrāntika Vasubandhu, who rejects the Vaibhāṣika interpretation.[20] The claim of the nonomniscient arhat that he has attained the same nirvāṇa as the omniscient Buddha has been suspect, therefore, only in later Buddhist schools, especially those which formulated the doctrine of Ekayāna. The authors of the *Saddharmapuṇḍarīkasūtra,* for example, do not hesitate to challenge openly the arhat's claim to nirvāṇa. They declare through the mouth of the Elder Śāriputra that the arhats were wrong and conceited in thinking that they had attained nirvāṇa, when what they had reached was only a state of rest (*viśrāma*), and conclude that there is no nirvāṇa without omniscient cognition (*sarva-*

jñatva).[21] Granted that the real aim of the Mahāyānists is to teach the realization of *sarvadharmaśūnyatā* (emptiness of all existents) when they talk of the Buddha's omniscience, it is nevertheless true that they place equal emphasis on the infinitude of his *saṃvṛtijñāna,* as if the two cognitions were inseparable. This is clear from several passages of the same sūtra, where the arhat is berated not only for his limited understanding of reality, but also for the infinitesimal range of his mental powers pertaining to worldy objects.[22]

It is debatable whether there is an invariable concomitance between the attainment of nirvāṇa and the possession of omniscience. Parallels to both models—that of the nonomniscient arhat and of the omniscient arhat (namely, the Buddha)—can be found in the Yoga and the Jaina traditions, respectively. The entire third book of the *Pātañjala Yogasūtra,* for example, is devoted to a description of the various powers of perfections (*vibhūtis*) that enable a yogin to acquire knowledge of the past and future (*atītānāgatajñāna*), of the speech of all beings (*sarvabhūtarutajñāna*), of his previous births (*pūrvajātijñāna*), of other people's minds (*paracittajñāna*), of regions (*bhuvanajñāna*), of the position of stars (*tārāvyūhajñāna*), and so forth. These knowledges are similar to the mundane *abhijñās* of the Buddhists.[23] All can be mastered prior to knowledge of the spirit (*puruṣajñāna*), the first stage in the yogin's progress toward isolation (*kaivalya*), and hence are comparable to the Buddhist *darśanamārga.* As a result of this *puruṣajñāna,* there arise unceasingly in the yogin vividness (*pratibhā*) and the organs of supernatural hearing, feeling, sight, taste, and smell. The commentator Vyāsa describes the first of these "knowledges," *pratibhājñāna,* as an intuitive knowledge of subtle (*sūkṣma*), concealed (*vyavahita*), or remote (*viprakṛṣṭa*) objects, whether past (*atīta*) or future (*anāgata*)—words that echo Vasubandhu's description of the Buddha's range of cognition.[24] Patañjali warns that these extraordinary perceptions are powers (*siddhis*) only for one whose mind is distracted (*vikṣipta*); otherwise they are obstacles (*antarāya*) in the way of samādhi.[25] When finally the yogin has attained full discernment into the difference between the matter (*prakṛti,* i.e., the *buddhi*) and the spirit (*puruṣa*), he attains "omniscience" (*sarvajñātṛtvam*) and there follows *kaivalya* or the nirvāṇa of the Sāṃkhya-Yoga system.

It is evident from these Yoga aphorisms that although possession of these knowledges and powers may be commendable, they are not prerequisites to *kaivalya.* The yogin is even advised to remain indifferent to them and treat some of them as inevitable byproducts of the practice of meditation. Commenting on the perfections a yogin acquires on his way to the goal of isolation, Vyāsa declares that it is immaterial whether the yogin has or has not attained these powers or knowledges, since one whose seeds of *kleśa* are burnt (*dagdhakleśabīja*) has no need of knowledge and the like.[26] This is the position followed in general by the Theravādins and the Vaibhāṣikas as well: the Buddha's omniscience is highly commendable, but the arhat's nirvāṇa is not dependent on overcoming the *akliṣṭa-ajñāna,* for the seeds of rebirth have been burnt forever equally by both.

The Jaina position appears to agree with the Ekayāna claim that nirvāṇa is inseparable from omniscience, and hence that only the Omniscient One gets the designation of an arhat or, as an Ekayānist would say, only the Buddha has attained nirvāṇa. I will not explain here the precise difference between the omniscience of the Buddha and that of the Jina, as I have dealt with this problem elsewhere.[27] Unlike the Buddhists, the Jainas maintained that ignorance of the true nature of things and other passions (e.g., delusion, attachment, aversion, etc., which correspond to the *anuśayas* in the Abhidharma) and ignorance of worldly objects (*ajñāna*) are two different kinds of defects caused by two distinct karmic forces, the *mohanīya* (deluding) and the *jñānāvaraṇīya* (knowledge-obscuring). The former is destroyed by the Jaina path called *guṇasthāna* (stages of spiritual progress), which is very similar to the *darśana* and *bhāvanā* mārgas of the Buddhists.[28] The consequent purity generated in the soul (*ātman*) affects its ignorance to some extent also, since the soul gains without any special effort certain supernatural knowledges called *avadhijñāna* (clairvoyance) and *manaḥparyayajñāna* (telepathy), comparable to some of the mundane *abhijñās* and *siddhis* mentioned earlier. With the total destruction of the *mohanīya,* the aspirant reaches the irreversible stage of liberation (*mokṣa*), appropriately called *kṣīṇamoha* (the stage of the destruction of delusion), comparable to the *āsravakṣayajñāna* attained by the Buddhist arhat. Yet this is not the final stage for the Jaina arhat; rather, with the destruction of the *mohanīya* the aspirant is for the first time able to engage in higher trances—an advanced stage of the Pure Meditation (*śukladhyāna*) that had commenced earlier—with which he is able to destroy the entire mass of the *jñānāvaraṇīyakarma* that had hitherto obstructed the soul's innate ability for omniscience. Thus he attains *kevalajñāna* (knowledge isolated from all karmic matter and freed from the constraints of the senses and mind) and is able to cognize all existents in their infinite aspects. He will remain in that state forever, even after his final death, which is called nirvāṇa in Jainism.[29]

All four schools discussed here appear to agree that although both *avidyā* and *ajñāna* are called ignorance, they do not necessarily spring from the same source and may partake of two different natures. *Avidyā* appears to be caused by some form of passion, whereas *ajñāna* seems to result from a certain lack of clarity, the cause of which cannot be easily determined. This probably explains the near unanimity in these schools' approaches to the problem of overcoming *avidyā* through almost identical paths. Their failure to devise an equally unanimous way to be rid of *ajñāna* probably derives from their inability to establish an invariable causal relationship between impurity and ignorance.

NOTES

1. *yaḥ sarvathā sarvahatāndhakāraḥ//Abhidharmakośa,* i, la. *pratyekabuddhaśrāvakā api kāmaṃ sarvatra hatāndhakārāḥ/kliṣṭasammohātyantavigamāt/ na tu sarvathā; tathā hy eṣāṃ buddhadharmeṣv ativiprakṛṣṭadeśakāleṣv anantaprabhedeṣu ca bhavaty evākliṣṭam ajñānam//Abhidharmakośabhāṣya,* Part I, p. 6. Dvārikadāsa Śāstrī, ed., *Abhidharmakośa and Bhāṣya of Ācārya Vasubandhu with Sphuṭārthā Commentary of Ācārya Yaśomitra* (Varanasi: Bauddha Bhāratī, 1970-1971), pts. 1-4.
2. *ajñānaṃ hi bhūtārthadarśanapratibandhād andhakāram/tac ca bhagavato buddhasya pratipakṣalābhena sarvatra jñeye punaranutpattidharmatvādd hatam; ato 'sau sarvathā sarvahatāndhakāraḥ// Abhidharmakośabhāṣya,* Part I, p. 6.
3. *pratipakṣalābhenety āryamārgalābhena/vipakṣaḥ kleśaḥ// vipakṣapratighātāya pakṣaḥ pratipakṣa iti kṛtvā/ ... athavā jñānam anāsravam ajñānapratipakṣaḥ, tasya lābhena// atyantaṃ sarvathā/ sarvatra jñeye punar anutpattidharmatvādd hatam/ asamudācāraprahāṇīkṛtam ity arthaḥ// Sphuṭārthāvyākhyā, Abhidharmakośabhāṣya,* Part I, p. 6.
4. *nanu ca sarvaṃ sāsravavastu śrāvakapratyekabuddhānām api buddhavat prahīṇam/ kim idam ucyate—kliṣṭasammohasya teṣām atyantavigama iti? ... tathā hy uktam— ..."nāham ekadharmam apy aparijñāyāprahāya duḥkhasyāntakriyāṃ vadāmi" iti/ tasmāc chrāvakapratyekabuddhānām api tad akliṣṭam ajñānaṃ cakṣurādivac chandarāga-prahāṇāt prahīṇam eva/ anyathā hi śrāvakapratyekabuddhānāṃ duḥkhāntakriyā na bhavet?* Ibid., Part I, pp. 6-7.
5. *satyam; asty etad evam/ prahīṇam eva teṣāṃ kliṣṭavad akliṣṭam apy ajñānam/ tat tu teṣāṃ cakṣurādivat prahīṇam api samudācarati/buddhasya tu prahīṇaṃ san na*

samudācarati/ ata eva viśeṣitaṃ—"punar anutpattidharmatvādd hatam" iti/ ... ye tu vyācakṣate—"śrāvakapratyekabuddhānāṃ kliṣṭasammohamātravigamāt saṃkleśavinivṛttiḥ" iti, tad apavyākhyānam eṣāṃ yathoktam iti pratyācakṣate// Ibid., Part I, p. 7.

6. *Ibid.*
7. *tāny etāni catvāry ajñānakāraṇāni bhavanti/ teṣāṃ kvacid ekam/ kvacid dve/ kvacit trīṇi/ kvacic catvārīti sambhavato yojyāni// Ibid.*, p. 8.
8. Shwe Zan Aung and Mrs. Rhys Davids, trans., *Points of Controversy* (*Kathāvatthu*), (London: Pali Text Society, 1960), pp. 114-119.
9. *Abhidharmakośabhāṣya,* Part IV, p. 1108.
10. Étienne Lamotte, "Passions and Impregnations of the Passions in Buddhism," L. Cousins, ed., *Buddhist Studies in Honour of I.B. Horner* (Dordrecht: D. Reidel, 1974), 91-104.
11. *kā punar iyaṃ vāsanā nāma śrāvakāṇām? yo hi yatkleśacaritaḥ pūrvaṃ tasya tatkṛtaḥ kāyavākceṣṭāvikārahetusāmarthyaviśeṣaś citte vāsanety ucyate/ avyākṛtaś cittaviśeṣo vāsaneti bhadant Ānantavarmā// Sphuṭārthāvyākhyā, Abhidharmakośabhāṣya,* Part IV, p. 1093.
12. *kasmād ete āveṇikā buddhadharmā ucyante? savāsanaprahāṇāt// Abhidharmakośabhāṣya,* Part IV, p. 1093.
13. *trīṇy āvaraṇāny uktāni bhagavatā/ karmāvaraṇaṃ kleśāvaraṇaṃ vipākāvaraṇaṃ ca//Ibid.*, Part II, p. 722.
14. I am indebted to Dr. Collett Cox for the information that the terms "*kleśāvaraṇa*" and "*jñeyāvaraṇa*" are found in the *Mahāvibhāṣā, T 27. 724b28.* Mr. Nobuyoshi Yamabe has kindly drawn my attention to a passage in the *Mahāvibhāṣā* (*T* 27. 42b24-c6) which seems to suggest that the concept of *mithyā-jñāna* (false knowledge—which may have some relation to *ajñāna*) was considered to be a form of *kliṣṭaprajñā* (defiled wisdom), and in the case of the arhat was applied only from the conventional (*saṃvṛti*) point of view.
15. It is not likely that the Vaibhāṣikas would have interpreted *jñeyāvaraṇa* as a *dauṣṭhulya* (depravity), as it is described by Asaṅga (*jñeyāvaraṇadauṣṭhulyaṃ sarvajñatāvipakṣaḥ,* i.e., a form of depravity that is the adversary of omniscience), since for the Vaibhāṣikas it would still constitute some form of *kleśa.* See Nathmal Tatia, *Abhidharmasamuccayabhāṣyam of Asaṅga,* Tibetan Sanskrit Works Series No. 17 (Patna: Kashi Prasad Jayaswal Research Institute, 1976), 93. It should be noted, however, that Sthiramati follows the Abhidharma tradition, since in his *Triṃśikāvijñaptibhāṣya* he does describe the term "*jñeyāvaraṇa*" as *akliṣṭa-ajñāna: jñeyāvaraṇam api sarvasmin jñeye jñānapravṛttipratibandhabhūtam akliṣṭam ajñānam//* Sylvain Lévi, *Vijñaptimātratāsiddhi* (Paris: Librairie Ancienne Honoré Champion, 1925), 15. But he fails to clarify the precise denotation of the term in this context. Our surmise is substantiated by Prajñākaramati's gloss on *jñeyāvaraṇa* as "*jñeyam eva samāropitatvāt āvṛtih,*" an oppositional *karmadhāraya,* in his commentary on the following: *kleśajñeyāvṛtitamaḥpratipakṣo hi śūnyatā/ śīghraṃ sarvajñatākāmo na bhāvayati tāṃ katham//* See P. L. Vaidya, *Bodhicaryāvatāra of Śāntideva together with Prajñākaramati's Pañjikā,* Buddhist Sanskrit Texts Series, No. XII (Darbhanga: Mithila Institute, 1960), chap. 9, v. 55.
16. *na dṛṣṭiheyam akliṣṭaṃ na rūpaṃ nāpy aśaṣṭajam// Abhidharmakośa, Abhidharmakośabhāṣya,* Part I, p. 110.
17. Ibid., Part IV, p. 1106.
18. Ibid., Part IV, p. 1113.

19. *buddhasya nāsti kiñcit prāyogikam/ tasya sarvadharmeśvaratvād icchāmātrapratibaddhaḥ sarvaguṇasampatsammukhībhāvaḥ// Abhidharmakośabhāṣya,* Part IV, p. 1106.
20. See ibid., Part III, pp. 986-1002.
21. *tathaiva śrāvakāḥ sarve prāptanirvāṇasaṃjñinaḥ/jino 'tha deśayet tasmai viśrāmo 'yaṃ na nirvṛtiḥ// upāya eṣa buddhānāṃ vadanti yad imaṃ nayam/ sarvajñtvam ṛte nāsti nirvāṇaṃ tat samārabha//* See P. L. Vaidya, *Saddharmapuṇḍarīkasūtra,* Buddhist Sanskrit Texts (Darbhanga: Mithila Institute, 1960), chap. 5, vv. 74-75.
22. Ibid., vv. 65-73.
23. Ram Shankar Bhattacharya, *Pātañjala-Yogadarśanam together with the Bhāṣya of Vyāsa and the Tattvavaiśāradīvyākhyā of Vācaspati* (Varanasi Bhāratiya Vidyā Prakāśana, 1963).
24. *tataḥ prātibhaśrāvaṇavedanādarśāsvādavārtā jāyante// prātibhāt sūkṣmavyavahitaviprakṛṣṭātītānāgatajñānam/ ... ity etāni nityaṃ jāyante//* Ibid., pp. 137-138.
25. *te samādhāv upasargā vyutthāne siddhayaḥ//*Ibid., p. 138.
26. *tārakaṃ sarvaviṣayaṃ sarvathāviṣayam akramaṃ ceti vivekajaṃ jñānam//* Ibid., p. 153. ... *prāptavivekajñānasyāprāptavivekajñānasya vā/ ... sattvapuruṣayoḥ śuddhisāmye kaivalyam iti// yadā nirdhūtarajastamomalaṃ buddhisattvaṃ ... dagdhakleśabījaṃ bhavati tadā ... śuddhiḥ/ etasyām avasthāyāṃ kaivalyaṃ bhavatīśvarasya vā vivekajñānabhāgina itarasya vā/ na hi dagdhakleśabījasya jñāne punar apekṣā kvacid asti ...* //Ibid., p. 154.
27. Padmanabh S. Jaini, "On the *Sarvajñatva* of Mahāvīra and the Buddha," in Cousins, ed., *Studies in Honour of I.B. Horner,* pp. 71-90.
28. For a description of the *guṇasthānas,* see Padmanabh S. Jaini, *The Jaina Path of Purification* (Berkeley: University of California Press, 1979), pp. 272-273.
29. *mohakṣayāj jñānadarśanāvaraṇāntarāyakṣayāc ca kevalam// mohanīye kṣīne jñanāvaraṇadarśanāvaraṇāntarāyeṣu kṣīṇeṣu ca kevalajñānadarśanam utpadyate/ ...mohakṣayād iti pṛthakkaraṇaṃ kramaprasiddhyarthaṃ yathā gamyeta pūrvaṃ mohanīyaṃ kṛstnaṃ kṣīyate tato 'ntarmuhūrtaṃ chadmasthavītarāgo bhavati/ tato 'sya jñānadarśanāvaraṇāntarāyaprakṛtīnāṃ tisṛṇāṃ yugapat kṣayo bhavati/ tataḥ kevalam utpadyate//* See Khubcandra Siddhāntaśāstrī, *Sabhāṣya-Tattvārthādhigamasūtra* (Agas: Rājacandra Jiana Śāstramālā, 1932), p. 437.

IV

ABHIDHARMA

CHAPTER 10

On the Theory of Two Vasubandhus*

Since the publication of Professor J. Takakusu's '*Life of Vasubandhu by Paramārtha*' in the year 1904,[2] several scholars have made attempts to determine the date and works of Vasubandhu. The problem is beset with several difficulties. Tradition gives three dates (A.N. 900, 1000, and 1100) based on different reckonings of the Nirvāṇa era. Vasubandhu, himself a Sautrāntika, is the author of the celebrated Vaibhāṣika work, viz., the *Abhidharma-kośa* (and its *Bhāṣya*), and is at the same time credited with the authorship of several major works of the Vijñānavāda school. The problem is rendered more complex by the mention in Yaśomitra's *Sphuṭārthā Abhidharma-kośa-vyākhyā* of an elder (Vṛddhācārya) Vasubandhu, leading to a recent theory of two Vasubandhus advocated by Professor E. Frauwallner.

Paramārtha gives two dates for Vasubandhu. In his 'Life of Vasubandhu' he gives A.N. 1100, and in his commentary on the *Madhyānta-vibhāga* (of Maitreya) he gives A.N. 900. Takakusu favoured A.N. 1100 and proposed A.D. 420-500 as the period of Vasubandhu. In 1911, P.N. Péri, after a thorough investigation of all available materials on the subject, proposed A.D. 350.[3] Over a period several scholars, notably Professor Kimura, G. Ono, U. Woghihara, H. Ui, and many others, contributed their views on this topic, which were summed up in 1929 by J. Takakusu,[4] who again tried to establish his previously proposed date of the fifth

*This article was originally published in *Bulletin of the School of Oriental and African Studies (=BSOAS)*, Vol. XXI, part 1, pp. 48-53, University of London, 1958. Reprinted with kind permission of Oxford University Press.

century A.D. Since then the problem received little attention until in 1951 when Professor Frauwallner published his monograph on Vasubandhu.[5]

Professor E. Frauwallner's views can be briefly stated as follows:

1. Of the three dates current in tradition, the first, viz. the A.N. 900, points to a time prior to A.D. 400, the last two, viz. the A.N. 1000 and 1100, refer to one and the same date, viz. the fifth century A.D. Thus there are only two dates for Vasubandhu.

2. These two dates refer not to one but to two persons bearing the same name. One Vasubandhu (the elder—fourth century A.D.) is the Vṛddhācārya Vasubandhu mentioned in the *Vyākhyā* of Yaśomitra, and the other Vasubandhu (the younger—fifth century A.D.) is the author of the *Abhidharma-kośa.*

3. Paramārtha in his 'Life of Vasubandhu' confuses these two and hence the difficulty of determining the date of Vasubandhu.

4. This biography can be divided into three distinct parts:

(i) Legend of the name of Vasubandhu's native city Puruṣapura, his father, the Brāhmin Kauśika, and of the three sons Asaṅga, Vasubandhu, and Viriñcivatsa.

(ii) Account of the council in Kāśmīr, arrival of the Sāṅkhya teacher Vindhyavāsin, and defeat of Buddhamitra the teacher of Vasubandhu. Vasubandhu's composition of the *Paramārthasaptatikā* in refutation of Vindhyavāsin. The composition of the *Abhidharma-kośa.* Saṃghabhadra's challenge to Vasubandhu for a disputation, declined by the latter on account of his old age.

(iii) Asaṅga's conversion of Vasubandhu to Mahāyāna. Vasubandhu's Mahāyāna works and death.

Of these the first and last sections deal with Vasubandhu the elder, the second part deals with Vasubandhu the younger.

5. From this it follows that Vasubandhu (elder) the brother of Asaṅga is not the Kośakāra Vasubandhu (younger). It is the elder Vasubandhu who was converted from Sarvāstivāda to Mahāyāna by Asaṅga. This is supported by Chi-Tsang's commentary on the *Śataśāstra,* where (this elder) Vasubandhu is said to have composed 500 Mahāyāna works (in addition to 500 Hīnayāna works composed by him prior to his conversion) and hence given the nickname of 'Master of the Thousand Manuals'.

The younger Vasubandhu, the author of the *Paramārthasaptatikā* and the *Abhidharma-kośa,* belonged to the Sarvāstivāda school, but leaned more and more towards the Sautrāntika school.

This in brief is a summary of Professor Frauwallner's thesis. The conclusion that would logically follow from his thesis is that the Kośakāra Vasubandhu was not a Mahāyānist and consequently, not the author of the Vijñānavāda works credited to him. These would necessarily have to be the works of the elder Vasubandhu, the brother of Asaṅga. But Professor Frauwallner avoids such conclusions by stating that the accounts of the life of Vasubandhu 'either do not give any information at all about these works, or mention them in passages where the two Vasubandhus are confused with each other' (p. 56).[6]

In this paper I propose to present some new evidence that throws some doubt on Professor Frauwallner's thesis and confirms the older and universal tradition about the conversion of the Kośakāra Vasubandhu to Mahāyāna, and his authorship of at least one work belonging to the Vijñānavāda school.

My evidence is based on the manuscript of the *Abhidharma-dīpa* (together with a commentary—the *Vibhāṣā-prabhā-vṛtti*), discovered in the Ṣhalu monastery in Tibet by Pandit Rāhula Sānkṛtyāyana in the year 1937. He brought back photographs of this work, which are treasured in the K.P. Jayaswal Research Institute of Patna.[7]

The MS discovered is incomplete. The last folio is numbered 150. The whole work might not have contained more than 160 folios. Of these, only 62 have been found. It contains two works, viz. the kārikā text (the *Abhidharma-dīpa*[8]) and a prose commentary (the *Vibhāṣā-prabhā-vṛtti*[9]). The work belongs to the Kāśmīra Vaibhāṣika school and appears, from internal evidence, to have been written either during or immediately after the time of the Kośakāra Vasubandhu. The name of the author is not mentioned in the work, but it is my conjecture that it was written by a rival of Vasubandhu, either Saṅghabhadra or one of his disciples.

The *Dīpa* and also its commentary (the *Vṛtti*) closely follow both in contents and in presentation, their counterparts, viz. the *Abhidharma-kośa*[10] and its commentary (the *Abhidharma-kośa-bhāṣya*[11]) of Vasubandhu. Of the 597 kārikās of the extant *Dīpa*, more than 300 have their parallels in the *Kośa*, and in many cases appear to be imitations of the latter. The *Vṛtti* has about 50 large passages almost identical with the *Bhāṣya*, 32 of which are directly borrowed from the latter. Thus to a large extent, the *Dīpa* and the *Vṛtti* are written in imitation of the *Kośa* and the *Bhāṣya*.

But what is more interesting to us is the fact that the extant

Vṛtti contains 17 hostile references to the Kośakāra (without mentioning the name Vasubandhu) criticizing his Sautrāntika views and at times accusing him of entering the portals of Mahāyāna Buddhism. I quote here a few such passages from the *Vṛtti*:

(i) *Idam idānīm abhidharma-sarvasvaṃ* Kośakāraka-*smṛti-gocarātītaṃ vaktavyam.* (Fol. 37b.[12])

(ii) Kośakāras *tv āha—'sarva-sūkṣmo rūpa-saṃghātaḥ paramāṇuḥ' iti. Tena saṃghāta-vyatiriktaṃ rūpam anyad vaktavyaṃ* ... (Fol. 43b.[13])

(iii) *Siddhā sabbhāgatā.* Kośakāraḥ *punas tāṃ Vaiśeṣika-parikalpita-jāti-padārthena samīkurvan vyaktaṃ pāyasa-vāyasayor varṇa-sādharmyaṃ paśyatīti.* (Fol. 47a.[14])

(iv) *Atra punaḥ* Kośakāraḥ *pratijānīte—'sacittikeyaṃ samāpattiḥ' iti ... Tad etad abauddhīyam.* (Fol. 47b.[15])

(v) *'Samādhibalena karmajaṃ jīvitāvedhaṃ nirvartya āyuḥ saṃskārā-dhiṣṭhānajam, āyur na vipākaḥ' iti* Kośakāraḥ. *Tatra kim uttaram iti? ...*Vaitulika-śāstra-*praveśa-dvāram ārabdhaṃ tena bhadantenety adhyupeksyam etat.* (Fol. 49a.[16])

In these passages the Kośakāra is criticized for his Sautrāntika views on the theory of atoms and the three *citta-viprayukta-saṃskāras,* viz. *sabhāgatā, nirodha-samāpatti,* and *āyu.* We may particularly note the last passage where the Kośakāra is said to have begun entering the portals of the *Vaitulika-śāstra.* The term *Vaitulika-śāstra* clearly refers to Mahāyāna scriptures. Asaṅga in his *Abhidharma-samuccaya* identifies *vaitulya* with *vaipulya* and explains the latter term as *Bodhisattva-piṭaka,*[17] which undoubtedly belongs to Mahāyāna. This is the first allusion to the Kośakāra's leanings not only towards Sautrāntika but also towards Mahāyāna Buddhism.

While dealing with a controversial question related to perception (whether the eye sees an object or the mind sees it) the *Vṛtti* quotes the following passage from the *Kośa-bhāṣya* and says:

Tatra yad uktaṃ Kośakāreṇa '*kim idam ākāśaṃ khādyate. Sāmagryāṃ hi satyāṃ dṛṣṭam ity upacāraḥ pravartate. Tatra kaḥ paśyatī' ti ?*[18] *Tad atra tena Bhadantena sāmagryaṅga-kriyā[paharaṇam?] kriyate. Abhidharma-saṃmohāṅkasthānenātmāpy aṅkito bhavaty ayoga-śūnyatā-prapātābhimukhyatvaṃ pradarśitam iti.*

The view of the Kośakāra quoted by our *Vṛtti* is what the *Kośa* gives as a Sautrāntika view. In the *Vṛtti* the Kośakāra is identified with the Sautrāntika. He is censured for his ignorance of *Abhidharma* and also accused of heading for the precipice of *ayoga-śūnyatā.*

The term *ayoga-śūnyatā* should put at rest any doubt about the real affiliations of the Kośakāra. The term certainly refers to a Mahāyāna doctrine.

In the fifth Adhyāya of the *Dīpa,* a fundamental principle of the Sarvāstivāda school, viz. the reality of the past and future elements, is discussed in opposition to the Sautrāntika arguments advanced by the Kośakāra in the fifth Kośa-sthāna of his *Bhāṣya.*[19] After dealing with the Sautrāntika, the *Vṛtti* criticizes the Vaitulika. He is described as *ayoga-śūnyatā-vādin* maintaining that nothing (i.e. the past, present, and future) exists,[20] and is, therefore, condemned as an annihilationist (*vaināśika*).[21]

The main Vaitulika doctrine criticized in the *Vṛtti* is the *niḥ-svabhāva-vāda,*[22] which is common to both the Yogācāra and the Mādhyamika schools. Both these schools are *śūnyavādins* in a real sense and would appear, to that extent, as Vaināśikas to a Realist Vaibhāṣika.

The term *ayoga-śunyatā* is not found in the traditional lists of 18, 19, or 20 kinds of *śūnyatās*[23] or in the Mādhyamika or the Yogācāra treatises. The *Vṛtti* does not explain the term. If this *vāda* could mean the doctrine of non-applicability of all predications, especially of *ātman* and *dharmas* (*ātma-dharmopacāraḥ*),[24] then it would be equivalent to the *niḥ-svabhāva-vāda,* accepted by both the Mādhyamika and the Yogācāra schools.

The passages quoted above from the *Vṛtti* indicate, in the view of the Vaibhāṣika, that the Kośakāra, even in the *Kośa-bhāṣya,* shows signs of more and more leanings towards Mahāyāna Buddhism. This in itself does not prove his conversion to Mahāyāna, but certainly indicates his inclination towards it. In the light of these findings we may now turn to further evidence which seems to anticipate his conversion and confirm his authorship of a Mahāyāna work.

After dealing with the *niḥ-svabhāva-vāda* of the Vaitulika, the *Vṛtti* again turns to the Kośakāra and says: 'The Vaitulika, apostate from the *Sarvāstivāda,* says: "We too advocate (imagine) three *svabhāvas*". To him we should reply: "The world is full of such illusions which please only fools. Rare are those imaginations that catch the hearts of the learned". These three *svabhāvas* imagined by you have been already rejected. Such other illusions should also be thrown away. This is one more occasion where the Kośakāra shows his ignorance of (the doctrine of) Time.'[25]

Three significant statements in this criticism may be noted: (i) The Vaitulika is called here *sarvāstivāda-vibhraṣṭiḥ* (one who has deviated from the *Sarvāstivāda*).

(ii) A reference is made to the doctrine of *tri-svabhāva-vāda.*

(iii) A reference is made to the Kośakāra in a manner which shows his responsibility in the formulation of this doctrine.

Of these, the last two statements most probably refer to the *Trisvabhāva-nirdeśa,*[26] a work of the Yogācāra-Vijñānavāda school, credited by tradition to Vasubandhu. It consists of 38 kārikās and marks the culminating point of the development of this doctrine found in the *Laṅkāvatāra-sūtra* and in the works of Maitreya and Asaṅga,[27] the chief founders of the Yogācāra school. The first statement saying that the Vaitulika deviated from the *Sarvāstivāda,* may be a general statement, referring only to the belief of the Vaibhāṣika that the Vaitulika branched off from the more orthodox Sarvāstivāda school. But read in the context of the above passage, it appears certain that the *Vṛtti* is alluding to the conversion of the Kośakāra to Mahāyāna Buddhism.

This in brief is our main evidence confirming Paramārtha's account of the Kośakāra Vasubandhu's conversion to Mahāyāna and his authorship of several Mahāyāna works. It does not contradict the fact of two (one elder and the other younger) Vasubandhus. The Vṛddhācārya Vasubandhu certainly existed, as is clear from the statements of Yaśomitra. He may well have been the author of a commentary to the *Abhidharma-sāra* of Dharma-śrī and also author of many Mahāyāna works.

But we certainly are not justified, in the light of the evidence of the *Dīpa,* in limiting the activities of the younger Vasubandhu to Hīnayāna alone, in crediting him only with the authorship of the *Kośa* and thus relating the last part of Paramārtha's biography to the life of Vasubandhu the elder. The date of the Kośakāra Vasubandhu and his relation to Asaṅga, however, still remains unsettled. But the confirmation of his authorship of the *Trisvabhāva-nirdeśa* might well lead us to accept the tradition preserved in Paramārtha's 'Life of Vasubandhu'.

NOTES

1. This paper was read before the XXIVth International Congress of Orientalists, Munich, 1957.
2. *T'oung Pao,* Serie II, Vol. v, 269-96.
3. 'À propos de la date de Vasubandhu', *BÉFEO,* xi, 1911, 339-90.
4. 'The date of Vasubandhu', in *Indian studies in honour of Charles Rockwell Lanman,* Cambridge, Mass., 1929, 79-88.
5. *On the date of the Buddhist master of the law Vasubandhu* (Serie Orientale Roma, III), Roma, 1951.
6. In his recent work *Die Philosophie des Buddhismus* (1956), Professor Frauwallner includes the *Viṃśatikā* and the *Triṃśikā vijñaptimātratāsiddhi* under the heading of 'Vasubandhu der Ältere', but is still hesitant about the ascription of these works: 'Meiner Ansicht nach ist Vasubandhu der Jüngere ihr Verfasser, doch kann diese schwierige Frage hier nicht weiter erörtert werden' (p. 351).
7. I am grateful to the K.P. Jayaswal Research Institute for entrusting me with the work of editing this MS. It will soon be published in the Tibetan Sanskrit Works Series, Patna. (Published in 1959.)
8. Henceforth called *Dīpa.*
9. Henceforth called *Vṛtti.*
10. Henceforth called *Kośa.*
11. Henceforth called *Bhāṣya.*
12. In this bold line the *Vṛtti* criticizes the Kośakāra for his omission of a topic dealing with cessation of *dhātus* through various stages of *anāsrava-mārga.*
13. See Poussin's *L'Abhidharma-kośa,* chapter II, kā. 22, and Yaśomitra's *Sphuṭārthā Abhidharma-kośa-vyākhyā,* p. 123 (ed. U. Woghihara).
14. See *L'Abhidharma-kośa,* Chapter II, kā, 41a, and *Vyākhyā,* pp. 157-9.
15. See *L'Abhidharma-kośa,* Chapter II, kā. 44d, and *Vyākhyā,* p. 169.
16. See *L'Abhidharma-kośa,* Chapter II, kā. 10a, and *Vyākhyā,* p. 104.
17. *Vaipulyaṃ katamat? Bodhisattva-piṭaka-samprayuktaṃ bhāṣitam. Yad ucyate vaipulyaṃ tad vaidalyam apy ucyate vaitulyam apy ucyate.* (Ed. P. Pradhan, p. 79.)
18. cf. 'Opinion du Sautrāntika.—Quelle discussion dans le vide! Le Sūtra enseigne: "En raison de l'organe de la vue et des visibles naît la connaissance visuelle" : il n'y a la ni un organe qui voit, ni un visible qui est vu; il n'y a là aucune action de voir, aucun agent qui voit; ce n'est que jeu de causes et effets. En vue de la pratique, on parle à son gré, métaphoriquement, de ce processus; "L'oeil voit; la connaissance discerne". Mais il ne faut pas se prendre à ces métaphores. Bhagavat l'a dit : il ne faut pas se prendre aux manières de dire populaires, il ne faut pas prendre au sérieux les expressions en usage dans le monde'. *L'Abhidharma-kośa,* chapter I, kā. 42.
19. See *L'Abhidharma-kośa,* chapter v, kā. 17-19.
20. *Tatra Sarvāstivādasyādhva-trayam asti ... Vibhajyavādinas tu, Dārṣṭāntikasya ca pradeśo vartamānādhva-saṃjñakaḥ. Vaitulikasyāyoga-śūnyatā-vādinaḥ sarvaṃ nāstīti. ...* (Fol. 108a.)
21. *Yaḥ Sarvāsti-vādākhyaḥ ... sadvādī. Tad anye Dārṣṭāntika*-Vaitulika-*Paudgalikāḥ ... Lokāyatika*-Vaināśika-*Nagnāṭa-pakṣe prakṣeptavyāḥ* (Fol. 108a.)
22. *Vaitulikaḥ kalpayati—*
Yat pratiya-samutpannaṃ
tat svabhāvān na vidyate/
Yat khalu niḥsvabhāvaṃ nirātmakaṃ hetūn pratītya jāyate tasya khalu svabhāvo

nāsti ... Tasmād alāta-cakravan niḥsvabhāvatvāt sarva-dharmā nirātmāna iti. Taṃ praty apadiśyate. ... (Fol. 111a.)

23. See Professor T. R. V. Murti's *The central philosophy of Buddhism,* Appendix.
24. I am indebted to Professor T. R. V. Murti for suggesting this interpretation of the term *ayoga-śūnyatā.*
25. *Atra Sarvāstivāda-vibhraṣṭir Vaituliko nirāha—vayam api trīn svabhāvān parikalpayiṣyāmaḥ. Tasmai prativaktavyam*
Parikalpair jagad vyāptaṃ
mūrkha-cittānurañjibhiḥ/
Yas tu vidvan-mano-grāhī
parikalpaḥ sa durlabhaḥ//
Te khalv ete bhavatkalpitās traya-svabhāvāḥ purvam eva pratyūḍhāḥ. Evam anye' py asat-parikalpāḥ protsārayitavyāḥ. Ity etad aparam adhva-saṃnohānkanā-sthānaṃ Kośakāraka*syeti.* (Fol. 112a.)
26. Sanskrit text and Tibetan version edited by Sujitkumar Mukhopādhyāya, Visvabharati, 1939.
27. See parallel passages collected by S. Mukhopādhyāya in the *Trisvabhāva-nirdeśa.*

Additional reading: "Landmarks in the History of Indian Logic" by Erich Frauwallner. In *Weiner Zeitschrift fur die Kunde Sud-und Ostasiens,* Band V, 1961.

CHAPTER 11

Buddha's Prolongation of Life*

The belief in immortality and the immeasurable life-span of a single existence is found in the earliest records of the Indian religions. The general trend of the Vedas, the epics, and the Purāṇas is towards immortalizing their devatās and deities. The *avatāras* of the Hindu Godhead, in spite of their earthly existence, were considered free from the laws of birth and death. In their case these incidents were spoken of as mere appearances, since such beings were but devices of the immortal God to work among mortals.

This extraordinary power over the laws of nature was in a limited way shared even by human beings. Certain great sages like Bhīṣma were endowed with powers known as *icchā-maraṇa* (death at one's own will). How this was accomplished is not stated. In the case of Bhīṣma, we are told that his great renunciation and his vow of celibacy won for him a boon of this kind from his father Śantanu.[1] How such a boon could control the causes of death is nowhere explained, but it is suggested that the laws of nature could be controlled by sheer force of character or strong will-power of the individual.

An attempt to explain the functioning of such will-power over the phenomena of death is made by the early Buddhists. Such power over death, i.e. the power of attaining an immeasurable life-span, is found attributed to the Buddha. The later Buddhists went a step further and advocated a doctrine of the immortal

*This article was originally published in *BSOAS*, Vol. XXI, part 3, pp. 546-552, University of London, 1958. Reprinted with kind permission of Oxford University Press.

Buddha, comparable to the *avatāras* of the Hindu God. The Buddhist texts, both Pali and Sanskrit, contain several controversies arising out of the criticism of this belief in the power of the Buddha. A study of this controversy sheds light not only on the various phases of the development of Buddhology, but also on the doctrine of Karma which explains the phenomena of life and death.

An account of the last days of the Buddha is preserved in the Pali and Sanskrit versions of the *Mahāparinirvāṇaṣūtra.* In both accounts it is said that the Buddha was 80 years old[2] when he attained *parinirvāṇa.* It is also said that three months prior to his death, he was overcome by a severe illness which he bore with great composure. Immediately after his recovery, during his sojourn in Vaiśālī, in the Cāpāla shrine, he declared to his intimate attendant, 'whosoever, Ānanda, has developed, practised ..., and ascended to the very heights of the four paths[3] to *ṛddhi* ...he, should he desire it, could remain in the same birth for an aeon (*kalpa*) or more than a *kalpa* (*kappāvasesaṃ*).[4] Now the Tathāgata has thoroughly practised them and he could, therefore, should he desire it, live on yet for an aeon or for more than an aeon'.[5]

This was indeed a hint to Ānanda that he should beg the Lord to remain during the aeon. But we are told that as the heart of Ānanda was possessed by the Evil Māra, he did not beg the Lord to exercise this power. The Buddha then repeated his declaration twice in vain, and asked Ānanda to leave him alone. In the meantime, the Māra appeared and reminded the Lord that it was time for the latter to attain *parinirvāṇa.* The Buddha promised that after a period of three months he would pass away. After the departure of the rejoicing Māra, it is said, the Buddha deliberately and consciously rejected the rest of his natural term of life.[6]

This account is given in identical terms in both the Pali and Sanskrit versions of the *Mahāparinirvāṇa-sūtra.* The Sanskrit version has a few more points of interest. It is said there that before rejecting the *āyuḥ-saṃskāra* (the force of life-duration),[7] the Lord thought that there were only two persons, viz. Supriya, the King of Gandharvas[8] and Subhadra, the parivrājaka, [9] who would be taught by the Buddha himself at their attaining maturity of insight within a period of three months. Thinking thus, the Lord attained that kind of *samādhi,* by which he mastered the forces of *jīvita* (new prolonged life) and rejected the forces of *āyuḥ* (the existing life-force).[10]

The Sarvāstivādins, on the basis of this, hold that the life of three months was indeed an extension of life. He prolonged his life for only this short period: there was no purpose in prolonging it further, as the two new converts mentioned above would have become his disciples by that time. Further, the Buddha did this to show his control over the forces of life and death.[11]

This episode in the *Mahāparinirvāṇa-sūtra* became a centre of several controversies among the Buddhists. The Sthaviravādins and the Sarvāstivādins agreed on the various miraculous powers of the Buddha. The prolongation of the life-span was indeed a splendid miracle which they would gladly have conceded to him. But when the Aṭṭhakathā-kāras and the Vibhāṣā-śāstrins set about explaining this sūtra-passage, they were confronted with several doctrinal difficulties. The main question was how to account for the new life and how to reconcile it with the accepted theories of the laws of karma.

According to the Buddhist karma theory, the life-span of any single existence (*nikāya-sabhāga*) is determined by the karma of the individual at the moment of his conception (*pratisaṃdhi*). This is illustrated by the analogy of an arrow. The destiny of an arrow and the time it will take to reach its destination are determined at the moment of its shooting. Similarly, karma determines the life-span of the individual (i.e., the five aggregates) at the moment of his conception. The karma, so to say, generates a force (*saṃskāra*) known as *āyuḥ* which keeps the series of the five aggregates intact for a certain period. When this particular force is exhausted, we call it *āyuḥ-kṣaya* or death. It is therefore maintained that *āyuḥ* is a *vipāka,* a result of some past karma. If the phenomenon of life-prolongation is accepted, we have to account for a new life-force. This, as suggested by the Buddha's declaration, is possible by assuming that the *ṛddhi* or the yogic potency produces such new life-force. Thus we find two kinds of life, the original one generated by the karma and the other by yogic powers.

The Sthaviravādins, despite the above-mentioned declaration of the Buddha in their sūtra, did not accept the theory of generating a new life by yogic practices. Consequently, they were not able to reconcile the text with their accepted theories of karma. They retained the passage, but gave it an interpretation to suit these theories. According to them the '*kalpa*' in this passage never meant a *mahākalpa,* i.e. an aeon, but an *āyuḥkalpa,* i.e. the duration of a man's life. Now the *āyuḥkalpa* is what people consider as the normal life-span of a human being. It is, as the Buddha himself said (in a different context), 'a hundred years, less or more'.[12] Since the Buddha had reached the normal limit, he did live for a *kalpa* or a portion of a *kalpa*. This indeed was a very poor explanation. The Sthaviravādins were aware of the doctrinal difficulties involved in this belief. Indeed, in the *Kathāvatthu,* where for the first time we meet with this controversy, the Sthaviravādin argues against the Mahāsānghika's claim that the Buddha could have lived for a *mahākalpa.* The main argument is whether the new life-span (*āyuḥ*), the new destiny (*gati*), the acquisition of a new individuality is a thing of magic potency.[13] This the Mahāsānghika cannot affirm, for he is committed to the theory that the *āyuḥ* is a *karma-vipāka* and not a result of magic potency.

Buddhaghosa, in his commentary on this controversy, maintains that the *kappa* here meant only *āyukappa.* He further explains that a person like Buddha, or anyone having mastery over the *iddhipādas,* can avert any obstructions to life, whereas others are not capable of this. When, therefore, the Buddha claimed that he could live for a *kappa,* what he really meant was that he had powers to avert any premature death.

We may note here that as yet there is no suggestion in the Pali works that the Buddha extended his life even for a short period of three months. It was a modified belief of the Sarvāstivādins. The *Milindapañha* accepts this Sarvāstivādin theory and maintains that the Buddha did extend his life for a period of three months and could have lived for a *kappa,* if only he had any desire for earthly life. While maintaining this, the author of the *Milindapañha* most inconsistently explains that the *kappa* here means only *āyukappa* and not the *mahākappa.*[15]

These explanations did not satisfy any one, least of all the Sthaviravādins. In the commentary on the *Mahāparinibbāna-sutta,* Buddhaghosa gives the view of one elder, Mahāsīvathera. This thera maintained that the Buddha did mean to live for an aeon by the powers of his magic gift. But be did not live because the physical body is subject to the laws of old age and the Buddhas pass away without showing any severe effects of it. Moreover, all his chief disciples would have attained nirvāṇa by that time and the Buddha living to the end of the *kappa* would have been left with a poor following of novices. Buddhaghosa dismisses this view without any comment and expressly states that according to the Aṭṭhakathās, the *kappa* here means only the *āyukappa* and not the *mahākappa*.[16]

These explanations of the Aṭṭhakathās do not seem to take notice of another Vinaya passage of the Sthaviravādins. In the *Cullavagga*, in the section dealing with the first council held under the presidentship of Mahākassapa, Ānanda is censured for his failure to request the Buddha to live for a *kappa* or *kappāvasesa*.[17] Surely if *kappa* meant only an *āyukappa*, and if the power of the Buddha was only limited to avert any premature death, there was no point in censuring Ānanda for his absentmindedness.

The Pali commentaries are silent on the manner in which the prolongation and the rejection of the life-force is accomplished. This topic is fully discussed in the works of the Sarvāstivāda School. Vasubandhu in his *Abhidharma-kośa-bhāṣya* gives several Vaibhāṣika views on this topic.[18] According to the Vibhāṣā-śāstra, karma is of two kinds. One is known as *āyur-vipāka-karma*, i.e. the karma which at the moment of conception determines the *āyuḥ*. The other kind is *bhoga-vipāka-karma*. This is a sum total of all past karmas, accumulated in the series of consciousness, which continuously yields its fruits (other than *āyuḥ*) during the phenomenal existence. A human arhat, having full mastery over the *ṛddhipādas*, can, by his strong resolution, transform the *bhoga-vipāka* karma into an *āyur-vipāka-karma*. This transformed karma then produces the new *āyuḥ*. If he wishes to reject his already established life-span (*āyuḥ-saṃskāra*), he transforms his *āyur-vipāka-karma* into the *bhoga-vipāka*.

This explanation is not satisfactory because at the time when the *āyuḥ* is rejected, the *āyur-vipāka-karma* is no longer potentially existent, for it has already yielded its fruit. Therefore, some ācāryas hold a different view. According to them, the karmas of the past birth, as yet unripe, are ripened and made to yield their fruit by the power of meditation. But the difficulty here is that in the case of an arhat, there is no possibility of any new potential *āyur-vipāka-karma*, since at the attainment of the arhatship, he has brought an end to all new births. In all these explanations we can see a sustained but unsuccessful attempt to relate the new (i.e., the prolonged) *āyuḥ* to some form of karma.

Ghoṣaka, a Vaibhāṣika ācārya, goes a step further. He holds that an altogether new body consisting of the material elements (*mahābhūtāni*) of the Rūpāvacara world is produced by the yogic powers. This body is capable of living for a *kalpa*. One can see here a veiled reference to the *nirmāṇa-kāya* or the assumed body of the Buddha. But it is not explained here how such a body can continue to exist when the original body would cease at the end of the *āyuḥ*.

Vasubandhu, after giving these views, gives his own. He says that such an arhat has such yogic potency that he can cut short or put aside the life-span cast by the past karma and produce a new life-span by the sole power of his meditation. Consequently, this new life-force would be a result of samādhi and not of karma.

This view takes us back to the controversy raised in the *Kathāvatthu*. The view of Vasubandhu is identical with the Mahāsānghika view condemned by the Sthaviravādins as contrary to the laws of karma.

This unorthodox view of Vasubandhu is severely criticized in a work of the fifth century A.D., known as the *Abhidharma-dīpa*,[19] representing the orthodox Vaibhāṣika school. The commentary on this work calls this view unbuddhistic, reaffirms the doctrine of karma, and accuses the Kośakāra of entering the portals of Mahāyāna Buddhism. 'For surely', says this work, 'if the Lord, by the powers of meditation could at will produce a new living personality or could cast a new life-span independent of karma, then indeed, the Buddha would be turned into a Nārāyaṇa. Moreover, he would never attain *parinirvāṇa*, such is his compassion for worldly beings. Therefore, this view deserves no consideration, as the Kośakāra here is following the Vaitulika-śāstra.'[20]

This statement is very significant. It anticipates the development of the avatāravāda in Mahāyāna Buddhism and reasserts the orthodox theory of the human Buddha. It also points to the Mahāyānistic origins of the belief in the Buddha's power of prolonging his life-span. We have already seen that the *Kathāvatthu* attributes this belief to the Mahāsānghikas, the forerunners of the Mahāyāna, who were the first to fall away from the orthodox church. The *Mahāvastu*, a Vinaya text of the Lokottaravādins, a branch of the Mahāsānghika, contains the earliest reference to the doctrine of the supermundane (*lokottara*) Buddha. It is said there that the Buddhas are not subject to the effects of old age. Nor are they subject to the laws of karma. The following verse[21] seems to refer to the belief in the Buddha's power of life prolongation and yet his passing away as a human being:

prabhūś ca karma vārayituṃ karmaṃ deśayanti ca jinā
aiśvaryaṃ vinigūhanti eṣā lokānuvartanā.[22]

The Pali commentators and the Vibhāṣā-śāstrins had to account for the laws of karma which even the Buddhas could not escape. Hence their argument that the Buddha wished to pass away while his body was still unaffected by old age. The Lokottaravādins placed the Buddha above the laws of karma and thus paved the way for the Mahāyānistic doctrine of a Transcendent Buddha.

Once the supremacy of the Buddha over the laws of karma was accepted, there remained no great difficulty in assuming a limitless life for the Buddha. The *Sukhāvatī-vyūha* opens with a similar and this time a far bolder declaration of the Buddha.[22] 'Should he desire, O Ānanda, the Buddha can live on a single morsel for one *kalpa,* or even a hundred, a thousand ..., or even millions of *kalpas,* or even beyond that and still his faculties will not diminish, nor will his complexion show any decay.' The *Sukhāvatī-vyūha* was indeed devoted solely to the glorification of this one aspect, symbolized by the glorious conception of the Buddha Amitāyu, the Buddha of immeasurable life.

The emergence of the absolutist schools like the Śūnyavāda brought a still greater revolution. Here the Buddha was considered not only a supermundane personality, but the very essence of phenomena, comparable to the Godhead of the Hindu religion. The theological conception of the *trikāya* of the Buddha is explained on the basis of this doctrine. It led to the doctrine of the identity of *saṃsāra* and *nirvāṇa.*[24] The statements in the *Prajñāpāramitās* or the *Saddharma-puṇḍarīka-sūtra,*[25] that the Buddha never attained *nirvāṇa* are to be understood in the background of this philosophical development. The historical or the human Buddha of the Hīnayāna was considered here as one of the many incarnations of the Absolute Buddha, his descent on earth in the *nirmāṇa-kāya* or the Assumed body.

Thus we see that the belief in the Buddha's power of prolongation of the life-span gradually led Buddhists to a higher conception of the Buddha of immeasurable life and to a still higher conception of the Transcendent and Immanent Buddha.

NOTES

1. *sa tena karmaṇā sūnoḥ prītas tasmai varaṃ dadau*
nākāma-maraṇaṃ tāta bhaviṣyati taveti ha.
na te prabhavitā mṛtyur yāvad icchasi jīvitum
svena kāmena martyo 'si nākāmas tvaṃ kathañcana.
Mahābhārata, I, 94, 75-6 (Southern rescension, ed. P.P.S. Shastri).
Also,
tad dṛṣṭvā duṣkaraṃ karma kṛtaṃ Bhīṣmeṇa Śantanuḥ
svacchanda-maraṇaṃ tasmai dadau tuṣṭaḥ pitā svayam.
Mahābhārata, I, 94, 94 (Poona edition).
2. For other traditions on this point, see E. Obermiller (tr.), *History of Buddhism by Bu-ston,* II, p. 70.
3. Will (*chanda*), effort (*vīrya*), thought (*citta*), and investigation (*vīmāṃsā*), each united to earnest thought.
4. The *Pali-English dictionary* (PTS) takes the word *kappāvasesaṃ* to mean '(for) the rest of the *kappa'.* But as Professor Edgerton has shown, this word probably means 'more than a *kalpa'.* See *BHSD,* 173.
5. *Tathāgatassa kho Ānanda, cattāro iddhipādā bhāvitā ... ākaṅkhamāno Ānanda, Tathāgato kappaṃ vā tiṭṭheyya, kappāvasesaṃ vā. Dīgha-nikāya,* XVI, 3, 3 ...; cf. *yasya kasyaci catvāra ṛddhipādā āsevitā ... ākāṃkṣamāṇaḥ sa kalpaṃ vā tiṣṭhet kalpāvaśeṣaṃ vā. Tathāgatasyānanda ... ākāṃkṣamāṇas Tathāgataḥ kalpaṃ vā tiṣṭhet kalpāvaśeṣaṃ vā. Mahāparinirvāṇa-sūtra,* ed. E. Waldschmidt, p. 204.
6. *Atha kho bhagavā Cāpāle cetiye sato sampajāno āyu-saṃkhāraṃ ossajji. Dīgha-nikāya,* XVI, 3, 9.
7. For the use of this expression, see Stcherbatsky, *The Central conception of Buddhism.*
8. There is no mention of Supriya in the Pali version.
9. Both versions contain an identical account of the conversion of this parivrājaka.
10. *Yannv ahaṃ tadrūpān ṛddhyabhisaṃskārān abhisaṃskuryāṃ yathā samāhite citte jīvita-saṃskārān adhiṣṭhāyāyuḥ-saṃskārān utsṛjeyam. Mahāparinirvāṇa-sūtra,* p. 210. Also *Divyāvadāna,* p. 203.
11. *Maraṇa-vaśitva-jñāpanārtham ... traimāsyam eva nordhvaṃ vineyakāryābhāvāt ....* Yaśomitra, *Abhidharma-kośa-vyākhyā,* p. 105.
12. *Ettha ca kappaṃ ti āyukappaṃ, tasmiṃ tasmiṃ kāle yaṃ manussānaṃ āyuppamānaṃ hoti taṃ paripuṇṇaṃ karonto tiṭṭheyya, kappāvasesaṃ ti : 'appaṃ vā bhiyyo' ti vuttavassasatato atirekaṃ vā. Sumaṅgalavilāsinī,* Vol. II, p. 554.
13. *Iddhibalena samannāgato kappaṃ tiṭṭheyyā'ti? āmantā. iddhimayiko so āyu,... sā gati ... so attabhāvapaṭilābho ti? na hevaṃ vattabbe .... Kathāvatthu,* XI, 5.
14. *Ko panettha iddhimato viseso, nanu aniddhimā pi āyukappaṃ tiṭṭheyyā ti? ayaṃ viseso, iddhimā hi ... akālamaraṇaṃ nivāretuṃ sakkoti, aniddhimato etaṃ natthi. Kathāvatthu-aṭṭhakathā,* XI, 5.
15. *'Kappāvasesaṃ vā' ti temāsaparicchedo ca bhaṇito. so ca pana kappo āyukappo vuccati ... vijjati ca taṃ mahārāja iddhibalaṃ bhagavato ... anatthiko mahārāja bhagavā sabbabhavehi ... Milindapañha,* pp. 141-2.
16. *Mahāsīvatthero panāha : Buddhānaṃ aṭṭhāne gajjitaṃ nāma natthi ... idaṃ bhaddaka-ppam eva tiṭṭheyya ... Evaṃ vutte 'pi so pana : ruccati, āyukappo ti idam eva Aṭṭhakathāyaṃ niyāmitaṃ. Sumaṅgalavilāsinī.* Vol. II, pp. 554-5.

17. The commentary on this section of the *Cullavagga* makes no reference to this point.
18. L. de la Vallée Poussin, *L'Abhidharma-kośa de Vasubandhu,* ch. II, kā. 10.
19. The original MS of this work was discovered in Tibet by Pandit Rāhula Sānkṛtyāyana, in the year 1937. It has been edited by the author of this article and will soon be published by the K. P. Jayaswal Research Institute, Patna, in their Tibetan Sanskrit Works Series. (Published 1959.)
20. *'Samādhibalena karmajaṃ jīvitāvedhaṃ nirvartyāyuḥ saṃskārādhiṣṭhānajam, āyur na vipākaḥ' iti Kośakāraḥ. tatra kim uttaram iti? na tatrāvaśyam uttaraṃ vaktavyam, yasmān naitat sūtre 'vatarati, vinaye na saṃdṛśyate, dharmatāṃ ca vilomayati ... tathāpi tu yuktimad uttaram ucyate. yadi Bhagavān samādhibalena svecchayāpūrvaṃ sattvaṃ ... utpādayet, svātmano vā jīvitam anākṣiptaṃ prāk-karmabhir yogabalenākṣipet, tato Buddho Bhagavān Nārāyaṇī-kṛtaḥ syāt, apūrva-sattvanirmāṇāt. sa ca kāruṇikatvān naiva parinirvāyāt ... tasmād Vaitulika-śāstra-praveśa-dvāram ārabdhaṃ tena bhadantenety adhyupekṣyam etat. Abhidharama-dīpa-vṛtti, kā.* 138.
21. *Mahāvastu,* I, p. 169.
22. 'Although they could suppress the working of karma, the conquerors let it become manifest and conceal their sovereign power. This is mere conformity with the world' (trans. by J.J. Jones, *The Mahāvastu,* Vol. I, p. 133). For other similar doctrines of the Lokottaravādins, see J. Masuda, 'Origin and doctrines of early Indian Buddhist schools', *Asia Major,* II, 1925.
23. *Ākāṃkṣann Ānanda, Tathāgata eka-piṇḍa-pātena kalpaṃ vā tiṣṭhet, kalpaśataṃ vā, ... tato vottari tiṣṭhet, na ca Tathāgatasyendriyāṇy upanaśyeyur na mukhavarṇsyānyathātvaṃ bhaven nāpi chavivarṇa upahanyeta. Sukhâvatî-vyûha* (Anecdota Oxoniensia. Aryan Series, Vol. I, Pt. 2), 1883, p. 4.
24. For a full exposition of this topic, see T. R. V. Murti : *The Central philosophy of Buddhism,* 284 ff.
25. *Nirvāṇabhūmiṃ cupadarśayāmi vinayārthasattvāna vadāmy upāyaṃ na cāpi nirvāmy ahu tasmi kāle ihaiva co dharmu prākāśayāmi.* Chapter XV (*Tathāgatāyuṣpramāṇaparivarta*), p. 323. Also cf. *Na Buddhaḥ parinirvāti dharmo 'ntarhīyate na ca, sattvānām paripākāya nirvāṇaṃ tūpadarśayet.* (Quoted in the *Abhisamayālaṃkārāloka,* p. 132.) For several views on this topic, see *Bu-ston,* II, pp. 67 ff.

(a) (b)

Borobudur Reliefs Nos. I, B, 17-18 Reproduced from N.J. Krom and T. van Erp. Beschrijving van Barabudur, 's-Gravenhagn Martinus Nijhoff, 1920, courtesy Martinus Nihoff.

CHAPTER 12

The Vaibhāṣika Theory of Words and Meanings*

Among the many controversies between the Sautrāntika and the Vaibhāṣika recorded in the *Abhidharma-kośa-bhāṣya* of Vasubandhu,[1] a large number are devoted to discussions of the reality of a Vaibhāṣika category called *citta-viprayukta-saṃskāras* (tr. 'pure forces' by Stcherbatsky).[2] The Vaibhāṣikas enumerate thirteen such *saṃskāras*[3] and declare them to be distinct from the traditional three categories of dharmas, viz. *rūpa* (matter), *citta* (mind), and *caitasikas* (mental concomitants).

Whereas the first ten of these *saṃskāras* have a bearing on the Buddhist theories of causation, unconscious trances, life-duration, and phenomenal existences, and thus are directly or indirectly related to the working of the traditional five *skandhas,* the last three *saṃskāras,* viz. the *nāma-kāya, pada-kāya,* and *vyañjana-kāya,* have a bearing only on the nature of words and meanings, as they are 'forces' that impart significance to words, sentences, and letters respectively. An influence of the theory of *sphoṭa* and also of the Mīmāṃsaka theory of eternal words in the formulation of these three Vaibhāṣika *saṃskāras* was long ago noted by Stcherbatsky in his *The Central Conception of Buddhism.*[4] A considerable amount of Ābhidharmika literature has been discovered since then, notably the *Abhidharma-samuccaya* of Asanga[5] and the *Abhidharma-dīpa*[6] (with its commentary the *Vibhāṣā-prabhā-vṛtti*[7]) which furnish us with valuable information on these last three *saṃskāras.*

---

*This article was originally published in *BSOAS,* Vol. XXII, part 1, pp. 95-107, University of London, 1959. Reprinted with kind permission of Oxford University Press.

The Pali scriptures make only incidental references to the problem of words and their meanings. The *Kathāvatthu* records no controversy on this theme. No Buddhist work prior to the *Bhāṣya* takes any serious note of this problem. It seems probable that the Buddhists made their entry into this field under the influence of their contemporary Mīmāṃsakas and Vaiyākaraṇas, who had developed their theories of eternal words and of *sphoṭa*.

For the Mīmāṃsakas, the problem of words and meanings was of primary importance, as all their metaphysical and ritual speculations were based on the doctrine of the validity of the Vedas. They, therefore, developed the doctrine of eternal words and their natural (*autpattika*) meanings. In parallel with this, the Vaibhāṣika theories of words and their meanings can also be traced primarily to their speculations on the nature of the words of the Buddha.

This can be seen from a controversy between the Sautrāntika and the Vaibhāṣika on the inclusion of the words of the Buddha in the formula of the five *skandhas*. Both these schools agreed that the words (which consisted of sounds—*śabda*) were made up of sound-atoms (*śabda-paramāṇu*) reposing on the eight *dravya-paramāṇus*. It was, therefore, only logical to treat all sounds (*vāk*) (and therefore all words) as material, and hence include them in the *rūpa-skandha*. Contrary to this Sautrāntika position, the Vaibhāṣikas maintained that the words of the Buddha are not of the nature of *vāk* (verbal sound) but are of the nature of *nāma* (non-material). The *Vṛtti* on the *Dīpa* quotes a scripture on this controversy : 'While the Lord lived, his words are of the nature of speech (*vāk*) as well as of the nature of *nāma* respectively in a secondary and primary sense. After his *parinirvāṇa*, however, his words are only of the nature of *nāma* and not of *vāk*. For, the Lord of the sages had a "heavenly sound" not comparable to any mundane speech'.[8]

Commenting on this controversy Yaśomitra says that according to the Sautrāntikas, the Buddha-*vacana* is of the nature of vocal expression (*vāgvijñapti*) and hence is included in the *rūpa-skandha*. Those who maintain the category of the *viprayukta-saṃskāras*, include the Buddha-*vacana* in the *saṃskāra-skandha*. The Ābhidharmikas, however accept both these views.[9]

In elaboration of this last statement, Yaśomitra quotes two passages from the *Jñāna-prasthāna* : 'What is a Buddha-*vacana*? The speech, speaking, talk, voice, utterance, range of speech, sound of speech, action of speech, vocal expression of the Tathāgata is Buddha-*vacana*'.[10] According to this view the Buddha-*vacana* is merely a *vāk-vijñapti,* i.e. verbal expression, which is identical with the '*vācā*' of the Theravādins, also defined in similar terms.[11]

This view, Yaśomitra says, is immediately followed by another view (supporting the Vaibhāṣika theory of *nāma-pada-vyañjana-kāyas*): 'What is this dharma called Buddha-*vacana?* The arrangement in regular order, the establishment in regular order, the uniting in regular order of the *nāma-kāya, pada-kāya,* and *vyañjana-kāya* (is called Buddha-*vacana*)'.[12]

This latter view is accepted by the Vaibhāṣikas. This passage suggests that the Buddha-*vacanas* are not verbal sounds but some other non-material dharmas put into order.

Yaśomitra does not name the Ābhidharmikas who accepted both these views. Apart from the *Bhāṣya* (representing the Neo-Vaibhāṣikas), the *Abhidharmāmṛta* of Ghoṣaka and the *Abhidharma-samuccaya* of Asanga (Yogācāra school) also enumerate the *nāma-pada-vyañjana-kāyas* in their *viprayukta* category. But their definitions are different from those of the Vaibhāṣikas. Ghoṣaka defines *nāma-kāya* as meaningful letters, the *pada-kāya* as naming a thing by an aggregate of *padas,* and the *vyañjana-kāya* as a collection of letters.[13] Asanga's definitions of the first two *saṃskāras* are altogether different. He says that when the own-natures of dharmas are designated or named there is a notion called *nāma-kāya.* When the peculiarities (or details) of dharmas are designated there is a notion called *pada-kāya. Vyañjana-kāya* is a notion for letters which are the support for the *nāma-kāya* and the *pada-kāya.*[14] The same definitions are given in Haribhadra's *Abhisamayālaṅkārāloka*[15] and the *Vijñapti-mātratā-siddhi* of Hiüan Tsang,[16] suggesting that the Yogācāra-Vijñānavādins did not interpret these terms in the sense in which they are understood in the Vaibhāṣika school. By Ābhidharmikas, therefore, Yaśomitra seems to refer to certain Vaibhāṣikas like our Dīpakāra who favoured the view that while the Buddha lived, his *vacanas* are of the nature of *nāma* as well as of *vāk* (albeit in a secondary sense) but after his death, they are only of *nāma-svabhāva.*

The Kośakāra deals with these *saṃskāras* rather briefly, concentrating more on their refutation and less on their explanation. We may here summarize the Vaibhāṣika position and the Sautrāntika refutation of this topic as contained in the *Bhāṣya.*[17]

The Vaibhāṣika maintains that verbal sound alone is not capable of conveying any meaning. A verbal sound (*vāk*) operates on the *nāman*, and the latter conveys the meaning. Thus it is the *nāman* which gives significance to a word, which is purely material. This *nāman* is a *viprayukta-saṃskāra*. In support of this theory, the Vaibhāṣika quotes a scripture which says that 'a stanza rests on *nāman*'.[18]

The Sautrāntika maintains that the *nāma-kāyas* do not play any part in conveying a meaning. It is true that all sounds or sounds alone (*ghoṣa-mātra*) do not convey a meaning. But verbal sounds (*vāk*) which are agreed upon by convention to mean a particular thing (*kṛta-saṅketa*) do convey their meanings. Since such a *saṅketa* is essential even in the assumption of the *nāma-kāya*, the latter is redundant and hence useless.

Moreover, the Vaibhāṣika theory that a *nāman* is operated on by verbal sounds (*vāk*) does not stand any scrutiny. For, if *nāman* is an entity, a real dharma, it can neither be produced nor revealed bit by bit by the verbal sounds, which come into existence only in series. Nor can it be said that it is produced or revealed only by the last sound, for in that case it should be sufficient to hear only the last sound in order to understand its *artha*.

If in order to avoid this dilemma the Vaibhāṣika thinks that, after the manner of a *viprayukta* like *jāti*, the *nāman* is also born with its object (*artha-sahaja*), then it would mean that there are no actual *nāma-kāyas* conveying past or future objects, or the *asaṃskṛta* dharmas which are not born.

Moreover to admit an entity in itself, called *nāman* (a word) or *pada* (a sentence) is a wholly superfluous hypothesis. We might as well argue that there exists distinct from ants a thing called 'line of ants'. One can understand the letters (*vyañjana*) being considered as real entities but it is absurd to treat their arrangements in an order like word or sentence as independent realities (*dravya*).

As regards the scripture quoted by the Vaibhāṣikas, the Sautrāntika points out that the '*nāman*' there means words on which men have agreed that they mean a certain thing. It does not refer to any additional *saṃskāra* as is postulated by the Vaibhāṣikas.

It is interesting to note that the scripture quoted by the Vaibhāṣikas also occurs in the Pali *Sagātha-vagga* of the *Saṃyutta-nikāya*. This deals with the composition of *gāthās*. To a question as to what is the origin and foundation of a verse, the Buddha says that letters are their origin and *nāmas* are their foundation.[19] Commenting on this, Buddhaghosa says that letters (*akkharas*) produce a *pada, padas* produce a *gāthā,* and the *gāthā* conveys a meaning.[20] As regards the term *nāma,* he says that it means names, such as 'ocean', 'earth', etc., which are designations of certain concepts.[21] From this it is clear that for the Theravādins the *nāma* is not a *saṃskāra.* But Buddhaghosa's explanation of *nāma* agrees with the Vaibhāṣika definition : *nāma-paryāyaḥ saṃjñā-karaṇaṃ yathā ghaṭa iti.*[22]

The Vaibhāṣika takes the term *pada* as a synonym of a sentence (*pada-paryāyo vākyam*).[23] This rather unusual meaning of the term *pada* can also be traced to Pali. In the suttas this term is often used in the sense of a sentence or a refrain of a verse or a line of a verse.[24] In the scripture quoted above dealing with *gāthā,* the term *pada* is not used. But the commentary says that *'akkharaṃ padaṃ janeti'*. Since *nāma* refers to a word, it is probable that by *padaṃ* here is understood a sentence (*pāda*) or a line of a *gāthā.* This seems to be the original meaning of the term *pada* in the expression *pada-kāya.* But a line of a verse may not necessarily be a complete sentence. The *Bhāṣya* defines the term *pada*—perhaps to make it conform to the Grammarian's definition of a sentence—as 'that by which the meaning is complete',[25] and quotes a line (*anityā vata saṃskārāḥ*) of a verse as an illustration. The *Vṛtti* also calls *pada* a synonym of *vākya* and quotes further an Ābhidharmika view: 'A *pada* (sentence) is a collection of significant words (*pada*) which fulfil the intended meaning'.[26]

The Vaibhāṣikas are not unaware of the fact that the term *pada* according to the Grammarians meant a word. In the Ābhidharmika view quoted above, *pada* is used side by side in both these meanings. Yaśomitra also quotes the Grammarian's definition '*sup-tiṅ-antaṃ padam*'.[27] The Theravādins also know this meaning as is evident from such expressions as *padaso* (word by word), *padattho* (meaning of a word), etc. The term *vyañjana* is also interpreted by the Theravādins as letters (*akkhara*) apparently including both the vowels and the consonants. Commenting on a sutta where *vaṇṇa* and *byañjana* occur together, Buddhaghosa says that these two terms are identical, and that the latter term could also mean only certain *vaṇṇas* (i.e. consonants).[28]

Thus it is clear that there was a pre-Vaibhāṣika tradition for the use of the terms *nāma, pada,* and *vyañjana* in the sense of word, sentence, and letter, respectively. Stcherbatsky's observation, therefore, that this is 'a case exhibiting clearly the desire to have a terminology of one's own'[29] overlooks the tradition noticed above.

Nor is this tradition limited only to a common use of these terms. One can even detect a certain correspondence between this Vaibhāṣika *saṃskāra* called *nāma-kāya* and a Theravādin dharma called *nāma-paññatti,* recognized more or less as an independent category by later Theravādins like Anuruddha.

The term *paññatti* occurs several times in the suttas, always referring to designations or concepts recognized as unreal in themselves, nevertheless used in common worldly parlance. In the *Poṭṭhapāda-sutta,* for instance, the Buddha while speaking on various speculations on the nature of self, says that a word like *atta-paṭilābha,* or expressions like past, present, future, or milk, curds, butter, ghee, etc. which he used in his discussion, are merely names, expressions, turns of speech, designations in common use in the world. The Tathāgata, although he makes use of these, is not led astray by them (i.e. knows them as unreal).[30]

The suttas do not contain further elaborations on the theme of *paññatti.* But the *Abhidhamma-piṭaka* and the *Aṭṭhakathās* offer several important speculations on the nature, scope, origin, and cognition of the *paññatti,* and treat it almost as a separate category like the *nāma* and *rūpa.* The *Puggala-paññatti,* for instance, is, as the name itself suggests, solely devoted to a description of various concepts arising about a central concept (*paññatti*) called a personality (*puggala*).

The *Suttanta-mātikā* contains three pairs (*dukas*)[31] dealing with dhammas respectively called *adhivacana, nirutti,* and *paññatti,* and the dhammas that are made known by them. Defining a dhamma which is *paññatti,* the *Dhammasaṅgaṇi* says : 'that which is an appellation, that which is a designation, an expression, a current term, a name, a denomination, the assigning of a name, an interpretation, a distinctive mark, a phrasing on this or that dhamma is a dhamma called *paññatti.* All dhammas are capable of being expressed'.[32] The other two terms, viz. *adhivacana* and *nirutti,* are described in identical terms.

Commenting on these *dukas,* the *Aṭṭhasālinī* dwells at length on one term, viz. the *nāma* [*paññatti*]. *Nāma* (name) is fourfold : that given on a special occasion, that given in virtue of a personal quality, that given by parents, and that which has spontaneously arisen (*opapātika-nāmaṃ*). Of these the last is more significant, as it points to a belief that certain names are eternal. 'In those cases where a former concept tallies with a later concept, a former current term with a later one, e.g. the moon in a previous cycle is [what we now call] moon, this name is called *opapātika-nāma*.'[33] It is suggested here that there are things which are not named by others, but name themselves, or are born with their names. The four (*arūpa*) *khandhas* are called *nāma,* because they make their own name as they arise. When they arise their name also arises.[34] No one names *vedanā,* saying 'Be thou called *vedanā*'. A *vedanā,* whether it is past, present, or future, is always called *vedanā.* This theory of the *opapāṭika-nāma* reminds us of the Vaibhāṣika theory that the *nāma-kāyas* are *artha-sahaja* (born with meanings) and also corresponds, as will be seen below, to what the Dīpakāra calls *apauruṣeya nāma-kāyas* conveying such dharmas as the *skandha, āyatana,* and *dhātu.*

Finally on the scope of this *nāma-paññatti,* the *Aṭṭhasālinī* says that this is a unique dharma which covers all dharmas, all dharmas come under its scope.[35] The *nāma-paññatti* is applicable to dharmas of all the three spheres. There is no being, nor thing that may not be called by a name.

The *paññatti* discussed above refers only to the *nāma-paññatti* or names. There is another kind of *paññatti,* called *attha-paññatti,* which can be roughly translated as 'ideas' or 'concepts' or 'reflexes' (*nimitta*). The Theravādins recognize several kinds of ideas.[36] There are ideas such as 'land', 'mountain', and the like referring to certain physical changes in nature; or ideas like 'man', 'woman', 'individual', referring to the fivefold set of aggregates; there are ideas of locality, time, and the like, derived from the revolutions of the moon, etc. These ideas are not real dharmas. Nevertheless, they become objects of knowledge. As Anuruddha says, 'they shadow forth the meanings [of things] and become objects of thought genesis [as our ideas]'. This idea is designated as *attha-paññatti.* It is called *paññatti,* because it is made known (*paññāpiyattā paññatti*) by the *nāma-paññatti.*[37] The names (*nāmas*) are called *nāma-paññatti,* because they make the ideas known (*paññāpanato paññatti*).[38] Thus the term *paññatti* includes both names and ideas.

Although its unreality was not lost sight of, the Theravādins on account of their recognition of the *paññatti* as an object of mind, had to show its place in the traditional formula of the five *skandhas.* They had to classify it either as *nāma* or *rūpa, saṃskṛta* or *asaṃskṛta, traikālika* (belonging to three times) or *kāla-vimukta* (transcending time). A few speculations on this problem are found in the *Abhidhammattha-saṅgaho* and its commentaries.

Anuruddha classifies all dharmas into three categories, viz. *rūpa, nāma,* and *paññatti.* Of these the first includes matter, the second includes *citta, cetasikas,* and *nibbāna.* The last includes names and ideas (i.e. *nāma* and *attha-paññatti*).[39] He describes *paññatti* as a *saṃkhata* dhamma since it is also produced by a cause, viz. by a certain worldly convention that a particular name refers to a particular object (*loka-saṅketa*).[40] Nevertheless, it is unreal, and hence cannot be predicated as past, present, or future. Therefore it is called *kāla-vimutta.*

After dealing with the nature of *paññatti,* Anuruddha explains the thought process involved in its cognition leading to an understanding of the thing meant (*attha*).[41] Following, i.e. making its object a vocal sound (*vacī-ghosa*) there arises a thought process called *śrotra-vijñāna* (auditory consciousness). In a subsequent thought process the verbal sound heard gives rise in the mind (*mano-dvāra*) to a corresponding *nāma-paññatti.* This is grasped in a subsequent process by a mind-consciousness (*mano-viññāṇa-vīthi*) which is already conversant with the *saṅketa*"[42] between this *nāma-paññatti* and the particular object it is conventionally taken to convey. When this mind-consciousness thinks on this *saṅketa* there follows the cognition of the object, i.e. the thing meant (*attha*).

The *nāma-paññatti* of the Theravādins offers several points of comparison with the *nāma-kāya* of the Vaibhāṣikas. Both these dharmas are different from verbal sounds (*vāk-śabda* or *vacī-ghosa*). Both are dependent on the verbal sounds for their origin. Both follow a verbal sound perceived by a hearer. Both serve the purpose of conveying a meaning (*artha*) by the help of *saṅketa.* The *nāma-paññatti* is enumerated as a separate category distinct from the *nāma* and *rūpa.* The *nāma-kāyas* also belong to the *viprayuktas,* different from the *nāma* and *rūpa.* But whereas the Theravādins recognize the *nāma-paññatti* as unreal and, therefore, a *prajñapti-dharma,* the Vaibhāṣikas treat the *nāma-kāyas* as a real *dravya-dharma.*

Although the Theravādins hold that *vacī-ghosa* gives rise to a *nāma-paññatti,* they do not offer any explanation on the difficulties involved in this operation. Nor do they show any acquaintance with the controversies that took place on this problem between the Sautrāntika and the Vaibhāṣika or between the Sphoṭavādins and their opponents. The Sautrāntikas were certainly acquainted with certain aspects of these controversies as can be seen from the Kośakāra's arguments against the revelation of the *nāman* by series of vocal sound—arguments which are not different from those of the Mīmāṃsakas and others against the theory of the revelation of *sphoṭa* by *dhvani.*[43] But neither the Kośakāra nor his commentator Yaśomitra makes any reference to the Mīmāṃsakas or the Sphoṭavādins. Both are content only with a brief refutation of the Vaibhāṣika. The Dīpakāra's treatment of this topic is more comprehensive. He refutes the Sautrāntika position, makes pointed reference to the theories of (verbal) sounds held by the Mīmāṃsaka and Vaiśeṣika, and briefly examines the *sphoṭa* theory of the Grammarians.

After briefly stating the Sautrāntika argument that the *nāma-kāyas,* etc. are not different from the verbal sounds (*vāk-śabda*) and, therefore, are unreal,[44] the Dīpakāra sets forth the Vaibhāṣika theory of these *saṃskāras.*[45] A verbal sound (*vāk-śabda*), he says, is synonymous with speech (*vāk*), utterance (*gīḥ*), and is, therefore, included in the *rūpa-skandha.* The *nāma-kāyas,* etc. are *viprayukta-saṃskāras,* and hence included in the *saṃskāra-skandha.* The *nāma-kāyas,* etc. are dependent for their origin on the verbal sound and manifest the meaning which is dependent on the utterance (or the individual word-shape) and thus are representatives of the thing meant (*artha*) as in the case of (the content of) a knowledge.[46] Just as the five sense cognitions are dependent on their corresponding five objects, similarly the *nāma-kāyas,* etc. are dependent for their origin on the verbal sound. It is said, therefore, 'A verbal sound (*vāk*) operates on the *nāman,* the *nāman* expresses the object (*artha*)'.[47]

Here the Sautrāntika raises the following objection: you say that along with the speech sound the letters (like *ka, ca, ṭa, ta, pa,* etc.) are produced, by the speech the *nāma-kāyas* are brought into operation. This being the case, the speech, following as it does each letter in turn, is subject to divisibility. Therefore, there can be no such thing as a *nāma-kāya* as a meaning conveyor (*abhidhāna*). (Since for this purpose a unitary entity is required.)

The Dīpakāra rejects this argument saying that when the aggregate of the sound parts are perceived, there is a possibility of its (*nāma-kāya*) having the capacity of being a meaning-bearer. Moreover, its existence is evident from its activity. Its activity is conveying its meaning. It conveys its own meaning, since the relation between *nāman*, and meaning is not created by any person (*apauruṣeyatvāt*).[48]

The Sautrāntika here brings forward the theory of *saṅketa*. He says that the *nāman*, etc. are not different from verbal speech. The verbal sound alone acting itself (*kṛtāvadhiḥ*) as the factor which gives rise to the cognition of the object, conveys the meaning to the listener when its constituent parts are grasped as a unit by memory. Why, therefore, postulate these separate *nāman*, etc.?[49]

The Dīpakāra points out that the verbal sounds, being atomic, are not capable of revealing the *artha*. A (verbal) sound being a collection of atoms can bring to light only those objects with which it has come into contact, like a lamp. Things which are not born or which are destroyed or are inaccessible (to the senses, like heaven, etc.) are not reached by sound. Naturally, therefore, a sound cannot convey these objects.

Moreover, the sounds cannot convey a meaning either serially or simultaneously. The stems of *balvaja* grass, for instance, which are individually incapable of being used in the action of dragging a piece of wood, become capable when they are put together and remain in the form of a rope. But the words of a sentence which consist of atoms of sound, and which come into existence in series, are merely conceptual unities of the constituent parts (*samudāya-saṃkṣepāḥ*) which are received by the mind. They are, therefore, incapable each part individually (of conveying the meaning), nor do they convey it if taken together, since they cannot stand in unity like the *balvaja* grass. Thus it is proved that the sounds do not convey the meaning either serially or simultaneously.[50]

Moreover, as in the case of a lamp, there is no relationship of revealed-revealer between the sounds and meanings (*artha*). Thus people who wish to see a pot take a lamp which has the capacity of revealing a pot and other things as well; and there are no speech sounds which have the predetermined activity of revealing (or acting) on any meaning taken at random by some particular relationship.

Nor is this particular relationship, viz. of revealed-revealer, appropriate in the case of the thing meant and a sound. For the sounds do not convey that which is not agreed upon by convention to mean a particular thing.[51]

Even if we accept the theory of *saṅketa* obtaining between a sound and *artha,* such a sound is still subject to the argument of seriality. If it is said that the memory of each sound conveys the meaning, then also it is subject to the same fault. And if it is maintained that the trace (*saṃskāra*) left by the sounds in the mind conveys the meaning,[52] then also we deny it as it is not proved.

The Dīpakāra further elaborates the atomic nature of sounds. He says that sound (*ghoṣa*) cannot be a unity as it consists of several *paramāṇus.* It is accepted that the diphthongs *e* and *ai* are produced in the throat and palate. But it is not correct to say that a sound consisting of only one atom operates in two different places. But this is possible in the case of aggregates of atoms.[53] Even then the atoms cannot convey a meaning individually, for their individual existence cannot be proved. Nor can they do so in a collection (*saṃghāta*). For a *saṃghāta* does not exist in reality apart from its constituent parts.

After thus showing that verbal sounds alone cannot convey a meaning, the Dīpakāra sums up his position. 'The correct form of exposition', he says, 'is that the letters which are past with reference to the last letter are grasped by a (single) mental effort (*mano-buddhi*) and then cause to arise the mental concept (*buddhi*) as directed towards the relevant meaning and thus (only in this fashion) convey the meaning'.[54]

As regards a common belief that a (verbal) sound conveys a meaning, the Dīpakāra says that this belief does not correspond to facts. 'In fact the speech (*vāk*) operates on the *nāman,* i.e. it expresses or speaks the *nāma,* i.e. it gives voice to it. The *nāma* brings to light the *artha.* Thus the speech passing over each letter in order, speaking or giving voice to the *nāma* and at the same time giving rise to (the perception of) its own form, but existing only in the form of series, is said to reveal the *artha* only by a process of metaphorical transfer. The meaning is not expressed or brought to light by the sound.'[55]

This exposition of the *nāma-kāya* offers several points of comparison with the *sphoṭa* theory of early Grammarians. *Sphoṭa* is defined as 'the abiding word, distinct from the letters and revealed by them, which is the conveyor of the meaning'.[56] The *nāma-kāya* is also distinct from letters (i.e. sound), is revealed by them, and is claimed as the conveyor of meanings. The Vaibhāṣika argument that sounds on account of their seriality cannot convey a meaning, is identical with the argument of the Sphoṭavādins against the Naiyāyikas who, like the Sautrāntika, maintained that verbal sounds (with the help of *saṅketa*) convey the *artha*.[56] But whereas the *sphoṭa* is called a *śabda* and described as one and eternal, the *nāma-kāyas* are nowhere designated as *śabda* and are declared to be many and non-eternal.

The Dīpakāra does not appear to be unaware of this similarity. As if anticipating an attack from the Sautrāntikas on this account, he raises a question as to whether the *nāma-kāya,* etc. are *nitya* or *anitya*.[57] Such a question is indeed unnecessary, for the *nāma-kāya* is a *saṃskāra,* and consequently *anitya.* The question raised, therefore, suggests that a similarity between the *sphoṭa* and *nāma-kāya* was present to the mind of the Dīpakāra. He is, therefore, unduly emphatic when he says that the *nāma-kāyas* are *anitya,* as they depend for their function on such causes as *ghoṣa* (sound), etc.[58]

Nor does he recognize the theory of *sphoṭa.* He examines a statement of Patañjali that *sphoṭa* (the unchanging substratum) is the word, the sound is merely an attribute of the word (*sphoṭaḥ śabdo dhvaniḥ śabda-guṇaḥ*).[59] The Dīpakāra does not admit any difference between a substratum and an attribute, and, therefore, says that these two being identical, even the sound (*dhvani*) will become eternal. For him *dhvani, śabda,* and *sphoṭa* are all synonyms like *hasta, kara,* and *pāṇi,* etc. The *sphoṭa* being thus identical with verbal sound is subject to the same fault of seriality and therefore incapable of conveying the *artha*.[60]

He further confirms his rejection of the theory of *sphoṭa* by openly favouring a view, which Patañjali calls naïve, that *śabda* is *dhvani.* Patañjali in his *Mahābhāṣya* gives two views on the nature of a word (*śabda*): (i) a word is that by means of which, when uttered (*yenoccāritena*), there arises an understanding of the thing meant; (ii) or a word is a sound capable of conveying a meaning (*pratīta-padārthako loke dhvaniḥ śabdaḥ*).[61] The expression *yenoccāritena* is traditionally held to refer to *sphoṭa*.[62] The Dipakāra does not refer to this view, but quotes the second view showing his preference for it. But this second view equally goes against his theory of *nāma-kāya.* He, therefore, says that the *nāma,* etc. are different from the *dhvani* (i.e. from the *śabda*), (because) they are *sarvārtha-viṣaya.*[63] The significance of this statement seems to be that whereas a sound refers to a particular thing, the *nāma-kāya* as a *saṃskāra* is capable of conveying all meanings. Taken as a dharma, this expression corresponds to what the Theravādins called *sabbe dhammā paññatti-pathā* or to the statement of the *Aṭṭhasālinī* that *ayaṃ hi nāma-paññatti eka-dhammo sabbesu catubhūmika-dhammesu nipatati.*[64]

The *sphoṭa* theory referred to by the Dīpakāra shows his acquaintance only with the Pātañjala school of grammar. He does not refer to the later developments of this theory as contained in the *Vākyapadīya* of Bhartṛhari. While dealing with the nature of sounds, he says that the Vaiyākaraṇas (together with the Mīmāṃsakas) do not recognize the atomic nature of sounds, and proceeds to show that the sounds are atomic, because they possess resistance. The *Vākyapadīya* refers to a view that some consider words (*śabda*) as consisting of atoms.[65] It is possible that the Dīpakāra was not aware of this view, or did not consider it an authoritative view of the Grammarians.

As seen above, the Sphoṭavādins understand the term *śabda* in the sense of *sphoṭa* and not in the ordinary sense of a sound. This *śabda,* therefore, is not perceived by the ears but only by the mind.[66] The Dīpakāra makes play with the ambiguity of this term and ridicules the Grammarians for maintaining a view that *śabda* (sound) is perceived by the mind.

The Dīpakāra further gives some more details about the *nāma-kāyas,* etc. The *nāma-kāyas* are two-fold: those which have a determinate meaning, and those which do not (in themselves) mean any particular thing (*yādṛcchika*). The former is again divided into two kinds: *apauruṣeya* (not created by any person) and *laukika* (mundane). The *nāma-kāyas* which convey the *dhātu, āyatana,* and *skandhas* are *apauruṣeya.* They are primarily perceived only by the Buddha. It is therefore said 'the *nāma-pada-vyañjana-kāyas* appear when the Tathāgatas appear (in the world)'.[67]

The *laukika* (worldly) *nāma-kāyas* are two-fold; those which convey a particular thing, and those which are *yādṛcchika.* Of these, the *apauruṣeya* as well as the *niyata-laukika nāma-kāyas* convey only those meanings for which there exists a *saṅketa.*[68]

The use of the term *apauruṣeya* for the *nāma-kāyas* which convey the Buddhist categories of dharma is significant. It reminds us of the *opapātika-nāma* of the Theravādins and shows a direct influence of the Mīmāṃsaka. For the latter, the Vedas are *apauruṣeya* and eternal. For the Vaibhāṣika, the Buddha-*vacanas* (i.e. *nāma-kāyas*) are *apauruṣeya,* but not eternal.

It appears from the above discussion that the Vaibhāṣika theory of the *nāma-kāyas* was a continuation and a development of an earlier tradition represented in the form of *nāma-paññatti* in the Pali *Abhidharma* and *Aṭṭhakathās.* As in the case of many other *prajñapti-dharmas,* the *nāma-kāyas,* etc., also came to be recognized by the Vaibhāṣikas as *dravya-dharmas,* and thus found a place in the *viprayukta* category. The lack of speculation on the nature of the Buddha-*vacana* in the Pali tradition and its presence in the Vaibhāṣika school suggests that this was a later development brought about by a certain influence of other schools, particularly the Mīmāṃsakas and the Vaiyākaraṇas, who, although for different reasons, had a primary interest in the problem of words and their meanings. The Vaibhāṣikas seem to have benefited from the arguments of the early Sphoṭavādin Grammarians. But the Mīmāṃsakas seem to have exercised a far greater influence on them as is evident from the use of such expressions as *apauruṣeya* for denoting the Buddha-*vacana.*

NOTES

1. *L'Abhidharma-kośa de Vasubandhu* (tr. L. de la Vallée Poussin), ch. I, kā. 35-48. Henceforth referred to as *Bhāṣya.*
2. *The central conception of Buddhism,* 23.
3. *Prāptiḥ, aprāptiḥ, nikāya-sabhāgatā, asaṃjñi-samāpattiḥ, nirodha-samāpattiḥ, jīvitendriyam, jātiḥ, sthitiḥ, jarā, anityatā, nāma-kāyaḥ, pada-kāyaḥ, vyañjana-kāyaḥ.*
4. p. 24, n. 1.
5. Ed. P. Pradhan, Santiniketan, 1950.
6. The MS of this work was discovered in Tibet by Rāhula Sānkṛtyāyana in the year 1937. It is a work written against the *Abhidharma-kośa* of (the Sautrāntika) Vasubandhu. It has been edited by the author of this article and will soon be published by the K.P. Jayaswal Research Institute, Patna, in their Tibetan Sanskrit Works Series. (Published 1959.)
7. Henceforth referred to as *Vṛtti.*
8. *'Jīvato bhagavato vāṅ-svabhāvaṃ Buddha-vacanaṃ gauṇa-mukhya-nyāyena. Parinirvṛtasya tu nāma-svabhāvam eva, na vāk-svabhāvam, brahma-svaratvān munīndrasya, loka-vācāṃ tat sādṛśyānupapatteḥ.'* *Vṛtti* on kā. 12.
9. *Yeṣāṃ Sautrāntikānāṃ vāg-vijñapti-svabhāvaṃ teṣāṃ tāni rūpa-skandha-saṃgṛhītāni. Yeṣāṃ nikāyāntarīyāṇāṃ citta-viprayuktaṃ nāmāsti teṣāṃ saṃskāra-skandha-saṃgṛhītāni .... Ābhidhārmikāṇāṃ tūbhaya-svabhāvam iṣṭam. Sphuṭārthā*

Abhidharma-kośa-vyākhyā (henceforth referred to as Sakv. Ed. U. Woghihara, 1936), p. 52.

10. *Katamad* Buddha-*vacanam? Tathāgatasya yā vāg vacanaṃ vyāhāro gīr niruktir vāk-patho vāg-ghoṣo vāk-karma vāg-vijñaptiḥ*. ibid.
11. *Yā ... vācā girā byappatho udīraṇaṃ ghoso ghosa-kammaṃ vācā vacībhedo, ayaṃ vuccati vācā ... Dhammasaṅgaṇi*, 637 (Poona edition, 1940).
12. *Punas tatraivānantaram uktaṃ* Buddha-*vacanaṃ nāma ka eṣa dharmaḥ? Nāma-kāya—pada-kāya—vyañjana-kāyānāṃ yā anupūrva-racanā anupūrva-sthāpanā anupūrva-samāyoga iti. Sakv.*, p. 52.
13. *Sārthakākṣarāṇi nāma-kāyaḥ. Pada-samuccayena vastu abhidhānaṃ pada-kāyaḥ. Vipula-samuccayaḥ* (=*varṇa-samāmnāyaḥ*) *vyañjana-kāyaḥ. Abhidharmāmṛta*, p. 130. (Text reconstructed from the Chinese by Śānti Bhikshu, Santiniketan, 1953.)
14. *Dharmāṇāṃ svabhāvādhivacane nāma-kāyā iti prajñaptiḥ. Dharmāṇāṃ viśeṣādhivacane pada-kāyā iti prajñaptiḥ. Tad ubhayāśrayeṣv akṣareṣu vyañjana-kāyā iti prajñaptiḥ. Abhidharma-samuccaya*, p. 11.
15. p. 495 (Gaekwad's Oriental Series, LXII, Baroda, 1932).
16. *La Siddhi de Hiüan Tsang*, by L. de la Vallée Poussin, I, pp. 68-70.
17. *L'Abhidharma-kośa de Vasubandhu*, ch. II, kā. 47. See *Sakv.*, pp. 181-5.
18. *'Nāma-sanniśritā gāthā'*. ibid.
19. *Chando nidānaṃ gāthānaṃ akkharā tāsaṃ viyañjanaṃ/ nāma-sannissitā gāthā kavi gāthānaṃ āsayo ti // Saṃyutta-nikāya*, I, p. 38.
20. *'Viyanjanaṃ' ti jananaṃ. Akkharaṃ hi padaṃ janeti, padaṃ gāthaṃ janeti, gāthā atthaṃ pakāsetīti. Saṃyutta-nikāyā-aṭṭhakathā*, I, pp. 94-5.
21. *'Nāma-sannissitā' ti samuddādi-paññatti-nissitā. Gāthā ārabhanto hi samuddaṃ vā paṭhaviṃ vā yaṃ kiñci nāmaṃ nissayitvā va ārabhati.* ibid.
22. *Vṛtti* on kā. 142.
23. ibid.
24. *Ekena padena sabbo attho vutto. Saṃyutta-nikāya*, II, p. 36. *'Ekena padenā'ti 'phassa-paccayā dukkhaṃ' ti iminā ekena padena. Saṃyutta-nikāya-aṭṭhakathā*, I, p. 57.
25. [*Vākyaṃ padaṃ*] *iti* .... [*Yāvatārtha-parisamāptis tad yathā 'anityā bata saṃskārā' ity evam ādi.*] *Sakv.*, p. 182.
26. *'Yāvadbhir arthavadbhiḥ padair vivakṣitārtha-paripūrir bhavati tāvatāṃ samūhaḥ padam' ity Ābhidharmikāḥ. Vṛtti* on kā. 142.
27. *Padaṃ tu sup-tiṅ-antaṃ padaṃ gṛhyate. ten' āha* ....*Sakv.*, p. 182.
28. *Tattha aparimāṇā vaṇṇā aparimāṇā byañjanā. Saṃyutta-nikāya*, V, p. 430. *'Aparimāṇā vaṇṇā' ti appamāṇāni akkharāni, 'byañjanā' ti tesaṃ yeva vevacanaṃ. Saṃyutta-nikāya-aṭṭhakathā*, III, p. 298.
29. *The central conception of Buddhism*, p. 24, n. 1.
30. *Imā kho Citta, loka-samaññā loka-niruttiyo loka-vohārā loka-paññattiyo, yāhi Tathāgato voharati aparāmasaṃ ti. Dīgha-nikāya*, I, p. 202.
31. *Dhammasaṅgaṇi, Mātikā* Nos. 128-30.
32. *Yā tesaṃ tesaṃ dhammānaṃ saṃkhā samaññā paññatti vohāro nāmaṃ nāma-kammaṃ nāmadheyyaṃ nirutti byañjanaṃ abhilāpo, ime dhammā paññatti. Sabbe'va dhammā paññatti-pathā.* ibid., 1308.
33. *Yā pana purima-paññatti apara-paññattiyaṃ patati, purima-vohāro pacchima-vohāre patati, seyyathīdaṃ purima-kappe cando cando yeva nāma, etarahi cando yeva...idaṃ opapātika-nāmaṃ. Aṭṭhasālinī*, V, 133. (Ed. P. V. Bapat, Poona, 1942.)
34. *Cattāro tāva khandhā nāma-karaṇaṭṭhena nāmaṃ. Vedanādayo hi ... attano nāmaṃ*

karontā va uppajjanti. Tesu uppannesu tesaṃ nāmaṃ uppannameva hoti... Atīte pi vedanā vedanā yeva, ... anāgate pi, paccuppanne pi .... ibid., v, 115.

35. *Eka-dhammo sabba-dhammesu nipatati, sabbe dhammā eka-dhammasmiṃ nipatanti. Kathaṃ? Ayaṃ hi nāma-paññatti eko dhammo, so sabbesu catu-bhūmikesu dhammesu nipatati. Satto pi saṃkhāro pi nāmato muttako nāma natthi.* ibid., v, 114.
36. See *Puggala-paññatti-aṭṭhakathā*, where in the beginning Buddhaghosa explains six *paññattis* occurring in the scriptures, six *paññattis* occurring only in the *Aṭṭhakathās*, and another twelve kinds of *paññatti* recognized in the tradition (*ācariya-naya*). Also see the *Abhidhammattha-saṅgaho*, VIII, 31-6, and the *Compendium of philosophy*, S. Z. Aung's introduction, pp. 4-6, 35.
37. *Paramatthato avijjamānā pi attha-cchāyākārena cittuppādānaṃ ārammaṇabhūtā taṃ taṃ ... kāraṇaṃ nissāya tathā tathā parikappiyamānā ... paññāpiyatīti paññatti. Abhidhammattha-saṅgaho*, VIII, 33. See *Compendium of philosophy*, 199.
38. *Paññāpanato paññatti pana nāma-nāmakammādi-nāmena paridīpitā. Abhidhammattha-saṅgaho*, VIII, 34.
39. *Iti tekālikā dhammā kālamuttā ca sambhavā/*
ajjhattaṃ ca bahiddhā ca saṃkhatāsaṃkhatā tathā//
paññatti-nāma-rūpānaṃ vasena tividhā ṭhitā/ Abhidhammattha-saṅgaho, VIII, 31.
40. *Sāyaṃ paññatti viññeyyā loka-saṅketa-nimmitā/* ibid., VIII, 36.
41. *Vacī-ghosānusārena sota-viññāṇa-vīthiyā/*
pavattānantaruppanna-mano-dvārassa gocarā//
atthā yassānusārena paññāyanti tato paraṃ/
sāyaṃ paññatti viññeyyā loka-saṅketa-nimmitā// ibid.
42. *Nāma-cintanākāra-pavattassa mano-dvārika-viññāṇa-santānassa idamīdisassa nāmaṃ ti pubbe yeva gahita-saṅketūpanissayassa ...Abhidhammattha-saṅgaho-vibhāvinīṭīkā*, VIII, 36.
43. See *Śābara-bhāṣya*, I, 1, 5, and the chapter on *Sphoṭavāda* in the *Mīmāṃsā Ślokavārttika* of Kumārila Bhaṭṭa.
44. *Nāmakāyādayo vaktavyāḥ. Na khalu vaktavyāḥ. Na hi te śabdād anye vidyante, svabhāva-kriyābhāvād iti. Tad upadarśanārtham idam ārabhyate* .... *Vṛtti* on kā. 142.
45. See *Vṛtti* on kā. 142-9.
46. *Viprayuktāḥ khalu nāmādayaḥ saṃskāra-skandha-saṃgṛhītāḥ. Vāk tu rūpa-skandha-saṃgṛhītā vāg gīr niruktir ity arthaḥ. Te ca tad adhīnotpattayo nirukty-adhīnārtha-pravṛttayaś ca jñānavad arthasya pratinidhi-sthānīyāḥ* ....ibid.
47. *'Vāṅ nāmni pravartate, nāmārthaṃ dyotayati' iti.* ibid.
48. *Svārtha-pratyāyanaṃ kriyā. Svaṃ svam arthaṃ pratyāyayaty apauruṣeyatvān nāmārtha-sambandhasya* ... ibid.
49. *Vāk chabda evārtheṣu saṃjñā-kartṛ-kṛtāvadhiḥ smṛtyā gṛhītāvayāva-samudāyaḥ śrotur arthaṃ pratyāyayatīti kim anyair nāmādibhiḥ parikalpitaiḥ.* ibid.
50. *Na caivaṃ vākyātmānaḥ śabdāḥ buddhy-upagṛhītāvayava-samudāya-saṃkṣepāḥ krama-labdha-janmānaḥ pratyekam artha-pratyāyana-samarthāḥ, nāpi saṃbhūya pratyāyayanti, saṃbhūyānavasthānād balvajavat. Vṛtti* on kā. 143.
51. ibid.
52. *Saṃskāra iti cet* .... ibid. This appears to be an allusion to the Mīmāṃsaka theory: *Pūrva-varṇa-janita-saṃskāra-sahito 'anto varṇaḥ pratyāyaka iti. Śābara-bhāṣya*, I, 1, 5.
53. *'Edaitau kaṇṭha-tālavyau' iti pratijñāyate. Na caikasyāna-*(read : °ṇu)-*vacanasya viśliṣṭa-sthāna-dvaye vṛttir upapadyate. Paramāṇu-saṃghātasya tūpapadyate* .... *Vṛtti* on kā. 145.
54. *Atīta-varṇa-samudāyas tvantya-varṇāpekṣo mano-buddhyopagṛhīta-svarūpaḥ*

sambandhiny arthe buddhim utpādayan pratyāyayatīti yukta-rūpo vyapadeśaḥ. ibid. It is curious to note that there is no reference to the *nāma-kāya* in this statement. Read without the context this line would appear to conform to the Sautrāntika view. Probably the term *buddhi* should here be understood as a concept, i.e. *nimitta*, another name for the *nāman*, which directs the mind towards the *artha*.

55. *Svarūpaṃ vedayaṃś cchabdo vyañjanādīni ca dhruvam/ artha-pratyāyakaḥ prājñair bhakti-kalpanayocyate//* Abhidharma-dīpa, kā. 144.
56. *Varṇātirikto varṇābhivyaṅgyo 'rtha-pratyāyako nityaḥ śabdaḥ sphoṭa iti tad vido vadanti*. Mādhava, *Sarvadarśanasaṅgraha* (ed. Abhyankar), p. 300.
57. It is precisely on this ground that Śāntarakṣita refutes the Vaibhāṣika theory of *nāma-kāya : 'Yo' pi Vaibhāṣikaḥ śabda-viṣayaṃ nāmākhyaṃ nimittākhyaṃ cārtha-cihna-rūpaṃ viprayuktaṃ saṃskāram icchati, tad apy etenaiva dūṣitaṃ draṣṭavyam. Tathā hi—tan nāmādi yadi kṣaṇikaṃ tadā anvayāyogaḥ, akṣaṇikatve krami-jnānānupapattiḥ ...'*. *Tattvasaṅgraha-pañjikā*, kā. 908. See S. Mookerji, *The Buddhist philosophy of universal flux*, Calcutta, 1935, 115.
58. *Anityās te tu vijñeyāḥ sāpekṣārtha-vibhāvanāt/* Abhidharma-dīpa, kā. 143cd.
59. *Mahābhāṣya*, I, 1, 70 (Kielhorn's edition, Vol. I, p. 181, lines 19-20).
60. *Sphoṭākhyo nāparo ghoṣāc chabdo nityaḥ prasiddhyati/ krama-vṛtter na śabdena kaś cid artho 'bhidhīyate//* Abhidharma-dīpa, kā. 146.
61. *Mahābhāṣya*, p. 1 (Kielhorn's edition, Vol. I).
62. On the validity of this tradition, see Professor J. Brough's article 'Theories of general linguistics in the Sanskrit Grammarians', *Transactions of the Philological Society*, 1951, 27-46.
63. *Tasmāt pratīta-padārthako loke dhvaniḥ śabdaḥ. Tataś cānye nāmādayaḥ sarvārtha-viṣayā iti sthāpanā. Vṛtti* on kā. 147.
64. *Aṭṭhasālinī*, v, 114.
65. *Vākyapadīya*, I, 107.
66. *Yad apy ucyate Vaiyākaraṇaiḥ 'śabdo buddhi-nirgrāhyaḥ' .... Vṛtti* on kā. Cf. *Śrotro-palabdhir buddhi-nirgrāhyaḥ prayogeṇābhijvalita ākāśa-deśaḥ śabdaḥ .... Vārttika* 12 on *Śivasūtra* 1. (Kielhorn's edition, Vol. I, p. 18, 1, 19.)
67. *Uktaṃ hi Bhagavatā 'Tathāgatānām utpādān nāma-pada-vyañjana-kāyānām utpādo bhavati' iti. ... Ye hy apauruṣeyā dhātvāyatana-skandhādy avadyotakās te prathamaṃ* Buddha-*viṣayā eva. Vṛtti* on kā. 148.
68. *Tatra ya āryayā niruktyā nirucyante dvādaśāyatana-viṣayās te niyatābhidheya-saṃbandhāḥ. Laukikyāś ca kecin niyatābhidheyā nirucyante. Ubhaye 'py ete kṛta-saṅketasyārthaṃ pratyāyayanti.* ibid.

CHAPTER 13

The Sautrāntika Theory of *Bīja**

Vasumitra in his famous work 'Origin and doctrines of early Indian Buddhist schools' (*Samaya-bhedoparacanacakra*)[1] enumerates the following four doctrines as characteristic of the Sautrāntika school: '(i) The *skandhas* transmigrate from one world to the other: hence the name Saṅkrānti-vāda; (ii) There are *mūlāntika-skandhas* and *eka-rasa-skandhas;* (iii) An average person (*pṛthagjana*) also possesses the potentiality of becoming a Buddha (lit. in the state of average man there are also divine things, *ārya-dharmas*); (iv) There are *paramārtha-pudgalas'*.[2]

Elucidating these doctrines and particularly the term *skandha,* J. Masuda says that a commentary on Vasumitra's work called *Shu-chi* interprets the term *skandha* as *bījas.* The *eka-rasa-skandhas* are interpreted as '*bījas* of one taste, which continue to exist from time immemorial without changing their nature'. The *ārya-dharmas* are interpreted as '*anāsrava-bījas*' (pure seeds),[3] which Masuda identifies with the *paramārtha-pudgalas.*[3]

Very little is known about these Sautrāntika doctrines or even about the origin and significance of the theory of *bīja.* Vasubandhu's *Abhidharma-kośa-bhāṣya*[4] and the *Sphuṭārthā Abhidharma-kośa-vyākhyā*[5] of Yaśomitra contain several references to the theory of *bīja,* but do not make any mention either of the *eka-rasa-skandha* or of the *ārya-dharma* of the Sautrāntika school.

In a newly discovered orthodox Vaibhāṣika work called the *Abhidharma-dīpa*[6] (with its commentary the *Vibhāṣā-prabhā-vṛtti*),[7]

---

*This article was originally published in *BSOAS,* Vol. XXII, part 2, pp. 236-249, University of London, 1959. Reprinted with kind permission of Oxford University Press.

primarily composed with a view to correct Sautrāntika bias exhibited by Vasubandhu in his *Bhāṣya,* we find valuable material that sheds light on several obscure doctrines of the Sautrāntika, and particularly on the theory of *bīja.* The author of the *Vṛtti* attributes to the Kośakāra the theory of a subtle and incorruptible pure element (*sūkṣma-kuśala-dharma-bīja*) which, as will be seen below, corresponds to the *eka-rasa-skandha* of the Sautrāntika, as well as to the *prabhāsvara-citta,* a cardinal doctrine of the Yogācāra-Vijñānavāda school.

This controversy on the validity of the theory of *bīja* between the Sautrāntika Kośakāra and the Vaibhāṣika Dīpakāra is fully developed in their discussions of the following three successive topics: (i) *manas-karma* and *kleśa,* (ii) *anuśaya* and *paryavasthāna,* (iii) the *kuśala-dharma-bīja.*

I. *Manas-karma* and *kleśa*

Three kinds of purely mental (evil) actions are spoken of in the sūtras. The *Sañcetanīya-sūtra,* for instance, says : 'How are the three kinds of volitional acts committed through mind? Here O monks, one becomes covetous (*abhidhyālu*), full of ill will (*vyāpanna-citta*), and a holder of a wrong view (*mithyā-dṛṣṭi*)'. According to this sūtra, the *abhidhyā, vyāpāda,* and *mithyā-dṛṣṭi* are purely mental acts. Since the Lord has said that *karma* is volition, the Dārṣṭāntikas (i.e. the Sautrāntikas) maintain that these three, being mental actions, are identical with volitions (*cetanā*).[8]

The Vaibhāṣikas do not agree with this Dārṣṭāntika view. According to them the *abhidhyā, vyāpāda,* and *mithyā-dṛṣṭi* are passions (*kleśas*) that produce an evil volition (*karma*), and not actions by themselves. They are not *manas-karma* (mental actions) but only *mano-duścarita.*[9] In the sūtra these three are identified with *cetanā* because the latter arises through them.

The Kośakāra, as usual, favours the Dārṣṭāntika viewpoint.[10] The Dīpakāra asserts the Vaibhāṣika position without advancing any new arguments in its favour, and criticizes the Kośakāra for favouring the Dārṣṭāntika interpretation of the *Sañcetanīya-sūtra.*[11]

The reason for the Vaibhāṣika treatment of *abhidhyā, vyāpāda,* and *mithyā-dṛṣṭi* as passions distinct from volitions is perhaps to be found in the Ābhidharmika theory that two volitions (*cetanās*) cannot operate in one moment. According to the Abhidharma all evil volitions (such as killing, theft, etc.) are prompted and sustained by one of these three, viz. *abhidhyā, vyāpāda,* or *mithyā-dṛṣṭi.* In the case of an evil act like *prāṇātipāta,* for instance, one of these three produces a *vadhaka-cetanā* (a volition to kill) which is essentially accompanied, till the accomplishment of the act of killing, by *vyāpāda* (ill will). If *vyāpāda* is also treated as a *cetanā* then there will be two volitions (*vyāpāda* and *vadhaka-cetanā*) operating in one moment. The Vaibhāṣika, therefore, maintains that these three are to be treated as *kleśas* (passions) and not as volitions (*karma*).

The Pali commentators also seem to recognize a similar theory. The *Aṭṭhasālinī* states that of the ten evil karmas (viz. *pāṇātipāta,* etc.) the first seven are *cetanā-dhamma* (i.e. identical with volition) whereas the last three, viz. *abhijjhā, vyāpāda,* and *micchā-diṭṭhi* are *cetanā-sampayuttā dhammā* (i.e. factors associated with the first seven volitions).[12]

This Ābhidharmika distinction between a volition (*karma*) and a passion (*kleśa*) has a close bearing on the theory of *bīja.* The *kleśas* are like roots which produce as well as sustain an evil volition. *Abhidhyā, vyāpāda,* and *mithyā-dṛṣṭi* are not called roots, but are recognized as intensive states of the three roots of evil (*akuśala-mūla*), viz. *lobha, dveṣa,* and *moha* respectively. All evil volitions are essentially rooted in and spring from one or other of these three basic passions (*mūla-kleśa*).

Corresponding to these three roots of evil, the Buddhists recognize three roots of good (volitions), viz. *alobha, adveṣa,* and *amoha.* All good volitions spring from these three *kuśala-mūlas,* the intensive states of which are called *anabhidhyā, avyāpāda,* and *samyak-dṛṣṭi* respectively. Thus the *kuśala-mūlas* and the *akuśala-mūlas* are incompatible in nature and exclude each other in their operation in a single moment.

Whereas their intensified states can be overcome by the attainment of the first three *lokottara* paths, the basic passions (*akuśala-mūlas*) are not completely annihilated until one attains arhatship. A *srota-āpanna,* for instance, overcomes *mithyā-dṛṣṭi,* but still possesses its root, viz. *moha.* A *sakṛdāgāmin* overcomes grosser forms of *vyāpāda,* but still possesses its root, viz., *dveṣa.* An *anāgāmin* completely overcomes *vyāpāda,* but he is not free from the *akuśala-mūlas.* Only an arhat brings an end to these roots of all evil volitions.[13]

If the *akuśala-mūlas* are not annihilated till the attainment of arhatship and if they are incompatible with the *kuśala-mūlas,* how are we to explain the operation of *kuśala-mūlas* or of *kuśala* volitions in a mundane (*laukika*) existence? Being incompatible they cannot operate simultaneously. Nor can they operate successively, for succession demands a certain element of homogeneity between the preceding and succeeding moments. If a *kuśala-citta* were to follow an *akuśala-citta,* then it will depend for its nature on a heterogeneous cause. This will amount to an admission of the unacceptable position that good springs out of evil or vice versa.

The Theravādins avoid this dilemma by postulating a theory that the *akuśala* and *kuśala-cittas* never follow each other without an intervening *avyākṛta* (indeterminate, i.e. *vipāka*) *citta.* An *akuśala-citta-vīthi* can be succeeded by a *kuśala-citta-vīthi* only after the intervention of a *bhavaṅga-citta,* which is necessarily a *vipāka-citta.*

The Vaibhāṣikas seek a solution by postulating a *citta-viprayukta-saṃskāra* called *prāpti,* a force which controls the collection of a particular kind of element, and another *saṃskāra* called *aprāpti* which prevents such a collection. Thus, for instance, when an *akuśala-citta* is followed by a *kuśala-citta* the latter is brought into operation by *prāpti* of the *kuśala* dharmas which is at the same time assisted by the *aprāpti* which prevents the rise of *akuśala* dharmas.

The Sautrāntikas reject both these theories. They do not accept the theory of the Theravādins presumably on the grounds that an *avyākṛta-citta* is not more helpful than the *akuśala-citta,* inasmuch as both are equally ineffective to produce a *kuśala-citta.* They reject the Vaibhāṣika dharmas called *prāpti* and *aprāpti* on the grounds that these in turn need to be produced by another *prāpti* and *aprāpti,* a position which leads to an infinite regress.

The Sautrāntikas explain the operation of *kuśala* and *akuśala* dharmas by postulating a theory of seeds. There are three kinds of seeds: seeds of evil and seeds of good, and those which are indeterminate. The seeds of evil (*akuśala-bīja*) are called *anuśaya;* the seeds of good are called *kuśala-dharma-bīja.* Before we proceed to an examination of the latter we shall note here views of several Buddhist schools on the nature of the *anuśayas,* a topic which holds a clue for the theory of seeds.

II. *Anuśaya*

The Pali scriptures as well as commentaries contain several references to and controversies on the *anuśayas*. The term *anuśaya*, derived from *śī*-(*śaya*-) 'to lie', connotes 'to live along with' or 'to cling to'. It is always used in the sense of a bias, a proclivity, a persistence of a dormant or latent disposition of mind leading to all kinds of evil volitions. Buddhaghosa says that a passion is called *anuśaya* because of its pertinacity. It ever and again tends to become the condition predisposing to the arising of new passions.[14] The Kośakāra calls it the root of existence.[15] The *Vṛtti* describes it as that which follows through the series of mind.[16] Seven such evil predispositions are enumerated in the scriptures: *kāma-rāga, pratigha, dṛṣṭi, vicikitsā, māna, bhava-rāga,* and *avidyā*. The three *akuśala-mūlas* as well as their accessory *kleśas* are included in these seven *anuśayas*.

The outbursts of these dormant passions are called *pariyuṭṭhāna* (Skt. *paryavasthāna*). There are seven *pariyuṭṭhānas* corresponding to the seven *anuśayas*, bearing the same names.[17] In the Vaibhāṣika tradition different *kleśas* are enumerated under the *paryavasthānas*. The *Vṛtti* enumerates ten: *mrakṣa, īrṣyā, ahrī, anapatrāpya, styāna, middha, auddhatya, krodha, mātsarya,* and *kaukṛtya*.[18] But this seems to be an Ābhidharmika tradition. The Sautrāntikas do not treat these ten as *paryavasthāna*. They agree with the Theravādin tradition (based on sūtra) in treating the *paryavasthāna* as outbursts of the latent *anuśayas*.

The relation between an *anuśaya* and a *pariyuṭṭhāna* is made clear in the *Mahā-Māluṅkya-sutta*.[19] This sutta deals with *saṃyojanas* (bonds or fetters) such as *kāma-cchanda, vyāpāda, vicikitsā,* etc., which chain all beings to the lower life. It is said there that heretic ascetics used to ridicule this theory of *saṃyojanas* by saying, 'An infant is not conscious of lusts of the flesh (*kāma*), much less can passion (*kāma-cchanda*) arise within it, its sensual propensities (*kāma-rāgo*) being latent only (*anuseti*)'.[20]

The implication of this criticism is not clear. According to the *Aṭṭhakathā* these ascetics believed that a person is associated with the passions (*kilesa*) only when they operate or beset him but at other times he is disassociated from passions.[21] Apparently the heretics believed that an infant is free from *kleśas*.

The Buddhists do not accept this position. According to them even an infant is in possession of *kleśas*, because the latter are present in him in their dormant state (*anuśaya*) and become active when there arise suitable conditions for their operation (*pariyuṭṭhāna*). This implies that when the passions are not operating they always remain in a dormant state. If they are always present in the mind then the latter is always *akuśala*, for a *kuśala* can neither co-exist nor operate simultaneously with an *akuśala*. Consequently, there will be no *kuśala-citta* as long as the latent passions are not removed, and they will not be removed without a *kuśala-citta*.

Different solutions are put forward by different schools to this problem.[22] The Theravādins (despite their objection to the heretical view noted above) and the Vaibhāṣikas denied the existence of *anuśayas* apart from the *paryavasthānas*. According to them a mind is *akuśala* only when passions are in operation. There is no such thing as purely latent passions. The Vātsīputrīyas maintained a difference between the *anuśayas* and *paryavasthānas*. But they said that the *anuśayas* are *citta-viprayukta-saṃskāras*, and hence could co-exist with *kuśala-dharmas*. But *paryavasthānas* are *citta-saṃprayukta-saṃskāras* and therefore cannot operate with *kuśala-dharmas*. They include the *anuśayas* in *prāpti*, a *viprayukta-saṃskāra* of the Vaibhāṣika list.

The Sautrāntikas maintained that the *anuśayas* as well as the *kuśala* elements (*bījas*) co-exist side by side in the form of subtle seeds, but only one of them operates at one time. When the *anuśayas* operate (i.e. become *paryavasthānas*), the mind is *akuśala*. When the seeds of *kuśala* operate the mind is *kuśala*.

All these views are well represented in a controversy on the meaning of a sūtra passage preserved in the *Kosá*, the *Vṛtti*, and also in the *Aṭṭhakathās*. A question is raised whether a term like *rāgānuśaya* should be taken as a *karmadhāraya* or as a genitive *tatpuruṣa*-compound. The former (i.e. *rāga eva anuśayaḥ*) goes against a sūtra passage which says: 'Here a person has a mind beset and obsessed (*paryavasthita*) by no sensuality (*kāma-rāga*); he knows the real escape therefrom; this obsession of sensuality (*kāma-rāga-paryavasthāna*) if vigorously combated is destroyed together with its propensities thereto (*sānuśayaṃ prahīyate*)'.[23]

By using the term *sānuśayaṃ* the sūtra makes it clear that *paryavasthāna* and *anuśaya* are not identical. The Vātsīputrīya here suggests that the term *sānuśayaṃ* means 'together with *anuśaya*, i.e. a *viprayukta-saṃskāra* called *prāpti*'. But this contention goes against Abhidharma where it is said that the *rāgānuśaya* is associated with three kinds of feelings. *Prāpti* being a *viprayukta* cannot associate with a *caitasika*. Therefore, *anuśaya* cannot be a *viprayukta*.[24]

Faced with this dilemma the Vaibhāṣika, regardless of the sūtra, states that the term *rāgānuśaya* should be taken as a *karmadhāraya* compound.[25] He resolves the contradiction of the sūtra by interpreting the term *sānuśaya* as *sānubandha,* i.e. together with its power of producing a new *kleśa.* He also gives an alternative suggestion that the sūtra identifies *anuśaya* with *prāpti* only figuratively; the Abhidharma is definitive when it says that *rāga* (*paryavasthāna*) is (identical with) *anuśaya*.[26]

The Theravādins also identify *pariyuṭṭhāna* with *anuśaya.* Commenting on the sūtra words *sānusayo pahīyati,* Buddhaghosa observes that some people on the basis of this expression maintain that the *saṃyojanas* (here identical with *pariyuṭṭhānas*) are different from *anuśaya.* They should be refuted, he says, by the simile of a person sleeping with his head covered. The person is not different from (his) head.[27] Buddhaghosa takes note of an objection that if *saṃyojanas* and *anuśayas* are identical then the Buddha's criticism of the heretic ascetics (for holding the view that an infant has no passions) is meaningless.[28] Buddhaghosa does not give any convincing answer to this criticism but asserts his position by repeating that the same passion is called *saṃyojana* because it binds, and is also called *anuśaya* because it is not renounced (*appahīna*).[29]

The *Kathāvatthu* records several controversies on the *anuśayas.* The Andhakas held that the *anuśayas* are different from *pariyuṭṭhāna*.[30] The Mahāsāṃghikas and the Sammitīyas maintained that the *anuśayas* are indeterminate (*abyākata*), without good or evil roots (*ahetukā*) and therefore *citta-vippayutta*.[31] The arguments of these schools are the same as noted above that if the *anuśayas* are *akuśala* and *citta-saṃprayukta* there will never be an occasion for the rise of *kuśala* consciousness.

Buddhaghosa's reply to these schools is the same, that the *anuśayas* are identical with *pariyuṭṭhānas.* He once more returns to this topic in his commentary on the *Yamaka.* There also he repeats the same arguments and adds that these passions are called *anuśaya* not because they are different from *pariyuṭṭhāna* but because they are strong passions (*thāmagata-kileso*) and because they arise on obtaining suitable conditions for their operation (*anusentīti anurūpaṃ kāraṇaṃ labhitvā uppajjantīti* ...).[32]

It is clear from these discussions that the Theravādin as well as the Vaibhāṣika interpretation of the term *sānuśaya,* and the subsequent identification of the *anuśayas* with *paryavasthāna* are contrary to the sūtra quoted above. They show a determined effort to uphold the Abhidharma in preference to the sūtra. The Sautrāntika takes strong exception to the Ābhidharmika theories and puts forth his theory of *bīja.* He says that the word *rāgānuśaya* should be taken as a genitive *tatpuruṣa,* i.e. *anuśaya* of *rāga.* Asked further if this *anuśaya* is a *saṃprayukta* or a *viprayukta,* the Sautrāntika says that it is neither, because it is not a separate *dravya* (reality).[33] When a *kleśa* (like *rāga*) is dormant, it is called *anuśaya.* When it is awakened, it is called *paryavasthāna.*[34] When it is dormant it does not appear but persists in the form of a seed. This form of seed is simply an inherent power of mind to produce a (new) passion which is itself born of a past passion. It is comparable to an inherent power of yielding rice found in a sprout which is also born of rice.[35]

The Kośakāra openly favours this Sautrāntika theory of *bīja* (attributed in the *Vṛtti* to the Dārṣṭāntika) in his *Bhāṣya.* The Dīpakāra borrows this whole controversy from the latter and remarks that he will expose the indolence of the Sautrāntika Kośakāra in properly grasping the clear sense (*nīti*) of the words of the Buddha. He refers to another work of his own called *Tattvasaptati,*[36] where he says he has dealt fully with this topic, and adds that the *bīja* imagined by the Sautrāntika, which is described as a mere power (*śakti*) or application (*bhāvanā*) or impression (*vāsanā*) of mind cannot stand any scrutiny. For this *bīja* could either be identical with or different from the mind. If the former, there is no point in speaking about it. If the latter, then it must be a *saṃprayukta* (associated) or *viprayukta* element, a position unacceptable to the Sautrāntika. If it is maintained that the *bīja* is neither identical with, nor different from the mind, and thus conforms to a middle course, this is also denied, for such a middle course is impossible in the case of a *bīja* which is an unreality like a stick made of sky-flowers.[37]

These brief arguments of the Dīpakāra are identical with Saṃghabhadra's criticism of the theory of *bīja.* We have noted above a Vaibhāṣika theory that a *viprayukta-saṃskāra* called *prāpti* brings into operation a particular set of dharmas (to the exclusion of others) in a given moment, and thus determines the nature of a *santati* either as impure (*akuśala*) or pure (*kuśala*). While dealing with this topic, the Kośakāra argues against the Vaibhāṣika that the seeds (*bījas*) of *kuśala* or *akuśala* accumulated in a *santati* determine the character of the latter. He defines the *bīja* as *nāma-rūpa*, i.e. the complex of the five *skandhas* capable of producing a fruit either immediately or mediately by means of a *pariṇāma-viśeṣa* of the *santati*.[38]

This theory of *bīja* advocated by the Kośakāra is subjected to a severe criticism in the *Nyāyānusāra* of Saṃghabhadra. Yaśomitra quotes a fairly long passage from the latter and defends the Sautrāntika position.[39] Saṃghabhadra's main criticism of the theory of *bīja* (as a *śakti-viśeṣa*) is that it could be either different from or identical with the mind. If it is a separate entity, then it is *prāpti*, for the dispute then is only on naming it. If, however, it is identical with mind, then it will result in the fault of mixture or confusion (*sāṅkarya-doṣa*) of good and bad seeds. For surely the Sautrāntika will admit that a mind possesses seeds of both the good (*kuśala*) as well as evil (*akuśala*), of *sāsrava* as well as *anāsrava* elements. If they are all accumulated in one *citta* what is there to determine the nature of a particular *citta* as *kuśala* or *akuśala* or *avyākṛta*? Yaśomitra's reply to this criticism is that the *sāṅkarya-doṣa* would arise only if the *bījas* were identical with the mind. But we maintain, he says, that a *bīja* is neither identical with, nor different from the mind, because a *bīja* is not a separate entity (*dravya*) but only a *prajñapti* (nominal) dharma.[40]

Yaśomitra further states that even if a *bīja* is considered identical with *citta*, there is no fault: for, a *kuśala-citta* which has arisen would in that case implant its seed in a (subsequent) *citta* of its own *santāna*, the latter *citta* being either of the same kind (*kuśala*) or of the opposite kind (*akuśala*). Thereafter (*tataḥ*), the (second) *citta* would arise as qualified (determined) by the first only in accordance with the principle that a specific effect arises from a specific cause (*kāraṇa-viśeṣa*) [i.e. if the second *citta* is *anya-jātīya*, the *bīja* lies dormant].... Nor does the fact that a specific *śakti* is implanted by a *kuśala-citta* in an *akuśala-citta* entail (*iti*) that the *akuśala* becomes *kuśala* or vice versa, since it is only a *specific śakti* [i.e. it cannot produce effects which, by its very nature, it is not competent to produce] also called *bīja* or *vāsanā*. These are all synonyms.[41]

Even the Vaibhāṣikas, he says, must resort to some such theory to explain the phenomenon of the succession of two heterogeneous *cittas*. They also believe that an *akuśala* can be succeeded by a *kuśala*. Do the Vaibhāṣikas here agree that the *kuśala* is produced by an *akuśala?* If they do not agree then they deny *samanantara-pratyaya*. If they agree then they must explain what kind of power (*śakti*) it is that produces a *kuśala-citta*. If this power is *akuśala* it cannot produce *kuśala*. If it is *kuśala* then it cannot on their terms remain in an *akuśala-citta*. It is, therefore, wrong of the Vaibhāṣikas to accuse us of maintaining that an *akuśala* seed would become the cause of a *kuśala-citta*. We do not maintain that a *kuśala* seed deposited in an *akuśala-citta* transforms the latter, but merely that this *kuśala* seed remains there and produces either immediately or in succession a corresponding *kuśala-citta*. This power of producing a new *citta* is what we call a *bīja*. It is not an independent entity but only a nominal thing (*prajñapti-mātra*).[42]

It appears from Yaśomitra's explanation that the theory of *bīja* was employed by the Sautrāntika primarily to replace the Vaibhāṣika dharma called *prāpti* in explaining the phenomena of immediate succession (*samanantarotpāda*) between two *cittas* of heterogeneous nature, and secondarily to reconcile the abiding nature of the *santati* with the momentary flashes of dharma. Their theory that the *bījas* are neither identical with nor different from the mind bears a close resemblance to the Vātsīputrīya theory of *pudgala* which is also described as neither different from nor identical with the five *skandhas*.[43] But whereas the Vātsīputrīya claims reality for his *pudgala*, the Sautrāntika insists on the nominality (*prajñapti-mātra*) of the *bījas* and thus escapes the heresy of which he accuses the former school. On the other hand his theory that the mind is a depository of good and bad seeds capable of yielding new seeds in the series of mind foreshadows the theory of *ālaya-vijñāna* (also called *mūla* or *bīja-vijñāna*) of the Vijñānavāda school.[44]

III. *Kuśala-dharma-bīja*

Although the Theravādins do not recognize this Sautrāntika theory of *bīja*, there is substantial evidence pointing to its origin in the suttas. The *Aṅg-nikāya* contains a long sutta dealing with the operation of *kuśala* and *akuśala-mūlas* in six kinds of persons.[45] In the case of the first three of these persons a comparison is made with good or bad seed (*bīja*) sown in a fertile or stony field. In the case of the first person, for instance, it is said: 'There is a person endowed with *kuśala* as well as *akuśala* dharmas. In course of time his *kuśala* dharmas disappear, and *akuśala* dharmas appear. But since his *kuśala-mūlas* are not completely annihilated, new *kuśala* dharmas appear from that (unannihilated) *kuśala-mūla.* Thus this person becomes in future one who does not fall (from the holy life). His *kuśala* is comparable to whole seeds (*akhaṇḍa bīja*) sown in a cultivated fertile field, capable of yielding abundant fruits'.[46]

This scripture is favourable to the Sautrāntika theory of *bīja.* It supports the contention that the *kuśala* and *akuśala* co-exist in the form of seeds which give rise in a subsequent time to their corresponding *kuśala* or *akuśala* thoughts, and thus determine the nature of a particular *santati* as subject to decay or subject to growth.

The Vaibhāṣikas also accept this sūtra, but maintain that it refers not to the theory of *bīja* but to their theory of *prāpti.* When, therefore, the sūtra says that a person is *samanvāgata* (endowed) with *kuśala* and *akuśala* dharmas,[47] it means that he has the *prāpti* of these dharmas, since *samanvāgama* and *prāpti* are synonyms.[48] A person cannot be endowed with *kuśala* and *akuśala* in one moment, because these two are *saṃprayukta* dharmas. But their *prāpti* being *viprayukta* can co-exist and thus cause the rise of *kuśala* and *akuśala* dharmas in favourable circumstances.

In support of this contention the Vaibhāṣika quotes the following passage from the same sūtra: 'A person is endowed with *kuśala* as well as *akuśala* dharmas. His *kuśala* dharmas disappear. But there is in him the root (*mūla*) of *kuśala* not destroyed. Even this *kuśala-mūla* is in course of time completely annihilated, whereupon he comes to be designated as a *samucchinna-kuśala-mūla*'.[49]

Here arises a problem regarding the rise of a new *kuśala-citta* in the *santati* of such a person. The Vaibhāṣika solves it by postulating the theory of *prāpti* which ushers in a new *kuśala-citta* independently of the seeds of *kuśala.* But according to the Sautrāntika a *kuśala-citta* can arise only out of its seeds. In the absence of the latter, therefore, a *samucchinna-kuśala-mūla* will have no possibility of having a *kuśala-citta.* Consequently he will be doomed to have only *akuśala-cittas* till eternity.

Indeed the Theravādins, on account of their view that a *kuśala* cannot succeed an *akuśala,* and because of their non-recognition of the theory of *prāpti,* arrived precisely at such a fateful conclusion. They maintained that a *samucchinna-kuśala-mūla* was incapable of producing a *kuśala-citta,* and sought to support this theory by the following scripture: 'Take the case, bhikkhus, of a person who is possessed with entirely black *akuśala*-states, he it is who once immersed, is immersed for ever'.[50] Commenting on this, Buddhaghosa says: 'The term *ekanta-kāḷaka* means those grave wrong views (*micchā-diṭṭhi*) (which deny the result of *karma*)—*natthikavāda, ahetukavāda,* and *akiriyāvāda.* A person like Makkhali Gosāla who holds these grave wrong views becomes the food of the fire of lower and lower hells. For such a person there is no emergence from worldly existence'.[51]

But neither of these alternatives (viz. of *prāpti* and of eternal doom) is acceptable to the Sautrāntika. The Kośakāra here puts forth a bold and original solution to this problem. He says that we should distinguish between two kinds of *kuśala* dharmas. There are some *kuśala* dharmas which are innate, which do not presuppose any effort (*ayatna-bhāvi*) but are always present in any given condition (*upapatti-lābhika*). Then there are other kinds of *kuśala* dharmas which are obtained only by effort or practice of meditations (*prāyogika*). The former, i.e. the innate *kuśala* dharmas, are never completely annihilated. When a person on account of holding a grave *mithyā-dṛṣṭi* becomes *samucchinna-kuśala-mūla,* he destroys only his *prāyogika-kuśala-mūlas.* His innate *kuśala* dharmas remain in the form of *bījas* intact in his *santati* from which arise new *kuśala* dharmas under favourable circumstances.[52]

The statement of the Kośakāra that even a *samucchinna-kuśala-mūla* possesses a subtle element of *kuśala* seems hardly satisfactory. The *Bhāṣya* naturally does not contain any criticism of this contradiction, and even Yaśomitra who defends the theory of *bīja* against Saṃghabhadra is silent on the point. Fortunately, a brief criticism of this major controversy has survived in the *Vṛtti.* The Dīpakāra gives the meaning of the term *samucchinna-kuśala-mūla* as understood in the Vaibhāṣika tradition, and criticizes the theory of *bīja* as propounded by the Kośakāra.

According to the Vaibhāṣikas, the *mithyā-dṛṣṭi* and the *kuśala-mūlas* both consist of three basic grades, viz. *mṛdu* (subtle or slight), *madhya* (of medium nature), and *adhimātra* (extreme). Each of these three grades is further divided into three, e.g. *mṛdu-mṛdu* ... *adhimātra-adhimātra.*

The *kuśala-mūlas* pertaining to the *arūpāvacara* and the *rūpāvacara* are destroyed by the *mṛdu* and *madhya mithyā-dṛṣṭis.*[53]

The *adhimātra mithyā-dṛṣṭi* destroys the *prāyogika-kuśala-mūlas* pertaining to the *kāma* world, leaving in such a person only the innate or the *upapatti-lābhika* roots of good. But when a person (like Maskarī Gośālīputra for instance) comes to hold such extremely grave (*adhimātra-adhimātra*) wrong views as *nāstika-vāda, ahetuka-vāda,* or *akriyā-vāda,* then he destroys even these innate and the most subtle (*upapatti-lābhika*) *kuśala-mūlas* pertaining to the *kāma-loka,* whereupon he is called a *samucchinna-kuśala-mūla.*

After stating this Vaibhāṣika theory of the loss of *kuśala* dharmas the Dīpakāra turns to the Kośakāra's definition of a *samucchinna-kuśala-mūla.*[54] This he condemns as contrary to the scriptures where it is specifically stated that the *kuśala-mūlas* are completely annihilated. He then criticizes the theory of *bīja,* arguing that the *kuśala* and *akuśala,* being incompatible like light and darkness, cannot co-exist at one time. Even if they co-exist, in the case of a *samucchinna-kuśala-mūla,* the *kuśala* elements are entirely lost. How can a new *kuśala* arise in this person? If it arises from the *akuśala* then one may as well argue that rice is obtained from barley seeds or that *mithyā-dṛṣṭi* is produced by right thinking.[55] Thus the Kośakāra's theory of *bīja* and the consequent wrong definition of a *samucchinna-kuśala-mūla* do not stand the test of either the scriptures or of reasoning.

The Kośakāra's definition of the term *samucchinna-kuśala-mūla* is identical with the Yogācāra definition of this term. In the *Mahāyāna-sūtrālaṃkāra* only the imminent liberation of a *samucchinna-kuśala-mūla* is denied.[56] This suggests that he may attain *parinirvāṇa* in the distant future. This would mean that according to the Yogācāras such a person is not completely devoid of a *kuśala-mūla.* The contention of the Kośakāra that the innate *kuśala-mūlas* are never entirely destroyed marks a still further departure from the orthodox Hīnayāna. It implies that unlike the *akuśala-bījas* which are completely annihilated, the elements of *kuśala* persist throughout the series of existence. This is a characteristically Mahāyānist view inasmuch as it holds an assurance of ultimate liberation even for a person like Maskarī Gośālīputra who comes to hold the gravest of wrong views.

The Kośakāra does not give further details of this incorruptible element of *kuśala.* Unlike the elements of *akuśala* which are only *sāsrava,* the *kuśala* elements are of two kinds, viz. *sāsrava* and *anāsrava.* The former pertains to the *kuśala kāma* and to the *rūpa* and *arūpa bhāvas*. The *anāsrava kuśalas* are those which produce the *lokottara* (super-mundane) states like arhatship or Buddhahood. Is it possible that the incorruptible *kuśala-bīja* spoken of by the Kośakāra represents the *anāsrava-kuśala-bīja* leading to *nirvāṇa*? We have noted above the Sautrāntika doctrines of *eka-rasa-skandha, ārya-dharma,* and the *paramārtha-pudgala*. All these are described as existing from time immemorial without changing their nature, transmigrating from one birth to another. In the *Shu-chi* they are interpreted as 'extremely subtle and incomprehensible *bīja*'. The *kuśala-dharma-bīja* propounded by the Kośakāra, which is also described as subtle (*sūkṣma*) and incorruptible (*na samudghāto*), offers a striking resemblance to the *eka-rasa-skandha,* the *ārya-dharma,* and the *paramārtha-pudgala*. None of these could mean a *sāsrava-kuśala-bīja,* for the latter is as much subject to destruction as are the *akuśala-bījas*. The *sūkṣma-kuśala-dharma-bīja* of the Sautrāntika, therefore, should be understood as an *anāsrava-kuśala-bīja* or *mokṣa-bhāgīya kuśala* leading to *parinirvāṇa*.

This conjecture is strengthened by the occurrence of such terms as *mokṣa-bīja* in the Sanskrit Buddhist scriptures. Of the ten extraordinary powers of the Buddha one is his power of fathoming the innate capacities of all beings for liberation. Illustrating this power, Yaśomitra quotes the case of a person desirous of obtaining the *pravrajyā* ordination. It is said that this person approached Śāriputra, but the latter could not see any roots of *kuśala-mūla* leading to liberation in him (*mokṣa-bhāgīya kuśala-mūla*), and therefore refused to admit him to the order. The Buddha, however, noticed it and said:

> *mokṣa-bījam ahaṃ hy asya susūkṣmam upalakṣaye/*
> *dhātu-pāṣāṇa-vivare nilīnam iva kāñcanam//* [57]

'I see his extremely subtle seed of salvation like a seam of gold hidden in metal-bearing rock'.

The simile of gold aptly describes an incorruptible element. The *mokṣa-bīja* thus described as extremely subtle (*susūkṣma*) and incorruptible seems to be identical with the *sūkṣma-kuśala-dharma-bīja* propounded by the Kośakāra. It is even possible that the word *dhātu* is used in the above verse with the express intention of evoking its other sense, as in the term *nānā-dhātu-jñāna-bala* (Pali *aneka-dhātu-nānā-dhātu-lokaṃ pajānāti*) where it is understood as *vāsanā, āśaya,* or a *gotra.*[58] The *sarvākārajñatā* of the Buddha consists in knowing the *gotra* of all beings. The doctrine of *gotra* is fundamental for Mahāyāna. It determines the 'family' of a person as belonging to the community of a *śrāvaka, pratyeka-buddha,* or a *Buddha.* Yaśomitra describes this *gotra* as *bīja,*[59] which could only be the *mokṣa-bīja* concealed in the midst of other *dhātus* or *bījas* such as *akuśala* and *sāsrava kuśala.*

The theory of an innate, indestructible, and pure (*anāsrava*) element existing in the midst of destructible, phenomenal, and impure elements shows an affinity with the Mahāyāna doctrine of *prakṛti-prabhāsvara-citta,* according to which mind is essentially and originally pure but becomes impure by only adventitious afflictions.[60] The *prakṛti-prabhāsvara-citta* is further described as identical with the *dharmatā, tathatā,* and, therefore, with the *dharmakāya* of the Buddha.[61]

The theory of a *prabhāsvara-citta* is not unknown to the Pali scriptures. It is said in the *Aṅg.-nikāya : 'pabhassaram idaṃ bhikkhave cittaṃ, taṃ ca kho āgantukehi upakkilesehi upakkiliṭṭhaṃ'* and *'...āgantukehi upakkilesehi vippamuttaṃ'.*[62] But the Theravādins interpret it as a *bhavanga-citta,*[63] i.e. a *paṭisandhi-citta* causing a rebirth. Now a *paṭisandhi-citta* can either be a *kuśala-vipāka* or an *akuśala-vipāka-citta,* accompanied by the *kuśala-*(*vipāka-*) *mūlas* like *alobha, adosa,* or *amoha,* or else *akuśala-vipāka-mūlas* like *lobha, dosa,* or *moha.* But according to the Theravādin Abhidhamma only the *kuśala-vipāka-cittas* are *sahetuka,* i.e. have the *mūlas.* The *akuśala-vipāka-citta* is considered to be *ahetuka,* i.e. devoid of any *mūlas.*[64] No reason for such a discrimination is given either in the *Aṭṭhakathās* or in the later *Ṭīkās.* Professor Dharmanand Kosambi, who noted this, explains that the *akuśala-vipāka-citta* is considered *ahetuka* because the *akuśala-mūlas* do not strengthen each other.[65] The real reason for such a discrimination is, perhaps, to be found in the Theravādin interpretation of the *pabhassara-citta,* as a *bhavanga-citta.* They must have thought that a *pabhassara-citta* can have the *kuśala-mūlas* (which are pure) but cannot possess the *akuśala-mūlas,* and hence formulated a rule that the *akuśala-vipāka-citta* is *ahetuka.*

NOTES

1. J. Masuda, *Asia Major,* II, 1925, 1-78.
2. ibid., 67-9.
3. ibid., notes to pp. 67-9.
4. *L' Abhidharma-kośa de Vasubandhu* (tr. L. de la Vallée Poussin). Henceforth referred to as *Bhāṣya.*
5. Henceforth referred to as *Sakv.* (Ed. U. Woghihara, 1936.)
6. Henceforth referred to as *Dīpa.* The MS of this work was discovered in Tibet by Rāhula Sānkṛtyāyana in the year 1937. It has been edited by the author of this article and will soon be published by the K.P. Jayaswal Research Institute, Patna, in their Tibetan Sanskrit Works Series. (Published 1959.)
7. Henceforth referred to as *Vṛtti.*
8. *Sañcetanīya-sūtre vacanād iti....abhidhyādaya eva manas-karmeti* Dārṣṭāntikāḥ Sautrāntika-*viśeṣā ity arthaḥ* (*Sakv.,* p. 400).
9. ibid. Cf. *Akarma-svabhavāny api tv abhidhyādīni mano-duścarita-svabhāvāni* (*Vṛtti* on kā. 188).
10. *L'Abhidharma-kośa,* ch. vi, kā, 65-6.
11. *Vṛtti* on kā. 188.
12. *Satta cetanā dhammā honti, abhijjhādayo tayo cetanā-sampayuttā* (*Aṭṭhasālinī,* iii, 158).
13. On these different *mārgas* (*darśana* and *bhāvanā-mārga*), see E. Obermiller, 'The doctrine of prajñā-pāramitā as exposed in the *Abhisamayālaṅkāra* of Maitreya', *Acta Orientalia,* XI, 1933, 21-5.
14. *Visuddhimagga,* XXII, 60.
15. *Mūlaṃ bhavasyānuśayāḥ* (*Abhidharma-kośa,* V, 1).
16. *Santānānugatā ity anuśayāḥ* (*Vṛtti* on kā. 261).
17. *Vibhaṅgappakaraṇa,* p. 383.
18. *Vṛtti* on kā. 373.
19. *Majjhima-nikāya,* I, p. 433.
20. *Daharassa hi kumārassa mandassa...kāmā ti pi na hoti, kuto pan' assa uppajjissati kāmesu kāma-cchando, anuseti tv ev'assa kāmarāgānusayo* (ibid).
21. *Ayaṃ hi tassa laddhi : samudācāra-kkhaṇe yeva kilesehi saṃyutto nāma hoti, itarasmiṃ khaṇe asaṃyutto ti...*(*Majjhima-nikāya-aṭṭhakathā,* III, p. 144).
22. Vaibhāṣika-*nayena paryavasthānam evānuśayaḥ.* Vātsīputrīya-*nayena prāptir anuśayaḥ.* Sautrāntika-*nayena bījam* (*Sakv.,* p. 442).
23. *Atha rāgādayo 'nuśayāḥ kathaṃ draṣṭavyāḥ? Kiṃ rāgādaya evānuśayāḥ, āhosvit rāgādīnām anuśayāḥ? Rāgādaya evānuśayāś cet sūtra-virodhaḥ : 'Ihaikatyo na kāmarāga-paryavasthitena cetasā bahulaṃ viharaty utpannasya kāmarāgaparyavasthānasyottara-nissaraṇaṃ yathābhūtaṃ prajānāti. Tasya tat kāmarāga-paryavasthānaṃ sthāmaśaḥ samyak susaṃvahataṃ sānuśayaṃ prahīyate' iti* (*Vṛtti* on kā. 261). Cf. *Majjhima-nikāya,* sutta 64, and *Aṅguttara,* III, p. 233.
24. ibid.
25. *Karmadhāraya eva parigṛhyate na ṣaṣṭhī-samāsa iti* Vaibhāṣikāḥ (ibid.).
26. *'Aupacāriko vā sūtre 'nuśaya-śabdaḥ prāptau...lākṣaṇikas tv abhidharme kleśa evānuśayaḥ* (ibid.).
27. *'sānusayo pahīyatī' ti vacanato panettha ekacce aññaṃ saṃyojanaṃ añño anusayo ti vadanti.... Te sasīsaṃ pārupitvā ādīhi paṭikkhipitabbā ...* (*Majjhima-nikāya-aṭṭhakathā,* III, p. 144).
28. ibid.

29. *Tasmā so yeva kileso bandhanaṭṭhena saṃyojanaṃ appahīnaṭṭhena anusayo ti idam atthaṃ sandhāya bhagavatā sānusayo pahīyatīti evaṃ vuttaṃ ti veditabbaṃ* (ibid.).
30. *Añño anusayo ti kathā* (*Kathāvatthu-aṭṭhakathā*, xiv, 5).
31. See *Tisso pi anusaya-kathā* and *Pariyuṭṭhānaṃ citta-vippayuttaṃ ti kathā* (ibid, xi, 1, and xiv, 6).
32. See *Yamaka-aṭṭhakathā*, p. 239 (Simon Hevavitarane Bequest Series, XL) and 'A dissertation on the *Yamaka*', by Ledi Sayadaw, *Yamaka*, II, pp. 258-9.
33. '*Evaṃ tu sādhu yathā* Dārṣṭāntikānāṃ' *iti Kośakāraḥ. Kathaṃ ca* Dārṣṭāntikānām? '*Kāmarāgasyānuśayaḥ kāmarāgānuśayaḥ. Na cānuśayaḥ saṃprayukto na viprayuktaḥ, tasyādravyāntaratvāt...*' (*Vṛtti* on kā. 261).
34. *Supto hi kleśa anuśaya ity ucyate, prabuddhaḥ paryavasthānam* (ibid.). This statement supports the Theravādin tradition where the same *kleśas* are enumerated under *anuśaya* and *pariyuṭṭhāna*.
35. '*Kā ca tasya prasuptiḥ? Asaṃmukhībhūtasya bīja-bhāvānubandhaḥ. Kaḥ prabodhaḥ? Saṃmukhībhāvaḥ. Ko 'yaṃ bīja-bhāvo nāma? Ātma-bhāvasya kleśajā kleśotpādana-śaktiḥ, yathā cāṅkurādīnāṃ śāli-phalajā śāli-phalotpādana-śakitiḥ' iti* (ibid.). See *Sakv.*, p. 444, and *L'Abhidharma-kośa*, ch. V, kā. 1.
36. *Tad etat Sautrāntikair antargataṃ Buddha-vacana-nīti-śravaṇa-kausīdyam āvirbhāvyate. ... Uktam atra karma-cintāyām uttaram, Tattva-saptatau ca ...* (ibid.). The *Tattva-saptati*, hitherto unknown, appears to be the title of a work by the author of the *Vṛtti* written on the model of the *Paramārtha-saptati* of Vasubandhu.
37. Sautrāntika-*parikalpite pratibījakalpe citta-śakti-bīja-bhāvanā-pakṣe nivṛttottaram anyānanyatvādi-doṣāt. Nānyānanya iti bīja-vāsanāvasthāne citta-vināśābhyupagame ca madhyamā-pratipat- siddhir iti cet. Na. Citta-svabhāva-śakti-kiryābhāve tad-anta-dvayāsiddhau madhyamā-pratipad-anupapatteḥ kha-puṣpamaya-daṇḍavat* (ibid.).
38. *Kiṃ punar idaṃ bījaṃ nāmeti...yan nāma-rūpaṃ phalotpattau samarthaṃ sākṣāt pāram-paryeṇa vā...*(*Sakv.*, pp. 147-8). See *L'Abhidharma-kośa*, ch. II, kā. 35-6.
39. ...*Ācārya*-Saṃghabhadraḥ ... *sa eva ca śakti-viśeṣa-lakṣaṇaṃ bījabhāvam ācāryeṇa vyavasthāpitaṃ dūṣayati. Kim ayaṃ śakti-viśeṣaś cittād arthāntaram utānarthāntaraṃ . . . Arthāntaraṃ cet, siddhaṃ prāptir astīti ... Anarthāntaraṃ cet, nanv akuśalaṃ kuśalasya bījam abhyupagataṃ bhavati akuśalasya ca kuśalaṃ ... iti sāṅkarya-doṣaḥ prasajyata iti* (*Sakv.*, pp. 147-8).
40. *Atra vayaṃ brūmaḥ. Anarthāntarabhāve sāṅkarya-doṣo bhavet. Tat tu bījaṃ na cittād arthāntaraṃ vaktavyaṃ, nāpy anarthāntaram. Upādāya-prajñpati-rūpatvāt...*(ibid.).
41. *Athāpy anarthāntarabhāvaḥ, tathāpy adoṣaḥ. Kuśalena hi cittenotpannena sva-jātīye 'nya-jātīye vā sva-santāna-citte bījam ādhīyeta. Tataḥ kāraṇa-viśeṣāt kārya-viśeṣa iti viśiṣṭaṃ tenetac cittam utpadyeta. ... Na ca kuśalenākuśale citte śakti-viśeṣa āhita iti tad akuśalaṃ kuśalatām āpadyate kuśalaṃ vā tad akuśalatāṃ śakti-viśeṣa-mātratvāt. Śaktir bījaṃ vāsanety eko 'yam arthaḥ* ...(ibid.).
42. ...*Na bhavanto bījārthaṃ jānate.... śakti-viśeṣa eva bījaṃ. Na bījaṃ nāmāsti kiñcit prajñapti-sattvāt* (ibid.).
43. See Stcherbatsky' *The conception of Buddhist nirvāṇa*, p. 30, n. 1, and S. Schayer's 'Kamalaśīla's kritik des Pudgalavāda', *Rocz. Orj.*, VIII, 1931-2, 68-93.
44. See J. Masuda, *Asia Major*, II, 1925, p. 68, n. 1; D. T. Suzuki, *Studies in the Laṅkāvatāra-sūtra*, pp. 176 ff. ; *La Siddhi de Hiüan Tsang* (tr. L. de la Vallée Poussin), I, pp. 100-23, and the following articles in the *Mélanges Chinois et Bouddhiques* : 'Notes sur l'Ālaya-vijñāna' (by la Vallée Poussin), III, 1935, 151; 'L'Ālaya-vijñāna dans le Mahāyāna-sangṅaha (by E. Lamotte), III, 1935, 208 ff.; 'Le Bouddhisme et le yoga de Patañjali' (by la Vallée Poussin), V, 1937, 231 ff.

45. *Aṅguttara-nikāya,* III, pp. 404-9.

46. *Idhāhaṃ Ānanda ekaccaṃ puggalaṃ evaṃ ... pajānāmi : imassa kho puggalassa vijjamānā kusalā pi dhammā akusalā pi dhammā. Tam enaṃ aparena samayena evaṃ ... pajānāmi: imassa kho puggalassa kusalā dhammā antarahitā, akusalā dhammā sammukhībhūtā, atthi ca khvā'ssa kusala-mūlaṃ asamucchinnaṃ, tamhā tassa kusalā kusalaṃ pātubhavissati. Evam ayaṃ puggalo āyatiṃ aparihāna-dhammo bhavissatītī. Seyyathā pi bījāni akhaṇḍāni ... sukhette suparikammakatāya bhūmiyā nikkhittāni ... vepullaṃ āpajjissanti...* (ibid.).

47. *Samanvāgato 'yaṃ pudgalaḥ kuśalair api dharmair akuśalair api yāvad asti cāsyāṇu-sahagataṃ kuśala-mūlam asamucchinnaṃ yato 'sya kuśala-mūlād anyat kuśala-mūlam utpatsyate. Evam ayaṃ pudgala āyatyāṃ viśuddha-dharmā bhaviṣyatīti ...* (*Sakv.,* pp. 188-9).

48. *Prāptir nāma samanvāgamo lābha iti paryāyaḥ* (*Vṛtti* on kā. 129).

49. *'Samanvāgato 'yaṃ puruṣaḥ kuśalair api dharmaiḥ' iti vistaraḥ .... Te 'sya pudgalasya kuśalā dharmā antardhāsyanti.... Asti cāsya kuśala-mūlam anu(°ṇu)-sahagatam anupacchinnam upapatti-lābhikam. Tad apy apareṇa samayeṇa sarveṇa sarvaṃ samucchetsyate. Yasya samucchedāt samucchinna-kuśala-mūla iti saṃkhyāṃ gamiṣyatīti* (*Vṛtti* on kā. 199).

50. *Idha bhikkhave ekacco puggalo samannāgato hoti ekanta-kāḷakehi akusala-dhammehi, so sakim nimuggo nimuggo va hotīti* (*Puggala-paññatti,* § 7, 1).

51. *'Sakiṃ nimuggo' ti eka-vāraṃ nimuggo. 'Ekanta-kāḷakehī' ti ekanteneva kāḷakehi natthika-vāda—ahetuka-vāda—akiriya-vāda-saṃkhātehi niyata-micchā-diṭṭhi-dhammehi. Evaṃ puggalo...nimuggo va hoti. Etassa hi puna bhavato vuṭṭhānaṃ nāma natthīti vadanti. Makkhali-gosālādayo viya heṭṭhā narakaggīnaṃ yeva āhārā honti* (*Puggala-paññatti-aṭṭakathā,* § 7, 1). In this connection see the following controversies recorded in the *Kathāvatthu* : *Kusala-citta-paṭilābha-kathā* (xiii, 2), *Kappaṭṭha-kathā* (xiii, 1), *Anantarāppayutta-kathā* (xiii, 3), *Niyatassa niyāma-kathā* (xiii, 4), *Kusalākusala-paṭisandhāna-kathā* (xiv, 1), *Accanta-niyāma-kathā* (xix, 7).

52. *Kuśalā api dvi-prakārā iti vistaraḥ. Yathā kliṣṭā dvi-prakārā iti api-śabdārthaḥ. Tad bīja-bhāvānupaghātād iti : teṣām utpatti-lābhikānāṃ bījaṃ ... samanvāgataḥ : kaiḥ? ayatna-bhāvibhiḥ kuśalaiḥ....Ko'sav ity āha : samucchinna-kuśala-mūlaḥ....Na tu khalu kuśalānāṃ dharmāṇāṃ bīja-bhāvasyātyantaṃ santatau samudghāto yathā kleśānām ārya-mārgeṇātyantaṃ santatau samudghāta ity abhiprāyaḥ ....* (*Sakv.,* p. 147). See *L'Abhidharma-kośa,* ch. ii, kā. 36.

53. The Kośakāra gives several views on the manner in which the *kuśala-mūlas* are destroyed. See *L'Abhidharma-kośa,* ch. iv, kā. 79, and *Vṛtti* on kā. 199.

54. *'Sūkṣmaṃ kuśala-dharma-bījaṃ tasminn akuśale cetasy avasthitaṃ yataḥ punaḥ pratyaya-sāmagrī-sannidhāne sati kuśalaṃ cittam utpadyate' iti* Kośakāraḥ. *Yukty-āgama-virodhāt tan neti* Dīpakāraḥ ... (*Vṛtti* on kā. 199).

55. ibid.

56. *Tat-kālāparinirvāṇa-dharmā ... duścaritaikāntikaḥ samucchinna-kuśala-mūlaḥ ...* (*Mahāyāna-sūtrālaṃkāra,* Vol. I, p. 12). See also *Studies in the Laṅkāvatāra-sūtra,* p. 220.

57. *Sakv.,* p. 644 *L'Abhidharma-kośa,* ch. vii, kā. 30, notes. *Sūtrālaṃkāra d'Aśvaghoṣa* (tr. Huber), p. 283. This story occurs in the *Mahāvagga* (*Vinaya-piṭaka,* I, p. 55), and the *Dhammapada-aṭṭhakathā,* vi, 1, vol. II, p. 105 (Rādhatthera-*vatthu*). In the Pali versions, however, Sāriputta ordains this person after recalling his charity of offering a spoonful of alms.

58. *Te punaḥ pūrvābhyāsa-vāsanā-dhātavaḥ ...* (*Vṛtti* on kā. 496).

59. Sautrāntikāḥ *punar varṇayanti—bījaṃ sāmarthyaṃ cetaso gotram iti* (*Sakv.*, pp. 583-4). On the Buddhist interpretation of the term *gotra* see among others, E. Obermiller's 'The sublime science of the great vehicle to salvation', *Acta Orientalia*, IX, 1931, 97 ff.

60. On *prabhāsavara-citta*, see K. Régamey's *Three chapters from the Samādhi-rāja-sūtra*, introduction, Warsaw, 1938.

61. *Mataṃ ca cittaṃ prakṛti-prabhāsvaraṃ*
sadā tad āgantuka-doṣa-dūṣitaṃ/
na dharmatā-cittam ṛte 'nya-cetasaḥ
prabhāsvaratvaṃ prakṛtau vidhīyate// Mahāyāna-sūtrālaṃkāra, ch. XIII, kā. 19.

62. *Aṅguttara-nikāya*, I, p. 10.

63. *Aṅguttara-nikāya-aṭṭhakathā*, I, p. 60.

64. *Akusala-vipākopekkhā-sahagata-santīraṇaṃ* (*Abhidhammattha-saṅgaho*, V, 10).

65. See *Abhidhammattha-saṅgaho-Navanīta-ṭīkā* (Benaras, 1941), i, 8; v, 10.

CHAPTER 14

The Origin and Development of the *Viprayukta-saṃskāras**

One of the most important factors which distinguish the Vaibhāṣika Abhidharma from the Theravāda Abhidharma is a category called the *viprayukta-saṃskāras*. The disputes on the reality of the dharmas included under this category dominate some of the major works on Abhidharma, especially the *Abhidharma-kośa-bhāṣya*[1] of Vasubandhu and the *Sphuṭārthā*[2] of Yaśomitra. An analysis of these dharmas is found in a few pioneering works like those of McGovern,[3] Stcherbatsky,[4] and others, but very little is known about their origin. Particularly the relation between these dharmas and the ones enumerated in the Pali Abhidharma as well as their correspondence to the *padārthas* (reals) of the non-Buddhist schools such as the Vaiśeṣika and the Mīmāṃsaka, are still in need of a more thorough investigation. There are valid reasons to believe that these *padārthas* exerted a strong influence on the Vaibhāṣika theory of reality and indirectly were responsible for the *dravya-vāda* of the neo-Vaibhāṣika school represented by Saṃghabhadra. The recent discovery of the *Abhidharma-dīpa*[5] (together with its commentary—the *Vibhāṣā-prabhā-vṛtti*[6]), a work belonging to the tradition of Saṃghabhadra, furnishes us with valuable information on certain aspects of the theory of *viprayukta* category in general and on the nature of some of the *viprayuktas* in particular.

In early Buddhism, *saṃskāra* is described by a solitary term, *cetanā* 'volition'. The *saṃskāra skandha* consists of six volitions cor-

---

*This article was originally published in *BSOAS*, Vol. XXII, part 3, pp. 532-547, University of London, 1959. Reprinted with kind permission of Oxford University Press.

responding to the six sense objects.[7] But as the Ābhidharmikas analysed the mental factors and differentiated their characteristics, they formulated long lists of dharmas which had to be accommodated in the traditional formula of the five *skandhas*. Instead of postulating new *skandhas*, they included these new dharmas in the *saṃskāra skandha*.

This addition of new dharmas in the group of *caitta* is justified by showing a functional co-ordination (*saṃprayoga*) between them and the *citta*. The *Abhidhammattha-saṅgaho* speaks of three kinds of uniformities that exist between a *citta* and 52 kinds of *cetasikas* (one *vedanā*, one *saṃjnā*, and 50 *saṃskāras*).[8] They arise and disappear at the same time, have the same object, and depend on the same base. The Vaibhāṣikas also speak of five kinds of *samatā* (uniformity).[9] There is between the *citta* and *caitta* uniformity as regards time, basis, objects, essential qualities, and function.

Both the Theravādins and the Vaibhāṣikas arrived at almost identical lists of these *saṃskāras*. The former enumerated 50, and the latter had 44 *saṃskāras*. In the formulation of these *saṃskāras*, the early Buddhists appear to have been influenced by the Yoga school, which also analysed various states of mind with reference to several *citta-bhūmis, samādhis, ṛddhis,* and *dhyānas* with their attendant *yogāṅgas* or the means of *yoga*.[10] In course of time, the Ābhidharmikas, and particularly the Vaibhāṣikas seem to have been much influenced by their contemporary realists like the Sāṃkhya, Vaiśeṣika, and Mīmāṃsaka schools.

Over a long period and particularly during the time of the *Mahāvibhāṣā*, the Ābhidharmikas were engaged in studying and criticizing the doctrines of these rival schools. Aśvaghoṣa's poems show an acquaintance with the Sāṃkhya system.[11] Vasumitra, a leading Vibhāṣā-śāstrin is extolled in the *Vṛtti* as the one who refuted the theory of 25 *tattvas* (of the Sāṃkhya) and demolished the (Vaiśeṣika) doctrine of the atomic structure of the cosmos.[12] We learn from Paramārtha's 'Life of Vasubandhu'[13] that a Sāṃkhya teacher Vindhyavāsin defeated Buddhamitra, the teacher of Vasubandhu, in a debate, whereupon the latter composed the *Paramārtha-saptatikā* in refutation of the Sāṃkhya. The *Bhāṣya,* as well as the *Vṛtti,* contain several criticisms of the Sāṃkhya and Vaiśeṣika theories.

A result of these criticisms and counter-criticisms was the acceptance not only of new theories but also of new dharmas and novel terms in the Vaibhāṣika school. The doctrine of the *Sarvāstivāda* bears a close resemblance to the *satkāryavāda.* The four traditional explanations of the *sarvāstivāda* can be treated as interpretations of the *pariṇāmavāda* of the Sāṃkhya. The atomic theory of the Vaiśeṣika too played a great part in formulating the Vaibhāṣika theory of the *dravya* and *saṃghāta paramāṇus.* The seven categories of the Vaiśeṣika greatly influenced the Vaibhāṣika analysis of the *nāma-rūpa* and even their theory of dharma. On account of their fundamental thesis of *anātmavāda* (non-substantialism), the Buddhists did not recognize the Vaiśeṣika distinction of *padārthas* as *dravya* (substance), *guṇa* (quality), *karma* (action), etc., but reduced all things to the status of dharmas, i.e. unique, momentary, ultimate elements. It is, therefore, not surprising to find that the term *dravya* is conspicuous by its absence from the Pali suttas and even from the Abhidhamma. In the Vaibhāṣika school, however, it almost replaces the Buddhist term dharma. Here all real dharmas are called *dravya.* Of the nine *dravyas* of the Vaiśeṣika, only five, viz. substances of earth, water, fire, air, and mind have their corresponding dharmas in the Theravāda Buddhism. The *ākāśa* was recognized by them only as a kind of matter (*ākāsa-dhātu* = *paricheda-rūpa*), and not as a *mahābhūta.* In the Vaibhāṣika school the four *mahābhūtas* came to be regarded as *dravya-paramāṇus,* as indivisible as the atoms of the Vaiśeṣika. The *ākāsa-dhātu* of the Theravāda was raised here to the status of an *asaṃskṛta* dharma, and made a *nitya-dravya* as in the Vaiśeṣika school. Of the remaining three *dravyas* of the Vaiśeṣika, viz. *kāla, dik,* and *ātman,* the first two were recognized by the Yogācāras as *prajñapti-dharmas.* Thus with the sole exception of the *ātman,* all the Vaiśeṣika *dravyas* came to be recognized in the later Ābhidharmika schools.

As in the case of the term *dravya* (substance), the term *guṇa* (quality) also is not found (in its technical sense)[14] in the Theravāda canon. But one can detect an influence of the Vaiśeṣika theory of *guṇa* and *dravya* in their enumeration of the derived matter (*upādāya-rūpa*).

The *Visuddhimagga* enumerates the following 24 kinds of derived matter: *cakkhu, sota, ghāṇa, jivhā, kāya; rūpa, sadda, gandha, rasa; itthindriya, purisindriya, jīvitindriya; hadaya-vatthu; kāyaviññatti, vacīviññatti; ākāsa-dhātu; rūpassa lahutā, rūpassa mudutā, rūpassa kammaññatā; rūpassa upacayo, rūpassa santati, rūpassa jaratā, rūpassa aniccatā,* and *kabaḷīkāro āhāro.*[15]

According to the Theravādins, all these 24 *upādāya-rūpas* are 'dhammas' and hence ought to be recognized as ultimate elements. But a large number of these can be treated rather as aspects, modes, or qualities than as separate entities. This is borne out by the description in the commentaries of some of these dhammas and a distinction drawn between the *nipphanna* and *anipphanna*[16] *rūpa*. Thus, for instance, the *ākāsa-dhātu* (element of space = vacuum) is called *pariccheda-rūpa* 'material quality of limitation'. The two *viññattis* (intimation by body and speech) together with the *lahutā, mudutā,* and *kammaññatā* (lightness, pliancy, and adaptability of matter) are called *vikāra-rūpas,* i.e. material qualities signifying special conditions. The *upacaya, santati, jarā,* and *aniccatā* (i.e. the integration, continuance, decay, and impermanence of matter) are called *lakkhaṇa-rūpas,* i.e. the and characteristics of matter. These ten kinds of *rūpa* are called *anipphanna* in order to distinguish them from the remaining 14 *rūpas* (and the four *mahābhūtas*) which are called *nipphanna-rūpa.* Thus in the *Aṭṭhakathās* Buddhaghosa explains the *nipphanna-rūpas* as those which 'transcend limits, change, and characteristics and which are to be seized in their intrinsic nature (*sabhāva*).[17] The *anipphannas* are contrary thereto. The *Visuddhimagga-ṭīkā* explains further that the *nipphanna-rūpas* have their own nature (*sabhāva*), whereas the *anipphannas* are devoid of their own nature and are known only in relationship to the *sabhāva-rūpas.*[18] The *anipphanna-rūpas* are nowhere in the suttas enumerated as *rūpa-dhammas.* Their inclusion in the Abhidhamma suggests an influence of the Vaiśeṣika school. It is certain that the commentators knew the theory of *guṇa.* Buddhaghosa criticizes a (Vaiśeṣika) theory according to which the *rūpa* (= *varṇa*) and *gandha* are qualities of *teja* and *pṛthivī,* respectively.[19] The words *nipphanna-rūpa* and *anipphanna-rūpa* do not occur in the canon. They are found only in the *Aṭṭhakathās.* It is, therefore, possible that the commentators introduced this division in order to separate the 'real' *upādāya-rūpas* from 'qualities', which in the later Sautrāntika terms could be designated as mere *prajñapti* (nominal) dharmas.[20]

A few of the so-called *nipphanna-rūpas* can also be placed in the category of the *anipphanna.* The *jīvitindriya,* for instance, does not consist of a separate *rūpa,* but is only a name given to the life of matter. The *itthindriya* and *purisindriya,* two 'material qualities of sex' can be treated as different aspects of the *kāya.*[21] The last *nipphanna-rūpa,* called *kabaḷīkāro āhāro* (edible food) is also not a separate entity but only a name given to the material quality of nutrition.

Thus out of the 24 kinds of *upādāya-rūpas,* only nine, viz. the five sense organs and four sense objects (the *phoṭṭhabba*—touch object—being included in the *mahābhūtas*) can be considered as dharmas having intrinsic nature (*sabhāva*) and, therefore real.[22] As a matter of fact, these ten are identical with the ten of the eleven dharmas enumerated in both the Vaibhāṣika and the Yogācāra lists of the *rūpa-dharma.*[23]

Although the Vaibhāṣikas did not enumerate the 'qualities' of *rūpa* in the *rūpa-dharma,* they certainly knew some of them. They recognized, for instance, the four *lakṣaṇas,* which were proclaimed in the sūtras as being universal characteristics of not only the *rūpa* but of all phenomenal elements. These were not enumerated as separate dharmas in the traditional formula of the five *skandhas.* If a large number of new *caitasikas* could be added under the *saṃskāra skandha,* there was no reason why these four *lakṣaṇas* could not also be accommodated under that heading, particularly when these were specifically called *'saṃskṛta-lakṣaṇas'* by the sūtra. But these *lakṣaṇas* were not exclusively *caitasika,* and could not, therefore, be treated as purely mental factors, inasmuch as they covered even the *rūpa-skandha.* The origin of a novel category called the (*rūpa*) *citta-viprayukta-saṃskāra* is perhaps to be traced to an attempt to include the *lakṣaṇas* and such other aspects or qualities in the traditional formula of the *pañca-skandha.*

Yaśomitra explains this term fully. These dharmas are disassociated from the *citta* but are more akin to it than to the *rūpa-skandha.* Hence they are included in the *nāma-skandha.* The term *viprayukta* is used for excluding the *caittas* which are *saṃprayukta.* The term *saṃskāra* is used to exclude the *asaṃskṛta* dharmas. Thus the *viprayukta* dharmas are distinct from the *rūpa, citta, caitta,* and *asaṃskṛta* dharmas.[24]

The term *citta-vippayutta* is known to the *Dhammasaṅgaṇi.* But there it refers only to the *rūpa-khandha* and *nibbāna.*[25] It is not recognized as a separate category as in the Vaibhāṣika school. The *Kathāvatthu,* however, shows acquaintance with the latter meaning. It contains a controversy where the opponent holds that the *pariyuṭṭhānas* ('outbursts' of *anusayas*) are *citta-vippayutta-dhammas.*[26] Buddhaghosa attributes this view to the Andhakas.[26a] In his commentary on another controversy on the *anusayas* he says that the Andhakas, Uttarāpathakas, Mahāsāṃghikas, and Sammitīyas hold that the *anusayas* are *citta-vippayutta*.[27] According to Yaśomitra, the Vātsīputrīyas also maintained the same view.[28] The *jīvitendriya* was also, according to Buddhaghosa, considered as a *citta-vippayutta-dhamma* by Pubbaseliyas and Sammitīyas.[29] The Yogācāra school of Asanga not only accepted this new category but added several dharmas of its own under that heading. Thus the category of the *citta-viprayukta-saṃskāra* was not necessarily a Vaibhāṣika invention; it was known as early as the time of the *Kathāvatthu* and was accepted by several major and minor schools.

There is no unanimity among different schools regarding the number of *saṃskāras* that were enumerated under this category. The lists of only two schools, viz. the Vaibhāṣika and the Yogācāra, have come down to us. Of the former, two lists are known. The older one is given in the *Abhidharmāmṛta*[30] of Ghoṣaka, and the later one is given in the *Bhāṣya* and the *Vṛtti*. The Yogācāra list is found in the *Abhidharma-samuccaya*[31] of Asanga.

Ghoṣaka enumerates the following 17 *saṃskāras:* (1) *prāptiḥ,* (2) *asaṃjñi-samāpattiḥ,* (3) *nirodha-samāpattiḥ,* (4) *asaṃjñi-āyatanam,* (5) *jīvitendriyam,* (6) *nikāya-sabhāgatā,* (7) *sthāna-prāptiḥ,* (8) *vastu-prāptiḥ,* (9) *āyatana-prāptiḥ,* (10) *jātiḥ,* (11) *jarā,* (12) *sthitiḥ,* (13) *anityatā,* (14) *nāma-kāyaḥ,* (15) *pada-kāyaḥ,* (16) *vyañjana-kāyaḥ,* (17) *pṛthagjanatvam.*

Asanga in his *Asm.* drops Nos. 7, 8, and 9 of the above list and adds the following nine, bringing his total to 23: (1) *pravṛttiḥ,* (2) *pratiniyamaḥ,* (3) *yogaḥ,* (4) *javaḥ,* (5) *anukramaḥ,* (6) *kālaḥ,* (7) *deśaḥ,* (8) *saṃkhyā,* (9) *sāmagrī.*

The *Kośa* and the *Dīpa* closely follow the list of Ghoṣaka. They enumerate only 13 dropping Nos. 2, 7, 8, 9, and 17 from his list, and adding one more item called *aprāpti.* The last nine *saṃskāras* of the Yogācāra list are omitted by them. Of these three, Ghoṣaka's list is undoubtedly the oldest as he represents the period of the *Mahāvibhāṣā.* The Yogācārins seem to have modified his list by including Nos. 7, 8, and 9 in No. 1 = (*prāpti*). The neo-Vaibhāṣikas like the Kośakāra modified it still further by including No. 2 in No. 4. They replaced the *pṛthagjanatva* (No. 17) by their new dharma, viz. *aprāpti,* since the former is only an *alābha* (non-obtainment) of *ārya-mārga.*

At least five items of these lists, viz. the four *lakṣaṇas* and the *jīvitendriya,* have corresponding dharmas in the *upādāya-rūpa* of the Theravāda. But the Theravādins enumerated the *lakṣaṇas* as 'qualities' devoid of *saṃskṛta-lakṣaṇas*[32] like the Vaiśeṣika *guṇas* which are *aguṇavat*. The Vaibhāṣikas enumerated them as *'dravya'*, i.e. having intrinsic nature, abiding in the three times and causing the origination, subsistence, decay, and extinction of all phenomenal existence. A logical conclusion of such a step was to postulate *upa-lakṣaṇas* (secondary characteristics) like *jāti-jāti, sthiti-sthiti,* etc., to these *lakṣaṇas*[32]; this was ridiculed by the Sautrāntikas as absurd and involving the fallacy of an infinite regress.

The same rule is applied in the case of the first two *saṃskāras,* viz. the *prāpti* and *aprāpti*. The former is a *saṃskāra* (force) which controls the collection or obtainment of certain dharmas in a given *santāna* (stream of life), as for instance, in the case of an *arhat* there is a *prāpti* of *aśaikṣa* dharmas. The *aprāpti* is a 'force' which prevents this *prāpti,* as for instance in the case of a *pṛthagjana,* there is a non-collection of the *ārya-dharmas*. As in the case of the *lakṣaṇas* the Vaibhāṣika here postulates such additional dharmas as *prāpti-prāpti* and *aprāpti-aprāpti* for explaining the obtainment of the *prāpti* and the prevention of *aprāpti,* respectively, again exposing his theory to the fallacy of regress.

One can detect an influence of the Vaiśeṣika in this *dravya-vāda* of the Vaibhāṣika. This influence is unmistakably seen in a few other *saṃskāras* of this list. The Vaiśeṣika category of *sāmānya* (generality), for instance, is unknown to the Pali canon. The Buddhists being pluralists, non-substantialists, and *vibhajya-vādins* always tended to oppose the reality of *sāmānya,* as the latter was a stepping-stone towards a unity, a substance, or even to the theory of *brahman* of the Advaita school. Their formulas of the *skandha, āyatana, dhātu,* etc., were primarily aimed at removing false notions of unity (*ekatva-grāha*).[34] In the later works on Buddhist logic the *sāmānya* is unanimously described as a mere conceptual construction (*vikalpa*) imposed on the discrete, unique, and momentary dharmas, and hence unreal.[35] But this *sāmānya* creeps up, in the Vaibhāṣika category of the *viprayukta,* under the guise of *sabhāgatā*. Like the *parā-sattā* and the *aparā-sattā* of the Vaiśeṣika, the Vaibhāṣika *sabhāgatā* is also divided into *sattva-sabhāgatā* (which is common to all beings—*abhinnā*) and dharma-*sabhāgatā* (which is found in smaller groups like men, women, laymen, monks, etc.).[36]

The Sautrāntika Kośakāra rightly observes that in recognizing the *sabhāgatā* as a *dravya,* distinct from the *skandha, āyatana,* or *dhātu* (which constitute a *sattva* or a dharma), the Vaibhāṣika has only supported the Vaiśeṣika category of *sāmānya*. The Vaibhāṣika seeks to support his *sabhāgatā* by a sūtra passage where the word *nikāya-sabhāga* is mentioned, and asks for an explanation of the notion of generality. The Sautrāntika points out that the sūtra does not warrant any recognition of the *sabhāgatā* as a distinct *dravya*. The generality is only a notion (*prajñapti*) and not a real dharma.[37] 'And if all notions were to be treated as real', continues the Kośakāra, 'why not assume distinct dharmas for the notions of number, magnitude, distinctness, conjunction, disjunction, remoteness, nearness, etc., which are treated as realities by the heretic schools ?'[38] Indeed, the last nine *viprayukta-saṃskāras* of the Yogācāra list seem to represent these notions treated as reals in the Vaiśeṣika school. Of these nine, the following six, viz. the *pravṛtti, java, kāla, deśa, saṃkhyā,* and *sāmagrī* correspond respectively to the *pravṛtti* (a kind of *prayatna*), *vega* (a kind of *saṃskāra*), *kāla* (a *dravya*), *dik* (a *dravya*), *saṃkhyā* (a *guṇa*), and *saṃyoga* (a *guṇa*).[39] The *anukrama*[40] can be taken to correspond to the *paratva* and *aparatva,* two *guṇas* of the Vaiśeṣika. Only two, viz. the *pratiniyama* (manifoldness) and *yoga*[41] (conformity of *hetu* and *phala*) have no corresponding reals in the Vaiśeṣika list.

The acceptance of these Vaiśeṣika reals exclusively by the Yogācāras did not, however, make them realists like the Vaibhāṣika. Unlike the latter, they treated all *viprayukta-saṃskāras* as mere notions (*prajñapti*). And in the case of the last nine *saṃskāras,* which directly correspond to the Vaiśeṣika *padārthas,* they interpreted them merely as different names of the *hetu-phala.*[42]

The Sautrāntikas also recognize these notions, but severely oppose the Vaibhāṣikas for accepting them as *dravya-dharmas* or reals. They point out that the so-called *viprayukta-saṃskāras* neither have own nature (*svabhāva*), nor are they preached in the sūtras. The second *kośasthāna* of the *Bhāṣya*[43] contains long and lively controversies between the Sautrāntika and the Vaibhāṣika on the validity of each and every item of the *viprayukta-saṃskāra.* The Kośakāra examines the scriptures quoted by the Vaibhāṣika, analyses their arguments, ridicules their dogmatic realism, and finally accuses them of supporting the heretical schools.

A counter-attack to this polemic of the Kośakāra is found in the *Vṛtti.* The Dīpakāra indirectly refers to the Kośakāra as an infant, ignorant of the Abhidharma, and boldly declares that he will prove the *svabhāvas* of these *saṃskāras,* and will also quote sūtras in his favour.[44] Unfortunately, a large number of folios containing these lively controversies are lost. Discussions on *prāpti* and *aprāpti* are entirely lost. The controversies on the *nirodha-samāpatti* are severely interrupted, since only a prima facie argument has survived which contains a view of the Kośakāra condemned as 'unbuddhistic' by the *Vṛtti.*[45] The treatment of *sabhāgatā* and *āsaṃjñika* is almost identical with the Vaibhāṣika explanations of these *saṃskāras* in the *Bhāṣya.* The *Vṛtti* here borrows several passages from the latter. The Dīpakāra does not advance any new arguments but contents himself with a remark that the Kośakāra in comparing the *sabhāgatā* with the Vaiśeṣika *sāmānya* has only made a futile attempt to see a similarity of the kind which we find obtaining between *pāyasa* (milk-porridge) and *vāyasa* (a crow).[46] The only important discussions available to us, therefore, are on the *jīvitendriya,* the four *lakṣaṇas,* and the last three *saṃskāras* called *nāma-kāya, pada-kāya,* and *vyañjana-kāya.*[47] Even in the case of these topics the Vaibhāṣika arguments of the Dīpakāra are not different from those given in the *Bhāṣya,* which are well known through Poussin's *L'Abhidharma-kośa* and Stcherbatsky's *The Central Conception of Buddhism.* We shall, therefore, concentrate here only on certain aspects of these controversies which are found only in the *Vṛtti.*

JĪVITENDRIYA

Although the term *jīvita* is known to the Pali suttas, the technical term *jīvitendriya* is mostly found in the Abhidhamma *Piṭaka.* In the suttas the term *āyu* is more commonly used in the sense of a principle signifying life-duration. The *Mahāvedalla-sutta* of the *Majjhima-nikāya* contains a conversation between Mahākoṭṭhita and Sāriputta on the mutual relation of the mind and mental concomitants. In this connection a question is asked on the basis of stability of the five *indriyas.* Sāriputta replies that their stability is on account of *āyu.* The latter, he says, depends on *usmā* (*ūṣmā,* heat generated by *karma*). Since *usmā* is also a part of the body, the *āyu* and *usmā* are inter-dependent like the flame and the light of a lamp. The light is seen by the help of flame, the flame is seen on account of the light.[48] As yet there is no indication here to show the place of *āyu* in the traditional formula of the five *khandhas.* Perhaps to elucidate this point, a further question is raised whether the *āyusaṃkhāras* (constituents of life) are identical with feelings (i.e. *vedanā*). Sāriputta says that they are not identical, for, if they were, a person undergoing the trance called *saññā-vedayita-nirodha* will not rise again from that trance.[49] It may be recalled here that according to the Theravādins, the four *nāma-skandhas* always rise and disappear in one time. The *nirodha* (cessation) of *vedanā* and *sañña* would, therefore, automatically mean *nirodha* of all the four. Consequently, if *āyu* is identical with any of them, it will also cease to be, resulting in the death of the yogin. Sāriputta further explains that when a person dies, three things abandon him, viz. the *āyu*, the *usmā* and the mind (*viññaṇa*). In the case of a person who has undergone the above *samādhi* the *āyu* and *usmā* still exist.[50] It appears from this passage that the sutta recognizes *āyu* as a factor which stabilizes the five *indriyas*, but does not include it in any of the *nāma-khandhas*. Its inclusion in the latter group would also go against the recognition of an existence called *asañña-bhava* which consists of only the *rūpa-khandha*. Nor could it be included in the *rūpa-khandha*, for in the *arūpa-loka*, in the absence of any *rūpa*, its operation will be impossible. Various speculations regarding its inclusion in the formula of the five *skandhas* can be traced to the above sutta and to the problems that arise on account of recognizing these two existences, one wholly material and another wholly mental.

The Theravādins solved this problem by postulating two *jīvitendriyas* (i.e. *āyu*), one physical (*rūpa*) and another mental (*arūpa*). Their Abhidhamma includes the former in the *upādāya-rūpas*, and the latter in the *saṃkhāra-khandha*.[51] The beings of the *asañña-bhava* and the *arūpa-bhava* live their life-span on account of these two dharmas, respectively. The beings of other existences possess both kinds of the *jīvitendriya*.

The Theravādin enumeration of *āyu* in the *rūpa-khandha* looks rather far-fetched. The sutta quoted above specifically raises the whole problem with reference to five *indriyas*, i.e. the five senses, and not matter in general. Death there spoken of refers not to a corpse but to a personality, i.e. a being led by his *karma* in different destinies (*gati*) or existences (*nikāya-sabhāga*) such as *naraka* (hell), *tiryañca* (animal), *preta* (spirit), *manuṣya* (human), and *deva* (god). The *āyuḥ* thus was directly related to *karma* or *cetanā* and not the *rūpa-skandha*. This seems to be the main reason for a criticism of the *rūpa-jīvitendriya* by Pubbaseliyas and Sammitīyas recorded in the *Kathāvatthu*.[52] They held that the *jīvitendriya* was essentially an *arūpa-dharma*. But these schools, as well as the Vaibhāṣikas, were equally committed to the theories of the *asaṃjña* and *arūpa-bhavas*, and hence could not include the *jīvitendriya* in the *nāma-skandha*. They, therefore, included it in their *viprayukta* category, distinct from both the *citta* and *rūpa*.

This conjecture is supported by the Vaibhāṣika description of this dharma. The *Vṛtti*[53] defines it as a (cause of) subsistence (*sthiti*) of the vital fire (*ūṣmā*) and mind (*vijñāna*). It is a basis for notions of different existences like human, animal, divine, etc., on account of its nature of being a result of the past *karma*. The Abhidharma describes it as a force of life-duration in all the three existences (viz. the *kāma*, *rūpa*, and *arūpa* worlds). The *Vṛtti*, in conformity with this Abhidharma, says that there is no faculty other than the *jīvita*, which is born of *karma*, covers all the three worlds, exists uninterrupted from the moment of birth, and thus becomes a basis for the notions of a particular destiny. The *Vṛtti* further quotes a scripture: 'when the *āyuḥ*, the *ūṣmā*, and *vijñāna* abandon this body, then (a person) lies discarded like a piece of wood devoid of consciousness'.[54]

But if the *āyuḥ* were to be always associated with the *ūṣmā* (matter) and *vijñāna* (mind), then it would not operate in the *arūpa-bhava* and in the *asaṃjña-bhava* respectively. Therefore, the *Vṛtti* says that the *āyuḥ* in the *kāma-dhātu* is always accompanied by the sense of touch, the *ūṣmā*, and *vijñāna*. It is not essential to have all the five senses for its operation. In the *rūpa-dhātu*, which includes the *asaṃjña-bhava*, the *āyuḥ* is always accompanied by the five senses, but not necessarily by mind. In the *arūpa-dhātu* it is accompanied only by *vijñāna*, with the exception of the *nirodha-samāpatti* (where even *vijñāna* is brought to a cessation).[55]

The Sautrāntika objection to this theory (as contained in the *Bhāṣya*)[56] is that if a separate dharma like *āyuḥ* is necessary to sustain the *ūṣmā* and *vijñāna*, then the *āyuḥ* itself will need to be sustained by another *āyuḥ*. The Vaibhāṣika, in conformity with the above sutta, says that the *āyuḥ*, *ūṣmā*, and *vijñāna* are interdependent. This gives rise to another problem as to which of these precedes the other two. The Vaibhāṣika, therefore, says that *karma* produces and sustains the *āyuḥ*. The Sautrāntika rightly argues that the *karma* alone should be efficient to sustain both the *ūṣmā* and *vijñāna*. There is no need to postulate a life-sustainer like *āyuḥ*. Moreover, the *āyuḥ* is a mere notion. Just as the destiny of an arrow and the time it will take to reach its destination are determined at the moment of its shooting, similarly the *karmas* of an individual, at the moment of a rebirth, fix the destiny (*nikāya-sabhāga*) and the duration of the *santāna* of the five *skandhas*. Therefore, concludes the Sautrāntika, the *āyuḥ* postulated by the Vaibhāṣikas is merely a notion and not a dharma separate from the *santati*.

The Dīpakāra does not take note of these arguments but asserts his position by saying that the *jīvitendriya*, being a basis of the notion of a destiny, is a *dravya*, a real dharma.[57] Otherwise, he says, what could prevent the death of a person who undergoes the *nirodha-samāpatti* or the *asaṃjñi-samāpatti*? Both are devoid of consciousness and hence require some real dharma which will be instrumental in the life-duration of these two states. That dharma is the *jīvitendriya*. These Vaibhāṣika arguments are, however, unconvincing to the Sautrāntika Kośakāra, for whom both *samāpattis* are conscious (*sacittika*), and which, therefore, do not require a separate dharma for sustaining the life-stream during those states.[58]

Whether the *āyuḥ* was accepted as a *dravya* or as a mere *prajñapti-dharma*, both the Vaibhāṣikas and the Sautrāntikas (together with the Theravādins) agreed that it was a *vipāka*, i.e. a result of some past *karma*. Being a *vipāka*, and being co-nascent with birth and coterminus with death, it functioned automatically, independent of any new *karma*. If a life-span (*āyuḥ*) was fixed it could neither be prolonged at will, nor could it be replaced by a new life-span to sustain the same *santati*. This unanimously accepted theory of *āyuḥ*, however, went against an equally well founded belief in the Buddha's power of prolonging his life-span for an indefinite period.

Various controversies relating to this belief and its bearing on the theory of *karma* are preserved in the Pali commentaries, the *Bhāṣya*, and the *Vṛtti*. The Kośakāra deals in detail with this problem and advances certain unorthodox solutions to this riddle. The Dīpakāra examines his arguments, declares them to be invalid, and accuses the Kośakāra of entering the portals of Mahāyāna Buddhism.[59]

SAṂSKṚTA-LAKṢAṆAS

The next four *viprayukta-saṃskāras* viz. *jāti* (origination), *sthiti* (subsistence), *jarā* (decay), and *anityatā* (extinction), are called *saṃskṛta-*

lakṣaṇas or phenomenalizing characteristics of all phenomena. According to the Vaibhāṣikas, these four simultaneously exercise their power on all phenomena causing the origination, etc., of the latter. They further maintain that these four *lakṣaṇas* are as real as the dharmas which they characterize. Consequently, they are also characterized by secondary characteristics (*upa-lakṣaṇas*) like *jāti-jāti,* etc. They seek to prove the reality of these four *lakṣaṇas* by the support of a sūtra which says 'of the *saṃskṛta* there is known the origin (*utpāda*), cessation (*vyaya*), and change of state (*sthityanyathātvam*)'.[60]

The Sautrāntika Kośakāra examines these *lakṣaṇas* at great length. His main arguments against their acceptance as real dharmas, distinct from the phenomena, are: (1) they cannot simultaneously work upon a momentary (*kṣaṇika*) dharma; (2) the theory of *upa-lakṣaṇas* results in the fallacy of regress; (3) the term *saṃskṛta* in the sūtra quoted by the Vaibhāṣikas does not refer to a momentary dharma but to a series of them (*pravāha*). 'The series or stream itself is called subsistence (*sthiti*), its origin is called *jāti,* its cessation is *vyaya,* and the difference in its preceding and succeeding moments is called *sthityanyathātva*.'[61] Therefore, concludes the Sautrāntika, the words like *jāti,* etc., have no corresponding realities: they are only names, like the word *pravāha* (series). The *saṃskṛta* is defined by the Lord in a different sūtra: 'Phenomenon is that which becomes having not been before, having once become it does not become again, and it is the series of which it forms a part which is called subsistence and which changes its state'.[62]

The Dīpakāra does not attempt a reply to these criticisms of the Kośakāra. He briefly deals with this topic concentrating only on two points, viz. the reality of *jarā* (decay) and *vināśa* (extinction).

The sūtra quoted by the Vaibhāṣikas speaks of only three *lakṣaṇas,* viz. *utpāda, vyaya,* and *sthityanyathātva.* In their Abhidharma, however, four are enumerated: *jāti, sthiti, jarā,* and *anityatā*.[63] Of these the first and last are identical with *utpāda* and *vyaya.* The sūtra term *sthityanyathātva* is differently explained in different schools. The Theravādins interpret it as *jarā*.[64] They do not recognize the *sthiti* as a separate *lakṣaṇa.* Although it is represented in their *upādāya-rūpas* as (*rūpassa*) *santati,* the *Dhammasaṅgaṇi* and the *Visuddhimagga* treat the latter term as a synonym of *jāti* (i.e. *upacaya*).[65]

The Vaibhāṣikas recognize both *sthiti* and *jarā*. They, therefore, interpret the term *sthityanyathātva* differently. The *Bhāṣya* gives two views.[66] Some *ācāryas* hold that the term *sthityanyathātva* means *jarā* only and not *sthiti*. The sūtra is only explanatory, and hence speaks only of *jāti, jarā,* and *nāśa,* whereas the Abhidharma is definitive and hence speaks of four. The sūtra does not refer to *sthiti,* because the Lord wanted to cause distress about the phenomena in the minds of his disciples. Moreover, *sthiti* (albeit not as a *saṃskāra*) is found even in the *asaṃskṛta* dharmas which are held to be eternal. In order to dispel any confusion between the *saṃskṛta* and *asaṃskṛta,* the sūtra speaks of only three. Other *ācāryas,* however, maintain that the term *sthityanyathātva* includes both *sthiti* and *jarā*. These two dharmas are like the goddesses of good luck and bad luck. The Lord combined *jarā* with *sthiti* in order to cause detachment from the phenomenal world.[67]

This second view alone is given by the Dīpakāra. He maintains that if a dharma were to be devoid of *sthiti* (subsistence), then it would be incapable of yielding any fruit, i.e. performing any action.[68] Consequently, it would not be a real dharma. But mere *sthiti* without *jarā* will also not be desirable. For in that case the dharma will go on performing more than one action and will never cease to be. Therefore, it is to be inferred that there is a force like *jarā* (decay) which reduces its strength (*śakti-hāni*) and hands it over to the last force, viz. *anityatā,* which brings an extinction of the dharma.

The Sautrāntika takes strong exception to this Vaibhāṣika theory of *śakti-hāni*. He points out that the change of a subsisting dharma into a decaying dharma corresponds to the *pariṇāma-vāda* of the Sāṃkhya,[69] where also a substance (*dharmin* or *dravya*) changes its aspects or qualities (*dharma*) without losing its identity.

The reply of the Dīpakāra to this criticism is brief. He says that according to the Sāṃkhya, when that which is characterized (*dharmin,* i.e. a substance), while remaining permanent, gives up one characteristic (or aspect=*dharma*) and assumes another, both these characteristics being identical (*svātmabhūta*) with the characterized, this is *pariṇāma*. According to the Vaibhāṣika, however, a characterized (*dharmin,* i.e. a *dravya*) is different from the characteristic (*dharma*), (in this case) *jarā*.[70]

Although brief, this statement of the Dīpakāra is significant. His definition of the Sāṃkhya ***pariṇāma*** corresponds to the one given by Vyāsa in his *Yoga-sūtra-bhāṣya.* Commenting on a sūtra[71] dealing with three kinds of mutations (*pariṇāma*), viz. *dharma* (of external aspects), *lakṣaṇa* (of time-variation), and *avasthā* (of intensity), Vyāsa defines a *pariṇāma* in the following words: 'What is a mutation? It is the rise of another external-aspect (*dharma*) in an abiding substance after an earlier external-aspect has come to an end'.[72]

It may be noted that these two definitions of the Sāṃkhya *pariṇāma* are almost identical, with the significant exception of the term *svātmabhūta* found only in the *Vṛtti.* The Dīpakāra uses this term to show that in the Sāṃkhya theory the *dharmas* and the *dharmin* are identical. This idea is also clearly enunciated by Vyāsa. After declaring that the three-fold mutation is in reality one mutation, Vyāsa says 'the external aspect (*dharma,* etc.) is nothing more than the substance itself'.[73]

Commenting on this, Vācaspati Miśra says that the three-fold mutation is based on the distinction between the substance and the external-aspects (*dharma*), etc. But as referring to the lack of distinction between them it is said that in the strict sense the external-aspects (*dharma,* etc.) are nothing more than the substance (*dharmin*) itself. [74] From this it is evident that the Sāṃkhya recognizes the identity as well as difference between the *dharma* and *dharmin.* Vyāsa further examines an objection of an opponent who, like the Dīpakāra, alleges absolute identity between the *dharma* and *dharmin.* Vācaspati Miśra refers to this opponent as a Buddhist.[75] The latter have always maintained that the *satkāryavāda* results in the identity of cause and effect and consequently in the denial of any action or change.[76] The Dīpakāra here represents this Buddhist thought.

The parallel development of almost identical speculations regarding the nature of a substance and its change in the Sāṃkhya-Yoga and the Vaibhāṣika schools has already been noted by many scholars, notably Stcherbatsky[77] and Poussin.[78] The Sāṃkhya admits one everlasting reality (*prakṛti-dravya*) along with its momentary manifestations. The Vaibhāṣika admits the reality of several distinct elements (*dravya*) potentially existing in the past as well as the future, but becoming manifest only in their efficiency moments, i.e. the present. The four traditional Vaibhāṣika explanations of the relation between a substance and its manifestations given by Dharmatrāta, Ghoṣaka, Vasumitra, and Buddhadeva have all been incorporated and harmonized by Vyāsa in his *Yoga-bhāṣya.*[79] The reality of the past and future is also proved in almost identical words in both the schools. Both admit that the mutations are not occasional, but perpetual. But whereas the Sāṃkhya holds it as the very nature of the substance to undergo these mutations,[80] the Vaibhāṣikas hold that there are external forces like the *saṃskṛta lakṣaṇas,* which bring about a mutation in the substance. The statement of the Dīpakāra that the Vaibhāṣika dharma (*jarā*) is distinct from the *dharmin* (i.e. a *saṃskṛta dharma*), and hence his position is different from the Sāṃkhya, confirms Stcherbatsky's observation that 'when accused of drifting into Sāṃkhya, the Sarvāstivādins justified themselves by pointing to these momentary forces, which saved the Buddhist principle of detached entities'.[81]

The Dīpakāra's use of such terms as *dharmin* and *dharma* respectively for a (*saṃskṛta*) dharma and (*saṃskṛta*) *lakṣaṇa* is also equally significant. It confirms our earlier hypothesis that the category of the *viprayukta-saṃskāras* was designed to accommodate 'qualities' or *guṇas* that qualified the substance (*dravyas*), i.e. non-*viprayukta-dharmas.* Had they been treated only as 'qualities' and, therefore, as mere names given to different aspects of a real dharma, the Sautrāntikas would have admitted them as *prajñapti-dharma.* The Vaibhāṣikas, however, did not stop only at enumerating different 'qualities', but proceeded to make them reals and ended in treating them as *dravyas* or substances.

The contention of the Dīpakāra that without a reduction of its strength (*śakti-hāni*) caused by *jarā,* a dharma will not be affected by *vināśa* (destruction) leads to another Vaibhāṣika theory that *vināśa* of a dharma is caused (*sahetuka*) and not inherent in it.

The Kośakāra deals with this topic in detail while explaining the momentary nature of all phenomena.[82] The Sautrāntika maintains that destruction is not caused. It is an inherent nature of a phenomenon to perish the moment it flashes into existence. It does not depend on any external agency to bring about its destruction. For, if a dharma were not to perish immediately and spontaneously after its birth, it might never perish, even afterwards. The Vaibhāṣika contention that it perishes on account of becoming different (*anyathībhūta*) by the loss of its power (*śakti hāni*) is wrong. For it is a contradiction to say that (a momentary thing) becomes different. A thing cannot be itself and yet appear different from itself. Therefore, destruction is uncaused. Moreover, *vināśa* is merely an absence (*abhāva*). An absence is not a reality, and being unreal it has no function to perform.

The Dīpakāra points out that this Sautrāntika position is not supported either by the scriptures or by reason: destruction of a thing is caused, because it depends on the origination of that thing. It conforms to the law that 'being this, that becomes'. If it were to operate without a cause, it will always exist, and consequently there will be no origination of any dharma.

Nor is destruction a mere non-existence. For the Vaibhāṣikas do not say that a substance is destroyed. It is only the efficiency (*kāritra*) of a substance that is destroyed by *vināśa*. 'What we call destruction', says the Dīpakāra, 'is the non-arising of a (new) activity (in a substance) when its efficiency is confronted by an opposite condition.'[83] Therefore, *vināśa* does not mean merely a non-existence (of a substance). Moreover, existence and non-existence are contingent upon each other. Denial of one means denial of another. If destruction is to be treated as uncaused, origination too will have to be treated similarly. The reasons for holding the origination as caused also obtain in the case of destruction. Hence *vināśa* is *sahetuka*. After advancing these arguments the Dīpakāra quotes the scriptures that support the Vaibhāṣika view: The Lord has said 'one must strive hard to destroy bad states that have arisen'. 'Here a person becomes a killer of life.' 'There are three periodical dissolutions by which the world is destroyed.' Finally it is said 'depending on birth, there arise decay and death'.[84]

It may be noted that these arguments of the Dīpakāra are almost identical with the traditional orthodox Vaibhāṣika views of *ācārya* Saṃghabhadra.[85] The central problem of this controversy rests, perhaps, on the meaning of a *kṣaṇa* and the simultaneous operation of these four incompatible *lakṣaṇas* on a *kṣaṇika* dharma. For the Sautrāntika, a *kṣaṇa* means a moment. For the Vaibhāṣika, however, it means that time which all the four functions, viz. origination, subsistence, decay and destruction take for their accomplishment.[86] Thus a *kṣaṇa* of the Vaibhāṣika corresponds to a *cittakkhaṇa* (mind-moment) of the Theravādins, which is really not a *kṣaṇa* but a unit of three moments.[87] The Dīpakāra does not fully discuss this problem, but from his other arguments on the reality of the *lakṣaṇas,* we can infer that he also subscribed to the same Vaibhāṣika concept of *kṣaṇa.*

NOTES

1. *L'Abhidharma-kośa de Vasubandhu* (tr. L. de la Vallée Poussin), ch. ii, kā. 35-48. Henceforth referred to as *Bhāṣya*.
2. *Sphuṭārthā Abhidharma-kośa-vyākhyā* (ed. U. Woghihara). Henceforth referred to as *Sakv.*
3. *A manual of buddhist philosophy*, I, 161-2.
4. *The central conception of Buddhism*, 23-4.
5. Henceforth referred to as *Dīpa.*
6. Henceforth referred to as *Vṛtti.*
7. See *The central conception of Buddhism*, 20.
8. *Ekuppāda-nirodhā ca ekālambana-vatthukā/ cetoyuttā dvi-paññāsa dhammā cetasikā matā//* (*Abhidhammattha-saṅgaho*, II, 1.)
9. *Pañcabhiḥ smatābhiḥ saṃprayuktāḥ....Tāḥ punar āśrayālambanākāra-kāla-dravyasamatākhyāḥ* (*Vṛtti* on kā. 126).
10. See Poussin's article 'Le bouddhisme et le yoga de Patañjali', *Mélanges Chinois et Bouddhiques*, v, 1937, 223 ff.
11. See Johnston's introduction to his translation of the *Buddha-carita.*
12. *Tad ebhyaś caturbhyaḥ sarvāstivādebhyaḥ sthavira*-Vasumitraḥ *pañcaviṃśati-tattva-nirāsī paramāṇu-saṃcaya-vādonmāthī ca* (*Vṛtti* on kā. 302).
13. *T'oung Pao*, Sér. II, Vol. v, 1904, 269-96.
14. The word *guṇa* occurs in the Pali scriptures only in the sense of 'string, a cord or a strand' (as in the case of *pañca kāma-guṇā*). It is sometimes used to mean a virtue but never in its technical sense of a quality as in the Vaiśeṣika or the Jaina schools.
15. Of these only 23 are enumerated in the *Dhammasaṅgaṇi*. The *hadaya-vatthu* is a later addition by the commentators. See *Aṭṭhasālinī*, iv, 112.
16. Also termed *parinipphanna* and *aparinipphanna* in *Aṭṭhasālinī*, iv, 119. In this connection compare the term *parinipphanna* with the Skt. *pariniṣpanna* (*svabhāva*) of the Yogācāra school.
17. *Catasso dhātuyo, cakkhādīni terasa, kabaḷīkārāhāro cā ti aṭṭhārasavidhaṃ rūpaṃ paricceheda-vikāra-lakkhaṇabhāvaṃ atikkamitvā sabhāveneva pariggahetabbato nipphannaṃ, sesaṃ tabbiparītatāya anipphannaṃ* (*Visuddhimagga*, xiv, 73). See *Aṭṭhasālinī*, iv, 119.
18. *Sabhāvenevā ti rūpassa paricchedo, rūpassa vikāro...ti ādinā aggahetvā attano sabhāveneva...gahetabbato* (*Visuddhimagga-ṭīkā*, pp. 457-8).
19. *Keci panettha, tejādīnaṃ guṇehi rūpādīhi anugayhabhāvato ti kāraṇaṃ vadanti. Te vattabbā : ko panevamāha, rūpādayo tejādīnaṃ guṇā ti?* (*Visuddhimagga*, xiv, 43).
20. This is further confirmed by the description in the commentaries of the *nipphanna* and *anipphanna rūpas*. The *nipphanna-rūpas* alone are called *rūpa-rūpa*, i.e. matter having the characteristic of *ruppana: Nipphanna-rūpaṃ panettha rūpa-rūpaṃ nāma ...* (*Visuddhimagga*, xiv, 77); *Yadettha ... nipphannaṃ ti vuttaṃ rūpaṃ, tadeva rūpa-lakkhaṇa-yogato rūpaṃ-ruppanaṃ rūpaṃ, taṃ etassa atthīti. ... Yadi evaṃ, ākāsadhātu-ādīnaṃ kathaṃ rūpabhāvo ti? Nipphanna-rūpassa paricceda-vikāra-lakkhaṇabhāvato taggatikamevā ti* (*Visuddhimagga-ṭīkā*, p. 460).
21. cf. *Kāyendriya-pradeśa eva hi kaścit strī-puruṣendriyākhyaṃ labhate...* (*Vṛtti* on kā. 73).
22. The Sautrāntikas go still further and enumerate only the four *mahābhūtas* and the four objects as real *rūpa-dharmas*. See *Ālambana-parīkṣā* (Adyar Library, 1942), Appendix D, p. 116.
23. The eleventh dharma of the Vaibhāṣika is *avijñapti* (unmanifested matter)

which the Yogācārins include in their eleventh category of *rūpa*, called *dharma-dhātu-paryāpanna* (matter included under *dharma-dhātu*). For details, see *A manual of Buddhist philosophy*, 118 ff.

24. *Citta-viprayuktā iti citta-grahaṇaṃ citta-samāna-jātīya-pradarśanārtham. Cittam iva cittena ca viprayuktāḥ ity arthaḥ. Kiṃ ca teṣāṃ cittena samāna-jātīyatvam? Yad arūpiṇo 'mī bhavanti. Rūpitvād eva hi viprayuktatve 'pi rūpaṃ na viprayuktatve nāma labhate. Yad vā amīṣāṃ nāma-rūpam iti nāmatvaṃ tat teṣāṃ cittena samāna-jātīyatvam. Caittā api cittena tulya-jātīyāḥ. Te tu cittena sahālambane saṃprayuktās tad viśeṣaṇārthaṃ viprayukta-grahaṇam. Asaṃskṛtam api tat-samāna-jātīyam anālambanatveneti tat-parihārārthaṃ saṃskāra-grahaṇam* (*Sakv.*, pp. 142-3).
25. *Sabbaṃ ca rūpaṃ, asaṃkhatā ca dhātu, ime dhammā citta-vippayuttā* (*Dhammasaṅgaṇi*, 1192).
26. *Pariyuṭṭhānaṃ citta-vippayuttaṃ ti kathā* (*Kathāvatthu*, xiv, 6).
26a. *Kathāvatthu-aṭṭhakathā*, xiv, 6.
27. ibid., xi, 1.
28. *Vātsīputrīya-nayena prāptir anuśayaḥ* (*Sakv.*, p. 442). See my article 'The Sautrāntika theory of *bīja*', *BSOAS*, XXII, 2, 1959.
29. *Tattha yesaṃ jīvitindriyaṃ nāma citta-vippayutto arūpa-dhammo...seyyathāpi* Pubbaseliyā*nañceva* Sammitīyā*nañca* (*Kathāvatthu-aṭṭhakathā*, VIII, 10).
30. Visvabharati Studies (Santiniketan), 17, 1953, p. 130.
31. Visvabharati Studies (Santiniketan), 12, 1950, p. 10. Henceforth referred to as *Asm.*
32. *Saṃkhata-lakkhaṇānīti saṃkhataṃ etanti sañjānana-kāraṇāni nimittāni ... uppādādayo saṃkhata-lakkhaṇā nāma...lakkhaṇaṃ na saṃkhataṃ saṃkhataṃ na lakkhaṇaṃ...* (*Aṅguttara-nikāya-aṭṭhakathā*, II, p. 252). See *Aṭṭhasālinī*, iv, 113-19.
33. *Jāti-jāty-ādayas teṣām te 'ṣṭa-dravyaika-vṛttayaḥ/* (*Abhidharma-kośa*, ii, 47.)
34. *Buddhy-aikatvādi-dhī-hānyai dhātūṃś cāṣṭādaśoktavān/* (*Dīpa*, kā. 6).
35. See S. Mookerji's *Buddhist philosophy of universal flux*, ch. vi.
36. *Sabhāgatā nāma dravyam. Sattvānām ekārtha-ruciḥ-sādṛśya-hetubhūtam. Nikāya-sabhāga ity asya śāstra-saṃjñā. Sā punar abhinnā bhinnā ca. Abhinnā sarva-sattvānāṃ sattva-sabhāgatā. Bhinnā punas teṣām eva sattvānāṃ...bheda-pratiniyama-hetuḥ* (*Vṛtti* on kā. 134).
37. *L'Abhidharma-kośa*, ii, kā. 41.
38. ibid., ii, kā. 46. *Yadi jātam-ity-evam-ādi-buddhi-siddhy-arthaṃ ... jāty-ādayaḥ kalpyante ... ekaṃ ...dve ...mahad aṇu pṛthak saṃyuktaṃ vibhaktaṃ param aparaṃ sad-rūpam iti...ādi-buddhi-siddhy-arthaṃ saṃkhyādayo 'pi Vaiśeṣika-parikalpitā abhuypagantavyāḥ...* (*Sakv.* p. 180).
39. *Hetu-phala-prabandhānupacchede pravṛttir iti prajñaptiḥ. Hetu-phala-āśu-pravṛttau java iti prajñaptiḥ. Hetu-phala-prabandha-pravṛttau kāla iti prajñaptiḥ. Daśasu dikṣu hetu-phala eva deśa iti prajñaptiḥ. Saṃskārāṇāṃ pratyekaśo bhede saṃkhyeti prajñaptiḥ. Hetu-phala-pratyaya-samavadhāne sāmagrīti prajñaptiḥ* (*Asm.*, p. 10). cf. *Prayatnaḥ saṃrambha utsāha iti paryāyāḥ. Vego....niyata-dik-kriyā prabandhahetuḥ. Kālaḥ parāpara-vyatikara-yaugapadyāyaugapadya-cira-kṣipra-pratyayaliṅgaṃ. Dik pūrvāparādipratyaya-liṅgā. Ekādi-vyavahāra-hetuḥ saṃkhyā. Saṃyogaḥ saṃyukta-pratyaya-nimittaṃ* (*Praśastapāda-bhāṣya* on the *Vaiśeṣika-sūtras*).
40. *Hetu-phalaikatye pravṛttau anukrama iti prajñaptiḥ* (*Asm.*, p. 10). cf. *paratvam aparatvaṃ ca parāparābhidhāna-pratyaya-nimittam* (*Praśastapāda-bhāṣya*).
41. *Hetu-phala-nānātve pratiniyama iti prajñaptiḥ. Hetu-phalānurūpye yoga iti prajñaptiḥ* (*Asm.*, p. 10).

42. ibid. Also see the refutation of the Vaibhāṣika theory of the *viprayuktas* in the *Vijñaptimātratāsiddhi;* v. *La Siddhi de Hiüan Tsang* (tr. L. de la Vallée Poussin), I, 53-72.
43. *L'Abhidharma-kośa,* II, kā. 35-48.
44. *Ke punas te viprayuktāḥ saṃskārāḥ?....Nahi vayam eteṣāṁ svabhāvam upalabhāmahe nāpi kṛtyam. Na caite dharmā loke prasiddhā nāpi* Buddha-*vacane....Tad atropavyāhriyate .... Yat tāvat svabhāva-kriyābhāvād iti. Tad atrobhayam abhidhāyiṣyate. Yad api* Buddha-*vacane na paṭhyanta iti. Tatrāpy āpta-vacanaṃ sārvajñaṃ vyāhariṣyate....Ye khalu sarvajña-viṣayā dharmāḥ buddhi-vṛtti-viṣayam āyānty ārya*-Maitreya-*sthavira*-Vasumitr*ācārya*-Aśvaghoṣa-*pramukhānāṃ... tejolpānāṃ stanandhaya-buddhīnām abhidharma-parokṣa-mati-vṛttīnāṃ ca kathaṃ sāndhakāreṣu manassu gocaratām āyāntīti* (*Vṛtti* on kā. 128).
45. *Atra punaḥ Kośakāraḥ pratijānīte sacittikeyaṃ samāpattir iti. Tad etad abauddhīyam* (*Vṛtti* on kā. 136).
46. *Siddhā sabhāgatā. Kośakāraḥ punas tāṃ* Vaiśeṣika-*parikalpita-jāti-padārthena samīkurvan vyaktaṃ pāyasa-vāyasayor varṇasādharmyaṃ paśyatīti* (*Vṛtti* on kā. 134).
47. These three *saṃskāras* have been separately dealt with in my article 'The Vaibhāṣika theory of words and meanings', *BSOAS,* xxii, 1, 1959.
48. *Imāni kho āvuso pañcindriyāni āyuṃ paṭicca tiṭṭhantīti....Āyu usmaṃ paṭicca tiṭṭhatīti....Seyyathāpi...acciṃ paṭicca ābhā paññāyati, ābhaṃ paṭicca acci paññāyati...* (*Majjhima-nikāya,* I, p. 295).
49. *Te ca kho āyu-saṃkhārā abhaviṃsu te vedaniyā dhammā, na-y-idaṃ saññā-vedayita-nirodhaṃ samāpannassa bhikkhuno vuṭṭhānaṃ paññāyetha* (ibid.).
50. *Yadā kho panāvuso imaṃ kāyaṃ tayo dhammā jahanti: āyu usmā ca viññāṇaṃ, athāyaṃ kāyo ujjhito seti yathā kaṭṭhaṃ acetanaṃ ti. ... yvāyaṃ ... mato ... yo cāyaṃ ... saññāvedayita-nirodhaṃ samāpanno, imesaṃ kiṃ nānākaraṇaṃ ti? Yvāyaṃ mato ... tassa ... āyu parikkhīṇo, usmā vūpasantā ... yvāyaṃ ... samāpanno tassa ... āyu aparikkhīṇo, usmā avūpasantā ...* (ibid.).
51. *Katamaṃ taṃ rūpaṃ jīvitindriyaṃ? Yo tesaṃ rūpīnaṃ dhammānaṃ āyu ṭhiti... jīvitaṃ...*(*Dhammasaṅgaṇi,* 635). *Yo tesaṃ arūpīnaṃ dhammānaṃ āyu...jīvitaṃ* (ibid., 19).
52. *Tattha yesaṃ jīvitindriyaṃ nāma citta-vippayutto arūpa-dhammo, tasmā rūpa-jīvitindriyaṃ natthīti laddhi, seyyathāpi* Pubbaseliyāna*ñceva* Sammitīyā*naṃ ca* (*Kathāvatthu-aṭṭhakathā,* viii, 10).
53. *Vṛtti* on kā. 138.
54. *Na cānyad indriyaṃ vipākajaṃ traidhātuka-vyāpy asti yaj janma-prabandhāvicchedena vartamānaṃ gati-prajñapty-upādānaṃ syāt, anyatra jīvitendriyāt....Āgamas tāvad ayaṃ:*
'Āyur ūṣmā' tha vijñānaṃ yadā kāyaṃ jahaty amī/
apaviddhas tadā śete yathā kāṣṭam acetanam//' (ibid.)
55. *Sarvaṃ hi jīvitendriyaṃ kāma-dhātāv avaśyaṃ kāyendriyoṣma-sahacariṣṇu. Tattv avaśyaṃ vijñāna-sahavarti nāpi cakṣurādīndriya-sahavarti. Rūpa-dhātau tu sarvaṃ kāyādi-pañcendriya-sahavarti. Na tv avaśyaṃ citta-sahacariṣṇu. Ārūpya-dhātau tu sarvaṃ vijñāna-sahavarti, anyatra nirodha-samāpatteḥ* (ibid.).
56. *L'Abhidharma-kośa,* ch. ii, kā. 45; *Sakv.*, p. 167.
57. *Jīvitendriyaṃ gati-prajñapty-upādānam astīti dravyam...* (*Vṛtti* on kā. 138).
58. See *L'Abhidharma-kośa,* ch. ii, kā. 44.
59. See my article 'Buddha's prolongation of life', *BSOAS,* XXI, 2, 1958.
60. *Trīṇīmāni bhikṣavaḥ saṃskṛtasya saṃskṛta-lakṣaṇāni. Katamāni trīṇi? Saṃskṛtasya....*

utpādo 'pi prajñāyate, vyayo..., sthity-anyathātvam apīti (*Sakv.*, p. 171). cf. *Tīnimāni...saṃkhatassa saṃkhata-lakkhaṇāni...uppādo paññāyati, vayo paññāyati, ṭhitassa aññathattaṃ paññāyati...*(*Aṅg.-nikāya*, I, p. 152).

61. *Jātir ādiḥ pravāhasya vyayac chedaḥ sthitis tu saḥ/ sthity-anyathātvaṃ tasyaiva pūrvāpara-viśiṣṭatā//* (*Sakv.*, p. 175.)
62. *L'Abhidharma-kośa*, ch. ii, kā. 47.
63. *Etāni khalu catvāri saṃskṛta-lakṣaṇāni bhagavatā 'bhidharme 'bhihitāni. Etāny eva vineya-prayojanavaśāt sūtre sthity-anyathātvam ekīkṛtya trīṇy uktāni* (*Vṛtti* on kā. 139).
64. *Uppādo ti jāti, vayo ti bhedo, ṭhitassa aññathattaṃ nāma jarā...* (*Aṅg.-nikāya-aṭṭhakathā*, II, p. 152).
65. *Ācaya-lakkhaṇo rūpassa upacayo,...pavatti-lakkhaṇā rūpassa santati...ubhayampetaṃ jāti-rūpassevādhivacanaṃ...* (*Visuddhimagga*, xiv, 66). See *Dhammasaṅgaṇi*, 643.
66. *Sakv.*, p. 176.
67. ibid.
68. *Yadi hi dharmasya sthitir na syāt, tasyātmany avasthitasya hetvākhyaḥ śakti-prabhāva-viśeṣo na syāt...* (*Vṛtti* on kā. 139).
69. *Naitad yuktam uktaṃ pariṇāma-doṣa-prasaṃgāt....bhavatā Sāṃkhyīyaḥ pariṇāmo 'bhuypagato bhavati* (ibid.).
70. *Anya eva hi no jarākhyo dharmo, anyaś ca dharmī.* Sāṃkhyasya *tv avasthitasya dharmiṇaḥ svātmabhūtasya dharmāntarasyotsargaḥ svātmabhūtasya cotpādaḥ pariṇāma iti* (*Vṛtti* on kā. 140).
71. *Etena bhūtendriyeṣu dharma-lakṣaṇa-avasthā-pariṇāmā vyākhyātāḥ* (*Yoga-sūtra*, iii, 13).
72. *Atha ko 'yaṃ pariṇāmo 'vasthitasya dravyasya pūrva-dharma-nivṛttau dharmāntarotpattiḥ pariṇāma iti* (*Yoga-sūtra-bhāṣya*, iii, 13).
73. *Paramārthatas tv eka eva pariṇāmo dharmi-svarūpa-mātro hi dharmaḥ...*(ibid.).
74. *So 'yam evaṃvidho bhūtendriya-pariṇāmo dharmiṇo dharma-lakṣaṇāvasthānāṃ bhedam āśṛtyāha. 'Paramārthatas tv' iti tu śabdo bheda-pakṣād viśinaṣṭi pāramārthikatvam asya jñāpyate...*(*Tattva-vaiśāradī*, iii, 13). See *Pātañjala-sūtrāṇi*, Bombay Sanskrit Series, XLVI.
75. *Nanu dharmiṇām dharmāṇām abhinnatve dharmiṇo 'dhvanāṃ ca bhede dharmiṇo 'nanyatvena dharmeṇāpīha dharmivad bhavitavyam ity ata āha...ekānta-vādinaṃ Bauddham utthāpayati* (ibid.).
76. See T.R.V. Murti, *The central philosophy of Buddhism*, 133-4, 168 ff.
77. *The central conception of Buddhism*, pp. 27, 47, notes, and 'The *dharmas* of the Buddhists and the *guṇas* of the Sāṃkhyas', *Indian Historical Quarterly*, x, 1934, 737-60.
78. 'Documents d'Abhidharma (Sarvāstivāda)', *Mélanges Chinoïs et Bouddhiques*, V, 1937, 1-158.
79. See *Yoga-sūtra-bhāṣya*, iii, 13 and 15.
80. *Guṇa-svābhāvyaṃ tu pravṛtti-kāraṇam uktaṃ guṇānām iti* (ibid.).
81. *The central conception of Buddhism*, 45.
82. *L'Abhidharma-kośa*, ch. ii, kā. 2-3. For full details and other Ābhidharmika references on this controversy, see 'Documents d'Abhidharma (Sarvāstivāda)', op. cit., 148-58.
83. *Kāritra-mātra-nāśāc ca. Viruddha-pratyaya-sānnidhye kriyā-mātraṃ nodeti, naśyati* (*Vṛtti* on kā. 141).
84. *'Utpannānām akuśalānāṃ dharmāṇāṃ nirodhāya', 'Ihaikatīyaḥ prāṇātipātiko bhavati', 'Tisraḥ saṃvartanyo...yāvac chubha-kṛtsnā vinaśyante', 'Jāti-pratyayaṃ jarā-maraṇam'...* (ibid.).

85. 'Documents d' Abhidharma (Sarvāstivāda)', op. cit., 149.
86. *Kṣaṇa-trayāvasthānāt* kṣaṇikatvaṃ bādhyata *iti.* Eṣa eva hi naḥ kṣaṇa *iti* kārya-parisamāpti-lakṣaṇo *na tūtpatty-anaṃtara-vināśa-lakṣaṇa ity arthaḥ* (*Sakv.*, p. 178). See *The central conception of Buddhism,* p. 41, notes, and 'Documents d'Abhidharma (Sarvāstivāda)', op. cit., 135-58.
87. *Uppāda-ṭṭhiti-bhaṅgavasena khaṇa-ttayaṃ eka-citta-kkhaṇaṃ nāma* (*Abhidhammattha-saṅgaho,* iv, 8).

Additional reading: *Disputed Dharmas: Early Buddhist Theories on Existence.* (An Annotated Translation of the Section on Factors Dissociated from Thought from Saṅghabhadra's *Nyāyānusāra*), by Collett Cox. Studia Philologica Buddhica Monograph Series XI, The International Institute for Buddhist Studies, Tokyo, 1995.

CHAPTER 15

*Abhidharmadīpa**

The palm-leaf manuscript of the *Abhidharma-dīpa* was discovered in Tibet by Rahul Sankrityayana in the year 1937. He brought the photographs of this MS. which are preserved in the K.P. Jayaswal Research Institute, Patna.[1]

The MS. is incomplete. The last folio is numbered 150. Of these only 62 folios have come down to us. The MS. contains two works, viz., the metrical *Abhidharma-dīpa* (here referred to as *Dīpa*) and a prose commentary on it known as the *Vibhāṣā-prabhā-vṛtti* (here referred to as *Vṛtti*).

The kārikā text, viz., the *Dīpa,* closely follows both in the contents and in presentation its counterpart, the *Abhidharmakośa* (here referred to as *Kośa*) of Vasubandhu. The eight *Adhyāyas* of the *Dīpa* correspond to the eight *Kośasthānas* of the *Kośa.* The number of the kārikās found in the extant *Dīpa* is 597. Of these a large number (about 300) correspond, almost one for one and sometimes word for word, to the kārikās of the *Kośa.* The commentary on the *Dīpa,* the *Vṛtti,* is also written more or less on the pattern of the *Abhidharma-kośa-Bhāṣya* (here referred to as *Bhāṣya*) of Vasubandu. It will be evident from the passages quoted below that this commentary was written solely for presenting the orthodox Vaibhāṣika viewpoint, encountering the criticisms levelled against it by the Kośakāra in his *Bhāṣya.* Although criticising it, the *Vṛtti,* in most parts, is an imitation of the *Bhāṣya.* It borrows about fifty large passages from the latter and presents the subject-matter in

*This article was originally published in *Encyclopaedia of Buddhism,* Fascicule: A-Aca, ed. G.P. Malalasekera, (Colombo: Ministry of Cultural Affairs, The Government of Sri Lanka, 1961), pp. 55-57. Reprinted with kind permission of the Editor-in-Chief, *Encyclopaedia of Buddhism.*

more or less identical words. At the end of the *Kośa,* Vasubandhu claims that he composed it in conformity with the Kāśmīra-Vaibhāṣika school.[2] But his *Bhāṣya* reveals that his real affiliation was with the Sautrāntika. He often uses the adverb *kila* to show his disagreement with the Vaibhāṣika view. On almost all controversial points between the two, he openly favours the Sautrāntika view-point. In his characteristically powerful style, Vasubandhu critically examines the *dravyavāda* of the Vaibhāṣikas, accuses them of being literalists, ridicules their dogmatism and compares them with such heretical schools as the Sāṅkhya and Vaiśeṣika. Yaśomitra rightly observes that Vasubandhu belongs to the Sautrāntika school.[3]

We learn from Paramārtha's 'Life of Vasubandhu'[4] that Ācārya Saṅghabhadra, a contemporary Vaibhāṣika, wrote two commentaries on the *Kośa,* called *Nyāyānusāra* and *Samaya-pradīpikā,* in order to present the orthodox Vaibhāṣika view and to correct the Kośakāra of his Sautrāntika bias. These works are available only in their Chinese translations. No other work written against the Kośakāra has come down to us. The discovery of the *Dīpa* (with its *Vṛtti*), therefore, is of great value as a sole surviving original work of the orthodox Vaibhāṣika school. Being an imitation of the *Kośa* (and the *Bhāṣya*) it does not add much to the subject-matter relating to the Abhidharma of the Sarvāstivāda school. But its references to the Kośakāra shed abundant light on the major points of dispute between the Sautrāntika and the Vaibhāṣika, and also on certain controversial aspects of the life of the Kośakāra Vasubandhu.

The extant *Vṛtti* contains the following sixteen hostile references to the Kośakāra:—

(1) *Kośakāras tvāha—anuśayānuśayanāt sāsravāḥ. tad etad abrahma (Fol. 32b).*

(2) *Tatra yad uktaṃ Kośakāreṇa—' kim idaṃ ākāśaṃ khādyate. sāmagryāṃ hi satyāṃ dṛṣṭam ity upacāraḥ pravartate. tatra kaḥ paśyati' iti. tad atra tena bhadantena sāmagryaṅga-kriyā (paharaṇaṃ?) kriyate. Abhidharma-sammohāṅka-sthānenātmāpy aṅkito bhavaty ayoga-śūnyatā-prapātābhimukhyatvaṃ pradarśitam iti (Fol. 35b).*

(3) *Kośakṛd ācaṣṭe—na hy atra kiñcit phalaṃ utprekṣyata iti. taṃ pratīdaṃ phalaṃ ādarśyate (Fol. 37a).*

(4) *Idam idānīm Abhidharma-sarvasvaṃ Kośakāraka-smṛti-gocarātītaṃ vaktavyam (Fol. 37b).*

(5) *Kośakārādayaḥ punar āhuḥ—'svārthopalabdhāv eva cakṣurādīnāṃ pañcānāṃ ādhipatyam'. tad etad Vaibhāṣikīyam eva kiñcid gṛhītam. nātra kiñcit Kośakārasya svaka-darśanam (Fol. 39a).*

(6) *Kośakāras tvāha—' sarvasūkṣmo rūpa-saṃghātaḥ paramāṇur' iti. tena saṃghāta-vyatiriktaṃ rūpam anyad vaktavyam (Fol. 43b).*

(7) *Tad idam atisāhasaṃ vartate yad viruddhayor api dvayor dharmayor ekatra citte samavadhānaṃ pratijñāyate. na hy etal loke driṣṭaṃ....iti Kośakāraḥ....tad idam andha-vilāsinī-kaṭākṣa-guṇotkīrtaṇa-kalpaṃ codyam ārbhyate (Fol. 45a).*

(8) *Siddhā sabhāgatā. Kośakāraḥ punas tāṃ Vaiśeṣika-parikalpita-jāti-padārthena samīkurvan vyaktaṃ pāyasa-vāyasayor varṇa-sādharmyaṃ paśyatīti (Fol. 47a).*

(9) *Atra punaḥ Kośakāraḥ pratijānīte—' sacittikeyaṃ samāpattiḥ' iti ....tad etad abauddhīyam (Fol. 47a).*

(10) *'samādhi-balena karmajaṃ jīvitāvedhaṃ nirvartyāyuḥ saṃskārādhishṭhānajam, āyur na vipākaḥ' iti Kośakāraḥ. tatra kim uttaram iti? na tatrāvaśyam uttaraṃ vaktavyam. yasmān naitat Sūtre' vatarati, Vinaye na saṃdṛśyate, dharmatāṃ ca vilomyati. tasmād bāla-vacanavad adhyupekṣyam etat..... tasmād Vaitulikaśāstra-praveśa-dvāram ārabdhaṃ tena bhadantenety adhyupekṣyam etat (Fol. 49a).*

(11) *Tasmāt pūrvokta-lakṣaṇa eva bhikṣur na yathāha Kośakāraḥ (Fol. 92b).*

(12) *'Abhidhyādaya eva karma-svabhāvāni' iti Sthiti-bhāgīyāh .... .Kośakāraḥ—'kotra doṣaḥ' ..... Sāṃkhyīyadarśanam abhyupagataṃ syāt (Fol. 94b).*

(13) *'Sūkṣmaṃ kuśala-dharma-bījaṃ tasminn akuśale cetasy avasthitaṃ yataḥ punaḥ pratyaya-sāmagrī-sannidhāne sati kuśalaṃ cittam utpadyate' iti Kośakāraḥ. yuktyāgama-virodhāt tan neti Dīpakāraḥ (Fol. 96b).*

(14) *'Evaṃ tu sādhu yathā Dārṣṭāntikānām' iti Kośakāraḥ .... .tad etat Sautrāntikair antargataṃ Buddha-vacana-nīti-śravaṇa-kausīdyam āvirbhāvyate (Fol. 104a).*

(15) *Tad atra Kośakāraḥ praśnayati—' ko vighnaḥ'. . . . .tatra vayaṃ prativadmaḥ—. . . . 'durbodhā khalu dharmatā' . . . . . (Fol. 111b).*

(16) *Atra Sarvāsti-vāda-vibhraṣṭir Vaituliko nirāha —vayam api trīn svabhāvān parikalpayiṣyāmaḥ. tasmai prativaktavyaṃ—. . . .*

.. *it etad aparam adhva-saṃmohāṅkanā-sthānaṃ Kośakārasyeti (Fol. 112a).*

Of these Nos. (3) and (4) refer to omissions of certain topics by the Kośakāra in his *Bhāṣya.* Nos. (2) and (5) deal with certain aspects of the Sautrāntika theory of perception. No. (6) deals with the Kośakāra's definition of *paramāṇu.* No. (7) refers to a controversy about the co-operation of *vitarka* and *vicāra* in a single moment of consciousness. Nos. (8), (9) and (10) deal with certain items of the much debated Vaibhāṣika categories called *citta-viprayukta-saṃskāras.* Nos. (1), (13) and (14) have a bearing on the Sautrāntika theory of *bīja* (seed). The last two references, Nos. (15) and (16), deal with the fundamental Vaibhāṣika doctrine of the reality of Three Times, i.e., the Sarvāstivāda.

It may be noted that these passages are all hostile and aim at exposing Vasubandhu's 'un-buddhistic' views. He is not only censured for his ignorance of the Abhidharma and his Sautrāntika leanings, but is also accused of entering the portals of Mahāyāna, of accepting the Vaitulika Śāstra and of following the *ayogaśūnyatā-vāda.* Finally, he is called an apostate from the Sarvāstivāda, and an advocate of the *trisvabhāva-vāda.* This doctrine is contained in Vasubandhu's *Tri-svabhāvanirdeśa,* a work of the Yogācāra-vijñānavāda school. All these references seem to allude to Kośakāra Vasubandhu's conversion to Mahāyāna,[5] accounts of which are preserved in Paramārtha's Life of Vasubandhu.

The name of the author of the *Dīpa* is not known. The *Vṛtti* calls him Dīpakāra. It also refers to his other work called *Tattva-saptati,* which is unknown to us. It may have been written on the model of the *Paramārtha-saptatikā* of Vasubandhu. From the internal evidence it would appear that the *Dīpa* as well as the *Vṛtti* were written by one and the same ācārya as in the case of the *Kośa* and *Bhāṣya.* The *Vṛtti* refers only to seven eminent Buddhists, viz., Aśvaghoṣa, (Ārya) Maitreya, Dharmatrāta, Ghoṣaka, Vasumitra, Buddhadeva and Kumāralāta. Saṅghabhadra is not mentioned, but several views of the Dīpakāra are identical with his views. We, therefore, can ascribe this work either to Saṅghabhadra or to one of his disciples, particularly Vimalamitra, who is said to have entertained a desire to write such śāstras "as will cause the learned men of Jambudvīpa to forget the name of the Great Vehicle and destroy the fame of Vasubandhu" and consequently to have "fallen into the deepest hell".[6]

NOTES

1. I am grateful to the K.P. Jayaswal Research Institute for entrusting me with the work of editing this MS. which has now been published in the Tibetan Sanskrit Works Series, Patna.
2. *Kāśmīra-Vaibhāṣika-niti-siddhaḥ prāyo mayā'yaṃ kathito'bhidharmaḥ*: *Kośa*. VIII. 40ab.
3. *Sautrāntika-pākṣikastvayam ācāryo nainam arthaṃ prayacchati*: *Spuṭārthā Vyākhyā*, p. 26.
4. By J. Takakusu, *T'oung Pao*, Serie II, Vol. V, 269-96.
5. For controversies on this point, see my article 'On the Theory of Two Vasubandhus" in the *BSOAS* 1958, xxi/i, pp. 48-53.
6. S. Beal: *Buddhist Records of the Western World*, I, pp. 196-7.

Additional articles on this topic:

1. "L'auteur de l' Abhidharmadīpa" by J.W. de Jong, in *T'ong Pao* lii (1966), p. 306.
2. "The Date of the Authorship of the *Abhidharmadīpavibhāṣāprabhāvṛtti*" by Kenyo Mitomo, pp. 676-88 in *Studies in Buddhology: A Collection of Articles in Honour of Professor Zuiryu Nakamura's Seventieth Birthday*, Shunjū-sha, Tokyo, 1985.

CHAPTER 16

Prajñā and *Dṛṣṭi* in the Vaibhāṣika Abhidharma*

The stress laid in Prajñāpāramitā texts upon the eradication of ignorance (*avidyā*) or attainment of perfect insight (*prajñā*) is of course well-known, often being cited as a distinguishing mark of that body of literature. Little has been said, however, about the concept of *prajñā* as it occurs among the so-called Hīnayāna doctrines, perhaps due to the generally held view that its role therein was a relatively unimportant one. Such a view is not, however, borne out by the textual evidence. Theravādin works, for example, refer to the Abhidharma teachings as *adhipaññāsikkhā*, "instruction in the highest insight;" similarly, Vasubandhu's opening remarks in his *Abhidharmakośa* define the very term *abhidharma* as *amalā* ("completely pure") *prajñā*. It must be admitted, furthermore, that in spite of the great attention paid to the subject by the authors of the Prajñāpāramitā materials, the precise meaning of *prajñā* itself remains obscure; one sometimes feels that nothing definite can be said beyond the statement that *prajñā* is something which was attained by the Buddha and is attainable by the bodhisattvas. Strangely enough, certain Hīnayāna materials are perhaps more useful in this regard than are their Mahāyāna counterparts. We will not claim here that these earlier sources provide complete clarification of the *prajñā* issue. It does seem to be true, however, that some investigation among Hīnayāna texts, supple-

*This article was originally published in *Prajñāpāramitā and Related Systems: Studies in Honour of E. Conze*, ed. L. Lancaster, Berkeley Buddhist Studies Series, (Berkeley: University of California, 1977), pp. 403-415. Reprinted with kind permission of The Regents of the University of California.

mented by a reasonable degree of inference, may well add greatly to our understanding of what the Buddhist *prajñā* is and is not. Light may be cast, moreover, upon heretofore unsuspected similarities between doctrines of the Hīnayānist Vaibhāṣika school and those of the Mahāyāna tradition.

Any discussion of *prajñā* and *avidyā* must begin by making clear precisely what is the object upon which these radically opposed modes of awareness are focused. Probably all Buddhist schools would designate this object as "the four noble truths," this expression here being a technical term for "things as they really are." Given that knowing "things as they really are" or failing to do so spells the difference between salvation and eons of suffering, we can see that the spiritual stakes here are of the highest order. Thus it is no surprise that the terms under discussion should have been subject to the closest scrutiny and generated a great deal of controversy among Buddhist thinkers. Consider for example, the following summary of certain points made in Chapter Three of the *Abhidharmakośabhāṣya*:[1]

> What is *avidyā?* Is it simply that which is not *vidyā?* Obviously not, for if so then even the eye and other sense-organs, for instance, would have to be called *avidyā*. Is it then the absence of *vidyā?* No, because in that case it would be nothing but an absence, i.e. not a positive existent (*dharma*). And such a theory cannot be accepted, for *avidyā* has time and again been referred to in the Sūtras as being a *dharma,* an adversary of *vidyā* which stands on its own. The (negative) prefix *a-* in *avidyā* is to be understood in the same way as that in *amitra,* which means "an enemy," not just "the absence of a friend." This must be so, for the term *avidyā* appears in various lists of *akuśala* ("unwholesome") *dharmas.* It cannot be considered merely a negative term showing the absence of something else; it must be understood as a positive *dharma.* (Someone else maintains, however, that) while the term *avidyā* does appear in the Sūtras, it is used there in a metaphorical sense, indicating not an absence of *vidyā* but rather a kind of defiled or wrong awareness (*kuvidyā*). Such expressions are common; a bad son (*kuputra*), for example, is often referred to as *aputra,* or an unfaithful wife (*kubhāryā*) as *abhāryā.* Thus, *avidyā* is nothing but *kuprajñā* ("wrong insight," here equivalent to *kuvidyā*). (The

Vaibhāṣika position is now given:) This cannot be, for *kuprajñā* is not *avidyā;* in fact it (i.e. *kuprajñā*) is nothing but a *dṛṣṭi* ("wrong view").

This exchange is not only interesting as an example of the content of the *Kośabhāṣya* and its style of argumentation; the final Vaibhāṣika remark, although delivered in a rather offhand manner, is in fact of great importance to our present investigation. First, in order to understand the Vaibhāṣika's point, we must recall the following tenets of the Abhidharma system: *Dṛṣṭi*[2], which refers most particularly to belief in the false notion of a permanent self, is destroyed by attainment of the *darśanamārga,* a moment of great insight which irrevocably establishes the aspirant upon the Buddhist path; *avidyā,* on the other hand, persists beyond the *darśanamārga,* eventually being overcome only at the level of arhatship through the extended meditational practices of the *bhāvanāmārga.*[3] It is clear that in this system *dṛṣṭi* and *avidyā* cannot be identical; thus, by equating *kuprajñā* with the former, the Vaibhāṣika denies his opponent's view.

Bearing this equation in mind for a moment, let us think a bit more about the term *dṛṣṭi* itself. One of the hallmarks of the Vaibhāṣika system is its enumeration of seventy-five *dharmas,*[4] a collection which supposedly comprises the totality of "reals" (i.e. existent-categories) in the universe. It is a characteristic of this list that many of the *dharmas* included thereon would be classified as "process" or "description" rather than "existent" by thinkers of other schools; in other words, the Vaibhāṣikas do not suffer from any tendency to "leave things out" simply because their identity as *dharmas* might be questionable. Thus it comes as no small surprise to the student of Vaibhāṣika thought to discover that *dṛṣṭi,* which plays such an important role in Buddhist soteriology, *does not appear* among the seventy-five *dharmas.* This is especially strange in light of the Vaibhāṣika doctrine that *dṛṣṭi,* following its destruction by the *darśanamārga,* is replaced by an *asaṃskṛta dharma* known as *pratisaṃkhyānirodha*[5] ("cessation resulting from the application of knowledge"). Now there are said to be several such *nirodhas,* special unconditioned "blanks" which correspond one-to-one with the six *anuśaya*-factors that they forever replace, viz. *vicikitsā, rāga, pratigha, māna, avidyā,* and *dṛṣṭi* itself. For some reason all of these six appear on the Vaibhāṣika *dharma* list except *dṛṣṭi.* Hence the Vaibhāṣikas might seem to have inadvertently committed an omission which calls the consistency of their whole schema into question. (This omission, strangely enough, elicits no comment from either Vasubandhu or Yaśomitra; such Abhidharma scholars as Stcherbatsky, moreover, have apparently failed to notice it.) Even the Theravādins, who are free of the *pratisaṃkhyānirodha* doctrine and thus have no pressing need to make *dṛṣṭi* a *dharma,* have seen fit to do so. It will not suffice, however, to simply suggest a Vaibhāṣika oversight here. Rather, we should assume a definite purpose in their manner of presentation, and thus seek to discover precisely what *dṛṣṭi* is understood to be and how this is connected to other aspects of Vaibhāṣika doctrine.

Returning to the passage cited above, a partial solution appears immediately: *dṛṣṭi* is for the Vaibhāṣikas a *type of prajñā* (viz. *kuprajñā*), and since *prajñā* already has a place among the *dharmas,* no new category need be created for *dṛṣṭi.* [6] But this of course means that the term *prajñā* itself cannot refer to a single kind of entity; it must have (at least) two varieties.

The situation is complicated still further when we examine the Vaibhāṣika classification of certain *dharmas* as *mahābhūmika,* "found in all moments of consciousness." The *dharmas* which fall into this category are given as follows: *vedanā* ("feelings"), *cetanā* ("will"), *saṃjñā* ("concepts"), *chanda* ("desire"), *sparśa* ("contact" "sensation"), *smṛti* ("memory"), *manaskāra* ("attention"), *adhimokṣa* ("inclination"), *samādhi* ("concentration"), and *prajñā.*[7] The inclusion of *prajñā* here seems very odd, for it means that even those mind-moments characterized by the presence of *avidyā* must contain the supposedly antithetical *prajñā* element. Even more significant, it suggests that *prajñā* is not something which must be *attained;* it is always present regardless of one's state of purity or defilement. The Theravādins avoid such difficulties by placing *prajñā* among twenty-five wholesome *caitasikas* found only in a few particular *cittas* ("mind-moments") and never in conjunction with *avidyā* (=*moha*)[8]. Similarly, Vasubandhu himself apparently did not agree with the Vaibhāṣika classification; one of his independent works, called *Pañcaskandhaprakaraṇa,*[9] groups *prajñā* with the *pratiniyataviṣayas, dharmas* associated only with certain *cittas* and then only when these are focused upon one of a given set of objects.

The Vaibhāṣikas themselves must have been aware of the problems accruing to their categorization of *prajñā* as a *mahābhūmika-dharma.* These problems can be circumvented, however, if *prajñā* is taken in a generic rather than specific sense, i.e. as a label designating two or more related but distinguishable entities. We have already seen this interpretation implied by the identification of *kuprajñā* with *dṛṣṭi,* above. The Vaibhāṣikas' further inclusion of *prajñā* among their "universal" *dharmas* leaves little room for doubt that such was indeed their understanding of the term.

How, then, shall we understand the relationship between *kuprajñā* and *prajñā?* In a similar context (viz. the discussion of *mithyāsamādhi* vs. *samādhi*), Yaśomitra uses the analogy of a rotten seed and a good seed; both are "seeds," and yet there is a definite difference between them.[10] At another point in the text, where *dṛṣṭi* is defined by Vasubandhu as *prajñāviśeṣa,* ("a special kind of *prajñā*"), Yaśomitra adds the following:

> *santīrikā yā prajñā, sā dṛṣṭiḥ* ("*dṛṣṭi* is that kind of *prajñā* which involves judgement").[11]

Our translation of the word *santīrikā* ("involving judgement") requires some expansion here. This seems to have been a Buddhist technical term which, along with the related *santīraṇa,*[12] denoted that stage of the cognitive process which followed perception and which comprised the making of discriminative decisions, i.e. "this is (an) x as opposed to (a) y." Now, it will be immediately apparent that the decision or judgement arrived at may be either incorrect or correct. In the former case we would have an example of *mithyādṛṣṭi,* "inaccurate view;" such views may be of various types, but as we have suggested earlier the term most often implies *satkāyadṛṣṭi,* belief in a permanent soul. (This is the most pernicious, hence most important, of *mithyādṛṣṭis.*) If, on the other hand, one's judgement is correct, i.e. made in accord with the Buddha's teachings ("that thing is nothing but the five *skandhas;* it is characterized by suffering; it is impermanent;" etc.), we have a *samyakdṛṣṭi,* "accurate view."

Lest some confusion arise here, we should point out the rather different use of these terms by Theravādin writers. They understand *dṛṣṭi,* first of all, only in the restricted sense of what has been called *mithyā-dṛṣṭi* above. *Samyakdṛṣṭi,* on the other hand, seems to be understood as the absence of *inaccurate* views, but not of *all* views. It is considered, moreover, the highest form of insight possible, the functional equivalent of *prajñā*.[13] This is very interesting, for it means that in this system there is no difference between the insight of the stream-winner (*srotāpanna*) and that of the *arhat;* both have experienced the *darśanamārga* and thus eliminated all but accurate views. The distinction between these two levels of the path, therefore, is here one of defilements overcome rather than of understanding attained.

Returning to the Vaibhāṣikas, it is obvious that they have gone beyond the simple Theravādin breakdown of cognition into "inaccurate" and "accurate" modes; as we have seen, Yaśomitra classifies *all* views based on decision making, regardless of their accuracy, as *dṛṣṭi* or *kuprajñā*. His notion of *santīrikaprajñā,* moreover, leaves open the possibility of another type of *prajñā* which is *asantīrikā,* totally free from any judgement whatsoever. This possibility is made explicit by Vasubandhu in the beginning of the seventh Kośasthāna; there he says that all *dṛṣṭis* are forms of knowledge (*jñāna*), but not all forms of knowledge are *dṛṣṭis,* and that those which are not can be described as "devoid of judgement" (*asantīraṇa*) and "devoid of investigation" (*aparimārgaṇa*). The *asantīraṇa-aparimārgaṇa* category, of course, refers to (pure) *prajñā* as opposed to *kuprajñā*[14].

With these distinctions in mind, it is possible to understand the otherwise perplexing role of *avidyā* in the Vaibhāṣika system. First, we can see that any instance of *avidyā* and *prajñā* coexisting in the same mind-moment must involve only *kuprajñā,* i.e. *dṛṣṭi,* for this factor is *not antithetical* to *avidyā.* Second, the idea that *avidyā* persists even after *dṛṣṭis* are destroyed by the *darśanamārga* makes sense when it is recalled that not all *dṛṣṭis,* but only those of the *mithyā* variety, are so destroyed. Thus, during the practice of the *bhāvanāmārga* the aspirant's consciousness is characterized both by *avidyā* and by the presence of *samyakdṛṣṭi;* the latter, though immeasurably *better* than *mithyādṛṣṭi,* is still a form of *kuprajñā.*

This brief discussion, growing out of the Vaibhāṣikas' "omission" of *dṛṣṭi* from their *dharma* list, has now led us back to our original field of inquiry: the Vaibhāṣika concept of pure *prajñā* itself. We have noted above Vasubandhu's reference to certain types of knowledge (*jñāna*) which are not *dṛṣṭis.* Such knowledges are two in number: *kṣayajñāna* ("knowledge of cessation") and *anutpādajñāna* ("knowledge of non-arising").[15] These are attained when, through the meditational disciplines of the *bhāvanāmārga,* the mind becomes totally free of discriminatory judgements, or, as later Mahāyāna texts would have it, of "concept formation" (*vikalpa*). *Samyakdṛṣṭi* and *avidyā,* in other words, are overcome simultaneously. (Indeed, it is not unreasonable to suggest that the investigative and judgemental functions of the former comprise nothing less than the sufficient conditions for existence of the latter.) Once this has taken place, there arises knowledge of the fact that all the *anuśayas* which remained after the *darśanamārga,* (viz. *rāga, pratigha,* and *māna,* in addition to *avidyā*) have now ceased to exist, and also that they will never arise again. Arhatship is thus achieved; the mind retains only a sort of "pure awareness" (*pratyavekṣaṇamātram*).[16]

Theravādins, as noted above, seem never to have considered this higher, non-discriminative level of *prajñā;* they simply equated the term with their version of *samyakdṛṣṭi.* But this means, as we have also seen, that the highest form of insight arises *prior* to the *bhāvanāmārga.* Even Theravādins themselves seem to have felt somewhat uncomfortable with this interpretation, for it raises serious questions about the very *raison d'etre* of the *samyakdṛṣṭi* (which is, after all, supposedly a functional *dharma*). The point is debated in the *Aṭṭhasālinī* in such terms as these:[17]

> If all sixty-two *dṛṣṭis* are left behind by the first path (i.e. the *darśanamārga*), there are none to be overcome by the three higher paths (i.e. the *bhāvanāmārga*). So how would you explain the purpose of *samyakdṛṣṭi* there? (The Theravādin says:) We would still call it *samyakdṛṣṭi,* in the same way that a medicine is still called by that name even when there is no poison against which it may be used. (The opponent suggests:) In that case it is nothing but a name, a totally non-functional thing. And if that is so, the limbs of the path (*mārgāṅga*) are not complete (i.e. if a *dharma* is mentioned in *sūtra* as an essential element of the path, as *samyakdṛṣṭi* is, it must be functional).

Pressed in this manner, the Theravādins offered a rather unconvincing explanation, namely that *māna* ("egocentrism"), one of the *anuśayas* not destroyed by the *darśanamārga,* takes the place of *dṛṣṭi* after the latter's removal; *māna,* in other words, takes over the role of *dṛṣṭi* as a "defiling element to be overcome by *samyakdṛṣṭi,* thereby giving *samyakdṛṣṭi* "something to do" on the path from stream-winner to *arhat.*[18] This suggestion is probably based upon the Pali Abhidharma doctrine that *māna* and *dṛṣṭi* never occur in the same *citta,*[19] perhaps because their respective functions (being both centered on ego) are similar enough so that the presence of one makes that of the other superfluous. Whether or not *māna* is indeed a proper "replacement" for *dṛṣṭi* as the object of *samyakdṛṣṭi's* "medicinal" effects, its use as such does restore some measure of consistency to the Theravādin system.

The Vaibhāṣikas, for their part, envisioned a much broader function for *samyakdṛṣṭi.* That function seems to have been removal of *all* the remaining *anuśayas.* By investigating the nature of his experiences over and over again from the correct standpoint ("this is only the five *skandhas,*" etc., as mentioned above,) the aspirant reaffirms the insight of the *darśanamārga* and weakens the unwholesome habits and tendencies produced when he was subject to *mithyādṛṣṭi.* For the Vaibhāṣikas, therefore, *samyakdṛṣṭi* is nothing less than the key element of the *bhāvanāmārga* itself; its application, together with that of the other "limbs" of the eight-fold path, entails the eventual eradication of all emotional attachments to the five *skandhas.* Once these attachments have been removed, even *samyakdṛṣṭi* itself can be allowed to pass out of existence; then, at last, pure *prajñā* is able to emerge.

A further point must be considered here. It was previously asserted that at the time when arhatship is attained, there is first an awareness of the destruction of the *anuśayas* (*kṣayajñāna*), then of the fact that they will never again arise (*anutpādajñāna*). Indeed this description conforms to the conventionally accepted, i.e. Theravādin, view of that event. Such a description cannot, however, be considered adequate for the Vaibhāṣikas, since it clearly involves the very sort of discriminative judgement (*santīraṇa*) which they have insisted must be absent from *prajñā.* Vaibhāṣika doctrine necessitates, therefore, that *kṣayajñāna* and *anutpādajñāna* be understood not as "knowledges" in the ordinary (discriminative) sense, but rather as those mind-moments wherein there occurs, respectively, *aprāpti* ("non-possession") of the *anuśayas* and *prāpti* ("obtainment") of *pratisaṃkhyānirodha*[20] (the "blank" *dharmas* referred to earlier.) Thus the traditional criteria of arhatship are met, but without the "taint" of *santīraṇa;* this is *anāsravā prajñā, prajñā* devoid of all defiling *dharmas.*

- Prajñā
  - (a) *dṛṣṭi (kuprajñā)*
    (Views characterized by investigation and judgement)
    - (a-1) *mithyādṛṣṭi* (inaccurate views)
    - (a-2) *samyakdṛṣṭi* (accurate views)
      - (a-2-a) *laukikīsamyakdṛṣṭi* (pre-*darśanamārga; dṛṣṭianuśaya* is still present)
      - (a-2-b) *śaikṣī sāsravā-samyakdṛṣṭi* (after the *darśana-mārga,* but prior to *arhatship*)
      - (a-2-c) *aśaikṣī anāsravā-samyakdṛṣṭi* (mode of awareness of the *arhat* living in the world.)
  - (b) non-*dṛṣṭi*
    - (b-1) *pañcavijñānakāyikā prajñā* (pure worldly perception, i.e. the first moment of any act of cognition, prior to investigation and judgement.)
    - (b-2) *aśaikṣī anāsravā prajñā* (pure non-worldly *prajñā* i.e. *kṣayajñāna* and *anutpā-dajñāna*).

It may well be asked here just how an *arhat,* ostensibly free from any tendency to discriminate or conceptualize, can function in daily life. The answer proceeds from understanding that the state of pure awareness, of *prajñā, does not continue;* it is a conditioned thing (*saṃskṛta*) and must therefore disappear after its moment of existence. Following that moment, the *arhat* once again makes identifications, judgements, etc. (of course in accord with the four noble truths), and to all appearances lives like any stream-winner (*srotāpanna,* i.e. one freed from *mithyādṛṣṭi*) until his death. The *effect* of his moment of pure *prajñā,* however, does *not* disappear; *pratisaṃkhyānirodha* is an unconditioned *dharma* which effectively precludes forever the arising of any defiling influences. In other words, the *arhat* seems to be operating in the context of *samyakdṛṣṭi,* but it is of a special sort, viz. unencumbered by *avidyā* or the other *anuśayas* and generating no attachment to anything, not even the five *skandhas.* Thus we have here still another form of awareness, another subcategory of *"prajñā;"* indeed, the significations given this term by the Vaibhāṣikas are so numerous that we should perhaps construct a small diagram to illustrate them (see p. 275).

If we have been correct in holding that the Vaibhāṣikas view pure *prajñā* as a condition of non-discriminative awareness accompanying the *kṣaya* and *anutpāda jñānas* (in their *aprāpti* and *prāpti* senses, as above), it would appear that their conceptualization of this supreme insight is not altogether different from that set forth in the Prajñāpāramitā literature. Most significantly, the *prajñā* of both traditions is said to be free from all conceptualizations, devoid of all *dṛṣṭis* (*śūnyatā sarvadṛṣṭīnām*). Even so, a major distinction remains between the systems, for while the Vaibhāṣikas did relegate even *samyakdṛṣṭi* to the level of *kuprajñā,* they never developed the implications of this move as the Mahāyānists did. Vaibhāṣika doctrine sees only *mithyādṛṣṭi* as *avastuka,*[21] "focused upon unreal or non-existent objects (e.g. a permanent soul);" *samyakdṛṣṭi,* while not considered pure *prajñā,* was nevertheless classed as *savastuka,* "focused upon actually existing objects (i.e. the five *skandhas*)". To apply Mahāyāna terminology, we may say that the Vaibhāṣikas believed in *pudgalaśūnyatā* ("non-existence of anything called 'the self'") but not in *dharmaśūnyatā* ("non-existence of *dharmas*"). The Prajñāpāramitā tradition, on the other hand, embraced both doctrines equally.

In the Buddha's famous sermon concerning the raft, it is stated that in addition to the obvious need for abandonment of non-*dharmas* (*a-dhammā*, i.e. the objects of *mithyādṛṣṭi*), eventually even *dharmas* (*dhammā*, i.e. the objects of *samyakdṛṣṭi*) must be left behind as well.[22] The full ramifications of this *sutta*, viz. that *dharmas* too are *avastu*, seem to have been lost on the Vaibhāṣikas. Although they understood that *samyakdṛṣṭi* was an inferior sort of *prajñā*, they were unable to translate that insight into a doctrinal rejection of the reality of the five *skandhas*.

NOTES

1. *athāvidyeti ko 'rthaḥ? yā na vidyā. cakṣurādiṣv api prasaṅgaḥ? vidyāyā abhāvas tarhi. evaṃ sati na kiñcit syāt; na caitad yuktam. tasmāt*
vidyāvipakṣo dharmo 'nyo 'vidyā 'mitrānṛtādivat//28//
yathā mitraviparyayeṇa tadvipakṣataḥ kaścid amitro bhavati, na tu yaḥ kaścid anyo mitrāt, nāpi mitrābhāvaḥ...evam avidyāpi vidyāyāḥ pratidvandvabhūtadharmāntaram iti draṣṭavyam....
samyojanādivacanāt,
saṃyojanaṃ bandhanam anuśaya ogho yogaś cāvidyocyate Sūtreṣu. na cābhāvamātraṃ tathā bhavitum arhati....
yathā tarhi kubhāryā abhāryety ucyate, kuputraś cāputraḥ, evam avidyā 'py astu?
kuprajñā cen na darśanāt/ 29 ab/
kutsitā hi prajñā kliṣṭā. sā ca dṛṣṭisvabhāvā iti nāvidyā yujyate.
yā tarhi na dṛṣṭiḥ sā bhaviṣyati? sāpi bhavituṃ nārhati. kiṃ kāraṇam
dṛṣṭes tat samprayuktatvāt/29 c/
avidyā cet prajñā 'bhaviṣyan na dṛṣṭis tayā yujyate.... dvayoḥ prajñādravyayor asamprayogāt. AKB. III, 28-29.
Commenting on the last part Yaśomitra says:
"*dṛṣṭes tat samprayuktatvāt*" *iti. avidyāsamprayuktatvād ity arthaḥ. kathañ ca dṛṣṭir avidyayā samprayuktā yasmād avidyālakṣaṇo mohaḥ kleśamahābhūmau paṭhyate, kleśamahābhūmikāś ca sarve 'pi mahābhūmikaiḥ saha samprayujyanta iti dṛṣṭyā satkāyadṛṣṭyādikayā prajñāsvabhāvayā avidyā samprayujyata iti gamyate. tasmān nāvidyā prajñā, dvayoḥ prajñādravyayor asamprayogāt. SAKV.* III, 29.
2. *dṛṣṭayaḥ pañca satkāyamithyāntargrāhadṛṣṭayaḥ*/
dṛṣṭiśīlavrataparāmarśāv iti punar daśa//
...ity ete...darśanaprahātavyāḥ, satyānāṃ darśanamātreṇa prahāṇāt. AKB. V, 3-4. [It should be noted that the *nirodha* of *vicikitsā* occurs together with that of *dṛṣṭi*.]
3. *catvāro bhāvanāheyāḥ: tad yathā—rāgaḥ, pratighaḥ, mānaḥ, avidyā ca. dṛṣṭasatyasya paścāt mārgābhyāsena prahāṇāt. AKB.* V, 5a.
4. See *CCB*, Appendix II (Tables of the Elements according to the Sarvāstivādins).
5. *yaḥ sāsravair dharmair visaṃyogaḥ sa pratisaṃkhyānirodhaḥ. duḥkhādīnām āryasatyānām....prajñāviśeṣas tena prāpyo nirodhaḥ....kiṃ punar eka eva sarveṣāṃ sāsravāṇāṃ dharmāṇāṃ pratisaṃkhyānirodhaḥ? nety āha. kim tarhi? pṛthak pṛthak*/

yāvanti hi saṃyogadravyāṇi tāvanti visaṃyogadravyāṇi. anyathā hi duḥkha-darśanaheyakleśanirodhasākṣātkaraṇāt sarvakleśanirodhasākṣākṣātkriyā prasajyeta. sati caivaṃ śeṣapratipakṣabhāvanāvaiyarthyaṃ syāt. AKB. I, 5cd.

6. *nanu ca dṛṣṭyadhikatvād ekaviṃśatir bhavanti? na bhavanti. yasmān mahābhūmika eva kaścit prajñāviśeṣo dṛṣṭir ity ucyate. AKB.* II, 29ab. Cf. *nanu ca dṛṣṭir adhikā? nādhikā, prajñāviśeṣa eva hi kaścit dṛṣṭir ity ucyate. ADV.* [123]

7. *vedanā cetanā saṃjñā cchandaḥ sparśo matiḥ smṛtiḥ/*
manaskāro 'dhimokṣaś ca samādhiḥ sarvacetasi//
ime kila daśa dharmāḥ sarvatra cittakṣaṇe samagrā bhavanti. AKB. II, 24. It should be noted that the *kārikā* actually employs the term *mati* rather than *prajñā* here. However, Vasubandhu glosses *mati* as *prajñā* (*matiḥ prajñā dharmapravicayaḥ*) in his *Bhāṣya,* and Yaśomitra is at pains to prevent any other interpretation when he says: *pratītatvāt prajñeti vaktavye ślokabandhānuguṇyena matir iti kārikāyām uktam. SAKV.* II, 24.

8. *...paññindriyena saddhim pañcavīsati 'me cetasikā sobhanā veditabbā. AbhS.* II, 7. *paññā, dvādasasu kāmāvacarasahetukacittesu, pannarasasu rūpāvacaracittesu, aṭṭhasu arūpāvacaracittesu, aṭṭhasu lokuttaracittesu cā ti sattacattāsīlacittesu sampayujjati. AbhS.* II. 16.

9. That Vasubandhu is indeed the author of this work is confirmed by Yaśomitra: *ime kileti. kilaśabdaḥ paramatadyotane. svamataṃ tu chandādayaḥ sarvacetasi na bhavanti. tathā hy anenaivācāryeṇa Pañcaskandhake likhitam...SAKV.* II, 24. For the complete *dharma* list of the *Pañcaskandhaka,* see *IAKB.* Part I, pp. XVI-XIX.

10. *...mahābhūmikatvā c ca samādheḥ sarvacittānām ekāgratāprasaṅgaḥ? na; durbalatvāt samādheḥ ....kliṣṭasya kathaṃ dhyānatvam? mithyopanidhyānāt. atiprasaṅgaḥ? na; tatpratirūpa eva tatsaṃjñāviniveśāt pūtibījavat. AKB.* VIII, ld.
"pūtibījavat". yathā kiñcid abījaṃ pāṣāṇādi atyantatajjātivilakṣaṇaṃ na pūtibījam ity ucyate, kiṃ tarhi? bījajātīyam evopahataṃ yad bhavati tasminn eva saṃjñāsanniveśaḥ 'pūtibījam' iti. SAKV. VIII, ld.

11. *yasmān mahābhūmika eva kaścit prajñāviśeṣo dṛṣṭir ity ucyate. AKB.* II, 29 ab.
"mahābhūmika eva kaścit prajñāviśeṣo dṛṣṭir" iti. santīrikā ya prajñā, sā dṛṣṭiḥ. SAKV. II, 29 ab.

12. *santīrikā hi dṛṣṭiḥ, upadhyānapravṛttatvāt. AKB.* I, 41cd.
santīraṇaṃ punar viṣayopanidhyānapūrvakaṃ niścayākarṣaṇam. SAKV. I, 41 cd. See *BHSD.* p. 556.

13. The *Dhammasaṅgaṇi,* for example, uses *sammādiṭṭhi* as a synonym for *paññindriya: katame dhammā kusalā* (*yasmiṃ samaye kāmāvacaraṃ kusalaṃ cittaṃ uppannaṃ hoti somanassasahagataṃ ñāṇasampayuttaṃ... tasmiṃ samaye ... paññindriyaṃ hoti ... sammādiṭṭhi hoti ... katamaṃ tasmiṃ samaye paññindriyaṃ hoti? yā tasmiṃ samaye paññā ... amoho dhammavicayo sammādiṭṭhi-idaṃ tasmiṃ samaye paññindriyaṃ hoti. katamā tasmiṃ samaye sammādiṭṭhi hoti? yā tasmiṃ samaye paññā ... paññindriyaṃ ... ayaṃ ... sammādiṭṭhi hoti. Dhs.* pp. 9-12.

14. *kṣayānutpādadhīr na dṛk/*
kṣayajñānam anutpādajñānaṃ ca na dṛṣṭiḥ, asantīraṇāparimārgaṇāśayatvāt.
tadanyobhayathāryā dhīḥ,
kṣāntikṣayānutpādaj ñānebhyo 'nyānāsravā prajñā, dṛṣṭiḥ jñānaṃ ca.
anyā jñānaṃ,
laukikī prajñā sarvaiva jñānam.
dṛśaś ca ṣaṭ//1//
pañca dṛṣṭayaḥ, laukikī ca samyagdṛṣṭiḥ. eṣā ṣaḍvidhā laukikī prajñā dṛṣṭiḥ, anyā na dṛṣṭiḥ. jñānaṃ tv eṣā vānyā ca. AKB. VII, 1.

15. ...*kṣayajñānam anutpādajñānaṃ ca na dṛṣṭih ity arthaḥ. yāvad ayam akṛtakṛtyaḥ, tāvad duḥkhādīni satyāny upanidhyāyati, parimārgayati vāśayato yathoktair anityādibhir ākāraiḥ... tasmān na te darṣṭisvabhāve ..."anye" ti. laukikī. sā sarvajñānamity avadhāraṇam. na sā prajñāsti yan na jñānam ity arthaḥ. kā punar asau prajñā? pañcavijñānakāyikā kuśalākuśalāvyākṛtā mānasīyā dṛṣṭisvabhāvakleśasamprayuktā, anivṛtāvyākṛtā ca. . . ."jñānaṃ tv eṣā cānyā ce" ti. eṣā ca ṣadvidhā dṛṣṭisvabhāvā prajñā, tato 'nyā ca pūrvoktā jñānam ity ucyate...yasmād etāḥ ṣaḍ jñānāni cocyante dṛṣṭayaś ceti. SAKV.* VII, 1. See also *AKB.* .I, 41.

16. ...*kṛtakṛtyasya punar yathā dṛṣṭeṣv eva duḥkhādiṣv āryasatyeṣu pratyavekṣaṇamātraṃ tābhyāṃ bhavatīti "duḥkhaṃ mayā parijñātaṃ na punaḥ parijñeyam" ity ādi. tasmān na te dṛṣṭisvabhāve. SAKV.* VII, 1.

17. ...*tattha paṭhamamagge sammādiṭṭhi micchādiṭṭhim pajahatī ti sammādiṭṭhi....evaṃ sante paṭhamamaggen' eva dvāsaṭṭhiyā diṭṭhigatānaṃ pahīnattā uparimaggattayena pahātabbā diṭṭhi nāma natthi. tattha sammādiṭṭhī ti nāmaṃ kathaṃ hotī ti? yathā visaṃ atthi vā, hotu mā vā, agado agado tv eva vuccati, evaṃ micchādiṭṭhi atthi vā, hotu mā vā, ayaṃ sammādiṭṭhi yeva nāma. yadi evaṃ nāmamattam ev' etaṃ hoti, uparimaggattaye pana sammādiṭṭhiyā kiccābhāvo āpajjati, maggaṅgāni na paripūrenti, tasmā sammādiṭṭhi sakiccakā kātabbā maggaṅgāni pūretabbānī ti. Dhs A.* 3.529.

18. *sakiccakā c' ettha sammādiṭṭhi yathālābhaniyamena dīpetabbā. uparimaggattayavajjho hi eko māno atthi, so diṭṭhiṭṭhāne tiṭṭhati. sā taṃ mānaṃ pajahatī ti sammādiṭṭhi. sotāpattimaggasmiṃ hi sammādiṭṭhi micchādiṭṭhim pajahati. sotāpannassa pana sakadāgāmimaggavajjho māno atthi. so diṭṭhiṭṭhāne tiṭṭhati... DhsA.* 3.530.

19. *diṭṭhi catūsu diṭṭhigatasampayuttesu* [*labbhati*]. *māno catūsu diṭṭhigatavippayuttesu* [*labbhati*]. *AbhS.* 2.13.

20. Cf."*ajitajayajitādhyavasānāt". yathā tadajitānigrāmanigamādīni jayati, jitāni cādhyāvasati, evam ānantaryamārgeṇājitān satkāyadṛṣṭyādīn kleśān jayati; tat prāpticchedāt. jitāṃś cādhyāvasati vimuktimārgeṇa; kleśavisaṃyogaprāptisahotpādāt. SAKV.* VI, 54d. On *prāpti* and *aprāpti,* see my article, 'Origin and development of the theory of *viprayuktasaṃskāras', Bulletin of the School of Oriental and African Studies,* University of London, Vol. XXII, Part 3, 1959, pp. 531-547.

21. ...*ity ete ..anuśayā darśanaprahātavyāḥ; satyānāṃ darśanamātreṇa prahāṇāt. AKB.* V, 4.

yo hi kleśo yasya satyasyāpavādāya pravṛttaḥ, sa tasmin dṛṣṭe prahīyate; sarpabhrāntir iva rajjudarśanāt. "satyānāṃ darśanamātreṇa prahāṇād" iti. nābhyāsena prahāṇād ity abhiprāyaḥ. SAKV. V, 4. *bhāvanāheyā hi kleśā dṛḍhāḥ, savastukatvāt. ato lokotterāṇāpi teṣāṃ na sakṛt prahāṇaṃ. SAKV.* VI, 1.

22. *kullūpamaṃ vo, bhikkhave, dhammaṃ desissāmi nittharaṇatthāya, no gahaṇatthāya. ...kullūpamaṃ vo, bhikkhave, dhammaṃ desitaṃ ājānantehi dhammā pi vo pahātabbā pageva adhammā. M.* I, 135.

"*dhammā pi vo pahātabbā" ti ettha dhammā ti samathavipassanā. bhagava hi samathe pi chandarāgaṃ pajahāpeti, vipassanāya pi. ... idha pana ubhayattha pajahāpento...āha. tatrāyaṃ adhippāyo:bhikkhave, aham evarūpesu pi santapaṇītesu dhammesu chandar āgappahānam vadāmi, kiṃ pana imsamim asaddhamme gāmadhamme ....MA.* Part II, p. 109. Cf. *tasmād iyaṃ tathāgatena vāg bhāṣitā "kolopamaṃ dharmaparyāyam ājānadbhir dharmā eva prahātavyāḥ prāg evādharmāḥ" iti. Vajra,* 6. Vasubandhu applies this *sūtra* to the *mārga: ...mārgasya kolopamatayā 'vaśyatyajanīyatvāt ... AKB.* VIII, 24d.

CHAPTER 17

Smṛti in the Abhidharma Literature and the Development of Buddhist Accounts of Memory of the Past*

Despite the extraordinary preoccupation of the ancient Buddhists in explaining the process of cognition, memory is conspicuous by its absence in the long list of mental events and concomitant mental factors (*citta-caitta-dharmas*). In the Theravādin Abhidhamma the word *sati* (*smṛti*) appears as a conditioning factor (*saṃskāra*) that occurs only in good (*kuśala*) consciousness and hence is invariably called "right-mindfulness" (*sammā-sati*).[1] The author of the *Dhammasaṅgaṇi* admits that even a person holding a wrong view can have a sort of "awareness," but seeks to reserve the term *sati* only for right-mindfulness.[2] The Vaibhāṣikas appear to have noticed some error here, for in their Abhidharma literature, *smṛti* is no longer restricted to good mental events, but is enumerated in the list of the factors invariably found in every mental event (*mahābhūmika-dharmas*), together with feeling (*vedanā*), thinking (*cetanā*), and conceptual identification (*saṃjñā*).[3] Vasubandhu (fourth or fifth century CE), in his *Abhidharma-kośabhāṣya,* defines *smṛti* as the "retention of" or "not letting drop the object" (*ālambana-asampramoṣa*).[4] He however does not specify

* This article was originally published in *In the Mirror of Memory: Reflections on Mindfulness and Remembrance in Indian and Tibetan Buddhism,* ed. J. Gyatso, (Albany: State University of New York Press, 1992), pp. 47-59. Reprinted with kind permission of State University of New York Press.

if the term *object* in this definition is past or present and thus leaves open the possibility that the term could be taken to mean either memory of the past or mindfulness of the present. Yaśomitra (eighth century) in his *Sphuṭārthābhidharmakośavyākhyā* is more specific and says: "*Smṛti* is that factor on account of which the mind does not forget the object; it is as if it repeats it."[5] The fact that *smṛti* is found in every mental event can only lead one to conclude that here too the term *smṛti* is understood to mean mindfulness and not memory of the past, for the latter is not a phenomenon that occurs at all times. Vasubandhu must have perceived some anomaly here, for in his *Pañcaskandhaprakaraṇa*, *smṛti* is not included in the group of mental factors that occur invariably, but in the next group of five factors that are found only in certain mental events (*viniyata-dharmas*). Other such occasional factors are zest (*chanda*), confidence (*adhimokṣa*), meditational concentration (*samādhi*), and insight (*prajñā*). There *smṛti* is defined as "the non-forgetting of a range of events towards which there is acquaintance and is a certain kind of discourse of consciousness (*citta*)."[6] This definition is almost identical with the one given by Sthiramati (*c.* 470-550) in his *bhāṣya* on Vasubandhu's *Triṃśikā* (verse 10), where *smṛti* is also classified with the factors that occur only in certain moments. According to Sthiramati *smṛti* is the nondropping (*asampramoṣa*) of a familiar entity; it is a mental repetition.[7] Sthiramati goes on to gloss the expression "familiar entity" as "a previously experienced object" (*vastu pūrvānubhūtam*), but even here the recollection of this past object is described in terms traditionally associated with meditative mindfulness. For example, he also glosses *smṛti* as "that which brings about nondistraction" (*avikṣepa-karmikā*). Why the Buddhists with their otherwise thorough analysis of the mental factors should have paid so scant attention to the phenomenon of memory of the past as such has remained a riddle and needs to be examined.

The term *asampramoṣa* in the above definitions of *smṛti* is derived from the root *muṣ* (of the ninth *gaṇa*) having the meaning "to release," or "to let go." *Asampramoṣa* therefore would be this root's opposite; namely, "retention" or "holding on to an object." In early Buddhist sources this referred primarily to a special kind of *smṛti* as one finds in the Buddhist term "applications of mindfulness" (*smṛtyupasthāna;* Pāli *satipaṭṭhāna*) that maintains awareness of one of the four objects; namely, the body (*kāya*), the feelings (*vedanā*), the mind (*citta*), and the remaining factors (*dharmas*), the foundation of all Buddhist meditation.[8]

This is not the meaning, however, in which other Indian philosophical schools understand the word *smṛti*. In the *Pātañjalayoga-sūtra,* for example, *smṛti* is defined as "not letting drop an object that has been experienced" (*anubhūta-viṣaya-asampramoṣa*),[9] almost identical with Sthiramati's gloss; "not letting drop ... a previously experienced object." The most ancient commentator Vyāsa (*c.* fifth century CE) was silent on the meaning of the term *asampramoṣa.* Vācaspati Miśra (ninth century), the foremost expositor of the Yoga system, however, in his *Tattvavaiśāradī* commentary interprets the word *asampramoṣa* in quite a different way. He derives the word from the same root *muṣ* as the Buddhists do, but having the meaning "to steal." *Asampramoṣa* thus comes to mean "not adding surreptitiously [to a once experienced object]." He explains this aspect further by saying that whereas other "fluctuations" (*vṛttis,* e.g., perception or inference) give access to a hitherto inaccessible object, memory does not go beyond the limits of previous experience. It corresponds with the previous experience or with less than that, but it does not correspond to any experience *in addition* to that. This is called *asampramoṣa,* (i.e., "not adding surreptitiously").[10] Vācaspati Miśra's derivation seems a trifle too artificial and suggests the possibility that in totally ignoring the alternative meaning of the root *muṣ,* he was showing his disagreement with the Buddhist explanation of the term *smṛti.*

Probably the first Theravādin to notice this omission of *smṛti* as memory in the Abhidharma Piṭaka is Nyanaponika Thera. Nyanaponika's transference of the function of *smṛti* to the aggregate of conceptual identification (*saṃjñā-skandha*), however, does not fully solve the problem of memory. We still need to account for the specific kind of cognition of the previous object alone that could be properly designated as memory of the past. Nevertheless, Nyanaponika's suggestion is worth noting because he asks us not to look for *smṛti* in that catch-all of dharmas called the *aggregate of conditioning factors* (*saṃskāra-skandha*), but in the act of cognition itself.

Nyanaponika's survey is limited to the Pāli Abhidharma texts and commentaries and does not cover the Sanskrit Abhidharma material, especially the *Abhidharmakośabhāṣya* of Vasubandhu. We already have referred to Vasubandhu's brief definition of *smṛti* and how it was understood as mindfulness by the Vaibhāṣikas. However, in his appendix to the *Abhidharmakośabhāṣya,* called the *Pudgalaviniścaya,*[11] Vasubandhu provides us with detailed material on *smṛti,* not as he defined it earlier as mindfulness, but as memory of the past. The context for his account of memory is provided by the Pudgalavādin Vātsīputrīya, the Buddhist heretic, who apparently uses the phenomenon of *smṛti* as a valid ground for his doctrine of a durable entity called *pudgala* (translated variously as "person," "self," or "soul"). Their debate on this particular point is highly informative in revealing Vasubandhu's understanding of the process involved in the event of memory (*smṛti*) and therefore may be briefly summarized here:

Pudgalavādin: If the self does not absolutely exist how can the momentary mental events (*cittas*) be capable of the remembrance or recognition of an object experienced (*anubhūta*) a long time ago?[12]

Vasubandhu: A special type of mental event connected (*anvaya*) with the conceptual identification (*saṃjñā*) of the object already perceived—which is hence called "object of memory"—produces memory and recognition.[13]

Pudgalavādin: What is this special condition of the mental event which is immediately followed by memory (*smṛti*)?[14]

Vasubandhu: The following conditions are required:[15]

1. *tadābhoga:* There should be "bending" (*ābhoga*) of the mental event, i.e. a turning of attention towards that object.
2. *sadṛśa-saṃjñā:* That mental event should have a conceptual identification which resembles the [conceptual identification of the past] object, should such a resemblance exist [e.g., a memory of a fire seen in the past aroused by its resemblance to the conceptual identification of a fire in the present.]
3. *sambandha-saṃjñā:* Or, that mental event should have a conceptual identification suggesting a relation (*sambandha*) to the past object [e.g., a memory of a past fire aroused by the conceptual identification of smoke seen in the present].[16]
4. *praṇidhāna:* The mental event should have a certain res-

olution (*praṇidhāna*) for example, "I shall remember this at a certain time."[17]

5. *anupahata-prabhāva:* There should be no impairment of the mental event on account of bodily pain, grief or distraction, etc.

These conditions are necessary but not adequate to produce a memory. If these conditions are fulfilled but the mental event is not connected with a previous concept of the object to be remembered then also there can be no memory. On the other hand, if the mental event is so connected but the above conditions are absent, it likewise is not able to produce the memory. Both factors, namely, connection to the previous conceptual identification and a suitable state of mind, are necessary for the emergence of a memory. A mental event which is not like this is incapable of evoking memory.[18]

Vasubandhu's stipulation that *smṛti* is a special type of mental event (*citta-viśeṣa*), a representative cognition of the past object, removes the necessity to postulate a separate dharma called *smṛti*. By being a type of mental event, *smṛti* thus already is included in the consciousness aggregate (*vijñāna-skandha*), and hence there is no need to postulate a new dharma by that name.

Vasubandhu's use of the term *connection* (*anvaya*) is extremely important here. In ordinary cognition, the object is a present one, and both the conceptual identification aggregate (*saṃjñā-skandha*) and the consciousness aggregate have the same object: the present object. But in the case of memory, the present consciousness with a present conceptual identification has to connect itself with a past concept, either on the basis of a resemblance (*sādṛśya*) or a relationship (*sambandha*) between the two concepts. If the Buddhist doctrine that all conditioned factors are momentary is to be valid, then the past concepts must be considered to have perished and thus be inaccessible to the present mental event. The Buddhist, therefore, must address the question of how the present can be linked with the past. This is the next stage in the debate.

Pudgalavādin: [If there were absolutely nothing permanent, it would mean that] one mental event has perceived the object and another remembers it. How could this possibly be? Surely it is not correct to say that Yajñadatta remembers an object perceived by Devadatta?[19]

Vasubandhu: There is no analogy here. Devadatta and Yajñadatta are not connected, whereas the two mental events are bound by the relation of cause and effect. Indeed, we do not say that one mental event sees an object and that [an altogether] different mental event remembers this object; for [although the two occur at different times] both mental events belong to the same series (*santāna*). What we do maintain is that one mental event of the past, which perceives a certain object and hence can be designated as a "seeing mental event" (*darśana-citta*) brings about the existence of another, namely the present mental event, which can be called "remembering mental event" (*smṛti-citta*) as it is capable of remembering this object. The two are causally related in the same manner of seed and its fruit, because both belong to the same series (*santati*).[20]

At this point we will not examine the validity of the doctrine of series or its alleged ability to explain the phenomenon of memory. It should be noted, however, that the use of the memory issue in defense of a theory of a person (*pudgala*) is not attested in the Pāli Nikāyas nor in the earlier Abhidharma works, including the *mātṛkā* texts, nor in the *Kathāvatthu,* which opens with the person theory as the main point of debate. The problem of memory of the past is a relatively new one, with perhaps its earliest appearance in the *Mahāvibhāṣā.*[21] That it was raised primarily in non-Buddhist circles is suggested even in the passage concerning the Pudgalavādins just mentioned. In that passage, the examination of *smṛti* begins at the end of the first section where Vasubandhu condemns the two heresies, namely the *pudgalagrāha* (the "dogma of a person" of the Vāstsīputrīya) and the *sarvanāstitāgrāha* (the "nihilism" of the Mādhyamika, according to Yaśomitra). Then Vasubandhu introduces the heterodox teachers, the Tīrthakaras (identified by Stcherbatsky with the Sāṅkhya and the Vaiśeṣika schools),[22] who maintain a doctrine of the self (*ātman*) as an independent substance.[23] But the arguments that are put in the mouth of the Buddhist Pudgalavādin in the following section employ the non-Buddhist word *self* (*ātman*), and not *person* (*pudgala*) as we might expect.[24] Thus Vasubandhu seems to be anticipating here not a Buddhist critique, but rather that of the Naiyāyika Vātsyāyana's (c. 400 CE) *Nyāyasūtrabhāṣya,* where the latter seeks to prove the existence of an eternal self (*ātman*) by pointing to the phenomenon of memory: "Memory is properly explained if it is [accepted] as a quality (*guṇa*) of the [abiding] self (*ātman*), for one does not remember [an object] seen [earlier] by some other person."[25] Vasubandhu's defense of the Buddhist theory of *smṛti* in his *Pudgalaviniścaya,* therefore, is a relatively novel one, unknown to the earlier Buddhist traditions prior to the Vaibhāṣika Abhidharma.

The only other Buddhist work of this period to address the problem of memory of the past in any detail is the *Abhidharmadīpavibhāṣāprabhāvṛtti.* This text is distinguished for its strident opposition to the Sautrāntika bias exhibited by Vasubandhu in his *Abhidharmakośa-bhāṣya.* The (*anonymous*) author of this work does not relegate the topic of *smṛti* to an appendix as does Vasubandhu, but introduces it in the first chapter of the *Abhidharmadīpa,* while expounding on the nature of the aggregate of consciousness (*vijñāna-skandha*). Having dealt with the varieties of the representative consciousness (*mano-vijñāna*) as listed in the *mātṛkā,* he embarks on a new topic in the following manner:[26]

> Now this must be discussed: How, in the absence of an eternal self (*ātman*) and in the absence of its quality (*guṇa*) called *smṛti,* can the consciousness (*vijñāna*) which cease momentarily and [hence] cannot establish a connection between each other, produce memory (*smṛti*) of an object experienced in the past?
>
> Answer: This doctrine [of the eternal self] has already been refuted;[27] even so we address this question as it is relevant to the topic at hand:
>
> Memory (*smṛti*) of an object experienced by a past consciousness is produced in the [present] consciousness on account of attention (*prayoga*), proximity of the causes (*aṅga-sānnidhya*), and the continuity of the same series (*sabhāga-santati*). [I, verse 27].
>
> When resolution, experience, expertise, repetition and other such efficient causes are present, memory arises of form and other objects, which have been experienced by a past consciousness belonging to the same series.
>
> Objection: Memory is produced on account of the impressions (*saṃskāra*) when there is a contact (*saṃyoga*) of the mind (*manas*) with the self (*ātman*).

> Answer: That is not so. The contact between the impressions, the mind and the soul is not proven because an eternal entity called self is like the horn of a hare and cannot be established ...[28]
>
> [And] when those conditions [of attention, proximity, etc.] are not obtained, and when one is overcome by indolence, passion and sickness, then non-remembrance (*vismṛti*) is produced pertaining to those objects which were known previously. [I, verse 28].

The *Abhidharmadīpa's* exposition of memory of the past is merely a restatement of Vasubandhu's description. But the terms appearing in the statement of the opponent, viz., *ātman, guṇa, saṃskāra, anubhava,* and so forth, reflect his familiarity with the Nyāya-Vaiśeṣika position, and their criticism of the Buddhist theory of memory perpetuated by a series of consciousness.

In this connection, Vātsyāyana's *Nyāyasūtrabhāṣya,* III. i. 14, dealing with *smṛti* may be compared with the arguments appearing in both Vasubandhu's *Abhidharmakośabhāṣya* and the *Abhidharmadīpavṛtti:*

> Now if the being (*sattva*) [who is the agent in all these several cognitions and re-cognitions] were a mere "series of impressions" (*saṃskāra-santati-mātre*) [as the Buddhist opponent holds], then inasmuch as every impression would [by its nature] disappear as soon as it has come into existence, there could not be a single impression which could do the apprehending (*anubhava*) of the cognition (*jñāna*) and the remembrance (*smṛti*), an apprehending that has been shown to pertain to all three points of time; and without such comprehending [by a single agent] there could be no recognition (*pratisandhāna*) [or recollecting] of cognition or of remembrance; and there would be no such conception of "I" or "my"; just in the same way as we have no such conception [as "I" and "mine"] with regard to the bodies of other persons.[29]

This single paragraph from Vātsyāyana's *bhāṣya* probably sums up the entire range of objections repeatedly raised by the Advaita Vedāntin[30] and the Jaina[31] teachers against the Buddhist doctrines of karma, its fruition (*vipāka*), the holy path, and the attainment of nirvāṇa. The problem of the evocation of memory is analogous to the problem of connecting the past agent of an action with the present experience of its result. The Buddhist must explain the mechanism whereby the past impressions (*saṃskāra*) of objects or the traces of the past actions are stored and await their fruition if everything in the series of consciousness is momentary.

In the case of actions, the Buddhists have maintained that the karmic potency (*phaladāna-śakti*) is carried unimpeded through the continuous chain of consciousness (*vijñāna-santati*).[32] The same principle seems to apply to the function of memory. Although there are no statements in the Abhidharma literature to the effect that the impressions of past objects are preserved in any concrete manner, a stray occurrence of the term *seed of memory* (*smṛti-bīja*) appearing in connection with the discussion of the latent passions (*anuśayas*) in the *Abhidharmakośabhāṣya* may be of interest here. Vasubandhu employs this term there in discussing his theory of the "seed" (*bīja*). The passions (*kleśas*) in their dormant stage are said to endure in the form of seeds in consciousness, just as the capacity to produce rice that belongs to the rice plant is engendered by the rice seed (*śāli-bīja*) and carried through various stages in between. Vasubandhu argues there that if the passions in their dormant state were to have any other substratum than the series of consciousness (e.g., a *citta-viprayukta-saṃskāra,* a factor which is distinguished from both mind and matter), then the opponent (the Vātsīputrīya) may also have to admit a similar substratum dharma, one totally dissociated from the mind, to account for the seeds of memory.[33] Vasubandhu does not develop this theory of seeds of memory beyond this laconic remark and his commentator Yaśomitra chose to ignore it altogether; but we may be certain that the Ābhidharmikas at some stage must have debated this problem of explaining the retention of past impressions through a series of momentary consciousnesses.

The Theravādin Abhidharma texts are totally silent on this matter, although their notion of the *bhavaṅga* (lit., "constituent of becoming") consciousness could have been exploited to serve this purpose.[34] As is well known, the Theravādins propose a theory of perception whereby a series (*vīthi*) of several mental events (*citta*) with the same object is maintained, after which the basic consciousness resumes until the next series begins. The series (of mental events) can be maintained for as many as seventeen moments when material objects are cognized (*pañca-viññāṇa*), or even longer for a mental cognition (*mano-viññāṇa*). Under certain circumstances there arises a mental event called "having the same object" (*tadārammaṇa*)[35] before the series is terminated. This regrasps the object for a moment before the object is lost, the series is terminated and the *bhavaṅga* instantaneously reemerges. It is conceivable that this having-the-same-object mental event could perform, in addition to reregistering the object, the function of passing on the mark (*nimitta*) of the vanishing object to the *bhavaṅga* consciousness where it could be stored. Of course, the Theravādins do not make any such claim, nor could they, given their rule that a consciousness or mental event (*citta*) can have only a single object at one time. Because the *bhavaṅga* consciousness already was provided with its object at the time of its first occurrence, that is, at the rebirth of a person, and that object remains the same for the entire duration of its successive appearances during one lifetime, it would not be correct to make the *bhavaṅga* a carrier of the countless impressions made by the other consciousnesses that repeatedly interrupted the *bhavaṅga*'s stream.[36] But, in any case, the concept of *bhavaṅga* clearly anticipates the emergence of the Yogācāra theory of the store consciousness (*ālaya-vijñāna*), and multilayered storehouse of all seeds (*sarva-bījaka*),[37] a convenient structure that traditionally is considered to explain adequately the operations of both action (*karma*) and memory (*smṛti*).

NOTES

1. *saranti etāya, sayaṃ vā sarati, saraṇamattam eva vā esā ti sati ...sati kusaladhamme apilāpeti—ime cattāro satipaṭṭhānā ....ime lokuttarā dhammā ti ...aparo pana nayo-apilāpanalakkhaṇā sati....ārammaṇe daḷhaṃ patiṭṭhitattā pana esikā viya.* Bapat and Vadekar, 1942. pp. 99-100.
2. *asaddhiyacitte pana sati n'atthī ti na gahitā. kiṃ diṭṭhigatikā attanā katakammaṃ naırantī ti? saranti. sā pana sati nāma na hoti. kevalaṃ tenākārena akusalacittappavatti. tasmā sati na gahitā. atha kasmā micchāsatī ti suttante vuttā? sā pana akusalakkhandhānaṃ sativirahitattā satipaṭipakkhattā ca micchāmaggamicchattānaṃ pūraṇatthaṃ taṭtha pariyāyena desanā katā. nippariyāyena pan' esā n' atthi.* Ibid., p. 202.
3. *vedanā cetanā saṃjñā cchandaḥ sparśo matiḥ smṛtiḥ,*
manaskāro 'dhimokṣaś ca samādhiḥ sarvacetasi.
Abhidharmakośa, II, 24. (Shastri, 1970, I, p. 186).

4. ... *saṃjñā saṃjñānaṃ viṣayanimittodgrahaḥ ... smṛtir ālambanāsampramoṣaḥ... samādhiś cittasyaikāgratā. Abhidharmakośabhāṣya*, II, 24.5 (ibid., I, p. 187).
5. *viśeṣanimittagrāha iti. viṣayaviśeṣarūpagrāha ity arthaḥ ... smṛtir ālambanāsampramoṣa iti. yadyogād ālambanaṃ mano na vismarati, tac cābhilapatīva, sā smṛtiḥ. Sphuṭārthā-Abhidharmakośavyākhyā*, II, 24 (ibid., p. 1870).
6. *Pañcaskandha-prakaraṇa*, Anacker, 1984, p. 67.
7. *smṛtiḥ saṃstute vastuny asampramoṣaś cetaso 'bhilapanatā. saṃstutaṃ vastu pūrvānubhūtam. ālambanagrahaṇāvipraṇāśakāraṇatvād asampramoṣaḥ. pūrvagṛhītasya vastunaḥ punaḥ punar ālambanākārasmaraṇam abhilapanatā. abhilapanam evābhilapantā. sā punar avikṣepābhāvād avikṣepakarmikā.* Lévi, 1925, pp. 25-26.
8. *tesu tesu ārammaṇesu okkhanditvā pakkhanditvā upaṭṭhānato upaṭṭhānaṃ. sati yeva upaṭṭhānaṃ satipaṭṭhānaṃ. kāyavedanācittadhammesu pan'assā... pavattito catudhā bhedo hoti: tasmā cattāro satipaṭṭhānā ti vuccanti. Visuddhimagga*, xxii, 34 (Warren, 1950, p. 583). For a detailed discussion of *smṛtyupasthāna*, see Cox's chapter in this book.
9. *pramāṇavikalpanidrāsmṛtayaḥ.* I, 6....*anubhūtaviṣayāsampramoṣaḥ smṛtiḥ.* I, 11. Bhattacarya, 1963, pp. 10 and 15.
10. *sampramoṣaḥ steyam. kasmāt? sādṛśyāt muṣa steye ity asmāt pramoṣapadavyutpatteḥ. etad uktaṃ bhavati—sarve pramāṇādayo 'nadhigatārthaṃ sāmānyataḥ prakārato vā 'dhigamayanti. smṛtiḥ punar na pūrvānubhavamaryādām atikrāmati. tadviṣayā vā tadūnaviṣayā vā na tu tadadhikaviṣayā. so 'yaṃ vṛttyantarād viśeṣaḥ smṛter iti.* Ibid., p. 15. See translation by Woods, 1914, p. 33.
11. Translated as *The Soul Theory of the Buddhists* by Stcherbatsky, 1920.
12. Shastri, 1973, p. 1215.
13. *smṛtiviṣayasaṃjñānvayāc cittaviśeṣāt.* Ibid., p. 1215.
14. *kīdṛśāc cittaviśeṣāt yato 'nantaraṃ smṛtir bhavati?* Ibid.
15. *tadābhogasadṛśasambandhisaṃjñādimato 'nupahataprabhāvād āśraya-viśeṣaśokavyākṣepādibhiḥ.* Ibid., p. 1216.
16. Added from the *Sphuṭārthāvyākhyā: sadṛśasaṃjñādimataḥ, yatra sādṛśyāt smṛtir bhavati. sambandhisaṃjñādimataḥ, yatrāntareṇāpi sādṛśyaṃ dhūmādidarśanāt smṛtir bhavati.* Ibid.
17. The term *praṇidhāna* is found in Yaśomitra's gloss on the word *ādi* ("and so forth") appearing in Vasubandhu's *bhāṣya.* See n. 15.
18. *tādṛśo 'pi hy atadanvayaś cittaviśeṣo na samarthas tāṃ smṛtiṃ bhāvayitum, tadanvayo 'pi cānyādṛśo na samarthas tāṃ smṛtiṃ bhāvayitum. ubhayathā tu samartha ity evaṃ smṛtir bhavati; anyasya sāmarthyādarśanāt.* Ibid.
19. *katham idānīm anyena cetasā dṛṣṭam anyat smarati, evaṃ hi Devadattacetasā dṛṣṭaṃ Yajñadattaḥ smaret?* Ibid.
20. *na, asambandhāt. na hi tayoḥ sambandho 'sti; akāryakāraṇabhāvād yathaikasantānikayoḥ. na ca brūmaḥ—anyena cetasā dṛṣṭam anyat smaratīti, api tu darśanacittāt smṛticittam anyad evotpadyate, santatipariṇatyā yathoktam iti ka evaṃ sati doṣaḥ?* Ibid., pp. 1216-17.
21. See Cox's chapter in this book, pp. 85-86.
22. Stcherbatsky, 1920 (reprint, 1970), p. 65.
23. *ye 'pi ca dravyāntaram evātmānaṃ manyante tīrthakarāḥ* ... Shastri, 1973, p. 1215.
24. *yadi tarhi sarvathā 'pi nāsty ātmā, kathaṃ kṣaṇikeṣu citteṣu cirānubhūtasya smaraṇaṃ bhavati? ...katham idānim anyena cetasā dṛṣṭam anyat smarati ... asaty ātmani ka eṣa smarati?* .... Ibid., p. 1215.
25. *yadi smṛtir ātmaguṇaḥ, evaṃ sati smṛtir upapadyate, nānyadṛṣṭam anyaḥ smaratīti*

... ekas tu cetano 'nekārthadarśī bhinnanimittaḥ pūrvadṛṣṭam arthaṃ smaratīty ekasyānekārthadarśino darśanapratisandhānāt smṛter ātmaguṇatve sati sadbhāvaḥ, viparyaye cānutpattiḥ ... saṃskārāsantatimātre tu sattve utpadyotpadya saṃskārās tirobhavanti. sa nāsty eko 'pi saṃskāro yas trikālaviśiṣṭaṃ jñānaṃ smṛtiṃ cānubhavet. na cānubhavam antareṇa jñānasya smṛteś ca pratisandhānam ahaṃ mameti cotpadyate, dehāntaravat. Nyāyasūtra-Bhāṣya, III, 1, 14. See Shastri, 1969, pp. 185-87.

26. Jaini, 1959a, p. 22.
27. *yady api dattotara eṣa vādaḥ*...Ibid. It is not clear whether the author of the *Vibhāṣāprabhāvṛtti* refers here to a refutation of his own (which is not extant) or to the *Pudgalaviniścaya* of Vasubandhu discussed earlier.
28. *ātmamanaḥsaṃyogāt saṃskārāpekṣā tadutpattir iti cet, na. ātmamanaḥ-saṃyogaḥ saṃskārāṇāṃ śaśaviṣāṇavad asiddhatvān nityasyātmanaḥ saṃskārāṇām anutpatteḥ.* Ibid., p. 22.
29. Quoted from Jha. 1939, p. 272.
30. *anusmṛteś ce.... anubhavam upalabdhim anūtpadyamānaṃ smaraṇam evānusmṛtiḥ, sā copalabdhyekakartṛkā satī sambhavati. puruṣāntaropalabdhiviṣaye puruṣāntarasya smṛtyadarṣanāt ... Brahmasūtra-Śāṅkara-Bhāṣya,* II. 25. See Dhundhiraj Shastri. 1929. pp. 535-58.
31. *kṛtapraṇāśākṛtakarmabhoga-bhavapramokṣa-smṛtibhaṅgadoṣān, upekṣya sākṣāt kṣaṇabhaṅgam icchan aho mahāsāhasikaḥ paras te. Anyayogavyavaccheda-dvātriṃśikā* of Hemacandra (1089-1172), xviii. See Dhruva, 1933, pp. 122-30; translation by Thomas, 1960, pp. 119-25.
32. For a detailed exposition, see Vasubandhu's *Pudgalaviniścaya* in Shastri 1973, pp. 1229-32.
33. *ko 'yaṃ bījabhāvo nāma? ātmabhāvasya kleśajā kleśotpādanaśaktiḥ, yathānubhavajñānajā smṛtyutpādanaśaktiḥ, yathā cāṅkurādīnāṃ śāliphalajā śāliphalotpādanaśaktir iti. yas tu* [*Sphuṭārthā—yas tv iti Vātsīputriyaḥ*] *kleśānāṃ bījārtham arthāntaraṃ viprayuktam anuśayaṃ kalpayati, teṇa smṛtibījam apy arthāntaraṃ kaplayitavyaṃ bhavati.* See Shastri, 1972, pp. 763—64. This discussion takes place in the context of a debate at *Abhidharmakośa,* v. I over the nature of the dharmas called the (six) *anuśayas*—beginning with sexual desire (*kāmarāga*) and ending with skepticism (*vicikitsā*)—that are eliminated through the supermundane (*lokottara*) path. The Sautrāntika believes that *anuśayas* are latent forces, which remain dormant (like seeds [*bījas*] of a plant) awaiting an opportunity for their outburst (*paryavasthāna*) when they are recognized as passions (*kleśa*). According to this view the *anuśayas* are always "present" in the stream of consciousness. Whether a dormant dharma can be called "present" in a given stream of thought forms the crux of the debate. The Vaibhāṣika rejects the theory of latency altogether on the grounds that the "presence" of these evil dharmas will preclude all possibility of having a wholesome (*kuśala*) mental event (*citta*) at any time, since the two are incompatible. The Vaibhāṣika therefore maintains that the *anuśayas* are identical with their so-called outbursts, the passions (*kleśa*). Another school (identified by Yaśomitra as the Vātsīputrīya) seeks to overcome this difficulty (of the incompatibility of the latent passion and the active purity in a single moment of mental event) by postulating that the *anuśayas* are dharmas of the category known as the *viprayukta-saṃskāras.* In this theory the anuśayas will be morally neither wholesome nor unwholesome, but neutral and thus can abide side by side with any kind of mental event. (For details on this debate, see Jaini, 1959b,

and 1959c.) Drawing on the similarity that exists between the latent forces (*anuśaya*) and the past impressions (i.e. the objects of memory), the Sautrāntika (Vasubandhu) retorts by asking if the Vātsīputrīya would also favour a theory of the "disassociated forces" to explain the operation of memory. Because the opponent remains silent, it can be presumed that the Vātsīputrīya does not pursue the matter further. This inconclusive debate shows the difficulty the various schools of Abhidharma encounter when, in the absence of an appropriate theory to account for past impressions, they try to explain the operation of passions or memories that spring from them.

34. For the canonical references to the *bhavaṅga-citta*, see Wijesekera, 1976, pp. 348-52.

35. ...*javanānubandhāni ca dve tadārammaṇapākāni yathārahaṃ pavattanti, tato paraṃ bhavaṅgapāto. Abhidhammatthasaṅgaho*, IV, 8. *javanānubandhānī ti paṭisotagāminiṃ nāvamiva udakaṃ, imāni tadārammaṇāni kiñci kālaṃ javanam anubandhanti. yasmā imāni bhavaṅgassa ārammaṇaṃ muñcitvā javanārammaṇe pavattanti, tasnā tadārammaṇānī ti vuccanti. Navanītaṭīkā*, IV, 8. See Kosambi, 1941, p. 69.

36. The object (*ālambana*) of the *bhavaṅga* will depend on the kind of consciousness at the time of one's rebirth. For example, if a being is to be born in the realm of desire (*kāmadhātu*), its *bhavaṅga* will be appropriate to the destinies within that realm (e.g., animal, human) and it will have any object available to the mindconsciousness (*mano-vijñāna*) at the time of conception. Similarly, if the rebirth took place in the realm of form (*rūpadhātu*), the *bhavaṅga* will be of a *rūpāvacara* variety and its object will have to be the meditational object appropriate to the particular *rūpa* heaven. Since the *bhavaṅga* does not change its quality for the duration of a particular life, its object (*ālambana*), with which it came into existence at the time of rebirth (*pratisandhi*), also remains the same. This precludes any possibility of endowing the current *bhavaṅga-citta* with a new object in midstream as it were, for that can only mean the beginning of a new life, a new *bavaṅga* with its own object.

37. *tatrālayākhyaṃ vijñānaṃ vipākaḥ sarvabījakaṃ. Triṃśikā*, 2cd. See Lévi, 1925, p. 18.

BIBLIOGRAPHY

Anacker, Stefan. 1984. *Seven Works of Vasubandhu* (trans. of the *Pañcaskandhaprakaraṇa*, pp. 49-82). Delhi: Motilal Banarsidass.

Bapat, P.V., and Vadekar, R. D., 1942. *Aṭṭhasālinī*. Poona: Bhandarkar Oriental Series, No. 3.

Bhattacarya, R. S. 1963. *Pātañjala-Yogadarśanam. Tattvavaiśāradī-saṃvalita-VyāsaBhāṣyasametam*. Banares: Bharatiya Vidya Prakashan.

Dhruva, A. B. 1933. *Malliṣeṇa's Syādvādamañjarī with Anyayoga-vyavavaccheda-dvātriṃśikā of Hemacandra*. Bombay Skt & Pkt. Series, No. 83.

Dhundhiraj, Shastri, 1929. *Brahmasūtra-śāṅkarabhāṣyam* (Pt. I). Kashi Sanskrit Series No. 71.

Jaini. P. S. 1959a, *Abhidharmadīpa with Vibhāṣāprabhā-Vṛtti*, Tibetan Sanskrit Works Series, No. 4. Patna: K. P. Jayaswal Research Institute (reprinted, 1977).

——.1959b, "The Sautrāntika theory of *bīja*." *Bulletin of the School of Oriental and African Studies* [University of London] 22, no. 2:236-49.

——.1959c, "The origin and development of the *viprayukta-saṃskāras*" *Bulletin of the School of Oriental and African Studies* [University of London] 22, no. 3:532-47.

Jha, Ganganath. 1939. *Gautama's Nyāyasūtras with Vātsyāyana's Bhāṣya* (trans.). Poona: Poona Oriental Series No. 59.

Kosambi, D. 1941. *Abhidhammatthasaṅgaho of Anuruddhācariya with Navanītaṭīkā.* Sarnath, Banares: Mahabodhi Society.

Lévi, Sylvain. 1925. *Vijñaptimātratāsiddhi: Deux Traites de Vasubandhu Viṃśatikā et Triṃśikā.* Paris: Librairie Ancienne Honoré Champion.

Nyanaponika Thera. 1965. *Abhidhamma Studies,* 2d ed. Kandy, Sri Lanka: Buddhist Publication Society.

Shastri, Dvarikadas. 1969. *VātsyāyanaBhāṣyasaṃvalitaṃ Gautamīyaṃ Nyāyadarśanam.* Banares: Bharatiya Vidya Prakashan.

——. 1970-73. *ĀcāryaVasubandhuviracitaṃ Svopajñabhāṣyasahitam Abhidharmakośa Yaśomitrakṛta Spuṭhārthāvyākhyopetam,* Pts. 1-4. (*Pudgala-Viniścayaḥ,* Pt. 4, pp. 1189-1234).

Stcherbatsky, T., 1920 (reprinted, 1970). *The Soul Theory of the Buddhists,* ed. Jaidev Singh. Banares: Bharatiya Vidya Prakashan.

Thomas, F. W. 1960. *The Flower-Spray of the Quodammodo Doctrine* (trans. of the *Syādvādamañjarī* of Malliṣeṇa). Berlin: Akademic-Verlag.

Warren, H. C. 1950. *Visuddhimagga of Buddhaghosācariya.* Cambridge, Mass.: Harvard Oriental Series, Vol. 41.

Wijesekera, O. H. De A. 1976. "Canonical References to Bhavaṅga." In *Malalasekera Commemoration Volume,* ed. O. H. De A Wijesekera. Colombo.

Woods, J. H. 1914. *The Yoga System of Patañjali.* Cambridge, Mass.: Harvard Oriental Series, Vol. 17.

Additional reading: For canonical references to the terms *bhavaṅga* and *tadārammaṇa,* see Cousins, L.S. 1981. "The *Paṭṭhāna* and the Development of the Theravādin Abhidhamma." *Journal of the Pali Text Society,* IX, pp. 22-46.

V

JĀTAKA & AVADĀNA LITERATURE

CHAPTER 18

The Story of Sudhana and Manoharā: An Analysis of Texts and the Borobudur Reliefs*

The story of Sudhana is one of the most popular of the *avadānas* of Northern Hīnayāna Buddhism. There are two main versions of this story, one adopted by the Mahāsāṅghika school and the other by the Mūla-Sarvāstivāda school. The former is preserved in the *Mahāvastu*[1] under the title *Kinnarī-jātaka,* and a similar version of this story is found in a Chinese collection called *Liu-tu-chi-ching* 'Collection [of tales to illustrate] the six *pāramitās*', said to have been translated in approximately A.D. 270 (*Taishō Tripiṭaka,* III, no. 152, 44 f.) and accessible to us in Chavannes' *Tripiṭaka* (*Cinq cents contes et apologues,* no. 80). The Mūla-Sarvāstivāda redaction is found in a Vinaya text of that school called the *Bhaiṣajya-vastu.*[2] It was translated by I-ching[3] and is referred to as *Ken pen chouo ...* by Chavannes (IV, 133). A Tibetan translation is also found in *Bkaḥ-hgyur,*[4] a translation of which is available in Schiefner's *Tibetan tales* (44-74). This redaction was bodily adopted by the *Divyāvadāna.*[5]

The Mahāsāṅghika version appears to have been generally superseded by redactions related to the Mūla-Sarvāstivāda version. One such appears in the *Avadānakalpalatā*[6] of Kṣemendra. Outside India, another is found in the Khotanese (Saka) Buddhist texts,[7] and towards the beginning of the fifteenth century, a much enlarged form is attested in Pali in recensions of the *Paññāsa-*

*This article was originally published in *BSOAS,* Vol. XXIX, part 3, pp. 533-558, University of London, 1966. Reprinted with kind permission of Oxford University Press.

jātaka, a collection of 50 'extra-canonical' *jātakas*[8] forming a major part of the popular Buddhist literature of the South East Asian countries. In later periods the story of Sudhana appears in several vernacular narrative poems (*pyo*) and dramas in Burma and Siam.

No other Buddhist story seems to have enjoyed such wide popularity and, with the possible exception of the *Vessantara-jātaka* and the *Suvaṇṇasaṅkha-jātaka* (*Paññāsa-jātaka,* no. 53), no other appears to have survived on a popular dramatic stage up to the present day in any Buddhist country.

The three Sanskrit redactions, viz. those of the *Mahāvastu* (*Mv.*), the *Divyāvadāna* (*Da.*) and the *Avadāna-kalpalatā* (*Ak.*), as well as the Chinese and Tibetan translations of it (through the translations of Chavannes ('Chinese A') and Schiefner), were already well known when Oldenburg in 1895 identified reliefs nos. I, b, 3–20 of the Borobudur[9] with the *Sudhanakumārāvadāna* of the *Divyāvadāna.* The Pali redactions of the *Zimmé Paṇṇāsa*[10] (*Zp.*) and *Paññāsa-jātaka*[11] (*Pj.*) were published later, but have remained comparatively unknown. With the publication of a translation of the Saka redaction[12] by Professor Sir Harold Bailey it is now possible to compare the Sanskrit, Saka, and Pali sources. In this article a comparison will be made of these different versions of this story in order to establish their mutual relationship and also to trace the main sources of the Borobudur reliefs (nos. I, b, 1-20) as well as of the popular vernacular versions prevalent in Burma and Siam.

Title: In *Mv.* the story is called *Kinnarī-jātaka,* in *Da. Sudhanakumārāvadāna.* In *Ak.* it is called *Sudhanakinnary-avadāna* suggesting a combination of the titles by Kṣemendra. Of the two Pali redactions *Zp.* has *Sudhanukumāra-jātaka* and *Pj.* has *Sudhana-jātaka.* The editor has kindly confirmed that the Saka text has no title.

Nidāna or 'moral of the story': In *Mv.* the *jātaka* is placed in the mouth of the Buddha who narrates it to the monks to illustrate how even in the past Yaśodharā his wife was won by him 'after great fatigue (*khedena*), great effort (*śrameṇa*), and great valour (*vīryeṇa*)'.[13] In *Da.* the Buddha narrates it to a king to illustrate his great charities, meritorious deeds, and the fulfilment of the *vīrya-pāramitā.*[14] There is no reference here to Yaśodharā. 'Saka' makes only a casual reference to Yaśodharā: 'He approached Kapilavastu.... For Yaśodharā's sake he there narrated a tale in illustration; he related his *pūrvayoga*' (Bailey, 'Sudhana poem', 506). *Ak.*, however, appears to resemble the *nidāna* of *Mv.*, introducing a novel incident in his personal life:[15] 'Whenever the Lord entered his capital city, Yaśodharā, confined to her palace, would, out of despair, try to throw herself from the terrace. The Lord would then save his loving ex-wife [by a glance of great pity]. One day being questioned by the monks out of curiosity the Lord said: Yaśodharā, O monks, on account of her separation from me is afflicted and resorts to such reckless acts. I too, O monks, in the past have experienced great calamities on account of my separation from her'. The Pali redactions give a long *nidāna* in full imitation of a *jātaka* story.[16] Both differ from the accounts given above. Here the Buddha narrates this story to a monk in love with a beautiful woman to show the dangers that a man in love may undergo to obtain his beloved, forsaking his parents, his kingdom, and even endangering his life.

The story: It will be convenient to summarize the *Mv.* and *Da.* redactions separately, as representatives of the two main versions. The variations found in 'Chinese A', closely related to the first version, and in the remaining redactions, associated with the second version, will be noted at the appropriate place.

***Kinnarī-jātaka* (*Mv.*)**

In Hastināpura there reigned a virtuous king named Subāhu. He had a son (the *bodhisattva*) named Sudhanu, the heir to the throne. His neighbour[17] a king named Sucandrima ruled in Siṃhapura. This king wishes to perform a sacrifice of all living beings.[18] Hunters gather all kinds of beings with the exception of a *kinnarī*. A competent hunter (name not given)[19] is sent to capture a *kinnarī*.

He goes up to the Himālaya, approaches a hermit in his hermitage where he hears celestial music. He learns from the hermit that it is the singing of the *kinnarīs*, daughters of a *kinnara* king called Druma.[20] He learns the name of one of them called Manoharā and also that she could be captured by uttering a truth (*satyavākyena*).[21] He utters her true name, thereby making her stand still, captures her, and brings her to the sacrificial enclosure of Sucandrima.

King Subāhu sends Sudhanu to attend the sacrifice. There he falls in love with Manoharā, preaches the doctrine[22] to king

Sucandrima, rescues her from the sacrifice, and brings her to his capital as his wife.

He is greatly attached to her and neglects his duties, and the citizens prevail upon the king to get rid of her. Consequently, the king bids her depart.[23] She leaves for the Himālaya.

There she meets two hunters called Utpalaka and Mālaka.[24] She gives them a ring and a garland, instructing them to give them to Sudhanu if he follows her.

Sudhanu leaves in search of her with a companion called Vasantaka,[25] meets the two hunters in the Himālaya, and obtains the ring and the garland from them. All four go in search of Manoharā. After crossing several mountains they come to the retreat of the hermit (this time his name is given as Kāśyapa) and beg him to guide them.

The hermit asks a king of monkeys[26] to guide them. All four mount him and ride to the city of Druma, called Nirati, on the summit of Mount Kailāsa.

As they all stand outside the city Sudhanu sees some *kinnarī* maids gathered to draw water for the purifying bath of Manoharā. The prince secretly puts the ring in one of the pitchers. Manoharā, while being bathed, finds the ring, recognizes it, and reports to her parents.

The prince is received by the king Druma and the lovers are reunited.[27] Sudhanu is anxious to return to his parents and is transported there with his wife by a group of Yambhara *yakṣas.*

Sudhanu's father orders funeral rites[28] to be performed for the supposedly dead prince. The arrival of the prince brings great happiness to all.

***Sudhanakumārāvadāna* (*Da.*)**

In *Da., 'Saka'*, and *Ak.* the king is called Dhana of Uttarapāñcāla (instead of Subāhu of *Mv.*). In 'Pali' he is called Ādiccavaṃsa. His son is Sudhana[29] the *bodhisattva.* The mother's name is not given in *Da.* In 'Saka' she is called Sūryaprabhā, in *Ak.* Rāmā, and in 'Pali' Candādevī.

In *Mv.* Subāhu's neighbour king Sucandrima is said to be his friend (in 'Chinese A' they are father and son) but in *Da.* etc. this neighbour is a rival of Dhana. His name is not given in *Da.* or 'Pali'. In 'Saka' as well as in *Ak.* he is called Mahendrasena.[30] He is a wicked king and his subjects desert him to take refuge in the kingdom of Dhana.

This exodus increases their rivalry and an element not found in *Mv.* and 'Chinese A' is introduced into the story. A *nāga* (dragon) called Janmacitraka (Citra in 'Saka' and *Ak.*[31] and Jambucittaka in 'Pali') protects the kingdom of Uttarapāñcāla and keeps it rich and full of food. The rival king sends a brahmin (only *Ak.* gives his name as Vidyādhara) to capture or kill this *nāga*. The *nāga* finds this out, seeks help from a hunter called Phalaka[32] (Utpalaka in 'Saka' and *Ak.*, Puṇḍarīka in 'Pali') who kills this brahmin and is honoured by the *nāga* with various presents. The hunter now approaches a hermit and tells him about his gifts obtained from the *nāga*. The hermit then asks him to get the *nāgapāśa* (called *amoghapāśa* 'unfailing noose').[33] The hunter returns to the *nāgabhavana,* persuades the *nāga* to part with the *nāgapāśa.*[34] On a subsequent occasion he visits a certain mountain, meets there another hermit, learns from him about the bathing *kinnarīs,* and captures Manoharā (without the aid of the *satyavākya* of *Mv.*) with his *nāgapāśa.* The Pali versions refer only to a single hermit but otherwise agree with *Da.* 'Saka' and *Ak.,* however, differ from *Da.* In these the hunter meets only one hermit and approaches him already armed with the *nāgapāśa.* Consequently he visits the *nāga* only once and not twice as in other versions.[35]

The subsequent flight of the other *kinnarīs* is described in only two lines in *Da. Zp.* here describes in nine verses their lamentation and the crying of Manoharā's mother. The latter is sent by the king Duma (*Da.,* Druma) in search of her.[36]

In *Da.,* 'Saka', and *Ak.* Manoharā hands over her magic crest-jewel (*cūḍāmaṇi*) to the hunter. In 'Pali' there is no direct reference to it but she hands over her shoes (*pādapūraṇa*) and all her jewellery (*alaṅkārabhaṇḍa*).[37] The hunter brings her to the capital where she is married to the prince. This new element, viz. their union in Hastināpura changes the scene of the sacrifice as well. In *Mv.* and also in 'Chinese A' it takes place outside Sudhana's capital.

In *Mv.* and 'Chinese A' the sacrifice takes place because of a foolish desire of the king to attain heaven, but in *Da.* etc. it is introduced as part of a court intrigue directly affecting the prince. Here we find a cunning *purohita* of the king intent on destroying the prince in order to get rid of a rival brahmin currently serving the prince. In *Da.* these two brahmins come from Jetavana; their names are not given. 'Saka' is silent on their names and their place of origin. *Ak.* states that they were *dākṣiṇātyas;* their names are given as Kapila and Puṣkara. In 'Pali' they are related as father and son, the father comes to know of his son's ambition and informs the king that the prince is trying to kill the latter to obtain the throne; the king, however, does not believe this and turns a deaf ear to him.

First the *purohita* sends Sudhana on a military expedition against a rebel. Sudhana goes to take leave of Manoharā but on seeing her he forgets all about the expedition. The *purohita* tries to bring him out of his harem. The king issues orders that the prince should not be allowed to see her again once he comes out.[38] This echoes the *Mv.* account[39] of his neglect of the royal duties for which he is detained by the king. Neither 'Saka' nor *Ak.* allude to this incident. In these and the Pali versions he simply assures Manoharā that he will return soon.[40]

Sudhana begs the king's leave to see his mother, approaches her to protect Manoharā, to guard the crest-jewel, and not to give it to her unless there was a danger to her life. Both 'Saka' and *Ak.* are identical on this point with *Da.,* the *Ak.* even repeating a verse in this connection found also in the latter.[41] The Pali versions are silent on this.

In *Da.,* Vaiśravaṇa the regent king instructs Pāñcika *yakṣa* to fight on behalf of the prince. In 'Saka' as well as *Ak.* he fights the war without any intervention by the *yakṣas.* In 'Pali' guardian deities (*ārakkhadevatā*) protect him in the battle.[42]

During his absence the wicked *purohita* is presented with a golden opportunity to destroy the prince by getting rid of Manoharā. The king has a bad dream[43] suggesting an impending disaster and the *purohita* urges him to undertake a sacrifice of all kinds of beings including a *kinnarī.* The *Da.* account of the subsequent pleading by the wicked *purohita*[44] differs considerably from the corresponding passages in 'Saka', *Ak.,* and the Pali versions

In *Mv.,* Manoharā leaves the capital at the order of the king her manner of departure is unspecified. In *Da.* she escapes from the palace by obtaining the crest-jewel from her mother-in-law. In 'Saka' she obtains the jewel, comes forth into the sacrificial enclosure (*maṇḍala-vāla-grāma*), recites a spell, and rises into the sky. In *Ak.* also she is given the jewel by her mother-in-law and asked to proceed first to the place of sacrifice (*yajñabhūmi*) and then to fly in the sky.[45] In 'Pali' Manoharā pleads with the queen to intervene, and when the latter tries to seek an audience with the king the men of the *purohita* prevent her. Manoharā then asks for her *pādapūraṇa* and the *alaṅkārabhaṇḍa*, adorns herself, and begs leave. When the king's men arrive to capture her she flies in the air.

In 'Pali' the story is interrupted here by scenes of lamentation during which Manoharā and Candādevī dwell upon the inevitability of *karma* which has brought about this separation.[46]

In *Mv.* and 'Chinese A' Manoharā meets Utpalaka and Mālaka, gives them the ring, and later proceeds to Kāśyapa's hermitage. In *Da.* as well as in 'Saka' and 'Pali', she directly approaches the hermit, gives him the ring, and also explains the dangers the prince will meet on his way if he follows her. In *Ak.*, however, after her flight she comes straight to her abode, is given a purifying bath, and then after a lapse of several days returns to the hermit to give him the ring.

Sudhana returns triumphant to his capital and is stricken with sorrow on not finding Manoharā. He obtains from Phalaka more information about the lake where she was captured and sets out alone in search of her. 'Saka' and *Ak.* do not refer to his meeting the hunter. In 'Pali' he takes the hunter with him (instead of Vasantaka as in *Mv.*), and makes an Act of Truth (*saccavacana*) declaring his determination not to return to the city without Manoharā.

On the way to the hermitage he laments for Manoharā asking various objects and birds the whereabouts of his beloved wife. The whole scene is reminiscent of a similar scene in the *Vikramorvaśīya* [47] where the king searches for his lost wife. *Mv.* and the Pali versions have nothing similar to this and 'Saka' deals with it in a single line: 'Whatever came before him, *tiryagyoni* and all the wild beasts, bowing down he asked from the heart, Have you seen Manoharā or not, where she has gone?' (Bailey, 'Sudhana poem', 512). *Ak.* devotes 12 verses to this scene.

As in *Mv.*, the hermit here also gives a monkey to guide the prince. But whereas he rides on the monkey (accompanied by companions) according to *Mv.*, in *Da.* he proceeds to his goal leaving the monkey behind him. On this point both 'Saka' and *Ak.* differ from *Da.* According to these the prince meets this monkey on a mountain called Kukūla, and rides on him. In 'Pali' he obtains this monkey from the hermit and makes him his guide but does not seem to ride on him.[48] Instead he comes across a group of birds[49] (called *hatthi-liṅga sakuṇa*) and learns from their talk about a great feast being arranged by king Duma for the purifying ceremony of Manoharā. The prince ties himself to the wings of a bird and is flown across the mountains to a lake where several maidens are gathered to fetch water for Manoharā's bath.

The incident of the recognition of the ring is identical in both *Mv.* and *Da.* But 'Saka' and *Ak.* give a slightly different account of Sudhana's attempt to place the ring in the pitcher. In *Da.* he places the ring secretly in the pitcher of a maiden. In 'Saka' he befriends an elderly maid: 'They lifted the jars to carry to the palace. One remained there, an aged woman, old, she could not lift the jar upon her shoulders....He went to her, he asked, Mother where is the water carried?' (Bailey, 'Sudhana poem', 513). In *Ak.* also it is said that he approached an elderly maid full of fatigue from lifting the pitcher and asked, 'O Mother, for whom is this being carried that you should disregard such great strain?' In both accounts the prince helps the old woman with her pitcher, obtains the news of Manoharā, and secretly throws the ring in the pitcher. It is interesting to note that the Pali versions also make use of this ruse but without making the *kinnarī* maid an old woman. Instead the prince resorts to an Act of Truth (*saccādhiṭṭhāna*) by the power of which one of the maidens becomes unable to lift the jar. She then approaches him and begs for his help.[50]

Only 'Saka' and 'Pali' refer at this stage to the years he spent in search of Manoharā. According to 'Saka' it took him 12 years to reach the abode of the *kinnaras,* but according to 'Pali' he accomplished this in a period of 7 years, 7 months, and 7 days.[51]

In *Mv.* the reunion takes place without any further incident. King Druma receives him with royal honours and the couple are united. In *Da.* the prince is brought secretly into the palace and kept in a guarded place.[52] He is then put to two tests by king Druma before he can claim her as his wife. Whereas this last episode is found in both *Ak.* and 'Pali', it is absent from 'Saka'. But 'Saka' is not in complete agreement with *Mv.* Rather it seems to allude to some kind of test: 'he (Druma) imposed upon him unlimited punishment, harsh threats, abusive speech. All that the *kinnara* king asked him the prince made known to him. He went out invincible as a *kesarin* lion. He so said to him, 'Son, on your part remain now here....' (Bailey, 'Sudhana poem', 513).

The first test consists of a feat of skill in archery reminding us of similar scenes in the *Rāmāyaṇa* and the *Mahābhārata,* with this difference that here the prince accomplishes this feat with the help of Śakra. *Ak.* agrees with *Da.* in its account of this test and repeats five verses found in the latter.[53] In 'Pali' the prince shows his skill in archery entirely on his own without the intervention of Śakra.[54]

The Pali versions here introduce an additional test of his strength by making him lift a huge sapphire stone. The prince now has recourse to an Act of Truth asserting his future attainment of the Buddhahood and lifts it on his shoulders with great ease.[55]

When he succeeds in his first test the king puts him to one more test of recognizing Manoharā in the middle of a thousand *kinnarīs* exactly like her reminding us of a similar scene in the Nala-Damayantī episode,[56] this time with the roles reversed. The prince, like Damayantī, has recourse to the utterance of a *satyavākya* (the first and the only time in *Da.*) and by the power of its truth Manoharā steps forward to meet him. *Ak.* treats this incident casually, simply stating that he recognized her and took her hand.[57] The Pali versions turn it into a more dramatic incident. He makes an Act of Truth (as in *Da.*) and begs the *devatās* to point her out (among seven other *kinnarīs*). According to *Pj.*, Sakka comes down in person, and tells him that he will create a golden fly which will hover around her head. According to *Zp.*, however, he comes down in the guise of a golden fly and tells him that he will indicate her to him by sitting on her hand.[58] Sudhana recognizes her and they are united.

As in *Mv.* the prince begins to feel homesick and wishes to see his parents, and the united couple are conducted to Hastināpura by the *kinnaras.* 'Saka' and *Ak.* do not refer to his longing to return home. The Pali versions give a long account of his sorrow; even king Druma accompanies them[59] (not found in any other version) and stays at Uttarapāñcāla for a week enjoying the hospitality of king Ādiccavaṃsa. The prince is now crowned and having ruled righteously for a long time enters Tusita heaven after his death.

In 'Pali' the *jātaka* is properly concluded with a brief sermon on the four Noble Truths, at the end of which the monk attains arhatship.[60]

Samodhāna: *Samodhāna* or identification of the characters of the story of the past (*atītavatthu*) with the persons connected with the story of the present (*paccuppannavatthu*) is one of the main features of a Pali *jātaka* and also of the *jātakas* in *Mv. Da.* identifies only Sudhana with the Buddha. *Ak.* identifies only Sudhana and Manoharā (with the Buddha and Yaśodharā) and 'Saka' only Sudhana and his parents (with the Buddha, Śuddhodana, and Mahāmāyā). The chart on pp. 307-08 summarizes the nomenclature of the characters in the various sources; divergence in the *samodhāna* of *Zp.* and *Mv.* is also noted, since the development of the *samodhāna,* like that of the *nidāna* and title, has some bearing on the genesis of the story as a whole.

The presence or absence of the last four characters in the story, viz. Janma-citraka, the *purohitas,* and Śakra, standing respectively for the episodes of the *nāgarāja,* the court intrigue, and finally the tests of valour, divides the story into its two main versions. Otherwise the subject-matter of the two versions including the names of the characters shows a virtually exact correspondence indicating a certain dependence of one on the other. The possibility of *Mv.* borrowing from the Mūla-Sarvāstivāda version is very remote: there is no reason why the narrator of the *Mv.* version should purge these major and inoffensive episodes from a good Buddhist *avadāna.* Rather it is probable that the simpler version reflected in *Mv.* has been re-edited with the introduction of the three new episodes. Since certain episodes are peculiar to *Mv.* (notably the closing funeral rites) or *Da.,* it will be necessary to distinguish between these redactions and the versions adopted by the Mahāsāṅghikas (*Mv.* V) and the Mūla-Sarvāstivādins (*Da.* V).

In this recasting the narrator had to make only two minor changes in the original story, viz. shifting the place (from Siṃhapura to Hastināpura) and time (after instead of before their marriage) of the sacrifice. The new episode of the *nāgarāja* merely culminates in procuring the noose with which the hunter captures Manoharā, a result as miraculously achieved in *Mv.* with a simple Act of Truth. The wicked *purohita* no doubt plays a central role in

Characters in the story		*Zp.*	*Mv.*
1. Subāhu	*Mv.*		
Nan-lo-shih	'Chinese A'		
Dhana	*Da.*, 'Saka', *Ak.*	Suddhodana	idem
Ādiccavaṃsa	'Pali'		('Chinese A' : Kāśyapa)
2. 'Sudhanusya mātā'	*Mv.*		
unnamed	'Chinese A'		
'Sudhanasya jananī'	*Da.*		
Sūryaprabhā	'Saka'	Mahāmāyā	idem
Rāmā	*Ak.*		('Chinese A': She-miao)
Candādevī	'Pali'		
3. Sudhanu	*Mv.*, *Zp.*		
Hsü-lo	'Chinese A'	the Buddha	idem
Sudhana	*Da.*, 'Saka', *Ak.*, *Pj.*		
4. The other king:			
Sucandrima	*Mv.*		
king of Ni-ho-pien ('le roi grand-pére')	'Chinese A'	not identified	idem
unnamed	*Da.*, 'Pali'		('Chinese A': Śuddhodana)
Mahendrasena	'Saka', *Ak.*		
5. Sorcerer brahmin:			
absent	*Mv.*, 'Chinese A'		
unnamed	*Da.*, 'Saka',	not identified	absent
Vidyādhara	'Pali' *Ak.*		
6. Druma	All except 'Pali'		
Duma	'Pali'	Sāriputta	Mahānāma
T'ou-mo	'Chinese A'		('Chinese A': not identified)
7. Manoharā	All except 'Chinese A'	Yasodharā	idem
'Devī'	'Chinese A'		('Chinese A' : Gopā)
8. Manoharā's mother:			
unnamed	All	not identified	idem
9. Utpalaka	*Mv.*, *Ak.*, 'Saka'		
Yu-pen	'Chinese A'	Ānanda	Rāhula
Phalaka or Halaka	*Da.*		('Chinese A' : Maudgalyāyana)
Puṇḍarīka	'Pali'		
10. Mālaka	*Mv.*		
'She-li'	'Chinese A'		
Sāraka	*Da.*		
Padamaka	'Saka'	absent	Ānanda
Padmaka	*Ak.*		('Chinese A' : Chandaka)
absent	'Pali'		

11. Kāśyapa	*Mv.*, *Da.*, 'Saka'		
unnamed	'Chinese A'	Kassapa	Mahākāśyapa
Kassapa	'Pali'		('Chinese A' : Śāriputra)
Valkalāyana	*Ak.*		
12. Vasantaka	only in *Mv.*	absent	Chandaka
13. The rebel:			
absent	*Mv.*, 'Chinese A'		
unnamed	*Da.*, 'Saka', 'Pali'	not identified	absent
Megha	*Ak.*		
14. The monkey:			
unnamed	*Mv.*, *Da.*, 'Saka', 'Pali'	Kāḷudāyī	Kaṇṭhaka
'Śakra in disguise'	'Chinese A'		('Chinese A': Kaṇṭhaka)
Vāyuvega	*Ak.*		
15. The *nāgarāja*:			
absent	*Mv.*, 'Chinese A'		
Janmacitraka	*Da.*		
Citra	'Saka', *Ak.*	Moggallāna	absent
Jambucittaka	'Pali'		
16. *purohita* no.1:			
absent	*Mv.*, 'Chinese A'	Devadatta	absent
unnamed	*Da.*, 'Saka'		
Kapila	*Ak.*		
Kusala	'Pali'		
17. *purohita* no. 2:			
absent	*Mv.*, 'Chinese A'	not identified	absent
unnamed	*Da.*, 'Saka', 'Pali'		
Puṣkara	*Ak.*		
18. Śakra:			
absent	*Mv.*, 'Chinese A', 'Saka'		
Śatakratu	*Da.*, *Ak.*	Anuruddha	absent
Sakko	'Pali'		

the new story, but the germs of a court intrigue were already provided in *Mv.* V and can be detected in the scene where the prince is detained by the king and Manoharā is ordered to return to her parents. Here the editor of *Da.* V had to make a slight change, sending the prince on an expedition on the one hand and making Manoharā a victim of the sacrifice on the other. The third innovation, the tests of valour, appears like an appendix, not entailing any alteration in the original story. It only demonstrates the practice of the *vīrya-pāramitā* by the *bodhisattva* amply achieved by *Mv.* V in its account of his crossing the mountains, etc., on his way to the abode of the *kinnaras*.

The remaining differences between *Mv.* V and *Da.* V also suggest that certain improvements have been effected by the latter on the former. The first of these concerns the two hunters. In *Mv.* V Manoharā meets them in the Himālaya and gives them the ring to be given to the prince. She then arrives at the hermitage of Kāśyapa, rests there for a while, and then proceeds to her abode. In *Da.* V she approaches the hermit directly and gives him the ring. *Da.* V would thus be more economical in eliminating two superfluous characters at this point and in making a better use of the hermit.

In *Mv.* V the prince takes Vasantaka as an attendant in his search for Manoharā. Vasantaka otherwise plays no part in the story. He also is absent in *Da.* V. Here the prince sets out alone on his arduous quest. The same motive of presenting the prince as a brave hero seems at work in the short scene connected with the monkey. In *Mv.* V the prince rides on him accompanied by three other attendants. In *Da.* he insists on going alone despite the pleading of the hermit.

While we may assume that *Da.* V has introduced these innovations and improvements into the *Mv.* V version, there is no question of direct borrowing from *Mv.* by *Da.* For despite the general similarity between these two versions *Da.* does not repeat even a single line or verse of *Mv.*, and presents its story in a very different style and language. On the other hand it is clear that the Mūla-Sarvāstivādins have drawn on some earlier *Da.* V text. Had there been a classical Pali *Sudhana-jātaka*[61] it would doubtless have thrown further light on the matter. The possibility of the existence of such intermediate versions is indicated by the 'Saka' which shares only two of the three major innovations (the episode of the *nāga* and the court intrigue) with *Da.* Were this to be the only difference between the two, 'Saka' could have been treated as merely an abridged version of *Da.* But there are in 'Saka' several other distinctive points, preserved in *Ak.*, suggesting an independent source for itself. In the order of their occurrence these can be listed as follows.

(1) Name of the wicked king: Mahendrasena (same in *Ak.*) [p. 539, n. 30].

(2) Name of the *nāgarāja*: Citra (same in *Ak.*) [p. 539, n. 31].

(3) Name of the hunter: Padamaka (Padmaka in *Ak.*) [p. 539, n. 32].

(4) The two hunters being father and son (same in *Ak.*) [p. 539, n. 32].

(5) Padmaka obtaining the *nāgapāśa* on his first visit to the *nāgarāja* (same in *Ak.*) [p. 540, n. 35].

(6) Description of the dream ('Saka' almost identical with *Ak.*) [p. 541, n. 43].

(7) Manoharā going through the *maṇḍala-vāla-grāma* before her flight (through *yajñabhūmi* in *Ak.*) [p. 542, n. 45].

(8) Sudhana's meeting with the monkey on the mount Kaukūlaka (Kukūla in *Ak.*) and riding on it (same in *Ak.*) [p. 543, n. 48].

(9) Account of a *rākṣasī* carrying the prince on the peak of a mountain (similar in *Ak.*) [p. 543, n. 49].

(10) Helping an old woman with her jar before putting the ring into it (same in *Ak.*) [p. 544, n. 50].

(11) Secret meeting of Sudhana and Manoharā before his arrival is revealed to king Druma (same in *Ak.*) [p. 544, n. 52].

There are also three scenes[62] found only in *Da.* but missing both in 'Saka' and *Ak.*

(1) Sudhana's reluctance to leave Manoharā before going on the expedition.

(2) The scene of the battle waged by Pāñcika *yakṣa* on behalf of the prince.

(3) Sudhana's meeting with the hunter before leaving in search of Manoharā.

It is very significant that all these distinctive points, and in the case of the *nāgarāja*[63] and the dream[64] even the phraseology used are reflected in *Ak.*, which in almost all other respects follows *Da.* (and repeats six verses[65] found in the extant version of the latter). This correspondence between 'Saka' and *Ak.* confirms our hypothesis of a source for the 'Saka' independent of both *Mv.* and *Da.*, and in content intermediate between these versions. The compilers of *Da.* must have used an intermediate version related closely to the common sources of 'Saka' and *Ak.*

That Kṣemendra had access to *Da.* and the source material of 'Saka' needs no further proof; but he may have used yet another version now lost to us. His title, as noted above, seems to combine the titles of *Mv.* V and *Da.* V. But there are certain names and a few minor scenes in *Ak.* that cannot be traced to any known version. Whereas two names, Mahendrasena and Padmaka, found otherwise only in the 'Saka' are also to be found in *Ak.*, the 'Saka' name of Sudhana's mother, Sūryaprabhā, is replaced here by Rāmā. Kāśyapa is the name of the hermit in both *Mv.* and *Da.* In the 'Saka' his name is not given. In *Ak.* he is called Valkalāyana. Names like Vidyādhara (for the sorcerer who comes to capture the *nāga*), Kapila and Puṣkara (for the two *purohitas*), Megha (for the rebel), and Vāyuvega (for the king of the monkeys) are found only in *Ak.*

Of the scenes we may note the following:

(1) In *Da.* the king is frightened at Manoharā's flight and is worried that the sacrifice might remain incomplete. The *purohita* simply says: *deva, siddhārtho 'pagatapāpo devaḥ sāmpratam iti* (*Da.*, 449). In *Ak.* the *purohita* is more convincing when he says:

Mantrair mayā samākṛṣṭaḥ Krūrākhyo brahmarākṣasaḥ/
nirvighnas te kratuḥ siddhaḥ sā hatā tena kinnarī// (*Ak.*, 196).

(2) In both 'Saka' and *Da.*, Manoharā first approaches the hermit (in *Mv.* the hunters) and gives him the ring before arriving at her abode. In *Ak.*, after the flight she comes straight to her parents, is given a purifying bath, and after a lapse of several days returns to the hermit to give the ring (*Ak.*, 198-202).

It is, of course, possible that these names and scenes (and possibly the one discussed above, p. 291, n. 53) are merely innovations employed by Kṣemendra in the course of re-editing the story from different versions.

Although the precise date of the composition of the Pali versions is not known, it is generally agreed that they are of a period later than all the versions hitherto discussed. Their relation to their predecessors therefore is of great importance in tracing their main sources, particularly as the works are extra-canonical, and originate (traditionally) not in India or Ceylon, but in the distant land of the Lao.[66]

With the single exception of the name Sudhanu (found only in *Zp.*) there is no indication that *Mv.* has been used by 'Pali'. Only one of the more important distinctive points common to *Ak.* and 'Saka' is found here. This relates to the scene of putting the ring in the pitcher. Both 'Saka' and *Ak.* make the maiden an old woman, unable to lift the jar. *Zp.* and *Pj.* employ an Act of Truth to make her unable to lift it instead of making her old.[67] There is another minor correspondence, viz. the length of the period of their separation. This point is mentioned only in 'Saka' and 'Pali'. In the former this period is of 12 years, in the latter it consists of 7 years, 7 months, and 7 days. Although evidently some common ground exists, it is not sufficient to suggest that use has been made of any version close to the extant 'Saka' and *Ak.*

Consequently, the only source left for 'Pali' would be *Da.* However, from the comparisons given above, it is clear that although the Pali versions have much in common with *Da.*, even more than 'Saka' and *Ak.*, they are by no means identical with it. The differences between 'Pali' and *Da.* tend rather to indicate an independent source for the former. These differences may be grouped under three heads.

(*a*) The absence of certain characters and scenes

(1) Only one hunter and one hermit (instead of two of each).

(2) The scene of Sudhana's lingering in the company of Manoharā before he sets forth on the expedition [pp. 288, nn. 38-40].

(3) The scene of Sudhana's lamentation while seeking for Manoharā [p. 289, n. 47].

(*b*) Additional scenes

(1) Lamentations by Manoharā's mother [p. 287, n. 36].

(2) Sudhana flying tied to the wings of a bird [p. 290, n. 49].

(3) Sudhana lifting the heavy stone by making an Act of Truth [p. 291, n. 55].

(4) The visit of king Druma to the capital of Uttarapāñcāla [p. 291, n. 59].

(*c*) Variations

(1) Sudhana taking the hunter with him (instead of merely obtaining information from him about Manoharā).

(2) Sudhana making the monkey his guide (instead of going alone) [p. 290, n. 48].

(3) Sudhana making an Act of Truth to make the maiden unable to lift the pitcher (instead of simply putting the ring into the pitcher) [p. 290, n. 50].

(4) Sudhana showing his skill in the feat of archery without help. (In *Da.*, Śakra orders *yakṣas* to perform this for him.) [pp. 291, n. 53, 54.]

(5) Sudhana recognizing Manoharā out of seven *kinnarīs* by the help of Sakka who comes down in person, and creates a golden

fly which hovers around Manoharā's head. (In *Da.*, Sudhana has to recognize her out of 1,000 (*Ak.* has 500) *kinnarīs*. Manoharā steps forward when the prince performs an Act of Truth) [p. 291, n. 58].

The last scene, the recognition of Manoharā by the prince with the help of Sakka, supplies, we believe, a clue to the main sources of the 'Pali'. Scholars like Oldenburg, Foucher, and Krom who studied the Borobudur reliefs depicting the story of Sudhana have considered that it was based on *Da.*[68] They had access only to *Mv.* and *Da.*, and the reliefs do indeed to a large extent agree with *Da.* But relief no. 18 (plate I (*b*)) depicting the scene of recognition, offered special difficulties in its interpretation and its identification with the *Da.* account. This relief shows seven maidens seated inside a pavilion (*maṇḍapa*). A young man with a halo is standing in front of them. Behind him there is a raised standard with a winged conch[69] mounted on it. At the other end another person, also with a halo, is seated on a pedestal with attendants crouching under it. The scene clearly depicts the recognition of Manoharā (among seven *kinnarīs*) in the presence of king Druma. Of the two nimbate persons, the seated one was rightly identified by Foucher with king Druma, the only person depicted with a halo on two other occasions (reliefs nos. I, b, 14 and 17)—distinguishable as a king of *kinnaras* (semi-divine beings) from the king of Uttarapāñcāla and all other human beings, including the prince. The standing nimbate figure could, on the basis of the *Da.* account, only be the prince. But as he does not appear with a halo in earlier or later scenes, Foucher assumed that the standing figure also depicted Druma granting his daughter to the Prince.[70] This obvious error was noticed by Krom who identified the standing figure with the prince.[71] The contrast, however, between the ornate splendour of the dress of this nimbate figure and the simplicity of that of the prince in the preceding relief (plate I (*a*)) escaped his notice, and although he observed the raised standard, he did not try to explain its presence in this scene.

The Pali versions, particularly *Pj.*,[72] afford us a more satisfactory explanation of both the halo and the raised standard found in this relief. The standing nimbate figure depicts neither Druma nor the *bodhisattva* but Śakra who according to *Pj.* comes down in person. The arrival of Śakra on the scene is denoted by this standard which appears nowhere else among these 20 reliefs. He would be invisible to all but the prince, an effect achieved by the sculptor in a most ingenious way. Not a single eye is turned towards him. By contrast, in the preceding scene (plate I (*a*)) where the prince is engaged in the first test (the feat of archery) he is keenly watched by a large number of the assembly present. The remaining story, which presumably involved Śakra's conversation with the prince and the hovering of the fly, is left to the imagination of the spectators.

Finally we may note yet another detail that agrees only with 'Pali'. *Da.* speaks of 1,000 *kinnarīs*[73] (*Ak.* of 500) among whom Manoharā is to be recognized. It is obvious that such a large number cannot be depicted on a relief and the sculptor would show only a few of them. Yet the fact that only seven maidens are shown is significant as this number exactly corresponds with the *satta-kaññāyo* of 'Pali'. This number is again repeated in 'Pali' in connection with the scene of Manoharā's bathing in the pond (prior to her capture) and relief no. I, b, 5, depicting this scene, also shows only seven *kinnarīs* (as against the 500 of *Da.*).[74]

It is true that the remaining three scenes (viz. the prince flying across the mountains tied to the wings of a bird,[75] the prince lifting the heavy stone, and Druma's visit to the human world) are not depicted on the Borobudur reliefs. These were perhaps not thought to be of any importance or more probably were later additions to the story. But there is not a single scene in all the 20 reliefs which could be shown to be at variance with the account in 'Pali'. It is therefore evident that the Borobudur reliefs of this story are not based on *Da.* but on some other hitherto unknown version which could also be the primary source for 'Pali'.

Whether this common unidentified source also belonged to the Mūla-Sarvāstivādins or to some other school popular in Java cannot be determined on the basis of 'Pali'. Nor is it possible to ascertain the precise date at which it became accessible to the Theravādins of the South East Asian countries who presumably adopted it with several additions of their own and rewrote it in Pali in perfect imitation of a classical *jātaka* for *Pj.* and *Zp.* Despite their apocryphal nature, these two versions became very popular among the Buddhists of Burma and Siam, and were adapted later for *pyos,* plays and theatrical performances composed in their own languages.

The earliest of these[76] appears to be the *Manoharī pyo*[77] by

Nawade dated 1579 based on *Zp.* This is followed by the *Sūjā pyo* by Padesarājā in the first half of the eighteenth century. In 1776 appeared a *Yagan* called *Ngwedaung*[78] by Shwedaung Nandathu. A play based on this story called *Dwe Me Naw pya zat*[79] (actually called *Ngwedaungthu* 'Girl of the Silver Hill') by Chan Mya was published in Rangoon in 1880. In 1878 A. Fytche published a translation 'The Silver Hill: a Burmese drama'.[80] Fytche does not mention the sources of his translation. It was probably based on an oral text, as in the case of J. Smith who in 1839 published a similar version of the story of Sudhana in his 'Specimen of the Burmese drama'.[81]

In Siam also the *Sudhana-jātaka* of the *Pj.* version became the source for many popular theatrical plays in Thai.[82] According to René Nicolas,[83] the generic term for a theatrical performance of the ancient 'chatri' type is *nōrā,* a southern Thai variant of central Thai *manōrā* (from Pali Manoharā). In the southern provinces of Siam the story of Manoharā has long been a favourite piece.

It is difficult to determine the extent of the dependence of these popular works in Burmese and Thai on the two Pali versions. Works like the *Manoharī pyo* are clearly based on *Zp.* But the English translations available to us indicate the possibility that independent popular oral traditions exist, directly connected with the Borobudur reliefs. The additions found in these two are of a minor nature, e.g. Manoharā giving birth to a child while the prince is away on the expedition, or king Druma subjecting the prince to an additional test of subduing a wild elephant and a horse. The omissions are more significant. The episode of the *nāgarāja* is only hinted at: the hunter obtains the noose from the hermit which had been presented to him by a dragon.[84] The second test of 'Pali', the lifting the heavy stone,[85] and the last scene, Druma's visit to Uttarapāñcāla, are missing here as also in the Borobudur reliefs.

But the more popular and distinctive scenes of 'Pali', e.g. the flight of the prince tied to the wings of a bird, the Act of Truth for making the maiden unable to lift the pitcher, and finally the intervention of Sakka in the scene of the recognition are all retained in both. The last scene undergoes a still further refinement in Fytche's version. Here the seven maidens expose their finger through a sevenfold screen and the prince has to recognize his bride by identifying her. The prince begs the 'Powers' to 'grant him a sign', and a bee settles on Manoharā's finger."[86]

The use of the screens is probably an afterthought suggested by the stylized hand-gestures of the Borobudur reliefs. But there is no doubt that Sakka plays an important role in this story as well as in a majority of these apocryphal *jātakas*. He appears in no less than 31 of the 50 *jātakas* of *Zp.*,[87] and on 30 occasions is identified with Anuruddha, renowned for his 'clairvoyant eye' (*dibbacakkhū ti pākaṭo*). This appears to be an imitation of the *Vessantara-jātaka* where also Sakka is identified with Anuruddha.[88] Otherwise in the Theravāda tradition, particularly that of Ceylon, Anuruddha plays a no more significant role than the other chief disciples of the Buddha. The prominence given to him in Burma and also in Siam[89] suggests the existence of a cult dedicated to Anuruddha and identified with Sakka, the chief of the 37 *nats* of Burma. It may not be without significance that the founder of the Pagan dynasty, the king responsible for placing Sakka at the head of the 37 *nats*, the first Buddhist king of Burma, should also be called Anuruddha[90] (A.D. 1044-1077). He might have been a royal patron of this cult and, in conformity with the concept of 'Devarājā' of those regions, might even have been identified with Sakka. Popular stories displaying Sakka's graceful interventions, originating even outside the Theravāda tradition, as in the case of the *Sudhana-jātaka*, might then have found a place among the orthodox Theravādins, forming a nucleus for the later apocryphal collections like *Zp.* and *Pj.*

In the light of the comparisons of the various texts given above it would appear that *Mv.* V is the oldest, that the redaction used by 'Saka' occupies a position intermediate between *Mv.* V and *Da.*, and that *Da.* is a subsequent, more developed redaction. Kṣemendra in his *Ak.* follows *Da.* in the main but appears to have had access to source materials connected with 'Saka'. An unidentified redaction belonging to the *Da.* V but differing in several details from the Indian and 'Saka' texts seems to have reached Borobudur where it became the source of reliefs nos. I, b, 1-20, and also of the apocryphal versions written in Pali, in imitation of the classical *Jātaka* book, by the Theravādins of South East Asia. These in turn, together with popular traditions surviving from the days of the Borobudur reliefs, appear to have inspired the composition of a large number of *pyos*, plays and theatrical performances based on this story popular even to this day in Burma and Siam.

NOTES

1. *Mahāvastu,* ed. Senart, II, 94-115.
2. N. Dutt (ed.), *Gilgit manuscripts,* III, 1, 123-49.
3. *Taishō Tripiṭaka,* XXIV, 59 ff. (C. A.D. 700).
4. *Tibetan Tripiṭaka,* XLI, 193-3-5 (Ge 190 b 5 ff.).
5. *Divyāvadāna,* ed. Cowell and Neil, XXX, 435-61.

As the *Bhaiṣajya-vastu,* the extant Mūla-Sarvāstivāda text where this story appears, is incomplete, and as the Tibetan translation of it, with the exception of six verses (see p. 288, n. 41, and p. 291, n. 53) and a few minor points (noted by Professor Dutt in *Gil. MSS*) is almost identical with the *Divyāvadāna* version it will not be wrong to treat the latter as an authoritative Mūla-Sarvāstivāda version. I-ching's translation of the *Bhaiṣajya-vastu,* in the light of random comparison made for me by Professor J. Brough, is based on a text not significantly different from the *Divyāvadāna* version (see p. 288, n. 41, and p. 291, n. 53).

On the sources of the *Divyāvadāna* in general, see Huber, 'Les sources du *Divyāvadāna*', *BEFEO,* VI, 1906, 1-37; Lévi, 'Les éléments de formation du Divyāvadāna', *TP,* Sér. 2, VIII, 1907, 105-22; Lévi, 'La Dṛṣṭânta-paṅkti et son auteur', *JA,* CCXI, juillet-sept. 1927, 103 ff.; J. Przyluski, 'Fables in the Vinaya-Piṭaka of the Sarvāstivādin school', *IHQ,* V, 1, 1929, 1-5. For a complete bibliography on this subject and a comparison of several versions of a similar story from the *Divyāvadāna* (XIII) see Kenneth K.S. Ch'en, 'A study of the Svāgata story in the *Divyāvadāna* in its Sanskrit, Pali, Tibetan, and Chinese versions', *Harvard Journal of Asiatic Studies,* IX, 3-4, 1947, 207-314.

6. *Avadānakalpalatā* of Kṣemendra, ed. with Tibetan text by S.C. Das and S.C. Vidyābhūṣaṇa (Bibliotheca Indica), II, 319-413. It consists of 337 verses.
7. H. W. Bailey (ed.), *Khotanese Buddhist texts,* 1951, nos. 7-12 (pp. 11-39). The Khotanese *Jātaka-stava* (*Khotanese texts,* I, 198-219) devotes eight verses (23 r 1-4) to this story.
8. The 'extra-canonical' nature of the *Paññasa-jātaka* was first established by L. Feer in his article "Les Jâtakas', *JA,* 7e Sér., V, 1875 (section 'Recueils extra-canoniques', pp. 417 ff.). In 1917 L. Finot published a complete concordance of the three recensions of this collection, one in Laotian and two in Pali. Of the last two, one is found in Burma and is called *Zimmé Paṇṇāsa,* and the other is the *Paññāsa-jātaka* found in Siam and Cambodia. For full details see 'Recherches sur la littérature laotienne', *BEFEO,* XVII, 5, 1917, 44-50. H. Deydier in his *Introduction á la connaissance du Laos* gives a brief description of the Laotian version and also states that the story of Sudhana is found in the paintings on the facade of a pagoda near Luang Prabang (p. 112). Both Finot and Deydier believe that these 'extra-canonical' works are of recent date and were composed in Chieng Mai during the fifteenth-eighteenth centuries by the local monks (see p. 284, n. 11).

Only one story of the entire collection has been critically edited and translated so far. This is found in Mme. G. Terral's 'Samuddaghosajātaka: conte Pali tiré du Paññāsa-jātaka', *BEFEO,* XLVIII, 1, 1956, 249-351. In her introduction Mme. Terral deals at length with the manuscript material of these collections and the peculiarities of their language.

There are three MSS of the Cambodian recension of the *Paññāsa-jātaka* in the Bibliothéque Nationale in Paris, one in Phnom Penh (Terral, op. cit., 266) and one in Colombo Museum Library (obtained from Cambodia in exchange—see *Catalogue of palm-leaf MSS*, I, 1938). Two Laotian *nissayas* of the *Paññāsa-jātaka* (entitled *Ha-sip-xat*) are listed in Pierre-Bernard Lafont's 'Inventaire des manuscrits des pagodes du Laos', *BEFEO*, LII, 2, 1963. The National Museum at Bangkok has a large number of palm-leaf MSS of the *Paññāsa-jātaka* (in Cambodian characters) hitherto unpublished. During my visit there in 1961, I was able to obtain, through the courtesy of the curator of the Museum, microfilm copies of eight (incomplete) MSS written during the post-Ayuthyan period and two MSS, one in Burmese (*jātakas* 1-17) and the other in Mon (*jātakas* 1-11) characters. I was also able to obtain microfilms of a MS in Laotian characters from the private collection of Dr. Christian Welder. This MS contains six stories and is dated Sakarāj 950 (A.D. 1589), perhaps the oldest MS of the *Paññāsa-jātaka* so far discovered.

9. Foucher in his 'Notes d' archéologie bouddhique (les bas-reliefs de Borobudur)', *BEFEO*, IX, 1909, 9-18, confirms Oldenburg's observation and adds that two more reliefs, nos. I, b, 1-2 also depicted the same story. For the purpose of this identification *Mv.* and *Da.* were compared but *Ak.* was not considered of any help as it was composed later than the Borobudur period. See N. J. Krom and T. van Erp, *Beschrijving van Barabudur*, 1920, 219-35, where details of 20 reliefs (Ser. I, b, 1-20, plates I-X) are given and compared with the corresponding story in *Da.* The Saka version was not then known and *Zimmé Paṇṇāsa*, although published in 1911, does not seem to have been consulted. As will be shown below (p. 314, nn. 71 and 75) certain scenes in reliefs nos. 15 and 18 can be satisfactorily identified only by means of the Pali versions.

10. *Zimmé Paṇṇāsa* (i.e. Chieng Mai 50) edited anonymously and published by the Hanthawaddy Press, Rangoon, 1911. The work, an octavo of 685 pp., has no introduction, critical apparatus, or variant readings.

MSS of *Zp.* are not found, to the best of my knowledge, anywhere outside Burma. In 1961, I was unable to find even a single MS of it in the libraries of Rangoon, Mandalay, and Pagan. I learnt from an elderly Mahāthera, chief abbot of Pagan, that, according to an oral tradition current in his young days, King Myndon of Mandalay (1853-78) had disapproved of this apocryphal work and consequently very few MSS of it were to be found in the monasteries of Burma. It is not found in Siam, not even in Chieng Mai, possibly the place of origin of this work as the title seems to indicate. In 1962, however, a MS of it consisting of 162 leaves was discovered by the Venerable U Wa Tha Wa in the Zetawun Monastery in Monyway (in Monywa district) near Mandalay. I have been able to obtain photographs of this rare MS by the courtesy of the Venerable U Wa Tha Wa and U Maung Maung Tin of the University of Mandalay. The MS is complete and is dated Sakarāj 1169, i.e. A.D. 1807. It is identical with the published *Zp.* and might have been the source of the latter.

11. Three parts containing 15 *jātakas* have been published by the Institut Bouddhique, Phnom Penh, 1953.

An abridged Siamese translation (with the original Pali verses) of the *Paññāsa-jātaka* was first published in Bangkok in 1926. It was published again in 1956 by the Fine Arts Department, and is entitled *Pannyāt Chādok* (*Paññāsa-jātaka*) *chabap hō, samut haeng chāt* (National Library version). In his preface to the first edition, Prince Damrong states that these stories were composed in Chieng Mai around A.D. 1467-1667. He also refers to the tradition that these stories were not approved of by a king of Burma. The second edition published in two volumes contains 61 stories instead of the traditional 50 found in the Cambodian version.

12. 'The Sudhana poem of Ṛddhiprabhāva', *BSOAS,* XXIX, 3, 1966, 506-32. I am deeply grateful to Professor Sir Harold Bailey for his kind permission to use the typescript of his translation in preparing this article.

13. *Na bhikṣavo idānīm eva Yaśodharā khedena labdhā anyadā pi eṣā mayā mahatā khedena mahatā śrameṇa mahatā vīryeṇa labdhā* (*Mv.*, II, 94). The first Chinese version (*liu-tu-chi-ching*—'Chinese A') gives a totally different *nidāna.* Here the story seems to illustrate not how Gautama obtained his wife, but Chandaka's former rendering of assistance to Sudhana which ultimately made him responsible for helping Gautama to become an ascetic. At the end of the story Chandaka is identified with one of the two monks (unlike *Mv.*, where Chandaka is identified with Vasantaka) who help the prince in his search for Manoharā. Chandaka plays a very minor role in the story, and it is likely that the source lacked the attested *Mv. nidāna.*

14. *Punar api mahārāja yan mayānuttarasamyaksambodhiprāptaye dānāni dattāni puṇyāni kṛtāni vīryapāramitā ca paripūritā anuttarā samyaksambodhir nārādhitā tac chrūyatām* (*Da.*,435).

15. *Tatsaṅgam āliṅganayor nirāśā bhrāntākhilāśā viṣamūrcchiteva/*
dhṛtiṃ vayasyām iva vārayantīṃ nirasya saudhāt tanum utsasarja//
Yadā yadā pallavapeśalāṅgī dehaṃ samutsṛṣṭavatī satī sā/
tadā tadā manmathamohitāṃ tāṃ dayārdracakṣur bhagavān rarakṣa// (*Ak.*, 4-5).
The words of Mv., *mahatā khedena labdhā,* find an echo in
Mayāpi tasyā viraheṇa pūrvaṃ janmāntare māravimohitena/
saṃsaktasantāpanimittabhūtaḥ khedaḥ prabhūtavyasano 'nubhūtaḥ// (*Ak.*, 8).

16. '*Kuto nu āgacchasi luddakā' ti. Imaṃ dhammadesanaṃ satthā Jetavane viharanto ekaṃ ukkaṇṭhitabhikkhuṃ ārabbha kathesi. So kira ekadivasamhi bhikkhāya caranto ekaṃ itthiṃ uttamarūpadharaṃ disvā paṭibaddhacitto hutvā tato nivattetvā ekaṃ antaṃ pattaṃ ṭhapetvā adhomukho dummano pajjhāyanto nisīdi. Tadassa sahāyakā(o) bhikkhu taṃ disvā 'bhante, tumhākaṃ aphāsukan 'ti pucchi. 'Avuso, na me aphāsukaṃ, hiyyo bhikkhācāratthāya caranto ekaṃ itthiṃ disvā paṭibaddhacitto hutvā tena me ukkaṇṭhitam eva āvuso 'ti. Te pi bhikkhū taṃ gahetvā bhagavato santike dassesuṃ. Te satthārā 'kiṃ nu kho bhikkhave anicchamānaññ eva bhikkhuṃ gahetvā āgacchathā' ti vutte taṃ attham ārocesuṃ. 'Saccaṃ kira tvaṃ bhikkhu ukkaṇṭhitosī' ti pucchitvā 'āma bhante' ti vutte, 'mā bhikkhu evarūpaṃ kareyyāsi, tvaṃ saddhāya pabbajito attano pitaraṃ chaḍḍetvā mama niyyānike sāsane pabbajitvā kathaṃ kilesarasaṃ gaccheyyāsi? Bhikkhu, mātugāmo nāma anatthakaro dujjayo tasmā hi bhikkhu sankiliṭṭhaṃ duccaritadhammaṃ vinodeyyāsi, kathaṃ ukkaṇṭhitaṃ gaccheyyāsi? Pubbe paṇḍitā mātugāmaṃ nissāya mahantaṃ rajjasiriṃ mātāpitūnañ ca anoloketvā attano jīvitañ ca agaṇetvā mātugāmarasena atidukkaraṃ agamaṃsū' ti vatvā tuṇhī ahosi. Tehi yācito atītaṃ āhari. Pj.*, 29-30.

The *Zp.* version of this passage is larger than *Pj.* by almost a half and is repetitive and elaborate, showing a certain interest in such items as *śamatha, vipassanā,* and *asubha-kammaṭṭhāna. Pj.* is as usual short and more to the point.

17. According to 'Chinese A' the two kings are related to each other as father and son, the latter (Nan-lo-shih) being the father of Sudhanu.

18. In 'Chinese A' the king of Ni-ho-pien (Siṃhapura?) learns from some selfish brahmins that it is possible to go to heaven alive by performing a sacrifice of all beings. The king undertakes this sacrifice. After four months the brahmins put up an impossible condition of including a *kinnarī* among the beings to be

sacrificed so that they can escape the blame if the sacrifice does not yield the desired result. In *Mv.* the *ṛṣis* who are invited by the king to inspect the sacrifice and point out any deficiencies suggest that it is incomplete without a *kinnarī* (*pratyavekṣantu bhagavanto yajñavāṭaṃ kiṃ paripūrṇaṃ na veti...Deva kinnarīye ūno...* (*Mv.*, II, 96)).

19. Later in the story *Mv.* mentions the names of two hunters, Utpalaka and Mālaka, whom the *kinnarī* meets on her way home in the Himālaya. In 'Chinese A', however, these two are referred to here as 'deux religieux' (p. 294); by an order of the king they are brought to the capital, are fêted, and requested to find a *kinnarī.*

20. This name is not noted in Pali, but appears frequently as a name of a king of the *kinnaras* in Buddhist Sanskrit works. A Mahāyāna text called *Druma-kinnara-rāja-paripṛcchā-sūtra,* translated into Chinese by Kumārajīva, is reported by Nakamura Hajime in his 'A Critical Survey of Mahāyāna and Esoteric Buddhism', *Acta Asiatica,* VI, 1964, 68.

21. *Ṛṣi āha. Satyavākyena etā badhyanti na śaknonti antarahāyituṃ ....*
Dhītā tvaṃ kinnararājasya Drumarājño yaśasvinī/
etena satyavākyena tiṣṭha baddhāsi kinnarī//
Yathā tvaṃ Drumarājasya dhītā Drumeṇa rājñā saṃvṛddhā/
satyavacanena bhadre Manohare mā padaṃ gaccha// (*Mv.*, II, 96).

On *satyavacana,* see E. W. Burlingame: 'The Act of Truth (saccakiriya)', *JRAS,* 1917, 429-67; W. Norman-Brown: 'Basis of the Hindu Acts of Truth', *Review of Religion,* v, 1, 1940-1, 36 ff.

In 'Chinese A' Manoharā is named 'Devī (à forme humaine)'. Nor is there any mention of the *satyavacana;* the two monks learn a spell from the hermit, pronounce it, and bring her in a bamboo cage to the capital.

22. *Mv.* lists here the ten *kuśala* and *akuśala karmapathas.* 'Chinese A' devotes several long passages to the condemnation of brahmins and their sacrifices.

23. *Rājñā Subāhunā Sudhanukumāro śabdāpito. Putra jānapadā oravanti. Arthārthāni na samanuśāsasi yathāpūrvaṃ, Manoharāye ... pramatto viharasi visarjehi putra etāṃ ....Rājñā ca gamanāya ... mātāpitṛṇāṃ sakāśaṃ ...* (*Mv.*, II, 101).

24. *Tahiṃ ... duve lubhdaputrā mṛgavyāṃ aṇvanti. Eko ... Utpalako nāma dvitīyo ....Mālako nāma* (ibid.).

'Chinese A' again refers to them as 'deux religieux' who had apparently returned to their abode after first having captured her.

25. *So dāni rājakulāto niryātvā sārdhaṃ Vasantakena ekinā paricārakena ...* (*Mv.*, II, 103).

This name occurs only in *Mv.* In 'Chinese A' the guardian deity of the palace shows him the way, but the prince leaves alone in search of the 'Devī'.

26. *...iha uddeśe vānarā prativasanti. Yo teṣāṃ yūthapati so mama abhiprasanno... tam ahaṃ vānararājaṃ adhyeṣiṣyaṃ....Ṛṣi āha. Imaṃ kumāraṃ ātmanā caturthaṃ Drumasya ... kinnaranagaraṃ tahiṃ nehi. Vānaro āha. Bhagavan nemi* (*Mv.*, II, 108).

In 'Chinese A' this monkey is Śakra in disguise : 'En ce moment, Śakra, roi des devas, prit la forme d'un singe dont le merveilleux prestige faisait trembler la montagne....' (p. 301).

27. *Evaṃ Sudhanu mahatā vibhūṣāye...kinnararājño nagaraṃ praveśito...Drumeṇa ca ... abhinandito utsange saṃveśito ...* (*Mv.*, II, 111).

28. *...Subāhunā mārgaṇā kāritā ...tasya bhavati mṛto bhaviṣyati kumāro....Tena rājñā kumārasya Sudhanusya mṛtasya kāryāṇi kṛtāni...*(ibid.).
This incident is not found in 'Chinese A' or any other version.

29. The names Dhana (only once Mahādhana, *Da.*, 435) and Sudhana in *Da.* are less convincing than their *Mv.* counterparts Subāhu and Sudhanu. Grammatically it is more likely that *-u* changed to *-a* than vice versa. In *Da.*, *ayaṃ dārako Dhanasya rājñaḥ putro bhavatu dārakasya Sudhano nāmeti* can account for the advent of Dhana. The name Subāhu appears only in *Mv.*, but Sudhanu reappears in *Zp.*; despite an explanation by the latter: *tassa pana jātadivase yeva tesu ṭhānesu tā pi nidhikumbhiyo bhūmito uṭṭhahitvā pākaṭā honti. Atha Ādiccavaṃsarājā pi taṃ acchariyam disvā...Sudhano tv eva nāmaṃ akāsi* (*Zp.*, 146). Thus *Zp.* introduces Sudhana but discontinues this in favour of Sudhanu. *Pj.* is consistent in calling him Sudhana, Sudhana-kumāra, and Sudhanarāja.

30. 'As a frontier king lived king Mahendrasena' (Bailey, 'Sudhana poem', 507).
cf. *Babhūva tasya bhūbhartur bhūpatir bhūmyanantaraḥ/*
mānī Mahendrasenākhyaḥ prakhyātapṛthuvikramaḥ//(*Ak.*, 13).

31. 'A meritorious *nāgarāja* by name Citra dwelt where in the ground at all times the seeds ripen' (Bailey, 'Sudhana poem', 507).
cf. *Viṣaye nāgarājo 'sti Citro nāma bahūdakaḥ/*
akāle śasyaniṣpattis tat prabhāveṇa jāyate/ (*Ak.*, 33a, 34a).

32. *Da.* gives the name of this hunter as Halaka but it is stated in the footnote (p. 283, n. 2) that MS C generally gives Phalaka. Professor Brough, who checked I-ching's transcription of this name, informs me that Phalaka is the correct reading in the Mūla-Sarvāstivāda version. This is also confirmed by the reading in the *Bhaiṣajya-vastu* (*Gil. MSS*, III, 1, 133).

Da. actually refers to two hunters called Sāraka and Phalaka. These might correspond to She-li and Yu-pen of 'Chinese A' (p. 294); *Mv.* in this context does not name the hunter, but on a subsequent occasion it refers to two hunters called Utpalaka and Mālaka (*Mv.*, II, 102). It is possible to conceive some relationship between Phalaka, Yu-pen, and Utpalaka, but we cannot determine which is the more original form. As for Sāraka (corresponding to She-li and Mālaka) his name is mentioned only once in *Da.* : *tatra ... dvau lubdhakau prativasataḥ Sārako Phalakaḥ. Sārako kālagato Phalako jīvati* (*Da.*, 437). It is not clear why his name should be introduced as he does not play any part in the story. This obscurity is removed in both 'Saka' and *Ak.* where the two hunters called Padmaka ('Saka' : Padamaka) and Utpalaka are related as father and son. The father obtains the *nāgapāśa* and when he dies it passes to his son who captures Manoharā:

'When he (Padamaka) passed away, after the son carried on, Utpalaka by name; the noose descended to him' (Bailey, 'Sudhana poem', 508).
cf. *Lubdhakaḥ Padmako nāma sa me saṃrakṣaṇakṣamaḥ/*
putrāyotpalakākhyāya pāśaṃ dattvā vyapadyata/ (*Ak.*, 48a, 65b).

33. *Ṛṣiḥ kathayati. Kiṃ ratnaiḥ ... tasya bhavane amogho nāma pāśas tiṣṭhati taṃ yācasva* (*Da.*, 439).

34. *...alaṃ mama ratnaiḥ kiṃ tv etaṃ amoghapāśaṃ prayacchatheti ... yadi asti kṛtam upakṛtaṃ cānuprayaccheti...*(ibid.).
cf. *Nāgapāsaṃ taṃ yācāmi, tenāhaṃ idha gacchāmi/*
tasmā taṃ detha taṃ sīghaṃ, nāgarājā mahiddhiko ti//
...bho nāgarāja, tvaṃ atipapañcaṃ avatvā nāgapāsaṃ va me dehī ti (*Zp.*, 153).

35. 'He (the *nāga* king) ... presented wealth to him. He for his part asked them for the *amogha-pāśa* ...' (Bailey, 'Sudhana poem', 508).
cf. *abhyaracamānaś Citreṇa kañcit kālam uvāsa saḥ//*
Kadācid atha nāgena pūjyamānaḥ savismayaḥ/
vidyuddāmopamaṃ pāśam amoghākhyaṃ dadarśa saḥ//(*Ak.*, 60b, 61).

36. *Zp.*, 154-5; also 156.

37. *Tayā śirasthaś cūḍāmaṇir datta uktaś ca. Eṣa cūḍāmaṇir yasya haste tasyāhaṃ vaśī bhavāmi* (*Da.*, 443). Cf. *Atha so luddako ... bhoti devī, tvaṃ tuyhaṃ pādapūraṇañ ca alankārabhaṇḍañ ca mayhaṃ dehī ti* (*Zp.*, 155).

For similar tales where bird-maidens were captured by stealing their feather-robes, see A. T. Hatto, 'The Swan Maiden: a folk-tale of north Eurasian origin ?', *BSOAS*, xxiv, 2, 1961, 326 ff.

38. *Gaccha kumāra ... kārvaṭikaṃ saṃnāmaya. Evaṃ deveti...antaḥpuraṃ praviṣṭo Manoharādarśanāc cāsya sarvaṃ vismṛtaṃ.... Rājā kathayati ... nirgataḥ kumāro 'ntaḥpurāt preṣayitavyo yathā Manoharāyāḥ sakāśaṃ na prativasatīti* ... (*Da.*, 446).

39. See p. 286, n. 23.

40. *Iti pitrā samādiṣṭaḥ samīhitaraṇotsavaḥ/*
kinnarīvirahālolaḥ so 'bhūd dolākulaḥ kṣaṇam//
Acirāgamanākhyānair yatnenāśvāsya vallabhām/ (*Ak.*, 153, 154a).
cf. *Mahāsatto, bhadde, tvaṃ mā socasi, mā paridevesi, mama gamanaṃ ciraṃ na hoti ... khippaṃ eva āyāmī ti taṃ samassāsetvā ... nagarato nikkhami* (*Zp.*, 161).

41. *So Manoharāsantakaṃ cūḍāmaṇim ādāya mātus sakāśaṃ ... kathayati ...*
Duhitā Śakrakalpasya kinnarendrasya māninī/
pālyā virahaśokārtā madvātsalyadhiyā tvayā// (*Da.*, 446).

This verse is not found in the extant *Bhaiṣajya-vastu* (*Gil. MSS*, iii, 1, 139) nor in its Chinese and Tibetan translations (see p. 291, n. 53). It is, however, found in *Ak.* :
jananīṃ svairam abhyetya praṇipatya jagāda saḥ//
Duhitā Śakrakalpasya ... madvātsalyadhiyā tvayā// (*Ak.*, 154b, 155).

42. *Tena khalu samayena Vaiśravaṇo mahārājo ... paśyati Sudhanakumāraṃ .... Tasyaitad abhavat. Ayaṃ bhadrakalpiko bodhisattvaḥ ... sahāyyam asya karaṇīyaṃ ... Pāñcikaṃ ... āmantrayate* ... (*Da.*, 447).
cf. *Tasmiṃ khaṇe sakalanagare ārakkhadevatāyo ... āhaṃsu :*
Bho devatā sabbe mayaṃ vasantā sabbaṭṭhānesu/
ārakkhāma tattha tattha gataṃ sasenaṃ Sudhanuṃ sadā// (*Zp.*, 161).

Both *Da.* and 'Pali' give long descriptions of the battle. The 'Saka' is very brief and *Ak.* devotes only half a line: *sa yayau tūrṇaṃ sainyācchāditadiṅmukhaḥ/* (157b).

43. *Da.* : *Dhanena ca rājñā svapno dṛṣṭaḥ. Gṛdhreṇāgatya rājña udaraṃ sphoṭayitvāntrāṇy ākarṣya tan nagaram antrair veṣṭitaṃ saptaratnāni gṛhaṃ praveśyamānāni dṛṣṭāni* (447).

'Saka': 'That night king Dada saw a dream that all his enemies had surrounded the city, they had burst open his belly, drawn out the intestines, had three times fastened it around the city' (Bailey, 'Sudhana poem', 510).
Ak. : *Dṛṣṭam adya mayā svapne niruddhaṃ śatrubhiḥ puram/*
pāṭitodarakṛṣṭaiś ca mamāntrair pariveṣṭitam// (164).
Zp. : *Evarūpo supino ahosi : rañño antaṃ kucchito nikkhamitvā sakalajambudīpaṃ tikkhattuṃ parivaṭṭetvā puna kucchiyaṃ pavisitvā aṭṭhāsī ti* (162).

These four accounts of the dream show a curious relationship between the four versions. The *gṛdhra* of *Da.* and the corresponding 'enemies' in both 'Saka' and *Ak.* are absent from 'Pali'. The 'three times' of 'Saka' is missing in *Da.* and *Ak.* but is found in 'Pali'. The reference to *saptaratnāni* is peculiar to *Da.*, while the words *gṛhaṃ praveśyamānāni* correspond to 'Pali' *kucchiyaṃ pavisitvā*. *Da.* agrees with 'Saka' -*Ak.* for the opening but with 'Pali' for the close.

44. *Tyajed ekaṃ kulasyārthe grāmasyārthe kulaṃ tyajed/*
grāmaṃ janapadasyārthe ātmārthe pṛthivīṃ tyajed// (*Da.*, 448).

This verse is found in the *Mahābhārata* and several other works. See Ludwik Sternbach: *Cāṇakya-nīti-text-tradition,* I, 1, Hoshiarpur, 1963, 109.
Tyajante jīvitasyārthe nijadeśapriyātmajāḥ/
jīvitād aparaṃ rājan jīvaloke 'sti na priyam// (*Ak.*, 193).
Suṇāhi me kathaṃ deva na thomenti paraṃ rakkhaṃ/
attānaṃ anurakkhā va thomenti yeva paṇḍitā//
Sasīse patati aggi puttaṃ pi jahati tadā/
kiṃ mocesi pare dukkhī tvaṃ gavesi sukhaṃ sadā// (*Zp.*, 164).

45. *Tat samanantaram eva Manoharā gaganatalam utplutya gāthaṃ bhāṣate ...* (*Da.*, 449). Cf. 'When she came forth into the *maṇḍala-vāla-grāma* (gathering of the circular sacrificial enclosure) she three times incanted, she rose into the air (Bailey, 'Sudhana poem', 511).
cf. *Śvaśvā dattaṃ samādāya baddhvā mūrdhni śikhāmaṇim/*
nṛpāhṛtā kratukṣetraṃ gatvā vyoma vyagāhata// (*Ak.*, 193).
Narānaṃ migapakkhīnaṃ viyogo te kato pubbe/
tena atthi vipākena viyogo t'ajja patinā//
Kiṃ karomi mama pubbe kareyya paraviyogaṃ/
tena kammavipākena viyogo hoti amhākan ti// (*Zp.*, 166).

47. These and other striking similarities have been noted by A. Gawroński in his *Notes sur les sources de quelques drames Indiens,* 1921, 18-39, where the author discusses at great length the relationship of *Sudhanakumārāvadāna* (*Da.*) to the legend of Purūravas and Urvaśī in general and to Act IV of *Vikramorvaśīya* in particular.

48. *Mv.*, II, 108 : *So dānī vānarādhipati tato eva āśramāto ātmanā caturthaṃ kumāraṃ pṛṣṭaṃ ārohayitvā* .... *Da.*, 455 : ... *tān apy atikramya Himavān parvatarājaḥ. Tat praveśena tvayā imāni bhaiṣajyāni samudānetavyāni ... vānaraḥ samudānetavyo* .... On p. 457: ...*tatas tena yathopadiṣṭāḥ sarve samudānītāḥ sthāpayitvā vānaraṃ. Alaṃ kumāra ... tvaṃ ekāki* ....

Schiefner's translation differs here from *Da.* : 'When he had obtained all but the monkey, he came back with them to the Rishi. The Rishi gave him a monkey and said, O youth, ... alone, without companions, ...' (*Tibetan tales,* 70). See *Tibetan Tripiṭaka,* XLI, 201-5-6 (Ge 204[a6]).

'Saka' (Bailey, 'Sudhana poem', 512): 'He will come to the Black Mountains called Kaukūlaka. There lives a king of monkeys, huge in limb. To him food is to be given, and he will take him on his back'.
Ak., 262b, 263 : *Himavantaṃ atikramya Kukūlādrim avāpa saḥ//*
Phalopahāraiḥ svīkṛtya tatra vānarayūthapam/
Vāyuvegākhyam āruyha sa taṃ śailam alaṅghayat//
Zp., 172: *Evañ ca vatvā mahāsatto attano magganāyakaṃ makkaṭapotakaṃ ādāya ... gamanam ārabhi.*

49. There is no reference to any bird helping the prince in *Mv. Da.* refers to a 'king of birds' which will convey him over a mountain called Vajraka, fourth in a list of nine mountains: (*Vajrake pakṣirājena praveśaḥ* (*Da.*, 450; 456)).

In 'Saka' (on the next mountain called Kāmarūpī) there is a *rākṣasī*: '... (he) will come to the *Kāmarupins.* In that place one amorous *rākṣasī* lives who through passion entices beings, at the last destroys them.... The *rākṣasī* carries him off, mounts him on the mountain peak. There he must promptly slay her .... Afterwards he will come to the mountain by name Ekadhvaja. There dwells a vulture-shaped *rākṣasī*. For her let him touch the *vīṇā* and surely he will escape without danger' (Bailey, 'Sudhana poem', 512).

Ak. is in close agreement here with the 'Saka' account except that here the prince uses the *vīṇā* not against the vulture-shaped *rākṣasī* on Ekadhvaja but against an ordinary *rākṣasī* on the mount Kāmarūpa. Here the 'vulture-shaped' *rakṣasī* appears on the mount Vajraka and carries him off to the peak of that mountain:

Vīṇāsvanair vaśīkṛtya rākṣasīṃ kāmarūpiṇīm/
Kāmarūpādrim ullaṅghya prayayau kinnarīpriyaḥ// (265).
Athogrataram āruyha Vajrakākhyaṃ sa parvatam/
gṛdhrarūpāṃ samālokya rākṣasīṃ piṣitaiṣiṇīm//(267).
Māṃsalubdhā tam utkṣipya gṛdhrarūpā niśācarī/
nidadhe śikharasyāgre bhoktuṃ bhīṣaṇavigrahā// (268).

Although some common basis exists for the incident of a *rākṣasa*-bird carrying the prince across the mountains, 'Pali' alone shows this bird to be friendly to the prince and refers to his flight (in the last stage of his journey) tied to the wings of it : *Tasmiṃ khaṇe bahū Hatthiliṅgasakuṇā taṃ vettavanaṃ āgantvā tatth' eva nisīdantā aññamaññaṃ pucchiṃsu. Bhonto, ajja mayaṃ kuhiṃ gocaraṃ gaṇhāmā ti.... Atha mahāsatto ekassa pakkhantamajjhe pavisitvā khaggarajjuyā pi attānaṃ bandhitvā nipajji* (*Zp.*, 173). See p. 554, n. 75.

50. *Mv.*: *Sudhanu pṛcchati. Kahiṃ udakaṃ imaṃ nīṣyati. Āhansu. Sā Manoharā snāpayiṣyati. Tasyā manuṣyagandhaṃ apanayiṣyati. Tena kumāreṇa aṅgulīyakā paścime udakaghaṭe prakṣiptā yathā tāhi kinnarīhi na dṛṣṭā. Manoharā snāyati ca aṅgulīyakā snāyantīye tato ghaṭakato utsaṅge patitā. Manoharāye sā aṅgulīyakā dṛṣṭvā parijñātā* (II, 110).

Da. : *Tenaikasyāḥ kinnaryā ghaṭe 'nālakṣitaṃ prakṣiptā sā ca kinnarī abhihitā anena tvayā ghaṭena Manoharā tat prathamataraṃ snāpayitavyā* (458).

Ak. : *Kumbhotkṣepe śramārtāyās tatraikasyāḥ sametya saḥ/*
hastālambena sāhāyyaṃ kṛtvā papraccha tāṃ śanaiḥ// (283).
Mātaḥ kasya kṛte toyamidaṃ yatnena nīyate/
yad bhaktyā gaṇyate nāyaṃ bhavatībhiḥ pariśramaḥ// (284).

Zp.: *Sace panāhaṃ tassa mama saccādhiṭṭhānapāramīpūraṇena tāya Manoharāya saddhiṃ samaggavāsaṃ labhissāmi tāsu ekikā kinnarīkaññā tam udakaghaṭaṃ ukkhiptuṃ asakkontī tatth' eva tiṭṭhatū ti adhiṭṭhahitvā ... aṭṭhāsi* (174).

51. 'During this interval twelve years had passed' (Bailey, 'Sudhana poem', 512). Cf; *Atha bodhisatto mahā ussāhena gacchanto sattavassāni sattamāsasattadivasādhikāni ...* (*Zp.*, 172).

52. *Gacchainaṃ pracchannaṃ praveśaya. Tayā praveśitaḥ sugupte pradeśe sthāpitaḥ. Tato Manoharā pituḥ pādayor nipatya kathayati...* (*Da.*, 458).

In 'Saka' they meet secretly before his arrival is announced to king Druma: 'They agreed with her thought, they brought him into the palace. They searched out a place, all were in the secret.... For many days they well honoured him. The *kinnarīs* secretly at night used to fetch him...' (Bailey, 'Sudhana poem', 513).

Ak. follows 'Saka' :

Tayā guptatare nyastaṃ kāntam udyānamandire/
kumudvatīva śaśinaṃ gatvāpaśyan Manoharā// (293).
Yad yat premṇaḥ sadṛśam ucitaṃ yad yat autsukyarāśe/
tat tat sarvaṃ praṇayasubhagaṃ dampatī cakratus tau//(295 cd).

53. *Āha ca :*
A *Tvayā kāntyā jitās tāvad ete kinnaradārakāḥ/*
saṃdarśitaprabhāvas tu divyasambandham arhasi//
B *Atyāyataṃ śaravanaṃ kṛtvoddhṛtya śaraṃ kṣaṇāt/*
vyuptam anyūnam uccitya punar dehi tilāḍhakaṃ//
C *Saṃdarśaya dhanurvede dṛḍhalakṣādi kauśalam/*
tataḥ kīrtipatākeyaṃ tavāyattā Manoharā// (*Da.*, 458).
These three verses are identical with *Ak.*, 313-15.
D *Śatakratusamādiṣṭair yakṣaiḥ sūkararūpibhiḥ/*
utpāṭite śaravane same vyuptaṃ tilāḍhakaṃ//
E *Ekīkṛtaṃ samuccitya Śakrasṛṣṭaiḥ pipīlikaiḥ/*
kumāraḥ kinnarendrāya vismitāya nyavedayat// (*Da.*, 459).
These two verses are preceded by the following three verses in *Ak.* :
F *Mithyāśramakleśaphale pravṛttaṃ śarapāṭane/*
taṃ vijñāya Sahasrākṣaḥ pakṣapātād acintayat//
G *Kiṃ bhādrakalpiko bodhisattvo 'yaṃ pārthivātmajaḥ/*
niyuktaḥ kinnarendreṇa niṣphale kleṣakarmaṇi//
H *Asyāsmin samyāyāse kāryaṃ sāhāyakaṃ mayā/*
iti sañcintya Śakro 'sya karmaniṣpattim ādadhe// (*Ak.*, 317-19).

Although verses A, B, C, D, and E, together with one more verse, viz. *Duhitā Śakrakalpasya* ..., cited above (p. 288, n. 41), appear in both *Da.* (in all MSS used by Cowell and Neil) and *Ak.*, they are not found in I-ching's translation of the *Bhaiṣajya-vastu.* (Professor Simon, who kindly checked this for me, found that several other verses—notably 12 of *Da.*, 455-7, from *Dṛṣṭvā sā* ... to *Candrasya khe* ...—although found in the Tibetan, are missing from I-ching's translation. Cf. *Taishō Tripiṭaka,* XXIV, 63b—64b.) The six verses in question are also missing from the Tibetan translation of the *Bhaiṣajya-vastu.* It is probable on the evidence of the Chinese and Tibetan translations, particularly of the latter, that these verses do not belong to the original *Bhaiṣajya-vastu.*

Verses A, B, and C appear to be quotations as they are preceded by the words *āha ca* in *Da.* These are followed by a prose passage containing a significant line : *Devatāś caiṣāṃ autsukyam āpatsyante avighnabhāvāya* (p. 459). At the end of this passage occur D and E which explicitly state that *yakṣas* performed the feat at the instruction of Śatakratu.

Whether this intervention by Śakra was introduced into the *Bhaiṣajya-vastu* story by the compilers of *Da.* (taking a clue from the line *devatāś caiṣāṃ*...) or whether *Da.* was following a different MS tradition of the *Bhaiṣajya-vastu* containing these verses cannot be determined on the available evidence.

Only these six, out of 44 verses found in this *avadāna* of *Da.*, are repeated (not as quotations) by Kṣemendra in his poem consisting of 331 verses of his own. It is not improbable that Kṣemendra was here introducing the intervention of Śakra either following some other version of the story or as one of his own innovations. His three verses (F, G, H) preceding D, E leave no doubt that the latter were also his own compositions. It seems likely, therefore, that the six verses in question were interpolated into the MSS of *Da.* at a later stage and have survived since then in all our known MSS of *Da.* The fact that Śakra's intervention at this stage of the story is not found in the Pali versions points to the same conclusion.

54. *Taṃ sutvā Sudhano...attano dhanuṃ āropetvā...vijjhati. Ātha so saro dhanujjiyā*

mutto sattatālarukkhe ca satta udumbararukkhaphalake...evaṃ paribhinditvā...puna Sudhanuss' eva hatthe patiṭṭhāsi (*Zp.*, 176).

55. *Mahāsatto...mahallapāsāṇaṃ nāma nīlavaṇṇapāsāṇaphalakaṃ upasaṃkamitvā tikkhattuṃ padakkiṇaṃ katvā... sace 'haṃ anāgate bodhirukkhamūle... nisinno mārabalaṃ vidhaṃsetvā ... anuttaraṃ sammāsambodhiṃ abhisaṃbujjhissāmi, api ca kho pana sace 'haṃ sakalalokasannivāsānaṃ sattānaṃ jātyādimānasaṅkhātamahāpabbataṃ sankamituṃ sakkomi, idāni idaṃ mahallapāsāṇaṃ nāma jātigarukaṃ lahukam eva hotū ti saccādhiṭṭhānaṃ adhiṭṭhahitvā taṃ ukkhipi...* (*Zp.*, 177).

56. *Yathā Drumasya duhitā mameha tvaṃ Manoharā/*
śīghram etena satyena padaṃ vraja Manohare// (*Da.*, 459).
cf. *Haṃsānāṃ vacanaṃ śrutvā yathā me Naiṣabho vṛtaḥ/*
patitve tena satyena devās taṃ pradiśantu me// (*Nalopākhyāna*, v, 17).

57. *Abhinnavarṇarūpānāṃ tulyābharaṇavāsasām/*
kinnarīṇāṃ sthitāṃ madhye gṛhāṇa nijavallabhām//
Ity uktaḥ sa punas tena kinnarīśatapañcakam/
tulyavarṇavayoveśaṃ dadarśa vyagram agrataḥ//
Tāsāṃ madhye parijñāya sa jagrāha Manoharām/
vallarīvanasaṃchannāṃ bhṛṅgaś cūtalatām iva// (*Ak.*, 327-9).

58. *Rājā attano sattadhītaro ... samānarūpā ... paṭipāṭiyā nisīdāpetvā 'bho Sudhanakumāra, passasi mama dhītarabbhantare tava bhariyā atthi udāhu' natthī' ti āha. Mahāsatto... ajānitvā upāyaṃ cintento...adhiṭṭhahanto āha* :
Yadi saccaṃ ahaṃ pubbe sabbasattahitaṃ karaṃ/
paradāraṃ na gacchāmi pūressāmi manorathaṃ/
na kiñci paradāresu ācikkhantu me devatā ti//

Evañ ca pana vatvā Sakkassa bhavanaṃ uṇhākāraṃ dassesi. Sakko āvajjanto taṃ kāraṇaṃ ñatvā ākāsena āgantvā santikaṃ mahāsattassa etad avoca : 'tāta, mahāpurisa, ahaṃ suvaṇṇamakkhikaṃ nimminitvā suvaṇṇamakkhikā yassa itthiyā sīsaṃ padakkhiṇaṃ katvā taṃ tava bhariyaṃ jānāhī' ti (*Pj.*, 71).

In *Zp.*, Sakka arrives in the guise of a golden fly and settles on Manoharā's hand : *Atha sakko āvajjanto taṃ kāraṇaṃ ñatvā suvaṇṇamakkhikena āgantvā bodhisattassa kaṇṇasamīpe samullapati : 'sāmi Sudhanu, ahaṃ Sakko va sañcaraṇamakkhiko hutvā tava bhariyahatthe patiṭṭhāmi, tvaṃ tāya saññāya etaṃ hatthaṃ gahetvā ayaṃ devī mama bhariyā ti vadesī'ti* (*Zp.*, 178).

For further changes in this scene made by the popular Burmese dramas see below (p. 315, n. 86).

59. *Tāta Sudhanu, ahaṃ pi idāni tayā saddhiṃ manussalokaṃ gamissāmī ti....Dumarājā bodhisattassa mātāpitūnaṃ nānappakārāni datvā āpucchitvā puna attano nagaram eva agamāsi* (*Zp.*, 180).

60. *Evañ ca pana vitthāretvā dhammadesanaṃ āharitvā bhikkhave, evem pi pubbe paṇḍitā mātugāmaṃ nissāya... pakkamiṃsū yevā ti. Saṅkhepen' eva... tesaṃ pi bhikkhūnaṃ cattāri saccāni pakāsento imaṃ gāthadvayam āha :*
Dukkhasaccaṃ samudayaṃ nirodhañ ca maggasaccaṃ/
iti hi taṃ catusaccaṃ sabbā tā kathitā mayā//
Tebhūmakaṃ dukkhasaccaṃ taṇhā samudayaṃ nāma/
nibbānaṃ nirodhasaccaṃ aṭṭhaṅgikaṃ maggasaccan ti//
Bhagavato desanāvasāne so ukkaṇṭhito bhikkhu arahattappatto nikkileso nibbhayo yeva ahosi. Aññe pi sampattaparisā sotāpattiphalādīni pāpuṇiṃsū ti (*Zp.*, 181).

61. The story of Sudhana is absent from the Pali *Jātaka* book and other *aṭṭhakathās*. The *Khaṇḍahāla-jātaka* (no. 542, *J*, VI, 129-57), however, offers several points of

comparison with both *Mv.* and *Da.* Here also the king wishes to undertake a sacrifice to attain heaven alive (as in *Mv.* and 'Chinese A'). Here also the king's credulity is exploited by a wicked brahmin minister (Khaṇḍahāla) who encourages the king to engage in human sacrifice with a secret plan to kill the prince Canda the *bodhisattva* (as in *Da.*) who has exposed his acts of injustice. In this as well as in *Mv.* and 'Chinese A' the *bodhisattva* gives long sermons on the evils of sacrifice, the main Buddhist message of the stories concerned. But whereas the story of Sudhana develops into a beautiful love story with all the ingredients of an epic, the *Khaṇḍahāla-jātaka* remains a purely didactic one being terminated by a rather premature intervention by Sakka at the performance of an Act of Truth by the wife of the prince.

62. We ignore a scene found only in *Da.* showing the lamentations of the childless king Dhana, his prayers to gods, the conditions (*pratyaya*) of conception, the treatment of the queen in her pregnancy, and the birth of the child. This stereotyped description (*tasya krīḍato ramamāṇasya na putro na duhitā...vardhate hradastham iva paṅkajaṃ* ...(*Da.*,439, 11, 26-30 to 441) is also found in the *Koṭikarṇāvadāna* and *Supriyāvadāna*. It is also found with slight variations in the following *avadānas* of the *Avadānaśataka*: *Kusīda, Maitrakanyaka, Hiraṇyapāṇi,* and *Gaṅgika*.

63. See p. 287, n. 31.

64. See p. 288, n. 43.

65. See p. 288, n. 41, and p. 291, n. 53.

66. See p. 284, n. 8.

67. See p. 290, n. 51.

68. See p. 284, n. 9.

69. On the significance of the winged conch in Indian (and Borobudur) sculpture, see F. D. K. Bosch, *The golden germ*, 115 ff., where a similar standard from the Borobudur reliefs is reproduced on pl. 52d. The conch is usually associated with Viṣṇu or his *avatāras*. In Theravāda Buddhism it is associated with Sakka, e.g. in the scene of Māravijaya : *Sakko devarāja Vijayuttarasaṅkhaṃ dhamamāno aṭṭhāsi, so kira saṅkho vīsaṃhatthasatiko hoti, sakiṃ vātaṃ gāhāpetvā dhamanto cattāro māse saddaṃ karitvā nissaddo hoti...* (*Jātaka*, I, 72).

70. '18 (L. 36). Il se résout enfin, ainsi qu'il est écrit et qu'on peut voir, à accorder au prince la main de sa fille ', *BEFEO*, IX, 1909, 16.

71. We cannot accept Krom's suggestion (*Beschrijving van Barabudur*, 234-5) that relief no. 18 is depicting the majesty of the *bodhisattva* by giving him a halo, since elsewhere in the reliefs the same prince appears without halo. As regards the trace of a halo on the figure of the prince in relief no. 20 which according to Krom may be faintly visible, this is certainly an illusion produced by a slight break in the relief above his head.

72. See p. 546, n. 58.

73. *Tataḥ kinnarīsahasrasya Manoharāsamānarūpasya madhye Manoharāṃ sthāpayitvā* ... (*Da.*, 459).

74. *Yāvan Manoharā kinnarī pañcaśataparivāritā avatīrṇā snātuṃ* (*Da.*, 443). Cf. *Atha tā sattakinnarikaññāyo Dumarājadhītāyo...kinnarīgaṇaparivutā ... tassa tīre otaritvā nisīdiṃstu...* (*Zp.*, 154). *Mv.* does not give any number: *Manoharā nāma dhītā bahūhi kinnarehi kinnarīhi ca parivāritā* ... (*Mv.*, II, 97).

75. In this connection, a pair of birds perched on the branch of a tree on the left-hand corner of relief no. I, b, 15 might be of some special interest. The relief depicts Sudhana's meeting with the hermit and his obtaining the ring from

the latter. From here onwards he starts on his journey through the forests and mountains until he arrives at the lake (relief no. 16). In the Pali versions alone he is brought there tied to the wings of a bird (see p. 290, n. 49). The fact that these two birds are seated and are not flying (unlike those in nos. 2, 3, 5, 11, and 16) suggests that their presence in this relief is probably linked with the story rather than merely forming a part of the scenery of the forest. There is, however, one more bird seated in the remote right-hand corner of this (no. 15) relief. But it is sitting right on top of a lake and may therefore have no other significance.

76. I am indebted to Mr. John Okell for furnishing me with a list of published Burmese works on Sudhana. Of the unpublished mention may be made of a Mon MS called *Lik bra rat iṇaṅ kaṅrī* 'The book of the diadem of the *kinnarī*' (124 pp.) found in the Bernard Free Library, Rangoon, a microfilm of which obtained by Mr. H. L. Shorto is in the Library of SOAS.

77. Mandalay, Hanthawaddy Piṭakat Press, 1929.

    I am grateful to Professor Hla Pe for comparing Nawade's work with *Zp.* and establishing their relationship.

78. See extracts in *Anthology of Burmese literature,* II, Rangoon, 1922, 131-4.

79. Rangoon, Bengalee Job-printing Press, 1880.

80. In his *Burma past and present,* 1878, II, 26-58. The translation is by Lieut. Sladen and Colonel Sparks made in 1856.

81. *Journal of the Asiatic Society of Bengal,* no. 91, 1839, 535-51.

82. See *Bot lakhōn khrang krung kao* 'Theatrical pieces of the Ayuthyan period': *Nāng manōrā* and *Sang thōng* version in the National Library, Bangkok, third ed., 1964, 130 pp. I am indebted to Mr. E. H. S. Simmonds for a comparison of *Nāng manōrā* with *Pj.* The Thai text contains only one scene depicting Manoharā's coming to bathe in the pond culminating in her capture by the hunter. (A miniature painting from a Thai MS of *Traiphūm* dated A.D. 1776, depicting the scene of Manoharā's capture by the hunter is reproduced by Klaus Wenk, *Thailändische Miniaturmalereien,* Wiesbaden, 1965, pp. 79-81 (plate XVI).) For brief theatrical extracts from eighteenth-century fragments based on this story, see Schweisguth, *Étude sur la littérature siamoise,* 146-52. Also see Jean Drans, *Histoire de Nang Manora et Histoire de Sang Thong,* Tokyo, 1947.

83. René Nicolas, 'Le lakhon nora ou lakhon chatri; et les origines du théatre classique Siamois', *Journal of the Siam Society,* XVIII, 1924, 85-110.

84. The Hermit: There is one way, and only one, my son,
    To gain the end you seek. A magic noose
    The King of Dragons gave himself to me....
    But take it, if you list, and snare your bird. Fytche, op. cit., 33.

    In Smith's translation the hunter captures Manoharā with his own noose: *JASB,* no. 91, 1839, 539.

85. The lifting of the heavy stone reminds one of a similar incident in the episode of two giants known as the Kāla brothers in the *Glass Palace Chronicle* : 'When they had eaten it they said, "Let us test whether what our teacher told us be true or no!" So they made assay, and lo! they could lift a stone slab ten cubits in length, eight cubits in breadth; and they put it at the foot of the stairs of the monastery' (tr. Pe Maung Tin and G. H. Luce, 1923, 76).

    The testing of enterprises by the lifting of stones is not unknown in present-day Burma as the following note kindly sent to me by Mr. H. L. Shorto would indicate: 'Omen stones or touchstones (Mon *tma' nimit*) are kept at various pagodas (in Lower Burma) in front of a particular image of the Buddha or of the guardian *nat* of the pagoda. After praying to the Buddha or *nat* the suppliant tries to lift the stone (about the size of a cannon-ball, of stone or metal); if he is successful he will be lucky. The formula is a sort of *saccakiriya*: "If I ..., may I lift this stone"'. See also Shway Yoe, *The Burman: his life and notions. Third ed.*, London, 1927, 240.

It is possible that this particular test in the Pali versions might have been introduced by the monks of Burma from some such popular tradition.

86. King: Before my daughters let a seven-fold screen
Of silk inwrought with gems suspended be,
And from within let each of them, in turn,
One taper finger carefully expose.
If he, who claims the lovely Dwaymenau,
By this can single her from the rest,
I will admit his title to her hand. Fytche, op. cit., 58.

87. Of the 31 stories not less than 23 are found in *Pj.* and there also Sakka is identified (in the *samodhāna*) with Anuruddha. The only story where he is identified with Moggallāna is *Akkharalikhita-jātaka* (*Zp.*, no. 43). Of the remaining 19 stories where Sakka does not play any part, 12 are to be found only in *Zp.* These could possibly be much later additions to the earlier collections of Sakka stories in both versions.

88. On Anuruddha, first cousin of the Buddha and one of his chief disciples, see *DPPN.* The Pali scriptures and *aṭṭhakathās* speak often of his *iddhi* powers and in 14 *jātakas* he is identified with Sakka. In Mahāyāna texts Anuruddha's name appears as Aniruddha: *tatas tāny ābharaṇāni cireṇa kālena Bhadrikasya Śākyakumārasya Mahānāmno Aniruddhasya cābadhyanta sma* (*Lalitavistara*, 229). See Edgerton's *BHSD.*

89. Mr. E. H. S. Simmonds to whom I owe the following note informs me that Aniruddha is mentioned along with the Buddha in theatrical invocation texts in Thai : 'In a shadow-play MS in the Library of the University of Edinburgh (Oriental collection, no. PL 42) Aniruddha appears immediately after the Buddha in the following passage:
I salute the Buddha the Supreme One,
compassionate towards innumerable creatures,
may we be raised to the state of Nirvāṇa.
I salute Aniruddha, he who sets all in being
the jungles of wood and water,
all streams that pour down from the hills'.

90. On Anuruddha (transcribed as Anawrahta in modern Burmese) king of Pagan, see the *Glass Palace Chronicle*, tr. Pe Maung Tin and G. H. Luce, 1923, 64-100. On p. 96 he is referred to as king Anuruddhadeva. See also Maung Htin Aung, *Folk elements in Burmese Buddhism;* H. L. Shorto, 'The 32 *myos* in the medieval Mon kingdom', *BSOAS*, XXVI, 3, 1963, 590.

Early terra-cotta plaques bearing the name of this king spelt Aniruddha are referred to in the *Report of the Superintendent, Archaeological Survey of Burma*, for 1906 (p. 10), 1912 (p. 19), and 1915 (p. 15). The last reads: *Eso bhagawā mahārāja sirī Aniruddhadevena kato vimuttattham sahatthenevā ti.*

But the same king's name with a different spelling Anuradhā occurs in an inscription (*Inscriptions of Burma*, portfolio II, pl. 160a) dated Sakarāj 609 (A.D. 1247) in the phrase *Cakkawatiy Anuradhā klon thu so kywan lay* (1.6).

CHAPTER 19

On the Buddha Image*

In discussing the origin of the Buddha-image, art historians, Coomaraswamy and Rowland among others[1], have alluded to accounts of the Chinese travellers Fa-Hian and Hiuen-Tsiang pertaining to the existence of a sandalwood image of the Buddha carved during the Buddha's lifetime. Both these accounts agree in substance but differ in certain minor details. Fa-Hian, for instance, reports that it was King Prasenajit of Kośala who commissioned this image, whereas Hiuen-Tsiang credits it to King Udayana of Kośāmbi. Fa-Hian's account, since it predates that of Hiuen-Tsiang by at least 200 years, is probably more accurate. In his description of the Jetavanārāma in Śrāvastī, which he visited, Fa-Hian gives the following account of the origin of the Buddha-image:

> When Buddha ascended into the Trāyastriṃshas heavens to preach for the sake of his mother, after ninety day's absence, King Prasenajit desiring to see him again, carved out of the sandalwood called Gośīrshachandana (*ox-head*) an image of the Buddha and placed it on Buddha's throne. When Buddha returned and entered the *vihāra*, the image, immediately quitting its place, went forward to meet him. On this Buddha addressed these words to it: 'Return, I pray you, to your seat. After my Nirvāṇa you will be the model from which my followers (four schools or classes) shall carve their images.' On this the figure returned to its seat. This image, as it was the very first made of

*This article was originally published in *Studies in Pali and Buddhism*, ed. A.K. Narain, (Delhi, 1979), pp. 183-188. Reprinted with kind permission of A.K. Narain, editor.

all the figures of Buddha, is the one which all subsequent ages have followed as a model.[2]

Whereas Fa-Hian was only reporting a tradition about the origin of the Buddha's image, Hiuen-Tsiang claims to have seen such an image in a large *vihāra,* not in Śrāvastī but in Kauśāmbī, the capital city of King Udayana. Referring to the origins of this image, he narrates the following legend:

> When Tathāgata first arrived at complete enlightenment, he ascended up to heaven to preach the law for the benefit of his mother, and for three months remained absent. This king (i.e., Udayana), thinking of him with affection, desired to have an image of his person; therefore he asked Maudgalyāyanaputra, by his spiritual power, to transport an artist to the heavenly mansions to observe the excellent marks of Buddha's body, and carve a sandalwood statue. When Tathāgata returned from the heavenly palace, the carved figure of sandalwood rose and saluted the Lord of the World. The Lord then graciously addressed it and said, "The work expected from you is to toil in the conversion of heretics, and to lead in the way of religion future ages".[3]

Both accounts agree that the first image of the Buddha was made in his absence while he was preaching in the Trāyastriṃśat heaven to his mother. They agree further that the image was made of sandalwood. Both maintain that the image became animated upon seeing the Buddha, and it was ordered by the Buddha to propagate his teachings upon his death.

While modern scholars have taken notice of this account, they have not given credence to this tradition of the alleged first image of the Buddha. This is primarily because no literary evidence supporting such a tradition has been attested to either in the Pali Tipiṭaka and its commentaries or in any other Buddhist literature originating in India, Sri Lanka or Southeast Asia. Spence Hardy reports in his *Eastern Monachism* that the legend of the first Buddha image commissioned by King Prasenajit of Kośala was known to the Buddhists of Sri Lanka, but that "It is rejected by the more intelligent of the priests, who regard it as an invention to attract worshippers to the temples".[4] In recent years U.P. Shah has published two articles pertaining to a sandalwood image of the Jaina teacher Mahāvīra, which was carved in his lifetime and thus called "Jīvantasvāmi".[5] In these articles Dr. Shah has proposed the possibility that the Buddhist traditions were perhaps imitations of the older Jaina tradition. We have no means of knowing whether the sandalwood image seen by Hiuen-Tsiang was indeed the first image of the Buddha, or whether it and other Buddha-images were, as suggested by Dr. Shah, modelled after an earlier image of the Jina. We have, however, come across a previously unnoticed piece of literary evidence in Pali, which for the first time lends some authenticity to the oral traditions reported by the Chinese travellers. We here refer to a certain Jātaka tale found in a collection known as the *Paññāsa Jātaka,* which probably originated in the 13th or 14th century in northern Chieng-Mai. These stories are known in Burma as "Chieng-Mai Fifty" (Burmese : *Zimmé Paṇṇāsa*).[6] The collection is "extra-canonical" and is unknown to Buddhist traditions anywhere outside of the countries of Southeast Asia.[7] Although the stories of this collection are modelled after those in the canonical Jātaka book, they were treated as apocryphal and were even reported to have been proscribed by the orthodox Buddhist king Myndon of Mandalay (1853-1872)[8]. They have, however, remained popular in Burma, Thailand and Cambodia and thus constitute an important source for our knowledge of the local Buddhist tradition which developed independently of both India and Sri Lanka.

The 37th Jātaka of this collection, entitled Vaṭṭaṅgulirāja-jātaka,[9] is historically of great importance as it contains a reference to the first image of the Buddha. It is a long story, comprising 204 verses. Being a Jātaka, the story is put in the mouth of the Buddha himself, who narrates an incident which occurred in one of his previous births as King Vaṭṭaṅguli. This king had once in a past life repaired the broken finger of a Buddha-image. As a consequence of this great deed, he was in his present life a king, and was able to subdue the army of his enemies literally by lifting and bending one of his fingers. (Hence the name "Vaṭṭaṅguli.") The story itself is not of great importance for our purpose, but the *nidāna,* or introductory, portion of the Jātaka introduces King Prasenajit (Pali : Passenadi) of Kośala and thus links the story with the tradition reported by Fa-Hian. The *nidāna-kathā* of this Jātaka may be briefly summarized as follows:

> Once upon a time the Lord journeyed from Sāvatthi to a distant place to preach the Law. At that time King Passenadi of Kośala, desirous of seeing the Enlightened One, went, surrounded by his large retinue, to the great monastery (*māhā-vihāra*) in Jetavana. Not seeing the Lord, his heart was filled with disappointment and, saying "Alas, alas, the Jetavana is empty without the Lord," he returned home greatly dejected. After some time, the Lord returned to Jetavana. The king heard the news and went with the citizens to pay his respects to the Buddha. Having worshipped the Master he said, "Lord, even while you are still alive, people feel extremely dejected when you are gone for a short time. How could they ever be happy and not feel extremely bereaved when indeed you will have entered *parinibbāna?* Therefore, O Lord, please allow me to make an image of you to be worshipped by both men and gods." Having heard these words of the king, the Lord, for the sake of the welfare of all beings and to insure the continuity of his teachings, gave his consent.

He then narrated the Jātaka of Vaṭṭaṅgulirāja referred to above, and the following account summarizes the events that then took place:

> Having heard this story, King Passenadi went to his residence and, selecting a beautiful sandalwood tree, had the image of the Buddha carved from it. Having covered the image with excellent robes, he placed it on an elevated seat in his palace. He then went to Jetavana and invited the Buddha to see the image. The Buddha consented by remaining silent. The next morning the Lord, accompanied by his chief disciples, entered the great pavilion in the palace of the king in order to see the Buddha-image. At that very moment, the sandalwood image, immediately upon seeing the Buddha, became animated, as if by the power of the Buddha, and thought thus: "When the great Buddha is alive and comes here it is not proper that I should be seated here on this high seat. Let me pay my respects to him." Thinking thus, the image lifted one foot from the pedestal in order to rise and welcome the Buddha. Having seen this, the Lord raised his right hand and said the following words: "Be seated, oh noble one. I shall be entering into

parinibbāna in a short time. May you sustain my *sāsana* (in the sense of teachings and order) for five thousand years to come....Beginning today I hand over my *sāsana* to you. May you stay in this *sāsana* for the welfare and benefit of the whole world.

The *Vaṭṭaṅgulirāja Jātaka* is of great interest on several accounts. It affirms the tradition reported by Fa-Hian, which predates that of Hiuen-Tsiang by 200 years, thereby giving credence to the earlier Buddhist tradition that an image of the Buddha was indeed commissioned by King Prasenajit of Kośala during the lifetime of the Buddha. Since this tradition is not attested to in any other literary work originating in South or Southeast Asia, one wonders about the source of the version found in the apocryphal Jātaka of a relatively later date. Is it possible that the writers of the *Paññāsa Jātaka* might have been aware of the accounts of the Chinese travellers? Such a possibility cannot be discounted. However, we have no evidence in support of such borrowing. Both Chinese accounts begin with a reference to the Buddha's visit to his mother in heaven, which necessitated the commissioning of the Buddha-image. It should be remembered that the Buddha's visit to heaven is a popular element of Buddhist belief in Burma and Thailand. Several architectural remains from the 14th century onwards portray this event by showing ladders which represent the Buddha's descent to earth from heaven. The omission of this popular motif in our version is therefore remarkable, and would tend to support the possibility that the *Paññāsa Jātaka* version had a source independent of that of the Chinese versions.[10]

Only through further research will the source of the *Vaṭṭaṅgulirāja Jātaka* be precisely identified. But the fact that the Buddhists of Southeast Asia preserved in their popular literature the story of the first image of the Buddha, should encourage art historians to give more credence to the accounts of the Chinese travellers which have been hitherto neglected for want of literary evidence.

II

Excerpts from the Vaṭṭaṅgulirājajātaka

...idaṃ Satthā Jetavane viharanto attano pubbakammavasena

katabuddhabimbam ārabbha kathesi. ekadivasaṃ hi Satthā imasmiṃ loke veneyyapuggale disvā te vinetuṃ disācārikaṃ pakkāmi. tadā Passenadi Kosalarājā mahājanakāyehi parivuto Sammāsambuddhaṃ passitukāmo c' eva attano purise gandhamālādīni pūjābhaṇḍāni gahāpetvā sakanagarato nikkhamitvā Jetavananāmake ārāme ṭhitaṃ mahāvihāram upāgami. so ca rājā sapariso tatth' eva Sugatālaye Sambuddham apassanto saṃvegajātahadayo evam āha: idaṃ hi bhonto Jetavanaṃ Sammāsambuddhena ca vinā suññam eva hotī ti. ...atha sabbe pi rājādayo mahājanakāyā mahāsaṃvegajātahadayā domanassappattā attano attano vasanaṭṭhānaṃ pakkamiṃsu. tadā pana Satthā nānādisāsu veneyyajane attano dhammadesanāya maggaphalaṃ bodhetvā Jetavane mahāvihāram upāgami. atha tappavattiṃ sutvā Passenadi Kosalarājā atiparamatuṭṭhacitto hutvā...Jetavanaṃ gantvā Bhagavantam upasaṅkamitvā taṃ vanditvā ekamantaṃ nisīditvā evam āha: hiyyo bhante Bhagavā, Sāvatthivāsino mahājanakāyā Sammāsambuddham apassantā atidukkhena yuttā attano attano vasanaṭṭhānaṃ gamissantī ti. evañ ca pana so rājā puna Bhagavantam evam āha: bhante Bhagavā, tava dharmāne aññasmiṃ ṭhāne gate cāyaṃ sattaloko tuyham rūpam apassanto anātho atidukkhito hoti; tayi pana anupādisesāya nibbānadhātuyā parinibbute yeva kuto panāyaṃ sattaloko satāṇo sukhito ca bhaveyya? tasmā pana mayham eva tumbe naradevapūjāsakkāratthāya ca tava seṭṭharūpaṃ kātum anujāneyyāthā ti. tass' eva rañño vacanaṃ sutvā Satthā sabbalokahitañ ca passanto niccakālam eva attano sāsanaṃ tiṭṭhanatthāya ca attano rūpaṃ kārāpetuṃ tass' eva rañño anujānamāno evam āha : mahārāja, yo koci naro saddhāya sampanno yathābalaṃ mattikādinā pi kenaci vatthuno khuddakaṃ vā mama rūpaṃ kareyyā ti. evaṃ ca pana vatvā Satthā pubbe pi mahārāja, porāṇakapaṇḍito ekass' eva buddharūpassa bhinnaṅguli ekasmiṃ nagare ṭhitapatitaṃ disvā tatth' eva pākaṭikam aṅguli sandhiyanto vipulasukham anubhuñjamāno mahātejānubhāvo c' eva ahosī ti vatvā tuṇhī ahosi. ten' eva yācito atītam āhari.

...evañ ca pana Bhagavato dhammadesanaṃ suṇanto sapariso Kosalarājā pītisomanassajātacitto sakalalokahitasukhāya buddhabimbakataṃ patthayanto tatth' eva gandhapupphādīhi Bhagavantaṃ pūjetvā attano vasanaṭṭhānaṃ gantvā candanarukkhavanato candanarukkhasāram ānayitvā samasamaṃ c' eva taṃ candanarukkhasāraṃ likkhāpetvā ten' eva candanarukkhasārena atimanoharaṃ buddhabimbaṃ kārāpeti. tadā so rājā siliṭṭhaṃ tam eva buddhabimbaṃ kārāpetvā punappunaṃ sena (?) rasena taṃ buddhabimbaṃ limpāpetvā lākhāra[sa]sadisena suravera (?) — cīvarayugena taṃ buddhabimbaṃ pārupetvā uccāsane nānāvidhe varavatthe taṃ buddhabimbaṃ nisīdāpesi. atha so rājā...tassa buddharūpassa pūjāsakkārañ ca katvā Jetavanārāme vasantaṃ Sammāsambuddham upasaṅkamitvā ekamantaṃ nisinno imaṃ gātham āha:

tayā Bhante, anuññātaṃ tava bimbaṃ me sukāritaṃ:
icchāmi gamanaṃ tuyhaṃ passituṃ tattha te rūpaṃ,
svātanāya te gamanaṃ ruccati mama sammā ti.

tass' eva rañño vacanaṃ sutvā Satthā tuṇhībhāvena adhivāsesi... punadivase pana Satthā attano sāvakehi parivuto tass' eva rañño mahāgehaṃ gantvā attano rūpam eva taṃ bimbaṃ dassanatthāya mahāmaṇḍapaṃ pāvisi. taṃ khaṇañ eva so buddhabimbo ten' eva candanarukkhasārena kato tatth' eva mahāmaṇḍape āgataṃ Sammāsambuddhaṃ passanto tass' eva Sammāsambuddhassa tejānubhāvena sagāravacittako viya jīvamānasarīro viya cintesi: evaṃ dharamāne Buddhaseṭṭhe idh' eva āgate idāni panāham ati ucce āsane nisinno mayham ayutto hutvā (hoti); tass' eva ādaram karomī ti. evañ ca pana cintento viya eso bimbo Sammāsambuddhass' eva gāravam karonto attano nisinnāsanā ekapādaṃ nikkhipitvā tatth' eva āgataṃ Sammāsambuddhaṃ paccuggamanākāraṃ dassesi. evañ ca katam eva buddhabimbaṃ disvā Satthā tatth' eva...attano cīvarato erāvaṇahatthino karākāraṃ viya atisobhaṇaṃ padakkhiṇahatthaṃ nīharitvā tam eva bimbaṃ nivārento gātham āha:

āvuso tvaṃ tiṭṭha, na ciren' evāhaṃ
nibbāyissāmi, 'nāgate pañcavassasahassāni
ciren' eva tvaṃ ca sabbadā tiṭṭheyyāsi sāsane mamā ti.

evañ ca vatvā Satthā tass' eva buddhabimbassa attano sāsanaṃ niyyādento imaṃ gātham āha:

ajj' ẹvāhaṃ niyyādemi mayhaṃ te sāsanaṃ tuyhaṃ,
sabbalokahitatthāya tiṭṭha tvaṃ sāsane mamā ti.

...evañ ca pana...Passenadi Kosalaraññā saddhiṃ kathaṃ niṭṭhāpetvā ...anāgatakāle tuyhaṃ c' eva atiuḷārasukhavipākadāyakaṃ bhavissatī ti vatvā jātakaṃ samodhānento osānagātham āha...

NOTES

1. A.K. Coomaraswamy, *The Origin of the Buddha Image* (2nd edition, Delhi 1972, p. 41) refers to Kern's opinion : "There is no lack of legends anent the origin of Buddha images, but it would be difficult to discover in those tales, which are wholly discordant, something like an historical nucleus." (*Manual of Indian Buddhism*, p. 94). See also, Benjamin Rowland, *The Evolution of the Buddha Image*, p. 5.
2. Samuel Beal, *Buddhist Records of the Western World*, Introduction xliv.
3. Ibid., vol. I, pp. 235-6.
4. Spence Hardy, *Eastern Monachism*, p. 199.
5. U.P. Shah, "A Unique Jaina Image of Jīvantasvāmi", *Journal of the Oriental Institute*, vol. I, i, pp. 71-79.
"Sidelights on the Life-time Sandal-wood Image of Mahāvīra", Ibid., vol. I, iii, pp. 358-367.
6. *Zimmé Paṇṇāsa* (i.e. Chieng Mai 50) edited anonymously and published by the Hanthawaddy Press, Rangoon, 1911. A critical edition of the Burmese version of the *Paññāsa Jātaka* is being prepared by me and is soon to be published by the Pali Text Society, London. (Published in 1983.)
7. See L. Feer, "Les Jātakas", *JA*, 7e Sér., v, 1875, pp. 417 ff.
8. See my article "The story of Sudhana and Manoharā : an analysis of the texts and the Borobudur reliefs", *Bulletin of the School of Oriental and African Studies*, University of London, vol. XXIX, Part 3, 1966, p. 534, n. 10.
9. *Zimmé Paṇṇāsa*, pp. 486-510.
10. As this article goes to the publishers, I learn from Professor H. Bechert that he is editing a volume entitled *Buddhism in Ceylon and Studies on Religious Syncretism in Buddhist Countries* which includes a paper by R.F. Gombrich on the Sinhalese *Kosalabimbavarṇanāva*. As this work originates from Sri Lanka it may have drawn on a source common to the *Vaṭṭaṅgulirāja-jātaka*.

Chapter 20

Some *nīti* Verses of the *Lokaneyya-pakaraṇa**

The very recent publication entitled *Pali Nīti Texts of Burma,*[1] by Professors Bechert and Braun, includes all of Ludwik Sternbach's research in this field[2] as well as all other material available in Southeast Asia. The only text conspicuously absent from Bechert and Braun's otherwise comprehensive work is the *Lokaneyya-pakaraṇa,* a Pali text of unknown authorship, which probably originated in northern Thailand during the post-Paññāsa-Jātaka[3] period.

Although it is a fairly long text, mostly in prose but containing more than six hundred verses (*gāthā*) as well, the *Lokaneyya-pakaraṇa* has never been cited in any catalogue of Pali manuscripts from Southeast Asia.[4] In 1960 I came across a single manuscript of this work in the National Museum of Bangkok and was able to obtain a photographic copy of it. This manuscript is written in Cambodian script and consists of 268 palm leaves, averaging 5 lines per page. It is complete, but there is no indication in the text of the author, date, or place of composition. Only the obverse of the first leaf is dated simply "Rāma IV", which appears to be the date of the copy (c. 1851-1868).

The term "Lokaneyya" is rather ambiguous and has not been explained in the text itself. However at the beginning the author refers to the text as *subhāsitaṃ vākyaṃ,* i.e. "well-spoken sentences", thus suggesting that the *Lokaneyya-pakaraṇa* falls in the genre of *nīti,* or aphoristic literature. But, unlike the *nīti* texts [namely

---

*This article was originally published in *Buddhist Studies in Honour of H. Saddhatissa,* ed. Dhammapala, (Nugegoda, Sri Lanka, 1984), pp. 116-122.

Dhammanīti, Lokanīti, Rājanīti, etc.] included in the *Pali Nīti Texts of Burma* the *Lokaneyya-pakaraṇa* is not merely a compilation of *nīti* verses; rather it is a work in which these verses have been integrated as a part of the narrative. In this respect the *Lokaneyya-pakaraṇa* may be said to imitate the style of the Pañcatantra and Hitopadeśa, the two classical Sanskrit *nīti* texts. Although Pali literature abounds in didactic poetry, as well as narrative prose, the *Lokaneyya-pakaraṇa* would appear to be the sole Pali work to have attempted a narrative, in which the prose merely serves as a context for presenting the *nīti* verses appropriate, however tenuously, to the occasion.

Although called a "pakaraṇa" the *Lokaneyya,* with a *nidāna, atītavatthu* and a *samodhāna,* reads like an "apocryphal" *jātaka* and, indeed, is modelled upon the Mahāummaggajātaka (Jātaka 546). Like the latter it is divided into several *Pañhas* (questions), through which the Bodhisatta, Dhanañjaya, imparts worldly wisdom to the King and at the same time defeats his rivals at the court. I do not propose to give a summary of the entire story here. The purpose of this short paper is to draw attention to the large number of *nīti* verses which abound in this text but are missing in the extant Pali *nīti* collections.

As mentioned earlier there are about 600 "gāthās" in the *Lokaneyya-pakaraṇa,* but only about a hundred of them can strictly be called "*nīti*" verses. As many as seventy-five of these can be traced to the various callections included in the *Pali Nīti Texts of Burma.* The remaining twenty-five verses still need to be traced to their original Pali sources. I reproduce here these twenty-five verses, together with their possible Sanskrit equivalents.[5]

1. atthā ghare nivattante susāne mittabandhavā/
sukataṃ dukkataṃ kammaṃ gacchantaṃ anugacchati/[58][6]

Cf. arthā gṛhe nivartante śmaśāne mitrabāndhavāḥ/
sukṛtaṃ duṣkṛtaṃ cāpi gacchantam anugacchati// VySS-7

2. anattho py attharūpeṇa attho py anattharūpato/
uppajjate vināsāya tasmā yuttaṃ parīkkhaṇaṃ//[17]

Cf. anartho' py artharūpeṇa tathārtho' nartharūpabhāk/
utpadyate vināśāya tasmād uktaṃ parīkṣayet//CNTT-49A

3. āpadāya dhanaṃ rakkhe dāre rakkhe dhanena pi/
attānaṃ satataṃ rakkhe dārehi pi dhanehi pi//[54]

Cf. āpadarthe dhanaṃ rakṣed dārān rakṣed dhanair api/

ātmānaṃ satataṃ rakṣed dārair api dhanair api//SCAGI-24

4. kaṇṭakānaṃ khalānañ ca duvidheva patikriyā/
pādukā mukhabhaggo vā dūrato vā vivajjanam//[202]

Cf. kaṇṭakānāṃ khalānāṃ ca dvividhaiva pratikriyā/
upānaṅmukhabhaṅgo vā dūrato vā visarjanam//VySS-9

5. khalo sāsappamattāni paradosāni passati/
attano hatthimattāni passanto pi na passati//[214]

Cf. khalaḥ sarṣapamātrāṇi paracchidrāṇi paśyati//
ātmano bilvamātrāṇi paśyann api na paśyati//SCAGI-59

6. khīrapānaṃ bhujaṅgassa kevalaṃ visavaḍḍhanaṃ/
upakāro'hi nīcānaṃ apakārāya vattate//[396]

Cf. upakāro' pi nīcānām apakāro' pi jāyate/
payaḥpānaṃ bhujaṅgānāṃ kevalaṃ viṣavardhanam//
SRB 81/11

7. gāvī satasahassāni vaccho anveti mātaraṃ/
evam eva kataṃ puññaṃ sāmikaṃ pariyesati//[378]

Cf. yathā dhenusahasreṣu vatso gacchati mātaram/
tathā yac ca kṛtaṃ karma kartāram anugacchati//SCAGI-173

8. te sādhavo bhuvanamaṇḍalamolibhūtā
ye sādhutaṃ nirupakārisu dassayanti/
atthappayojanavasīkatakhīṇadeho
pubbopakāriṇi khalo pi hi sādhukappo//[208]

Cf. te sādhavo bhuvanamaṇḍalamaulibhūtā
ye sādhutāṃ nirupakāriṣu darśayanti/
ātmaprayojanavaśīkṛtakhinnadehaḥ
pūrvopakāriṣu khalo' pi hi sānukampaḥ//SV-2475

9. dūreṇa nāvamantabbā rājāno dīghabāhukā/
gaṇhanti sahasā daḷhaṃ disa(ā?) loko va pīḷakaṃ//[150]

Cf. paṇḍitena viruddhaḥ san dūre' smīti na viśvaset/
dīrghau buddhimato bāhū yābhyāṃ dūre hinasti saḥ//
SV-2765

10. dvijivhaṃ utrāsakaraṃ kharaṃ ekantaniṭṭhuraṃ/
khalassāhissa ca mukham apakārāya kevalaṃ//[200]

Cf. dvijivham udvegakaraṃ krūram ekāntadāruṇam/
khalasyāheś ca vadanam apakārāya kevalam//CNTT-498

11. na yāti kopaṃ sujano nāsakāle patiṭṭhite/
chedo(e) pi candanataru surabhī c' eva vāsiyā//[121]

Cf. sujano na yāti vairaṃ parahitabuddhir vināśakāle' pi/
chede' pi candanataruḥ surabhayati mukhaṃ kuṭhārasya//
SCAGI-236

12. na vinā parāpavādena rammante dujanā khalu/
kāko sabbarasaṃ bhutvā vinā mīḷhe na tussati //[199]

Cf. na vinā parāpavādena ramate durjano janaḥ/
kākaḥ sarvarasān bhuṅkte vinā medhyaṃ na tṛpyati//
CNTT-562

13. paradāraṃ paradhanaṃ parihāsañ parassa ca/
niccaṃ paranivesanañ ca na kareyya kadāci pi//[310]

Cf. paradārān paradravyaṃ parivādaṃ parasya ca/
parihāsaṃ guroḥ sthānaṃ cāpalyaṃ ca vivarjayet//CNTT-639

14. pāpaṃ samācarati vītaghaṇo jaghañño
patvāpadaṃ sakaruṇo pi [hi] majjhabuddhī/
pāṇaccaye pana na sādhujano suvutti
velaṃ tasantari (? samudda-r-iva?) vitikkamituṃ samattho//
[320]

Cf. pāpaṃ samācarati vītaghṛṇo jaghanyaḥ
prāpyāpadaṃ saghṛṇa eva tu madhyabuddhiḥ/
prāṇātyaye'pi na tu sādhujanaḥ suvṛttaṃ
velāṃ samudra iva laṅghayituṃ samarthaḥ//SV-272

15. madhuraṃ nipphalaṃ kiccaṃ naṭṭham abbhantaraṃ bhave/
tādiso no ca seveyya visamissaṃ guḷaṃ yathā//[111]

Cf. madhuram aruciraṃ vacaḥ khalānām
amṛtam aho prathamaṃ pṛthu vyanakti/
atha kathayati mohahetum antar-
gatam iva hālāhalaṃ viṣaṃ tad eva//SRB 87/142

16. miyate mānam āpanno na ca yāti paraṃ natiṃ/
silāthambho' tibhāreṇa bhijjate n' eva namyate//[119]

Cf. mriyate mānam āpanno na ca yāti parābhavam/
śilāstambho' tibhāreṇa bhidyate naiva namyate//VySS-80

17. mukhen' ekena vijjhanti pādam ekassa kaṇṭakā/
dūrā mukhasahassena lokapāṇaharo khalo//[201]

Cf. mukhenaikena vidhyanti pādam ekasya kaṇṭakāḥ/
dūrān mukhasahasreṇa sarvaprāṇaharaḥ khalaḥ//SV-375

18. yathā gajo parisanto chāyaṃ nissāya vissame/
vissamma taṃ dumaṃ hanti tathā nīco sanissayaṃ//[384]

Cf. yathā gajapatiḥ śrāntaś chāyārthī vṛkṣam āśritaḥ/
viśramya tu drumaṃ hanti tathā nīcaḥ svamāśrayam//SV-354

19. yad' anatthesu sāmatthaṃ atthesu pi ca vijjate/
hatthatthaṃ nu bhave tassa sabbaññutaṃ na saṃsayo//[10]

Cf. yady anartheṣu sāmarthyam artheṣv api ca vidyate/
hastasthaṃ na bhavet kasya sarvīyaṃ saugatam padam//
VySS-p. 27, n. 69

20. rukkhaṃ khīṇaphalaṃ cajanti vihagā daḍḍhaṃ vanāntaṃ migā/
mālā milātā cajanti simagaṇā(bhamarā?) sukkaṃ saraṃ sārasā//
dhananaṭṭhaṃ purisaṃ cajanti vanitā [bhaṭṭha]
manussa (bhūpassa) mantiṇo/
sabbākāravasā jano' bhiramate kasyātra ko vallabho//[165]

Cf. vṛkṣaṃ kṣīṇaphalaṃ tyajanti vihagāḥ śuṣkaṃ saraḥ sārasāḥ/
nirdravyaṃ puruṣaṃ tyajanti gaṇikā bhraṣṭaṃ nṛpaṃ mantriṇaḥ//
puṣpaṃ paryuṣitaṃ tyajanti madhupā
dagdhaṃ vanāntaṃ mṛgāḥ/
sarvaḥ kāryavaśāj jano' bhiramate
tat kasya ko vallabhaḥ//CNTT-958

21. lobhā pamādā vissāsā puriso tabyatthite (?vyathite?) tihi/
lobhaṃ pamādaṃ vissāsaṃ na kareyya budho tato//[153]

Cf. lobhapramādaviśvāsaiḥ puruṣo naśyate tribhiḥ/
tasmāl lobho na pramādaḥ kasmin hi na viśvaset//SCAGI-195

22. virodhā bahavo n' eva dujjeyyo hi mahājano/
mahantam api nāgindaṃ bhakkhayanti kipillikā//[370]

Cf. bahubhir na viroddhavyaṃ durjanaiḥ svajanair api/
sphurantam api nāgendraṃ bhakṣayanti pipīlikāḥ//
SRB 269/593

23. sakkarāmadhusaṃyutto vijjuppanno pi (? ujupaññehi?) sa(i)ñcito/
khīrakumbhasahassehi nimbo kiṃ madhurāyate//[117]

Cf. na durjanaḥ sajjanatām upaiti bahuprakārair api sevyamānaḥ/
bhūyo' pi siktaḥ payasā ghṛtena na nimbavṛkṣo madhuratvam eti//CNTT-542

24. sabbattha sabbe va guṇā na santi
guṇekadesaṃ guṇāyanti santo/
yaṃ ketakīkaṇṭakalaṃkapattaṃ
siromaṇiṭṭhānaṃ upeti loke//[206]

Cf. kasyāpi ko' py atiśayo' sti sa tena loke
khyātiṃ prayāti na hi sarvavidas tu sarvaḥ/
kiṃ ketakī phalati kiṃ panasaḥ supuṣpaḥ
kiṃ nāgavally api ca puṣpaphalair upetā//SRB 288/1031

25. sasī divasadullabho vigatayobbanā kāminī
saro vigatavārijo mukham anakkhararuciraṃ/
pabhū dhanaparāyaṇo satataduggato su(a)j[j]ano
narādhipati yo khalo manasi satta sallāni me//[197]

Cf. śaśī divasadhūsaro galitayauvanā kāminī

saro vigatavārijaṃ mukham anakṣaraṃ svākṛteḥ/
prabhur dhanaparāyaṇaḥ satatadurgataḥ sajjano
nṛpāṅgaṇagataḥ khalo manasi sapta śalyāni me//SV-3458; SRB 291/1070

TRANSLATION

1. Wealth is left behind in the home; friends and relatives come back from the cremation ground; but good and bad deeds follow the departing one.
2. [Sometimes] something meaningless turns out to have meaning; and [sometimes] something meaningful turns out to be destructive. One should therefore examine [what has been said]. (Skt. *uktaṃ* is rendered *yuttaṃ* in Pali?)
3. Save your wealth for the bad times ahead. Give up your wealth to protect your women; but regardless of wealth and women, always protect yourself.
4. Thorns and wicked men are alike, only two ways to deal with them: Either smash their face with your shoes or keep them at a distance.
5. A wicked man sees the faults of others be they as small as a mustard seed. But his own, as large as elephants, although he looks, he cannot see.
6. Give milk to a snake; its poison merely increases. Do a mean fellow a favour; and he will only do you evil in return.
7. From 100,000 cows a calf chooses its mother. Likewise a good deed done always finds its doer.
8. Those are saints, crest-jewels of the earth's orb, who show kindness to ones who have done them evil. For surely a wicked man, who only mortifies his body for selfish ends, is saintly towards those who already have done him good. (Pali *sādhukappo* seems to be a misprint for Skt. *sānukampo.*)
9. Don't insult kings, even from a distance, for they have long arms indeed. Those who harm them they will seize quickly and firmly, like light [reaching] the four directions. (Reading of last line is doubtful and meaning unclear.)
10. Forked-tongued, terrifying, harsh and cruel, through and through, the mouths of wicked men and snakes are only good for doing evil!
11. A good man does not resort to anger even when his downfall is

at hand. Even when cut, the sandalwood tree bestows its fragrance on the axe's blade.

12. The wicked are not happy unless finding fault with others. Although he has enjoyed delicious flavours, a crow is not content without [the taste of] dung.
13. To covet the wives and wealth of others, to mock others, or to live too long in another's house—one should never do these things.
14. The basest man, devoid of compassion, does evil deeds. A man of average intellect, even when calamity befalls him, still maintains compassion. But a truly good man, though his life be endangered, can no more abandon his good conduct than an ocean overflow its shore.
15. Like treacle mixed with poison, one should not partake of pleasurable action, which is fruitless and rotten to the core.
16. A man too proud to submit to others, dies just as a stone pillar, unbending, breaks under a heavy load.
17. Thorns, with their single point, pierce but one person's foot. The wicked man, though far away, with his thousand tongues robs everyone of his life.
18. Just as a weary elephant rests in the shade, and having rested, destroys the tree, thus a vile man destroys his very refuge.
19. If one's ability to do good were as great as one's ability to do evil, he no doubt would have omniscience in his hand.
20. Birds abandon trees devoid of fruit, deer abandon forests which have burned down, bees abandon garlands which have faded, and Sārasa birds a desiccated lake. A harlot abandons one who has lost his wealth, and ministers a king who has been overthrown. Impelled by thoughts of gain one enjoys the company of others. Thus who is the friend of whom?
21. Through greed, carelessness, and trust a man comes to grief. Threfore let not a wise man be greedy, careless, or trusting [i.e. gullible].
22. Never anger the multitude; a large number of men are difficult to defeat. [For] ants devour even the mighty king of snakes!
23. Does the Margosa (neem) tree become sweet, even if it is sprinkled by wise men with hundreds of pitchers of milk mixed with sugar and honey? (*vijjuppanno' pi* does not make sense. My emendation to *ujupaññehi* is merely a guess.)
24. Not all virtues are found in all places; good men cause even a

little virtue to multiply. Doesn't the screw-pine (ketakī), although its leaf is marred by thorns, achieve the status of "crest-jewel" in the world?

25. The moon, difficult to see in daytime; the beloved, who has lost her youth; a lake bereft of lotuses; a sweet face, without learning; a good man, who is always poor; and a wicked king—these are the seven thorns in my heart. (The Skt. *nṛpāṅgaṇagataḥ khalaḥ* has been changed in Pali to *narādhipati yo khalo*; this seems deliberate, since the author of the *Lokaneyya-pakaraṇa* wants to make the king in the story seem wicked.)

These verses, many of them of unusual meters, reveal the erudition of the Buddhist monk who composed the *Lokaneyya-pakaraṇa* and his familiarity with Sanskrit literature. The discovery of this manuscript should reopen our search for further material concerning *nīti* verses. Due to the prevalence of Sanskrit in court circles in Southeast Asia, there is undoubtedly a wealth of hitherto unknown Pali verses awaiting us.

NOTES

1. *Pali Nīti Texts of Burma, Critical Edition and Study,* H. Bechert and H. Braun, PTS 1981.
2. See particularly *The Spreading of Cāṇakya's Aphorism over "Greater India"* (SCAGI) L. Sternbach,* Calcutta 1969 (Calcutta Oriental Book Agency).
3. *Paññāsa-jātaka or Zimme Paṇṇāsa* (*in the Burmese Recension*), ed. P. S. Jaini, Vols. I and II, PTS 1981-83. The Bahalaputtajātaka, No. 33 of this collection has been reproduced (with minor changes) in the *Lokaneyya-pakaraṇa,* thus suggesting the dependence of the latter on the former. The compilation of the *Paññāsajātaka* probably took place around the 15th century. See Introduction, Vol. II, xlv.
4. Mention may be made here of a Laotian work by the mame of Lokavinaya reported by Louis Finot in his 'Recherches sur la littérature laotienne', in *BEFEO,* XVII, 5, pp. 44-50 and more recently by H. Saddhātissa in his article 'Pali Literature from Laos' in *Studies in Pali & Buddhism,* ed. A. K. Narain, Delhi 1979, pp. 327-340. The name of the bodhisatta in this as well as in the *Lokaneyya-pakaraṇa* is Dhanañjaya. H. Saddhātissa also refers to another text, the prose Dhanañjayajātaka, in his 'Pali Literature in Cambodia' in JPTS IX, 1981, p. 189. Here he states: "On the basis of this prose work, a Pali poem in ten chapters (*khaṇḍas*) has been composed, entitled *Gāthālokaneyya.*" All these three texts, namely the *Lokavinaya,* the *Dhanañjayajātaka* and the *Gāthālokaneyya,* judged by their contents, appear to be abridged vernacular versions of our Pali *Lokaneyya-pakaraṇa.*

5. The following signs and abbreviations have been used:
Additions in [ ] Emendations in ( )

CNTT *Cāṇakya-Nīti-Text-Tradition* ed. L. Sternbach, 2 vols. with 5 pts., Hoshiarpur 1962-1970 (Vishveshvaranand Indological Series 27-29).

SCAGI *The Spreading of Cāṇakya's Aphorisms over "Greater India"*, Calcutta 1969 (Oriental Book Agency).

SRB *Subhāshita-Ratna-Bhāṇḍāgāraṃ*, ed. K. P. Parab, Bombay 1886 (The Nirnayasagara Press).

SV *The Subhāṣitāvalī of Vallabhadeva*, ed. P. Peterson, Bombay 1886 (Bombay Sanskrit Series 31); second edition, Poona 1961.

VYSS *The Vyāsa-subhāṣita-saṃgraha*, ed. L. Sternbach, Benares 1969 (Kashi Sanskrit Series 193).

6. These are the serial numbers of the *gāthās* in the *Lokaneyya-pakaraṇa* added by the present editor.

*See also his study of *Subhāṣita, Gnomic and Didactic Literature* (A history of Indian literature, IV, Wiesbaden, 1974) and paper delivered to the second conference of the International association of Buddhist studies at the Nava Nalanda Mahāvihāra, Bihar, on 18.1.80, "Non-Buddhist elements in Buddhist collections of wise sayings" which included a discussion of Burmese Nīti literature.

CHAPTER 21

Political and Cultural Data in References to Mathurā in the Buddhist Literature*

The Buddhist literary sources for the cultural history of ancient Mathurā can be grouped, in the traditionally accepted chronological order, as following:

A. *The Pāli Tripiṭaka and the Aṭṭhakathās*[1]
This consists of one sutta from the Majjhimanikāya,[2] three suttas from the Aṅguttaranikāya,[3] one *Jātaka*[4] and a single reference in the Vimānavatthu-Aṭṭhakathā.[5] To this list we may add such non-canonical Pāli texts as the Milindapañha,[6] the Cūlavaṁsa[7] and the Dīpavaṁsa,[8] which provide one reference each to the city of Madhurā. Finally, a reference to the city of Verañjā, a place in the vicinity of Madhurā, appearing in the Vinayapiṭaka[9] and the Aṅguttaranikāya,[10] may also be included under this heading.

B. *The Sanskrit Avadāna Literature*
The twenty-sixth *avadāna* (viz. the Pāṁśupradānāvadāna) of the Divyāvadāna[11] is our primary source for the history of the spread of Buddhism in the region of Mathurā. This *avadāna* prophesies the founding of a monastery called Naṭabhaṭa-vihāra in the vicinity of Mathurā and relates the legends associated with the monk Upagupta who is claimed as the spiritual teacher of the Mauryan

*This article was originally published in *Mathurā: The Cultural Heritage,* ed. Doris Srinivasan, (New Delhi: American Institute of Indian Studies, 1988), pp. 214-222. Reprinted with kind permission of American Institute of Indian Studies.

Emperor Aśoka. The *Avadānakalpalatā*[12] of Kṣemendra (*circa* 12th century) which repeats these legends should also be included in this group.

C. *The Vinaya texts of the Mūla-Sarvāstivādins*

The *Bhaiṣajyavastu* section of the Vinayavastu[13] of the Mūla-Sarvāstivādins is probably the last canonical source on Mathurā available to us. In addition to repeating the avadāna prophecies about the Naṭabhaṭa-vihāra and Upagupta's missionary activities, the Vinayavastu relates several incidents which took place during the Buddha's alleged visit to Mathurā, notably the conversion of a large number of yakṣas and the building of numerous vihāras to commemorate the event. Of equal interest, for an insight into the lives of the affluent section of the city, is the Cīvaravastu[14] story of the royal physician Jīvaka who makes a fortune in Mathurā because of his skill as a surgeon.

D. *Accounts of the Chinese Pilgrims*

The textual references to the Buddhist establishments in ancient Mathurā find their partial corroboration in the accounts of Fa-hsien and Hsüan-tsang, the two celebrated Chinese pilgrims who visited that city. The topographical descriptions of the various monasteries and stūpas found in their accounts provide the only link between the literary sources mentioned above and modern archaeological discoveries at Mathurā. We should also include under this heading references to Mathurā found elsewhere in the Chinese literature; of special interest are those references which mention Aśvaghoṣa the great poet in the court of Kaniṣka, and Mahādeva, a brahman of Mathurā, who is said to have propounded a pro-Mahāyānist dogma prior to the council of Vaiśālī.

E. *The Buddhist Inscriptions at Mathurā*

Our final and probably the most reliable source for the study of ancient Mathurā is the group of Buddhist inscriptions discovered there. These inscriptions are invaluable not only for the knowledge they provide on contemporary Buddhism (namely, the vihāras and the saṅgha there), but also for the information they impart about the citizens of Mathurā (namely, the kings, the donors, the merchants, etc.), and the visitors from the neighbouring countries to that famous city.*

We should point out at the outset that Mathurā is always referred to as Madhurā in the Pāli texts. It is difficult to ascertain whether the Pāli suttas retain the original name of the city or only a variant spelling of the same. Mathurā appears in all of our Sanskrit sources, and the Chinese accounts also seem to know that city by that name. The Pāli commentaries, including the *Jātakaṭṭhakathā*, however, know only Madhurā and often refer to it as Uttara Madhurā.[15] Since the latter is not attested in the *Milindapañha*[16] (which originates in the North and knows Madhurā) it may be correct to assume that the name Uttara Madhurā was introduced by the Sinhalese authors to distinguish Madhurā of the *suttas* from the city of the same name (the modern Madurai) in South India.[17] Whatever the original spelling, there is no doubt that all these references are to the famous city of Mathurā on the river Yamunā.

The Pāli sources enumerate Śūrasena in the traditional list of the sixteen *janapadas* and include Madhurā within that kingdom, but there is no specific mention of it as a capital city. The Mūla-Sarvāstivāda Vinayavastu places Mathurā between Bhadrāśva and Otalā, all within the territory of the Śūrasena kingdom. It designates the latter as the first kingdom (*ādi-rājya*) because the 'first King' [of our aeon] was elected here and hence was known as Mahāsammata, 'the Great Elected'.[18] The legend certainly points to a belief that this country was the cradle of civilization and was once ruled by a popular monarch.

More credible perhaps is the information provided by the Madhurasutta of the Majjhimanikāya. We read here that a king of Madhurā called Avantiputta once visited the Elder Mahā Kaccāna when the latter was residing in the Gundāvana, a park in that city. The king, after listening to the sermon of the Elder, was greatly distressed to hear that the Buddha had passed away.[19] This event evidently took place not long after the *parinirvāṇa* of the Buddha and hence the sutta may be referring to a real person of the name of Avantiputta. The *Aṭṭhakathā* on this sutta states that this Avantiputta was the son of the daughter of the king of Avanti.[20] There is thus a possibility that the king of Madhurā was related to the royal house of Ujjeni. Nothing is known about the descendents of this king. The Dīpavaṁsa account that 'in the past, Sādhīna and twenty-two of his descendents, the last of whom was Dhammagutta, reigned in Madhurā'[21] stands by itself and hence is not verifiable.

It is noteworthy that the Buddhist canonical texts, both Pāli and Sanskrit, are silent on the legends of Vāsudeva Kṛṣṇa so intimately associated by the Brahmanical epics and purāṇas with the city of Mathurā. By the time of the *Aṭṭhakathās*, however, these legends seem to have reached the Buddhists of Śri Lanka as can be seen from the *Ghaṭajātaka*. This *jātaka* names one Mahāsāgara as the king of Uttara Madhurā whose younger son Upasāgara comes to the kingdom of Uttarāpatha ruled by Kaṁsa. Upasāgara marries Kaṁsa's sister Devagabbhā (cf. Devakī) and they live together in the neighbouring village called Govaddhamāna (cf. Govardhana). There Devagabbhā gives birth to ten sons of whom Vāsudeva and Baladeva are the two eldest. They grow up concealed in the household of a servant woman Nandagopā and her husband Andhakaveṇhu. Eventually, Vāsudeva and Baladeva kill Muṭṭhika and Cāṇūra, the two wrestlers of that city as well as the king, Kaṁsa, and rule that city. They then aspire to conquer the whole of India and after capturing Ayojjhā proceed to Dvāravatī.[22] Since Mathurā figures in this jātaka merely as the birthplace of Kṛṣṇa's father the story is of little value to us.

Turning our attention to the cultural data, it would be correct to assume that the Pāli canonical texts are our oldest available Buddhist sources and hence provide us with a description of Mathurā which is closest to the time of the Buddha and his immediate disciples. The *suttas* do not mention that the Buddha ever visited the city itself, although one passage does say that he journeyed along the highway between Madhurā and Verañjā.[23] The latter city was probably in the neighbourhood of Madhurā and hence the conditions obtaining in Verañjā were probably present in Mathurā as well. A certain tree, called Naḷerunimba, figures several times in these *suttas* as a sacred spot on this highway.[24] According to the commentaries, this tree was sacred because of a yakṣa named Naḷeru. Yakṣa-worship seems to have been quite prevalent in Mathurā from ancient times and these are probably the first references to it.

Several brahmans from Mathurā and Verañjā figure in the *suttas*. The Aṅguttaranikāya[25] mentions one named Kandarāyaṇa and refers to one brahman from Verañjā (probably identical with the person mentioned in the Vinayapiṭaka). All these passages are concerned with the Buddha's refusal to show the customary respect to the aged brahmans or to uphold the doctrine of their superiority in the caste hierarchy. Even Avantiputta, the king of Mathurā, thought it fit, while visiting the Elder Mahā Kaccāna, to raise questions regarding the alleged superiority of brahmans by virtue of their birth.[26] These references reflect the great agitation in the minds of the members of the upper castes caused by the Buddhist practice of opening the doors of the saṅgha even to the śūdras who were customarily barred from entry into monastic orders.

Turning now to the merchant castes, they appear to be active and affluent in and around Mathurā. The Aṅguttara passage quoted above states that a large number of householders were also on the Madhurā-Verañjā highway when the Buddha was travelling there with 500 monks.[27] The fact that as many as 500 monks stayed in Verañjā for a period of the rainy season indicates that a large mercantile community, that would have the means to support many monks, was active in that area.

The Vinayapiṭaka gives a full account of a famine in Verañjā during the Buddha's visit to that place. The text says: 'At that time Verañjā was short of almsfood, which was difficult to obtain; it was suffering from famine and people subsisted on blades of grass. Nor was it easy to keep oneself going by gleaning or by favour. At that time some horse dealers of Uttarāpatha arrived at the rain-residence of Verañjā with 500 horses. In the horse-rings they prepared *pattha*-measures after *pattha*-measures of steamed grains for the monks. The monks went into the horse-rings for food. Having brought the *pattha*-measures of steamed grain back to the park, they pounded them and ate them.'[28] We are told that the Buddha was also offered a *pattha*-measure and he accepted it. This particular *sutta* indirectly tells us a great deal about the economic conditions of Mathurā. The fact that 500 horses were brought there indicates that Mathurā was a prominent market place. Furthermore, since horses were used primarily for military purposes, Mathurā also must have been a strategically important center, being situated between the Uttarāpatha and the Madhyadeśa. The food which was served during the famine was called *pulaka* which, according to the commentaries, meant unhusked, steamed barley and rice. Barley and rice appear then to have been a staple food of the people. The *pattha* seems to have been the smallest measure of grain. It was equal to one *nāḷi* or a small bamboo piece and according to the Vinaya commentary four such pieces made one *āḷhaka*.[29]

Apart from this description of Verañjā during the famine, the Pāli suttas yield very little information about the conditions in and around Mathurā. The Buddha seems to have viewed the city with distinct disfavour. In one sutta he says: 'Monks, there are five disadvantages in Madhurā. What five? The ground is uneven; there is much dust; there are fierce dogs; bestial *yakkhas;* and alms are got with difficulty.'[30] There is no doubt that the experience of famine in Verañjā deterred the early disciples of the Buddha from frequenting Mathurā. The same sentiment is preserved in the Mūla-Sarvāstivādins' Vinayavastu as will be seen below.

The Buddha's dislike for Mathurā, however, did not completely dissuade the monks from visiting that city and spreading the faith there. We have already seen that Mahā Kaccāna came to Mathurā after the death of the Buddha and converted the king, Avantiputta, to Buddhism. The next piece of evidence for such missionary activity is to be found in the Divyāvadāna, a collection of some 38 stories which describe the noble deeds of various people. This text belongs to the Mūla-Sarvāstivāda school and although the extant version of the text is dated between 200 and 350 A.D., the compilers of it were drawing upon earlier sources which were closer to the times of the Mauryan Emperor Aśoka, *circa* 260 B.C. Four *avadānas* of this text, Nos. 26-29, deal with the events which allegedly took place during the lifetime of Aśoka and according to the 26th *avadāna,* the Pāṃśupradānāvadāna, which makes a specific reference to Mathurā, these events occurred 100 years after the Buddha's death. This *avadāna* prefaces the story of the emperor's conversion to Buddhism with a narrative about his teacher, *sthavira* Upagupta. We are told that the Buddha, just before attaining his death, having subdued Upalālanāga and also having instructed the potterwomen named Caṇḍālī and Gopālī, arrived in the city of Mathurā. There he called his disciple, Ānanda, and pointed out to him the nearby blue hills of Urumuṇḍa. He then prophesied that two merchant brothers from Mathurā, named Naṭa and Bhaṭa, would establish a vihāra on that hill which would be known as Naṭabhaṭavihāra, a favourite haunt of meditation-loving monks. There the Elder Śāṇakavāsi (a 100 years after the *parinirvāṇa* of the Buddha) would ordain Upagupta.[31] The latter would become a second Buddha, as it were, and would preach the doctrine in such a way that all his mendicant disciples would attain arhatship. Following this prophecy, the *avadāna* relates the story of Upagupta, a native of Mathurā, and thus indirectly tells us something about the merchant caste of Mathurā. We learn that Upagupta was born in the family of a perfume dealer (*gandhika*—the modern equivalent of *gāndhī*—) known by the name of Gupta. The Elder Śāṇakavāsi perceived by means of his supernatural knowledge that Upagupta (the third of three brothers, Aśvagupta and Dharmagupta being his elder brothers) was the one destined to be the great preacher. Upagupta's father agrees to relinquish his youngest son to the saṅgha for ordination at the proper time (i.e. when there will be neither loss nor gain in the business). The narrative tells us that Upagupta received instructions from Śāṇakavāsi to cultivate only wholesome thoughts and to always conduct his business lawfully. His reputation for honesty reaches a rich courtesan of Mathurā, Vāsavadattā, whose charges were 500 'old' (gold?) coins (*purāṇaśata*) for one night. She falls in love with Upagupta and invites him to spend the night with her. He refuses, saying that this is not the 'right time' for him to see her. Thinking that he cannot afford the 500 'old' coins Vāsavadattā sends word that she is not interested in even a single copper coin (*kārṣāpaṇa*), and that she truly loves him. Once again Upagupta sends back the same reply. Vāsavadattā would appear then to be a courtesan cultivated enough to want lovers only for the sake of love. However, she was equally greedy and cruel. We are told that a son of a merchant was in her chambers one night. A certain member of a caravan arrives in Mathurā from Uttarāpatha that same night bringing with him enough money to buy 500 horses. He proceeds to the courtesan's chamber with the 500 'old' coins and many valuable presents as well. Vāsavadattā, greedy for the man's riches, has the merchant's son killed and thrown into a trunk and spends the night with the other man. The relatives of the merchant's son later find him, remove him from the trunk and inform the king. Vāsavadattā is punished by the cutting off of her ears and nose and the severing of her hands and feet and she is thrown onto the cremation grounds. The story then tells at length how Upagupta goes to see the courtesan, as this was the 'right time' to see her and preach the law to her. She takes refuge in the Buddha, Dharma, and Saṅgha just before dying and she is reborn in a heaven. We are told that the devatās or fairies of the city proclaim that she has been reborn in a heaven. Upon hearing this, the people of Mathurā cremate her body and worship her remains.[32] Eventually, Upagupta is ordained as a monk and preaches the doctrine of the Buddha. His fame reaches far and wide and even the Emperor Aśoka wants to visit him in Mathurā. Perceiving that such a royal visit will cause a great deal of harassment to the people of Mathurā, Upagupta offers to visit the Emperor and proceeds by boat to Pāṭaliputra.[33]

The account of the courtesan Vāsavadattā was probably introduced by the Buddhist authors in order to illustrate the doctrine of suffering, etc. Nevertheless, it is of great value to us as it reveals Mathurā as a prosperous city boasting such courtesans and frequented by wealthy foreign merchants who were both willing and able to pay their price. The story also tells us something about the crimes and punishments known to the people of Mathurā. The fact that the guilty courtesan was not put to death for her crime suggests the existence of a criminal code which prohibited capital punishment for women. The final episode of the story provides valuable information about the religious beliefs of the people. Normally one would expect a criminal like Vāsavadattā to remain unburied in the cemetery and to be devoured by wild animals. The fact that the people performed a *pūjā* for her remains (*śarīra*) after learning of her conversion to Buddhism, shows the esteem in which Buddhism was held. Liberal attitudes prevailed even in the case of a criminal like Vāsavadattā who was awakened to faith at her death.

The latter part of the *avadāna* describes the career of Upagupta as a preacher of the Law. We are told that Māra, the Evil One, was subdued by him, when the former tried to prevent his preaching at an assembly and even dared to tie a garland of flowers on the monk's head, a substance forbidden to the Buddhist ascetics. Upagupta in return created by his magic powers three dead bodies, respectively, of a snake, a dog and a man, and tied them to Māra's body. Māra, unable to shake off the dead bodies, confessed his defeat and agreed to do the bidding of Upagupta. The latter asked Māra to manifest the form of the Buddha by his supernatural powers. The story tells us that Māra entered a thick forest and having taken the guise of the Buddha, like a *naṭa* (stage actor) who has been made up properly in the green room (*naṭa rva suruciranepathyaḥ*), came out of the forest and appeared before Upagupta. He presented the grand scene of the Lord, adorned with his circle of rays, with Śāriputra on his right side and

Maudgalyāyana on his left and the venerable Ānanda behind him holding the Buddha's almsbowl.[34] This miraculous event led to the conversion of hundreds of thousands of brahmans in Mathurā, many of whom attained to arhatship. The above story of Māra may well be an invention. Nevertheless, it alludes to dramatic performances by skilled artists; the people of Mathurā seem to have been well acquainted with this art.

The story of Upagupta ends with one more interesting detail. We are told that on Urumuṇḍa hill there is a cave (18' long and 12' wide).[35] Upagupta is said to have instructed all those of his disciples who had attained arhatship to place a four-inch stick (*kaṭikā*) in the cave. Consequently, in one day 10,000 sticks were placed in that cave. According to another tradition, Upagupta's body was cremated with these sticks.[36] Whatever the purpose of such a practice of throwing sticks in a cave, this cave became a pilgrimage site. It was visited by Hsüan-tsang in the seventh century.

Our next canonical source, the Mūla-Sarvāstivāda Vinayavastu, repeats the prophecy of the Buddha regarding the founding of the Naṭabhaṭavihāra and the advent of Upagupta in Mathurā. However, unlike the previous sources, the *Vinayavastu* mentions the Buddha entering the city of Mathurā proper and relates the events which followed his arrival. We read that the Buddha arrived in Mathurā while journeying in the country of the Śūrasenas. The brahmans of Mathurā, learning of his arrival, were extremely distressed. They feared that if he entered Mathurā and preached his doctrine of spiritual salvation of all *varṇas*, their social superiority would be in jeopardy.[37] They therefore contrived to have him insulted by a prominent man of Mathurā and thus prevent his entrance. They approached a brahman named Nīlabhūti, who was learned in all the Vedas and quite competent in philosophical debate, and begged him to revile the Buddha. Nīlabhūti was a man of unquestioned integrity. He therefore told the brahmans that he would neither praise nor blame the Buddha, but would express only the impartial truth. When he approached the Buddha surrounded by the brahmans, he praised him with 500 verses. The Buddha then entered the city to beg for alms.

That same day was also a holiday in honour of a certain constellation (*nakṣatra*). The goddess of Mathurā, the recipient of worship on that night, thought to herself, 'If the ascetic Gautama enters Mathurā, the festivities will certainly be hindered.' Thus, in order to turn him away, she appeared naked in his presence. The Buddha addressed the goddess as follows: 'A woman looks bad enough when poorly dressed, what to speak of without clothing!' She, very embarrassed, disappeared. The Buddha then stepped away from the path, sat down in a quiet place and proclaimed to the assembly of monks the following five defects of Mathurā: 'The ground is uneven, it is covered with stones and brickbats, it abounds in prickly shrubs, the people take solitary meals and there are too many women.'[38]

Following this incident, the Buddha decided not to enter Mathurā and instead proceeded to the abode (*bhavanaṁ*) of a yakṣa named Gardabha (lit. a donkey). He sat in the yakṣa's courtyard under a tree for the rest of the day. The brahmans and some other householders of Mathurā, upon hearing that the Buddha and his retinue had not entered the city and consequently had not eaten, brought large amounts of food to the courtyard and begged the Buddha to accept their food. The Buddha had his company of monks gather in a residence hall (*upasthānaśālā*) for the meal. When they had finished, the devout brahmans and householders entreated the Buddha as follows: 'The Lord has subdued many cruel nāgas and wicked yakṣas. This Gardabha yakṣa has for a long time undeservedly been hostile to us. He takes away our newborn children. It would indeed be a great blessing of the Lord if he would subdue this yakṣa also.' The Buddha then sent for Gardabha yakṣa and admonished him to refrain from his evil deeds. The yakṣa agreed to do so only on the condition that the people of Mathurā establish in his name a vihāra for the Buddhist saṅgha. Thus took place the conversion of Gardabha yakṣa together with his retinue of 500 minor yakṣas. The people of Mathurā built 500 vihāras in their name. The Buddha also subdued at this time two other yakṣas, Śara and Vana and one yakṣiṇī named Ālikavendā Maghā residing outside the city. Finally, the Buddha by his magic powers entered the city and there he converted the yakṣiṇī Timisikā (with a following of 500) in whose name 500 vihāras were built. The text concludes by saying that during his sojourn in Mathurā, the Buddha subdued 2,500 yakṣas in and around the city and that the same number of vihāras were built by the devout (*śrāddha*) laymen in the name of those yakṣas.[39]

We have seen that the Pālī *suttas* mentioned only the yakṣa

Naḷeru, who was associated with the neem tree. The *Divyāvadāna* passages do not refer to yakṣas at all, showing thereby that they were drawing upon an older tradition. The Mūla-Sarvāstivāda text reflects a period when the brahmans of Mathurā became increasingly hostile to the spread of Buddhism there, and also a time when the yakṣa worship increased enormously in that region. The names of the yakṣas and yakṣiṇīs mentioned probably refer to beings actually worshipped in the city at the time of the compilation of the *Vinayavastu*. We should note however that neither Fa-hsien nor Hsüan-tsang refer to these yakṣas in their accounts and also that their names are conspicuously absent from the inscriptions found in Mathurā.

The Verañjā of the Pāli scriptures is probably identical with the Vairambhā of the *Vinayavastu*. We learn from the latter that the Buddha, having left Mathurā came to Otalā and from there proceeded to Vairambhā. The king of Vairambhā was a brahman named Agnidatta. He was not a follower of the Buddha but out of courtesy invited the Buddha to spend a period of three months in his city. He ordered the ministers to prepare plenty of food but failed to mention that the food was for the benefit of the Buddha and his monks. Seeking to be the sole donor, he forbade others from offering alms to the saṅgha on the pain of death![40] On the same night the king had a dream full of ill omens and he was advised to remain in complete seclusion for three months. The king retired in haste and thus could neither command that the monks be fed nor rescind his order prohibiting offerings by his subjects. No one dared to approach the king to tell him that the monks were facing starvation. The Buddha himself asked Ānanda to contact the citizens to come forward with food offerings but there were no volunteers as they were all scared of the 'wicked' king (*kali-rājā*). The situation was saved by the arrival from the Northern country (Uttarāpatha) of a caravan leader who camped in Vairambhā with five hundred horses and enough food to feed them. He heard the misdeeds of the hated king, but thinking to himself, 'I am not a subject of this kingdom, what can the king do to me?'[41] he offered Ānanda to give the surplus from his horse food to the saṅgha. We are told that the Buddha and his monks (a total of 448 monks who showed their willingness to eat that food by picking up a śalākā or a piece of stick) then subsisted for the entire period on a measure (called *prastha*, cf. Pāli *pattha*) of *yava* (barley) each supplied every day by the caravan leader. At the end of the third month the Buddha sent word to the king that he was leaving. The king was astonished and was full of grief over his negligence and prevailed upon the Buddha to forgive him and accept his alms. We should probably not treat this story too seriously: it is very likely a recast of the Pāli *Vinaya* story of the famine in Verañjā where the saṅgha was saved from starvation by the charity of visiting merchants to that city.

Notwithstanding the hardships endured by the saṅgha due to famine, Mathurā in normal times would appear to have been an affluent and pleasant city as evidenced by the story of the courtesan Vāsavadattā in the Divyāvadāna. Several narratives in the Mūla-Sarvāstivāda Vinaya also depict Mathurā as being highly prosperous. Especially noteworthy is the *Cīvaravastu* section. Here we are told of the famous physician Jīvaka and his exploits as a skillful surgeon. Having completed his education in Takṣaśilā, he arrived in Mathurā on his way to Rājagṛha. There he saw a wrestler, apparently dead, having been felled by a rival. Jīvaka, we are told, placed a crystal jewel on his forehead and peered into the mangled intestines of the fallen wrestler. He then placed a certain powder in a reed pipe and blew it into the patient's mouth.[42] When the powder reached his intestines, he was cured. We should note here that wrestling appears to have been a popular sport in Mathurā; the Ghaṭajātaka referred to earlier also mentions two wrestlers, Cāṇūra and Muṭṭhika, who were killed by Kṛṣṇa and Baladeva. We understand from the present story that Jīvaka earned 500 *kārṣāpaṇas* (copper coins?) from the wrestler for his surgery.

A second episode concerns the treatment of a young widow afflicted with a certain type of venereal disease. She had been the wife of a merchant and became widowed while still young. Her husband greatly attached to her, died, and was reborn as a worm (*kṛmi*) in her yoni. All men, who had intercourse with her, died, apparently bitten by that worm, and thus, no one would approach her. She heard that Jīvaka was in Mathurā and went to see him for a treatment. Jīvaka, finding her very attractive, listened to her story. He agreed to treat her only on the condition that she sleep with him. She was disconcerted but realizing that she needed to be cured, agreed and bared herself to him. Jīvaka then inserted a piece of meat into her yoni. When the worm had attached itself to the meat, Jīvaka pulled it out and discarded it. The lady, now cured, was desirous of the physician, but he refused her, saying 'you are a sister to me. This was necessary in order to treat you'.[43] She also gave Jīvaka 500 *kārṣāpaṇas* and he left Mathurā for the banks of the Yamunā. The story speaks for itself regarding the beliefs about venereal diseases and the cures thereof. It reveals the morals of rich, young widows of respectable families, and certainly provides a unique insight into the scruples of a young physician in his relationship with his patients. The amount of 500 *kārṣāpaṇas* appears to have been the standard fee of a royal surgeon.

The Pāli and the Buddhist Sanskrit sources quoted above cannot be dated with any certainty. Exact chronology is however possible for our two remaining sources, the records of the Chinese pilgrims and the Buddhist inscriptions at Mathurā. Although these are not included in the 'Literary sources', they are nevertheless valuable for confirming the canonical accounts particularly of institutions said to have been established in Mathurā in those times.

Turning to the Chinese sources, Fa-hsien was in India around 400 A.D., as is well known. He mentions that he visited Mathurā on his way from the Punjab to Saṅkīsa. His visit there was apparently very short. We learn from his account that there were some 20 monasteries with 3,000 monks on both banks of the Yamunā river. He does not seem to have visited any of the sacred places mentioned in the canonical texts, i.e. the Naṭabhaṭavihāra and the cave of Upagupta. Fa-hsien states, however that near the vihāras, there were pagodas in honour of Śāriputra, Maudgalyāyana and Ānanda, and that special offerings were made to the latter by nuns. There were also pagodas in honour of the *Sūtras,* the *Vinaya* and the *Abbidharma.* Fa-hsien also mentions the Mahāyāna, whose followers, he says, made offerings to Mañjuśrī, Avalokiteśvara and Prajñāpāramitā.[44]

The second account is by Hsüan-tsang who visited Mathurā more than 200 years after Fa-hsien, around 630 A.D. By this time Buddhism seems to have declined in Mathurā since, according to his description, there were 20 monasteries with only about 2,000 monks of both vehicles. There were also five *deva* temples of non-Buddhist sects. In addition to confirming Fa-hsien's account of the pagodas, Hsüan-tsang says that 'there are three topes all built by Aśoka; very numerous traces left by the Four Past Buddhas...'.[45]

Hsüan-tsang also probably visited the Naṭabhaṭavihāra and the cave of Upagupta: 'going east from the capital five or six *li* one comes to a "hill monastery" the chamber of which was quarried in a steep bank, a narrow defile being used to form its entrance. This monastery has been made by the venerable Upagupta and it enclosed a tope with a finger-nail relic of the Buddha. Through the north rock-wall of the monastery was a cave about 20 feet high by 30 feet wide, within which were piled up fine four-inch slips of wood (that is, tallies). When the Venerable Upagupta was preaching and converting, every married couple that attained arhatship put down a tally here, but for single members of families although they became arhats no record of the fact was kept.'[46]... 'to the south-east of the cave (that is, the cave monastery) and 24 or 25 *li* from it was a large dried-up pond beside which was a tope...'.[47] Doubt has been cast on the veracity of Hsüan-tsang's descriptions of Mathurā. Watters is of the opinion that he did not travel to the capital but only made a hurried journey across part of the Śūrasena country. Even so, in the absence of any other eye-witness accounts of Mathurā, these two Chinese records can aid in searches for the exact locations of the Naṭabhaṭavihāra and the cave monastery associated with the name of Upagupta.

We may mention in passing that certain Chinese (and also Tibetan) sources have claimed that Aśvaghoṣa, the great poet and author of the *Buddhacarita* and the *Saundarananda,* was the spiritual counselor of king Kaniṣka.[48] Assuming that Kaniṣka was ruling in Mathurā around the first century A.D., Aśvaghoṣa may well have lived in that city even though such residence is not mentioned in any of his extant works.

One more piece of information, derived from the Chinese sources, may be pertinent here. According to Vasumitra's treatise on the eighteen schools, translated by Hsüan-tsang, a brahman named Mahādeva, a Buddhist from Mathurā, propounded a doctrine which cast doubt on the attainment of salvation by an arhat.[49] Mahādeva maintained that an arhat may commit a sin by unconscious temptation and also that he may have doubts in matters of doctrine. It was believed that the council of Vaiśālī was at least in part convened to debate this controversy regarding the status of an arhat. Mahādeva's points certainly indicate the beginnings of the Mahāyāna doctrine (of the Saddharmapuṇḍarīka-sūtra) that the path of arhat was only a stepping-stone to the final goal of nirvāṇa attained by the bodhisattva path. If indeed the views attributed to Mahādeva originated in Mathurā, then the city would have to be considered as the place where the Mahāyāna doctrine of *ekayāna* came to be formulated.

NOTES

*It is beyond the scope of this paper to consider in detail these inscriptions for which the chief source is Heinrich Lüders, *Mathurā Inscriptions,* ed. by K. L. Janert, Göttingen 1961. Briefly it may be noted that the excavation sites have not so far yielded the localities of the Naṭabhaṭvihāra nor the cave of Upagupta. Instead we learn the existence of several vihāras unknown to the canonical texts or to the Chinese pilgrims. Most important of these is the Mahārāja-Devaputra-vihāra named after the king Huviṣka. The inscriptions mention several Buddhist schools that flourished in Mathurā. The Mahāsāṅghikas appear to have the largest following; they are associated with three vihāras, namely, the Ālanakavihāra, the Cūtakavihāra, and the Kāṣṭikīyavihāra. The Sammitīyas lived at Sirivihāra. The Sarvāstivādins and the Dharmaguptakas are also mentioned and must have had a vihāra of their own. Several vihāras are gifts of guilds, as for example, the Prāvārikāvihāra (of cloakmakers), Suvarṇakāravihāra (of goldsmiths), and the Kāṣṭikīyavihāra (of timber merchants). Individual donors come from different strata of society. The inscriptions mention donations from a barber, a trooper, and sons of actors (known as the Candraka Brothers of Mathurā). The management of the caityas and vihāras appears to have been in the hands of a group of laymen called *saṅghaprakṛta* ('Commissioners of the Community') drawn mostly from the merchant community (*vyavahārī*). The inscriptions confirm the canonical accounts of the visits of foreigners to Mathurā; one records the gift of a pillar-base by a native of Oḍīyana and the other relates to the donation of a similar gift by a resident of Nagarahāra (Nagarakīyasya), a son of Mitravarmā. The inscriptions abound in names of monks and nuns who resided in Mathurā; but the two most famous names, viz. Śāṇakavāsa and Upagupta, are conspicuously absent. There is a solitary inscription which records a gift to a vihāra specifically associated with 'practicers of meditation' (*prahāṇika*), monks who appear to have kept the tradition of Upagupta alive.

1. The Pāli texts referred to are publications of the Pali Text Society, London.
2. *Majjhimanikāya,* ii, p. 83.
3. *Aṅguttaranikāya,* i, p. 67; ii, 57, iii, p. 256.
4. *Jātaka,* iv, pp. 79 ff.
5. *Vimānavatthu-Aṭṭhakathā,* pp. 118 ff.
6. *Milindapañha,* p. 331.
7. *Cūlavaṁsa,* xciii, 23 ff.
8. *Dīpavaṁsa,* iii, 21.
9. *Vinayapiṭaka (Suttavibhaṅga),* i p. 1.
10. *Aṅguttaranikāya,* ii, p. 57; iv, p. 117.
11. P. L. Vaidya, *Divyāvadāna,* Patna 1959, pp. 216-241.
12. P. L. Vaidya, *Avadānakalpalatā,* Patna 1959, ii, pp. 447-453.
13. N. Dutt and S. Sharma, *Gilgit Manuscripts,* Srinagar, iii, pt. 1.

14. Dutt and Sharma, *Gilgit Manuscripts,* iii, pt. 2. (Srinagar 1942).
15. *Jātaka,* iv, p. 79.
16. *...Pāṭheyyakā, Koṭumbara-Mādhurakā Ālasanda-Kāsmīra-Gandhārā...*, *Milindapañha,* p. 331.
17. The *Vimānavatthu-Aṭṭhakathā* and the *Cūlavaṁsa* references given above are all to the Uttara Madhurā. The former tells the story of a woman of Uttara Madhurā who gave alms to the Buddha and was reborn in heaven, while the latter text tells the story of a king called Mahāsena of Pāṭaliputra who went to Uttara Madhurā in disguise as a labourer and gave alms to monks with the wages earned there.
18. *atha bhagavān Śūraseneṣu janapadeṣu cārikaṁ carann Ādirājyam anuprāptaḥ. ...asminn Ānanda pradeśe Mahāsammato rājā prathamato rājyenâbhiṣiktaḥ. abhiṣikto 'yaṁ ca rājñām ādir ato 'syâdirājya ādirājya iti saṁjñā saṁvṛttā. Gilgit Manuscripts,* iii, pt. 1, p. 3. The Pāli tradition claims this honour for the original ancestor of the Śākyan family reigning at Kuśāvatī. See *Mahāvaṁsa,* ii, 1-15.
19. *ekaṁ samayam āyasmā Mahā Kaccāno Madhurāyāṁ viharati Gundāvane. assosi kho rājā Mādhuro Avantiputto... 'kahaṁ pana bho Kaccāna, etarahi so bhagavā viharati ...? 'parinibbuto kho, mahārāja, etarahi so bhagavā...'. Majjhimanikāya,* ii, p. 84-90.
20. *Majjhimanikāya-Aṭṭhakathā,* iii, p. 319.
21. *Dīpavaṁsa,* iii, 21.
22. *Jātaka,* iv, pp. 79 ff. It should be noted that Ghaṭapaṇḍita (the ninth brother), the bodhisattva of this jātaka is assigned a very minor role of consoling Vāsudeva at the loss of his son.
23. *Aṅguttaranikāya,* ii, p. 57.
24. *Aṅguttaranikāya,* iv, p. 198.
25. *Aṅguttaranikāya,* i, p. 67.
26. *...rājā Mādhuro Avantiputto āyasmantaṁ Mahā Kaccānam etad avoca: brāhmaṇā, bho Kaccāna, evam āhaṁsu—'brāhmaṇo va seṭṭho vaṇṇo, ...brāhmaṇā va sujjhanti, no abrāhmaṇā,' ...idha bhavaṃ Kaccāno kim akkhāyī ti. Majjhimanikāya, ii, p.* 84.
27. *Aṅguttaranikāya,* ii, p. 57.
28. I. B. Horner, *The Book of the Discipline,* London 1938, i, p. 11.
29. Horner, *Discipline,* p. 12, n. 2.
30. *pañc' ime, bhikkhave, ādīnavā Madhurāyaṁ, katame pañca? visamā, bahurajā, caṇḍasunakhā, vāḷayakkhā, dullabhapiṇḍā. Aṅguttaranikāya, ii, p.* 256.
31. *eṣa Ānanda U(or R)urumuṇḍo nāma parvataḥ. atra varṣaśata parinirvṛtasya Śāṇakavāsī nāma bhikṣur bhaviṣyati. so 'tra...vihāraṁ pratiṣṭhāpayiṣyati, Upaguptaṁ ca pravrājayiṣyati. Mathurāyām Ānanda Naṭo Bhaṭaś ca dvau bhrātarau śreṣṭhinau bhviṣyataḥ tau U(or R)urumuṇḍaparvate vihāraṁ pratiṣṭhāpayiṣyataḥ. tasya Naṭabhaṭikêti saṁjñā bhaviṣyati. etad agram me bhaviṣyati śamathānukūlānāṁ śayyāsanānāṁ yad idaṁ Naṭabhaṭikāraṇyāyatanam. Divyāvadāna,* p. 217.
32. *Devataiś ca Mathurāyām ārocitaṃ...deveṣûpapannêti. śrutvā ca Mathurāvāstavyena* janakāyena Vāsavadattāyāḥ *śarīre pūjā kṛtā. Ibid,* p. 221. It may be noted that Kṣemendra's *Avadānakalpalatā,* mentioned above, agrees substantially with the *Divyāvadāna* account of Vāsavadattā.
33. Whether Aśoka visited Mathurā or not must remain an open question. Our text however is emphatic in stating that the Sthavira himself visited him in Pāṭaliputra: *tato rājñā sthavirôpaguptasyârthe nauyānenāgamiṣyatîti yāvac ca Mathurāṁ yāvac ca Pāṭaliputraṁ antarān nausaṅkramo 'vasthāpitaḥ. atha sthavirôpagupto rājño 'śokasyânugrahārtham aṣṭādaśabhir arhatsahasraiḥ parivṛto nāvam abhiruhya Pāṭaliputram anuprāptaḥ. Divyāvadāna,* p. 245.

34. *Divyāvadāna*, p. 226.
35. *tatra côrumuṇḍaparvate guhā aṣṭādaśahastā dairghyeṇa dvādaśahastā vistāreṇa. Divyāvadāna*, p. 228.
36. *...caturaṅgulamātrā śalākā prakṣeptavyā...ekasmin divase daśabhir arhatsahasraiḥ śalākāḥ prakṣiptāḥ. Divyāvadāna. Cf. ... parinirvṛtaṁ cainaṁ tābhir evārhatkaṭikābhiḥ sametya te dhmāpayiṣyanti. Gilgit Manuscripts*, iii, pt. 1, p. 4.
37. *aśrauṣur Māthurā brāhmaṇāḥ śramaṇo Gautamo Mathurām anuprāptaḥ. so 'tyarthaṁ cāturvarṇaviśuddhiṁ rocayati...yady asau Mathurāṁ pravekṣyati asmākaṁ lābhāntarāyo bhaviṣyati. Gilgit Manuscripts*, iii, pt. 1, p. 7.
38. *pañcême bhikṣava ādīnavā Mathurāyāṁ. katame pañca? utkūlanikūlāḥ sthāṇukaṇṭakapradhānā bahupāṣāṇaśarkarākaṭhallā uccandrabhaktāḥ pracuramātṛgrāmā iti. Gilgit Manuscripts*, iii, pt. 1, p. 14. (See note 30 above.)
39. *Gilgit Manuscripts*, iii, pt. 1, p. 17.
40. *Vairambhye ca ghaṇṭāvaghoṣaṇaṁ kāritaṁ—nânyena śramaṇo Gautamas traimāsīṁ bhojayitavyaḥ. yo bhojayati tasya vadho daṇḍa iti. Gilgit Manuscripts*, iii, pt. 1, p. 26.
41. *nâham asya rājño nivāsī. kiṁ mama rājā kariṣyati. Gilgit Manuscripts*, iii, pt. 1, p. 29.
42. *tato Jīvakena sarvabhūtaprasādakamaṇiḥ śirasi sthāpayitvā pratyavekṣitaḥ. ...tena nāḍikāyāṁ cūrṇaṁ prakṣipya mukhe vāyunā preritaṁ. cūrṇena antrāṇi spṛṣṭāni. svasthībhūtaḥ. Gilgit Manuscripts*, iii, pt. 2, p. 35.
43. *...bhaginī tvaṃ mama. tavaiṣā cikitsêti mayaivaṁ kṛtam iti. Gilgit Manuscripts*, iii, pt. 2, p. 36.
44. H. A. Giles, *The Travels of Fa-hsien*, Cambridge 1923, p. 23.
45. T. Watters, *On Yuan Chwang's Travels in India*, London 1904, i, p. 302.
46. Watters, *Travels*, p. 306.
47. Watters, *Travels*, p. 309
48. S. Beal, *The Fo-Sho-Hing-Tsan-King*, Sacred Books of the East, Vol. XIX, Intro. xxx-xxxii.
49. J. Masuda, *Origin and Doctrines of Early Indian Buddhist Schools*, Liepzig 1925. See also, P. V. Bapat, *2500 Years of Buddhism*, New Delhi 1956.

CHAPTER 22

Padīpadānajātaka: Gautama's Last Female Incarnation*

The *Paññāsa Jātaka* occupies an important place in the history of Pali narrative literature originating from Southeast Asia. It is a collection of fifty (*Paññāsa* or *paṇṇāsa*) "birth-stories" (*jātaka*) of the Buddha Gautama, composed in imitation of the canonical *Jātakatthavaṇṇanā*.[1] More than a hundred years ago L. Feer, in his article, 'Les Jātakas', established the 'extra-canonical' nature of these stories and suggested that they may have originated in Chieng Mai (Northern Thailand) in the fifteenth century A.D.[2] In 1911 the Hanthawaddy Press, Rangoon, published a volume entitled *Zimme Paṇṇāsa* (literally 'Chieng-Mai Fifty') comprising the Pali text of the Burmese recension of the *Paññāsa Jātaka*.[3] In 1917 L. Finot compared this version with manuscripts of three collections of these stories, two in Pali (originating in Thailand and Cambodia) and one in Laotian (from Laos)[4]. In recent years Madame Terral has critically edited and compared the Burmese and Cambodian versions of a major story from the *Paññāsa Jātaka* collection, namely the *Samuddaghosajātaka*, and has made a significant contribution to the study of the linguistic peculiarity of the Pali language used in these two texts.[5]

During my visit to Burma in 1960 I was able to obtain photographs of a unique manuscript of the *Zimme Paṇṇāsa* version, which facilitated the preparation of a critical edition of the *Paññāsa Jātaka*. This work has been completed, and the first volume, con-

*This article was originally published in *Amalā Prajñā: Aspects of Buddhist Studies, Professor P.V. Bapat Felicitation Volume*, eds. N.H. Samtani and H.S. Prasad, (Delhi: Indian Books Centre, 1989), pp. 33-39.

taining the first 25 *jātakas*, has been published by the Pali Text Society[6]. The second volume is in press and includes an unusual story of the past life of Gautama Buddha, even prior to his commencement of the bodhisattva career.

It is well-known that Buddhist doctrine does not allow a woman to become Buddha, and the Theravādins even require that, during the pursuit of the *pāramitās*, the bodhisattva not be born as a female.[7] There is no reference in the Pali scripture to the bodhisattva being a female, even in an animal existence. The *liṅga-sampatti*, or the endowment of male gender, is one of the prerequisites for the prediction by a Buddha of a *bodhisattva's* attaining Buddhahood, as when Dīpaṅkara made the prophecy that the recluse Sumedha would one day become a Buddha named Siddhārtha Gautama. Since the *Nidānakathā*, which stipulates the eight prerequisites,[8] does not mention Sumedha's career before the time of Dīpaṅkara, we have no means of knowing if he ever engaged in those activities which were conducive to the attainment of any of those eight conditions, especially that of *liṅga-sampatti.*

The *Nidānakathā* alludes to an *aṭṭhakathā* tradition that Dīpaṅkara was not the first Buddha of this *kalpa* (aeon), but that he was preceded by three other Buddhas, namely, Taṇhaṅkara, Medhaṅkara, and Saraṇaṅkara. It further states that the *Buddhavaṃsa* does not mention their names while discussing the career of Gautama, since he had not received a prophecy (*byākaraṇa*) from them as he did from Dīpaṅkara and subsequent Buddhas.[9] It is likely that the lack of mention of our *bodhisattva* during the period of these three Buddhas might have led to the composition of a new story which would show how our Gautama, when he was still an ordinary layman (*puthujjana*), was able to leave behind forever birth as a female, the major impediment to commencing the *bodhisattva* career. The *Padīpadānajātaka*, No. 35 of the *Paññāsa Jātaka*, seems to be an attempt to explain why the *Buddhavaṃsa* tradition is silent about any activity of the *bodhisattva* during the time of the first three Buddhas of this aeon. A story, which places him in heaven during this period, and also accounts for *liṅga-sampatti*, neatly explains the tradition of the *bodhisattva's* career commencing during the time of Dīpaṅkara.

The story takes us back to the ancient time prior to this *Bhaddakappa* during the *sāsana* of Buddha Porāṇa-Dīpaṅkara. The

Dīpaṅkara of our aeon (called in the story 'Pacchima-Dīpaṅkara') was at that time born as a *brahman* named Rāma who had become a monk under the Buddha Porāṇa-Dīpaṅkara. Because of his great erudition, he was also known as Tipiṭakadharathera and had received the prophecy that he would become the Buddha Dīpaṅkara in the future.

During this time our Gautama, "due to some unwholesome acts," was born as a woman (*itthi jāto*) in a royal family, the daughter of the Buddha Porāṇa-Dīpaṅkara's mother's younger sister. One day the Tipiṭakadharathera came to her door to collect alms. She had a golden vessel filled with sesame (*siddhattha*) oil and offered it to him, and making a firm resolve in her heart to become a Buddha in future, begged the following: "Venerable sir, please worship the Buddha on my behalf by burning a lamp with this oil, and then convey to him that his cousin-sister ardently desires to become a Buddha in the future as a result of this gift of lamps."

The thera did as he was asked but was told by the Buddha that his cousin, being a woman, had not yet fulfilled the eight conditions required for obtaining a prophecy regarding her attaining the Buddhahood. He then enumerated the eight conditions in a verse—identical with the *Buddhavaṃsa*, i, 207—and pointed out that the princess had not yet fulfilled the conditions of *liṅga-sampatti* and *pabbajjā*. However, the Buddha added that the princess would indeed receive such a prophecy in the distant future, during the time when the Elder Tipiṭakadhara would have become the Buddha Pacchima-Dīpaṅkara, from the Buddha himself. In the meantime, Porāṇa-Dīpaṅkara predicted that the princess, the donor of the oil, as a result of lighting a lamp to worship the Buddha, would be reborn as a male god in the *Tusita* heaven.

Establishing a causal connection between *padīpa-dāna* and the elimination of female existence, a hindrance to the attainment of the status of a *bodhisattva*, would appear to be the main aim of this 'extra-canonical' *jātaka*. There is nothing in this story which may be considered being at variance with the traditional Theravāda doctrine. The birth of the princess in the *Tusita* heaven in the past aeon and the subsequent rebirth as the hermit Sumedha during the time of the Pacchima-Dīpaṅkara is also most convenient to explain the conspicuous absence of Gautama's name even as an ordinary layman (or laywoman) during the time of the first three Buddhas of the present *kalpa* mentioned above. One would indeed expect the narrator of the *Nidānakathā* to provide some such version of an *atidūre-nidāna*, a task so eminently accomplished by the author of the *Padīpadānajātaka*. Are we to assume that the Buddhists of Southeast Asia invented such a story entirely on their own? Or, is it likely that they had before them a scriptural source, which they skillfully employed in composing this *jātaka?*

To the best of our knowledge, there is no Pali text which talks of our Gautama prior to the time of his incarnation as the *tāpasa* Sumedha. But a story, linking him with a Buddha of the previous *kalpa*, is to be found in the Chinese translation of the Sanskrit *Aṅguttarāgama*[10]. In the Chinese version, our Gautama is called Princess Munī, who lived during the time of the Buddha Ratanākara. His attendant was an old monk (name not given) who had received the prophecy that he would become a future Buddha by the name of Dīpaṅkara. This monk used to collect oil and other requisites, employing them in his worship of the Buddha. One day the princess Munī heard of the prediction made about this Elder and went to ask the Buddha himself if she could also become a Buddha in the future. Buddha Ratanākara replied that a woman cannot become a Cakravartin, Indra, Brahmā, Māra, or a Tathāgata. However, he said that in the future there would be a Buddha by the name of Dīpaṅkara, who would be her *kalyāṇamitra*, who would then make a prophecy of her becoming a Buddha.

The similarities between the two versions are rather striking. The princess Munī of the Chinese version and the anonymous princess of the Pali version are both recipients of a promise that the Buddha Dīpaṅkara would make a *vyākarana* about them as soon as they permanently cease to be born as females. The old monk of the Chinese story is identical to the Elder Tipiṭakadhara of the Pali version. As to the name of the Buddha, the two traditions differ. Buddha Ratanākara is found in the Mahāyāna tradition[11] but is unknown to the Theravādins. Porāṇa-Dīpaṅkara is a device employed by the author of Pali version, which saves his inventing a new name for a Buddha outside of the tradition. These similarities encourage one to think that the author of the Pali version had some access to the Sanskrit *Aṅguttarāgama*, the original source of the Chinese version. Since two stories from the *Paññāsa Jātaka* collection, namely the stories of Sudhanu and

Surūpa have been traced to the *Divyāvadāna*[12] and *Avadānaśataka*[13], respectively, there is a good possibility that a similar textual tradition was available to the author of the *Padīpadānajātaka.*

Below are extracts from the Pali original which illustrate the story and make it available for further research in this field. The text reproduced is considerably abridged and all variant readings have been omitted.

Extracts from the *Padīpadānajātaka*

"iminā padīpadānenāti"...idaṃ Satthā Jetavane viharanto padīpadānaṃ ārabbha kathesi.

...atīte bhikhave ito bhaddakappato kappasatasahassādhikānaṃ vīsati-asaṃkheyyānaṃ matthake Porāṇa-Dīpaṅkaro nāma sammāsambuddho imasmiṃ loke udapādi. tasmiṃ pana kāle jāto Pacchima-Dīpaṅkaro nāma sammāsambuddho bodhisattabhūto Amaravatī nāma nagare brāhmaṇa-mahāsālakule nibbatto Rāmabrāhmaṇo māma ahosi. tadā so Rāma-brāhmaṇo ...Porāṇa-Dīpaṅkarabuddhasāsane pabbajitvā...Tipiṭaka-dharathero ti nāmena pākaṭo ahosi... ath' ekadivasaṃ hi so thero...telapiṇḍāya caritvā... telaṃ ānetvā anekehi padīpehi ca Porāṇa-Dīpaṅkarasammāsambuddhassa... padīpaujjalanaṃ katvā ..paṇidhānam karonto paṭhamaṃ gāthaṃ āha:

1. *iminā padīpadānena sacitte vippasanno sadā/*
   sabbalokahitatthāya 'haṃ Buddho hessāmi 'nāgate ti//

evañ ca padīpadānena buddhapaṇidhānaṃ karonto so thero Porāṇa-Dīpaṅkarabuddhassa santike nisinno sirasi añjaliṃ paggaṇhanto dutiyaṃ gāthādvayam āha:

2. *yath' eva tvaṃ mahāvīra nāyako sammāsambuddho/*
   aggo jeṭṭho anuttaro lokanātho 'si adhunā//

3. *tath' evāhaṃ loke buddho anuttaro lokanātho/*
   sattaloke maggaphalaṃ bodhayissāmi 'nāgate ti//

taṃ sutvā Porāṇa-Dīpaṅkaro bhagavā pi anāgataṃ saññāṇaṃ pesetvā tass' eva therassa buddhabhāvapatthanāya samiddhabhāvaṃ disvā taṃ eva theraṃ byākaronto bhikkhūnaṃ majjhe āvikaronto imā...gāthāyo āha:

4. *passatha bhikkhave tumhe imaṃ bhikkhuṃ pūjākataṃ/*
   idha mayhaṃ padīpena ujjalitena adhunā//

5. *imass' eva buddhapatthanāya samijjhissati anāgate/*
ito soḷasa-asaṅkheyyakappasatasahassādhike//
6. *tadā jāto eso bhikkhu lokanātho mahāyaso/*
Dīpaṅkaro ti nāmena buddho loke bhavisatī ti//

...evañ ca pana imaṃ atītavatthuṃ pakāsetvā amhākaṃ satthā idāni tesaṃ bhikkhūnaṃ attano atītatavatthuṃ pakāsento atītaṃ āhari:

atīte bhikkhave tasmiṃ Porāṇa-Dīpaṅkarabuddhakāle jāto ahaṃ puthujjanabhāve ṭhito attanā pubbakammena aparāpariyavedaniyanāmena akusala-kammena itthi jāto Porāṇa-Dīpaṅkarabuddhassa mātuyā kaniṭṭhabhaginiyā puttī jāto rājakule viharāmī ti. ath' ekadivasañ hi so Tipiṭakadharathero nagare telatthāya vicaritvā kiñci pi telaṃ aḷabhitvā rājaṅgaṇaṃ pavisitvā tatth' eva rājaṅgaṇe aṭṭhāsi. tasmiṃ khaṇe sā rājadhītā ...attano vātapānena rājaṅgaṇaṃ oloketvā ...tattha gantvā...theraṃ vanditvā... tuṭṭhamānasā hutvā taṃ theraṃ...paññatte āsane nisīdāpetvā sayaṃ eva ekaṃ suvaṇṇasarakaṃ ādāya suvaṇṇavaṇṇena siddhatthatelena suvaṇṇasarakaṃ pūretvā attano ubhohi hatthehi sīsamatthake taṃ sarakaṃ ṭhapetvā attano cittabbhantare yeva buddhapaṇidhānaṃ akāsi: yathā sammāsambuddho mama bhātiko imasmiṃ loke sabbalokahitatthāya buddho hoti, tathā cāhaṃ pana anāgate buddho bhavissāmi, iminā va siddhattha-teladānena mama buddhabhūtakāle Siddhatthanāmena mama nāmaṃ hotū...ti. evañ ca pana sā rājadhītā...buddhapaṇidhānaṃ katvā sakasīsato taṃ sarakaṃ otāretvā therassa patte telaṃ pakkhipitvā añjaliṃ paggaṇhitvā taṃ theraṃ namassamānā evaṃ āha: bhante tvaṃ pana iminā va siddhatthateladānena mama bhātikassa padīpapūjaṃ karohi, katvā ca pana tvaṃ bhante mama bhātikassa buddhassa vadeyyāsi: bhante bhagavā tumhākaṃ kaniṭṭhabhaginī sā rājadhītā mayhaṃ imaṃ siddhatthatelaṃ datvā iminā va siddhatthateladānena anāgate buddhabhāvāya icchati. ekanten' eva bhante tvaṃ mayhaṃ vacanaṃ tuyhaṃ satthuno bhagavato vadeyyāsīti...sāsanavacanaṃ datvā taṃ theraṃ vanditvā uyyojesi.

tadā pana so thero Porāṇa-Dīpaṅkarassa bhagavato santikaṃ āgantvā ten' eva siddhatthatelena tass' eva bhagavato padīpapūjaṃ katvā vanditvā evaṃ āha: bhante...sā rājadhītā... anāgate buddhabhāvāya icchatī ti. taṃ sutvā Porāṇa-Dīpaṅkaro bhagavā taṃ theraṃ evaṃ āha: idāni bhikkhu mayā na sakkā mama kaniṭṭhabhaginibhāvaṃ taṃ rājadhītaṃ byākaritun ti. atha so thero bhagavantaṃ pucchi: kasmā pana bhante tayā na sakkā...byākaritum ti. taṃ sutvā bhagavā taṃ theraṃ āha:...itthibhāve ṭhitattā...aṭṭhadhamma-samodhānena apripuṇṇattā ti...atha... aṭṭhadhamma-samodhāne pakāsento imā gāthāyo āha:

8. *manussattaṃ purisaliṅgattaṃ tihetukaṃ satthāradassanaṃ/*
   pabbajjitañ ca guṇasampattiṃ adhikāro ca chandatā cā ti/
   aṭṭh' ime sammā ekato pi ca dhammasamodhānā ti nāmakā//

...āvuso tassa rājadhītāya santānabbhantare ime aṭṭhadhamma-samodhāne apripuṇṇattā yeva taṃ itthibhāvaṃ mayā na sakkā byākaritun ti.

...taṃ sutvā so thero bhagavantaṃ pucchi: tena hi bhante tumhākaṃ kaniṭṭhabhaginiyā patthitapatthanā kiṃ nu kho samijjhissati no nu kho ti. atha so Porāṇa-Dīpaṅkaro bhagavā atītabhave anukkamena atītaṃ saññāṇaṃ pesetvā tīsu attabhavesu tassa rājadhītāya sakacittabbhantare yeva buddha-paṇidhānaṃ sañjānitvā puna pi anāgatabhave anāgataṃ saññāṇaṃ pesetvā tassā rājadhītāya anāgate yeva buddhakāraṇa-dhammakatasabhāvañ ca sañjānitvā Tipiṭakadharatheraṃ āha: yadā pana tāta Tipiṭakadharabhikkhu tvaṃ anāgate sammā sambuddho bhavissasi tadā esā rājadhītā tuyhaṃ eva...santike sammāsambuddha-byākaraṇaṃ labhissatī ti. evañ ca pana vatvā eso Porāṇa-Dīpaṅkaro bhagavā etaṃ Tipiṭakadharatheraṃ āha: tāta Tipiṭaka-dharabhikkhu esā rājadhītā tena siddhatthateladānānisaṃsaphalena itthibhāvato cavitā Tusitadevaloke dibbapāsāde suvaṇṇavaṇṇo devaputto hutvā nibbattissatī ti.

...evañ ca pana imaṃ atītavatthuṃ āharitvā amhākaṃ satthā Gotamo nāma sammāsambuddho idāni Jetavane sannipatitānaṃ bhikkhūnaṃ pākaṭabhāvatthāya padīpadānānisaṃsaṃ desento imā gāthāyo abhāsi:

29. *tasmā hi paṇḍito naro patthento sukhaggaṃ varaṃ/*
    dadeyya telandānañ ca padīpañ ca tiratane ti//

tadā so Porāṇa-Dīpaṅkaro sammāsambuddho yāvatāyukaṃ ṭhito parinibbāyanto anupādisesāya nibbānadhātuyā parinibbāyi. sā pana rājadhītā siddhattha-teladāyakā yāvatāyukaṃ ṭhitā āyuhapariyosāne tato cutā Tusitapure yeva nibbattatī ti.

satthā pana imaṃ dhammadesanaṃ āharitvā jātakaṃ samodhānento osānagāthaṃ āha:

30. *tadā thero Tipiṭako karonto padīpapūjaṃ/*
Pacchimo-Dīpaṅkaro sambuddho nibbuto tadā//
32. *yā sā rājadhītā tadā siddhatthateladāyakā/*
sambuddho 'haṃ tathāgato lokanātho idāni 'si//

33. *sabbe pi tumhe patthentā tividhaṃ sukhaṃ attano/*
atigāravacittena evaṃ dhāretha jātakan ti.
Padīpadānajātakaṃ niṭṭhitaṃ.

NOTES AND REFERENCES

1. *The Jātaka* (Together with its Commentary), ed. V. Fausboll, 7 volumes, 1877-87. Second edition by the Pali Text Society, London, 1962-64.
2. 'Les Jātakas', *Journal Asiatique*, V, 1875, pp. 417 ff.
3. *Zimme Paṇṇāsa*, edited anonymously, Hanthawaddy Press, Rangoon, 1911.
4. 'Recherches sur la littérature laotienne', *Bulletin de L'Ecole Francaise de L'Extreme Orient* (BEFEO), XVII, 5, 1917, pp. 44-50.
5. G. Terral, 'Samuddaghosajātaka: conte Pali tiré du Paññāsa-jātaka', BEFEO, XLVIII, 1, 1956, pp. 249-351.
6. *Paññāsa-Jātaka or Zimme Paṇṇāsa* (in the Burmese Recension), Vol. I, [*Jātakas* 1-25], ed. P.S. Jaini, Pali Text Society Text Series No. 172, London, 1980.
7. *itthibhāvaṃ na gacchanti, ubhatovyañjanapaṇḍakā,*
na bhavanti pariyāpannā bodhiyā niyatā narā.
Jātaka (Nidānakathā), I, p. 45.
8. *yasmā pana buddhattaṃ patthentassa*
manussattaṃ liṅgasampatti hetu Satthāradassanaṃ,
pabbajjā guṇasampatti adhikaro ca chandatā,
aṭṭhadhammasamodhānā abhinīhāro samijjhati.
Jātaka (Nidānakathā), I, p. 14.
9. *yasmiṃ pana kappe Dīpaṃkaradasabalo udapādi tasmiṃ aññe pi tayo Buddhā ahesuṃ. Tesaṃ santikā Bodhisattassa vyākaraṇam n'atthi tasmā te idha na dassitā, Aṭṭhakathāyaṃ pana tamhā kappā paṭṭhāya sabbe Buddhe dassetuṃ idaṃ vuttaṃ:*
Taṇhaṃkaro ca Medhaṃkaro atho pi Saraṇaṃkaro,
Dīpaṃkaro ca sambuddho Koṇḍañño dipaduttamo.
Jātaka (Nidānakathā), I, p. 43.
10. *Aṅguttarāgama*, chapter 38, *Taisho Tripiṭaka*, Vol. 2, pp. 757b-758c. I am grateful to Professor Y. Kajiyama for drawing my attention to this reference.
11. This name is spelt as Ratnākara in F. Edgerton's *Buddhist Hybrid Sanskrit Dictionary*, p. 452.
12. See P.S. Jaini, "The story of Sudhana and Manoharā: an analysis of the texts and the Borobudur reliefs", *Bulletin of the School of Oriental and African studies*, University of London, XXIX, 3, 1966, pp. 553-558.
13. Compare *Surūparājajātaka* (*Paññāsa Jātaka*, No. 14) with the *Avadānaśataka*, (No. 35), ed. P.L. Vaidya, Darbhanga, 1958, pp. 85-87.

CHAPTER 23

The Apocryphal Jātakas of Southeast Asian Buddhism*

In the first centuries of their history, the Theravāda Buddhists launched a major expansion of their *Tipiṭaka* as they raised to canonical status a number of independent Pali works—notably *Milindapañha, Nettipakaraṇa* and *Paṭisambhidāmagga,* and even the massive *Jātaka* collection—by including them in the large miscellany known as the *Khuddakanikāya.* This practice seems only to have come to an end with the writing down of the ancient Singhalese *Aṭṭhakathās* long before the time of Buddhaghosa (*ca.* 425 A.D.). While all Pali works composed subsequently were not considered to be canonical, their adherence to recognized doctrines and orthodox traditions did lend them a certain authority which made them what might be termed "semicanonical." Works having such status included the commentaries (*aṭṭhakathā*) to the texts of the *Tipiṭaka,* philosophical exegeses like the *Visuddhimagga* of Buddhaghosa, and historical chronicles such as *Mahāvaṃsa* or *Jinakālamālī.* No new *suttas* or *vinaya* rules were allowed to be added to the fixed stock of material; and while later Abhidhamma treatises, as for example, *Abhidhammatthasaṅgaha,* might contain theories (e.g., the theory of the process of perception, or *vīthis*) that were not found in the canon, their claims to legitimacy were nevertheless based on their adherence to canonical precedents. The same rule was applied with great scrupulousness to the vast

*This article was originally published in *The Indian Journal of Buddhist Studies,* Vol. I, pp. 22-39, (ed. A.K. Narain), Bhikkhu Jagdish Kashyap Institute of Buddhist and Asian Studies, Sarnath, Varanasi, 1990. Reprinted with kind permission of A.K. Narain, editor.

amount of later Pali narrative literature, like the *Dhammapadaṭṭhakathā*, and such minor collections as *Sīhaḷavatthu* or the much-later *Dasbodhisattuppattikathā*. While both the narrators of such tales as well as their audiences would have acknowledged that few of the stories included in these literary collections were part of the canon proper, it was generally recognized that most of their source-material was adapted from the inexhaustible storehouse of the *Tripiṭaka*.

Given the penchant of Buddhist storytellers to embellish old canonical tales with new elements drawn from the indigenous cultures of their own native regions, it is no small wonder that the Buddhists of Southeast Asia should have eventually been parties to the growth of a popular kind of narrative literature that developed sometime during the twelfth and thirteenth centuries in the devout circle of Buddhist monks in the area surrounding the present-day city of Chieng-mai in northern Thailand. It is almost one hundred years since a French scholar, L. Feer, first drew attention to a compilation of Pali narrative tales, entitled *Paññāsa Jātaka* (Chieng-mai Fifty; hereafter *PJ*), which he recognized as being a collection of what he termed "extracanonical Jātakas."[2] He reported that there were at least three Pali recensions of these stories, one found in Burma, one in Cambodia and one in Siam/Laos. In 1917, L. Finot (1917: 44-50) prepared a concordance of the titles of the stories included in that collection and discovered that, while each recension claimed only fifty stories each, not all these stories were identical; in fact, there were almost one hundred independent stories that could be considered part of the *PJ* collection. He also determined that in almost all cases where the titles were identical, the stories differed, thus indicating that there were regional variations of what once must have been a core story, which subsequently underwent various accretions or omissions.

That *PJ* was considered extracanonical even by the chronicles of Burma and Siam is evident from the fact that neither the sixteenth-century dynastic chronicle *Jinakālamālī* nor the nineteenth-century ecclesiastical chronicle *Sāsanavaṃsa* referred to this work, even though it is hard to imagine that they would not have been familiar with it. While there is no evidence of any formal proscription of this book, an oral tradition has persisted that King Myndon of Mandalay (r. 1853-1878) disapproved of the work (Jaini 1966: 553-4, n. 10; 1981-3: vol. I. p. V.); such royal displeasure apparently prompted many monasteries to dispose of the book, until there were few manuscripts remaining anywhere in Burma. Apparently, the collection was not in such disfavour in the royal courts of Siam or Cambodia, for a large number of palm-leaf manuscripts of their recensions of *PJ* were still to be found in the Bangkok Museum as well as in the monasteries of Phnom Penh before the Vietnamese war. As a matter of fact, royal patronage of *PJ* is implied by the fact that an abridged Thai translation of the work was made by Prince Damrong (1926). The pre-war Cambodian government also looked favourably on the collection and twenty-five of its fifty stories in the Cambodian recension were published by the Institut Bouddhique beginning in 1953. Only in Burma does the work seem to have all but vanished. Even so, an edition of the Burmese recension was published by the Hanthawaddy Press in 1911, but without any information as to the editor or the source of the manuscript. Unfortunately, a great many of these copies were destroyed during World War II, together with the original manuscript, and the text dropped once more into obscurity. In the meantime, almost all the known Pali works originating in Sri Lanka and Burma had been published under the aegis of the Pali Text Society, London; but since the manuscripts of these extracanonical *Jātakas* were unavailable outside the monastic libraries of Southeast Asia, they remained virtually unknown to Western Pali scholarship. In our days, the credit for bringing them to light again goes to Madame G. Terral, who published in 1956 the Pali text of both the Burmese and Thai recensions of one story from *PJ*, entitled *Samuddaghosa-jātaka*, together with their French translations (1956: 249-351). Her translation and grammatical notes introduced to scholarship a beautiful love story not found in the Theravāda canon or its commentaries. Her work led me to search for manuscripts of *PJ* in Southeast Asia, and in 1961 I was able to obtain photographs of a single manuscript of the Burmese recension of the work that had been found in a monastery in the vicinity of Pagan. A critical analysis of one story in this collection, *Sudhanukumāra-jātaka* (*PJ* no. 11), revealed that this love story concerning the Bodhisatta Sudhanu and his fairy-queen Manoharā was based on such non-Theravāda sources as the *Kinnarī-jātaka* of the *Mahāvastu* and the *Sudhanāvadāna* of *Divyāvadāna*. But this story did not merely copy verbatim from those two sources; in addition, it also included many folk elements drawn from the autochthonous culture of the region, which still survive in the theatrical plays, called Manora, common to Burma and Thailand. This discovery showed the great importance of the full collection for the study of Buddhism in Southeast Asian culture, where the Theravāda religion had interacted with the heterodox traditions of the area. Certain episodes in this Pali story were also helpful in interpreting some of the Borobudur reliefs which depicted scenes from the Mūla-Sarvāstivāda recension of the *Divyāvadāna.*[3] For all intents and purposes, this tale can be called an "apocryphal *Jātaka*", for while its material was not drawn from the Pali *Jātaka* book, *Jātakatthavaṇṇanā* (Fausboll, 1896) itself, its careful adherence to the standard forms employed in that genre of literature justify its inclusion among the *jātaka* literature.

The apocryphal *jātakas* included in *PJ* conform both in form and content to the canonical *jātakas* of the Pali *Tripiṭaka*. A *jātaka,* literally "birth-story," is more than an ordinary folktale with a moral message attached. It is instead the story of Siddhattha Gotama, narrated by himself, pertaining to his manifold past lives— whether as an animal or a human being— when, as a buddha-to-be (*bodhisatta*), he practiced to perfection (*pāramī*) certain virtues, notably charity (*dāna*), forbearance (*khanti*), and wisdom (*paññā*). A certain incident happening in the present provides the Buddha with a context (*nidāna*) for narrating the story as it took place in one of his previous births. This story of the past (*atītavatthu*) is what constitutes the *jātaka* proper. The tale concludes by correlating (*samodhāna*) the main characters of the past with the known persons of the present. The apocryphal *jātakas* adhere closely to these three main stages of the tales, namely *nidāna, atītavatthu,* and *samodhāna.*

The *Jātaka* book in its extant form consists of verses (*gāthās*) as well as prose narrative.[4] According to the Theravāda tradition, the canonical part of the *Jātaka* consists of the verses only; the prose narrative is considered to be a "commentary" (*aṭṭhakathā*) added at some later time.[5] The *nidāna,* or the present context of the story, therefore always begins with a quotation of the first line of the first verse of that particular *jātaka* and then proceeds to ask such questions as where, when, and in what context the Lord uttered that verse. The apocryphal *jātakas* also scrupulously follow this scheme.

Thematically as well, the apocryphal *jātakas* follow canonical models and exemplify one or another of the *pāramitās* cultivated by the Bodhisatta. In this regard, the *Vessantara-jātaka,* (Fausboll, 1896, Vol.6: 479-596) one of the largest and most poignant tales of the *Jātaka* book, seems to have been the prime source of inspiration for a number of *jātakas* in *Paññāsa Jātaka.* The extraordinary perfection in charity attained by Gotama in his incarnation as the Bodhisatta Vessantara exercised a deep and enduring influence upon the Buddhists of the Southeast Asian countries. More than half of the stories found in that collection are variations on its theme of extreme charity. The high points of such stories are the giving away of one's wife and children; the pathos that attends such an event; the appearance of Sakka, the king of the gods, to test the Bodhisatta's resolve; and the subsequent reunion of the royal family. Such stories illustrating the Bodhisatta's chairty abound: our hero is never content with freely giving away either his wealth or his wife (as in *Arindama-jātaka, PJ* no. 4), but must submit to cutting his body to pieces (e.g. *PJ* nos. 17, 18, 29) only to be restored to life by Sakka. With the exception of a couple of stories which introduce a slightly different motif—i.e., saving monks from persecution at the risk of one's life (*PJ* nos. 2, 31)—the *jātakas* of this type have virtually no plot at all other than to praise the offerings of robes (*kaṭhinadāna*) and other requisites (*parikkhāradāna*) to monks (e.g., *PJ* nos. 7, 12, 15, 18).

PJ also includes a great many love stories where the hero and heroine suffered separation on account of such calamities as shipwreck, and are reunited by the goddess Maṇimekhalā, an indigenous Southeast Asian deity. In addition to showing the bravery of the hero-Bodhisatta in the travails he suffers to find his wife, such stories also serve to emphasize the karmic consequences of deeds done previously which brought about this separation. These tales of past deeds cannot be traced to the canonical narratives and contain motifs that are peculiar to Southeast Asian society. In several of the shipwreck stories, we are told that the couple had previously rocked the flimsy boat of a novice (*sāmaṇera*) on his almsround, causing it to capsize; this misdeed caused them to suffer a comparable calamity. Such an island motif would never have been found in the canonical *Jātaka* stories originating on the Indian mainland.

There are also several unusual tales involving animals, which include features unknown to the *Jātaka* book. These are, for example, the stories of the white mouse, called Setamūsika, or the truthful cow, Bahalagāvī. The former tale resembles the canonical *Sasa-jātaka* (*Jātaka* no. 316), and the latter compares well with the *Suvaṇṇamiga-Jātaka* (*Jātaka* no. 359), but both introduce a new element: Sakka, the king of the gods, who advents before them to test their virtue, physically transports them to heaven and later returns them to earth. In the Theravāda *Tripiṭaka,* one comes across such stories as that of the Buddha's nephew, Nanda, whom the Buddha escorted to heaven in order to teach the futility of sensual pleasures. But in the canon, only humans are known to have the capacity to visit the heavens; there are no cases where animals are similarly transported. Our stories, however, seem to indicate a peculiar Southeast Asian belief that animals too have such supernatural abilities.

A similar motif stressing the capacity to rise to heaven in one's own physical body seems to be at work in another story, the *Sirasākumārajātaka* (*PJ* no. 38). This is the extraordinary tale of an infant bodhisatta whose peculiar birth caused both him and his mother to be banished from the kingdom. Without uttering a single word, he causes many miracles to occur before his premature death, when he is physically lifted to heaven by two maidens. A Bodhisatta dying so young is itself a unique event, but his physical ascent to heaven is even more peculiar. This tale probably has its origin in some Southeast Asian folktale concerning a baby who was wrongly punished, and thence became deified as a Bodhisatta. This could be an extension of the stories of men and women turned into spirits, as is well documented for the *nāṭ* legends of Burma. (Shorto, 1963: 572-91; Spiro, 1967: 40-63, 91-142).

There are also a few stories which by their very nature could not have been included among the canonical *jātakas.* These pertain to the making of a Buddha-image and its consecration. The first of these tales is the *Vaṭṭaṅgulirāja-jātaka* (*PJ* no. 37), the story of a Bodhisatta who, having once repaired the broken finger of a Buddha-image, was reborn as a king and was able to subdue a hundred enemy kings by simply bending his finger. This story is of historical importance since it is the only Pali literary source which confirms the reports of the Chinese pilgrims, Fahsien and Hsüan-tsang, that the first image of the Buddha was made during the Lord's own lifetime by King Pasenadi of Kosala, and that this sandalwood image was instructed by the Buddha himself to sustain the dispensation.[6] The recently discovered *Kosalabimbavaṇṇanā* (Gombrich 1978: 281-303) a short Pali text of twenty-six verses, also gives an account of this event. It, however, considerably postdates the *Vaṭṭaṅgulirāja-Jātaka* which is not only much longer (203 verses), but also gives graphic details concerning the consecration of the image that are not found in the Sri Lankan work. According to that *jātaka*, the consecration ceremony is preceded by a scene in which the image comes alive and stands itself up at the approach of Gotama Buddha. That an image of a Buddha can become so animated is itself a novel idea, which in this particular story, is explained as taking place through the majesty of the Buddha himself. However, in another story included in *PJ*, called *Viriyapaṇḍita-jātaka* (*PJ* no. 25), a newly-consecrated Buddha-image is possessed by its guardian-spirit (*buddhabimbārakkhadevatā*), who then speaks to the Bodhisatta through the image. Whereas this belief in a spirit entrusted with the duty of guarding a Buddha-image is all but universal in Buddhist circles, the possession of such an image is most peculiar, and owes its origin to the shamanistic practices which have been assimilated into Southeast Asian Buddhism.

There are also some conspicuous story elements which prove that the *PJ jātakas* are apocryphal, but nevertheless make important contributions to Pali Buddhist literature. This is especially so with a story called *Padīpadāna-jātaka* (*PJ* no. 35), which speaks of a time when Gotama was female and had not yet received the prophecy (*byākaraṇa*) of future Buddhahood from the Buddha Dīpaṅkara. With the solitary exception of the later *Jinakālamālī*, there is no other Pali text which mentions the lives of Gotama prior to his incarnation as the ascetic (*tāpasa*) Sumedha, when he met Dīpaṅkara. Being endowed with male gender (*liṅgasampatti*) is one of the eight prerequisites of the prediction of Buddhahood, (Fausboll, vol. 1:14) but the canonical Pali texts make no mention of Sumedha's previous career during which time he would have developed that requirement. *Nidānakathā*, the Introduction to the *Jātaka* book, alludes to an ancient *aṭṭhakathā* tradition (ibid: 43) that the Buddha Dīpaṅkara was not the first Buddha of our present kalpa, and that he was preceded by three more Buddhas, namely Taṇhaṅkara, Medhaṅkara, and Saraṇaṅkara. It adds further that their names were not mentioned in the *Jātaka's* recital of the career of Gotama because he had not received *byākaraṇa* from them. The *Nidānakathā* begins its account of Gotama with Dīpaṅkara of the present *kalpa*, from whom Gotama finally did receive his prophecy. The *Padīpadāna-jātaka* thus is an attempt to fill this gap in our knowledge of Gotama's previous lives, by showing how the future Buddha, while he was still an ordinary laywoman, was able to free himself forever from female rebirths, the major impediment to commencing the bodhisatta path, by making offerings of lamps (*padīpadāna*). Through this offering, the woman was reborn in Tusita heaven, where the lifespan is immeasurably long, which accounts for Gotama's conspicuous absence during the entire period of the first three Buddhas of this eon. It is very much to the credit of the author of this story that he was thus able to improve on the *Nidānakathā* without in any way violating the spirit of the canonical account. While there are no other Pali texts which mention Gotama prior to his rebirth as Sumedha, we do find a story linking him with a Buddha earlier than Dīpaṅkara in the Chinese translation of the *Ekottarāgama*, thought to be the Mahāsāṃghika recension.[7] There, Gautama was called princess Munī, the Buddha was named Ratnākara, and that Buddha's attendant was an anonymous senior monk who had received the prophecy that he would become the future Buddha Dīpaṅkara. The Buddha tells her that the senior monk would later serve as her *kalyāṇamitra* and give her the prophecy of future Buddhahood. The strong similarities between these two stories seem to indicate that the author of *Padīpadāna-jātaka* drew upon a Sanskrit recension of the *Ekottarāgama* in the composition of his *jātaka*-tale (Jaini, 1989).

So far, only the Burmese recension of *PJ* has been critically edited. Only portions of the Siamese and Cambodian recensions have been published; complete critical editions of those texts will be certain to further our knowledge of the Buddhist traditions of those regions of Southeast Asia. Independent of the stock of stories included in *PJ*, however, there is another major apocryphal narrative work in Pali language also originating from the Chiengmai region, at approximately the same period of time. This work is known by two titles, *Mahāpurisa-jātaka* or the more-common *Lokaneyya-pakaraṇa* (*Treatise for the Guidance of the World*; hereafter *LP*) (Jaini, 1986). As well as being another apocryphal *Jātaka* collection, it also is a treatise (*pakaraṇa*) dealing with worldly wisdom. To the best of our knowledge, there is but a single manuscript of this work in the National Museum, Bangkok. Although fragments of a Thai translation of the text are also to be found in the same museum, the book has remained totally unknown in the Buddhist circles of Sri Lanka and Southeast Asia. Written primarily in prose, *LP* includes 550 verses of which 141 can be identified as *nīti* verses, most of them traceable to Sanskrit correlates. As its alternate titles suggest, *LP* is a *nīti* text in the style of a *Jātaka*, a unique compilation in the history of Pali and Sanskrit Buddhist literature. Whereas the stories in *PJ* are separate and distinct, *LP* instead forged a coherent story-line. This its anonymous author accomplished by combining the substances of two canonical *Jātakas*, *Mahāummagga-Jātaka* (*Jātaka* no. 546) and *Kurudhamma-Jātaka* (*Jātaka* no. 267), with more than 130 *nīti* verses, almost all Pali renderings of original Sanskrit verses. The use of *Mahāummagga-Jātaka* allowed the author of *LP* to establish the superiority of the Bodhisatta Dhanañjaya, the hero of this narrative, in worldly matters, by having the Bodhisatta compete successfully against such eminent rivals as royal chaplains, court pandits, and enemy kings in answering questions on secular matters. This afforded an excellent opportunity to incorporate into his text the available store of floating *nīti* verses, most of which were said to derive from the collection of the sage Cāṇakya, which were considered to be the essence of secular wisdom (Sternbach, 1969). The majority of these verses had been rendered from Sanskrit into Pali long before they were compiled in their extant forms in *Lokanīti*, *Dhammanīti*, *Mahārahanīti* and *Rājanīti* (Bechert and Braun, 1981) and were thus readily available to any Buddhist author. After thus establishing the Bodhisatta's superiority in conventional concerns, the author moved on in the last few chapters to a consideration of Dhanañjaya's ability to legislate on the duties of the king and the members of the royal court. There, the author drew upon the *Kurudhamma-jātaka*, which related the scrupulous practice of the five Buddhist lay precepts (*pañcasīla*) by devout members of the royal court. Instead of resorting to such texts on polity as *Rājanīti* in order to detail the duties of court officials, the author of *LP* drew partly upon his own creative genius and partly upon additional textual sources that are no longer extant. In this wise, *LP* admirably synthesized both of these *Jātakas* with widely-known *nīti* verses, and offered a narrative full of worldly wisdom which would be relevant to both royalty and commoners. The compilation has legitimate claims to the title of *pakaraṇa* (treatise), but can also be accepted as a *Jātaka*, since its stories conformed to the classical *Jātaka* form, as was shown above in the case of *PJ* as well, and demonstrated the Bodhisatta's perfection of wisdom (*paññāpāramī*).

There are several features which distinguish *LP* from a regular *Jātaka* tale or *nīti* text. Of course, the canonical *Jātaka* book abounds in verses which are quite similar to *nīti* verses in that they discuss about worldly ways of wisdom. But in the context of *LP*, the word *nīti* has a specific meaning, for it applies only to those verses which are Pali renderings of Sanskrit aphoristic verses originating from generally non-Buddhist sources. In this respect, *LP* can be compared to *Pañcatantra* or *Hitopadeśa*, where *nīti* verses and the prose narrative mutually support one another, however tenuously. Of the more than 130 *nīti* verses found in *LP*, only some fifty are the author's own renderings, the remainder traceable to the Pati *nīti* collections mentioned above. Our author's Pali renderings of those verses show his skill in versification, for some twenty-five include a number of complex Sanskrit meters that are not normally used in Pali poetry, such as *śārdulavikrīḍita, pṛthvī,* and *vasantatilakā.* What is of some interest is that one of these verses in *vasantatilakā* (*LP*, no. 326), which is attributed to a Buddhist named Bhadantaśūra (identical with Āryaśūra, the author of *Jātakamālā?*), appears in the fourteenth-century Sanskrit collection entitled *Subhāṣitāvalī* (Petetson: 43). *LP* is apparently the only Pali work which had access to Vallabhadeva's verse-anthology.

Other than the two core *Jātakas* used in *LP* which were mentioned above, this text also borrows some forty verses from fifteen other *Jātakas* in the *Jātaka* book. It also presents virtually the whole story of *Ulūka-Jātaka* (*Jātaka* no. 270) and *Amba-Jātaka* (*Jātaka* no. 474), albeit in greatly modified form. Of course, no acknowledgement is made of the original source of such borrowings, since *LP* purports to give the Buddha's own narration of his story and he certainly would not be expected to cross-reference his own tales. Our author similarly draws upon two stories from the *PJ* collection of apocryphal *Jātakas.* One is its story of Bahalagāvī, which corresponds to the *Bahalaputta-Jātaka* (*PJ* no. 39). In these cases as well, *PJ* is not mentioned by name, though the similarities are so striking that direct borrowing is clearly suggested. These affinities between *LP* and *PJ* would seem to indicate that *LP* was written sometime after the composition of the stories that comprise *PJ*, but before their compilation into the formal *PJ* collection.

While it is rather extraordinary that *LP* does not mention the *Jātaka* book by title it does refer to the title of a minor Pali text, the *Majjhimaṭṭhakathā*. In his narration of the story of Soṇa Hatthipāla, whose life is saved by the recitation of three-refuges litany, the *LP* author remarks that his narration is only an abridged version of the story of Soṇa, the full details of which appear in the *Majjhimaṭṭhakathā*. This is the only Pali text mentioned by name in the entire *LP*. Be that as it may, the story of Soṇa [Hatthipāla] cannot be traced to the extant edition of that text, nor is that layman known elsewhere in Pali literature. Assuming that the author's attribution is not incorrect, a great leap of faith in itself, it could be possible that the author of *LP* had before him a different recension of *Majjhimaṭṭhakathā* that is no longer extant, perhaps even the ancient *Sīhaḷa-aṭṭhakathā* itself, which was otherwise known since the time of Buddhaghosa (Norman: 122).

In this connection, we may also refer briefly to the author's interesting use of the liturgy *iti pi so bhagavā* ("So he is the Lord") which is universally known in Theravāda countries. While presenting this litany during his account of a discourse given by the Bodhisatta to a yakkha, our author composes an acrostic using each syllable of the formula. These seven verses are certainly extraordinary to Pali literature, and show our poet's poetic genius. Given the popularity of this liturgy, one might expect that the Buddhists of South and Southeast Asia would also be familiar with these verses. Surprisingly, however, the acrostic is neither quoted anywhere nor is it known in any Buddhist community in those regions. This again suggests that *LP* had little currency anywhere among the Theravāda centres of learning.

Turning to the story elements themselves, the *Mahāumaggajātaka* provides a framework within which our author builds a tension between a Brahmin court-chaplain (*purohita*) who is identified as an adherent of the Śiva-sāsana (Śaivism) and the Bodhisatta Dhanañjaya, the son of a merchant, who although very young, stands up for the Buddha-sāsana. One major purpose of *LP* would thus appear to be to show the conflict between the eventual triumph of Buddhism over the Śaivism of the Śaivite court brahmans of Siam and Burma that took place during the fourteenth century.[9] In our story, the vanquished court-chaplain finally forsakes the Śiva-sāsana and declares his allegience to the Buddha-sāsana instead, begging the Bodhisatta to teach him his duties as a *purohita* according to the Buddhist teachings. Since these duties are of a worldly nature, but need to be performed in a Buddhist spirit of keeping the precepts, the Bodhisatta is able to edify him through the recitation of appropriate *nīti* verses, as supplemented by the message of the *Kurudhamma-jātaka.*

In domonstrating the superior wisdom of the Bodhisattva, our author has spared no one, not even the venerated community of monks. In the second section of *LP*, called *Malatarapañha* ("On unwholesome acts"), there is related a confrontation that took place between the king and the Saṅgha. While on a hunting expedition in the forest, the king arrived at the grove of a yakkha named Nandi who threatens to kill him unless he could successfully answer his questions regarding the most unwholesome acts within a period of seven days. Upon his return to the capital, the king first asked his ministers for the answer. When they failed, the king approached the Bhikkhusaṅgha, headed by the "King of the Saṅgha" (Saṅgharāja). When they too were unable to respond, he chided them: "Oh venerable ones! Surely mendicants like you who are *ganthadhura,* experts in the scriptures, should be able to understand this! Why don't you ?'' He then departed, swearing to return to them seven days later for the answer. On that night, the king pompously approached the Saṅgha once again, and rebuked them, "Oh sirs! What good to me are dull-witted people like you, if you are unable to answer these questions?" Petrified, the whole Saṅgha sat in silence until the king finally departed in disgust. This confrontation is of course introduced to show the difficulty of the questions asked, thus to enhance the prestige of the young Bodhisatta who would eventually supply the answers. Even so one rarely meets in Pali texts such an explicit denunciation of the Saṅgha, and especially of the Saṅgharāja, regardless of literary or narrative concerns served thereby.

As in the above example, our author often shows considerable audacity in his choice of scenes by which to display his creativity. This is particularly noticeable in his startling defense of the superiority of monogamy over polygamy. *LP* is the only place in Pali literature where a Bodhisatta refuses to accept the king's offer of a royal princess for a second wife, the Bodhisatta declining because he is already happily wedded to his first bride, Kalyāṇī. Kalyāṇī then narrates a story of her own past life when she was also married to the Bodhisatta. During that life, she had suffered greatly at the hands of her co-wives, and the Bodhisatta is said to have vowed then never again to take a second wife. Of course, this attitude collided with the practice of polygamy that was so common in all the Buddhist countries of Southeast Asia, and particularly in Siam and Burma. In such an environment, it was certainly a unique innovation that a Buddhist storyteller would have upheld monogamy as a virtue befitting a great Bodhisattva. This innovation would seem to have been suggested by Gotama's own example of keeping only a single wife, Yasodharā, during his final lifetime.

Perhaps the most important contribution of *LP*, however, is its long discourse on the duties of the royal court, in the section entitled "Kurudhammapañha." As was noted earlier, the short *Kurudhamma-jātaka* of the canonical *jātaka* book provided the framework for this section. In that *jātaka*, the word "Kurudhamma" was applied to the keeping of the five precepts by laymen, and it relates how the eleven members of the royal court—king, queen-mother, queen, crown-prince (*uparāja*), chaplain (*purohita*), land-surveyor (*rajjuka*), charioteer (*sārathi*), treasurer (*seṭṭhi*), revenue-collector (*doṇa*), gatekeeper (*dovārika*), and courtesan (*gaṇikā*)—diligently kept their precepts, but still thought they were not scrupulous enough in observing them. The duties of these court members is developed at great length by the author, and his information is unattested elsewhere in Pali literature. Especially noteworthy are the sections on the treasurer, which include a long exegesis on the coinage (*kahāpaṇa*). Of equal importance is the treatment of the duties of the land-surveyor and revenue-collector, both of whom were cautioned to exercise great caution in applying the tax laws equitably, without infringing on the rights of the populace, on the one hand, or the needs of the royal court, on the other. Finally, mention must also be made of the duties of the courtesan. According to *Kurudhamma-jātaka*, she was able to keep the five precepts while engaging in her sordid occupation only by maintaining absolute equanimity toward all her clients. But no other Pali text attempts to defend her capacity to refrain from immoral sexual conduct (*kāmesu micchācāra*), the fourth precept. The author of *LP* boldly raises this question, and notes that wives of the men who frequent her often denounce the courtesan for laxity in proper sexual conduct. Our author replies that she cannot be faulted on this account. Her role is compared to that of a ferryman who owns the ferry and pilots it quietly, but is not thereby responsible for any fighting that might take place between the passengers. Similarly, regardless of whatever infighting might take place between spouses because of her, she is not to be held censurable on that account. Hence, she is capable of maintaining her precepts as well as any other layperson.

Both *PJ* and *LP* are by anonymous authors, which is to be expected since anyone purporting to write a new *jātaka* would have had to cover all traces of authorship and provenance that might betray the apocryphal nature of such a story. Indeed, the names of such major cities of that region as Pagan, Thaton, Haripuñjaya, and Sukhothai are conspicuously absent, and even smaller towns appearing in the Pali chronicles of Burma and Siam are missing. Neither do the stories mention the names of any kings of Burma or Thailand nor allude to events of any historical importance, such as the wars which continuously racked the region or the arrival of eminent monks from Lanka (as was reported in such chronicles as *Jinakālamālī* and *Sāsanavaṃsa.*) A stray reference to Sīhaḷadīpa, the Island now known as Sri Lanka, in the *Suvaṇṇakumāra-jātaka* (*PJ* no. 40), harkens back to a time when that island was ruled by the non-Buddhist king, Bhaṭosura, and probably recalls the legendary connections of Lanka with the demon-king, Rāvaṇa. This reference seems to be of no historical value, however. There may be a possibility that the island was mentioned because of a major event—perhaps the establishment of the Sīhaḷa sect called the Lankāvaṃsa—which took place in Chieng-mai around 1430 (Le May, 1954: 187). Even so, there is no mention in either *PJ* or *LP* of the Sīhaḷa Saṅgha or the famous Sīhaḷa Buddha-image. Both texts do refer to Suvaṇṇabhūmi, the legendary name of Burma, and *LP* refers specifically to a kingdom called Bhaṅgaraṭṭha,(alt. Ābhaṅgaraṭṭha) which is probably identical with Biṅgaraṭṭha, another name for Chieng-mai. *LP* refers (implausibly, of course) to the king of that country, Ābhaṅgirājā, as being the founder of the ancient cities of Haṃsavatī and Dvāravati. While this is of course impossible, it does show that the memory of the founding of these two ancient cities was still fresh in the mind of the author of our work.

Conclusion

Since the publication of the Siamese Pali chronicle, *Jinakālamālī* (Buddhadatta: 1962) we have learned a great deal about the intercourse between the ecclesiastical orders of Sri Lanka and the countries of Southeast Asia that took place in the thirteenth and fourteenth centuries. That text provided valuable information about both the miraculous Buddha-image, called the Sīhaḷabimba, which was brought from Ceylon, and the revival of the cult worship centered on such images which supported the legitimacy of royal authority. Thus, considerable new information was gleaned about the religious and political exegencies of the various Buddhist dynasties that flourished both in Burma and in the kingdoms of Laos, Cambodia, and Siam. These contacts brought about a great resurgence in literary activities, both in the courts as well as in the rejuvenated monastic establishments, as is evidenced by Bechert and Braun's *Pāli Nīti Texts of Burma.* That collection shows that the monks of those countries not only studied avidly the Sanskrit aphoristic literature deriving from India, but even rendered them into Pali and assimilated their own writings.

The discovery of *PJ* and *LP*, the two major apocryphal narratives of the Southeast Asian Buddhism, take us even beyond the erudite court and monastic circles. In those texts we find stories, both secular and religious in nature, which are of value not only to students of Buddhism, but also to scholars of Southeast Asian culture in general. Indeed, one may venture to suggest that they are the only extant sources of authentic information for understanding a variety of unique aspects of the indigenous culture: their native legends and mythical beings, their passionate love stories arising out of the tensions produced by a heavily monogamous society, their fratricidal wars and dangerous seafaring adventures, their court hierarchies and the spiritual aspirations that prompted royalty to cultivate the Buddhist virtues of charity and truthfulness, and their unshakable faith in the Three Jewels (*tiratana*). The revived missionary zeal of the Buddhists demanded that a great deal of individual leeway be allowed for monks who were engaged in proselytizing activities among the laity. For this purpose, monks were given the freedom to exploit fully in their popular sermons the enormous quantities of narrative material found in the *Jātaka* book, and in particular the *Vessantara-jātaka.* The Buddhist monks took such canonical *jātakas* as models for their repetitive literary endeavours, much in the same way that they reduplicated Buddha-images or *stūpas ad infinitum* as an expression of their deep faith. The Buddhist belief in the power of actions repeated with ardour and vigour (*saṃskāra*) goes beyond the purely verbal action of repeating the Three Refuges (*tisaraṇa*) litany or *pañcasīla* formula, which were administered daily to the laypeople by the monks; it also accounts for the credence given by Buddhist laypeople of all periods that erecting a new Buddha-image or building a new *stūpa* was an act that accumulated new merit. It is this same idea that appears to be at work in the composition of these new *jātaka* tales, and especially those which were modelled directly on the *Vessantara-jātaka*. That canonical tale seems to have constituted the nucleus for the formation of the apocryphal *jātaka* collections. But for those monks who wrote such *jātakas*—for it would be extraordinary indeed if it were laypeople who were their composers—and those laypeople who heard and even enacted them, those stories were no more spurious than newly-constructed Buddha-images or *stūpas*. Once that nucleus had been fixed, other tales that the Buddhists found circulating in their native areas would gradually have been assimilated into the growing collections. These external sources could be Brahmanical fables, such as taken from *Pañcatantra* and *Hitopadeśa*, or Buddhist stories originating from Theravāda schools. One might even find material drawn from the folklore of the indigenous regions of Southeast Asia, such as might be associated with a certain locale, period, or personage. These new elements would gradually have enriched those collections and increased the floating mass of popular *Jātakas*.

Despite being clearly outside the orthodox canonical collection, the respectability of these apocryphal *jātaka* collections was not demeaned in the eyes of the laypeople. We might therefore ask how it was that Buddhist traditions as concerned with maintaining the traditional orthodoxy as were those of Southeast Asia would have allowed such obviously spurious works to circulate. The structural and thematic similarities with the canonical *jātakas* of the stories included therein would not *per se* have been a sufficient reason for them to enjoy such a prerogative. To my mind, these tales were made an exception primarily because they did not violate the spirit of the Buddhist teachings (*satthusāsana*), the ultimate standard set by the Buddhists themselves to judge the authenticity of a text. It is true that these tales could not be traced to the canonical *Jātaka* book itself. They also were not found in the *Sutta* or *Vinaya piṭakas*, the primary condition that must be satisfied in order for a suspect text to be accepted as canonical, a standard laid down by the Buddha himself in his discussion on the four standards of authenticity (*mahāpadesa*) in the *Mahāparinibbā-nasuttanta* of the *Dīghanikāya* (Rhys Davids and Carpenter, 1975: 123-4). Notwithstanding the diverse sources from which these tales drew, because the spirit of their teachings remained distinctly Buddhist, they were acceptable as complements to the canonical *Jātakas*. In this wise, these apocryphal *Jātakas* came to be venerated by the laity, if not the ordained Saṅgha proper. Indeed, the monks were undoubtedly aware of their spurious nature, and seem never to have made any attempt to integrate them into the canonical *Jātaka* book. Even so, as long as the hero of these tales remained the Bodhisatta, and as long as nothing blatantly contrary to the Buddha's teachings was allowed to corrupt their message, their value in the edification of devout laypeople remained unchallenged.

NOTES

1. This paper was presented at the VIth World Sanskrit Conference, Section 17: Buddhist and Jaina Studies, Philadelphia, Pennsylvania, USA, October 16, 1984.
2. L. Ferr, (1875: 417). The Burmese recension of the text has been edited by the author (Jaini: 1981-83). An English translation was begun by I.B. Horner, which was completed by the present author (Jaini and Horner: 1985-86).
3. For further information, see Jaini (1966: 553-8).
4. Generally speaking, the number of *gāthās* appearing in a *Jātaka* tale is indicative of its length. The canonical *Jātaka* is classified into twenty-three books (*nipāta*) on the principle of the ascending order of the *gāthās* found in a given tale e.g., five *gāthās* constituting the Fifth Book, stories of 20 verses making up the Twentieth Book, and so on. The compilers of *PJ* do not seem to have followed any such order in arranging the sequence of their stories.
5. On the controversy over what exactly constitutes a *Jātaka* and whether the commentary should be accepted as authentic, see L. Feer (1875); M. Winternitz (1933 Vol. 2: 113-25), W.B. Bollee (1970: Introduction).
6. For the accounts of the Chinese pilgrims, see Samuel Beal, xliv, 235-5; also the discussion in Jaini, 1979, 183-188.
7. See *Tseng-i A-han Ching* 38, I: 125.2.757 b-758c.
8. Who these Śaivite Brahmans were remains something of a mystery. A single passage in *LP* (verse no. 70) mentions Damiḷas, an apparent reference to South Indian Dravidians. This would tally well with our knowledge that the

Brahman *purohitas* of the Siamese court used Tamil language in some of their liturgies; see Quaritch Wales (1931: Ch. V).

9. This is the period described in *Jinakālamālī* as taking place after the founding of Chieng-mai (*ca.* 1296) and probably during or soon after the introduction of Sīhaḷasaṅgha in that region around the end of the fourteenth century. See Jayawickrame (1969: XXIV).

ABBREVIATIONS

JA	:	*Journal Asiatique, Paris.*
BEFEO	:	*Bulletin de l'Ecole francaise d'extreme orient, Paris.*
BSOAS	:	*Bulletin of the School of Oriental and African Studies, London.*

REFERENCES

Beal, Samuel, 1888. *Buddhist Records of the Western World,* Vol. 1. Reprint ed. New York: Paragon Book Reprint Corp., 1968.

Bechert, Heinz and Braun, Heinz (eds.) 1981. *Pali Nīti Texts of Burma,* London: Pali Text Society.

Bollee, W.B. (ed. and trans). 1970. *Kuṇāla Jātaka,* London: Pali Text Society.

Buddhadatta, A.P. Ven. (ed.). 1962. *Jinakālamālī,* London: Pali Text Society.

Damrong, Prince. 1956. *Pannyāt Chadok,* 2 Vols. Bangkok: National Library.

Fausboll, V. (ed.). 1896. *The Jātaka* (*Together with its commentary*), 6 Vols. London: Pali Text Society.

Feer, L. 1875. "*Les Jātakas*", *JA,* 7e Ser., V: 417 ff.

Finot, L. 1917. "Recherches Sur la littérature laotienne". BEFEO, 17-5: 44-50.

Gombrich, R.F. 1978. "Kosala-Bimba-Vaṇṇanā" in Heinz Bechert (ed.), *Buddhism in Ceylon and Studies on Religious Syncretism in Buddhist countries,* Gottingen.

Institut Bouddhique (ed.) 1953-62. *Paññāsa-Jātaka,* 5 Vols. Phnom Penh.

Jaini, P.S. 1966. "The story of Sudhana and Manoharā. An analysis of the texts and the Borobudur reliefs", *BSOAS,* 29:533-58.

Jaini, P.S. 1979. "On the Buddha Image", in A.K. Narain, (ed.), *Studies in Pali and Buddhism,* Delhi; B.R. Publishing Co.

Jaini, P.S. 1981-83. *Paññāsa Jātāka* or *Zimme Paṇṇāsa,* 2 Vols. London: Pali Text Society.

Jaini, P.S. (ed.), 1986. *Lokaneyyappakaraṇaṃ,* London: Pali Text Society.

Jaini, P.S. 1989. "Padipadāna-Jātaka, Gautama's last female incarnation", in N.H. Samtani and H.S. Prasad (eds.), *Amalā Prajñā, Aspects of Buddhist Studies* (P.V. Bapat Felicitation Vol. Delhi: Sri Satguru Publications.

Jaini, P.S. and Horner, I.B. 1985-86. *Apocryphal Birth-Stories,* 2 Vols. London: Pali Text Society.

Jayawickrame, N.A. 1969. *The Epochs of the Conqueror,* London: Pali Text Society.

Le May, Reginald, 1954. *The Culture of South-East Asia,* London: Pali Text Society.

Norman, K.R. 1983. *Pali Literature. A History of Indian Literature,* Vol. 8, Fasc. 2, Wiesbaden.

Peterson, Peter (ed.) 1961. *Subhāṣitāvalī of Vallabhadeva,* Bombay Sanskrit and Prakrit series, No. 32. Poona: Bhandarkar Oriental Research Institute.

Quaritch Wales, H.G. 1931. *Siamese State Ceremonies.*

Rhys Davids T.W. and Carpenter, J.E. (eds.) 1903. Reprint 1975. *Dīgha Nikāya,* Vol. 2. London: Pali Text Society.

Shorto, H.L. 1963. "The 32 myos in the Medieval Mon Kingdom" *BSOAS* 36: 572-91.

Spiro, Melford, E. 1967. *Burmese Supernaturalism,* Englewood Cliffs, New Jersey: Prentice Hall.

Sternbach, Ludwig, 1969. *The Spreading of Cāṇakya's Aphorism over greater India,* Calcutta: Calcutta Oriental Book Agency.

Terral, G. 1956. "Samuddaghosa Jātaka: Conte Pali tire du Paññāsa Jātaka," *BEFEO* 48: 247-51.

Winternitz, M. 1933. *A History of Indian Literature,* Vol. 2, Calcutta: University of Calcutta.

VI

MAHĀYĀNA

CHAPTER 24

The *Ālokā* of Haribhadra and the *Sāratamā* of Ratnākaraśānti: A Comparative Study of the Two Commentaries of the *Aṣṭasāhasrikā**[1]

Of the several commentaries on the *Aṣṭasāhasrikā-prajñā-pāramitā-sūtra*, the *Abhisamayālaṅkāra-ālokā* of Haribhadra (ninth century) and the *Sāratamā* of Ratnākaraśānti (eleventh century) are the only two works that have survived in the original Sanskrit. The *Ālokā* is well known through the editions of Tucci and Wogihara, and critical works in this field by Obermiller and Conze. The Sanskrit text of the *Sāratamā* is now awaiting publication in the Tibetan Sanskrit Works Series, Patna. It is based on two incomplete MSS photographed by the late Rāhula Sāṃkṛtyāyana in the year 1937 and preserved in the library of the Bihar Research Society, Patna.

A brief description of these MSS appears in Rāhula's article 'Second search of Sanskrit palm-leaf MSS in Tibet', *JBORS*, XXIII, 1, 1937, 24-5. We may note here a few interesting details. MS No. 201 is in Kuṭilā script. It bears no date but appears likely to have been written towards the end of the thirteenth century. The total number of leaves found by Rāhula is 103. The last folio is, how-

*This article was originally published in *BSOAS*, Vol. XXXV, part 2, pp. 271-284, University of London, 1972. Reprinted with kind permission of Oxford University Press.

ever, numbered 85. This is because the numbering is not continuous. There are signs of fresh numberings at three places at least. From the uniform writing of all three sections it appears that they originate from the same scribe. The other MS (No. 200 of Rāhula's list) is also in Kuṭilā script (of an earlier variety) and is incomplete. The first leaf is missing but the last leaf is preserved and bears the date of the MS. The colophon states that the MS belongs to one Paṇḍita Jīvandhara Siṃha of the Kāyastha family, in the province of Guṇḍigulma, in the reign of Śrī Harṣadevarāja. The date reads *saṃvat ā to 3*, which as noted by Rāhula stands for 213 of the Nepalese era, and corresponds to A.D. 1093. The last leaf is numbered 103. As the numbering is continuous the whole work contained only 103 leaves of which 49 (1-21, 51-55, 57-79) were missing when Rāhula found it in Tibet.

Photographs of both these MSS were made available to me by the Bihar Research Society as early as 1957, and a brief notice of the *Sāratamā* appeared in the annotated bibliography prepared by Dr. Conze in his *The Prajñāpāramitā literature*, 's-Gravenhage, 1960, 56. The illegibility of a great many photographs and the disorderly nature of MS 201 prevented any serious progress in editing this work. Then in 1966 excellent photographs of a 'new' MS of the *Sāratamā* were obtained through the kind courtesy of the Director of the Namgyal Institute of Tibetan Studies, Sikkim. To my great surprise the 'new' MS happened to be identical with our MS No. 200 which Rāhula had photographed in 1937 and which had now reached Sikkim through the refugees who had migrated from Tibet into India. The Sikkim MS had 11 more leaves which were missing in Rāhula's collection. Thus only 38 leaves (1-21, 51-55, 57-58, 63-72) were now missing out of a total of the 103 leaves of MS 200. A few of these missing portions were supplemented from MS 201. As a result, our text lacks only two entire *parivartas* (Nos. 13 and 14) and parts of six *parivartas* (Nos. 1, 8, 9, 10, 11 and 12) out of the 32 *parivartas* of the original text.

The name of the work as given in both MSS, at the end of *parivartas* and in the colophon, is *Sāratamā*. It is called *Sāratarā* once in MS 201—at the end of *parivarta* 8. This may well have been a scribal error. However, the Tibetan translation of this work ascribed to Subhūtiśānti (*mdo-'grel* x, 1—253a, no. 3803 in Hakuju Ui and others (ed.), A *complete catalogue of the Tibetan Buddhist canons*, Sendai, 1934) calls it *Sārottamā*. Although *Sārottamā* would appear to be a better title we have followed the evidence of our MSS and have accepted *Sāratamā* as the original title of this work. The full title, however, is *Āryāṣṭasāhasrikāyāḥ prajñāpāramitāyāḥ Sāratamā nāma pañjikā.*

The MSS as well as the Tibetan translation and the Tibetan historian Bu-ston[2] (A.D. 1290-1364) ascribe the *Sāratamā* to *Ratnākaraśānti.* We learn from the Tibetan historian Tārānātha[3] that Ratnākaraśānti was a disciple of Nāropā and a contemporary of such famous *ācāryas* as Prajñākaramati and Vāgīśvarakīrti, and presided over the Vikramaśīla monastery. He was succeeded there by (his disciple?) the celebrated Atīśa, better known as Dīpaṅkara Śrījñāna. The date of the latter is A.D. 982-1054. Ratnākaraśānti thus lived in the first half of the eleventh century A.D. Besides the *Sāratamā* he is also the author of a commentary on the *Abhisamayālaṅkāra* called the *Śuddhamatī* (var. lect. *Śuddhimatī*), and possibly also of the *Prajñāpāramitā-piṇḍārtha-pradīpa*[4], now available only in their Tibetan translations.[5]

Because of the loss of a large number of commentaries, notably the *Tattvaviniścaya* of Asaṅga, the *Paddhati* of Vasubandhu, and the *Vārttika* of Bhadanta Vimuktisena (not to speak of the ancient *Prajñāpāramitā-upadeśa-śāstra* ascribed to Nāgārjuna) in their original Sanskrit, the *Ālokā* of Haribhadra was hitherto our only major source for the study of the co-ordinated texts of the *Prajñāpāramitā-sūtras* and the *Abhisamayālaṅkāra-śāstra.*[6] The handy edition by Dutt of the first *parivarta* of the *Pañcaviṃśati-sāhasrikā* (*Abhisamayālaṅkārānusāreṇa saṃśodhitā*—rearranged to conform to the scheme of the *Aa.*), and the recent edition by Pensa of the first *abhisamaya* of Ārya-Vimuktisena's *Aa.-vṛitti* have greatly advanced our knowledge in this field. The discovery of the *Sāratamā* takes us one step further as it is probably the only (and the last) commentary of both the *Sūtra* and the *Śāstra* written on the model supplied by Haribhadra in his *Ālokā.*

As indicated above, the *Sāratamā* is a *pañjikā* which analyses and explains difficult words of the *Aṣṭasāhasrikā.*[7] Haribhadra too calls his *Ālokā* a *pañjikā,*[8] but as a matter of fact it is a great deal more than a mere 'perpetual commentary'. His introductory verses take due notice of the works of the great masters like Asaṅga, Vasubandhu, Ārya Vimuktisena, and Bhadanta Vimuktisena, while the text is replete with copious quotations from these as well as from the works of Nāgārjuna, Āryadeva, Diṅnāga, and scores of other *sūtras* and *śāstras* including the *Pañcaviṃśatisāhasrikā* and the *Aa.* He gives a brilliant summary of the entire *Aa.* in the first *adhikāra* (W, 1—21) and treats at length a large number of controversial problems, e.g.

(1) The rebirth of the *śrāvaka* and the *pratyeka-buddha* =*triyāna—ekayāna* (W, 133-4).

(2) The Buddha's *parinirvāṇa*= death of the *nirmāṇa-kāya* only (W, 145-50).

(3) Whether the *darśana-mārga* consists of 15 or 16 moments (W, 170-1).

(4) The nature of the *māyopama-advaya-jñāna* of the Buddha (W, 268-70).

(5) Omniscience and the limits of the *jñeya* (W, 531-6).

(6) The *sarva-dharma-abhinna-svabhāvatva* of *Tathatā* examined in view of the distinction between a *bodhisattva* and a *Tathāgata* (W, 624-42).

(7) The true nature of *saṃvara* and *asaṃvara* (W, 730—1).

(8) The nature of *kṣaya-jñāna* and the *anutpāda-jñāna* (W, 883—5).

(9) The simultaneous appearance of two *Tathāgatas* in one *loka-dhātu* (W, 960-61).

(10) Examination of the theory that totality of causes (*sāmagrī*) produces effect (W, 969-76).

Compared with this masterly work, the *Sāratamā* leaves much to be desired both in its contents and in its scope. The introductory verses speak only of Maitreya. Names like Asaṅga, Vasubandhu, Vimuktisena,[9] and even Haribhadra, and indeed of any other *ācārya*, are conspicuous by their absence from the text. The work abounds in quotations from the two larger *Prajñāpāramitā-sūtras*, almost invariably referred to as '*Mahatyor bhagavatyoḥ*', as if the two were identical in their readings! The only other quotations are one each from the following texts (mentioned by their names): (1) *Daśabhūmikasūtra*, (2) *Sūtrālaṅkāra*, (3) *Ārya-Vimalakīrtinirdeśa*, (4) *Buddhabhūmi-sūtra*, (5) *Dharmadāna-sūtra*. As regards the 10 major controversies listed above where Haribhadra leads a vigorous attack on his opponents, Ratnākaraśānti chooses to make a few casual comments on only two of them: the 'eventual' attainment of Buddhahood by an *arhat* (No. 1); and the simultaneous appearance of two Buddhas in one *loka-dhātu* (No. 9). Nor does he appear anxious to give any information on his date and place;

in this respect, as in others, one cannot but admire Haribhadra for giving (in the concluding verses) elaborate descriptions not only of his guru and the king, but also of the *vihāra* where the *Ālokā* was composed.

This does not, however, detract from the value of the *Sāratamā* as a *pañjikā* of the combined texts of the *Aṣṭasāhasrikā-sūtra* and the *Aa.-śāstra.* In this respect, the *Sāratamā* can certainly be considered an improvement upon the *Ālokā.* The latter is content to place the *kārikās* of the *Aa.* at the end of the *parivartas* as a mere quotation (*tathā coktam*) to serve as a conclusion to the chapter. The *Sāratamā* opens its *parivartas* with the *Aa.* text, weaves in with it the relevant portions of the *Aṣṭasāhasrikā-sūtra,* and gives a word for word explanation not only of the *sūtra,* but (unlike the *Ālokā*) also of the *Aa.* text. It also abounds in etymological and grammatical analyses of unusual words and forms, understandably omitted by the Tibetan translator.

Since the *Aa.* was primarily composed with specific reference to the *Pañcaviṃśati-sāhasrikā,* it is evident that modifications to the former would be necessary in applying it to a shorter text of the *Aṣṭasāhasrikā.* Haribhadra, whether he was responsible for adapting the *Aa.* to the *Aṣṭasāhasrikā* or not, does not show any awareness of this need for modification. On the contrary, he appears to be indignant at any attempt to tamper with the *Aa.* text as can be seen from his concluding remarks towards the end of the 29th *parivarta*— the *Anugama*[10]:

> 'The meaning of the *grantha* (i.e. the *sūtra* text) should be explained in a manner that corresponds to the order of the *abhisamayas* on the authority of the *Kārikā-śāstra* (and the spirit of the text). A certain commentator, having made numerous changes in the readings of the *kārikās* of the *Aa.*, has given irrelevant explanations of this Mother (=the *Aṣṭasāhasrikā*)... because of an improper understanding of the purport of the partial and the whole text. We have not undertaken a refutation of this exposition (*vyākhyāna*) as we leave the judgement in this matter to the wise'.[11]

We will probably never know the name of the commentator who is rebuked by Haribhadra, nor if Ratnākaraśanti had access to the *Ālokā.* If he did, as seems likely, he certainly chose not to heed

Haribhadra's admonition against changing the *kārikā* text. The extant *Sāratamā* preserves not less than eight such instances of deliberate modifications of the *Aa.* to suit the text of the *Aṣṭasāhasrikā*. We may note some of these.

The first instance occurs in the second *parivarta* and relates to *kārikās* 3-5 of the *Mārgajñatā-adhikāra* dealing with 'the aids of penetration' (*nirodhabhāgīyas*) of a *śrāvaka*:

rūpādi-skandha-śūnyatvāc chūnyatānām abhedataḥ/
ūṣmaṇo 'nupalambhena teṣāṃ mūrdhagataṃ mataṃ// II, 3
kṣāntayas teṣu nityādiyogasthānaniṣedhataḥ/
daśabhūmīḥ samārabhya vistarāsthānadeśanāt// II, 4
agradharmagataṃ proktam āryaśrāvakavartmani/
tat kasya hetor buddhena buddhvā dharmāsamīkṣaṇāt// II, 5

Haribhadra applies the four terms (*ūṣman, mūrdhan, kṣānti,* and *agradharma*) described in these verses to the relevant passages of the *Aṣṭasāhasrikā*, and quotes these *kārikās* in support (*tathā coktaṃ*) of his explanation. Ratnākaraśānti's endeavour is directed to the derivation not only of the items *ūṣman*, etc., but also of the wordings of the *kārikās* from the text of the *Aṣṭasāhasrikā*. He therefore finds it necessary to change the above *kārikā* text to suit this *sūtra* (*tasmād asyāṃ Bhagavatyām anyathaiva śāstrapāṭha unnetavyaḥ*) as follows:

asthānam ūṣmā rūpādau, mūrdhā tad iti hīti yat/
kṣāntir na nityaṃ nānityaṃ rūpādīty asthitidvaye//
phala[ṃ] puṃsām ihāryāṇāṃ viśeṣeṣv asthitis tu yā/
saivāgradharmo vijñeya āryaśrāvakavartmani//

It will be observed that the modified *kārikā* text directly corresponds to the text of the *Aṣṭasāhasrikā*:

(1) *na rūpe sthātavyaṃ...na buddhatve sthātavyaṃ* (W, 140) (=*asthānam ūṣmā rūpādau*);

(2) *iti hi rūpam iti na sthātavyaṃ...iti hi buddhatvam iti na sthātavyaṃ* (W, 140) (=*mūrdhā tad iti hīti yat*);

(3) *rūpaṃ nityam anityam iti na sthātavyaṃ...vijñānaṃ śūnyam upalabhyate veti na sthātavyaṃ* (W, 141-2) (=*kṣāntir na nityaṃ nānityaṃ rūpādīty asthitidvaye*);

(4) *srotāpattiphalam asaṃskṛtaprabhāvitam iti na sthātavyaṃ...*

pratyekabuddho dakṣiṇīya iti na sthātavyaṃ (W, 142-3) (*=phalaṃ puṃsām ihāryāṇāṃ...).*

We may further note that the first three lines of the modified *kārikā* text have a close resemblance to the first three lines of *Aa* II, 3-4. The real difference is seen only between the last line of the modified text and the last three lines of *Aa.* II, 4-5. Since the context is that of the *mokṣabhāgīyas* of a *śrāvaka* (and not of a *bodhisattva*), Ratnākaraśānti might have judged the last three lines of *Aa.* II, 4-5 irrelevant to the topic and not supported by the text of the *Aṣṭasāhasrikā.* The text of the *Pañcaviṃśati* probably justified the *Aa.* text; we have no means of finding out the precise difference between the readings of these two *sūtras,* as the second book of the *Pañcaviṃśati* has not been published yet.

The second case of modification also occurs in the second *parivarta* (and the second *adhikāra*) in connection with the first seven *kṣaṇas* of the *darśanamārga* of a *bodhisattva.* This is given in *Aa.* II, 12-13:

ādhārādheyatā'bhāvāt tathatābuddhayor mithaḥ/
paryāyeṇānanujñānaṃ, mahattā, sāpramāṇatā// II, 12
parimāṇāntatā'bhāvo, rūpāder avadhāraṇam/
tasyāṃ sthitasya buddhatve, 'nugrahātyāgatādayaḥ// II, 13

In *kārikā* 12 the first *kṣaṇa* is explained as 'no consent (to the separate existence of dharmas), because the foundation (Suchness) and that which is founded on it (the Buddha) are not (ultimately distinct)... and because (the Suchness of the *skandhas*) and the Buddha are in turn identical'.[12] The particular *Aṣṭasāhasrikā* passage to which Haribhadra applies this *kārikā* lacks the words *ādhāra, ādheya, tathatā,* etc. Instead it raises the question: *...prajñāpāramitā ...kuto gaveṣitavyā* and answers:.... *na rūpād gaveṣitavyā, nānyatra rūpād gaveṣitavyā...vijñānād gaveṣitavyā* (W, 173). Ratnākaraśānti quotes *Aa.* II, 12-13, but finds it necessary to modify:

imāṃ tu Bhagavatīm adhikṛtyādyaṃ pādatrayam anyathā kartavyam:
rūpādito dhīr nānanyā na cānyā paramārthataḥ/
tasyāś catuṣṭayaṃ yat tu mahattā sāpramāṇatā//
parimāṇāntatā'bhāvau rūpāder avadhāraṇaṃ/

The change in the third line is a minor one. The dual form

parimāṇāntatā' bhāvau refers to the following readings of the *Aṣṭasāhasrikā*: *aparimāṇapāramiteyam ārya Subhūte...anantapāramiteyam ārya Subhūte yad uta prajñāpāramitā/* (W, 174). The modified version of the *kārikās* truly reflects the readings of the *Aṣṭasāhasrikā*.

The third case of modification relates to *Aa.* III, 10b, which describes the tenth 'endeavour' of a *bodhisattva:*

(*aparapratyayo yaś ca*) *saptadhā khyātivedakaḥ/*[13]

As noted by Haribhadra, the *Pañcaviṃśati* mentions all the seven aspects, but only the last aspect, viz. the *pratiśrutka*, is read in the *Aṣṭasāhasrikā*. Haribhadra is content with the explanation that the latter is a brief text and also that the mention of the middle aspect (No. 4) indicates the inclusion of the remaining aspects as well.[14] Ratnākaraśānti, however, deems it necessary to change the *kārikā* text: *Mahatyor bhagavatyor saptadhā khyātiḥ paṭhyate/ ...sā ekenāpi dṛṣṭāntena śakyā darśayituṃ/ ...tasmād asyāṃ Bhagavatyāṃ pratiśrutkopamataiva paṭhyate/ ata enāṃ prati śāstrapāṭho 'nyathā kartavyaḥ:*

yo 'paro khyātivedakaḥ/ iti/

The fourth change, also a minor one, relates to the sixth of the 16 marks (*lakṣaṇas*) of the cognition of *sarvajñatā*. This mark consists of the cognition of that aspect (*ākāra*) due to which the thoughts of beings are not extinguished, as expressed by the words *akṣayākāratāyāṃ* in *Aa.* IV, 15.[15] The wording of the *Aṣṭasāhasrikā* is *aprameyākṣayāṇi cittāni* (W, 541) and not *akṣayāṇi cittāni*. Ratnākaraśānti has noted this change and states that the *Aa.* reading (*akṣayāṇi*) is correct for the two larger *sūtras*; but with reference to the *Aṣṭasāhasrikā* we should read instead *ameyākṣaratāyāṃ* as our text reads *aprameyākṣayāṇi cittāni.*[16] Haribhadra is aware of the different readings, but does not suggest any amendments to the *Aa.*: *cittasyākṣayākārajñānaṃ vaktum āha: aprameyākṣayāṇi cittānīty ādi.*[17]

The fifth change pertains to the topic of *prayoga-samatā* 'the sameness of endeavours' as given in *Aa.* III, 10cd:

caturdhā 'mananā tasya rūpādau samatā matā/

Ratnākaraśānti explains that the *prayoga-samatā* consists of four kinds of *amananās* 'absence of preconceptions', and quotes the following passage from the 'Larger *sūtras*' (*Mahatyoḥ*): *rūpaṃ na manyate, rūpeṇa na manyate, rūpaṃ mameti na manyate, rūpe 'pi na manyate, evaṃ vedanādiṣv iti.* The corresponding passage of the *Aṣṭasāhasrikā,* however, lists eight kinds of *amananās*: *sa ca tān na manyate na samanupaśyati na jānāti na saṃjānīte te ca dharmā na vidyante na saṃdṛśyante na saṃvidyante nopalabhyante iti viharati* (W, 431). Ratnākaraśānti notices this discrepancy and comments that the *Aṣṭasāhasrikā* text has eight kinds of *amananās,* viz. four pertaining to the *grāhya* and four pertaining to the *grāhaka.* He therefore recommends an amendment to the *Aa.* text: *imāṃ tu Bhagavatīṃ prati śāstrapāṭho 'nyathā kartavyaḥ*—

aṣṭadhā 'mananā tasya rūpādau samatā matā/

It is interesting to note that Haribhadra fails to notice any discrepancy between the two readings. His interpretation[18] of the *Aṣṭasāhasrikā* passage (quoted above) also differs from that of Ratnākaraśānti (who in addition gives a *pañjikā* on all the eight words of that passage). What is far more intriguing is that Ratnākaraśānti's quotation from the '*Mahatyoḥ*' (on which is based his understanding of the 'four' *mananās*) does not agree with the fourfold *mananās* (*padārtha, nimitta, prapañca, adhigama*) as laid out by Haribhadra evidently on the basis of the *Pañcaviṃśatisāhasrikā.*[19]

We may note one more instance of a similar nature where a particular *kārikā* comes to be applied to two different passages of the *Aṣṭasāhasrikā.* This pertains to *Aa.* II, 29:

kleśajñeyatrimārgasya śiṣyakhaḍgajinaurasām/
hānād viśuddhir, ātyantikī tu buddhasya sarvathā//

This *kārikā* describes four forms of 'purity', viz. the purity of the *śrāvakas,* of the *pratyekabuddhas,* of the *bodhisattvas,* and the 'perfect purity' of the Buddha. Haribhadra derives all these four kinds of 'purities' from a single line: *yā rūpaviśuddhiḥ sā sarvajñatāviśuddhiḥ* . . . (W, 408) by interpreting the word *sarvajñatāviśuddhiḥ* as *tri-sarvajñatāviśuddhiḥ.*[20] Ratnākaraśānti does not quote this *kārikā* in the *Sāratamā,* for, as he explains, 'the fourfold "purities" are enumerated in the two larger *sūtras* (*Mahatyoḥ*) as the latter are comprehensive of all three paths; they are not spoken of in the *Aṣṭasāhasrikā* as it is devoted solely (in this context) to the path of the *bodhisattva*. Consequently he understands the word *sarvajñatā* to mean only the *sarvākārajñatā* of the Buddha.[21]

These two different interpretations have a bearing upon the application of the next *kārikā* which describes the nine grades of the *viśuddhi*:

> *mṛdumṛdvādiko mārgaḥ śuddhir navasu bhūmiṣu/*
> *adhimātrādhimātrāder malasya pratipakṣataḥ//* II, 30

The next *sūtra* passage (following the one quoted above with the word *sarvajñatāviśuddhiḥ*) has nine words describing the 'purity' of the *prajñāpāramitā*. Śāriputra says that the *prajñāpāramitā* is *gambhīrā, avabhāsakarī, ālokaḥ, apratisaṃdhiḥ, asaṃkleśaḥ, aprāptiḥ, anabhisamayaḥ, anabhinirvṛttiḥ,* and *atyantānupapattiḥ*. Haribhadra takes these nine terms to be indicative of the nine stages described in *kārikā*, II, 30.[22] In doing this he ignores the fact that the *sūtra* text gives two terms, *aprāpti* and *anabhisamaya,* together in one sentence,[23] and also that the last word, *atyantānupapattiḥ,* is followed by the words *kāmadhātu-rūpadhātv-ārūpyadhātuṣu*. Ratnākaraśānti is aware of both these and hence has a different explanation. He derives the first two[24] of the nine stages from the word *sarvajñatāviśuddhiḥ* appearing in the previous passage. He therefore needs only seven terms to account for the remaining seven stages. These he derives from the next passage by counting the two words (*aprāpti* and *anabhisamaya*) as one in conformity with the *sūtra* text, and by taking the last word (*atyantānupapattiḥ*) not to refer to the ninth stage but to the next *kārikā* which deals with the *tri-dhātu-pratipakṣatva*,[25] and which corresponds to the *sūtra* expression: *atyantānupapattir Bhagavan prajñāpāramitā kāmadhātu-rūpadhātv-ārūpyadhātuṣu.*

It is clear from these examples that Ratnākaraśānti is consistent in his adherence to the text of the *Aṣṭasāhasrikā* in preference to the '*Śāstra*'— a digest of the two larger *sūtras*. It is, of course, understood that there are no doctrinal differences between the three *sūtras*: the larger ones are broader in their scope, whereas the *Aṣṭasāhasrikā* is essentially a brief text (*saṃkṣiptā ceyaṃ*

Bhagavatī). Nonetheless, Ratnākaraśānti has no hesitation in pruning the text of the *Aṣṭasāhasrikā* if he finds it at variance with the larger *sūtras.* Fortunately one such example has survived in our extant text, and is singularly valuable as it also reveals Ratnākaraśānti's predilection for the *tri-svabhāva* theory of the Yogācāra school.

The passage in dispute, which consists of a single word, is found towards the end of the first *parivarta* of the *Aṣṭasāhasrikā.* It corresponds to the text of the *Pañcaviṃśatisāhasrikā* (ed. Nalinaksha Dutt, Calcutta Oriental Series, 28, London, 1934), p. 252, and pertains to the topic of *prāpti-niryāṇa*[26] (sixth of the eight *niryāṇas*) listed in *Aa.* I, 72-3.[27]

According to Haribhadra, the *prāpti-niryāṇa* consists in the rejection of the *prāpya* (i.e. the own nature—*svabhāva*—to be attained), the *prāpaka* (the person—*a bodhisattva*—who attains it), and the relationship between the two in conformity with the law that no *dharma* exists apart from the *Dharmadhātu.*[28] This definition corresponds to the scheme adopted in the *Pañcaviṃśati-sāhasrikā,* where the section on the *prāpti-niryāṇa* (p. 244) is followed by three more sections: *iti prāpti-niryāṇe prāpyapratiṣedhaḥ* (p. 247),... *prāpaka-pratiṣedhaḥ* (p. 250), and ... *prāpya-prāpaka-sambandha-pratiṣedhaḥ* (p. 256). In the *Aṣṭasāhasrikā* the *prāpti-niryāṇa* occupies only 12 small paragraphs (W, 109-14). Haribhadra's treatment of this section is brief and confined to the summary given above. Ratnākaraśānti, however, seems to attach great importance to the analysis of the text on this *niryāṇa,* and avails himself of the opportunity to expound on the 'threefold nature' (*tri-svabhāva*) of the *prāpya* for which he uses the better-known term *grāhya.* He also points out that the 12 'sentences' (*vākya*) of the *Aṣṭasāhasrikā* deal with the 12 characteristics of the *prāptiniryāṇa.*[29] The first five *vākyas* reject (*pratiṣedha*) the obtainment (*prāpti*) of the 'imputed' (*kalpita*) from the point of view of the *dharma-nairātmya,* whereas the sixth *vākya* rejects the *prāpti* of the same from the point of view of the unreality of the *pudgala.* The seventh *vākya* rejects even the obtainment (*prāpti*) of the 'relative reality' (*paratantra-svabhāva*). The eighth, ninth, and tenth *vākyas* explain the 'absolute reality' (*pariniṣpanna-svabhāva*), viz. the *śūnyatā* of both the *grāhya* and the *grāhaka.* The last two establish the 'non-duality' (*advaidhībhāva*) between the two.[30]

The controversial reading alluded to occurs in the seventh *vākya,* which according to Ratnākaraśānti denies the *paratantra-svabhāva.* This *vākya* in Haribhadra's version of the *Aṣṭasāhasrikā* reads as follows: *evam asvabhāvānāṃ sarva-dharmāṇāṃ katamat tad rūpaṃ yad agrāhyaṃ anabhinirvṛttaṃ/ katame te vedanā...vijñānaṃ yad agrāhyam anabhinirvṛttaṃ/* (W, 112). Haribhadra's comment on this passage is brief: 'since it is "devoid of own nature" (*asvabhāva*), it is not produced (*anabhinirvṛtta*); therefore, free from the nature of being either object or subject, the *rūpa* is only by *saṃvṛti* (appearance)'.[31]

Ratnākaraśānti cites a different reading of the above text: '*evam abhāvasvabhāvāḥ sarvadharmāḥ*' *iti.* The modification of the text *asvabhāvānāṃ* into *abhāva-svabhāvāḥ* and also the change of the case (from the genitive to the nominative) is evidently not based on the authority of any variant reading of the MSS of the *Aṣṭasāhasrikā.*[32] Rather, the change is deliberate as Ratnākaraśānti himself questions the authenticity of this reading and proceeds to give a lengthy justification: 'Whence this reading? This reading is found in the *Pañcaviṃśati* (lit. the two larger *sūtras*). In that *sūtra* Subhūti sets forth his exposition (of the *prāpti-niryāṇa*) in 12 *vākyas.* There follow 12 corresponding questions by Śāriputra asking Subhūti the reason for his statements [*kena kāraṇenāyuṣman Subhūte evaṃ vadasi...*]. Subhūti answers these questions in due order. In his reply to the seventh question "for what reason, O Subhūti, do you say that all *dharmas* are of the nature of *abhāva* (*abhāvasvabhāvāḥ*)", Subhūti then states his reason and concludes: "in this manner, O Śāriputra, are all *dharmas* of the nature of *abhāva* (*abhāva-svabhāvāḥ sarvadharmāḥ*)" '.[33]

It must be noted that the text of the *Pañcaviṃśati* shows a great deal of inconsistency between the *uddeśa,* the question of Śāriputra, and the answers of Subhūti at the end. The *uddeśa-vākya,* for instance reads: *evam abhāvasvabhāvānāṃ dharmāṇāṃ katamad rūpaṃ yad anabhinirvṛttaṃ?* (Dutt, 245). The full text of Śāriputra's question is lost in the above edition due to the abridgement effected by the editor. But it is repeated again in Subhūti's speech: *punar aparaṃ yad āyuṣman Śāriputra evam āha 'abhāvasvabhāvāḥ sarvadharmā' iti.* The answer by Subhūti shows the source of confusion: *evam etat. tat kasya hetoḥ? tathā hy āyuṣman Śāriputra, nāsti sāṃyogikaḥ svabhāvaḥ... anenāyuṣman Śāriputra paryāyeṇa asvabhāvāḥ sarvadharmāḥ* (ibid., 252). Yet in answer to a subsequent question of Śariputra, *kena kāraṇenāyuṣman Subhūte akūṭasthā 'vināśinaḥ sarvadharmāḥ?*, Subhūti says: *rūpam āyuṣman Śāriputrākūṭastham avināśi... anena paryāyeṇa...abhāvasvabhāvāḥ sarvadharmāḥ* (ibid., 253).

Curiously enough, Dutt's edition of the *Pañcaviṃśati* reports both readings —*abhāva-svabhāvānāṃ* in the text and *asvabhāvānāṃ* in footnote 3 (based on the Asiatic Society MS)—in the seventh *uddeśa-vākya* of Subhūti. Probably Ratnākaraśānti's text of the *Pañcaviṃśati* had only the latter reading—*asvabhāvānāṃ*— as can be seen from his comments: 'It is not the *uddeśa* but the questions (of Śāriputra), and the concluding answers of Subhūti which should be considered as authoritative in this context. The *uddeśa* of the seventh *vākya* has suffered corruption. Three errors have in course of time arisen: first, [a desire to establish] identity with the subsequent text; second, the adoption of the genitive case in the place of the nominative to achieve this identity; and third, the removal of [the original reading] *abhāva-svabhāva* in preference to the [new] reading *asvabhāva*.'[34]

Whatever the original reading—whether *asvabhāvānāṃ* or *abhāva-svabhāvāḥ*— Haribhadra's brief comment that the *dharmas* (*rūpa*, etc.) exist only by *saṃvṛti* indicates that as a Mādhyamika[35] he probably saw no real difference between the two expressions. For Ratnākaraśānti, however, the two terms stand respectively for the *kalpita* (by implication), and the *paratantra-svabhāvas*, and cannot therefore be treated as synonyms. This is clear from the following where he seeks to support his interpretation by quoting the text of the *Pañcaviṃśati*: *evam iti paratantreṇa svabhāvena. abhāva-svabhāva eṣām ity abhāva-svabhāvāḥ sarvadharmāḥ. yad āha: 'nāsti sāṃyogikaḥ svabhāvaḥ pratītya-samutpannatvāt'* [*Pañcaviṃśati*°, 252] *iti*. He explains further the *sūtra* term *sāṃyogika-svabhāva*:

> 'Coming together of the causes is *saṃyoga*. That which comes into existence only in the presence of this *saṃyoga* is called *sāṃyogika*. The own nature which is thus *sāṃyogika* is non-being (*abhāva*), as that nature cannot exist upon the disappearance of the causes (that produced it by coming together). Moreover, that which is produced by the causal dependence (*pratītya-samutpanna*), being momentary, is of the nature of "subsequent non-existence" (*paścād-abhāva*). The latter cannot be the nature of that which exists, otherwise there will be contradiction. Therefore, that which is of the nature of being (*bhāva*) in one

moment has the nature of non-being (*abhāva*) in the subsequent moments. Therefore *abhāva* is the *svabhāva* of these [*rūpa*, etc.]. And also: that which is momentary is suffering (*duḥkha*); suffering is that which should be destroyed. Even for this reason *abhāva* is the own nature of these'.[36]

Ratnākaraśānti thus concludes: 'It is the meaning of the seventh *vākya* that the *bodhisattva* is not obtained even by the *paratantra-svabhāva*'.[37]

In keeping with this scheme, he takes the term *anabhinirvṛtti* (appearing in the last three *vākyas*) as identical with the *pariniṣpanna-svabhāva*.[38] It is evident from these brief portions of the *Sāratamā* that Ratnākaraśānti was writing his *pañjikā* in conformity with the *tri-svabhāva* doctrine of the Yogācāra school.

His affiliation to the Yogācāra school is further confirmed by his comments on yet another *sūtra* passage which pertains to the next *niryāṇa*, called the *sarvajñatā-niryāṇa*.[39] The *sūtra* passage introducing this *niryāṇa* takes up the (apparent) contradiction in a previous statement of Subhūti that all *dharmas*, including the *bodhisattva* and the *sarvajñatā*, are *anutpāda* (unproduced), and yet the *bodhisattva* strives hard to attain the enlightenment of the Buddha. Śāriputra poses a question that if both these are *anutpāda*, surely the *bodhisattva* has already attained the *sarvajñatā*, and without any effort![40] Subhūti's answer to this objection is that there indeed is no attainment (*prāpti*) of the [*sarvajñatā* which is] *anutpanna* by a *dharma* [=a *bodhisattva*] which is *anutpanna*.[41] Ratnākaraśānti comments on this *sūtra* in the light of the doctrine of *prabhāsvara-citta*, another major tenet of the Yogācāra school:

'It is proper to reject the attainment of *anutpanna* by *anutpanna*. The *Dharmadhātu* is the true reality of all *dharmas*. This *Dharmadhātu* by virtue of its being without a beginning and an end, and on account of its being essentially pure (*prakṛti-prabhāsvara*), is neither to be attained, nor is attained, but is only to be realized. Its realization itself is the non-apprehension of all *dharmas* which are imagined (*kalpita*). That realization itself is the supreme *prajñāpāramitā*...Therefore the *Dharmadhātu* bearing the designation of *bodhisattva*, although essentially pure, is (said to be) soiled by adventitious hindrances. When these adventitious coverings are destroyed, the resultant purity is (said to be) attained by the *bodhisattva*. Like, for instance, space which attains purity when the adventitious coverings like cloud, smoke, etc., depart from it...'[42]

Haribhadra's comment on the same passage is brief and free from any reference to the doctrine of the *prabhāsvara-citta*. As a Mādhyamika he refers to the *saṃvṛti* and the *paramārtha satyas* and concludes that at the time of realization (*abhisamayakāle*) that which is realized is devoid of both the *śāśvata* and the *uccheda*.[43]

Some 40 years ago, Obermiller, on the basis of his observations of the Tibetan *Śuddhimatī*, pointed out that Ratnākaraśānti was a follower of the Yogācāra system although he had supported the Mādhyamika opinion on the *gotra* being identical with the Absolute (*Dharmadhātu*).[44] Our brief study of the *Sāratamā* has confirmed Obermiller's conclusion about Ratnākaraśānti's adherence to the Yogācāra school. On the doctrine of the *gotra* also, the *Sāratamā* would seem to support Obermiller. It must, however, be noted that whereas Haribhadra openly favours the theory of the *ekayāna*[45] and advocates with great vigour his conviction that there are not three *gotras* in reality, Ratnākaraśānti appears rather mild in his treatment of the same problem,[46] particularly on the possibility of the attainment of Buddhahood by the *arhat* and the *pratyekabuddha*. This would indicate that the later Yogācārins were not committed to the dogma of the *ekayāna* but merely allowed it as an alternative to the *triyāna* concept advocated by earlier Yogācārins like Asaṅga.[47]

It is hoped that this brief comparison of the two commentaries on the *Aṣṭasāhasrikā* written by two eminent *ācāryas* representing the two rival schools will open a new avenue for future research on the precise differences between the Mādhyamika and the Yogācāra, and also between the manifold versions of the *prajñāpāramitā-sūtras*, a common heritage of both these schools.

NOTES

1. This paper was read before the twenty-eighth International Congress of Orientalists, Canberra, 1971.
2. *History of Buddhism*, translated by E.E. Obermiller, Heidelberg, 1931-2, I, p. 31 and n. 284.
3. *Geschichte des Buddhismus in Indien*, translated by F.A. von Schiefner, St. Petersburg, 1869.

4. E. Conze, *The Prajñāpāramitā literature* (Indo-Iranian Monographs, VI), 's-Gravenhage, 1960, 113.
5. Several other works on the doctrine of the *citta-mātra*, and in the field of Tantra are ascribed to Ratnākaraśānti and survive in the Tibetan translation. Professor Alex Wayman informs me that the following works are included in the *citta-mātra* section of the Tibetan Tanjur: 'The *Madhyamakālaṅkāravṛttimadhyamapratipadāsiddhi-nāma*, two little works both entitled *Prajñāpāramitābhāvanopadeśa*, the *Prajñāpāramitopadeśa*, and the *Madhyamakālaṅkāropadeśa*, five in all. He has also written three commentaries on the *Guhyasamāja-tantra* and has composed a number of lesser Tantric commentaries and works, such as the *Khasmāna-nāma-ṭīkā*, the *Abhiṣekanirukti*, and a number of *sādhanas*'.
6. Henceforth referred to as *Aa.* or *Śāstra.*
7. We have used Wogihara's edition of this text together with the *Ālokā* (*Abhisamayālaṃkār' ālokā-prajñāpāramitāvyākhyā* (Toyo Bunko Publications, Ser. D, II), 2 vols., Tokyo, 1932-5). Henceforth indicated by W.
8. *tattv'āloka-vidhāyinī viracitā sat-pañjikeyaṃ mayā//* (W, 994.)
9. It should be noted here that Ratnākaraśānti refers to Vimuktisena in the introductory verses of his *Śuddhimatī*. I am indebted to Professor Alex Wayman for this information and for the following translation of the Tibetan verses.
   'The *Abhisamayālaṅkāra* of the gentle Mother, was
   composed by Ārya Maitreya. The *Śuddhimatī*
   commentary of mine was written by myself, Ratnākara.
   Thinking that Vimuktisena had not completely
   explicated the meaning of the extended Mother
   (=*prajñāpāramitā*), it was understood by me according /
   to the *Prakaraṇa* in the manner of discourse.'
10. This is the last *parivarta* of the original version of the *Aṣṭasāhasrikā* as opposed to the 32 *parivartas* of the extant version. See Conze, *The Prajñāpāramitā literature*, 15.
11. *evam eva Kārikā-śāstraprāmāṇyād bhāvādhyāhārādipadādibhir abhisamaya-kramānurūpo granthārtho vācyah. tataś ca kenacid Abhisamayālaṅkāra-kārikā-pāṭhaṃ bāhulyenānyathā kṛtvā pratibhātu te Subhūta ity-ādi vākyam ārabhyāsyā Mātur yad asambaddhaṃ samyak-samudāyāvayavārthānabhidhānād vyākhyānaṃ kṛtaṃ tat santa eva jñātum arhantīti nopanyasya nirākṛtaṃ* (W, 925-6).
12. Conze's translation, *Abhisamayālaṅkāra* (Serie Orientale Roma, VI) Rome, 1954.
13. '(Finally one considers) the one who experiences it in the seven aspects in which (the dharmas which constitute him and his training) resemble (a dream, a magical illusion, a mirage, an echo, a reflex, a city of the gandharvas, a fictitious magical creation)' (Conze, *Abhisamayālaṅkāra*, 46).
14. *...hetuvirahād akāraka-khyātyā...bhāvā jñātā bhavantīty evaṃ Pañcaviṃśatisāhasrikāyām uktaṃ. atra tu saṃkṣepasya vivakṣitatvāt pratiśrutkopamāḥ sarva-dharmā iti vacanena madhyamasya nirdeśād ādy-anta-trika-nirdeśa iti pratipattavyaṃ* (W, 431).
15. *akṣayākāratāyāṃ ca sarāgādau pravistṛte/*
    mahadgate 'pramāṇe ca vijñāne cānidarśane// (*Aa.* IV, 15)
16. *'akṣayākāratāyāñ ca 'iti kṣayapāṭho Mahatyau prati. imāṃ tu prati 'ameyākṣayatāyāñ ca' iti pāṭhaḥ. asyāṃ hi paṭhayate 'aprameyākṣayāni cittāni 'iti.*
17. W, 541.
18. *samatā-dvāreṇa prayogo bhāvanīya iti samatām āha sa ca tān na manyata ity ādinā.*

tatra samāhitena cittena tān na manyate yato na samanupaśyati. te ca dharmā na vidyante yato na saṃdṛśyante, samāhitena manasā na jānāti yato na saṃjānīte, te ca dharmās taj-jñāna-gamyā na saṃvidyante yato nopalabhyanta iti yojyaṃ (W, 432).

19. *tad evaṃ rūpādipadārthamananā-nīlādinimittamananā-rūpadvidhāviṃśatidhetyādiprapañcamananā-nirvedhabhāgīyādyadhigamamananānāṃ pratiṣedhena jñātṛjñeya-dharmānupalabdhiś caturdhoktā vijñeyā* (W, 432).

20. *sāmānyena śuddhim evam abhidhīya viśeṣeṇāha: punar aparam ity ādi. sarvajñatāviśuddhir iti trisarvajñatāviśuddhir ity arthaḥ...mārgajñatādhikāre viśuddhikathanaprasaṅgāt ātyantikī cetarā ca tathāgatānāṃ śrāvakādīnāṃ ca yathākramaṃ viśuddhiḥ kathitā* (W, 408).

21. *viśuddhibhedāś catvāro Mahatyor bhagavatyor uktāḥ sarvasaṅgrahārtham, asyāṃ tu noktā bodhisattvamārgādhikārāt...sarvajñateti sarvākārajñatā...*(*parivarta* 8).

22. *gambhīrā...atyantānupapattir iti...nava-padārthāni yathākramaṃ mṛdumṛdvādi navaprakāra-bhāvanā-mārgatvena vācyāni...*(W, 409).

23. *āha/ aprāptir anabhisamayo Bhagavan prajñāpāramitā/* (W, 409).

24. *sarvajñateti sarvākārajñatā. tasyā viśuddhir dvividhā. yā skandhānām ekaśo viśuddhiḥ pāramitānāṃ ca sā sarvākārajñatāviśuddhiḥ. yā ca tasyāḥ sā teṣām ity ekā sarvākārajñatāviśuddhiḥ. ...sarvam etad abhinnam acchinnam iti dvitīyā sarvākārajñatāviśuddhiḥ. yad asyāṃ na paṭhyate upalakṣaṇatvāt tad grāhyam iti mṛdumṛdumārgo madhyamadhyaś ca* (*parivarta* 8).

25. *tridhātupratipakṣatvaṃ samatā mānameyayoḥ/* (*Aa.* II, 31 ab).

26. 'the going-forth which has the mark of (leading to) the attainment (of the achievements open to all the three vehicles)' (Conze, *Abhisamayālaṅkāra*, 29).

27. *uddeśe samatāyāṃ ca sattvārthe yatnavarjane/*
atyantāya ca niryāṇaṃ niryāṇaṃ prāptilakṣaṇam// (*Aa.* I. 72.)
sarvākārajñatāyāṃ ca niryāṇaṃ mārgagocaram/
niryāṇapratipaj jñeyā seyam aṣṭavidhātmikā// (*Aa.* I. 73.)

28. *tac ca prāpti-niryāṇaṃ prāpya-prāpaka-tadubhaya-sambandha-pratiṣedhalakṣaṇam ataḥ...āha...rūpāparyantatayety ādi.*
dharma-dhātu-vinirmukto yasmād dharmo na vidyata/
iti nyāyād dharmadhātuvat tat-svabhāvībhūtānāṃ yasmād rūpādīnām aparyantatayā rūpādīnām aparyantatā. tasmād bodhisattvaṃ nopaitīti bhāvaḥ (W, 109-10).

29. *atra śikṣitvety ādinā prāpti-niryāṇaṃ prastauti...prāpti-niryāṇam adhikṛtya tasyāṃ prāptau dvādaśaviśeṣān dvādaśabhir vākyair āha...*(*parivarta* 1).

30. *evaṃ tāvat pañcabhir vākyair dharma-nairātmyamukhena nāmadheyamukhena ca kalpitasya prāptiḥ pratiṣiddhā. pudgala-nairātmyamukhenāpi tat pratiṣedhāya ṣaṣṭhaṃ coktaṃ...paratantrasvabhāvam adhikṛtya saptamaṃ coktaṃ...aṣṭamād ūrdhvaṃ trīṇi vākyāni pariniṣpannaṃ svabhāvam adhikṛtya...* (*parivarta* 1).

31. *yady evaṃ nyāyenāsvabhāvatve sarva-dharmāṇāṃ katamat tad rūpam ity āśaṅkyāha: yad ity ādi. yasmād anabhinirvṛttaṃ tasmād yad grāhya-grāhaka-bhāva-vigataṃ tattvena tad avicāraikamanoharaṃ saṃvṛtyā rūpaṃ* (W, 112).

32. It may be noted that Wogihara's edition (both of the *Aṣṭasāhasrikā* and of the *Ālokā*) does not report a variant reading for the word *asvabhāvānāṃ*.

33. *paratantra-svabhāvam adhikṛtya saptamaṃ coktaṃ: evam abhāva-svabhāvāḥ sarvadharmāḥ iti. kuta etat? yato Mahatyor bhagavatyor dvādaśabhir vākyair uddeśaḥ Subhūtinā kṛte tata eṣāṃ dvādaśānāṃ abhidhāna-kāraṇa-praśneṣu Śāriputreṇa kṛteṣu sthavira-Subhūtiḥ kāraṇāni krameṇa bruvāṇaḥ saptama-sthānakena kāraṇena 'abhāva-svabhāvāḥ sarvadharmāḥ' iti praśnam anudyābhāva-svabhāvatāyāṃ kāraṇam uktvā 'anena paryāyeṇa Śāriputra, abhāva-svabhāvāḥ sarvadharmāḥ' ity upasaṃhāraṃ kṛtavāṇ. tata eṣa pāṭhaḥ pratīyate.* (*parivarta* 1). Cf. *Pañcaviṃśati*, p. 252.

34. *Subhūteḥ praśnānuvādakāraṇākhyānatadupasaṃhārā iha jñāpakā na tūddeśaḥ. uddeśe 'pi saptamavākyasya prāyeṇa pāṭhabhraṃśāt. yataḥ saptamavākye trayo viplavāḥ kālena jātāḥ. uttareṇa granthena sahaikavākyatā prathamo viplavaḥ. ekavākyārthe prathamām vibhaktim apanīya ṣaṣṭhīvibhaktiḥ kṛteti dvitīyo viplavaḥ. abhāva-svabhāvatāṃ cāpanīya asvabhāvatā paṭhiteti tṛtīyo viplavaḥ. arthaṃ brūmaḥ...*(*parivarta* 1).

35. Although a Mādhyamika, Haribhadra gives due recognition to the *tri-svabhāva* doctrine, as can be seen from the following comment on the *sūtra* passage: *evaṃ hi...ādikarmiko bodhisattvaḥ anupūrveṇa prajñāpāramitāyām avatārayitavyaḥ: anupūrveṇety ādāv ātmādinirākaraṇena bāhye 'rthe pratiṣṭhāpya, paścāt kalpita-paratantra-pariniṣpanna-svabhāvakathanena traidhātukacittamātrāvagame niyojya, tadanu samyagarthakriyāsu yogyam ayogyaṃ tathyātathyabhedena saṃvṛtisatyadvayam avicāraikaramya-pūrvapūrva-svakāraṇādhīnaṃ nirdiśya, tathya-saṃvṛtau sthitvā yathādarśanaṃ māyāpuruṣeṇeva dānādy ācaritavyaṃ paramārthato 'nutpādaś ca bhāvayitavyaḥ. ity evaṃ krameṇa prajñāpāramitāyām avatārayitavyaḥ* (W, 594).

36. *kāraṇasaṃnidhiḥ saṃyogaḥ. tasmin saty eva bhavatīti sāṃyogikaḥ. sāṃyogiko yaḥ svabhāvaḥ so 'bhāvaḥ kāraṇaviyoge saty abhāvāt. api ca yaḥ pratītyasamutpannaḥ so 'nityatvāt paścādabhāvaḥ. na ca vidyamānasya paścād-abhāvo ghaṭate virodhāt. tasmād ekakṣaṇa eva yo bhāvaḥ sa ekakṣaṇāntareṣv abhāvaḥ. tasmād abhāva eṣāṃ svabhāvaḥ. kiñca, yad anityaṃ tat duḥkhaṃ, duḥkhaṃ ca prahātavyaṃ. tato 'py abhāvasvabhāva eṣāṃ.*

37. *tasmāt paratantreṇāpi svabhāvena bodhisattvo na prāpnotīti saptamasyārthaḥ* (*parivarta* 1).

38. *asyāṃ tu Bhagavatyāṃ grāhyatāpi kalpitasya pratiṣiddhā bālagrāhyatvāt tasya. aṣṭamād ūrdhvaṃ trīṇi vākyāni pariniṣpannaṃ svabhāvam adhikṛtya evam ity ādi. evam iti kalpitena svabhāvena. eteṣām iti paratantrarūpāṇāṃ yā asvabhāvatā śūnyatā sā 'nabhinirvṛttir iti sa pariniṣpannasvabhāva ity arthaḥ* (ibid).

39. *sarvākārajñatāyāṃ ca niryāṇaṃ.../* (*Aa.* I, 73) 'the going-forth (which leads to) the knowledge of all modes (peculiar to a Buddha)' (Conze, *Abhisamayālaṅkāra,* 29).

40. *yady āyuṣman Subhūte bodhisattvo 'py anutpādo...sarvajñatā 'py anutpādaḥ...nanv āyuṣman Subhūte anuprāptaivāyatnena bodhisattvena....sarvajñatā bhavati...*(W, 120). Cf. *Pañcaviṃśati*[b], 259.

41. *nāpy anutpannena dharmeṇānutpannā prāptiḥ prāpyate* (W, 121).

42. *tasmāt sādhūktaṃ nāpy anutpannena dharmeṇānutpannā prāptiḥ prāpyata iti yuktaḥ prāptivikalpapratiṣedhaḥ. tasmāt sarvadharmāṇāṃ paramārtho dharmadhātuḥ. sa ca prakṛtiprabhāsvaratvād anādinidhanatvāc ca na prāpyate nāpi prāpnoti. kevalaṃ draṣṭavyaḥ. yat tasya darśanaṃ saiva kalpitānāṃ sarvadharmāṇām anupalabdhiḥ. saiva niratiśayā prajñāpāramitā ...tataḥ prakṛtiprabhāsvaro 'pi bodhisattvākhyo dharmadhātur āgantukair āvaraṇamalair malinīkṛtaḥ. tena teṣāṃ kṣaye sati tatra kṣayalakṣaṇā viśuddhir apūrvatvāt prāpyate. tad yathā prakṛtyā viśuddham ākāśam āgantukair dhūmādibhir āvaraṇamalair malinīkriyate. paścāt tad apāye ...viśuddhis tena prāpyate. sarvavibhramanivṛttau ca suviśuddhasarvadharmadharmatājñāna-lakṣaṇā sarvākārajñatā yā 'pūrvatvāt bodhisattvena labhyate. saiva tasyā viśuddher ātmabhūtāyāḥ saṃvedanāprāptyabhisamayaḥ saṃpadyata iti siddhāntaḥ* (*parivarta* 1).

43. *tattvena prāpyaprāpakayor asattvāt kuto 'yatnena prāptiḥ. saṃvṛtyā 'pi...kathaṃ prāptiḥ ...atyantaṃ pratibhātīty apagataśāśvatoccheda-rūpaṃ pratibhāsate* (W, 121-3).

44. 'The sublime science of the great vehicle to salvation', *Acta Orientalia*, IX, 2-3, 1931, p. 103, n. 4.
45. See W, 133-4.
46. *śrāvakair api bodhipariṇatikaiḥ samyaksambodhau cittasyotpādanāt. te hi svāṃ bodhim adhigamyāpi buddha-bodhisattvānāṃ lokottarāṃ vibhūtiṃ dṛṣṭvā vañcitam ivātmānaṃ manyamānās tathāgatair adhiṣṭhitās tad bodhau cittam utpādyācalyabhūmikabodhisattvavan nirmitābhir upapattibhir bodhicaryāṃ caritvā parāṃ bodhim adhigacchantīti vyāptiḥ* (*parivarta* 1).
47. *nānā-nayāvādinas tv ārya-Asaṅga-pādās tan matānusāriṇaś cānyathā vyācakṣate* ...(W, 134).

CHAPTER 25

The Sanskrit Fragments in Vinītadeva's *Triṃśikā-Ṭīkā**

Scholars conversant with the history of the Yogācāra/Vijñānavāda school are familiar with the names of Vasubandhu and his renowned commentator, Sthiramati; the Buddhist logicians Dignāga and Dharmakīrti, who are also associated with that school, are equally well known for their scholastic achievements. A later commentator important in both schools is Vinītadeva (*c.* 645-715), who has received a great deal of attention in recent years. No less than a dozen of his commentaries, most of them called *ṭīkās*, are preserved in Tibetan translation.[1] Sylvain Levi's publication in 1925 of Sthiramati's *Triṃśikāvijñaptibhāṣya* first aroused scholarly interest in Vinītadeva's commentaries.[2] The eminent buddhologist, Theodore Stcherbatsky, was probably the first scholar to study Vinītadeva's work in depth; Stcherbatsky utilized the Tibetan translation of Vinītadeva's *Nyāyabinduṭīkā* in his pioneering translation of the *Nyāyabindu* which appeared in 1930 in his massive two-volume publication, *Buddhist logic.*[3] The first complete translation of the Tibetan rendering of two of Vinītadeva's *ṭīkās*, namely, the *Viṃśatikā-ṭīkā* and the *Triṃśikā-ṭīkā* was undertaken by Yamaguchi Susumu and Nozawa Josho, respectively; this appeared in Japanese in 1953.[4] More recently, in 1971, M. Gangopadhyaya published a Sanskrit reconstruction with English translation of Vinītadeva's *Nyāyabindu-ṭīkā.*[5] A still more recent work appears in

*This article was originally published in *BSOAS,* Vol. XLVIII, part 3, pp. 470-492, University of London, 1985. Reprinted with kind permission of Oxford University Press.

the 1975 Ph.D. thesis of Dr. Leslie Kawamura of the University of Saskatchewan.[6]

Both Professors Yamaguchi and Kawamura have helped to establish the relative chronology of major Yogācāra/Vijñānavāda scholars, such as Dignāga (*c.* 480-540), Dharmapāla (*c.* 530-561), Dharmakīrti (600-660), and Vinītadeva (645-715). They have also accepted the Tibetan historian Tārānātha's account that Vinītadeva was an ācārya at Nālandā University, and was indeed the author of the works attributed to him. The research of Nozawa, Yamaguchi and Kawamura concentrates on the *Triṃśikā-ṭīkā,* probably the most studied of Vinītadeva's commentaries. Its popularity undoubtedly derives from the tremendous importance of Sthiramati's *Bhāṣya* to Vasubandhu's *Triṃśikā* text, which was the fundamental treatise of the Vijñaptimātratā school. Even so, Vinītadeva's *ṭīkā* falls a great deal short of what one would expect from a commentary which claimed to elucidate so profound a work as Sthiramati's *Bhāṣya.*

In view of the historical importance of Vinītadeva's *ṭīkās,* which not only help in determining the textual accuracy of the original works commented upon but also are occasionally illuminating in their own right, it is unfortunate that not one of his works should have been preserved in the original Sanskrit. While I was teaching at the School of Oriental and African Studies, University of London, in 1966, it was therefore a matter of great gratification that a visitor from Darjeeling, who prefers to remain anonymous, delivered a bundle to me containing 13 fragile palm-leaves, which were eventually determined to be fragments of Vinītadeva's *Triṃiśikā-ṭīkā.* The folios of the manuscript were in complete disarray, but a chance reading of a rubricated line of the third folio of the bundle revealed the words *srotasaughavat,* which immediately established that this was a commentary on the *Triṃśikā,* that line being the last quarter of verse no. 4 of Vasubandhu's text. The remainder of the first line of that folio disclosed that the text being commented upon was Sthiramati's *Triṃśikābhāṣya.* My colleague at the School, Dr. Ishi Yamada, who is now at Northwestern University, suggested to me that the text might be Vinītadeva's *Triṃśikā-ṭīkā,* and his reading of the Tibetan translation of that commentary, *Sum-cu-pa'i 'grel-bshad,*[7] confirmed his surmise. With the help of the rubrications, it was possible to collate the manuscript. The original order of the folios, and the corresponding verses in the *ṭīkā* were as follows:

folio	*verse no.*	*folio*	*verse no.*
1	17-18	8	11
2	13-14	9	12
3	4-5b	10	14
4	15, 16	11	5cd, 6cd
5	8, 9, 10	12	6, 7a
6	10	13	30
7	10		

Once the folios were collated, it was found that only the following fragments of the *ṭīkā* were extant. The last line of the fourth verse through to verse 14 (corresponding to S. Levi's ed., p. 21, last line, to p. 30, 1.25: *Tibetan Tripiṭaka* Peking ed., vol. 114, p. 20b, 1.7, to p. 41b, 1.2) survived. There was a folio missing after this (corresponding to Levi ed., p. 30, 1.26, to p. 31, 1.22: Peking ed., vol. 114, p. 41b, 1.2, to p. 43b, 1.3). The text then continued uninterrupted up to verse 18 (Levi ed., p. 36, 1.15: Peking ed., vol. 114, p. 51b, 1.2). After this, there was only a single leaf (no. 13) remaining, which commented on a line in Sthiramati's *Bhāṣya, 'dvidhā dauṣṭhulyahānitaḥ'* (Levi ed., p. 44, 1.9: Peking ed., vol. 114, p. 67a, 1.5).

Unfortunately, the fourth line of fol. 13b strayed completely from the *Triṃśikābhāṣya* and contained material that was extraneous to Sthiramati's commentary, both in the original Sanskrit as well as in the Tibetan translation. Vinītadeva's text thus ended on the fourth line, with the words *dharmakāya iti ucyate* (Levi ed., p. 44 last line). The remainder of the manuscript, beginning with *atraiva vyākhyānāntaraṃ kurvann āha* and continuing through to *utpadyante iti aṅgāni,* could not be traced to any of Vinītadeva's works and, with the assistance of Dr. Leslie Kawamura, was finally discovered to be a fragment from Sthiramati's commentary, the *Madhyāntavibhāgaṭīkā* (Yamaguchi Susumu's ed., p. 92, 1.15, to p. 93, 1.8). There is no clear reason why these extraneous lines were copied into the manuscript. Thus, the first three verses of the *Triṃśikā* dealing with *vijñānapariṇāma* and vv. 19-29 on the *trisvabhāvas*—perhaps the sections of the text most important for understanding Vijñānavāda thought— were missing: the majority of the extant text (vv. 9-17) dealt with the Abhidharma classifications of dharmas, and particularly with the *caitasika-dharmas.* These extant sections should be of special interest to students of Yogācāra Abhidharma.

The fragmentary nature of the manuscript notwithstanding, its importance cannot be denied, since it is the only work by Vinītadeva that has even partially survived in its original language. The task of comparing the Sanskrit text with the Tibetan translation and Yamaguchi's Japanese rendering was kindly undertaken at my request by my esteemed friend and colleague, Professor Kajiyama Yuichi, during his sabbatical stay at U.C. Berkeley in 1975. These comparisons have been useful in preparing the annotation that appears under the text below. In making the edition, I have taken the liberty of adding in full only the verses of the *Triṃśikā* so as to maintain some kind of continuity in the discussion: these additions are printed in capital letters in square brackets. Sthiramati's *Bhāṣya*, which Vinītadeva reproduces verbatim, has been italicized: these quotations invariably end with the words *ity ādi*. On many occasions, Vinītadeva has appropriated Sthiramati's words as part of his own *ṭīkā*: these have been allowed to stand as Vinītadeva's own comments.

Welcome as it would have been to find the entire text, and deplorable as it is that perhaps the most crucial portions of the commentary are missing, we must still be grateful that at least some portions of Vinītadeva's work have survived. Because of the fragmentary nature of the text, I have not found it feasible to produce an English translation. For fuller treatments of Vinītadeva's thought, using the comprehensive Tibetan sources, the reader may refer to the works of Nozawa, Yamaguchi and Kawamura.

TEXT[8]

...[9] [ĀTMADHARMOPACĀRO HI VIVIDHO YAḤ PRAVARTATE/
VIJÑĀNAPARIṆĀMO 'SAU PARIṆĀMAḤ SA CA TRIDHĀ//1//
VIPĀKO MANANĀKHYAŚ CA VIJÑAPTIR VIṢAYASYA CA/
TATRĀLAYĀKHYAṂ VIJÑĀNAṂ VIPĀKAḤ SARVABĪJAKAM//2//
ASAṂVIDITAKOPĀDISTHĀNAVIJÑAPTIKAṂ CA TAT/
SADĀ SPARŚAMANASKĀRAVITSAṂJÑĀCETANĀNVITAM//3//
UPEKṢĀ VEDANĀ TATRĀNIVṚTĀVYĀKṚTAM CA TAT/
TATHĀ SPARŚĀDAYAS TAC CA VARTATE SROTA] [*1a][10] SAUGHAVAT[//4//]

iti/ tac cālayavijñānam oghavat srotasā vartate na tv ekam abhinnam/ padārthaṃ[11] darśayann āha/ *tac cālayavijñānam ity ādi/* subodhaṃ etat/ srotaḥsvabhāvaṃ darśayann āha/ *tatra srota ity ādi/* hetuphalayor nairantaryeṇa prabandhena pravṛttiḥ srota ucyate/

oghasvarūpaṃ darśayann āha/ *udakasamūhasyety ādi/* udakasamūhasya hi purvāparayor bhāgayor avicchedena yaḥ pravāhaḥ sa ogha ucyate/ evaṃ padārtham ākhyāya sūtrārthaṃ darśayann āha/ *yathaugha*[12] *ity ādi/* yathā khalv oghas tṛṇādīn karṣayan[13] gacchati, evam ālayavijñānam api puṇyādikarmavāsanā[nu]gataṃ sparśādīn karṣa[ya]t prabandhenānuparataṃ pravartate/

punar api paraḥ pṛcchati/ *tasyaivaṃ srotasety ādi/* tasyālayavijñānasyaivaṃ prabandhena pravartamānasya kasyām avasthāyāṃ vyāvṛttir iti vaktavyam/ siddhāntavādy āha/

TASYA VYĀVṚTTIR [ARHATVE]

ity ādi/ arhatvapratipattikāle tasya vyāvṛttir bhavati/ apara ajānan pṛcchati/ *kiṃ puna[r a]rhatvam iti/* siddhāntavādy āha/ *yad yogād ity ādi/* yasya dharmasya yogād ayam prāṇī arhann ity ucyate tad arhatvam ucyate/ paras tad dharmam ajānan pṛcchati/ *kasya punar ity ādi/* ka[ta]masya dharmasya yogād arhann ity ucyate/ siddhāntavādy āha/ *kṣayajñānety ādi/* kṣayajñā[nānutpāda]jñānayor lābhād asāv arhann ity ucyate/ kim iti tadālayavijñānaṃ vyāvartata ity āha/ *tasyām avasthāyām* ālayavijñānāśritaṃ yat kiñcid dauṣṭhulyam āsīt tat sarvaṃ niravaśeṣaṃ prahīyate/ tasmād *ālayavijñānaṃ vyāvṛttaṃ bhavati/* kleśabījā[śrayaṃ] tad asyāpagataṃ bhavatīty arthaḥ/ yasyām avasthāyām ālayavijñānām vyāvartate saivārhad avasthocyate/ yasmād vimuktikāye vā [dharmakāye vā] labdhe arhan vyapadiśyate/

evaṃ vistareṇa vipā[kā]khyaḥ pariṇāma uktaḥ/ *savibhaṅga iti* savistara ity arthaḥ/

dvitīyapariṇāmā[bhisandhiṃ darśaya]nn āha/ *idānīṃ mananākhyam ity ādi/* subodham etat/ katamaḥ sa ity āha/ *tadāśrityety ādi/* asya paścād vyākhyānaṃ kariṣyati/ adhunā tu kārikābhisambandhaṃ darśayann āha/ *tatra[yathā] cakṣurādivijñānānām ity ādi/* cakṣurādivijñānādīnām āśrayālambane prasiddhe naivaṃ kliṣṭasya manasas tayoḥ prasiddhiḥ/ [*lb][14] nāśrayālāmbananirapekṣasya pravṛttir yujyate/ tasmād asyāśrayālambanapratipādanārthaṃ nirvacanapratipādanārthaṃ ca.

TADĀŚRITYA [PRAVARTATE/
TADĀLAMBAṂ MANONĀMA VIJÑĀNAṂ
MANANĀTMAKAM//5//]

ity ādi kārikam āha/ ālayavijñānam āśrityālambya ca kliṣṭaṃ manaḥ pravartate/ tac ca mananātmakatvād mano 'bhidhīyata iti sūtrārthaḥ/ avayavavyākhyānam āha/ *tadāśritya pravartata ity ādi/* tac chabdenātrālayavijñānaṃ sambandhanīyam ity arthaḥ/ kathaṃ punar asyālayavijñānam āśrayam i[yam i]ty āha/ *tadvāsanāśrayo hīty ādi/* yasmāt kliṣṭasya manasaḥ yā vāsanā tasyā mūlavijñānam āśrayaḥ, tasmāt kliṣṭam manaḥ ālayavijñānam āśritya pravartate/ *pravartata ity* etasya vyākhyānaṃ *santānenotpadyate* kṣaṇaparamparāyogena sahotpadyata *ity arthaḥ/*

atraiva vyākhyān[āntar]aṃ kurvann āha/ *atha vā yasmin dhātāv ity ādi/* yasmin kāmādike dhātau yasyāṃ vā prathamadhyānādikāyāṃ bhūmau ālayavijñānaṃ vipāka upalabhyate tad api [kliṣṭaṃ manaḥ] yasmāt taddhātukaṃ tadbhūmikaṃ vā bhavati tasmād ālayavijñānapratibaddhavṛttitvāt tad āśritya pravartata ity ucyate/

ālambanam asya darśayann āha/ *tad ālambanam ity ādi/* etad vivṛṇvann āha/ *ālayavijñānālambanam evety ādi/* yasmāt kliṣṭaṃ manaḥ satkāyadṛṣṭyādibhiḥ samprayujya[te tasmā]d ahaṃ [ma]mety anenākāreṇālayavijñānam evālambate/ āśrayam evālambanam ity etat paraḥ sambhāvayan pṛcchati/ *kathaṃ punar yata evety ādi/* yata āśrayabhūtāc cittād utpadyate kliṣṭaṃ manaḥ kathaṃ tad evāsyālambanaṃ bhavati? anyo hy ālambanārtho 'nyaś cāśrayārthaḥ, tat kathaṃ dvayaṃ yokṣyate? siddhāntavādī sāmyam āpādayann āha/ *yathā tad anicchatāṃ keṣāṃcid ity ādi/* ye hi kliṣṭaṃ mano necchanti teṣām/ yathā kasyāṃcid anantaraniruddhe svacittapratyavekṣaṇāvasthāyām/ yata eva cittāt samanantarapratyayabhūtāt manovijñānam utpadyate, tadd[15] hīnam (tat kṣīṇam?) eva,[15] yathaiva tan manovijñānaṃ svāśrayālambanaṃ bhaviṣyati/ yad etat svāśrayālambanaṃ vijñānaṃ tat kin nāmadheyam ity āha/ *mano nāmety ādi/* su[bodham eta]t/

evaṃ padārthaṃ vyākhyāya sūtrārthaṃ darśayann āha/ *tad ālayavijñānam ity ādi/* yad etan mano nāma vijñānam uktaṃ [*2a][16] tac cālayavijñānam āśritya pravartate, ālayavijñānālambanaṃ ca/ manaḥśabdasya vyavacchedyam anena darśayati/ tathā hi manograhaṇenālayavijñānāt pravṛttivijñānāc cāsya vyavacchedaṃ karoti/

svabhāvam asya pṛcchann āha/ *tat punaḥ kiṃ svabhāvam ity ādi/ mananātmakam iti/* aham iti mameti ca nityaṃ manyate tasmāt mananasvabhāvaṃ tat/ niruktim asya kurvann āha/ *evaṃ ca mananātmakatvād ity ādi/* yasmān mananātmakaṃ tasmān mana[17] ity ucyate/ *nairuktena vidhinā iti* nirvacananyāyena/

kārikābhisambandhaṃ kurvann āha/ *vijñānasvarūpatvād ity ādi/* subodham etat/

caitasikasvarūpasaṃkhyākālapratipattyartham āha/

KLEŚAIŚ CATURBHIḤ [SAHITAṂ NIVṚTĀVYĀKṚTAIḤ SADĀ/]

ity ādi/ kliṣṭaṃ manaḥ kleśair nivṛtāvyākṛtasavbhāvaiḥ samprayuktam iti sūtrārthaḥ/ kleśagrahaṇasya vyacchedyaṃ darśayann āha/ *caittā hīty ādi/*subodham etat/

saṃkhyāviśeṣasya vyavacchedyaṃ darśayann āha/ *kleśā 'pi ṣaḍ ity ādi/* etad api subodham/ sahitaśabdena rasiko 'py ucyata ity āha/ *sahitam ity ādi/* etad api subodham/

kasmān nivṛtāvyākṛtais tat samprayujyata ity āha/ *na hi nivṛtenety ādi/* nivṛtāvyākṛtaṃ hi kliṣṭaṃ manaḥ, tasmān nivṛtena vijñānenākuṣalānāṃ samprayogo na yujyata ity āha/ *nivṛtāḥ kliṣṭatvāt/* yasmāt kliṣṭās tasmān nivṛtā ity arthaḥ/ yadi nivṛtāḥ kim ity avyākṛtā ity āha/ *avyākṛtā ity ādi/* yasmāt kuśalatvenākuśalatvena ca na vyākriyante tasmād avyākṛtā ucyante/

kālam asya darśayann āha/ *sadety ādi/* yāvat kliṣṭaṃ mano 'sti tāvat taiḥ sarvakālaṃ samprayujyate/

kārikāsambandhaṃ kurvann āha/ *sāmānyanirdeśād ity ādi/* kleśaiś caturbhir iti sāmānyena nirdeśaḥ kṛto viśeṣato na vijñāyate katamaiś caturbhir iti/ ato viśeṣeṇa darśayann āha/

[*2b][18] ĀTMADṚṢṬYĀTMAMOHĀ[TMAMĀNĀTMASNEHA-SAṂJÑITAIḤ//6//]

ity ādi/ ātmadṛṣtyā ātmamohenātmamānenātmasnehenety ebhiś caturbhir iti sūtrārthaḥ/ ātmadṛṣṭyādīn darśayann āha/ *upādānaskandheṣv ity ādi/* pañcopādānaskandheṣu ya ātmeti grāhaḥ, so 'trātmadṛṣṭiḥ/ tam eva prasiddhena paryāyeṇa darśayati/ *satkāyadṛṣṭir ity* anena/ ajñānaṃ mohaśabdenocyate/ ātmaviṣayo mohaḥ ātmamohaḥ/ ātmani yo māna utpadyate sa ātmamāna ucyate/ tam eva prasiddhena paryāyeṇa darśayati/ *asmiṃ māna ity anena*/ ātmani yaḥ sneha utpadyate sa ātmasneha ucyate/ asya prasiddhaṃ paryāyaṃ darśayati/ *ātmaprema ity anena*/

katham eṣām ālayavijñānam ālambanam ity āha/ *tatrālayavijñanasvarūpe sammoha*[19] *ity ādi*/ yo hy ālayavijñānasyānityādisvarūpaṃ na jānīte, sa tatrātmagrāhaṃ karoti/ eṣa me aham ātmeti yat tad ajñānaṃ[20] sa ātmamohaḥ/ ya ātmagrāhaḥ sā satkāyadṛṣṭiḥ/ ātmadarśanottarakālaṃ ca dharmatāvaśena yā cittasyonnatiḥ upajāyate so' smimāna ucyate/ *etasmiṃs traye* mohāditraye saty uttarakālam *ātmābhimate vastuni yo 'bhiṣvaṅgo jāyate sa ātmasneha* ucyate/

uktārthasaṅgrahaślokam āha/ *āha cety ādi*/ yan mananālakṣaṇaṃ manas tad avidyādibhiś caturbhiḥ kleśaiḥ saṃkliṣṭam iti ślokārthaḥ/ *saṃkliṣṭam iti* malinīkṛtaṃ/ dvitīyena ślokena kliṣṭasya manasaḥ astitve yuktiṃ darśayann āha/ *viparyāsanimittam tv ity ādi*/ yasmāt kliṣṭamanaḥ sarvakālaṃ viparyāsasya nimittaṃ tasmāt tad astīti mantavyam/ katamasya viparyāsasyety āha/ *kuśalāvyākṛte citta ity ādi*/ kuśalacittāvasthāyām ahaṃkāro nimittam, ahaṃ dānaṃ dadāmīty ādeḥ/ avyākṛtacittāvasthāyām ahaṃkāro nimittam, ahaṃ patracchedyāni karomīti/ tataś cānātmany ālayavijñāne ātmaviparyāso yas tan nimittam ity uktaṃ bhavati/

[*3a][21] kārikābhisambandhaṃ kurvann āha/ *ete hy ātmamohādaya ity ādi*/

navabhūmayo 'tra kāmadhātuḥ, catvāri dhyānāni, catvāraś cārūpyā veditavyāḥ/ pariśiṣṭaṃ subodham/

sandehanivṛttyartham āha/

YATRAJA[S TANMAYAIR]

ity ādi/ etad vivṛṇoti *yatra jāta ity ādinā*/ yasmin dhātau yasyāṃ vā bhūmau jāto bhavati prāṇī tad dhātukais tadbhūmikair eva satkāyadṛṣṭyādibhis tat samprayujyate, nānyadhātukair nānyabhūmikaiḥ/

sūtraṃ darśayann āha/ *kiṃ punaś caturbhir evety ādi*/ subodham etat/ bhāṣyakāra āha/ *nety āhety ādi*/ etad vivṛṇvann āha/

ANYAIḤ SPARŚĀDYAIŚ CA

ity ādi/ etad api subodham/

caśabdārthaṃ darśayati/ *caśabda ity ādi*/ tataś ca na kevalam ātmadṛṣṭyādibhiḥ samprayujyate manaḥ kiṃ tarhi? sparśādibhiś cānyaiḥ samprayujyata ity uktaṃ bhavati *sparśādyair ity ādinā/* ādyaśabdārthaṃ darśayati/ ādau bhavā ādyāḥ/ kiṃ punaḥ kāraṇam etat sparśādibhiḥ samprayujyata ity āha/ *ete hi pañcadharmā ity ādi/* yasmād ete pañca sparśādayaḥ dharmāḥ sarvatragā iṣyante, tasmāt sarvavijñānaiḥ samprayujyante/ eṣām api dhātubhūminiyamaṃ darśayann āha/ *etair apīty ādi/* gatārtham etat/

atraiva vyākhyānāntaraṃ kurvann āha/ *yadi tat kliṣṭaṃ mana ity ādi, athavā anyair ity ādi/* ye mūlavijñānena samprayuktāḥ sparśādayas tebhyo vyavacchedārtham anyaiḥ sparśādyair ity uktam/ tathā hi mūlavijñāne 'nivṛtāvyākṛtāḥ sparśādaya iṣyante, kliṣṭe punar manasi manovat nivṛtāvyākṛtāḥ/ sūtrasambandhaṃ kurvann āha/ *yadi tat kliṣṭaṃ mana ity ādi/* yadi sarvāsu kliṣṭāvyākṛtāvasthāsv aviśeṣeṇa kliṣṭaṃ manaḥ pravartate, na tasya nivṛttir astīti prāptam/ yāvac ca tan na nivartate tāvat kuto mokṣaḥ? tasmāt mokṣābhāvaḥ prasajyate prāṇīnām/ siddhāntavādy āha/ *na prasajyata ity ādi/* na mokṣābhāvaḥ prasajyate, *yasmād.*

[ARHATO NA TAT/
NA NIRODHASAMĀPATTAU MĀRGE LOKOTTARE[22] NA[22] CA//7//]

arhataḥ kliṣṭaṃ mano na vidyate, nirodhasamāpattyavasthāyāṃ na vidyate, 'lokottare ca mārgeṇa(mārge na)',[23] vajropamasamādhyākhyena prahīyate/ evaṃ kliṣṭaṃ manas tenaivānantaryamārgeṇa sarveṇa sarvaṃ prahīyate/[*3b][24] tataś ca yathā saṃkleśā arhato na vidyante evaṃ tadā api na vidyate/ atha anāgāminaḥ kasmān nāstīty āha/ *ākiñcanyāyatanavītarāgasyāpīty ādi/* yaḥ khalv ākiñcanyāyatanavītarāgo 'nāgāmī nirodhasamapāttilābhī tasya nirodhasamāpattyavasthāyāṃ kilṣṭaṃ mano na vidyate/ yasmān mārgabalena nirodhasamāpattir labhyate, tasmān mārgavat tatrāpi tatkālamātraṃ na vidyate/ atha vyutthitasya kutas taj jāyata ity āha/ *nirodhāc cety ādi/* yadā nirodhasamāpatter vyutthito bhavati tadālayavijñānād eva punar utpadyate/ tatra hy asya vāsanā astīti/ mārgasthasyābhāvaṃ darśayann āha/ *mārge* lokottaro bhavati/ vyākhyātārtham etat/

nanu ca '*mārge na ca*' ity evam vaktavyaṃ, kimarthaṃ lokottaragrahaṇaṃ kṛtam ity āha/ lokottaragrahaṇaṃ laukikād vyavacchedārtham iti/ subodham etat/ kimarthaṃ laukiko vyavacchidyata ity āha/ *laukike tv ity ādi/* tuśabdo yasmād arthe, yasmāl laukike mārge kliṣṭasya manasaḥ pravṛttir iṣyata eva/ kasmāl lokottare na pravartata ity āha/ *nairātmyadarśanasyety ādi/* yasmān nairātmyadarśanam ātmagrāhasya pratipakṣas tasmāl lokottare mārge kliṣṭaṃ mano na pravartitum utsahate/ na hi vipakṣapratipakṣau yugapad bhavataḥ/ tataś ca vipakṣapratipakṣayor yaugapadyābhāvāt lokottare mārge tatkālamātraṃ kliṣṭaṃ mano na pravartate/ yadā tu lokottarāt mārgād vyutthito bhavati tadālayavijñānād eva punar utpadyate/ upasaṃharann āha/

DVITĪYAḤ PARIṆĀMO 'YAṂ

ity ādi/ yaḥ pūrvam uddiṣṭa āsit sa idānīṃ nirdiṣṭa ity arthaḥ/ tṛtīyapariṇatisambandhaṃ darśayann āha/ *dvitīyapariṇāmānantaram ity ādi/* subodham etat/ katamaḥ sa ity āha/

TṚTĪYAḤ ṢAḌVIDHASYA YĀ/
[VIṢAYASYOPALABDHIḤ SĀ]

ity ādi/ ṣaḍvidhasya viṣayasya yā upalabdhiḥ sā tṛtīyo vijñānapariṇāma iti sūtrārthaḥ/ vijñānapariṇāmo 'tra vyāhartavyaḥ/ padārthādhigamapūrvako vākyārthādhigama iti padārthaṃ darśayann āha/ *ṣaḍvidhasyety ādi/* subodham etat/

sā punar ity ādināsyāḥ prabhedaṃ pṛcchati/ siddhāntavādī prabhedaṃ darśayann āha/

KUŚALĀKUŚALĀDVAYĀ [//8//]

iti/ etad vivṛṇvann āha/ *kuśalety ādi.* [*4a][25] advayagrahaṇenāvyakṛtocyate/ pariśeṣaṃ subodham/ kuśalādisvarūpaṃ darśayann āha/ *alobhādveṣāmohair ity ādi/*

etad api caitasikasvarūpe tat saṃkhyāyāṃ ca sandihyamānaḥ pṛcchati/ *sā punaḥ kīdṛśair ity ādi/* sandeha[dvayaṃ] nirākurvann āha/

SARVATRAGAIR [VINIYATAIḤ KUŚALAIŚ CAITASAIR ASAU/
SAMPRAYUKTĀ TATHĀ KLEŚAIR UPAKLEŚAIS TRIVEDANĀ
[//9//]

ity ādi/ sarvatragādibhiḥ samprayujyata iti saṃkṣiptaḥ sūtrārthaḥ/ sarvatragādiṣv api paraḥ sandihyamānaḥ pṛcchati/[26] *ya eta ity ādi/* subodham/ siddhāntavādī tat pradarśanārtham āha/

ĀDYĀḤ SPARŚĀDAYAḤ

sarvatragā abhipretāḥ/ kasmāt sarvatragā ādyā ucyanta ity āha/ *ādau nirdiṣṭatvād ādyā iti/* etad vivṛṇvann āha/ *tathā hi sarvatragā ity ādi/* yasmāt sarvatragā anantarakārikāyāṃ prathamaṃ nirdiṣṭāḥ tasmād ādyā ucyante/ yais tu sparśādaya ādyā iti vyākhyānaṃ kriyate te atyantāsambaddhaṃ vyācakṣate/ tathā hy anantarakārikāyāṃ sarvatragā ādau nirdiṣṭā na sparśādayaḥ/ sparśādaya ity atra samāsaṃ kurvann āha/ *sparśa ādir eṣām*[27] *ity ādi/* gatārtham etat/

atha kasmād ete sarvatragā ucyanta ity āha/ *te punar ity ādi/* yasmād ete sparśādayaḥ sarvaṃ cittam anugacchanti tasmāt sarvatragā ucyante/ kathaṃ jñāyata ity āha/ *tathā mūlavijñāna*[28] *ity ādi/* yasmād ālayavijñāne 'pi, tasmāt sarvacittam anugacchantīti siddham/

viniyatān adhikṛtyāhety anena kārikābhisambandhaṃ darśayati/

CHANDĀDHIMOKṢASMṚTAYAḤ [SAHA/ SAMĀDHIDHĪBHYĀṂ NIYATĀḤ]

ity adinā viniyatān darśayati/ chandādayaḥ pañca viniyatā iti sūtrārthaḥ/ kasmād ete viniyatā ucyanta ity āha/ *viśeṣa ity ādi/* yasmād ete viśeṣe niyatā ucyante/ tathā hy eṣāṃ viśeṣa eva viṣayo na sarvaḥ/

ko 'yaṃ chando nāmety āha/ *tatra chanda ity ādi/* abhimate vastuni yo 'bhilāṣaḥ sa chandaḥ/ abhipretagrahaṇena pratiniyataviṣayatvam jñāpitaṃ bhavati/ yasmād anabhiprete chando na jāyate/ kiṃ punar abhipretam ity āha/ *darśanādīn ity ādi/* subodham etat/ chandasya paryāyaṃ darśayann āha/ *tatra darśanety ādi/* darśanaśravaṇādīnāṃ yathārthatā sa chandaś cocyate 'bhilāṣaś ca/ karmāsya darśayann āha/ *sa ca vīryārambhety ādi/* vīryārambhasya nimittabhāvopagamanaṃ karmāsyety arthaḥ/

atha ko 'yam adhimokṣa ity āha/ *adhimokṣo niścita ity ādi/* pramāṇaparidṛṣṭe vastuni yaḥ sampratyayaḥ so 'dhimokṣa iti saṃkṣiptārthaḥ/ niścitagrahaṇaṃ kimartham ity āha/[*4b][29] *niścitagrahaṇam ity ādi/* subodham etat/ kim idaṃ niścitam ity āha/ *yuktita ity ādi/* pratyakṣānumānābhyām āptāgamena vā yad vastu niḥsaṃdigdhaṃ kṛtaṃ tan niścitam ucyate/ yenaiva cānityādyākāreṇa tad vastu niścitaṃ tenaivākāreṇa tasya vastunaś cetasi sanniveśanam, evam etan nānyatheti yad avadhāraṇam, so 'dhimokṣa ity ucyate/ karmāsya darśayann āha/ *sa cāyam ity ādi/* svasiddhāntād anapaharaṇaṃ karmāsyety arthaḥ/ katham etat karmāsyety āha/ *adhimuktipradhāno hīty ādi/* yasmād yo 'dhimuktipradhānaḥ sa svasiddhāntād paravādibhir apahartuṃ na śakyate tasmād etat karmāsya/

atha keyaṃ smṛtir ity āha/ *smṛtiḥ saṃstute*[30] *vastunīty ādi/* pūrvānubhūtasya vastuno yaś cittād aprabhraṃśaḥ punar āmukhīkaraṇam, tasmāt smṛtiḥ/ kim idaṃ saṃstutaṃ nāmety āha/ *saṃstutaṃ vastu ity ādi/* subodham etat/ kasmāt smṛtir asampramoṣa ucyata ity āha/ *ālambanety ādi/* ālambanasya grahaṇaṃ yat pūrvam āsīt tasya yasmād avipraṇāśakāraṇaṃ smṛtis tasmād asaṃpramoṣa ucyate/ tataś cāyam avipraṇāśakāraṇatvād asaṃpramośa ity uktaṃ bhavati/

abhilapanasvarūpaṃ darśayann āha/ *pūrvagṛhītasyety ādi/* yat pūrvagṛhītaṃ vastu tasya puna ālambanākārasya smaraṇaṃ yat sābhilapanatā/ svārthe bhāvapratyayaṃ darśayann āha/ *abhilapanam evety ādi/* subodhaṃ/ karmāsya darśayann āha/ *sā punar ity ādi/* ālambanavikṣepaṇaṃ karmāsyāḥ/ yasmād yadā cittasyālambanaṃ punaḥ punar āmukhīkaraṇam, [31] tadā ālambanāntare ākārāntare vā cittasyāvikṣepo bhavati/ tasmād avikṣepakarmikā smṛtir ucyate/

ko 'yaṃ samādhir ity āha/ *samādhir upaparīkṣya ity ādi/* nirūpayitavye vastuni yā cittasyaikāgratā sā samādhiḥ/[31] kenākāreṇopaparīkṣyam ity āha/ *upaparīkṣyaṃ vastv ity ādi/* guṇata upaparīkṣyaṃ doṣato vā/ nirodhamārgasatye śāntapraṇītādibhir ākārair guṇata upaparīkṣitavye/ duḥkhasamudayasatye 'nityādibhir ākārair doṣata upaparīkṣitavye/ etasmin [*5a][32] yā ekālambanatā saikāgratocyate/ karmāsya darśayann āha/ *jñānasanniśrayety ādi/* jñānanimittabhāvopagamanaṃ karmāsya yasmāt samāhite citte yathābhūtaprajñānaṃ sambhavati/

keyam dhīr ity āha/ *dhīḥ prajñeti/* etad vivṛṇvann āha/ *sāpy upaparīkṣitavyety ādi/* upaparīkṣitavye eva vastuni yogavihitaḥ, ayogavihito 'nyathā vā, yaḥ pravicayaḥ sā prajñā/ vyutpattiṃ kurvann āha/ *prat(v)icinotīty ādi/* pravicayārthaṃ darśayann āha/ *saṅkīrṇasvasāmānyalakṣaṇeṣv ivety ādi/* saṅkīrṇasvasāmānyalakṣaṇeṣv iva dharmeṣu yaḥ samyaṅgmithyā vā vipākāvabodhaḥ sa pravicayaḥ/ kaḥ punaṛ yogavihita ity āha/ *yuktir yoga iti/* yogaśabdena yukir abhidhīyata iti/ tam eva prabhedena darśayann āha/ *sa punar āptopadeśa* ity ādi/ subodham etat/ vihitārthaṃ darśayann āha/ *tena triprakāreṇety adī/* upaparīkṣye vastuni yaḥ pravicayo janitaḥ sa yogavihita ucyate/ tasya prabhedaṃ darśayann āha/ *sa punaḥ śrutamaya ity ādi*/ subodham etat/

śrutamayādīnāṃ svarūpaṃ darśayann āha/ *tatrāptavacanety ādi*/ āptasya vacanaṃ pramāṇīkṛto(-kṛtya) yo 'vabodho jāyate sa śrutamaya ucyate/ yuktyā nirūpayatāṃ yo jāyate sa cintāmaya ucyate/ yaḥ samādhibalena jāyate sa bhāvanāmaya ucyate/ pramāṇabhūtaḥ puruṣa āpta ucyate/ nidhyānaṃ nirūpaṇam/

ayogasya prabhedaṃ darśayann āha/ *ayoga ity ādi*/ asamyakpravartitaḥ samādhir mithyāpraṇihita ucyate/ pariśiṣṭaṃ subodham/ vihitārthaṃ darśayann āha/ *tenāyogenety ādi*/ gatārtham etat/

tṛtīyaṃ prakāraṃ darśayann āha/ *upapattipratilambhikety ādi*/ yaḥ sahajayā prajñayā padārthāvabodho yaś ca laukikavyavahārasya krayavikrayāder avabodhaḥ sa na yogavihito nāyogavihito ucyate/ upapattipratilambhika iti/ upapattyā pratilambha upapattipratilambhaḥ, so 'syāstīty upapattipratilambhikaḥ/ sahaja ity arthaḥ/ [*5b][33] vihita iti janitaḥ kṛta iti yāvat/ karmāsya darśayann āha/ *eṣa cety ādi*/saṃśayavyāvartanaṃ karmāsyāḥ/ tathā hi prajñayā dharmān pravicinvatas teṣu niścayaṃ pratilabhate/ niścayalābhāc ca saṃśayavyāvartanam/

kim ete sahopajāyante, uta pratyekaśa ity āha/ *ete hi pañca dharmā ity ādi*/ parasparaṃ vyatiricyāpy ete pañca dharmā vartante[34] na saha evety arthaḥ/ evaṃ ca yatra citte adhimokṣas tatra nāvaśyam itarair bhavitavyam/ evam anyeṣv api vaktavyam/ abhipretaniścitasaṃstutopaparīkṣyagrahaṇenaiṣāṃ pratiniyataviṣayatvaṃ jñāpitam/ tathā hy anabhiprete chando nāsti/ aniścite 'dhimokṣo nāsti/ asaṃstute smṛtir nāsti/ anupaparīkṣye samādhiprajñayor abhāvaḥ/

kecit punar enaṃ grantham anyathā paṭhanti/ ete hi pañca dharmā na parasparaṃ vyatiricya vartante, avaśyaṃ ca yatrādhimokṣas tatrāvaśyam itarair api bhavitavyam iti/ evaṃ te vinaṣṭaṃ paṭhanti/ tathā hy anāgate vastuni yad[ā]bhilāṣo jāyate tadā tasmin smṛtir nāsti, anubhūtaviṣayatvāt tasyāḥ/ yadā cānupaparīkṣye vastuni chandādayo bhavanti tadā tatra samādhir nāsti, upaparīkṣyavastuviṣayatvāt tasya/ yadā vā 'niścite vastunie chandādayo bhavanti tadā tatrādhimokṣo nāsti, niścitavastuni viṣayatvāt tasya/ tataś ca kathaṃ parasparato na vyati[ri]cya vartante/ vakṣyamāṇenābhisambandhaṃ darśayann āha/ *uktā viniyatā ity ādi*/ subodhaṃ etat/

taṃ(sad? kuśalān?) darśayann āha/

ŚRADDHĀTHA HRĪR
APATRAPĀ[//10//
ALOBHĀDITRAYAṂ VĪRYAṂ PRASRABDHIḤ SĀPRAMĀDIKĀ/
AHIṂSĀ KUŚALĀḤ]

ity ādi/ eṣāṃ saṃkhyāṃ darśa[ya]nn āha/ *ete ekā[da]śa ity ādi/* subodham etat/

śraddhāsvarūpaṃ darśayann āha/ [*tatra śraddhety ādi/*][35] śubhāśubheṣu karmasu, iṣṭāniṣṭeṣu phaleṣu, duḥkhādiṣu satyeṣu, sambuddhādiṣu ca ratneṣu, yaḥ sampratyayo yaḥ prasādo yo 'bhilāṣaḥ sā śraddhā/ tathā hi śraddhā triprakārā paravartate/ sampratyayādīnāṃ viṣayavibhāgaṃ darśayann āha/ *sati guṇavatīty ādi/* guṇavad aguṇavad vā yad vastu vidyate tatrāstitva-[*6a][36] sampratyayākārā śraddhā/ yat pu[na]r vastu vidyate guṇavac ca tatra prasādākārā/ yat punar vastu vidyate guṇavac ca, prāptum utpādayituṃ vā śakyā, tatrābhilāṣākārā/ prasādasvarūpaṃ darśayann āha/ *cetasaḥ prasāda ity ādi/* yasmāc chraddhā cittakāluṣyeṇa saha virudhyate, tat samprayoge sati kleśopakleśasaṃjñitamala-kāluṣyavigamāc cittaṃ śraddhām āśritya prasīdati, tasmāc cetasaḥ prasāda ucyate/ cittakāluṣyaśabdena kleśavāsanocyate/ karmāsyā darśayann āha/ *sā punaś chandety ādi/* pravṛttyabhilāṣasaṃjānana-karmakā/ tathā hi jātasampratyaye(-yaḥ) śakye vastuni utpannābhilāṣapravṛttiś chandaṃ kurute/

hriyaḥ svarūpaṃ darśayann āha/ *hrīr ity ādi/* ātmānaṃ dharmaṃ cāpekṣamāṇasyāvadyena yā lajjopajāyate, sā hrīr ity ucyate/ kiṃ punar anavadyam ity āha/ *sadbhir garhitatvād ity ādi/* yasmāt sadbhir garhitam aniṣṭavipākajananaṃ pāpam evāvadyam ucyate/ tena cāvadyena kṛtena yaś cittasya sankoca upajāyate sā lajjā/ saiva ca hrīr ity ucyate/ karmāsyā darśayann āha/ *iyaṃ cety ādi/* duścaritanivāraṇakarmakety arthaḥ/

apatrāpyasvarūpaṃ darśayann āha/ *apatrāpyam ity ādi/* yā lokāpekṣayā 'vadyena lajjā tad apatrāpyam/ yasmād etal loke garhitam, maṃ caivaṃ karmakāriṇaṃ viditvā loko garhāṃ kariṣyatīti, tasmād akīrtibhayāvadyena lajjate/ garhā nindā/ akīrtir aślokaśabdenocyate/ karmāsya darśayann āha/ *idam apīty* ādi/ gatārtham etat/

alobhaḥ ka ity āha/ *alobha ity ādi/* lobhasya pratipakṣabhūto yo dharmaḥ so 'trālobha[ḥ]/ [ko lobha][37] ity āha/ *lobho nāmety ādi/* saṃsāre saṃsāropakaraṇeṣu ca yā saktiḥ prārthanā ca sa lobhaḥ/ tasya pratipakṣabhūta alobhaḥ/ tataś ca saṃsāre tad upakaraṇeṣu ca hastyaśvādiṣv asaktir[38] vaimukhyam aspṛhā anutkaṇṭhā 'lobha ity uktam bhavati/

adveṣam āha/ *adveṣa ity ādi/* dveṣasya pratipakṣabhūto maitrīsvabhāvo dharmaḥ adveṣaḥ/ dveṣa eva tāvat ka ity āha/ *dveṣo hīty ādi/* apakāriṣu sattveṣu duḥkhe duḥkhahetuṣu ca viṣakaṇṭakādiṣu ya āghātaḥ sa dveṣaḥ/ adveṣas tu dveṣapratipakṣatvāt sattveṣu duḥkhaduḥkhahetuṣu cānāghātarūpo draṣṭavyaḥ/ karmāsya darśayann āha/ *ayam apīty ādi/* gatārtham etat/

amohaṃ darśayann āha/ *amoha ity ādi/* mohasya pratipakṣabhūto yathābhūtā-[*6b][39] vabodhasvabhāvo dharmaḥ so 'trāmohaḥ/ moha eva tāvat ka ity āha/ *moha iti karmaphala ity ādi/* karmādiṣu yad ajñānaṃ sa mohaḥ/ amohas tu tatpratipakṣatvāt satyādiṣu sampratipattisvabhāvo draṣṭavyaḥ/ karmāsya darśayati/ *ayam apīty ādi/* gatārtham etat/

vīryasvarūpam āha/ *vīryam ity ādi/* kausīdyapratipakṣabhūtaḥ kuśalakarmaṇi yaś cetasa utsāhaḥ tad vīryam, na tu kliṣṭe karmaṇi/ yaḥ punaḥ kliṣṭe karmaṇy utsāhaḥ, sa kutsitatvāt kausīdyam eva, na vīryaṃ; kutsite vastuni sīdatīti kṛtvā tad api kausīdyam eva/ tataś ca dvividhaṃ kausīdyam ālasyalakṣaṇaṃ kliṣṭaś cotsāhaḥ/ karmāsya darśayann āha/ *etac cety ādi/* kuśalapakṣasya paripūraṇaṃ pariniṣpādanaṃ ca karmāsya/

prasrabdhiḥ katamety āha/ *prasrabdhir ity ādi/* dauṣṭhulyasya pratipakṣabhūtā kāyacittayor yā karmaṇyatā sā prasrabdhiḥ/ kim idaṃ dauṣṭhulyam ity āha/ *dauṣṭhulyam ity ādi/* kāyacittayor akarmaṇyatā dauṣṭhulyam ucyate/ yadi vā sāṃkleśikānāṃ dharmāṇāṃ bījaṃ dauṣṭhulyam/ kuta etad ity āha/ *tad apagama ity ādi/* yasmāt sāṃkleśikadharmabījāpagame sati prasrabdhir bhavati tasmāt tad api dauṣṭhulyam/

atha keyaṃ kāyakarmaṇyatā ity āha/ *tatra kāyakarmaṇyatety ādi/* kāyasya svakāryeṣu laghusamutthānatā yato bhavati sā kāyakarmaṇyatocyate/ laghusamutthānateti pāṭavam/

cittakarmaṇyatāṃ darśayann āha/ *cittakarmaṇyatety ādi/* samyagmanasikāraprayuktasya yogino yac cittaṃ tasyālhādalāghavanimittaṃ yac caitasikaṃ dharmāntaraṃ sā cittakarmaṇyatā/ ālhādaḥ sukham/ lāghavaṃ pāṭavam/ kuta ity āha/ *yad yogāc cittam ity ādi/* yasmāt tasya caitasikasya dharmasya yogāc cittam ālambane pravartate, atas tac cittakarmaṇyatety ucyate/

yadi nāmātra caitasikaṃ dharmāntaraṃ prasrabdhir iti keyaṃ kāyaprasrabdhir ity āha/ *kāyasya punar ity ādi/* kāyasya spraṣṭavyaviśeṣa eva kaścit prītyā hṛtaḥ kāyaprasrabdhir veditavyā/ kuta etad ity āha/ *prītamanasa ity ādi/* yasmāt prītaṃ yadā mano bhavati tadā kāyaḥ prasrabhyata ity uktam sūtre/ karmāsya darśayann āha/ *iyaṃ ca tad vaśenety ādi/* yasmāt prasrabdhivaśeṇāśrayaparāvṛttir bhavati tasmād aśeṣasya kleśāvaraṇasya niṣkarṣaṇaṃ karmāsyāḥ/

sāpramādikety etad vivṛṇvann āha/ *sāpramādikety ādi/* subodham etat/ vyutpattimātreṇa svarūpam asyā na vijñāyata iti pṛcchati/ *kā punar asāv ity ādi/* siddhāntavādy āha/ *upekṣeti/*[*7a][40] upekṣātra sāpramādikā 'bhipretety arthaḥ/ paraḥ kāraṇaṃ pṛcchann āha/ *kuta etad iti/* siddhāntavādī kāraṇaṃ darśayann āha/ *ekāntakuśalatvād ity ādi/* yasmād ekāntakuśalā upekṣā kuśalāś ca caitasikāḥ sarvā eveha nirdeṣṭum adhikṛtāḥ/ na t(c)āsyāḥ śraddhādivat sākṣān nirdeśaḥ kṛtaḥ/ ekādaśakuśalacaitasikavyatirekeṇa cānye kuśalāś caitasikā na sambhavanti/ ataḥ pāriśeṣyād upekṣaiva sāpramādikāśabdenābhidhīyate/ etad uktaṃ bhavati/ sarveṇa sarvam upekṣayā sahaikādaśa kuśalāḥ/ tatra daśānāṃ śṛṅgagrāhikayā nirdeśaḥ kṛtaḥ/ upekṣātra svanāmnā na nirdiṣṭā/ tasmāt saivātra sāpramādikāśabdenocyate/

kaḥ punar apramāda ity āha/ *tatrāpramāda ity ādi/* etad eva vivṛṇvann āha/ *yān alobhādīn*[41] *ity ādi* yāṅkāṃścid alobhādīn āśrityākuśalān dharmān prajahāti, akuśaladharmapratipakṣabhūtān kuśalān dharmān bhāvayati, te 'lobhādayo 'pramādaśabdenocyante/ ata evāsau pramādapratipakṣo bhavati, yasmāt pramāda etadviparītaḥ/ vaiparītyaṃ cāsya vakṣyati/ karmāsya darśayann āha/ *sa punar ity ādi/* sarveṣāṃ laukikalokottarāṇāṃ guṇānāṃ sampadaḥ paripūraṇam asya karma/

upekṣā katamety āha/ *upekṣā cittasamatety ādi/* layauddhatyavigamād yā cittasya samatā, vinā prayatnena yā cittasya svarasavāhitā, layauddhatyapratipakṣeṣu prāmodyasaṃvejanīyamanaskāreṣv ābhogam akurvataś ca yā cittasyānābhogatā sopekṣā/

kiṃ punar etāvadbhiḥ padaiḥ prayojanam ity āha/ *ebhis tribhiḥ*[42] *padair ity ādi/* subodham etat/

atha keyaṃ cittasamatety āha/ *tatra layauddhatyaṃ cety ādi/* yadā cittaṃ līnaṃ bhavati, uddhataṃ vā, tadā viṣama ucyate/ layauddhatyayor abhāvāt prathamataś cittaṃ na līnaṃ nāpy uddhataṃ bhavati tadā samatety ucyate/ itīyaṃ cittasamatā/

cittapras(ś)aṭhatāṃ pradarśayann āha/ *tato 'nabhisaṃskāreṇety ādi/* cittasamatottarakālaṃ vinaiva prayatnena samāhitasya cetaso yogānurūpyeṇa samasyaiva yā anuvṛttiḥ sā cittasya pras(ś)aṭhatā/ tasyāṃ punar avasthāyāṃ yogino layauddhatyaviṣayā āśaṅkā samatottarakālaṃ[*7b][43] vidyate/ sā nāmaiṣā durātmanī punar api bhaviṣyatīty evaṃrupā/ tathā hy eṣā sama[tā]vasthā idānīm eva saṃprāptā na tu cirakālam abhyastā/ tasmād asti śaṅkāsambhavaḥ/

cittānābhogatāṃ darśayann āha/ *tato bhāvanety ādi/* tata uttarakālaṃ yadā sā bhāvanā prakarṣaṃ gatā bhavati tadā tad vipakṣayor layauddhatyayor dūrīkṛtatvāt tadviṣayā śaṅkā na jāyate tataś ca layauddhatyapratipakṣanimitteṣu pra(ā)modyasaṃvejanīyamanaskāreṣu yogī ābhogaṃ na karoti/ ābhogam akurvato 'nābhogāvasthitacittasya yogino yāvasthā sā cittānābhogatocyate/[44] karmāsya darśayann āha/ *iyam cety ādi/* sarveṣāṃ kleśopakleśānām anavakāśasya sanniśrayadānaṃ karmāsyāḥ/

avihiṃsā katamety āha/ *avihiṃsety ādi/* etad vivṛṇvann āha/ *vadhabandhanādibhir ity ādi/* vadhabandhanādibhir upaghātakāraṇaiḥ sattvānām anupatāpanam aviheṭhanam avihiṃsocyate/ sā ca sattveṣu kāruṇyasukhaṃ ruṇaddhi/ vyutpattim asyā darśayann āha/ *kaṃ ruṇaddhīty ādi/* kaṃśabdena sukham ucyate, tataś ca sukhaṃ ruṇaddhīty uktam bhavati/ ruṇaddhīty āvṛṇoti/ katham etaj jñāyate? yasmāt kāruṇikaḥ paraduḥkhaduḥkhī bhavati tasmāt kāruṇyasukhaṃ ruṇaddhi/ karmāsya darśayann āha/ *iyam cety ādi/* sattvānām aviheṭhanaṃ karmāsyāḥ/

vakṣyamāṇasyābhisambandhaṃ kurvann āha/ *uktā ekādaśety ādi/* gatārtham etat/

kleśān darśayann āha/

KLEŚĀ RĀGAPRATIGHA [MŪḌHAYAḤ//11//
MĀNADṚGVICIKITSĀŚ CA]

ādaya ity ādi/ samāsaṃ darśayann āha/ *rāgaś cety ādi/* gatārtham etat/ rāgaḥ katama ity āha/ *tatra rāga ity ādi/* bhave bhogeṣu ca yad adhyavasānaṃ yā ca prārthanā sa rāga ucyate/ pratyutpanneṣv adhyavasānam anāgateṣu prārthanā/[45]

pratighaḥ katama ity āha/ *pratighaḥ sattveṣv ity ādi/* yaḥ sattveṣv āghāto yā sattveṣu rukṣacittatā yena cāviṣṭaḥ sattvānāṃ vadhabandhanādikam anarthaṃ cintayati sa pratighaḥ/ karmāsya darśayann āha/ *sa pu[na]r ity ādi/* etad vivṛṇvann āha/ *sparśaḥ sukham ity ādi/* subodham etat/ katham etaj jñāyata ity āha/ *āghātacittasyety ādi/* yasmād dviṣṭacittasyāvaśyaṃ duḥkhadaurmanasye samudācarataḥ/ tat samudācārāc cittaṃ tapyate, [*8a][46] upatapte ca cetasi tad anuvidhānāt kāyasyāpy upatāpo bhavati/ tataś ca sarveṣv evāsyeryāpatheṣu saduḥkhasavighāto vihāro bhavati/ viharaṇaṃ vihāraḥ/ yaś ca pratihatacittasya na kiñcid duścaritaṃ dūre tasmāt pratighasya/ etad yathoditaṃ karmākhyātam/

mohaḥ katama ity āha/ *moho 'pāyeṣv ity ādi/* apāyādiṣu yad ajñānaṃ sa mohaḥ/ aviparīte hetuphalasambandha iti/ śubhasyetaṃ phalam aśubhasyāniṣṭaṃ phalam ity aviparītatā/ karmāsya darśayann āha/ *ayam cety ādi/* etad vivṛṇvann āha/ *tatra kleśakarmajanmātmaka ity ādi/* kleśātmakaḥ karmātmako janmātmakaś ca trividhas saṃkleśaḥ/ tasya trividhasya saṃkleśasya pūrvapūrvasaṃkleśanimittād uttarottarasya saṃkleśasyātmalābha utpattir abhidhīyate/ asyās tūtpatteḥ sanniśrayadānam eva veditavyam/ yasmān mūḍhasyaiva mithyājñānādikaḥ saṃkleśa pravartate, nāmūḍhasya/

mānaḥ katama ity āha/ *māna ity ādi/* etad vivṛṇvann āha/ *māno hīty ādi/* sarva eva hi mānaḥ satkāyadṛṣṭiṃ niśritya[47] pravartate/ svabhāvas tv asya cittonnatisvābhāvyam/ satkāyadṛṣṭyāśrayo māna iti/ kuta etad ity āha/ *tathā hy ātmātmīyabhāvam ity ādi/* yasmāt skandheṣv ātmātmīyatvam adhyāropyāyam aham, aham itthaṃ paṇḍitaḥ,[48] idaṃ mamaiva dharmaiśvaryam, ity ādinā viśeṣeṇātmānam unnamayati, anyebhyo 'dhikaṃ manyate/ tasmān mānaḥ satkāyadṛṣṭisanniśraya ucyate/ karmāsya darśayann āha/ *sa cāgauravety ādi/* agauravasya duḥkhotpatteś ca sanniśrayadānaṃ karmāsya/

kim idam agauravam ity āha/ *agauravaṃ guruṣv ity ādi/* ācāryādiṣu guruṣu tad anyeṣu ca guṇavatsu pudgaleṣu yā stabdhatā kāyavācayor apraśṛtatā[49] tad agauravam/ stabdhateti praṇativaidhuryam/ apraśṛtate[50] ti kāyenānabhyutthānaṃ vācā svāgatādy akaraṇam/ keyaṃ duḥkhotpattir ity āha/ *duḥkhotpattiḥ punar ity ādi/* yā anyasya janmana utpattir iyaṃ duḥkhotpattir abhipretā/ prabhedam asyā darśayann āha/ *sā punaś cittonnatir ity ādi/* yady api cittonnatisvarūpaṃ na bhidyate[51] tathāpi tan nimittabhedena saptadhā bhidyate/ *māno 'timāna ity ādinā* taṃ prabhedaṃ darśayati/ mānaḥ katama ity āha/ *hīnāt kulavijñānavittādibhir ity ādi/* kulād iti hināc chreyān asmi/ sadṛśena kulādibhiḥ sadṛśa iti [*8b][52] yā cittasyonnatir ayaṃ mānaḥ/ kulādibhis tu sadṛśāt tyāgaśīlādibhiḥ śreyān asmi/ śreyasā vā kulādibhiḥ sadṛśo 'smi vijñānavittādibhir[53] ity evaṃ yā cittasyonnatir atimānaḥ/ kulādibhiḥ śreyaso 'ham eva śreyān vijñānavittādibhir[54] ity evam yā cittasyonnatir ayaṃ mānātimānaḥ/ ete ca trayo 'pi vastukāḥ/ tathā hy ete satsv eva kulādiṣu pravartante/ anyathā mithyāmānān na bhidyeran/[55] kevalaṃ tv eko hīnāpekṣayā, dvitīyaḥ sadṛśāpekṣayā, tṛtīya utkṛṣṭāpekṣayātmānam utkarṣayatīti viśeṣaḥ/ vijñānaśabdenātra citrakarmādiṣu kauśalyam ucyate/ vittaśabdena dravyam ucyate/ *asmimāna ity ādi/* pañcasūpādānaskandheṣu bhūtārthenātmīyarahiteṣv api, ātmātmīyābhiniveśād yā cittasyonnatir upajāyate so 'smimāna ucyate/

ūnamānaḥ katama ity āha/ *ūnamāna ity ādi/* bahunāntareṇa kulādibhir viśiṣṭād alpenāntareṇa kulādibhiḥ hīno 'smīti yā cittasyonnatir upajāyate 'yam ūnamāna ucyate/

mithyāmānaḥ katama ity āha/ *mithyāmāna ity ādi/* aguṇavataḥ sato guṇavān asmīti yā cittasyonnatir upajāyate sa mithyāmānaḥ/ kim ity ayam mithyāmāna ity āha/ *aguṇā hīty ādi/* dauḥśīlyādayo 'trāguṇāḥ/ te yasya vidyante puruṣa sa aguṇavān/ tataś ca guṇavān asmīty anena dānaśīlādyabhāve 'pi yasmād guṇavatvam abhyupagataṃ bhavati tasmān nirvastukatvān mithyāmāna ucyate/ yady api doṣā nibandhanaṃ bhava(n)ti te guṇā na bhavantīti guṇāpekṣayā nirvastukatvaṃ vidyata eva/ nirvastukatvād iti nirv(n)ibandhanatvād ity arthaḥ/

dṛṣṭiḥ katamety āha/ *drśī(dṛg i)tyādi/* yady api drśī(dṛg i)ti sāmānyena nirdeśa kṛtas tathāpi pañcaiva satkāyadṛṣṭyādikā dṛṣṭayaḥ sambadhyante yasmād iha kleśā adhikṛtāḥ, tāś ca kleśasvabhāvāḥ/ na tu laukikī samyagdṛṣṭir gṛhyate anāsravā vā/ kiṃ kṛto 'yam āsāṃ bheda ity āha/ *āsāṃ tv ity ādi/* yady apy āsāṃ kliṣṭatvena nitīraṇākāratvena[56] ca viśeṣo nāsti, tathāpy ālambanabhedād ākārabhedāc ca parasparato bhedaḥ/ nitīraṇaṃ nirūpaṇam/

satkāyadṛṣṭiḥ katamety āha/ *tatra satkāyadṛṣṭir ity ādi/* yat pañcasūpādānaskandheṣv ātmātmīyākāreṇa ca darśanaṃ sā satkāyadṛṣṭiḥ/ sāsravāḥ skandhā upādānaskandhā ucyante/

antagrāhadṛṣṭiḥ katamety āha/ [*9a][57] *antagrāhadṛṣṭir ity ādi/* pañcasūpādānaskandheṣv ātmātmīyatvena pūrvagṛhīteṣūttarakālam ucchedākāreṇa śāśvatākāreṇa yad darśanaṃ sā 'ntagrāhadṛṣṭiḥ/ grāhapūrvikā dṛṣṭir grāhadṛṣṭiḥ satkāyadṛṣṭir ity arthaḥ/ antayor grāhadṛṣṭiḥ antagrāhadṛṣṭiḥ/

mithyādṛṣṭiḥ katamety āha/ *mithyādṛṣṭir ity ādi/* yayā dṛṣṭyā datteṣṭahutasucarita[duścarita][58] lakṣaṇaṃ hetum apavadate, phalavipāke [iha]paralokalakṣaṇaṃ phalañ cāpavadate, pitroḥ kriyāṃ vā 'pavadate, sad vastv arhadādikaṃ yayā dṛṣṭyā nāśayati, sā sarvadarśanebhyaḥ pāpataratvān mithyādṛṣṭir ity ucyate/

dṛṣṭiparāmarśa katama ity āha/ *dṛṣṭiparāmarśa ity ādi/* pañcasūpādānaskandheṣu agraviśiṣṭaśreṣṭhaparamākāreṇa yad darśanaṃ sa dṛṣṭiparāmarśaḥ/ prādhānyād agrata anyebhyo viśiṣyamāṇatvād viśiṣṭataḥ/ adhikābhāvāc chreṣṭhaḥ/ samābhāvāt paramataḥ/

śīlavrataparāmarśaḥ[59] katama ity āha/ *śīlavrataparāmarśa*[60] *ity ādi/* pañcasūpādānaskandheṣu śuddhimuktinairyāṇikākāreṇa yad darśanaṃ sa śīlavrataparāmarśaḥ/ pāpamalaprakṣālanāc chuddhitaḥ/ kleśabandhanavigamān muktitaḥ/ nirvāṇāvāhakāryatvān nairyāṇikataḥ/

vicikitsā katamety āha/ *vicikitsety ādi/* karmasu phaleṣu satyeṣu ratneṣu ca yā vimatiḥ sā vicikitsā/ vyutpattiṃ darśayann āha/ *vividhā matir ity ādi/* subodham etat/ yadi vividhā matir vimatir evaṃ sati prajñā prāpnotīty āha/ *prajñātaś ced ity ādi/* prajñā hi pravicayasvabhavā/ iyaṃ tu dvedhākāreṇa pravartate/ tasmād arthāntaraṃ prajñātaḥ/

vakṣyamāṇenābhisambandhaṃ kurvann āha/ *uktāḥ ṣaṭ kleśā ity ādi/* gatārtham etat/

upakleśān darśayann āha/

KRODHOPANAHANE PUNAḤ

[/MRAKṢAḤ PRADĀŚA ĪRṢYĀTHA MĀTSARYAṂ SAHA MĀYAYĀ//12//

ŚĀṬHYAṂ MADO 'VIHIṂSĀ HRĪR ATRAPĀ STYĀNAM UDDHAVAḤ/

ĀŚRADDHYAM ATHA KAUŚĪDYAṂ PRAMĀDO MUṢITĀ SMṚTIḤ//13//

VIKṢEPO 'SAMPRAJANYAṂ CA KAUKṚTYAṂ MIDDHAM EVA CA/

VITARKAŚ CA VICĀRAŚ CETY UPAKLEŚĀ DVAYE DVIDHĀ //14//]

ity ādi/

dvaye dvidheti/ dve dvike dviprakāre/ tataś catvāro dvividhā ity uktaṃ bhavati/

krodhaḥ katama ity āha/ *tatra krodha ity ādi/* vartamānam apakāram āśritya yaś cetasa āghāta upajāyate sa krodhaḥ/ ayaṃ ca krodha āghātasvabhāvatvāt pratighasya sakāśān na bhidyate/ kiṃ tu tasyaiva pratighasya kasmiṃścid avasthāviśeṣe prajñapyate/ tathā ca pratighāṃśikapaṭhane pṛthag bhidyate/[61] katamasminn avasthāviśeṣe prajñapyata ity āha/ *vartamānam apakāram ity ādi/* yāvad apakāro na nivartate tāvad eva yaś cetasa āghātaḥ sattvāsattvaviṣayo jāyate [sa] āghātaviśeṣaḥ krodha iti prajñapyate/ tasya ca daṇḍādānādīnāṃ sanniśrayadānaṃ karma/ *sattvāsattvaviṣaya iti/* prāṇiviṣayaḥ [viṣa]śastrakaṇṭakādiviṣayaś cety arthaḥ/ daṇḍādānaśabdena daṇḍanam ucyate/ ādiśabdena vadhabandhanādayaḥ/

upanāhaḥ katama ity āha/ *upanāha ity ādi/ krodhād ūrdhvam ity ādi/* krodhe nivṛtte mamaivaṃvidhasyānenāyam apakāraḥ kṛto dhiṅ mama jīvitam, yady aham asya pratīpakam apakāraṃ na karomi nāhaṃ manuṣyanāma dhārayāmīty asyaivaṃvidhasya vairātmakasyāśayasya yo 'nutsargaḥ prabandhena pravartanaṃ sa upanāhaḥ/ karmāsya darśayann āha/[*9b][62] *ayaṃ cety ādi/* akṣāntihetutvaṃ karmāsya/ akṣāntiṃ darśayann āha/ apakārasyāmarṣaṇaṃ pratyapakārecchā akṣāntir abhidhīyate/ prajñaptisattvam asya darśayann āha/ *ayam apīty ādi/* subodham etat/

mrakṣaḥ katama ity āha/ *mrakṣa ity ādi/* etad vivṛṇvann āha/ *chandadveṣabhayādīn ity ādi/* yaś codakaś chandādibhir agatiṃ na gacchati codyamānasya ca hitaiṣī tena tathāvidhena codanakālaṃ jñātvā tvam evaṃkārīti paryanu[yu]ktasya codyamānasya yā mohāṃśikī avadyapracchādanā jāyate sa mrakṣa ucyate/ katham asya mohāṃśikatvam ity āha/ *mohāṃśikatvam tv ity ādi/* yasmān mrakṣaś chādanākāraḥ tasmāt mohāṃśikaḥ/ karmāsya darśayann āha/ *ayam cety ādi/* etad vivṛṇvann āha/ *dharmataiṣety ādi/* prakṛtir iyaṃ janasya dharmāṇāṃ vā yat pāpaṃ pracchādayataḥ puruṣasya kaukṛtyam utpadyate/ kaukṛtyaṃ cāvaśyaṃ daurmanasyena samprayujyate/ tato daurmanasyasamprayogād asparśavihāro bhavati/

pradāśaḥ katama ity āha/ *pradāśa ity ādi/* caṇḍair vacobhir daśanaṃ pradāśaḥ/ caṇḍaṃ vaco darśayann āha/ *caṇḍaṃ vācā ity ādi/* marmaghaṭṭanayogena yat pragāḍhaṃ pāruṣyaṃ tac caṇḍaṃ vacaḥ/ pragāḍham iti tīkṣṇam/ dāśitāṃ darśayann āha/ *daśanaśīla ity ādi/* daśanaprakṛtir ayaṃ caitasikas tasmād dāśī, tasya bhāvo dāśitā/ svārthenāyaṃ bhāvapratyaya utpannaḥ/[63] tataś ca sa eva caitasikaś caṇḍena vacasā daśatīti caṇḍavacodāśitāśabdenocyate/ prajñaptisattvam asya darśayann āha/ *ayaṃ cety ādi/ krodhopanāhapūrvaka iti/*[64] krodhopanāhanimittakaḥ/ pariśiṣṭaṃ subodham/ karmāsya darśayann āha/ *tadvata ity ādi/* yaḥ pradāśavān pudgalaḥ tena saha[vāsāt] yasmād duhkham utpadyate tasmāt pradāśo 'sparśavihārakarmakaḥ/

īrṣyā katamety āha/ *īrṣyety ādi/* etad vivṛṇvann āha/ *lābhasatkārādhyavasitasyety ādi/* svakīyalābhasatkāre ca saktasya pareṣāṃ lābhasatkāraṃ kuśalādīṃś ca guṇaviśeṣān upalabhya yo dveṣāṃśiko 'marṣakṛtaś caitasiko vyāroṣo dveṣo jāyate [sā] īrṣyā/ vyutpattiṃ darśayann āha/ *svamāśrayam ity ādi/* subodham/ karmāsya darśayann āha/ *daurmanasyety ādi/* yataḥ daurmanasyena samprayujyate, yasmāc ca daurmanasyapūrvako 'sparśavihāraḥ, tamsād ubhayakarmikocyate/

mātsaryaṃ katamad ity āha/ *mātsaryam ity ādi/* dānaviruddho āgrahas tan mātsaryam/ dānaṃ darśayann āha/ *upāttam vastv ity ādi/*[65]

[*10a][66] [ā]ha/ *styānam ity ādi/* cittasya yā akarmaṇyatā yat staimityaṃ tat styānam/ kim idaṃ staimityam ity āha/ *staimityam ity ādi/* stimitasya bhāvaḥ staimityam/ pravṛttinimitto bhāvapratyayaḥ/ tathā hi [ya]d yogā[t] cittaṃ jaḍatvāt stimitaṃ bhavati, ālambanaṃ pratipattuṃ notsahate, tat staimityam ity ucyate/ karma darśayann āha/ *etac cety ādi/* gatārtham etat/ prajñaptikatām asya darśayann āha/ *mohāṃśika ity ādi/* subodham etat/

auddhatyam katamad ity āha/ *auddhatyam ity ādi/* cittasyāvyupaśamo yas tad auddhatyam/ kuta etad ity āha/ *vyupaśamo hīty ādi/* yasmād vyupaśamaśabdena śamatha ucyate tad viruddhaś[67] cāvyupaśamaḥ/[67] sa punar eṣa rāgānukūlaṃ pūrvahasitaramitakrīḍitādikaṃ samanusmarataḥ cetaso 'vyupaśamahetutvād avyupaśamaḥ auddhatyam ity uktam/ karma darśayann āha/ [*śamathaparipanthakarmakaḥ/*][68] śamathaḥ samādhis tasmai tad āvaraṇaṃ karoti/

āśraddhyaṃ katamam ity āha/ *āśraddhyam ity ādi/* karmādiṣv asampratyayaḥ śraddhāvipakṣabhūto dharmaḥ āśraddhyam/ vipakṣa iti kuta etad ity āha/ *śraddhā hīty ādi/* gatārtham etat/ aśraddhā *tadviparyayeṇety ādikam/* etad api subodham/ karma darśayann āha/ *kausīdyam ity ādi/* etad vivṛṇvann āha/ *aśraddadhānasyety ādi/* yasmād yāvat kasmiṃścid rūpe sampratyayābhilāṣau na jāyete tāvat prayogāya chanda eva na jāyate tasmāt kausīdyahetutvaṃ karmāsya/

kausīdyaṃ katamad ity āha/ *kausīdyam ity ādi/* etad vivṛṇvann āha/ *kuśale kāyavāṅ[manaḥ]karmaṇīty ādi/* nidrāsukhaṃ pārśvaśayanasukhaṃ cāsya hetuḥ/ lakṣaṇavākye 'pi kuśale kāyādikarmaṇi yo mohāṃśikaś cetaso 'nabhyutsāho jāyate tat kausīdyam/ karma darśayann āha/ *etac cety ādi/* kuśalapakṣe yaḥ prayogas tasyāvaraṇaṃ karoti/

pramādaḥ katama ity āha/ *pramāda ity ādi/* yair lobhādibhir grastaḥ kleśād rāgādikāc cittaṃ na pariharati, kuśalaṃ ca rāgādipratipakṣabhūtaṃ nābhyasyati, teṣu lobhamohakausīdyeṣu pramādaprajñaptiḥ kriyate/ karma darśayann āha/ *ayaṃ cety ādi/* akuśalavṛddheḥ kuśalahāneś ca hetutvaṃ pratipadyate/

muṣitasmṛtiḥ katamety āha/ *muṣitasmṛtir ity ādi/* kleśasamprayuktā yā smṛtiḥ/ karma darśayann āha/ *iyaṃ cety ādi/* subodham etat/

vikṣepaḥ katama ity āha/ *vikṣepa ity ādi/* etad vivṛṇvann āha/ *vividha[ṃ] kṣipyata ity ādi/* bahubhiḥ prakāraiś cittam ālambane kṣipyate 'neneti cittavikṣepaḥ/ prajñaptisattvam asya darśayann āha/ *yai rāgadveṣamohair ity ādi/* yai rāgādibhiḥ samādhyālambanāc[*10b][69] cittaṃ bahir nīyate teṣu yathāsambhavaṃ vikṣepaprajñaptiḥ kriyate/ karma darśayann āha/ *eṣa cety ādi/* vairāgyasyāvaraṇaṃ karoti, vikṣiptacittasya vairāgyābhāvāt/

asamprajanyaṃ katamad ity āha/ *asamprajanyam ity ādi/* kliṣṭā prajñā asamprajanyam ucyate/ kliṣṭāṃ prajñāṃ darśayann āha/ *yayā 'saṃviditety ādi/* āgamanagamanādiṣu yayā prajñayā asaṃviditā kāyavāk[citta]caryā[70] bhavati sā kliṣṭā prajñocyate/ sā cāsamprajanyam/ karma darśayann āha/ *karaṇī[ye]ty ādi/* asamprajñānakarībhiḥ kartavyākartavyaṃ nālocayati/ tataś cāpattihetutvaṃ karmāsya/

kaukṛtyaṃ katamad ity āha/ *kaukṛtyam ity ādi/* etad vivṛṇvann āha/ *kutsitaṃ kṛtam ity ādi/* yad vastu yathā kartavyaṃ tad yadā 'nyathā kriyate tadā kukṛtam ucyate/ tasya yataḥ kutsitaṃ karaṇaṃ tad bhūtārthena kaukṛtyam/ iha tu punaḥ kukṛtavastuviṣayaś cetaso yo vilekho vipratisāras tat kaukṛtyam, yasmāc caitasikā ihādhikṛtāḥ/ karmāsya darśayann āha/ *etac cety ādi/* cittasthitiḥ samādhiḥ/ tasyāvaraṇaṃ karoti/

middhaṃ katamad ity āha/ *middham ity ādi/* etad vivṛṇvann āha/ *vṛttir ālambana ity ādi/* yad vaśāc cittam ālambane 'svatantraṃ pravartate tan middham ity ucyate/ atraiva vyākhyānāntaraṃ kurvann āha/ *kāya[citta] sandhāraṇety ādi/*[71] yayā cetovṛttyā[72] kāyo na sandhāryate, sā asvatantrā yad vaśād bhavati tan[73] middham/ abhisaṃkṣepaṃ darśayann āha/ cakṣurādīndriyadvāreṇa yadā vijñānāni [na] pravartante, sa teṣām abhisaṃkṣepaḥ/ asvatantragrahaṇena samādhito viśeṣaṃ darśayati, abhisaṃ[kṣe]peṇa ca styānāt/ prajñaptisattvam asya darśayann āha/ *etac cety ādi/* gatārtham etat/ karma darśayann āha/ *kṛtyātipattīty ādi/* śayitasya hi kāryahānir bhavati/

vitarkaḥ katama ity āha/ *vitarka ity ādi/* kim etad ity evaṃ nirūpaṇākārapravṛttaḥ prajñācetanāviśeṣātmako yo manojalpaḥ sa vitarkaḥ/ manojalpaṃ darśayann āha/ *manasa ity ādi/* subodham etat/ jalpasvarūpaṃ darśayann āha/ *jalpo 'rthakathanam iti/* cittenārthakathanam ity arthaḥ/ katham asya cetanāsvābhāvyam ity āha/ *cetanāprajñāviśeṣa*[74]*ity ādi/* yasmāc cetanā cittaparispandarūpā, prajñā ca guṇadoṣanirūpaṇākārapravṛttā, tayoś ca vaśena cittaṃ pravartate, tasmāt kadācic cittacetanayor vitarkaḥ prajñāpyate, yadā na kiñcid abhyūhyate, kadācit prajñācittayoḥ, yadā 'bhyūhyate/

atraiva vyākhyānāntaraṃ kurvann āha/[75]

[*11a][76]...[PAÑCĀNĀṂ MŪLAVIJÑĀNE YATHĀPRATYAYAM UDBHAVAḤ/
VIJÑĀNAṂ SAHA NA VĀ TARAṄGĀṆĀṂ YATHĀ JALE//15/
/]...

[yathā] pratiniyataś cakṣurvijñānasya rūpam eva, śrotravijñānasya śabda evety evam ādi/ naivaṃ cakṣurvijñānādīnām samanantarapratyayo niyata iṣyate/ yasmāc cakṣurvijñānasyotpattau ṣaḍ api vijñānāni paryāyeṇa samanantarapratyayabhāvaṃ pratipadyante, evaṃ yāvan manovijñānasya ṣaḍ api paryāyeṇa samanantarapratyaya ity abhyupapattavyam/ [ta]taś caikasmād api samanantarapratyayād yady ālambanapratyayaḥ sannihito bhavati tadā dvayor bahūnām vā vijñānānām utpattir na virudhyate/ athaivaṃ neṣyate, tadā vaktavyaṃ kiṃ cātra kāraṇaṃ yat samanantarapratyayasya niyamābhāve 'pi pañcānāṃ yugapad ālambanapratyayasānnidhye 'pi ekenaiva vijñānenotpattavyam, na tu pañcabhir apīti/ yata evam atra niyamakāraṇaṃ kiñcid api na dṛśyate tasmād ālambanasadbhāve sati yadi vā pañcānām api vijñānānām utpattyā bhavitavyam, yadi vā naikasyāpīti/

bhūyaḥ prasaṅgāntaraṃ kurvann āha/ *idam idānīṃ vaktavyam ity ādi*/ praśnārthaḥ subodhaḥ/ siddhāntavādy āha/

MANOVIJÑĀNASAMBHŪTIḤ [SARVADĀSAṂJÑIKĀD ṚTE/
SAMĀPATTIDVAYĀN MIDDHĀN MŪRCHANĀD APY ACITTAKĀT//16//]

ity ādi/ āsaṃjñikān varjayitvā sarvakālaṃ manovijñānaṃ sambhavatīti sūtrārthaḥ/ padārthaṃ darśayann āha/ *sarvadety ādi*/ subodham etat/ yatra manovijñānaṃ neṣyate tatra nivārayann āha/ *asyotsargasyety ādi*/ yady api manovijñānasya sarvakālaṃ sambhavo 'bhyupagataḥ, tathāpy āsaṃjñikaṃ varjayitvā, nirodhāsaṃjñisamāpattidvayaṃ varjayitvā, acittakaṃ middhaṃ varjayitvā, mūrchām cācittikāṃ varjayitvā manovijñānasambhava eṣṭavyaḥ/ samāne vidhāna utsarga ucyate/ viśeṣeṇa vidhānam apavādaḥ/

atha kim idam āsaṃjñikam ity āha/ *tatrāsaṃjñikam ity ādi*/ a[saṃ]jñisattvāḥ kecid devāḥ paṭhyante/ teṣūpapannasya yaś cittacaittānāṃ nirodhas tad āsaṃjñikam ucyate/[77]

samāpattidvayaṃ katamad ity āha/ *samāpattidvayam ity ādi/* subodham etat/

keyam asaṃjñisamāpattir ity āha/ *tatrāsaṃjñisamāpattir ity ādi/* tṛtīyād dhyānād vītarāgasya yogina[ḥ] [na] ūrdhvam avītarāgasya, yo mokṣamārgasaṃjñāpurvakeṇa manaskāreṇa manovijñānasya tena ca samprayuktānāṃ caitasikānāṃ[*11b][78] yo nirodhaḥ sātra pravacane asaṃjñisamāpattir ity ucyate/ vyutpattiṃ darśayann āha/ *nirudhyate anenety ādi/* nigadavyākhyānam etat/

kaḥ sa tādṛśa ity āha/ *sa punaḥ* [*sa*]*sam*[*pra*]*yogasyety*[79] *ādi/* saparivārasya manovijñānasya samudācāro yena nirudhyate sa nirodha ucyate/ sa cāśrayasyāvasthāviśeṣaḥ kaścin na tu dravyaṃ yathā kaiścit parikalpyate/

nanu ca kuśalādicittaikāgratā samādhir ity ucyate, tat kathaṃ cittacaittanirodhaḥ samapāttir ity āha/ *samāpatticittād ity ādi/* yasmāt samāpatticittasyānantaraṃ cittāntarotpattiviruddha āśrayaḥ prāpyate tasmāt sa cittacaittanirodhaḥ samāpattir ity ucyate/

dvitīyaṃ darśayann āha/ *nirodhasamāpattir ity ādi/* ākiñcanyāyatanād vītarāgasya yogi[naḥ] śāntavihārasaṃjñāpūrvakeṇa manaskāreṇa saparivārasya manovijñānasya kliṣṭasya ca manaso yo nirodhaḥ, sā nirodhasamāpattir ity ucyate/ śāntavihārasaṃjñāpūrvakeṇeti śānto 'yaṃ vihāra ity evaṃvidhāṃ buddhiṃ pūrvaṃ kṛtvā paścāt tāṃ samāpadyata ity arthaḥ/ asyā api prajñaptisattvaṃ darśayann āha/ *iyam apīty ādi/* yathā asaṃjñisamāpattir āśrayasyāvasthāviśeṣa prajñapyate evam iyam apīty arthaḥ/

kathaṃ middham acittakaṃ bhavatīty āha/ *acittakam ity ādi/* yadā gāḍhena middhenāśraya upahato bhavati tadā tāvat kālaṃ yasmāt manovijñānaṃ na pravartate tasmād acittakam ity ucyate/

katham acittikā mūrcchā bhavati kva vā vyavasthāpyata ity āha/ *acittikety ādi/* āgantukenābhighātena[80] yadi vā dhātuvaiṣamyeṇa manovijñānasya tāvat kālaṃ samudācāraviruddhatvād āśrayavaiṣamyaṃ yad bhavati tatrāśrayavaiṣamye 'cittikā mūrcchopacaryate/ upasaṃhṛtya darśayann āha/ *etā eva* [*pañca*][81] *avasthā ity ādi/* upasaṃhārārthaḥ subodhaḥ/

manovijñānam adhikṛtya pṛcchann āha/ *evam āsaṃjñikādiṣv ity ādi/* yadā āsaṃjñikādaya apagacchanti tadā kutaḥ punas tad vijñānam utpadyate, yena tasya yoginaḥ kālakriyā na bhavatīti/ siddhāntavādy āha/ *tat punar ālayavijñānād evety ādi/* āsaṃjñikādibhyo vyutthitasyālayavijñānād eva tan manovijñānam utpadyate/ yasmāt tad ālayavijñānaṃ sarvavijñānabījānuṣaktam/ vakṣyamāṇādisambandhaṃ kurvann[*12a][82] āha/ *yatra vijñānapariṇāma ity ādi/* subodham etat/

ātmā dharmāś ca vijñānapariṇāmān na bahir bhavantīti yat pratijñātaṃ tasyedānīṃ prasādhanāyāha/

VIJÑĀNAPARIṆĀMO 'YAṂ [VIKALPO YAD VIKALPYATE/ TENA TAN NĀSTI TENEDAṂ SARVAṂ VIJÑAPTIMĀTRAKAM//17//]

ity ādi/ yo 'yaṃ vijñānapariṇāmaḥ sa vikalpaḥ/ tena vikalpena yat kiñcid vastu vikalpyate tat sarvam nāsti/ tasmāt sarvam idaṃ jagad vijña[pti]mātrakam iti sūtrārthaḥ/ avayavārthaṃ darśayann āha/ *yo 'yam ity ādi/* gatārtham etat/

vikalpasvarūpaṃ darśayann āha/ *adhyāropitārthākārā ity ādi/* ye traidhātukāś cittacaittā adhyāropitākāreṇa pravartante te vikalpaśabdenocyante/ atra *Madhyāntavibhāgaṃ*[83] jñāpakam āha/ *yathoktam ity ādi/* tatra hy uktaṃ traidhātukāś cittacaittā abhūtaparikalpā iti/ kimiti vijñānapariṇāmo vikalpaśabdenocyata ity āha/ *tena trividhenety ādi/* yasmād anena trividhenālayavijñānādikena sasamprayogeṇa yad vastu vikalpyate bhājanādikaṃ tad bhūtārthena nāsti, tasmāt sa vijñānapariṇāmo vikalpa ucyate/ yasmād asyālambanaṃ vastuto nāsti/

bāhyārthavādy asambhāvayan pṛcchati/ *kathaṃ punar etad ity ādi/* vikalpālambanaṃ vastu san na bhavatīti katham etat jñāyate? siddhāntavādy āha/ *yadd hi yasyety ādi/* yad yasya kāraṇam iṣyate tasmin samagre tad utpadyate/ aviruddhe ca nānyathā(nānyataḥ?)[84] itīyaṃ tāvan nītir evam avasthitā/ vijñānaṃ ca māyādiṣu vināpy arthena jāyate tena manyāmahe nārthapratibaddho vijñānasyotpādaḥ/ yadi hy[85] ālambanapratibaddho vijñānasyotpado 'bhaviṣyat tadā māyādiṣv artho nāstīti vijñānaṃ notpatsyeta/ upasaṃhāravyājena vijñānasya kāraṇaṃ darśayann āha/ *tasmāt pūrva[kā]n niruddhād ity ādi/* yata evaṃ bāhyārthapratibaddhaṃ vijñānaṃ na bhavati tasmāt pūrvasmād eva tulyākārād vijñānād vijñānam utpadyate/ na tu bāhyārthāt, yasmād asaty api bāhye 'rthe tad vijñānaṃ bhavati/ evaṃ tāvad vaikalyaṃ darśitam/

virodhaṃ darśayann āha/ *dṛṣṭā cety ādi/* ekarūpe 'py arthe pratipat[t]ṛṇāṃ kuṇapakāminīmāṃsādyākāreṇa parasparaviruddhāḥ pratipattayo dṛśyante/ tatraitat syāt/ ekam eva vastv anekākārayuktaṃ bhaviṣyatīti/ ata āha/ *na caikasyety ādi/* na khalv ekasya padārthasya parasparaviruddhātmakatvaṃ yujyate/ yata evaṃ tasmād adhyāropitākāratvād vikalpasyālambanam asad iti pratipattavyam/

upasaṃhāraṃ darśayann āha/ *anena tāvad ity ādi/* vikalpaviṣayasya nāstitvavacanena samāropāntaḥ parihṛtaḥ/

adhunā apavādāntaṃ[*12b][86] parihartukāma āha/ '*tenedaṃ sarvam' ity ādi/* etad vivṛṇvann āha/ *teneti tasmād ity ādi/* yasmāt pariṇāmasvabhāvena vikalpena yad vastvādikaṃ vikalpyate tad bhūtārthena nāsti, sa tu vikalpo vidyate/ tasmād viṣayasyābhāvād vikalpasyāstitvāt sarvaṃ '*vijñaptimātrakam*'/ avayavārthaṃ darśayann āha/ *sarvam ity ādi/* traidhātukam asaṃskṛtaṃ ca sarvaśabdenoktam ity arthaḥ/ yas tu mātraśabdaḥ sa vijñaptito 'dhikasya viṣayasya vyavacchedārthaḥ/ [kakāraḥ] punar atra nālpahrasvakutsā-praśaṃsārthaḥ/ kiṃ tarhi? ślokaparipūraṇārthaḥ/ parasya paṭhana(praśnā)vakāśam āśaṅkyāha/ *yadi sarvabījam ity ādi/* yadi sarvaṃ bhūtārthena vijñaptimātrakam eva, na tu tato vijñaptimātrād anyaḥ kartā karaṇam vā vidyate, tat kathaṃ mūlavijñānāt kenacit kartranadhiṣṭhitāt karaṇam antareṇa nānāprakārā vikalpāḥ pravartanta iti vaktavyam/ atra siddhāntavādy āha/

SARVABĪJAṂ HI [VIJÑĀNAṂ PARIṆĀMAS TATHĀ TATHĀ/
YĀTY ANYONYAVAŚĀD YENA VIKALPAḤ SA SA JĀYATE//
18//]

ity ādi/ ālayavijñānam evānyonyabalena tathā pariṇāmaṃ yāti yena te te vikalpā jāyante vinā kartṛkaraṇād iti sūtrārthaḥ/ vṛttikāro 'vayavārthaṃ darśayann āha/ *tatra sarvadharmotpādenety ādi/* yasmād ālayavijñānaṃ sarvadharmotpādakasamarthaśaktibhir anugataṃ tasmāt sarvabījakam ity ucyate/ viśeṣaṇadvayopādāne prayojanaṃ darśayann āha/ *vijñānaṃ hīty ādi/* yasmād asarvabījakam api vijñānam asti pravṛttivijñānakhyātaṃ, tasmāt sarvabījakam ity etad viśeṣaṇaṃ tad vyavacchedārthaṃ kṛtam/ vijñānavyatirekeṇāpi kaiścit pradhānādikaṃ sarvabījakaṃ parikalpyate, tasmāt tad vyavacchedārthaṃ vijñānagrahaṇam/

atraiva vyākhyānāntaraṃ kurvann āha/ *athavaikapadety ādi/* yathā nīlotpalam ity atrobhayapadaviśeṣaṇaviśeṣyabhāvo bhavati naivaṃ sarvatra, kiṃ tarhi? kvacid ekapadavyabhicāro(e) 'pi, viśeṣaṇaviśeṣyatvam bhavati yathā pṛthvīdravyam iti/ atra hy āpodravyatvaṃ na vyabhicarati, atha ca dravyaṃ viśeṣaṇam upādīyate/ evam ihāpi yady api sarvabījaṃ vijñānatāṃ na vyabhicarati, tathāpi vijñānena viśeṣyate/ avayavārthaṃ vyākhyāsyann āha/ *pariṇāma ity ādi/* purvāvasthāvailakṣaṇyaṃ pariṇāmaḥ/ sa ca tasya vikalpasyānantarotpādanasamarthāvasthāprāptilakṣaṇaḥ/ anyonya-vaśād ity etat *tathā hīty ādinā vyācaṣṭe/* cakṣurādivijñānaṃ hi yadā svaśaktiparipoṣaṇāya pravartate tadā śaktiviśiṣṭasyālayavijñānasya nimittabhāvaṃ pratipadyate/ so 'py ālayavijñāna[pariṇāmas] tasya cakṣurādivijñānasya nimittaṃ bhavati/ evaṃ .../[87]

...[KARMAṆO VĀSANĀ GRĀHADVAYAVĀSANAYĀ SAHA/
KṢĪṆE PŪRVAVIPĀKE 'NYAD VIPĀKAṂ JANAYANTI TAT//
19//
YENA YENA VIKALPENA YAD YAD VASTU VIKALPYATE/
PARIKALPITA EVĀSAU SVABHĀVO NA SA VIDYATE//20//
PARATANTRASVABHĀVAS TU VIKALPAḤ
PRATYAYODBHAVAḤ/
NIṢPANNAS TASYA PŪRVEṆA SADĀ RAHITATĀ TU
YĀ//21//
ATA EVA SA NAIVĀNYO NĀNANYAḤ PARATANTRATAḤ/
ANITYATĀDIVAD VĀCYO NĀDṚṢTE 'SMIN SA DṚŚYATE
//22//
TRIVIDHASYA SVABHĀVASYA TRIVIDHĀṂ NIḤSVA-
BHĀVATĀM/
SAṂDHĀYA SARVADHARMĀṆĀṂ DEŚITĀ NIḤSVA-
BHĀVATĀ//23//
PRATHAMO LAKṢAṆENAIVA NIḤSVABHĀVO 'PARAḤ
PUNAḤ/
NA SVAYAṂ BHĀVA ETASYETY APARĀ NIḤSVABHĀVATĀ
//24//
DHARMĀṆĀṂ PARAMĀRTHAŚ CA SA YATAS TATHATĀPI
SAḤ/
SARVAKĀLAM TATHĀBHĀVĀT SAIVA VIJÑAPTIMĀTRATĀ
//25//
YĀVAD VIJÑAPTIMĀTRATVE VIJÑĀNAṂ NĀVATIṢṬHATI/
GRĀHADVAYASYĀNUŚAYAS TĀVAN NA VINIVARTATE
//26//
VIJÑAPTIMĀTRAM EVEDAM ITY API HY UPALAMBHATAḤ/
STHĀPAYANN AGRATAḤ KIÑCID TANMĀTRE NĀVA-
TIṢṬHATE//27//
YADĀTVĀLAMBANAṂ VIJÑĀNAṂ NAIVOPALABHATE
TADĀ/.
STHITAM VIJÑĀNAMĀTRATVE GRĀHYĀBHĀVE
TADAGRAHĀT//28/...
[*13a][88] [ACITTO 'NUPALAMBHO 'SAU JÑĀNAṂ

LOKOTTARAṂ CA TAT/
ĀŚRAYASYA PARĀVṚTTIR DVIDHĀ DAUṢṬHULYA-HĀNITAḤ//29//
SA EVANĀSRAVO DHĀTUR ACINTYAḤ KUŚALO DHRUVAḤ/
SUKHO VIMUKTIKĀYO 'SAU DHARMĀKHYO 'YAṂ MAHĀMUNEḤ//30//]

...[prāpya]te/ dvaividhyaṃ darśayann āha/ *dvidhety ādi/* kleśāvaraṇadauṣṭhulyaṃ jñeyāvaraṇadauṣṭhulyaṃ cātra dvividhaṃ dauṣṭhulyam abhipretam/ kim iti dauṣṭhulyam ity āha/ *dauṣṭhulyam ity ādi/* āśrayasyākarmaṇyatā dauṣṭhulyam ucyate/ bhūtārthena punas tad dauṣṭhulyaṃ kleśajñeyāvaraṇayor bījam ity ucyate/ prabhedam asyā darśayann āha/ *sā puna āśrayaparāvṛttir ity ādi/* ekā śrāvakapratyekabuddhagotragatadauṣṭhulyahānyā prāpyate, yad āha *vimuktikāya iti/* dvitīyā bodhisattvagatadauṣṭhulyahānyā prāpyate, yad āha *dharmākhyo 'yaṃ mahāmuner iti/* tad evam atra dvividhāvaraṇaprahāṇabhedena sottarā niruttarā cāśrayaparāvṛittir uktā veditavyā/

dvividhāvaraṇapratipādanārthaṃ jñāpakam āha/ *atra gāthēty ādi/* dvayāvaraṇasvabhāvam ādānavijñānaṃ bandho jñeyaḥ/ kasya bandha ity āha/ *dvayor iti/* tenālayavijñānenāvaraṇalakṣaṇena dvayoḥ śrāvakādigotrabo[dhi]sattvayor bandha ity arthaḥ/ sarvabījaṃ kleśabījam ity anenāvaraṇadvayaṃ darśitam/ dvayāvaraṇaṃ lakṣaṇaṃ yasyālayavijñānasya tat tathoktaṃ sarvaṃ yasmin kleśānāṃ bījaṃ yasminn ālayavijñāne tad evam ucyate/ vṛttikāro 'vayavārthaṃ darśayann āha/ *dvayor*[89] *ity ādi/* śrāvakādigotrasya kleśabījaṃ bandhaḥ/ bodhisattvasya dvayāvaraṇabījaṃ bandhaḥ/ dvayāvaraṇabījaśabdena sarvabījam uktam/ kasmād bodhisattvasyaivetad āvaraṇam ity āha/ *tat samudghātād*[90] *ity ādi/* yasmād āvaraṇadvayaprahāṇāt sarvajñatā prāpyate 'taḥ tasyaivāvaraṇaṃ bandhaḥ/

gāthāṃ vyākhyāya pūrvaprakṛtaṃ śeṣaṃ vyākhyāsyann āha/ *sa evānāsrava ity ādi/* sa evāśrayaparāvṛttiviśeṣo 'nāsravo dhātur ity ucyate/ yasmān nirdauṣṭhulyatvāt sarvāsravavigataḥ[91] tasmād anāsravaḥ/ sarvāryadharmahetutvād dhātur uktaḥ, yasmādd hetutvārtho 'tra dhātuśabda upāttaḥ, tan nimittā hi sarve āryadharmāḥ/

katham acintya ity āha/ *acintya ity ādi/* yasmāt tarkasya gocaro na bhavati, yasmāc ca pratyātmavedya āryāṇām, yasmāc ca dṛṣṭānto 'tra nāsti, tasmād acintyaḥ/

kathaṃ kuśala ity āha/ yasmād viśuddher ālambanaṃ nāma, yasmāc ca ya[ḥ] kṣema yasmāc cānāsrava[dharmamayaḥ],[92] tasmāt kuśalaḥ/

kathaṃ dhruva ity āha/ yasmān nityo na kṣīyate sugatasya(-taḥ), tasmād dhruvaḥ/

kathaṃ sukha ity āha/ *sukha ity ādi/* yasmān nityas tasmāt[93] sukhaḥ/ [*13b][94] tathā hi yad anityaṃ tad duḥkham, ayaṃ tu nityaḥ tasmāt sukhaḥ/

pudgalabhedenāśrayaparāvṛttibhedaṃ darśayann āha/ *kleśāvaraṇaprahāṇād ity ādi/* sa āśrayaparāvṛttiviśeṣaḥ śrāvakāṇāṃ vimuktikāya ucyate/ yasmāt teṣāṃ kleśāvaraṇamātraṃ prahīyate/ tāvan mātreṇaiva te vimuktim āsādayanti/ tataś ca vimukter āśrayo vimuktikāya ity uktaṃ bhavati/ mahāmunes tu sa evāśrayaparāvṛtti-lakṣaṇo dharmakāya ity ucyate/ kiṃ kāraṇaṃ bhagavataḥ sa dharmakāya ity ucyata ity āha/ *bhūmipāramitābhāvanayety*[95] *ādi/* yasmād bhumīnāṃ pāramitānāṃ ca bhāvanayā kleśajñeyāvaraṇa-prahāṇaṃ bhavati, āśrayaparāvṛttiś ca samudāgacchati, tasmān mahāmuner dharmakāya ity ucyate/ etad uktaṃ bhavati/ yasmād bhūmipāramitādharmaiś cīyate tasmād dharmakāya ity ucyate/

atraiva vyākhyānāntaraṃ kurvann āha/ ...[96]

NOTES

1. The works of Vinītadeva preserved in Tibetan: To. 4065 *Prakaraṇaviṃśakaṭīkā;* To. 4070 *Triṃśikāṭīkā;* To. 4114 *Vinayavibhaṅgapadavyākhyāna;* To. 4126 *Triśatakārikāvyākhyāna;* To. 4137 *Vinayastotrapadavyākhyāna;* To. 4140 *Samayabhedoparacanacakre nikāyabhedopadeśanāsaṃgrahaḥ;* To. 4230 *Nyāyabinduṭīkā;* To. 4234 *Hetubinduṭīkā;* To. 4236 *Sambandhaparīkṣāṭīkā;* To. 4238 *Saṃtānāntarasiddhiṭīkā;* To. 4240 *Vādanyāyaṭīkā;* To. 4241 *Ālambanaparīkṣāṭīkā.*
2. Sylvain Levi, ed.; *Vijñaptimātratāsiddhi: Viṃśatikā* (La *vingtaine*) *et Triṃśikā* (La *trentaine*) (Paris: Librairie Ancienne Honoré Champion, 1925); S. Levi, tr. *Matériaux pour l'étude du système Vijñaptimātra* (Paris: Librairie Ancience Honoré Champion, 1925).
3. Theodore Stcherbatsky, *Buddhist Logic* (1930; repr. New York: Dover Publications, 1962).
4. Nozawa Josho and Yamaguchi Susumu, *Seshin Yui-shiki no Genten Kaimei* (Kyoto: Hozokan, 1953), 133-408. Sections of their translation originally appeared in instalments in *Otani gakuho* and *Mikkyo bunka* between 1944 and 1952.
5. M. Gangopadhyaya, *Vinītadeva's Nyāyabindu-ṭīkā* (Indian Studies Past and Present, Calcutta: R. D. Press, 1971).
6. Leslie Kawamura, 'Vinītadeva's contribution to the Buddhist mentalistic trend', Ph.D. thesis, University of Saskatchewan, 1975.

7. *Sum-cu-pa'i 'grel-bshad, Tibetan Tripiṭaka* (Peking edition), vol. 114, no. 5571, pp. 1-69a. The Tibetan translation is by Jinabhadra, Śīlendrabodhi, and Dānaśīla as in Derge vol. Hi.
8. Abbreviations and symbols used in the text:
   [*] =folio No. of MS.
   [ ] =additions
   ( ) =emendations
   L. Sylvin Lévi, ed.: *Vijñaptimātratāsiddhi: Deux Traités de Vasubandhu: Viṃśatikā et Triṃśikā* (Paris: Librairie Ancienne Honoré Champion, 1925).
   MS The present manuscript of the Sanskrit *Triṃśikā-ṭīkā.*
   T *Tibetan Tripiṭaka, Peking edition,* Vol. 114, folios 1-69a. no.5571, pp. 175, 1.1 to pp. 203, 1.5, letter 6. This corresponds to *Derge,* Vol. Hi, p. 20b, 1.7 to p. 61b, 1.7.
   J Japanese translation by Yamaguchi Susumu and Nozawa Josho: *Seshin Yui-shiki no Genten Kaimei* (Kyoto: Hozoken, 1953) 133-408.
9. The *Ṭīkā* covering the *Bhāṣya* on the first four *kārikās* of the *Triṃśikā*, corresponding to L., p. 15, 1.1 to p. 21, 1.27—up to *tac ca vartate*—is missing. We have reproduced the kārikās for the sake of maintaining the continuity of the text.
10. The beginning corresponds to L., p. 21, 1.27; T., p. 20b, 1.7, letter 20; J., p. 228, 1.2.
11. MS reads: *padārthavad.*
12. L. reads: *yathā hy oghas.*
13. L. reads *ākarṣayan.*
14. Corresponds to L., p. 22, 1.17; Ṭ, p. 25a, 1.7.
15. Not found in T, 26a, 1.4.
16. Corresponds to L., p. 22, 1.27; T, 26a, 1.6.
17. MS reads: *manana-.*
18. Corresponds to L., p. 23, 1.11; T, 26a, 1.6.
19. L reads: *saṃmūḍhāḥ.*
20. MS reads *ātmajñānaṃ* which is not supported by T: *mi śes pa gaṅ yin pa de bolag tu rmoṅs paho* (*yat tad ajñānaṃ sa ātmamohaḥ*), T, 26b, 1.5.
21. Corresponds to L., p. 23, 1.23; T, 28a, 1.2.
22. L. (p.24, n. 1) gives *lokottareṇa ca* as a variant reading.
23. The reading: *mārge na* is supported by T, 28b, 1.7 to 29a, 1.1.
24. Corresponds to L., p. 24, 1.16; T, 29a, 1.1.
25. Corresponds to L., p. 25, 1.5; T, 29b, 1.7.
26. MS reads: *pṛcchann āha/*
27. L. reads: *sparśa eṣām ādir iti.*
28. L. reads: *tathā hy eta ālayavijñāne* ...p. 25, 1.17.
29. Corresponds to L., p. 25, 1.26; T, 31a, 1.1.
30. MS reads: *samprayukte* which is an error. The word *saṃstute* appears immediately below.
31. In the MS this portion is repeated and subsequently bracketed for omission by the scribe.
32. Corresponds to L., p. 26, 1.6; T, 31b, 1.6.
33. Corresponds to L., p. 26, 1.16; T, 32b, 1.4.
34. L. (p. 26, 1.18) reads: *ete hi pañca dharmāḥ parasparaṃ vyatiricyāpi vyāvartante.* Our reading *vartante* is correct and supported by T: *tha da du gyur nas skye ba yin gyi* (32b, 1.6).

35. Addition supported by T.
36. Corresponds to L., p. 26, 1.26; T, 33b, 1.1.
37. Addition supported by T.
38. L. reads: *anāsaktiḥ vaimukhyam,* p. 27, 1.6.
39. Corresponds to L., p. 27, 1.10; T, 34b, 1.1.
40. Corresponds to L., p. 27, 1.23; T, 35a, 1.8.
41. L. notes this reading (p. 27, n. 5) but amends it to *yair alobhādīn* in agreement with T.
42. MS reads: *trabhiḥ.*
43. Corresponds to L., p.28, 1.3; T, 36a, 1.5.
44. Here the MS crosses out five letters (*tato bhāvanā*) not found in T.
45. T has four more lines here covering L., p. 28, II. 14-16 (from *sa punar* to *nirdiśyate*) which is not found in our MS.
46. Corresponds to L., p. 28, 1.20; T. 37a, 1.7.
47. MS reads: *niśritya.*
48. MS reads: *paṇḍitaṃ.*
49. MS reads: *apraśritatā.*
50. MS reads: *apraśritatā.*
51. MS reads: *vidyate* which is wrong. Cf. *cittonnatisvarūpābhede 'pi* (L., p. 29, 1.3).
52. Corresponds to L., p. 29, 1.6; T, 38a, 1.5.
53. MS reads: *vijñānacittādibhiḥ.*
54. MS reads: *vijñānacittādibhiḥ.*
55. MS reads: *vidyeran.*
56. MS reads: *nītīraṇākāratvena.*
57. Corresponds to L., p. 29, 1.21; T, 39a, 1.5.
58. Found in T: *ñes par spyod pa.*
59. MS reads: *-parāmarṣaḥ.*
60. MS reads: *-parāmarṣaḥ.*
61. T reads: *na pṛthag vidyate* (*de ltar khoṅ khro baḥi ihar gtogs pa de ñid de bud na med do*).
62. Corresponds to L., p. 30, 1.8; T, 40b, 1.1.
63. This line is missing in T.
64. MS repeats this line.
65. Folios corresponding to L., p. 30, 1.25 through to p. 31, 1.22 (T, 41b, 1.2 through to 43, 1.3; and J, p. 298, 1.14 through to p. 307, 1.7) are missing.
66. Corresponds to L., p. 31, 1.25; T, 41b, 1.2.
67. MS reads: *viruddhatvavyupaśamaḥ.*
68. MS reads: *katamaṃ cety ādi,* which is an error. T reads instead: *źi gnas kyi bar du gcod paḥi las can no źes by ba smras so.* 43b, 1.8.
69. Corresponds to L., p. 32, 1.8; T, 44b, 1.4.
70. The word *citta* is found in both L. and T.
71. The word *citta* is found in both L. and T.
72. MS reads: *vṛtyā.*
73. MS reads: *tadvān* (*tad vā?*). Both L. and T read *tat* only.
74. *cetanāprajñaptiviśeṣaḥ,* which is not supported by L. or T.
75. Folios corresponding to L., p. 32, 1.24 through to p. 34, 1.8(T, 45b, 1.4 through to 47b, 1.7; J, p. 317, 1.12 through to p. 331, 1.4) are missing.
76. Corresponds to L., p. 34, 1.8; T, 47b, 1.7.
77. Here the T has the following lines not found in our MS: *sus ḥdod paḥi khams su ḥdu śes med paḥi sñoms par ḥjug pa baskyed pa de ni ḥdu śes med paḥi lha rnams kyi*

nan du skyeḥo// sus ḥdod paḥi khams su ḥgog paḥi sñoms par ḥjug pa bskyed pa de ni srid paḥi stse skyeḥo// ḥdu śes med pa ni ci yaṅ mi śes te/ don med par gnas so// (T, 48b, II. 1-3; compare J, p. 331, II. 5-7).

78. Corresponds to L., p. 34, 1.21; T, 48b, 1.5.
79. L. reads: *sasamprayogasya*, p. 34, 1.24.
80. L. reads: *āgantunā-*, p. 34, 1.29.
81. L. reads: *pañca*, p. 35, 1.1.
82. Corresponds to L., p. 35, 1.5; T, 49b, 1.4.
83. *abhūtaparikalpaś ca cittacaittās tridhātukāḥ/ tatrārthadṛṣṭir vijñānaṃ tad viśeṣe tu caitasāḥ//8// Madhyānatavibhāga-bhāṣya* (ed. Nagao, Tokyo, 1964) 20.
84. L. reads: *nānyataḥ*, p. 35, 1.18.
85. L. reads: *ca*, p. 35, 1.19.
86. Corresponds to L., p. 35, 1.27; T, 50b, 1.4.
87. Folios corresponding to L., p. 36, 1.16 through to p. 44, 1.9 (T, 51b, 1.3 through to 67a, 1.4; J, p. 342, .4 through to p. 403, 1.14) are missing.
88. Corresponds to L., p. 44, 1.9; T, 67a, 1.5; J, p. 403, 1.15.
89. L. reads: *dvayāvaraṇabījaṃ*, p. 44, 1.17.
90. L. reads: *tad ughātād;* T supports L. (*deḥi phyir de dag bcom pa źes bya* ba).
91. L. reads: *sa tv āsravavigataḥ*, p. 44, 1.20; T (68a, 1.2) supports *sarvāsrava* (*zag pa thams* cad).
92. L. reads: *anāsravadharnamayatvāc ca*, p. 44, 1.22.
93. L., p.44, 1.24 reads: *asmāt*, which is wrong.
94. Corresponds to L., p. 44, 1.24; T, 68a, 1.6.
95. L. reads: *bhūmipāramitādi* ...p. 44, 1.26.
96. As pointed out in the Introduction, our MS at this point contains a long passage from Sthiramati's commentary to *Madhyāntavibhāga*, corresponding to Yamaguchi Susumu's edition, p. 92, II. 15 through to p. 93, 1.8. We reproduce this portion as it appears in our MS:
[line 4] mokṣabhāgīyānām āropaṇam indriyeṣv āvaraṇam uktam/ kim ity (atra) āvaraṇam/ yo(e)nopakleśe[na] mokṣabhāgīyaṃ nākṣipati/ sā punarbhavasaktir nirvāṇe trāsaś ceti/ baleṣu teṣām evendriyāṇāṃ daurbalyam āvaraṇam iti prakṛtam/ kathaṃ punar indriyāṇām daurbalyam ity [line 5] ata [āha/] *vipakṣavyavakiraṇād* iti/ āśraddhyakausīdyamuṣitasmṛtivikṣepadauḥprajñātmakena vipakṣeṇābhibhavād ity arthaḥ/ūṣmagatamūrdhaprabhāvitānīndriyāṇi/ etac ca dvividham api nirvedhabhāgīyaṃ durbalam āśraddhyādivipakṣābhibhavād ata eva tasmin parihā[ṇi][line6]sambhavaḥ/ nirjitavipakṣatvāt tu śraddhādīni kṣāntyagradharmayor balākhyāṃ pratilabhante/ atas teṣām eva śraddhādīnām ūṣmagatamūrddhāvasthānāt(-sthāyāṃ?) yad vipakṣābhibhavād daurbalyaṃ tad balānām āvaraṇam/ tasmin sati balāvasthā 'sambhavād iti/ kim atrāvaraṇam/ sa evāśraddhyā[diko] vipa[kṣaḥ]/ [line 7] bodhyaṅgeṣu dṛṣṭidoṣaḥ/ āvaraṇam ity atra vartate/ bodhir atra darśanamārgo 'bhipretaḥ/ tasyaitāni smṛtidharmavicayaprītiprasrabdhisamādhyupekṣātmakāni sapta bodhyaṅgāni darśanaheyaprahāṇakāle utpadyanta ity aṅgānīty [ucyante] .../ MS ends here.

CHAPTER 26

Stages in the Bodhisattva Career of the Tathāgata Maitreya*

Introduction

Although considerable differences exist in Buddhist thought concerning the nature of a Buddha and the number of bodhisattvas for whom a prophecy has been made concerning future Buddhahood, Buddhists are unanimous in declaring the bodhisattva Maitreya to be the next Tathāgata,[1] the immediate successor to the Buddha Śākyamuni. One would expect such an heir apparent to have been a historical person closely associated with the Buddha, someone like the elder (*thera*) Ānanda (before he disqualified himself by becoming an arhat!), the chief attendant of the Teacher during his lifetime and transmitter of his sermons after his *parinirvāṇa.* Or one would suppose him to have been a contemporary king emulating the noble example of the bodhisattva Prince Vessantara, who could be singled out by Gautama publicly for such an honour. Maitreya, at least in the Theravāda canon, is neither, and hence there has lingered the suspicion that this legendary figure was added to the earlier genealogy of the Buddhas under the influence of a foreign cult of the Messiah (e.g., the Zoroastrian Saošyant or the Persian-Greek Mithras Invictus)[2]. Whatever the source of the cult of Maitreya, it is certain that his

---

*This article was originally published in *Maitreya, the Future Buddha*, eds. Sponberg and Hardacre, (Cambridge: Cambridge University Press, 1988), pp. 54-90. Reprinted with kind permission of Cambridge University Press.

Quotations from the Sanskrit and Pali texts were not reproduced in the original article. Here we have included them in an Appendix at the end of the article for easy access. They are referenced by roman numerals in the respective notes.

unanimous elevation to the position of successor to Śākyamuni, over the heads of other equally legendary but more powerful bodhisattvas (e.g., Mañjuśrī and Avalokiteśvara), could not have been possible unless he was fully integrated into the traditional structure of the bodhisattva path.[3] The aim of this chapter is to trace the stages, as depicted in the Pali and Sanskrit literature, in the bodhisattva career of Maitreya, culminating in the prophecy of his future Buddhahood.

The only surviving South Asian texts that deal exclusively with Maitreya, the Pali *Anāgatavaṃsa* and the Sanskrit *Maitreya-vyākaraṇa*, are both noncanonical, and their date and authorship are uncertain. In the canonical literature of the Theravādins, Maitreya is mentioned only once, and rather casually, in the *Cakkavattisīhanāda-sutta* of the *Dīghanikāya*. Among the Mūla-Sarvāstivādins, Maitreya receives a less casual, yet not complete treatment in the *Maitreyāvadāna* of the *Divyāvadāna*. The *Mahāvastu*, the canonical text of the Lokottaravādi-Mahāsāṅghikas, which developed the concept of bodhisattvas as supernatural beings, was apparently responsible for initiating a list of future Buddhas with Maitreya at its head. It therefore serves as an excellent starting point for the study of Maitreya's career as a bodhisattva.

Turning to the Mahāyāna Sūtras, one finds Maitreya mentioned in almost all the Vaipulyasūtras, and in some of these he is active either as an interlocutor or as a preacher, enjoying a status similar to that of the bodhisattva Mañjuśrī. In the postcanonical period, the Theravādins appear to have lavished greater attention on Maitreya. The *Anāgatavaṃsa* draws exclusively upon the *Dīghanikāya* passage found in the *Cakkavattisīhanāda-sutta*, as does its complementary *Maitreya-vyākaraṇa* (together with a Khotanese recension of it called *Maitreya-samiti*) upon the *Divyāvadāna*. At a still later date, around the fourteenth century, the Theravādins too found it necessary to establish a line of future Buddhas, as evidenced by the *Dasabodhisattuppattikathā*, in which nine other persons known to the Pali canon (including King Pasenadi of Kosala) were selected to follow Maitreya in succession as Buddhas. There is also a small southeast Asian Pali text called the *Pañcabuddhabyākaraṇa* that narrates an unusual story about Maitreya's birth as a lion in the company of four other bodhisattvas of our eon. Finally, mention should be made of two popular works, one in Sinhalese called *Śrī Saddhammāvavāda-saṅgrahaya* and the other in Thai called the *Phra Pathomsomphōthikathā,* which contain new episodes leading to the prophecy of Maitreya's future Buddhahood. This, then, is the textual material available to us in the South and Southeast Asian traditions, which can be studied to identify the stages of Maitreya's bodhisattva career.

The *Mahāvastu* itself talks of four stages in the career of a bodhisattva.[4] The first is called *prakṛti-caryā,* or "natural career," during which a future bodhisattva leads a righteous life, worships the Buddhas, and cultivates the roots of merit (*kuśala-mūla*). The second stage is called *praṇidhāna-caryā,* "the resolving stage," during which he vows to attain enlightenment (*bodhi*). This is always done in the presence of a Buddha, who prophecies (*vyākaraṇa*) the aspirant's future Buddhahood, whereupon he comes to be designated as a bodhisattva. The third stage is called *anuloma-caryā,* "the conforming stage," during which the bodhisattva progressively approaches the goal through various *bhūmis* by fulfilling the ten *pāramitās.* The final stage is called *anivartana-caryā,* "the preserving career," or the point at which it becomes impossible for the bodhisattva to turn away from the path; he then becomes destined (*niyata*) for Buddhahood. Once he attains this stage, he will be anointed (*abhiṣeka*) by a Buddha as his immediate successor and will be reborn in the Tuṣita Heaven. The bodhisattva's final incarnation from Tuṣita will be his last birth, when he will become a Tathāgata and will attain *parinirvāṇa* at the end of his life.

***Prakṛti-caryā* of Maitreya**

The literary material available to us on Maitreya is varied, and there is no unanimity among Buddhists concerning the events of his bodhisattva career. Only the *Mahāvastu* provides a glimpse into the prebodhisattva stage of Maitreya. As a matter of fact, this stage in the career of a bodhisattva is of little consequence, and there are no canonical narratives dealing with it even for Siddhārtha Gautama. Only a pair of Southeast Asian "extracanonical" Pali texts narrate an event concerning a female incarnation of Siddhārtha in which she offered oil to a monk so that he would worship a Buddha named Porāṇa-Dīpaṅkara as described in the *Buddhavaṃsa.*[6] One would have expected to meet with a similar story about Maitreya, but no such account has come down to us.[7] The *Mahāvastu* account referred to above appears in the first book when Śākyamuni narrates to Mahā-Maudgalyāyana his countless previous births during which he served thousands of Buddhas. In the middle of this narration, there is a reference to Maitreya, which, being out of context, seems likely to be a later addition. While speaking about a Buddha called Suprabhāsa, Śākyamuni says:

> "Suprabhāsa was the name of the Tathāgata when bodhisattva Maitreya, as the universal king (*cakravartin*), Vairocana, was aiming at the perfection of enlightenment in the future, and thus first acquired the roots of goodness. And when Suprabhāsa was the Tathāgata, the measure of man's life was four times 84,000 crores of years, and men lived more or less to this age ...
>
> "Then Mahā-Maudgalyāyana, when the *cakravartin* King Vairocana had seen the exalted Suprabhāsa, he experienced a supreme thrill, ecstasy, joy and gladness. For ten thousand years he honored... Then he conceived the thought: 'May I become in some future time a Tathāgata... as this Exalted Suprabhāsa now is. Thus may I preach dharma... as the Exalted Suprabhāsa now does."[8]

Normally, such a resolution made in the presence of a Buddha brings forth a prophecy (*vyākaraṇa*) such as the one that the brahman Sumedha obtained from the Buddha Dīpaṅkara regarding his future Buddhahood. In this case, however, the Buddha Suprabhāsa did not respond to the wish of the *cakravartin* Vairocana. As if he were explaining this strange phenomenon, Śākyamuni adds, "Even so, Mahā-Maudgalyāyana, there is something to add to this, for it was after forty-four *kalpas* that Maitreya conceived the thought of enlightenment."[9]

Whatever the reason for the long delay, it is clear from this statement that Maitreya's *prakṛti-caryā* lasted at least from the time of his meeting with the Buddha Suprabhāsa until his *bodhicitta praṇidhāna*. The *Mahāvastu* does not specifically mention the name of the Buddha who accepted his *praṇidhāna* and confirmed it by a prophecy (*vyākaraṇa*) concerning its fulfillment. This event probably occurred at a much later time, under the Buddha Ratnaśikhi, as described in the *Divyāvadāna*.

Praṇidhāna-caryā of Maitreya

In the *Divyāvadāna* account, the would-be Buddha Maitreya is not a *cakravartin* but an ordinary king named Dhanasammata who lived during the time when the Buddha Ratnaśikhi was born in Jambudvīpa. The father of this Buddha was a king named Vāsava, who was waging war against King Dhanasammata. Perceiving his imminent defeat, King Vāsava approached his son, the Buddha Ratnaśikhi, and asked him, "O Lord, at whose feet do all kings prostrate themselves?" The Buddha replied, "At the foot of a *cakravartiṇ*". Hearing this, King Vāsava made a resolution: "May I become in a future life a *cakravartin.*" He then received a prophecy from the Buddha that he would become a *cakravartin* by the name of Śaṅkha. Later, his opponent, King Dhanasammata, the victorious king, asked the Buddha, "At whose feet do the *cakravartins* prostrate themselves, Sir?" And when told that they prostrate themselves at the feet of a Tathāgata, King Dhanasammata made a solemn resolution that he would himself become a Tathāgata. The Buddha Ratnaśikhi then prophesied, "O King, you will become a Tathāgata by the name of Maitreya, when the life span of men would have reached 80,000 years."[10] Thus according to the *Divyāvadāna,* Maitreya entered his bodhisattva career under the Budha Ratnaśikhi.

Anuloma-caryā of Maitreya

Having made a *praṇidhāna* to become a Buddha, Maitreya must have performed heroic deeds similar to those of Gautama in his past lives. During this period, Maitreya may have been born as an animal and practised the perfection of keeping the precepts or giving away his life. Unfortunately, no such story is known, nor does Maitreya play any part in the 547 birth stories of Gautama as described in the *Jātakatthavaṇṇanā.* There is, however, a single story, called the *Pañcabuddhabyākaraṇa,* originating in Chieng Mai/ Laos (ca. the fifteenth century), which commemorates a holy place called Duṅ Yaṅ, sacred to the memory of the bodhisattva Maitreya. According to this extracanonical *jātaka,* Maitreya was born in Duṅ Yaṅ as a lion in the company of four other bodhisattvas, namely, Kakusandha, Koṇāgamana, Kassapa, and Gotama, who were born, respectively, as a rooster, snake, tortoise, and bull.[11] They kept the precepts (*sīla*) together at Duṅ Yaṅ and resolved that whoever among them attained Buddhahood should revisit that spot and leave behind a strand of hair as a relic. The story does not give details of the *pāramitās* fulfilled by Maitreya in this rebirth as a lion, but the *jātaka* is indicative of the Southeast Asian belief that all five bodhisattvas of the present eon, called the *bhaddakappa* (Skt. *bhadrakalpa*), had been playmates and that Gautama himself acted more as a colleague than as a teacher of Maitreya in his past life.

The next story referring to Maitreya's fulfillment of the *pāramitās* (or failure to do so) occurs in the *Divyāvadāna*, no 22. In this story a bodhisattva called Candraprabha wishes to cut off his head and offer it to a brahman named Raudrākṣa, but the guardian deity of the royal park prevents the brahman from approaching the bodhisattva. When Candraprabha learns of this, he orders the deity not to hinder his fulfillment of the *dāna-pāramitā* and cites the example of Maitreya, who suffered a great setback because of a similar obstruction:

> "This is [the spot], O guardian deity, where Maitreya had turned away. [How?] Maitreya, the bodhisattva, who had [once] abandoned himself to a tigress and had proceeded [on the bodhisattva course] for forty *kalpas*, had been compelled to turn his back upon [his career because of a similar obstruction] in once giving away his head."[12]

This story of Maitreya is not attested to elsewhere, but the Pali *Dasabodhisattuppattikathā* continues the theme with a similar motif. According to this text, Maitreya was born in the past in the kingdom of Kurus, in the city of Indapatta, as a *cakravartin* king named Saṅkha. He was the first *cakravartin* to appear in that eon, and the Buddha of that *kalpa* had not yet appeared. The *cakravartin* proclaimed that he would give away his kingdom to anyone who would bring him the good news of the appearance of a Buddha in the world. In the course of time, there appeared the Buddha Sirimata, and he arrived within the kingdom of Saṅkha. A poor man informed the *cakravartin* of the arrival of the Buddha in his kingdom, and after relinquishing his throne to him, the *cakravartin* started out on foot to meet the Buddha. Lord Sirimata, knowing the aspirations of the *cakravartin*, decided to appear before him. He took on the guise of a young man riding a chariot, drove to where Saṅkha was walking, and asked him to mount the chariot.

When they arrived at the assembly, the Buddha miraculously appeared before Saṅkha, seated in full glory. The Buddha then gave a sermon on *nirvāṇa*, and Saṅkha, wanting to worship the Buddha with the best gift that he could give, cut his head off at the neck with his bare nails and presented it to the Buddha with the words, "May this gift of mine result in omniscience." With this heroic deed he fulfilled the perfection of giving and was born in the Tuṣita Heaven, where he was known as Saṅkha Devaputta.[13]

These are the only references that one finds in non-Mahāyāna works pertaining to Maitreya's *anuloma-caryā*. The *Anāgatavaṃsa*, the Theravāda text on the lineage of the future Buddha, only casually mentions that Maitreya had served under four Buddhas, namely, Sumitta, (a former) Maitreya, Muhutta, and Gotama.[14] The names of the first three Buddhas are not attested to elsewhere, and the text furnishes no details concerning Maitreya's service under Gautama.

Maitreya, Manjuśrī, and Gautama

The Mahāyānists, of course, were not lax in compiling their own biographies of the Buddhas. The entire *Lalitavistara* is devoted to the life of Siddhārtha Gautama, and the *Sukhāvatīvyūha* describes how a monk named Dharmākara, practising under the direction of the Buddha, Lokeśvararāja, became the Buddha Amitābha by the sheer power of his ardent aspiration. One would expect that, in view of the extraordinary position held by Maitreya, the Mahāyānists would have produced a similar work to demonstrate the reasons for his anointment as the next Buddha. Surprisingly, however, no biography devoted exclusively to Maitreya has come down to us. There are nevertheless a number of references, in texts as early as the *Saddharmapuṇḍarīka-sūtra* and as late as the *Suvarṇaprabhāsa-sūtra* to incidents that bring Maitreya and Mañjuśrī together and relate them to Gautama in some incarnation. The "Vyāghrī-parivarta" of the *Suvarṇaprabhāsa-sūtra* seems to allude to a period long before either Mañjuśrī or Maitreya had entered the bodhisattva path. The story narrates how Gautama, as a bodhisattva, gave away his life to a hungry tigress. The bodhisattva was once born as the youngest son of King Mahāratha and was known as Mahāsattva. His two elder brothers were Mahāpraṇāda and Mahādeva, identified, respectively, with Maitreya and Mañjuśrī. One day the three brothers went to a forest and saw a tigress who had recently given birth to five cubs and was extremely hungry. Mahādeva (Mañjuśrī) saw her and wondered how she would ever be able to search for food. Mahāpraṇāda (Maitreya) lamented, saying, "Alas! It is extremely difficult to sacrifice oneself!"[15] Mahāsattva (Gautama), however, went fearlessly into the forest and offered his body to the tigress. This story is not contained in the *Jātakatthavaṇṇanā*, but found its way, via the *Jātakamālā* of Āryaśura,[16] into the *Jinakālamālī* in a greatly revised form. In both the *Jātakamālā* and the *Jinakālamālī* Mañjuśrī is omitted from the story altogether and Maitreya is made the chief disciple of the brahman mendicant Gautama. When the latter sees the hungry tigress, he orders Maitreya to scavenge some meat from a lion's kill to feed her. But before Maitreya can return, the bodhisattva, overcome by compassion, gives his life to the tigress and saves the cubs from being eaten by her.[17]

The connection between Mañjuśrī and Maitreya persists in their *anuloma-caryā*, as is illustrated in the "Nidāna-parivarta" of the *Saddharmapuṇḍarīka-sūtra*. It is said that Maitreya saw a great miracle of a ray emanating from the forehead of the Buddha Śākyamuni and was overwhelmed by it. He wanted to know the reason for the display of such a miraculous power. He decided that Mañjuśrī must have witnessed similar signs from earlier Tathāgatas and should therefore be able to explain it to him. Responding to his request, Mañjuśrī addressed Maitreya by his first name Ajita and said:

> "I remember that, in the days of yore,... more than a countless eons ago, there was born a Tathāgata called Candrasūrya-pradīpa. Training under the aforesaid Lord there was a bodhisattva named Varaprabha, who had 800 pupils. It was to this bodhisattva that the Lord ... taught the sermon called the *Saddharmapuṇḍarīka*, which was also preceded by a similar display of a ray issuing from his *ūrṇā-kośa* ... Eventually the Lord Candrasūryapradīpa entered into *parinirvāṇa*....
>
> "The monk who then was the preacher of the law and the keeper of the law, Varaprabha, expounded it for full eighty intermediate *kalpas* ....
>
> "Among the pupils of Varaprabha ... was one who was slothful, covetous, greedy for gain and clever.
>
> "He was also excessively desirous of glory, but very fickle, so

that the lessons dictated to him and the reciting done by him faded from his memory as soon as they were learned.

"His name was Yaśaskāma.... He propitiated a thousand *koṭis* of Buddhas, to whom he rendered ample honour. He went through the regular course (*anuloma-caryā*) of duties and saw the present Buddha Śākyasiṃha.

"He shall be the last [i.e., the next] to reach supreme enlightenment and become a Lord known by the family name of Maitreya, who will educate thousands of *koṭis* of creatures."[18]

After narrating this story, Mañjuśrī revealed the identity of the characters involved to Maitreya:

"He who then, ... was so slothful, was thyself, and it was I who then was the preacher of the law.

"As on seeing a foretoken of this kind, I recognize a sign such as I have seen manifested before. Therefore, for that reason I know,

"That decidedly the chief of the Jinas ... is about to pronounce the excellent sūtra which I have heard before."[19]

That Mañjuśrī was a teacher of Maitreya eons ago and that the latter was his slothful pupil need not be a revelation. What is astonishing is that the author (or the compiler) of the *Saddharmapuṇḍarīka-sūtra* should not have noticed any anomaly in presenting Mañjuśrī as more knowledgeable about the Buddha rays than Maitreya, who was acknowledged as the "anointed" one and should therefore have been far more advanced toward Buddhahood than the former!

Bodhisattva Maitreya's *Anivartana-caryā*

The apprenticeship of Maitreya under different Buddhas must have come to an end by the time Gautama himself had achieved Buddhahood. We have seen how Gautama and Maitreya met in their past lives, as in the "Vyāghrī-parivarta" of the *Suvarṇaprabhāsa-sūtra.* We now move forward to the time when Maitreya encountered Gautama after the latter's attainment of Buddhahood. The encounter is alluded to in a passage of the *Mahākarmavibhaṅga* in which Gautama praises Maitreya for undertaking noble actions that befit a bodhisattva. While illustrating a category of actions called *maheśākhaya-saṃvartanīya-karmas* (actions resulting in exalted births as a *cakravartin* or a Buddha) the text quotes from the *Purvāparāntaka-sūtra* (the sūtra of the past and future), in which the Buddha is said to have uttered the following words of inspiration on behalf of the bodhisattva Ajita: "Truthfully, O Ajita, this [act] prepares your mind for the noble aspiration, to leave the Sangha [and seek solitude]."[20] The passage is rather enigmatic, since quitting the community of monks should not be considered an appropriate action for a bodhisattva. But if we recall Mañjuśrī's statement in the *Saddharmapuṇḍarīka-sūtra* that Ajita was desirous of fame and hence delinquent in his career as a bodhisattva, then Maitreya's present action would seem to be highly commendable.[21] We may assume that Ajita's ardent exertions on his own would have led him into the irreversible (*anivartika*) phase of his career. He would have then obtained his much awaited *abhiṣeka* (anointment) as the next Tathāgata from the Buddha Gautama himself. The precise circumstances leading to their meeting, however, as well as the crucial scene of Gautama's public anointment of Maitreya as his immediate successor, are for some reason never revealed in any canonical text.[22]

In the *Cakkavattisīhanāda-sutta* of the *Dīghanikāya*[23] as well as the *Maitreya-vyākaraṇa*, the Buddha addresses the monks and tells them that in the future there will appear a Buddha named Maitreya. There is no indication in either text that the two had ever met or that Maitreya was ever known by any other name. In the *Mahāvastu*, where Maitreya is referred to as many as eleven times, his personal name is given as Ajita and he is fifth in the list of the one thousand Buddhas who are destined to appear[24] (according to the Mahāsāṅghikas, as opposed to only five in the Theravāda tradition) in the current *bhadrakalpa*. But at no time does the text describe the two meeting or engaging in conversation.[25]

The name Ajita, however, seems to have gained recognition among the Theravādins toward the end of the sixth century, since it is known to the *Anāgatavaṃsa*, and its *Aṭṭhakathā*, the *Samantabhaddikā*, as well as to the *Dasabodhisattuppattikathā* mentioned above. The *Anāgatavaṃsa* appears to be the first Pali text to refer to Maitreya by his name Ajita, who was said to have been a son of King Ajātasattu of Magadha, a contemporary of the Buddha.[26] According to the *Anāgatavaṃsa-Aṭṭhakathā* Ajita became a monk and was the recipient of two priceless pieces of cloth that

Mahāpajāpatī Gotamī, the foster mother of Gautama, had presented to the Buddha himself.[27] The author of the *Samantabhaddikā* is here undoubtedly drawing upon the canonical *Dakkhiṇāvibhaṅga-sutta* of the *Majjhimanikāya*. In this *sutta*, Gotamī presents two pieces of cloth to the Buddha, but the Lord asks her thrice to donate them not to himself but to the community (Sangha) of monks.[28] There is no mention in this *sutta* of any particular monk being chosen for the honour of receiving them.

Further elaboration of this story is to be found in a (sixteenth-century?) Sinhalese work called *Śrī Saddhammāvavāda-saṅgrahaya*.[29] According to this work Ajita was the son of a rich merchant named Sirivaḍḍhana of Saṃkissa, in the neighbourhood of Sāvatthi. He witnessed the Buddha's descent from the Tāvatiṃsa Heaven (after preaching Abhidhamma to his mother there) at Saṃkissa and decided to renounce the world. He joined the Sangha and became a very learned monk and an expert in the Tipiṭaka. In recognition of his erudition, Gautamī, after listening to the aforementioned *Dakkhiṇā-vibhaṅga-sutta*, offered him two lengths of cloth. The elder Ajita, however, made canopies out of them for the chamber occupied by the Buddha. Knowing his true disposition, the Buddha called the monks together and announced to them that the monk Ajita would, in this very *bhaddakappa*, become a Buddha by the name of Metteyya. Since according to the Theravāda tradition only five Buddhas may appear in a *bhaddakappa*, and since Gautama was the fourth, it followed that Ajita would be the next Buddha, even if Gautama had not specifically used such expressions as "the next" or "my successor."

The Thai *Phra Pathomsomphōthikathā* (nineteenth century) introduces still more innovations to the Sinhalese version. It follows the *Anāgatavaṃsa* in maintaining that Ajita was a son of King Ajātasattu and furnishes the name of his mother as Kañcanadevī. It differs, however, from the Sinhalese tradition in several details. Here Ajita is said to be a *sāmaṇera* (novice) and not a fully ordained monk. After narrating the story of Mahāprajāpatī's request to the Buddha to accept the pieces of cloth she had brought and his admonition to present them not to him but to the Sangha, the Thai version adds that Gotamī became very unhappy with the thought that the Lord had rejected her gift and went around the Nyagrodhārāma monastery offering her gift first to Sāriputta, Moggallāna, and then the other great elders. Each of them, however, refused her offer, pleading that they were unworthy of so great a gift. Gotamī finally had no choice but to give it to a novice, who happened to be none other than the novice Ajita, who accepted it quietly. Gotamī's heart was filled with sorrow, and she shed tears thinking that her store of merit was so low that a mere novice was the appropriate recipient of her gift. When the Buddha saw her weeping, he called Ānanda and asked him to fetch his alms bowl. Addressing the congregation of the great disciples, he said, "Disciples, do not carry this alms bowl of the Tathāgata; let this young Ajita carry it." He then threw it up in the air, whereupon the alms bowl disappeared into the clouds. At that point Sāriputta obtained the permission of the Buddha to retrieve it and floated up into the air to find it but returned empty-handed. All the other great disciples also tried to recover it, each equally unsuccessful. Then the Tathāgata commanded Ajita to bring back the alms bowl. Ajita realized that he lacked the miraculous power to fly, but with his heart filled with joy, he made an asseveration of truth (*sacca-adhiṭṭhāna-kiriyā*): "If I am leading the holy life (*brahmacariya*) as a novice in order to attain the Enlightenment which can destroy the Four Deadly Floods ... then may the alms bowl of the Tathāgata descend into my hands!" Instantly, the alms bowl descended and, as if it were a sentient being, declared to the assembly of the elders: "I did not come into the hands of the *mahāsāvakas*, but I come to the novice monk, because he will become not a *sāvaka*, nor a *paccekabuddha*, but a *sammāsambuddha*." Gotamī was greatly pleased by this miracle and worshipped Ajita with deep reverence. Ajita thought, "What good are these high gifts for me?" and made a canopy over the ceiling of the Buddha's residence with one piece of cloth and curtains with the other. The Buddha watched this act of worship and looked down upon the novice with a smile. Then the venerable Ānanda, perceiving the smile of the Buddha, inquired as to the cause, and the Buddha replied: "Lo! Ānanda, the novice Ajita will become a lion among the Jinas, a Buddha by the name of Metteyya in this *bhaddakappa*."[30]

These extracanonical stories of the monk Ajita have led scholars to search for an individual among the known disciples of the Buddha with whom he could be identified.[31] There are indeed two monks by the name of Ajita and Tissametteyya, both mentioned in the "Pārāyaṇavagga" of the *Suttanipāta*.[32] They were formerly pupils of the brahman Bāvari living on the banks of the Godāvarī (in the South), who later visited the Buddha and became his disciples. However, both attained arhatship during that lifetime[33] and hence could not be identified with a future Buddha.

Maitreya's *Vyākaraṇa* in the Mahāyāna Sūtras

As already stated, Maitreya's name appears in almost all of the Mahāyāna Sūtras. In some of them he is side by side with Mañjuśrī and participates in the discourses and is looked upon by everyone as the heir apparent to the Buddha Śākyamuni. We saw that he figures prominently in the introductory section, the "Nidāna-parivarta," of the *Saddharmapuṇḍarīka-sūtra.* He appears subsequently in four more Parivartas: the fourteenth, fifteenth, seventeenth, twenty-sixth. In the fourteenth, a large number of bodhisattvas appear from other Buddha fields and beg Lord Śākyamuni's permission to write down the *Saddharmapuṇḍarīka-sūtra.* But the Buddha tells them that they need not engage in this task, since he has at his service a great many bodhisattvas of his own Buddha field. At once, from all sides of the Sahā world, countless bodhisattvas materialize in a miraculous fashion and surround the Buddha. Maitreya is puzzled at the sudden appearance of this large congregation of bodhisattvas and, expressing his perplexity (*vicikitsā*), begs the Lord to dispel his doubts concerning this matter.[34] The sight also produces doubts in the minds of the lay disciples of the countless Buddhas from other worlds, and they too want to know how so many bodhisattvas could manifest from the Sahā world. The Buddhas then call their disciples to attention and ask them to remain silent, saying:

> "O sons of good families, wait a while. Maitreya bodhisattva, who has been proclaimed to be the successor to the Lord Śākyamuni, is asking questions concerning this matter to the Lord Śākyamuni. He will explain this matter. Listen to him."[35]

Two significant points are noticeable in this passage: (1) Maitreya's prophecy is alluded to as if that event had taken place long ago; (2) Maitreya is still subject to doubts and perplexities and hence has a long way to go before the prophecy of his Buddhahood is fulfilled. Maitreya, for example, wonders how

Gautama could have brought so many bodhisattvas to maturity in the less than forty years since his own attainment of Buddhahood.[36] The fifteenth Parivarta, called the "Duration of Life of a Tathāgata," is a sermon preached in answer to this question. The sixteenth and seventeenth parivartas, called, respectively, "The Merits" and "The Meritoriousness of Joyful Acceptance," are also addressed to Maitreya and describe in detail the merit accumulated by listening to the *Saddharmapuṇḍarīka-sūtra.*

Maitreya's induction into the Tantric tradition must have taken place several centuries after his appearance in the *Saddharmapuṇḍarīka-sūtra.* Even a casual look at Tantric literature shows that he plays a very minor role compared with such peers as Mañjuśrī and Avalokiteśvara. He is not mentioned at all in such major works as the *Hevajra-tantra,* and ritual manuals like the *Sādhanamālā* devote only a paragraph to him.[37] One significant passage in the *Guhyasamāja-tantra* shows that Maitreya was considered even by the Tantric tradition to be undeveloped in the mysteries of the Vajrayāna. The passage occurs in the seventeenth chapter, the "Sarvasiddhimaṇḍalavajrābhisambodhi," in which several Tathāgatas give short sermons on the nature of the *vajra-citta,* at the end of which the Lord Sarvatathāgatakāyavākcittavajra enters into a *samādhi* called *sarvatathāgatasamatāvihāra* and falls silent. It is at this stage that Maitreya greets all Tathāgatas and asks, "O Lords! How should a Vajrācārya, who has been anointed (*abhiṣikta*) by the Guyhasamāja consisting of all the Tathāgatas who have transformed their body, speech, and mind into *vajra* be seen by all the Tathāgatas and all the bodhisattvas?"[38]

All the Tathāgatas reply:

> "O son of good family, the *bodhicitta* should be seen as *vajra* by all the Tathāgatas. And why is that? *Bodhicitta* and the [Vajra]ācārya are not two; there is no duality between them ... All those Buddhas and bodhisattvas who live in the ten directions of the Lokadhātu visit the *ācārya* three times each day and worship him with the honour due to all the tathāgatas, and utter these potent words: 'He is the father of all of us Tathāgatas; he is the mother of all of us Tathāgatas.' Moreover, O son of good family, the amount of the aggregate of merit born of the *vajras* of the lords, the Buddhas who live in the ten directions, does not surpass the amount of the aggregate of merit that

occupies a single strand of hair of that [Vajra]ācārya. And why is that? O son of good family, the *bodhicitta* is the essence of the cognition of all the Buddhas and the source of the omniscient knowledge of all the Buddhas."[39]

These solemn words must have come as a great shock to Maitreya, who obviously considered himself to be an anointed person, and the text tells us that he became frightened (*bhītaḥ*) and deeply agitated (*saṃtrasta-mānasaḥ*) and remained silent after hearing these words.[40]

Maitreya suffered from doubts and perplexities unbecoming a truly advanced bodhisattva in the above episodes of the *Saddharmapuṇḍarīka-sūtra* and the *Guyhasamāja-tantra.* That he lacked confidence in his achievements and also needed to be reeducated in the deep mysteries of the Mahāyāna is made clear by his encounter with the indomitable Vimalakīrti described in the celebrated *Vimalakīrtinirdeśa.* It is understandable that the Great Disciples (*mahāśrāvakas*) would recognize their inferiority to the bodhisattva Vimalakīrti with regard to their achievement of wisdom (*prajñā*) and, therefore, would decline to visit him to inquire about his illness. It is extraordinary, however, that Maitreya as well hesitated and begged to be excused from performing this task when specifically ordered to do so by the Buddha. In disobeying the Buddha's command, Maitreya related to him an account of his past encounter with Vimalakīrti. He was once discoursing on the irreversible stage of a bodhisattva with the gods of the Tuṣita Heaven. At that time Vimalakīrti approached him and respectfully addressed him concerning his prediction:

> "Honourable Maitreya, the Blessed One predicted to you that after only one birth you will come to supreme and perfect enlightenment. With regard to which birth (*jāti*) did you receive this prediction (*vyākaraṇa*)? Is it the past (*atīta*) birth, the future (*anāgata*), or the present (*pratyutpanna*) one? If it is the past birth, it is already exhausted; if it is the future birth, it has yet to come; if it is the present birth, it is without foundation ... How then, O Maitreya, would you receive the prediction?"[41]

Maitreya, we are told, was reduced to silence and could not reply. He therefore pleaded with the Lord that he was incapable of inquiring about Vimalakīrti's illness. The revelation that Maitreya did not consider himself fit to visit Vimalakīrti must come as a surprise, since Maitreya, as Vimalakīrti admitted, was predicted to be the next Buddha. Even so, it is significant that, in the last chapter, the bodhisattva Maitreya is summoned to take over the task of transmitting this noble sūtra to future generations. In this connection, the Buddha narrates to Śakra, the king of gods, his own story of the distant past when he served the Buddha Bhaiṣajyarāja. At that time the bodhisattva Gautama was known as Candracchatra and was one of the one thousand sons of the *cakravartin* king Ratnacchatra. Describing the bodhisattva career of all those one thousand sons, the Buddha declares that they were destined to be the one thousand Buddhas of this *bhadrakalpa* and entrusts Maitreya with the guardianship of this sūtra.[42] The story appears to be an attempt to legitimize Maitreya's successorship and to place him in the exalted family of the Buddhas.

Maitreya in the *Prajñāpāramitā-sūtra*

The next important canonical text in which Maitreya matures as a propounder of the perfection of wisdom doctrine is the *Aṣṭasāhasrikā-Prajñāpāramitā-sūtra.* In the sixth Parivarta of this sūtra, called "The Supreme Merit of Dedication and Jubilation," Maitreya engages in a long discussion with the venerable Subhūti on the merit accumulated by others, the jubilation of a bodhisattva over that merit, and his dedication of the merit produced by that jubilation to the attainment of perfect enlightenment by all beings. Subhūti raises some important metaphysical questions concerning the foundations — that is, the "objective supports" (the *skandhas*) and points of view (*dṛṣṭis*) — that underlie the meritorious actions of others, over which the bodhisattva rejoices. He then points out that, if the bodhisattva rejected those subjective supports as non-existent, there would arise the perverted perception of rejoicing over something that does not exist. If, however, he accepted these supports as real, he would be no better than an ordinary person who is devoid of even rudimentary wisdom. Maitreya's words to Subhūti in this context are spoken in the spirit of skill in means:

> "O Subhūti, this should not be taught or expounded in front of a bodhisattva who has newly set out in the faith, for he will lose what little faith he has, and what little affection, serenity,

and respect which are his. In front of an irreversible bodhisattva should this be taught and expounded."[43]

Maitreya then proceeds to expound at length on the proper way in which a bodhisattva can skilfully transform the meritorious work founded on jubilation into omniscience.

Hitherto we have examined texts in which Maitreya participates in various discussions instigated by others, for example, by Subhūti or Vimalakīrti. But there are certain Mahāyāna Sūtras in which he initiates a dialogue by asking the Buddha a question or propounds a doctrine with great confidence on his own, as if he were vindicating his claim to future Buddhahood. In the *Samādhirāja-sūtra*, for example, the householder Candraprabha makes a resolution (*praṇidhāna*) to become a Buddha in the presence of Śākyamuni, and the latter, in his characteristic manner, bestows a smile upon him. Normally in sūtras it is the privilege of Ānanda to question the Lord concerning the reason for his smile and thus provide an occasion for the elucidation of an extraordinary event. In the *Samādhirāja-sūtra*, however, Maitreya is accorded this honour and elicits the Lord's prophecy (*vyākaraṇa*) about Candraprabha's future Buddhahood as described in the "Smitavyākaraṇa-parivarta" (no 15).[44] Similarly, in the last chapter of the *Lalitavistara*, called the "Dharmacakrapravartana," it is Maitreya who is singled out to request the Tathāgata Gautama to display a miracle called the Turning of the Wheel of Law on behalf of the countless bodhisattvas who were gathered at the Deer Park of Vārāṇasī. Using several hundred adjectives, the Tathāgata describes to Maitreya the true nature of the *dharmacakra*, which was not revealed to his earlier audience of the group of five monks.[45] The *Lalitavistara* itself does not allude to Maitreya as the successor to Gautama, but in the last Parivarta the Buddha specifically entrusts this sūtra to Maitreya, thus elevating him to a higher status than other bodhisattvas.[46]

The Bodhisattva Maitreya as a Preacher of the Doctrine

To be acceptable as a bodhisattva to both the Hīnayāna and the Mahāyāna schools, Maitreya would have to be an advocate of teachings that are free of sectarian bias. The *Śālistamba-sūtra* is a perfect example of such a teaching, since it is devoted entirely to the doctrine of *pratītya-samutpāda* (conditioned coproduction). The sūtra begins as follows. Once when the Lord was living in Rājagraha at Vulture's Peak, the venerable Śāriputra approached the place where the bodhisattva Maitreya was mindfully pacing back and forth (*caṅkrama*). They exchanged greetings and sat down together on a stone slab. Then the venerable Śāriputra spoke:

> "O Maitreya, having seen today a sheaf of corn (*śālistamba*) the Lord uttered the following: 'Whosoever, O monks, perceives the *pratītya-samutpāda* perceives the Dharma, perceives the Buddha.' Having spoken thus the Lord fell silent. O Maitreya, what is the meaning of these words of the Lord? What is *pratītya-samutpāda*? What is Dharma? Who is the Buddha? How is seeing *pratītya-samutpāda* [the same as] seeing the Dharma? How is seeing the Dharma [the same as] seeing the Buddha?"[47]

When asked thus, Maitreya expounded at great length on the doctrine of the *pratītya-samutpāda* and explained how perceiving the Dharma was identical to perceiving the Buddha. Although it is considered to be a Mahāyāna Sūtra, the *Śālistamba-sūtra* contains no doctrine that would be unacceptable to non-Mahāyāna schools and indeed was considered canonical by the Sarvāstivādins and the Mahīśāsakas, as we know from Yaśomitra's eighth-century commentary on Vasubandhu's *Abhidharmakośa-bhāṣya*, the *Sphuṭārthā-vyākhyā*. The *Kośa-bhāṣya* examines a view (attributed to the Mahīśāsakas by Yaśomitra) that the *pratītya-samutpāda* itself was an unconditioned (*asaṃskṛta*) dharma like *nirvāṇa*. This view was said to have been supported by the following sūtra passage:

> Whether the Tathāgatas appear or whether the Tathāgatas do not appear, the Law [of *pratītya-samutpāda*] does exist, the Thatness, the Dharmaness, the invariable nature of dharmas, the unchangeableness of the Law.[48]

Yaśomitra in his *Vyākhyā* identifies this text as the *Śālistamba-sūtra* and states that these were the words of Lord (Bhagavān) Maitreya spoken to Śāriputra.[49] Although this passage is missing in the extant editions of the *Śālistamba-sūtra*, it has a parallel in the Pali *Saṃyuttanikāya*[50] and is quoted by Candrakīrti in his *Prasannapadā*[51] commentary on Nāgārjuna's *Mādhyamikakārikā*. It may certainly be regarded as a great utterance spoken by a future

Buddha on the impersonal nature of the Law that prevails regardless of his appearance! It is significant that, at the conclusion of his discourse, Maitreya tells Śāriputra that whosoever understands properly the *pratītya-samutpāda* receives the prophecy of his future Buddhahood from the Lord: "You shall become a fully enlightened Buddha."[52] Such an utterance claimed to have issued from Maitreya seems to be an attempt on the part of the compiler of the sūtra to vindicate his claim to future Buddhahood.

The most important scripture revealing the true majesty of Maitreya's insight into the Law and his mastery over the meditational trances is the *Gaṇḍavyūha-sūtra.* An entire chapter (no. 54), some sixty pages long, describes his meeting with the pilgrim Sudhana. Following Mañjuśrī's command, Sudhana had travelled all over the South (Dakṣiṇāpatha) and had visited more than fifty *kalyāṇa-mitras* in search of instruction in the bodhisattva path. Finally, he arrived at Samudrakaccha, probably a port city, where Maitreya was residing in a gabled palace called Vairocanakūṭālaṃkāra-garbha. He approached Maitreya and sang his praises in 55 beautiful verses, calling him the eldest son of the Jina, the "anointed one" (*abhiṣeka-prāpta*). Maitreya received him with honour and instructed him in the bodhisattva career in no less than 121 verses. At the conclusion of his speech Sudhana respectfully addressed Maitreya:

> "The Noble Maitreya has been proclaimed by all the Buddhas to be the one who will attain to Buddhahood after only a single rebirth. Such a person must have passed through all the stages (*caryā*) of a bodhisattva, must have fulfilled all the *pāramitās*; ... he is anointed (*abhiṣikta*) for omniscient cognition ... May he please instruct me: How should a bodhisattva conduct himself in following his career?"[53]

Then Maitreya praised Sudhana for his aspirations, took him to the gate of his gabled palace, opened its gates with a snap of his fingers, and led Sudhana in. By the majesty of Maitreya's resolution (*adhiṣṭhāna*) Sudhana was able to see instantly all the halls and chambers of that great palace. He witnessed in a trance state the place where Maitreya had first conceived the thought of enlightenment (*bodhicitta-utpāda*) and saw the numerous Buddhas under whom he had practised the *pāramitās.* He also saw the place where Maitreya had initially attained mastery over the Maitrasamādhi, which earned him the name Maitreya,[54] a derivation supported by the *Samādhirāja-sūtra*[55] and accepted by Haribhadra in his *Ālokā*[56] commentary on the *Abhisamayālaṅkāra* and the *Prajñāpāramitā-sūtra*. He then saw those places where, in the course of his manifold transmigrations, Maitreya had been born as a *cakravartin* king, as Śakra, the king of gods, and the place where he would be reborn, namely, the Tuṣita Heaven. He also witnessed the extraordinary scenes of Maitreya's birth in Jambudvīpa out of the petals of a lotus flower, his first seven steps as an infant, his youth in the harem, his renunciation, his self-mortification followed by his partaking of food, his approach to the *bodhi* tree, his victory over the forces of Māra, his enlightenment and finally his turning of the Wheel of the Law at the request of Brahmā. When Maitreya realized that Sudhana had the vision of the entire bodhisattva career of the future Buddha, he withdrew his magic power, snapped his fingers, and awakened Sudhana from his trance.

Sudhana then discovered that the palace was no longer there and that everything he had seen was nothing more than a supernatural vision. He then begged Maitreya to reveal the true location of the palace and of Maitreya himself who had conjured it. Maitreya engaged for a while in enigmatic answers but finally returned to a more conventional level and, apparently anticipating that future generations would be curious about his place and parentage, told Sudhana that his birthplace (*janma-bhūmi*) was called Kuṭigrāma in the country of Mālada in the South (Dakṣiṇāpatha). There, he had chosen to be born in a family of brahmans in order to remove their vanity of high birth. While living in his hometown he had established his parents, a large number of his clansmen, and a merchant named Gopālaka in Mahāyāna. He had left that area recently and was now living in Samudrakaccha in his gabled residence called the Vairocanavyūhālaṁkāra-garbha.[57] He added that after his death he would "display" his rebirth in the Tuṣita Heaven in order to bring to maturity both the gods of that abode and those who would arrive there later through the inspiration of the Lord Śākyamuni. He assured Sudhana that, in the company of Mañjuśrī, he would see Maitreya again after the latter had attained buddhahood.[58] Maitreya then bid Sudhana farewell and directed him to return to Mañjuśrī for further instructions.

The Bodhisattva Maitreya and the Buddha Amitābha

The last Mahāyāna text that sheds light on the irreversible aspect of Maitreya's career before his rebirth in the Tuṣita Heaven is the *Sukhāvatīvyūha.* This sūtra, as is well known, is preached by Śākyamuni to the venerable Ānanda and contains a glorious description of the Land of Bliss (Sukhāvatī) presided over by the Buddha Amitābha. As the sūtra comes to a close, Ānanda expresses a wish to have a vision of the Lord Amitābha and of the bodhisattvas inhabiting his land. His wish is instantly granted by the Lord Amitābha, who produces a ray of light by which the entire Buddha land shines with great splendour. Maitreya, the only other person privileged to share the vision, also sees this miracle.

The Lord Śākyamuni addresses him, saying:

> "Do you see, O Ajita, the perfection of that Buddha country and the bodhisattvas who never stop meditating, as well as those gods and men who are dwelling within the calyx of lotus flowers and others who are born miraculously sitting cross-legged in the lotus flowers?"[59]

Ajita Maitreya saw all these and spoke to the Lord:

> "O Lord, will the bodhisattvas who have left this Buddha country or departed from the company of other blessed Buddhas be born in the world Sukhāvatī?"[60]

The Lord's answer to Maitreya's question is an emphatic one. He even gives a list of hundreds of crores of bodhisattvas who at different times and different places served different Buddhas and managed by their devout faith to be born in the blessed land of the Buddha Amitābha. We are not told whether Śākyamuni wished Maitreya also to be born there. In all probability, Maitreya could have chosen to be reborn in Sukhāvatī, in the presence of the Buddha Amitābha. The sūtra is silent on this matter, and the Buddha is content merely to ask Maitreya to guard the sūtra and not let it perish or disappear. The Mahāyāna tradition agrees unanimously that Maitreya did not seek Amitābha's company, but instead was born in the Tuṣita Heaven, awaiting the time for his descent to earth as the next Buddha.

Lest we wrongly assume, however, that the path of Maitreya will not lead to Amitābha's paradise, it must be added that at least one text, the *Samādhirāja-sūtra*, declares emphatically that, by worshipping Maitreya and by holding to the good law, a person may be reborn in Sukhāvatī, presided over by the Buddha Amitābha. Then, having served Lord Amitābha, he will strive for the attainment of perfect enlightenment.[61] Consequently, these two goals are not in conflict.

The Bodhisattva Maitreya in the Tuṣita Heaven

Buddhists recognize a law (*dharmatā*) that an "anointed" bodhisattva must be born in the Tuṣita Heaven before descending to earth for his final incarnation. Since Maitreya is such a person, it is assumed by all Buddhists that he is at present dwelling in Tuṣita, although there is no canonical reference to his death while in the company of the Buddha Śākyamuni. The first canonical reference to his residence in Tuṣita is to be found in the *Saddharmapuṇḍarīka-sūtra*, in the twenty-sixth chapter called the "Samantabhadra-utsāha-parivarta." This Parivarta describes the arrival of the bodhisattva Samantabhadra and a great congregation of other bodhisattvas at the assembly of the Buddha Śākyamuni after the latter has completed his preaching of the *Saddharmapuṇḍarīka-sūtra*. The bodhisattva Samantabhadra approaches the Lord and announces to him that his congregation has arrived from the eastern Buddha country of Lord Ratnatejābhyudgatarāja for the purpose of listening to the sermon called the *Saddharmapuṇḍarīka*. He begs Śākyamuni to explain in detail once more the entire sūtra. The Lord gives a brief exposition to the new audience, at the end of which Samantabhadra responds by saying:

> "O Lord, in the future I shall protect those who recite this sūtra and those who write it down ... Such people will never be born in purgatories nor in lower destinies. They will certainly be born in the company of the heavenly beings in Tuṣita, where the bodhisattva Maitreya, the great being, resides, endowed with the 32 marks, and surrounded by hundreds and thousands of other bodhisattvas and heavenly damsels (*apsaras*), preaching the Law."[62]

We saw earlier that Maitreya figures prominently in the first

Parivarta as well as in several of the middle Parivartas of the *Saddharmapuṇḍarīka-sūtra.* This reference to his residence in the Tuṣita Heaven, coming in the last Parivarta, would indicate that Maitreya had died at some point before the conclusion of the twenty-fifth Parivarta (called the "Pūrvayogaparivarta"). It is likely, however, that the twenty-sixth Parivarta was a much later addition and that the compilers took the opportunity to introduce Maitreya's birth in Tuṣita by means of this Parivarta. The *Mahākarma-Vibhaṅga*[63] and the *Mañjuśrī-Mūlakalpa*[64] are the only two other Mahāyāna texts surviving in Sanskrit that mention, though in no more than a single line, Maitreya's residence in Tuṣita.

Among the Pali texts, the earliest reference to Maitreya's heavenly abode is to be found in the noncanonical *Mahāvaṃsa.* In this chronicle of the island of Sri Lanka, king Duṭṭhagāmaṇi Abhaya (101-77 B.C.), the hero of that island and the builder of the great stūpa at Anurādhāpura, is said to have been reborn in the Tuṣita Heaven, "where the bodhisattva Maitreya, the Compassionate One, awaits his time [to descend on earth] for attaining buddhahood."[65]

In the late medieval period, the cult of Maitreya must have gained great popularity among the Theravādins of Sri Lanka and Thailand, as witnessed by the story of a monk named Malaya-Mahādeva, who is said to have visited heaven and gained an audience with Maitreya. According to the eleventh-century Pali narrative entitled *Rasavāhinī,*[66] by means of his supernatural powers the elder Malaya-Mahādeva took a devout layman to the Tāvatiṃsa Heaven to worship at the Cūḍāmaṇi-cetiya. There they met Maitreya, who was also paying his respects to the shrine, and the bodhisattva very graciously presented the layman with a set of divine clothes. The elder and the layman then returned to the island, where the layman enshrined the divine clothes in a *cetiya* and was subsequently reborn in Tuṣita in the company of the bodhisattva.

A similar story about the elder Malaya-Mahādeva's encounter with the bodhisattva Maitreya appears in the Thai *Phra Malai sutta,* written in Chieng Mai in the sixteenth century. Here the elder questions the bodhisattva concerning the means by which beings can ensure meeting him when he comes into the world. Maitreya advises the elder that recitation of the *Vessantarajātaka* will provide the necessary merit to yield a human birth that coincides with the auspicious occasion of the advent of the new Buddha![67]

Maitreya the Tathāgata

The bodhisattva career of Maitreya, leading to his birth in the Tuṣita Heaven, is of importance to the Buddhist tradition because it establishes his succession to Gautama after the latter's teaching (*śāsana*) disappears from the world. This apocalyptic event is believed to take place five thousand years after Gautama's *parinirvāṇa*[68] (circa A.D. 4456!), as the world regresses toward evil days, when human beings will live no longer than ten years.[69] But the advent of Maitreya will not take place immediately after the end of the five-thousand-year period.[70] Buddhists envisage a long interval of thousands of chaotic years before the world gradually moves into the ascending half of its cycle. It will reach its apex when human beings will have attained a life expectancy of more than eighty thousand years.[71] The conditions will have improved so much by then that the earth will be a paradise, with wish-fulfilling trees yielding fruits and the people needing no government to rule over them.[72] In the course of time, with the increase in population, evil and greed will increase, longevity will begin to decrease, and the production of food and protection of the weak will become necessary. Such a time is considered to be most auspicious for the rise of a universal monarch, the *cakravartin* king, the first lawgiver, who will set in motion the Wheel of Command by Law (*dhammena eva cakkaṃ vatteti*)[73] and bring the world under his domain (*āṇaṃ pavatteti*).[74] With the rule of law firmly established, there will appear a Buddha who, by turning the other wheel, the Wheel of the Sacred Law (*dharmacakra*), will usher in a new period in which human beings will follow his noble path.[75] The turning of these two wheels at the same time is an extraordinary event that takes place once in a long while, at the start of each new ascension within an intermediate eon (*antarkalpa*) in a given time cycle (*mahākalpa*).[76] At other times, a Buddha may arise without a *cakravartin* preceding him, as in the case of our own Buddha, who appeared at the tail end of an *antarkalpa*, which is moving rapidly toward a minor apocalypse. Maitreya's advent is distinguished from that of Gautama because he resolved to become a Buddha precisely at a time when human beings will live for eighty thousand years, as we have seen in the *Mahāvastu* and the *Divyāvadāna*. Moreover, his way will be paved by a *cakravartin* who, according to the *Divyāvadāna* account, also resolved to attain that high office. The karmic forces generated by their volitions will thus combine to inaugurate in the distant future a civilization supported by the two wheels of law, one leading by way of meritorious deeds to heaven, and the other by way of renunciation to *nirvāṇa,* the two complementary goals of human life.

Despite the unanimity of the Buddhist tradition concerning Maitreya's succession as the next Buddha, no Mahāyāna text has even given the details of the future Buddha's place of appearance or of his family life. Our sources of information on these points are exclusively non-Mahāyānist. The *Dīghanikāya* (*Cakkavattisīhanāda-sutta*), the *Divyāvadāna,* the *Mahāvastu,* the *Anāgatavaṃsa,* the *Maitreya-vyākaraṇa,* and the still later Sinhalese and Thai texts treat this topic very seriously and seem to draw upon a common tradition, unmarred by sectarian dissensions. Because Maitreya's advent, for the reasons outlined earlier, must be preceded by that of a *cakravartin* king, the canonical accounts of Maitreya the Tathāgata uniformly begin with a narrative of the *cakravartin* Śaṅkha, who will rule from his capital city of Ketumatī (the present Vārāṇasī). Because a *cakravartin* must be a kshatriya, it is apparently imperative that the Buddha be a brahman, and Maitreya is made the son of the *cakravartin's* chaplain, the brahman named Brahmāyu, and his wife Brahmavatī. In some accounts his family (*gotra*) name is Maitreya and his first name is Ajita. According to the *Anāgatavaṃsa,* the bodhisattva Maitreya will live a householder's life for eight thousand years with his wife Candramukhī and will have a son named Brahmavaḍḍhana. His renunciation will parallel that of Gautama, but after seeing the four sights, he will spend only a week practising the austerities, in contrast to Gautama's six years.[78] According to the *Divyāvadāna,* on the day of his enlightenment the seven royal gems (the wheel gem, etc.) of the *cakravartin* will disappear, and King Śaṅkha will renounce his kingdom and become a disciple of Lord Maitreya.[79] Subsequently, surrounded by the vast multitude of his disciples, Maitreya will visit a mountain named Gurupādaka, where the remains of the venerable Mahākāśyapa are lying undisturbed. After the mountain pass opens by itself, the Lord will approach the remains of the elder; taking them in his hands, he will address his congregation:

> "O monks, these are the bones of the elder Mahākāśyapa, who was born when the Lord Śākyamuni appeared in this world, when the life expectancy of men was no more than a hundred

years. This elder has been declared to be the chief among those who are satisfied with little, content with little, foremost in ascetic practices (*dhutaguṇa*). When the Lord Śākyamuni entered into *parinirvāṇa,* this elder held a recitation of the teaching of the Lord (*śāsana-saṅgītiḥ*)."[80]

The *Divyāvadāna* story of the Tathāgata Maitreya's noble act of honouring the remains of the elder Kāśyapa was no doubt motivated by a desire to establish a physical connection, if not a direct line of transmission, between the Buddha of the present and the Buddha of the future. This narrative, however, is conspicuously absent in the *Dīghanikāya,* the *Mahāvastu,* the *Maitreya-vyākaraṇa,* and in the later Theravāda literature.[81] Is it possible that the Mūla-Sarvāstivādins, who inhabited Kashmir and Gandhāra, introduced this story into the Maitreya legend through the influence of the Indo-Greeks and the Persians who ruled these lands? This conjecture is strengthened by the evidence of a further elaboration of this story that is found in both the Khotanese *Maitreya-samiti* and a *Maitreya-sūtra,* extant only in several Chinese translations closely related to it.

According to the *Maitreya-samiti,* after becoming the Buddha, Maitreya will climb a mountain called Kukkuṭapāda. Thereupon, the elder Mahākāśyapa, who has apparently sat in meditation (probably a *samādhi* called *nirodhasamāpatti*) on that very spot since the time of the Buddha Gautama, will arise from his trance and, having bowed to the Buddha Maitreya, will say:

> "Never before has there been a monk who, like me, has known two Buddhas and who experiences as much happiness as I am now at being able to impart these words of the Buddha... The former Ahur Mazda (whose name was Śākyamuni) has disappeared from all regions ...Śākyamuni asked me just before his death to tell you [that]...an evil age his risen, which is devoid of Buddhist monks. I have a few more moments of my life to spend." ...[And Śākyamuni said further,] "At the beginning of this eon Krakucchanda was the Buddha. He was followed by Kanakamuni, and then by Kāśyapa. Those who became monks in their *śāsana* but were not able to attain perfection will achieve release through me, the fourth [successor]. The fifth will be Maitreya, my equal; may he too release many beings."[82]

Having uttered these words, the text adds, the elder Mahākāśyapa will perform many miracles and will then enter *parinirvāṇa.*

The Chinese translation of the *Maitreya-sūtra* provides an additional detail about the episode. It relates that the elder Mahākāśyapa will offer Maitreya a robe (*saṃghāṭī*) of the Buddha Śākyamuni, saying that the Lord had entrusted it to him to be given to the future Buddha. When Lord Maitreya takes the *saṃghāṭī,* it will barely cover two fingers of his right hand and two fingers of his left. All will then marvel, "How small the past Buddha must have been!" The Lord Maitreya will then ask the elder to demonstrate his supernatural powers and to teach the *Sūtra of the Past Buddha.*[83]

The Theravādins, as noted earlier, have no canonical tradition of any such contact between a disciple of Gautama and the Buddha Maitreya. They have aspired, however, to establish a close connection between the two dispensations by claiming a family relationship between their Sinhala hero, King Duṭṭhagāmaṇi Abhaya, and the future Buddha Metteyya. According to the *Mahāvaṃsa,* Kākavaṇṇatissa and Vihāramahādevī, father and mother of Duṭṭhagāmaṇi, will be Metteyya's parents, Duṭṭhagāmaṇi himself will be the chief disciple of the Buddha, and his son Prince Sāli will be the Buddha's son.[84] The great lay devotees of the Buddha will be fortunate to have a vision of the Lord Maitreya, and the benefactor Anāthapiṇḍika will even redonate the sacred Jetavana to the new Lord![85] Both the *Anāgatavaṃsa* and the *Maitreyavyākaraṇa* promise that anyone who has served the Sangha, repaired a *cetiya,* or even raised a flagpole will meet and serve the future Buddha. Although the texts do not mention them specifically, there need be no doubt that the great commentators like Buddhaghosa[86] or the noble kings like the imprisoned Burmese monarch Siritibhuvanādicca of Pagan[87] or the numerous scribes and copyists of the Tipiṭaka, who have fervently aspired to be reborn during the time of the Buddha Metteyya, will do so and will be blessed with his vision and will attain *nibbāna.*

The Concept of a Future Buddha and a Future Jina

This survey of the South and Southeast Asian literature on Maitreya helps us to trace the traditional stages of his bodhisattva career, which culminates in his attainment of Buddhahood. No survey, however, can turn a legendary figure into a historical person, regardless of the number of Mahāyāna Sūtras or Theravāda apologists who have tried to present him as a contemporary of the Buddha Gautama. His overwhelming presence in the Mahāyāna Sūtras seems to imply that it was the Mahāyānists who were responsible for anointing him as Śākyamuni's successor. But a close examination of the material discussed in this chapter does not bear this out. It must be remembered that of the dozen or so great Mahāyāna bodhisattvas, including Mañjuśrī and Avalokiteśvara, who have been described as *ekajātipratibaddha* (those who are able to attain Buddhahood in a single rebirth),[88] only Maitreya is accepted as a bodhisattva by the non-Mahāyāna traditions. His investiture as the future Buddha, overriding the claims of all other bodhisattvas, suggests that Maitreya might originally have been a bodhisattva of the non-Mahāyāna variety, or was at the very least introduced by a pre-Mahāyāna school. This idea could not have originated in the Theravāda school, however, if only because no more than a single paragraph in the entire Pali Tipiṭaka is dedicated to Maitreya, and that, too, in the context of a long narrative concerning the future *cakravartin* Śaṅkha. The Mahāsāṅghika *Mahāvastu* is far more likely to have been the source of the cult of Maitreya. Although it refrains from mentioning Mañjuśrī, Avalokiteśvara, or any other bodhisattvas, it refers to Maitreya as many as eleven times, recognizes his first name Ajita, alludes to his past *caryās*, and proclaims his future Buddhahood through the mouth of the Buddha Gautama. But whereas the bodhisattva Gautama of the *Mahāvastu* stands out as a supernatural being (*lokottara*), the depiction of Maitreya is surprisingly free of any Lokottaravāda influence. Maitreya's succession could therefore be accepted unreservedly by the Theravādins of the South, as well as the Mūla-Sarvāstivādins of the North and correlated with their legend of the future *cakravartin* Śaṅkha. But apparently neither school made any attempt to make Maitreya a contemporary of the Buddha Gautama by introducing him as the latter's disciple in the existing sūtras. Only the Mahīśāsakas appear to have been bold enough to proclaim this, by first making Maitreya the chief preacher of the *Śālistamba-sūtra* and by then making the further claim that Maitreya was anointed by the Tathāgata as the future Buddha because he had correctly understood the doctrine of *pratītya-samutpāda*. Having assimilated Maitreya into the canon, the Theravādins (as well as *ācāryas* of other schools) must have found it necessary to identify him with a canonical person worthy of this singular honour. Who could such a person be who would answer to the name Ajita? The *mahāśrāvakas,* because of their having attained arhatship, were disqualified from receiving the title of bodhisattva. Nor would it have been proper to confer so great an honour on a layman, even if he were one as generous as Anāthapiṇḍika, because monks would then have been obligated to treat a layman deferentially. Given these parameters, the choice of a young novice must have appeared an attractive compromise for the position of bodhisattva. The Theravādins therefore came up with the most plausible story of a novice named Ajita,[89] who received first a gift of cloth meant for the Buddha and then a prophecy of his future Buddhahood. The name Metteyya itself, which expressed mastery over the *mettā-bhāvanā,* a favourite form of meditation among the Theravādins, might have also contributed to the popularity of this bodhisattva among the mendicants and the laity alike.

The hypothesis that the legend of the bodhisattva Maitreya was a Mahāsānghika innovation is supported by his portrayal in the Mahāyāna Sūtras. Despite his status as the "anointed one," Maitreya is repeatedly shown to be inferior not only to the bodhisattva Mañjuśrī, but even to the householder Vimalakīrti. His image improves gradually, however, and is fully matured in his encounter with the pilgrim Sudhana. Thanks to the author of the *Gaṇḍavyūha,* we are allowed a brief glimpse of Maitreya, the human being, emerging out of the legendary mist. It is significant that the author of the *Gaṇḍavyūha* chose to make him not a resident of Kashmir or Gandhāra, which might have suggested possible western influences, but of the South (Dakṣiṇāpatha). By his own account, as he tells Sudhana, Maitreya was a South Indian brahman born in a small place called Kuṭigrāma (Hut Village), in the (as yet unidentified) Mālada country. At the time Sudhana met him, he was living in Samudrakaccha, probably a port city. Before he left his native place, he had converted his parents and a large number of clan members to the Mahāyāna. Such a statement could very well be taken to mean that he was born in a non-Mahāyāna family and was himself a convert to Mahāyāna, a significant piece of information that adds credence to his assimilation into Mahāyāna from the Mahāsāṅghika.[90]

We will never know if the novice Ajita of the Pali texts and the brahman Maitreya of the *Gaṇḍavyūha* are identical, or if they are both purely legendary figures. One thing, however, is certain: The idea of a future Buddha need not be attributed to foreign influence. Buddhist canonical texts, as well as the texts of other Śramaṇa sects, such as the Ājīvikas and the Jainas, are full of references that anticipate the rise of a new Tīrthaṅkara, Jina, or Tathāgata. As is well known from the *Sāmaññaphala-sutta* of the *Dīghanikāya*, at the time of the Buddha there were six other prominent leaders of ascetic communities who had long established themselves as *tīrthakas*, the builders of bridges (for the crossing of the river of *saṃsāra*).[91] Makkhali-Gosāla, the Ājīvika saint, a senior contemporary of Gautama, was probably the first to proclaim himself a Jina (spiritual victor), a claim that was hotly disputed by his rival, the Nigaṇṭha Nātaputta, popularly known by his title Mahāvīra (the Great Hero), who was and still is recognized by his followers, the Jainas, as the twenty-fourth and last Tīrthaṅkara of the current cycle.[92] The first book of the *Vinayapiṭaka*, which describes the events following the Buddha's enlightenment, indicates that the Buddha himself must have been aware of the existence of such rivalries for the title of saviour. We are told that the Buddha was in search of disciples who might be able to accept him as a teacher (*satthā*), and so proceeded from Bodhgayā to Vārāṇasī on foot. The first person to encounter him was the naked ascetic Upaka, a member of the Ājīvika community, who accosted him and asked not so much about him as about his teacher: "On account of whom have you, your reverence, gone forth? Who is your teacher? Whose *dhamma* do you profess?"[93] This question brought a most extraordinary reply from the Lord: It was he himself who was an omniscient person without a teacher, who had no equal in the world, who was the Perfected Being, the Teacher Supreme, the One who had attained to *nirvāṇa*.[94] Upaka seems to have taken this claim as the boast of an upstart, for as he departs he says tauntingly, "According to your claim, your reverence, you ought to be Anantajina?"[95] The last term, which is attested to nowhere else in the entire Buddhist canon, has been explained by the commentators as "a victor of the unending, namely, of *nibbāna*."[96] It is more likely that the term referred to an exalted Jina, the founder of a new mendicant community and, if taken literally, to an eternally free soul (*sadā-mukta*), someone like the Īśvara of the *Yoga-sūtras* of Patañjali.[97] The title Jina was the one most coveted at that time and was claimed by all three historical teachers, Makkhali-Gosāla, Nigaṇṭha Nāṭaputta, and Siddhārtha Gautama. It is therefore quite likely that there was an anticipation at that time of the appearance of a Jina, Tīrthaṅkara, or Tathāgata to coincide with the approaching end of a great eon. As a matter of fact, the Jainas believed that the long period stretching across countless eons that witnessed the rise of the twenty-four Tīrthaṅkaras of the current descending (*avasarpiṇī*) half of the time cycle ended exactly three years, eight and a half months[98] after the death of Mahāvīra in 527 B.C. They also believed that no new Tīrthaṅkara would arise during the remainder of the *antarkalpas*, until the world began its ascendancy, and reached a state identical to the one described in the Buddhist texts as the time destined for the arrival of the Buddha Maitreya.[99] The Jainas have even compiled a list of the twenty-four Tīrthaṅkaras of the future time cycle, and their first Tīrthaṅkara of that period will be known as Mahāpadma, who will no doubt be a contemporary of the Buddha Maitreya.[100]

It is not merely adventitious that this Mahāpadma, the future Jina, was identified by the Jainas with a historical person who was a contemporary of both Mahāvīra and the Buddha. This person belongs to a royal family and is known as Śreṇika Bimbisāra,[101] the father of King Ajātasattu of Magadha. It is well known, as the Pali *Sāmaññaphala-sutta* relates, that Ajātasattu was a patricide, who subsequently became a lay follower of the Buddha.[102] The Jainas have claimed that Śreṇika had become a devout Jaina through the influence of his wife Celanā, an aunt of Mahāvīra. As a great devotee of Mahāvīra, he had accumulated enough meritorious karma to be the first Jina of the next cycle. Unfortunately, he was imprisoned by his son Ajātasattu, who kept him in chains and even lashed him daily himself. Later, Ajātasattu had a change of heart and approached his father, carrying an iron club, in order to free him from his chains. But the old king, misunderstanding his son's motives for approaching him with club in hand and fearful that he would cruelly inflict upon him an ignominious death, ingested poison and died instantly.[103] Despite his status as a future Jina, he was reborn, as retribution for this act of suicide, in hell, where he awaits his time to appear on earth as the next Jina, as surely as does the bodhisattva Maitreya in the Tuṣita Heaven.[104]

It is no small irony that the author of the *Anāgatavaṃsa*, allegedly an Indian Theravādin,[105] should choose a person from King Śreṇika Bimbisāra's family as the future Buddha. Members of the royal family, as is well known from the court histories of Buddhist kingdoms, were destined for high honours, especially when they embraced the yellow robes in their youth. The novice Ajita, as described in the *Anāgatavaṃsa*, was a prince, the son of the King Ajātasattu. The Buddhists could not be expected to appoint Śreṇika, a *sotāpanna* and victim of patricide, as suitable candidate for bodhisattvahood. As for Ajātasattu, his act of patricide disqualified him from claiming any such honour. Whether or not there was indeed a prince named Ajita, there seems little doubt that this royal house, which has been credited with destroying several small "republics" (*janapadas*) of the Gangetic Valley and with founding the Magadhan empire, stood in some special relationship to both Buddhists and Jainas and was probably regarded by all as a family of minor *cakravartins* (*dhammarājās*; see note 104) ruling at the termination of a great salvific era that had seen the advent of numerous Buddhas and Jinas.

NOTES

1. The terms "Buddha" and "Tathāgata" are virtually synonymous in Buddhist materials. In choosing to refer to Maitreya as a Tathāgata rather than as a Buddha, however I am following a distinction first noted in *Dharmasaṃgraha*, ascribed to Nāgārjuna. This work distinguishes between the five Buddhas — Vairocana, Akṣobhya, Ratnasambhava, Amitābha, Amoghasiddhi— and the seven Tathāgatas —Vipaśyi, Śikhī, Viśvabhū, Krakucchanda, Kanakamuni, Kāśyapa, and Śākyamuni. The former are celestial Buddhas who never appear on earth, whereas the latter advent from heaven for the weal of human beings in Jambudvīpa. Although Amitābha is referred to as Tathāgata in the *Sukhāvatīvyūha* and elsewhere, this does not negate the reasons for the classification itself. Hence, Maitreya is called Tathāgata to indicate his direct salvific role.
2. For example, "Among the doctrines of Zoroastrianism, which has strongly influenced other religions both East and West, is that of the savior (Saošyant), who, at the end of the world, will lead the forces of good and light against those of evil and darkness. Under the invading rules of N.-W. India Zoroastrianism and Buddhism came in contact, and it was probably through this that the idea of the future Buddha became part of orthodox belief" (A.L. Basham, *The Wonder That Was India* [New York: Grove Press, 1954], 274). For a discussion of the possible connection between Ajita Maitreya and Mithras Invictus, see Etienne Lamotte, *Histoire du bouddhisme indien des origines á l'ère Śaka* (Louvain, 1958). 782 *ff*.

3. It is difficult to determine the period during which Maitreya would have been fully accepted by both the pre-Mahāyāna schools. He must have reached his status as the successor to the Buddha Gautama by the time of the Kuṣāṇa King Kaniṣka (*ca.* 125 A.D.), since he is depicted in one of the king's copper coins bearing the Greek inscription "Metrauo Boudo." See Joe Cribb, "Kaniṣka Buddha Coins — The Official Iconography of Śākyamuni & Maitreya," *Journal of the International Association of Buddhist Studies,* 3, no. 1 (1980): 79-87.
4. *Mahāvastu,* 1:46 (See Appendix - i)
5. See *Paññāsa-jātaka* (no. 35, "Padīpadāna-jātaka"), 2: 396-402, and *Jinakālamālī,* 5.
6. *Buddhavaṃsa,* 2:60-66 (See Appendix - ii)
7. Maitreya is mentioned in the *Buddhavaṃsa* only in an appendix called the "Buddhapakiṇṇakakhaṇḍa" in the list of the five Buddhas of this *bhaddakappa. Buddhavaṃsa,* xxvii, 18-19.(See Appendix - iii)
8. *Mahāvastu,* 1:67-8. (See Appendix - iv)
9. Ibid., 1:69. (See Appendix - v)
10. *Divyāvadāna* (no. 3, "Maitreyāvadāna"), 40. (See Appendix - vi)
11. For a pictorial depiction of these five Buddhas with their animal emblems in a Cambodian temple, see the *Pañcabuddhabyākaraṇa,* plate 14.
12. *Divyāvadāna,* 202 (See Appendix - vii)
13. *Dasabodhisattuppattikathā,* 127. The rebirth of King Śaṅkha in Tuṣita need not necessarily refer to Maitreya's present (and final birth) in that heaven, because one can be born any number of times in world of gods (*devaloka*) by deeds of merit. (See Appendix - viii)
14. The editor of the *Anāgatavaṃsa* (Professor J. Minayeff) does not reproduce the text pertaining to Maitreya's past career but summarizes it as follows: "Then follows a history of the previous existence of Metteyyo, with the three Buddhas, Sumitto, Metteyyo, and Muhutto, during twenty-seven Buddhas, and finally at the time of the Buddha Gotama, when he was born as son of Ajātasattu, prince of Ajita" (*Anāgatavaṃsa,* 34).
15. *Suvarṇaprabhāsa-sūtra,* 108, 122. (See Appendix - ix)
16. The *Jātakamālā* does not mention Maitreya but calls the attendant (of the bodhisattva) by the name Ajita (*Jātakamālā* [no. 1, "Vyāghrī-jātaka"], 1-6).
17. *Jinakālamālī,* 4. (See Appendix - x)
18. *Saddharmapuṇḍarīka-sūtra,* 1: 57, 90-4. (See Appendix - xi)
19. Ibid., 1:95-6. (See Appendix - xii)
20. *Mahākarmavibhaṅga,* 39-40, See p. 39, n.6, where Sylvain Lévi observes that the *Purvāparāntaka-sūtra* survives only in Chinese translation and that this passage is not found there. (See Appendix - xiii)
21. A very interesting discussion of the virtue of leading the Sangha is recorded in the *Milindapañha* in connection with the Buddha's prediction regarding the Lord Metteyya's leadership of a large Sangha consisting of thousands of monks (*Milindapañha,* 159). Note that this is the only reference to Metteyya in the *Milindapañha.* (See Appendix - xiv)
22. The only canonical text surviving in Sanskrit in which the Buddha directly addresses Maitreya and predicts his future Buddhahood is to be found in the "Pudgala-viniścaya" chapter at the end of the *Abhidharmakośa-bhāṣya* of Vasubandhu. There the Vātsīputrīya states that the Buddha does not make declarations regarding future existences lest he be accused of admitting the doctrine of eternalism (*śāśvatavāda*). The Vaibhāṣika encounters the Pudgalavādin by quoting the following passage, in which the Buddha does

indeed speak of a future existence: idaṃ tarhi kasmād vyākaroti — "bhaviṣyasi tvaṃ Maitreyānāgate 'dhvani tathāgato 'rhan samyaksambuddhaḥ" iti? evam api hi śāśvatatvaprasaṅgaḥ? (*Abhidharmakośa-bhāṣya,* 9:471). Unfortunately, both Vasubandhu and his commentator Yaśomitra fail to indicate the source of this quotation, and it has yet to be traced in the extant canonical texts.

23. *Dīghanikāya,* 3:76.
24. *Mahāvastu,* 3:130. (See Appendix - xv)
25. Several passages in the *Mahāvastu* refer to the Buddha's prediction of Maitreya's future Buddhahood (e.g., *Mahāvastu,* 1:51). (See Appendix -xvi)
26. See note 14.
27. *Anāgatavaṃsa-Aṭṭhakathā,* p. 38. (See Appendix - xvii)
28. *Majjhimanikāya* (no. 142, *Dakkhiṇāvibhaṅga-sutta*), 3:253. (See Appendix - xviii)
29. See M. Saddhatissa's summary of this version in his introduction to the *Dasabodhisattuppattikathā,* 31.
30. *Phra Pathamsomphōthikathā,* chap. 20. I am indebted to Christopher Court, instructor of Thai at the University of California, Berkeley, for a summary of this chapter, entitled "Metteyabyākaraṇa-parivatta."
31. See Lamotte, *Historie du bouddhisme indien,* 776.
32. Ajitamāṇavapucchā and Tissametteyyamāṇavapucchā (*Suttanipāta,* 197-9).
33. *Suttanipāta-Aṭṭhakathā,* 5:2. (See Appendix - xix)
34. *Saddharmapuṇḍarīka-sūtra,* 182. (See Appendix - xx)
35. Ibid., 84. (See Appendix - xxi)
36. Ibid., 186. (See Appendix - xxii)
37. In an iconographic depiction of the bodhisattva Maitreya in a *maṇḍala,* he has three faces, three eyes, and four arms of golden hue; he is seated in a cross-legged position with his two upper arms in the teaching (*vyākhyāna*) *mudrā,* his lower right hand in the *abhaya-mudrā,* and his lower left hand holding a blossom of *nāgakeśara* flowers; cf. *Sādhanamālā* (no. 283, "Maitreyasādhanam"), 560. (See Appendix - xxiii)

    For a sketch of Maitreya based on the *Sādhanamālā,* see B. Bhattacharya, *The Indian Buddhist Iconography,* 2d ed. (Calcutta: Firma K.L. Mukhopadhyay, 1958). figure 47. It should be noted that the description of Maitreya given here is conspicuously silent on the characteristic feature of Maitreya's image as found in Tibet: the depiction of a stūpa in his crown. Nor does it make even the slightest hint of the depiction of Maitreya in Korean images, in which he has a huge square platform stūpa on top of his head. Even later tantric texts like the *Niṣpannayogāvalī* by Abhayākaragupta of Vikramaśīla monastery, which is dated *ca.* 1114 A.D., are silent on this prominent feature of Maitreya's iconography, indicating that this style of depiction may not be of Indian origin.
38. *Guyhasamāja-tantra,* 137. It should be noted that this is the only occasion where the term *vajrācārya* occurs in the *Guyhasamāja-tantra.* (See Appendix - xxiv)
39. Ibid., 138. (See Appendix - xxv)
40. Ibid., 138.
41. *Vimalakīrtinirdeśa,* 85-8.
42. Ibid., 265-70.
43. *Aṣṭasāhasrikā-Prajñāpāramitā-sūtra,* 71. (See Appendix - xxvi)
44. *Samādhirāja-sūtra,* 14:41, 74. (See Appendix - -xxvii)

45. *Lalitavistara* (no. 26, "Dharmacakrapravartanaparivarta"), 306-13. (See Appendix - xxviii)
46. Ibid. (no. 27, "Nigamaparivarta"), 318.
47. *Śālistamba-sūtra,* 100 (i.e., a, 1-2). (See Appendix - xxix)
48. *Abhidharmakośa-bhāṣya* (chap. 3, v. 28a), 137. (See Appendix - xxx)
49. *Sphuṭārthā-Abhidharmakośa-Vyākhyā* (chap. 3, v. 28a), 293. (See Appendix - xxxi)
50. *Saṃyuttanikāya,* 2:25. (See Appendix - xxxii)
51. *Prasannapadā (Mādhyamika-Kārikā-Vṛtti),* 40. (See Appendix - xxxiii)
52. *Śālistamba-sūtra,* 106 (i.e., a, 19). (See Appendix - xxxiv)
53. *Gaṇḍavyūha-sūtra,* 392-3. (See Appendix - xxxv)
54. Ibid., 408. (See Appendix - xxxvi)
55. *Samādhirāja-sūtra* (tenth Parivarta), 1:121-2. (See Appendix - xxxvii)
56. *Abhisamayālaṅkār Ālokā-prajñāpāramitā-vyākhyā,* 385. For references to a *Maitreyavimokṣa-sūtra* (named after Maitreya?), see *Śikṣāsamuccaya,* 9, 177. For a discussion of the derivation of the name "Maitreya," see Sylvain Lévi, "Maitreya le Consolateur," in *Etudes d'Orientalisme publiées par le Musée à la mémorie de Raymonde Linossier* (Paris, 1932), 2:355-402. (See Appendix - xxxviii)
57. *Gaṇḍavyūha-sūtra,* 416-17. (See Appendix - xxxix)
58. Ibid., 418. (See Appendix - xl)
59. *Sukhāvatīvyūha,* 65. (See Appendix - xli)
60. Ibid., 69. (See Appendix - xlii)
61. *Samādhirāja-sūtra* (18th Parivarta), 271. 52—3. (See Appendix - xliii)
62. *Saddharmapuṇḍarīka-sūtra,* 266. (See Appendix - xliv)
63. *Mahākarmavibhaṅga,* 40. (See Appendix - xlv)
64. *Mañjuśrī-Mūlakalpa,* 489. (See Appendix - xlvi)
65. *Mahāvaṃsa,* 32, 73. (See Appendix - xlvii)
66. *Rasavāhinī,* pt. 2, 163. (See Appendix - xlviii)
67. See Frank E. Reynolds, "Buddhism as Universal Religion and as Civic Religion," in *Religion and Legitimation of Power in Thailand, Laos and Burma,* ed. B. Smith (Chambersburg, Pa.: Anima Books, 1978).
68. *Anāgatavaṃsa,* 34-6. (See Appendix - xlix)
69. *Dīghanikāya,* 3: 73. For a Theravādin description of the destruction of the *mahākappa,* see F.E. Reynolds and M.B. Reynolds, *Three Worlds According to King Ruang: A Thai Buddhist Cosmology* (Berkeley, Calif.: Asian Humanities Press, 1982), chap. 10. For the Vaibhāṣika view, see the *Abhidharmakośa-bhāṣya* (chap. 3, v. 89-93), 178-81.
70. Contrary to the canonical tradition, Burmese and other Southeast Asian Buddhists often appeared to have anticipated the advent of the new Buddha soon after the 5,000th anniversary of the Buddha's *parinirvāṇa,* as noticed by E. Michael Mendelson: "In Burmese history, roughly from the time of King Bodawpaya onward, we can observe the interplay of two contradicting beliefs: one in the inevitable decline, and another in the nativistic and revivalistic forces that a messianic dispensation would be granted much sooner than the texts would have it" (*Sangha and State in Burma,* [Ithaca, N.Y.: Cornell University Press, 1975], 276).
71. *Dīghanikāya,* 3: 76 and *Ārya Maitreya-vyākarṇam* (Verse restored from the Tibetan). (See Appendix - L)
72. *Dasabodhisattuppattikathā,* 121. On the millenarian visions linked to the future Buddha Metteyya in the political life of the Southeast Asian Buddhist coun-

tries, see S.J. Tambiah, *World Conqueror and World Renouncer* (Cambridge University Press, 1976), chap. 19. (See Appendix - Li)

73. *Aṅguttaranikāya*, 1:109—10. For a full discussion of the ethic of *dharma* in early Buddhist thought, see S. J. Tambiah, *World Conqueror and World Renouncer* (Cambridge University Press, 1976), chap. 4. (See Appendix - Lii)

74. Compare "*yathā, mahārāja, mahiyā rājāno honti samajaccā, samajaccānam pi tesaṃ eko sabbe abhibhavitā āṇaṃ pavatteti* ...." (*Milindapañho*, 189). (See Appendix - Liii)

75. For further discussions of the interplay between the monarchy and the Sangha in India and Sri Lanka, see Frank Reynolds, "The Two Wheels of Dhamma: A Study of Early Buddhism" in *The Two Wheels of Dhamma*, ed. G. Obeyesekere, F. Reynolds, and B.L. Smith, American Academy of Religious Studies in Religion, Chambersburg, Pa., 1972; and Bardwell L. Smith, "Kingship, the Sangha, and the Process of Legitimation in Anuradhapura, Ceylon: An Interpretative Essay," in *Buddhism in Ceylon and Studies on Religious Syncretism in Buddhist Countries*, ed. Heinz Bechert (Abhandlungen de Akademie der Wissenschaften in Gottingen, 1978), no. 108.

76. The *Divyāvadāna* begins the account of Maitreya with the question, What is the reason for the simultaneous appearance of these two jewels? (*ko bhadanta hetuḥ ko pratyayo, dvayo ratnayor yugapal loke prādurbhāvāya? bhagavān āha: praṇidhānavaśāt*, p. 37). The text then narrates the story of the two kings, Vāsava and Dhanasammata, who had in the past resolved to become a *cakravartin* king and a Buddha, respectively (see note 10 above). According to the Vaibhāṣikas, a *cakravartin* king arises only when the life span of human beings remains above eighty thousand years, and parallel to the rule pertaining to the appearance of the Buddhas, only one *cakravartin* king may rule at one time: *atha cakravartinaḥ kadotpadyante?... amite cāyuṣi manuṣyāṇāṃ yāvad aśītisahasrake cotpattiś cakravartināṃ, nādhaḥ, tasyāḥ sasyasampadas tadūnāyuṣāṃ abhājanatvāt .... na ca dvau saha buddhavat* (*Abhidharmakośa-bhāṣya* [chap. 3, v. 95], 184).

77. *Anāgatavaṃsa*, v. 47, 54. According to the *Divyāvadāna*, Maitreya will attain enlightenment on the same day he renounces the world: *yasminn eva divase vanaṃ saṃśrayiṣyati, tasminn eva divase ... anuttaraṃ jñānam adhigamiṣyati* (*Divyāvadāna*, 61).

78. *Ārya Maitreya-vyākaraṇam*, 18, v. 54. This explains the association of the *nāgakeśara* flower with the iconographic representation of the bodhisattva Maitreya.

79. *Divyāvadāna*, 37. From this account, as well as that in the *Cakkavattisīhanāda* of the *Dīghanikāya*, it would appear that according to the Mūla-Sarvāstivādins even a Buddha and a *cakravartin* king cannot coexist! The role of the *cakravartin* king would seem to be solely that of establishing the rule of law and thus pave the way for the commencement of a Buddhist community at the beginning of the descending half of a new eon. (See Appendix - Liv)

80. Ibid. (See Appendix - Lv)

81. H. Saddhatissa notes that there is an unpublished Pali work named *Mahāsampiṇḍinidāna* in the Colombo Museum that contains a description of the cremation of the elder Mahākassapa's dead body in the presence of the future Buddha Metteyya. See *Dasabodhisattuppattikathā*, 43.

82. *Maitreya-samiti*, vv. 282-92.

83. Dr. K. Watanabe's translation of the *Maitreya-sūtra* in *Maitreya-samiti*, 227. For further discussions of the legend of the elder Mahākassapa's exchange of robes with that of the Buddha Gautama, see G.P. Malalasekera, *Dictionary of*

Pali Proper Names (London: Pali Text Society, 1960), 2: 478. For further discussion of this legend, see Lamotte, *Histoire du bouddhisme indien*, 226, and H. Saddhatissa's introduction to the *Dasabodhisattuppattikathā*, 43-5.

84. *Mahāvaṃsa*, 32: 81-3. The Pali *Anāgatavaṃsa* appears to be unaware of this Sinhalese tradition; according to this text Aśoka and Brahmadeva would become the two *agga-sāvakas* of the Buddha Metteyya: *Asoko Brahmadevo ca aggā hessanti sāvakā* (v. 97). The *ĀryaMaitreya-vyākaraṇa* does not contain any information on the chief disciples of the Buddha Maitreya. (See Appendix - Lvi)
85. *Avadānakalpalatā* (no. 21, "Jetavanapratigrahāvadānam"), 1:158, v. 83.
86. *Visuddhimagga*, 614. (See Appendix - Lvii)
87. G.H. Luce, "The Shewgugyi Pagoda Inscription, Pagan, 1141 A.D.," *Journal of the Burma Research Society*, 10, no. 2 (1920); 67-72. (See Appendix - Lviii)
88. *Samādhirāja-sūtra* (10th Parivarta), 119. (See Appendix - Lix)
89. The *Dhammapada-Aṭṭhakathā* (2: 240) narrative of Sāriputta's disciple Saṃkicca the Novice (*sāmaṇera*), who is said to have attained arhatship the moment the razor touched his hair, might have served as a model for the story of Ajitasāmaṇera's elevation to future Buddhahood.
90. Though we cannot be sure of his original religious affiliation, at the very least this information confirms that Maitreya was not a follower of Mahāyāna by birth.
91. The six *titthiyas*, namely, Pūraṇa Kassapa, Makkhali Gosāla, Ajita Kesakambali, Pakudha Kaccāyana, Sañjaya Belaṭṭhiputta, and Nigaṇṭha Nāṭaputta (the last identified with the Jaina teacher Mahāvīra), are all described in the following manner: *ayaṃ deva ... saṅghī c'eva gaṇī ca gaṇācariyo ca ñāto, yasassī, titthakaro, sādhusammato bahujanassa, rattaññū, cirapabbajito, addhagato, vayo anuppatto* (*Dīghanikāya* [*Sāmaññaphala-sutta*], 1:48. (See Appendix - Lx)
92. For a detailed account of Makkhali Gosāla's claim to the status of a Jina and to "omniscience," leading to his confrontation with the Jaina teacher Mahāvīra, see A.L. Basham, *History and Doctrine of the Ājīvikas* (London, Luzac, 1951), chap. 4.
93. *Vinayapiṭaka-Mahāvagga*, 1.8. (See Appendix - Lxi)
94. Ibid. (See Appendix - Lxii)
95. Ibid. The Buddha retorts with words that explain why he is entitled to be a Jina: *mādisā ve Jinā honti ye pattā āsavakkhayaṃ / jitā me pāpakā dhammā tasmā 'haṃ Upaka, jino ti //* (ibid): "Like me, they are victors indeed, /Who have won to destruction of the cankers; / Vanquished by me are evil things, / Therefore am I, Upaka, a victor" (*Book of Discipline*, 1:12). (See Appendix - Lxiii)
96. I.B. Horner's note: "*anantajina. Vinaya-Aṭṭhakathā* merely says, 'You are set on becoming a victor of the unending.' *Ananta*, the unending, may refer to *dhamma*, also to nibbāna" (*Book of Discipline*, n. 4).
97. *kleśakarmavipākāśayair aparāmṛṣṭaḥ pursuṣaviśeṣa īśvaraḥ/ ... sa tu sadaiva muktaḥ sadaiveśvara iti* (*Pātañjala-Yogasūtra* with the *Vyāsabhāṣya*, 1:24). (See Appendix - Lxiv)
98. *imīse osappiṇīe dusamāsusamāe [samāe] bahuvīikkantāe tīhiṃ vāsehiṃ aḍḍhanavamehi ya māsehiṃ sesehiṃ Pāvāe ... kālagae ... parinivvuḍe* (*Kalpa-sūtra*, no. 146. See Hermann Jacobi, *Jaina Sūtras*, Sacred Books of the East, vol. 22, pt. 1, London, 1884, p. 269. (See Appendix - Lxv)
99. For a description of the Jaina cosmology and the Jaina belief regarding the

appearance of twenty-four Jinas in the ascending and descending halves of each time cycle, see P.S. Jaini, *The Jaina Path of Purification* (Berkeley and Los Angeles: University of California Press, 1979), 29-33.

100. For a list of seventy-two Jinas (the twenty-four of the past, present, and future), see Jinendra Varni, *Jainendra-siddhānta-kośa* (Varanasi: Bharatiya Jnanapitha, 1944), 2: 376-91.

101. The *Jaina Mahāpurāṇa* (of the ninth-century Guṇabhadra) contains the following prediction about King Śreṇika's future Jinahood: "*Ratnaprabhāṃ praviṣṭaḥ san tatphalaṃ madhyamāyuṣā / bhuktvā nirgatya bhavyāsmin Mahāpadmākhyatīrthakṛt // āgāmyutsarpiṇīkālasyāditaḥ kṣemakṛt satām / tasmād āsannabhavyo 'si mā bhaiṣīḥ saṃsṛter iti*" // (*Mahāpurāṇa*, bk. 2, chap. 74, vv. 451-2). (See Appendix - Lxvi)

In the Theravāda tradition King Śreṇika is known by the name of Bimbisāra; he is considered to be a devotee of the Buddha. See Malalasekera, *Pali Proper Names,* 2: 284—9. For further details on Śreṇika in the Śvetāmbara Jaina canon, see "Seṇiya," in M.L. Mehta and K.R. Chandra, eds., *Prakrit Proper Names* (Ahmedabad: Institute of Indology, 1971-2), 2: 856-7.

102. *Dīghanikāya,* 1:80. In the Jaina tradition, King Ajātasattu is known by the name of *Kūṇika.* See Mehta and Chandra, *Prakrit Proper Names,* 1:196. (See Appendix - Lxvii)

103. Hemacandra describes the last days of Śreṇika in the *Triṣaṣṭiśalākāpuruṣacaritra,* 10: 12. 161-7. The Theravādins, however, have preserved a different version of the king's death. According to them, he was a *sotāpanna* (one who has "entered the stream") and submitted patiently to the torture perpetrated upon him by the men dispatched by his patricide son; he died peacefully and was reborn in the Cātummahārājika Heaven in the company of the regent king Vessavaṇa. See Malalasekera, *Pali Proper Names.* (See Appendix - Lxviii)

The Jaina claim that King Śreṇika committed suicide and the Buddhist claim that his son confessed to the crime of killing him cannot be easily reconciled. Is it possible that the Jainas considered it politically advantageous to absolve the new King Kūṇika (i.e., Ajātasattu) of patricide or that the Buddhists found it doctrinally unacceptable to allow a *sotāpanna* to commit suicide? Whatever the case, there is no doubt that both traditions considered the dead king a righteous ruler, the Buddhists going as far as calling him *dhammiko dhammarājā,* a designation normally applied in the canon only to a *cakravartin* king.

104. Ordinarily the Jainas also depict their would-be Jinas as being born in the heavens before their final incarnations as human beings. The case of Śreṇika is treated therefore as an extraordinary event that may take place only once in a long while. What is remarkable, however, is the Jaina refusal to make an exception to the operation of the laws of karma, even for so distinguished a person as a would-be Jina! Even assuming that Śreṇika had resorted to suicide only to save his son from his *ānantarya-karma,* an act that would seem appropriate for a bodhisattva, the Jainas cannot accept the taking of life in any form and had no choice but to consign him to purgatory. For a comparison of the careers of a bodhisattva and a would-be Jina, see P.S. Jaini, "Tīrthaṅkara-prakṛti and the Bodhisattva path," *Journal of the Pali Text Society,* 9 (1981): 96 104.

105. Attributed to an elder named Kassapa, an inhabitant of the Coḷa country. See Malalasekera, *Pali Proper Names,* 1:66.

BIBLIOGRAPHY

TEXTS AND TRANSLATIONS

Abhidharmakośa-bhāṣya of Vasubandhu, Sanskrit text ed. by P. Pradhan. Patna: K.P. Jayaswal Research Institute, 1967.

Abhisamayālaṅkar Ālokā-Prajñāpāramitā-vyākhyā of Haribhadra, 2 vols., ed. U. Woghihara. Tokyo, 1932-5.

Anāgatavaṃsa, ed. J.Minayeff. *Journal of the Pali Text Society*. London, 1886, 33-53.

Anāgatavaṃsa-Aṭṭhakathā, ed. J. Minayeff. *Journal of the Pali Text Society*, London, 1886, 33-53.

Ārya Maitreya-vyākaraṇam, ed. P.C. Majumdar. Calcutta: K.L. Mukhopadhyaya, 1959.

Aṣṭasāhasrikā-Prajñāpāramitā-sūtra, ed. P.L. Vaidya. Buddhist Sanskrit Texts, nos. 22—3. Darbhanga, 1959.

Buddhavaṃsa, ed. R. Morris. London: Pali Society, 1882.

Dasabodhisattuppattikathā, text ed. together with trans. entitled *The Birth-Stories of the Ten Bodhisattvas*, by H. Saddhatissa. Sacred Books of the Buddhists, no. 29. London: Pali Text Society, 1975.

Dhammapada-Aṭṭhakathā, 4 vols., ed. H.C. Norman, London: Pali Text Society, 1914.

Dharmasaṃgraha, ed. M. Muller and H. Wenzel. Anecdota Oxoniensia, Aryan Series, vol. 1, pt. 1. Oxford, 1855.

Dīghanikāya, 3 vols. ed. T. W. Rhys Davids and J.E. Carpenter. London: Pali Text Society, 1890-1911.

Divyāvadāna, ed. E. B. Cowell and R.A. Neil. Cambridge, Eng., 1886.

Gaṇḍavyūha-sūtra, ed. P.L.Vaidya. Buddhist Sanskrit Texts, no. 5. Darbhanga, 1960.

Guyhasamāja-tantra, ed. B. Bhattacharya. Gaekwad's Oriental Series, no. 53, Baroda, 1967.

Hevajra-tantra, ed. and trans. by D. Snellgrove. London Oriental Series, no. 6. London, 1959.

Jātakamālā of Ārya Śūra, ed. by H. Kern. Harvard Oriental Series, no. 1. Cambridge, Mass., 1890.

Jātakatthavaṇṇanā, 2d ed., 6 vols., ed. V. Fausboll. London: Pali Text Society, 1964.

Jinakālamālī, ed. A.P. Buddhadatta. London: Pali Text Society, 1962. Translated as *The Epochs of the Conqueror*, by N.A. Jayawickrama. Translation Series, no. 36. London: Pali Text Society, 1968.

Kalpa-sūtra (Prakrit Kappasuttaṃ). Jayapur: Prakrit Bharati, 1977. Translated as *Lives of the Jinas*, by H. Jacobi in *Jaina Sutras*, Sacred Books of the East, no. 22, pt. 1. London, 1895, 217-311.

Lalitavistara, ed. P.L. Vaidya. Buddhist Sanskrit Texts, no. 1. Darbhanga, 1958.

Mahākarma-vibhaṅga, ed. and trans. S. Lévi. Paris, 1932.

Mahāpurāṇa of Guṇabhadra, ed. P. Jain. Varanasi: Bharatiya Jnanapitha, 1965.

Mahāvaṃsa, ed. W. Geiger. London: Pali Text Society, 1958.

Mahāvastu, 3 vols., ed. E. Senart (Paris, 1882-97). Translated as *The Mahāvastu*, 3 vols., by J.J. Jones. Sacred Books of the Buddhists, nos. 16, 18 and 19, London: Pali Text Society, 1949-56.

Maitreya-samiti, ed. and trans. E. Leaumann. Strasbourg, 1919.

Maitreya-sūtra, trans. by Watanabe, in the *Maitreya-samiti*, 227-80.

Maitreya-vyākaraṇa, ed. and trans. S. Lévi, "Maitreya le Consolateur," in *Etudes d'Orientalisme publiées par le Musée Guimet á la mémorie de Raymonde Linossier*. Paris, 1932, vol. 2.

Majjhimanikāya, 3 vols., ed. V. Trenckner and R. Chalmers. London: Pali Text Society, 1888-1902.

Mañjuśrī-Mūlakalpa, ed. T.Ganapati Shastri. Reprinted in the Buddhist Sanskrit Texts, no. 18. Darbhanga, 1964.

Milindapañho, ed. V. Trenckner. London: Pali Text Society, 1880.

Niṣpannayogāvalī, ed. B. Bhattacharya. Gaekwad's Oriental Series, no. 109. Baroda: Oriental Institute, 1949.

Pañcabuddhabyākaraṇa, ed. and trans. G. Martini, in *Bulletin de l'Ecole Francaise d'Extréme-Orient*, 55 (1969): 125-44.

Paññāsa-Jātaka or Zimme Paṇṇāsa (in the Burmese Recension), 2 vols. ed. P.S. Jaini. London: Pali Text Society, 1980-1.

Phra Malai sutta (known by the title *Dika Malaideva sut*). Bangkok: Thambanakhan Press, 1971.

Phra Pathomsomphōthikathā, by Paramanuchit Chinorot (1790-1853). Bangkok: Ministry of Education, 1962.

Prasannapadā-Mādhyamikakārikā-vyākhyā by Candrakīrti, in *Madhyamakaśāstram*, ed. P. L. Vaidya. Buddhist Sanskrit Texts, no. 10. Darbhanga, 1960.

Rasavāhinī of Vedeha, ed. by Saranatissa Thera, 2 parts. Colombo: Jinalankara Press, 1928.

Saddharmapuṇḍarīka-sūtra, ed. P.L. Vaidya. Buddhist Sanskrit Texts, no. 6. Darbhanga, 1960.

Sādhanamālā, 2 vols., ed. B. Bhattacharya. Gaekwad's Oriental Series, nos. 26 and 41. Baroda, 1925-8.

Śālistamba-sūtra, no. 8 in the *Mahāyāna-sūtrasaṅgraha*, ed. P.L. Vaidya. Buddhist Sanskrit Texts, no. 17. Darbhanga, 1961, 100—6.

Samādhirāja-sūtra, 2 vols., ed. N. Dutt, *Gilgit Manuscripts*, vol.2, pts. 1 and 2. Srinagar, Kashmir, 1941 and 1953.

Saṃyuttanikāya, 4 vols., ed. Leon Feer. London: Pali Text Society, 1884-98.

Śikṣāsamuccaya, ed. C. Bendall. Indo-Iranian Reprints. The Hague: Mouton, 1957.

Sphuṭārthā-Abhidharmakośa-vyākhyā of Yaśomitra, 2 vols., ed. U. Woghihara. Tokyo, 1932—6.

Śrī-Saddharmāvavāda-saṅgrahaya, by Siddhartha Buddharakshita. Panadura, 1930.

Sukhāvatīvyūha, ed. M. Muller and B. Nanjio. Anecdota Oxoniensia, Aryan Series, no. 1, part 2. Oxford, 1883.

Suttanipāta, ed. D. Anderson and H. Smith. London: Pali Text Society, 1948.

Suttanipāta-Aṭṭhakathā (*Paramatthajotikā*). ed. H. Smith. London: Pali Text Society, 1916-18).

Suvarṇaprabhāsa-sūtra, ed. S. Bagchi. Buddhist Sanskrit Texts, no. 8. Darbhanga, 1967. Translated as *The Sūtra of Golden Light*, by R.E. Emmerick. Sacred Books of the Buddhists, no. 27, London, 1970.

Triṣaṣṭiśalākāpuruṣacaritra of Hemacandra. Bombay, 1956, chap. 10. Translated *as The Lives of Sixty-three Illustrious Persons*, by H.M. Johnson. Gaekwad's Oriental Series, no. 140. Baroda, 1962.

Vimalakīrtinirdeśa or the teaching of Vimalakīrti, by E. Lamotte. Sacred Books of the Buddhists, no. 32. London, 1976.

Vinayapiṭaka, 3 vols., ed. H. Oldenberg. London: Pali Text Society, London, 1979-83. Translated as *The Book of the Discipline*, 6 vols. by I.B. Horner. Sacred Books of the Buddhists, vols. 10, 11, 13, 14, 20, 25. London, 1938-66.

Visuddhimagga of Buddhaghosācariya, by H.C. Warren and D. Kosambi. Harvard Oriental Series, no. 41. Cambridge, Mass., 1950.

Yoga-sūtras of Patañjali with Vyāsa-bhāṣya: See *Pātañjala-Yogadarśanam,* ed. by R.S. Bhattacharya (Bharatiya Vidyaprakashana). Varanasi, 1963.

MODERN WORKS

Basham, A.L. *History and Doctrine of the Ājīvikas.* London, 1951.

The Wonder That Was India. New York: Grove Press, 1954.

Bhattacharya, B. *The Indian Buddhist Iconography,* 2d ed. Calcutta: Firma K.L. Mukhopadhyay, 1958.

Cribb, J. "Kaniṣka's Buddha Coins — The Official Iconography of Śākyamuni & Maitreya." *Journal of the International Association of Buddhist Studies,* 3, no. 1 (1980): 79-87.

Jaini, P.S. *The Jaina Path of Purification.* Berkeley and Los Angeles: University of California Press, 1979.

"Tīrthaṅkara-prakṛti and the Bodhisattva Path." *Journal of the Pali Text Society,* 9 (1981): 96-104.

Lamotte, E. *Histoire du bouddhisme indien des origines á l'ére Śaka.* Louvain, 1958.

Lévi, S. "Maitreya le Consolateur," in *Etudes d'Orientalisme publiées par le Musée Guimet á la mémoire de Raymonde Linossier.* Paris, 1932, vol. 2.

Luce, G.H."The Shwegugyi Pagoda Inscription." *Journal of the Burma Research Society,* 10, no. 2 (1920): 67-72.

Malalasekera, G.P. *Dictionary of Pali Proper Names,* 2 vols. London: Pali Text Society, 1960.

Mehta, M.L., and Chandra, K.R. *Prakrit Proper Names,* 2 vols. Ahmedabad: L.D. Institute of Indology, 1971-2.

Mendelson, E.M. *Sangha and State in Burma.* Ithaca, N.Y.: Cornell University Press, 1975.

Reynolds, F.E. "The Two Wheels of Dhamma: A Study of Early Buddhism." In *The Two Wheels of Dhamma,* ed. G. Obeyesekere, F. Reynolds, and B.L. Smith. American Academy of Religous Studies in Religion, Chambers, Pa., 1972.

"Buddhism as Universal Religion and as Civic Religion." In *Religion and Legitimation of Power in Thailand, Laos, and Burma,* ed. B. Smith. Chambers, Pa.: Anima Books, 1978.

Three Worlds According to King Ruang: A Thai Buddhist Cosmology. Berkeley, Calif.: Asian Humanities Press, 1982.

Smith, B. "Kingship, the Sangha, and the Process of Legitimation in Anuradhapura Ceylon: An Interpretative Essay." In *Buddhism in Ceylon and Studies on Religious Syncretism in Buddhist Countries,* ed. H. Bechert. Abhandlungen de Akademie der Wissenschaften in Gottingen, no. 108. 1978.

Tambiah, S.J. *World Conqueror and World Renouncer.* Cambridge University Press, 1976.

Varni, Jinendrá. *Jainendra-siddhānta-kośa,* 4 vols. (in Hindi). Varanasi: Bharatiya Jnanapitha, 1944.

Appendix: Citations from Pali & Sanskrit Texts indicated by Roman numerals in the notes.

(i) catasraḥ iha Mahāmaudgalyāyana bodhisatvacaryāḥ. katamāś catasraḥ? tad yathā prakṛticaryā praṇidhānacaryā anulomacaryā anivartanacaryā. *Mahāvastu*, I, p. 46.

(ii) Dīpaṅkaro lokavidū āhutīnaṃ paṭiggaho /
ussīsake maṃ ṭhatvāna idaṃ vacanam abravī//
passatha imaṃ tāpasaṃ jaṭilam uggatāpanaṃ/
aparimeyye ito kappe buddho loke bhavissati// ...
imassa janikā mātā Māyā nāma bhavissati/
pitā Suddhodano nāma ayaṃ hessati Gotamo// *Buddhavaṃsa*, ii, 60-66.

(iii) imamhi Bhaddke kappe tayo āsiṃsu nāyakā/
Kakusandho Koṇāgamano Kassapo cāpi nāyako//
aham etarahi sambuddho Metteyo cāpi hessati/
ete pi 'me pañca buddhā dhīrā lokānukampakā// *Buddhavaṃsa*, xxvii, 18-19.

(iv) Suprabhāso nāma Mahāmaudgalyāyana tathāgato 'rhaṃ samyaksambuddho yatra Maitreyeṇa bodhisatvena prathamaṃ kuśalamūlāny avaropitāni, rājñā Vairocanena cakravartibhūtena āyatiṃ sambodhiṃ prārthayamānena ... rājño Vairocanasya taṃ bhagavantaṃ Suprabhāsaṃ dṛṣṭvā udāraharṣam udāravegaprītiprāmodyam utpadye .... so taṃ bhagavantaṃ satkāresi ... taṃ cāyuḥpramāṇam anugṛhṇanto evaṃ cittam utpādesi: aho punar ahaṃ bhaveyam anāgate 'dhavni tathāgato 'rhaṃ ... yathāyaṃ bhagavān Suprabhāso etarahi. *Mahāvastu*, I, pp. 67-68.

(v) ato ca bhūyo anyaṃ:— catucatvāriṃśatkalpasamprasthitasya khalu punar Mahāmaudgalyāyana Maitreyasya bodhisatvasya paścā tāye bodhāye cittam utpāditam. *Mahāvastu*, I, p. 69.

(vi) atha Dhanasammato rājā ... sarvam imaṃ lokaṃ maitreṇāṃśena sphuritvā praṇidhānaṃ kartum ārabdhaḥ:—anenāhaṃ kuśalamūlena śāstā loke bhaveyaṃ tathāgato 'rhan samyaksambuddha iti. Ratnaśikhī samyaksambuddhaḥ kathayati—bhaviṣyasi tvaṃ mahārāja aśītivarṣasahasrāyuṣi prajāyāṃ Maitreyo nāma tathāgato 'rhan samyaksambuddha iti. *Divyāvadāna* (No. 3, Maitreyāvadāna), p.40.

(vii) tato rājā Candraprabha udyānadevatā nivārayati:— mā devatā mama śiroyācanakasyāntarāyaṃ kuruta. tat kasya hetoḥ? ...eṣa eva devate sa pṛṣṭhībhūto Maitreyo yo vyāghryā ātmānaṃ parityajya catvāriṃśatkalpasamprasthito Maitreya bodhisattva ekena śiraparityāgenāvapṛṣṭhīkṛtaḥ. *Divyāvadāna*, p. 202.

(viii) atha kho Sāriputta, so Saṅkho cakkavattirājā ... eted avoca: '...bhante Sirimata Buddha, ...idaṃ sabbaññutañāṇassa paccayo hotū ' ti vatvā nakhena sīsaṃ chindi. ... ayaṃ kho ... sīsadānaṃ paramatthapāramī nāma ahosi, jīvitapariccāgo va. tato cuto Tusitapure nibbattitvā mahiddhiko mahānubhāvo Saṅkho nāma devaputto ahosi. evaṃ, Sāriputta, Metteyassa ekā pāramī pākaṭā ahosi.

Dasabodhisattuppattikathā, p. 127.

(ix) Mahādeva uvāca: ihaiṣā kṣuttṛṣāparītaśarīrā ... na śakyam anyasthāne bhojanam anveṣṭuṃ. ko 'syāḥ prāṇaparirakṣaṇārtham ātmaparityāgaṃ kuryād iti. Mahāpraṇāda uvāca: bho duṣkara ātmaparityāgaḥ. ....
...Mahāpraṇādas tatha Maitriyo 'bhūt/
Mahādeva āsīd atha rājaputro
Mañjuśrīr abhūd vīrakumārabhūtaḥ// *Suvarṇaprabhāsa-sūtra*, pp. 108 and 122.

(x) Mahāsattassa sissānam isīnaṃ sabbajeṭṭhakasisso Metteyyabodhisatto ahosi. ath' ekadivasaṃ bodhisatto ... attano putte khāditukāmaṃ ekaṃ vyagghiniṃ disvā ... "samma, sīhādīnaṃ vighāsaṃ pariyesitvā imissā vyagghiniyā dassāmā" ti jeṭṭhsissam āha. *Jinakālamālī*, p. 4.

(xi) atītamadhvānam anusmarāmi, acintiye aparimitasmi kalpe/
yadā jino āsi prajāna uttamaś, Candrasya Sūryasya Pradīpa nāma//
...yaś cāsi tasyo sugatātmajasya, Varaprabhasyo tada dharma bhāṣataḥ/
siṣyaḥ kusīdaś ca sa lolupātmā, lābhaṃ ca jñānaṃ ca gaveṣamāṇaḥ//
yaśorthikaś cāpy atimātra āsīt, kulākulaṃ ca pratipannam āsīt/
uddeśa svādhyāyu tathāsya sarvo, na tiṣṭhate bhāṣitu tasmi kāle//
nāmaṃ ca tasyo imam evam āsīd, Yaśakāmanāmnā diśatāsu viśrutaḥ/
sa cāpi tenākuśalena karmaṇā, kalmāśabhūtena 'bhisaṃskṛtena//
ārāgayī buddhasahasrakoṭyaḥ, pūjaṃ ca teṣāṃ vipulām akārṣīt/
cīrṇā ca caryā vara ānulomikī, dṛṣṭaś ca buddho ayu Śākyasiṃhaḥ//
ayaṃ ca so paścimako bhaviṣyati, anuttarāṃ lapsyati cāgrabodhim/
Maitreyagotro bhagavān bhaviṣyati, vineṣyati prāṇasahasrakoṭyaḥ//

Saddharmapuṇḍarīka-sūtra, I, 57 and 90-94.

(xii) kausīdyaprāptas tada yo babhūva, parinirvṛtasya sugatasya śāsane/
tvam eva so tādṛśako babhūva, ahaṃ ca āsīt tada dharmabhāṇakaḥ//
imena haṃ kāraṇahetunādya, dṛṣṭvā nimittam idam evarūpam/
jñānasya tasya prathitaṃ nimittaṃ, prathamaṃ mayā tatra vadāmi dṛṣṭam//

Saddharmapuṇḍarīka-sūtra, I. 95-96.

(xiii) yathoktaṃ bhagavatā, Vārāṇasyāṃ *Pūrvāparāntaka-sūtre*'jitasya bodhisattvasya samuttejanaṃ kṛtam." mahate khalu te 'jita autsukyāya cittaṃ damayati yad idaṃ saṅghaparihāpaṇāya." *Mahākarma-Vibhaṅga*, pp. 39-40.

(xiv) bhante Nāgasena, bhāsitaṃ p' etaṃ bhagavatā:— "tathāgatassa kho Ānanda na evaṃ hoti—ahaṃ bhikkhusaṅghaṃ pariharissāmī ti .... puna ca Metteyassa bhagavato sabhāvaguṇaṃ paridīpayamānena evaṃ bhaṇitaṃ— so anekasahassaṃ bhikkhusanghaṃ pariharissati seyyathā pi aham etarahi anekasataṃ bhikkhusaṅghaṃ pariharāmī ti". *Milindapañha*, p. 159.

(xv) Puṣpiko nāmāyaṃ bhikṣavo bhadrakalpo, bhadrakalpe ca buddhasahasreṇa bhavitavyam. trīṇi pratītāni, ahaṃ caturtho. *Mahāvastu*, III, p. 130.

(xvi) Of the several passages in the *Mahāvastu* which refer to the Buddha's prediction about Maitreya's future Buddhahood, the following may be noted:

...pañca buddhakāryāṇi avaśyaṃ kartavyāni. katamāni pañca? dharmacakraṃ pravartayitavyaṃ...yuvarājā abhiṣiñcitavyo:— eṣa mamātyayena buddho loke bhaviṣyati, yathā etarhi ahaṃ tathā eṣa Ajito bodhisatvo mamātyayena buddho loke bhaviṣyatīti Ajito nāmena Maitreyo gotreṇa. *Mahāvastu*, I, p. 51.

(xvii) ayaṃ pana *Anāgatavaṃso* kena desito...ti. tatr' idaṃ visajjanaṃ. kadā desito ti *Buddhavaṃsā*vasāne. kassa pucchā ti Dhammasenāpatinā. kam ārabbha desito ti. Mahāpajāpatiyā Gotamiyā bhagavato upanītadussayugesu ekadussa-paṭiggāhakam Ajitattheram ārabbha desito. *Anāgatavaṃsa-aṭṭhakathā*, p. 38.

(xviii) ekaṃ samayaṃ bhagavā Sakkesu viharati Kapilavatthusmiṃ Nigrodhārāme. atha kho Mahāpajāpatī Gotamī navaṃ dussayugaṃ ādāya ... bhagavantam etad avoca: idaṃ me bhante navaṃ dussayugaṃ bhagavantam uddissa sāmaṃ kataṃ sāmaṃ vāyitaṃ. taṃ me bhante bhagavā paṭigaṇhātu anukampam upādāyā ti. evaṃ vutte bhagavā Mahāpajāpatiṃ Gotamim etad avoca:— saṅghe Gotamī dehi, saṅghe te dinne ahaṃ c' eva pūjito bhavissāmi saṅgho cā ti. *Majjhimanikāya* (No. 142, Dakkhiṇāvibhaṅga-sutta), III, p. 253.

(xix) evaṃ bhagavā arahattatikūṭena desanaṃ niṭṭhapesi; desanāpariyosāne Ajito arahatte patiṭṭhāsi ...desanāpariyosāne ayam pi (Tissametteyyo) brāhmaṇo arahatte patiṭṭhāsi.... *Suttanipāta-Aṭṭhakathā*, 5:2.

(xx) atha khalu Maitreyo bodhisattva mahāsattva ātmanā vicikitsaṃ kathaṃkathaṃ viditvā...bhagavantaṃ...etam evārthaṃ pṛcchati sma. *Saddharmapuṇḍarīka-sūtra*, p. 182.

(xxi) evaṃ ukte te tathāgatāḥ... tān svān svān upasthāyakān etad ūcūḥ:— āgamyadhvaṃ yūyaṃ kulaputrā muhūrtam. eṣa Maitreyo nāma bodhisattvo...bhagavataḥ Śākyamuner anantaraṃ vyākṛto 'nuttarāyāṃ samyaksambodhau, sa etaṃ ... arthaṃ paripṛcchati... eṣa ca bhagavān vyākariṣyati. tato yūyaṃ śroṣyatheti.

Saddharmapuṇḍarīka-sūtra, p. 84.

(xxii) atha khalu Maitreyo bodhisattvo....bhagavantam eted avocat:— katham idānīṃ bhagavaṃs tathāgatena kumārabhūtena ...samyaksambodhir abhisambuddhā, tasyādya bhagavan kālasya sātirimkāṇi catvāriṃśadvarṣāṇi. tatkathaṃ bhagavaṃs tathāgatena iyatā kālāntareṇedam aparimitaṃ tathāgatakṛtyaṃ kṛtaṃ... yo 'yaṃ bodhisattvagaṇo...anuttarāyāṃ samyaksambodhau samādāpitaḥ paripācitaś ca?

Saddharmapuṇḍarīka-sūtra, p. 186.

(xxiii) purvoktavidhānena candramaṇḍalopari pītam alaṅkārapariṇataṃ viśvakamalasthitaṃ trimukhaṃ trinetraṃ caturbhujaṃ kṛṣṇaśukladakṣiṇa-vāmamukhaṃ suvarṇagauraṃ sattvaparyaṅkinaṃ vyākhyānamudrādharakaradvayam aparadakṣiṇavāmabhujābhyāṃ varadapuṣpitanāgakeśaramañjarīdharaṃ nānālaṅkāradharam ātmānaṃ Maitreyarūpam ālambya mudrāṃ bandhayet. hastadvayena pṛthak muṣṭiṃ baddhvā tarjjanyau aṅguṣṭhamadhyotthāpite puṣpākāreṇa mīlayet. tato jāpamantraḥ:— oṃ maiṃ Maitreya svāhā. *Sādhanamālā* (No. 283, Maitreyasādhanam), p. 560.

(xxiv) atha khalu Maitreyabodhisattvo mahāsattvaḥ sarvatathāgatān praṇipatyaivam āha:— sarvatathāgatakāyavākcittavajraguyhasamājābhiṣikto bhagavān vajrācāryaḥ sarvatathāgataiḥ sarvabodhisattvaiś ca kathaṃ draṣṭavyaḥ? *Guyhasamāja-tantra*, p. 137.

(xxv) sarvatathāgatā prāhuḥ:— bodhicitto vajra iva kulaputra sarvatathāgataiḥ draṣṭavyaḥ. tat kasmāt hetoḥ? ...yāvanto daśadiglokadhātuṣu buddhāś ca bodhisattvāś ca tiṣṭhanti ...sarve te triṣkālam āgatya tam ācāryaṃ sarvatathāgatapūjābhiḥ sampūjya svasvabuddhakṣetraṃ prakrāmanti, evaṃ ca vāgvajrākṣarapadaṃ niścārayanti:— pitāsmākaṃ...mātāsmākaṃ sarvatathāgatānām. ...buddhānām bhagavatāṃ yāvat...puṇyaskandha... ācāryasyaiva romakūpāgravivare viśiṣyate. *Guyhasamāja-tantra*, p. 138. atha khalu Maitreya bodhisattvo mahāsattvo bhītaḥ santrastamānasaḥ tūṣṇīm abhūt. *Guyhasamāja-tantra*, p. 138.

(xxvi) atha khalu Maitreyo bodhisattvo mahāsattva āyuṣmantaṃ Subhūtiṃ sthaviram eted avocat:— nedam ārya Subhūte navayānasamprasthitasya bodhisattvasya mahāsattvasya purato bhāṣitavyaṃ nopadeṣṭavyam. tat kasya hetoḥ? yad api hi syāt tasya śraddhāmātrakaṃ premamātrakaṃ prasādamātrakaṃ gauravamātrakaṃ tad api tasya sarvam antardhīyeta. anivartanīyasyedam ārya Subhūte bodhisattvasya mahāsattvasya purato bhāṣitavyam upadeṣṭavyaṃ.

Aṣṭasāhasrikā-Prajñāpāramitā-sūtra, p. 71.

(xxvii) Maitreyu pṛcchi daśabalajyeṣṭhaputraṃ
kasyārthi etaṃ smitu kṛtu nāyakena//
na hy akāraṇakā jinā vināyakā
darśayanti smitam agrapudgalāḥ/
muñca ghoṣa vara dundubhisvara
kasya arthi smitu etu darśitam// *Samādhirāja-sūtra*, XIV, 41 and 74.

(xxviii) atha khalu Maitreyo bodhisattvo mahāsattvo bhagavantam etad avocat:— ime bhagavan daśadiglokadhātusaṃnipatitā bodhisattvā mahasattvā bhagavataḥ sakāśād dharmacakrapravartanavikurvaṇasya praveśaṃ śrotukāmāḥ. tat sādhu bhagavan deśayatu tathāgato 'rhan...kiyadrūpaṃ tathāgatena dharmacākraṃ pravartitam? bhagavān āha:— gambhīraṃ Maitreya dharmacakraṃ grāhakānupalabdhitvāt. ...tat khalu punar Maitreya dharmacakraṃ sarvadharmaprakṛtisvabhāvaṃ ...tathāgata ity ucyate...cakrāṅkitapādatala ity ucyate...idaṃ tan Maitreya dharmacakrapravartanaṃ tathāgataguṇavarṇapra-deśasya yat kiñcid avatāramātraṃ saṃkṣepeṇa nirdeśitaḥ. *Lalitavistara* (XXVI, Dharmacakrapravartanaparivarta), pp. 306-313.

(xxix) evaṃ mayā śrutam. ...athāyuṣmān Śāriputro yena Maitreyasya bodhisattvasya mahāsattvasya caṅkramas tenopasaṅkrāmīt. upasaṅkramya anyonyaṃ samodanīyaṃ kathaṃ bahuvidhaṃ vyatisārayitvā ubhau śilātale upāviśatām. athāyuṣmān Śāriputro Maitreyaṃ bodhisattvaṃ mahāsattvam etad avocat:— adyātra śālistambam avalokya Maitreya bhagavatā bhikṣubhyaḥ sūtram idam uktam:— "yo bhikṣavaḥ pratītyasamutpādaṃ paśyati sa dharmaṃ paśyati. yo dharmaṃ paśyati sa buddhaṃ paśyati. ity uktvā bhagavāṃs tūṣṇī babhūva. atha Maitreya sugatoktasūtrāntasya arthaḥ katamaḥ? dharmaḥ katamaḥ? buddhaḥ katamaḥ? kathaṃ pratītyasamutpādaṃ paśyan dharmaṃ paśyati? kathaṃ dharmaṃ paśyan buddhaṃ paśyati?" *Śālistamba-sūtra*, p. 100 (i.e. A 1-2).

(xxx) asaṃskṛtaḥ pratītyasamutpāda iti nikāyāntarīyāḥ, "utpādād vā tathāgatānām anutpādād vā tathāgatānāṃ sthitaiveyaṃ dharmatā" iti vacanāt. tad etad abhiprāyavaśād evaṃ ca na caivam. *Abhidharmakośa-bhāṣya* (iii, 28a).

(xxxi) "nikāyāntarīyāḥ" iti āryaMahīśāsakāḥ. ...āyuṣmān Śāriputro Maitreyaṃ bodhisattvam etad avocat. śālistambam avalokya bhikṣubhyaḥ sūtram idam uktam: yo bhikṣavaḥ...paśyati. idaṃ cābhisandhāyedam uktaṃ tatra sūtre:— "utpādād vā tathāgatānām anutpādād vā tathāgatānāṃ sthitaiveyaṃ dharmatā dharmasthititā dharmaniyāmatā tathatā avitathatā ananyatathatā bhūtatā satyatā tattvam aviparītatā aviparyastatā" ity evam ādi bhagavanMaitreya-vacanam. *Sphuṭārthā-Abhidharmakośa-Vyākhyā* (iii, 28a), p. 293.

(xxxii) uppādā vā tathāgatānaṃ, anuppādā vā tathāgatānaṃ, ṭhitā va sā dhātu dhammaṭṭhitatā dhammaniyāmatā idappaccayatā. *Saṃyuttanikāya*, II, p. 25.

(xxxiii) tathā:— utpādād vā tathāgatānām anutpādād vā tathāgatānāṃ sthitaivaiṣā dharmāṇāṃ dharmatā, ...evaṃ ...pratītyasamutpādo deśito bhagavatā.... *Prasannapadā (Mādhyamika-Kārikā-Vṛtti)*, p. 40.

(xxxiv) yo bhadanta Śāriputra, evaṃvidhadharmakṣāntisamanvitaḥ pratītyasamutpādaṃ samyag avagacchati, tasya tathāgato 'rhan samyaksambuddho...buddho bhagavān samyaksambodhiṃ vyākaroti:— samyaksambuddho buddho bhaviṣyasī ti. Maitreyeṇa bodhisattvena mahasāttvena evam uktam. *Śālistamba-sūtra*, p. 106 (i.e. a, 19).

(xxxv) ārya Maitreyo vyākṛtaḥ sarvatathāgatair ekajātibaddhatayā anuttarāyāṃ samyaksambodhau. yaś caikajātipratibaddho ... so 'vakrānto bodhisattvaniyāmam, tena paripūritāḥ sarvapāramitāḥ ...so'bhiṣiktaḥ sarvajñajñānaviṣaye ...tad vadatu me āryaḥ:— kathaṃ bodhisattvena bodhisattvacaryāyāṃ śikṣitavyam ..... *Gaṇḍavyūha-sūtra*, pp. 392-93.

(xxxvi) yatra Maitreyeṇa bodhisattvena prathamo maitrasamādhiḥ pratilabdhaḥ, yata upādāya asya Maitreya iti saṃjñodapādi tad adrākṣīt. *Gaṇḍavyūha-sūtra*, p. 408.

(xxxvii) dakṣiṇato Ajita sthitu tasya Maitraku nāma anantaguṇāḍhyaḥ/
yo 'sya anantaru bheṣyati buddhaḥ puṇyajñānaparipūritabhāraḥ//
maitryupekṣamudabhāvitakāyo karuṇayā ca janitaḥ sa mahātmā/

dharmamayāparyantaguṇebhiś cintayamānu munīndraguṇāni// *Samādhirāja-sūtra,* (Xth Parivarta), I, p. 121-22.

(xxxviii) "atha khalu Maitreya" ity ādi. tatra maitreyo nāma samādhiḥ ... tena maitrīvimokṣaprabhāvitatvād arjita yenāsau maitreyo jātaḥ iti Maitreyaḥ. *Abhisamayālaṅkāra-Ālokā-Prajñāpāramitā-vyākhyā,* p. 385. tathā hi śrūyate:-- ...ĀryĀsaṅgaḥ punaruktabāhulyena... *Prajñāpāramitā*rtham unnetum aśakto daurmanasyam anuprāpatḥ. tatas tam uddiśya Maitreyeṇa bhagavatā *Prajñāpāramitā-sūtram* vyākhyātam, *Abhisamayālaṅkārakārikāśāstram* ca kṛtam. tac chrutvā punar ĀryĀsaṅgena ĀcāryaVasubandhuprabhṛtibhiś ca vyākhyātam iti. *Ibid.,* p. 75.

(xxxix) api ca kulaputra, yad vadasi:—kiyad dūrāt tvam āgacchasī ti. aham asmin, kulaputra, āgacchāmi janmabhūmer Māladebhyo janapadebhyaḥ Kuṭigrāmakāt. tatra Gopālako nāma śreṣṭhī. taṃ buddhadharmeṣu pratiṣṭhāpya janmabhūmakānāṃ ca manuṣyāṇāṃ yathābhājanatayā dharmaṃ deśayitvā mātāpitṛjñātisambandhinaś ca brāhmaṇagṛhapatīn Mahāyāne samādāpya. ...Jambudvīpe ca Māladeṣu janapadeṣu Kuṭigrāmake brāhmaṇakuleṣūpapannānāṃ mātāpitṛjñātisambandhināṃ vinayārthaṃ brāhmaṇakulajātiviśeṣeṇa caiṣāṃ jātyabhimānikānirabhimānatāyai tathāgatakule saṃjananārtham ihopapannaḥ...so 'ham ihaiva...sattvānāṃ ... paripākavinayaṃ kurvan ihaiva Vairocanavyūhālaṅkāragarbhe kūṭāgāre prativasāmi. *Gaṇḍavyūha-sūtra,* pp. 416-17.

(xl) itaś cāhaṃ cyutaḥ Tuṣitabhavane saṃdarśayiṣyāmi ...sahaparipācitānāṃ ca tatropapattisaṃgrahaṇatāyai, Śākyamunisampreṣitānāṃ ca vineyakānāṃ prabodhanatāyi. kāle paripūrṇābhiprāyasarvajñatām adhigamiṣyāmi. bodhiprāptaṃ ca māṃ kulaputra tvaṃ punar api drakṣyasi sārdhaṃ Mañjuśriyā kalyāṇamitreṇa. *Gaṇḍavyūha-sūtra,* p. 418.

(xli) tatra khalu bhagavān Ajitaṃ bodhisattvam āmantrayate sma:— paśyasi tvam Ajita amuṣmin buddhakṣetre... yenaite bodhisattvā nityam avirahitā buddhānusmṛtyā? ...padmeṣu paryaṅkaiḥ prādurbhavanti...? ...Ajita āha:— paśyāmi bhagavan .... *Sukhāvatīvyūha,* p. 65.

(xlii) evamukte Ajito bodhisattvo bhagavantam etad avocat:— kiṃ punar bhagavan bodhisattvā ito buddhakṣetrāt pariniṣpannā anyeṣāṃ vā buddhānāṃ bhagavatām antikāt Sukhāvatyāṃ lokadhātāv upapatsyante? bhagavān āha:— ito hy Ajita buddhakṣetrād dvāsaptatikoṭinayutāni bodhisattvānāṃ ... yāni ...Sukhāvatyāṃ lokadhātāv upapatsyante. *Sukhāvatīvyūha,* p. 69.

(xliii) Maitreyasya ca buddhasya pūjāṃ kṛtvā niruttarām/
saddharmaśreṣṭhaṃ dhāritvā gamiṣyanti Sukhāvatīm//
yatrāsau virajo buddho Amitāyus tathāgataḥ/
tasya pūjāṃ kariṣyanti agrabodhīya kāraṇāt// *Samādhirāja-sūtra* (XVIII Parivarta), p. 271, vv. 52-53.

(xliv) ahaṃ bhagavan paścime kāle ...evaṃrūpāṇāṃ sūtrāntadhārakāṇāṃ bhikṣuṇāṃ rakṣāṃ kariṣyāmi, ... na ca durgativinipatagāmī bhaviṣyati, itaś cyutaś ca Tuṣitānāṃ devānāṃ sabhāgatāyopapatsyate, yatra sa Maitreyo bodhisattvo mahāsattvas tiṣṭhati, dvātriṃśadvaralakṣaṇo bodhisattvagaṇaparivṛto 'pasaraḥkoṭīnayutaśatasahasrapuraskṛto dharmaṃ deśayati.

Saddharmapuṇḍarīka-sūtra, p. 266.

(xlv) Maitreyas Tuṣitasurālayādhivāsī
prāpatavyā divi bhuvi ceha yena pūjā/
sa śrīmān daśabalatām avāpya śīghraṃ
lokānāṃ bhavatu śaśīva nityapūjyaḥ// *Mahākarma-Vibhaṅga,* p. 40.

(xlvi) bhinnadeho tato rājā kālaṃ kṛtvā diviṃ gataḥ/
devā Tuṣitavarā nāma Maitreyo yatra tiṣṭhati// *Mañjuśrī-Mūlakalpa,* p. 489.

(xlvii) buddhabhāvāya samayam olokento mahodayo/
Metteyyo bodhisatto hi vasate Tusite pure// *Mahāvaṃsa,* xxxii, 73.

(xlviii) tass' evaṃ sallapante Metteyyo bodhisatto āgantvā rathā oruyha theram upasaṅkamitvā pañcapatiṭṭhitena vanditvā ṭhito kim atthāy' ettha bhante āgatatthā ti pucchi. ...bodhisatto tassa [upāsakassa] tadanurūpaṃ dibbasāṭakayugalaṃ datvā appamatto hohī ti ovaditvā upāsakena ca therena ca saddhiṃ Cuḷāmaṇicetiyaṃ gantvā vandāpesi. *Rasavāhinī,* part 2, p. 163.

(xlix) ...mama 'ccayena paṭhamaṃ pañca antaradhānāni bhavissanti. katamāni pañca antaradhānāni? adhigama-antaradhānaṃ: tattha adhigamo ti bhagavato parinibbānato vassasahassam eva bhikkhū paṭisambhidaṃ nibbattetuṃ sakkhissanti. ...paṭipatti-antaradhānaṃ nāma jhānavipassanāmaggaphalāni nibbattetum asakkonto catupārisuddhisīlamattam pi rakkhissanti. ...pariyatti-antaradhānaṃ nāma tepiṭake buddhavacane sāṭṭhakathā pāḷi yāva tiṭṭhati tāva pariyatti antarahitaṃ nāma na bhavissati. ...liṅga-antaradhānaṃ nāma...pacchimakā bhikkhū ...kāsāvakhaṇḍaṃ chaḍḍetvā araññe migapakkhino vihed(-heṭh?)essanti. etasmiṃ kāle liṅgam antarahitaṃ nāma bhavissati. tato sammāsambuddhassa sāsane pañca vassasahasse sakkārasammānam alabhamānā dhātuyo sakkārasammānaṃ labhamānaṭṭhāne gacchissanti... idaṃ Sāriputta dhātu-antaradhānaṃ nāma. *Anāgatavaṃsa,* pp. 34-36.

(l) asītivassasahassāyukesu, bhikkhave, manussesu Metteyyo nāma bhagavā loke uppajjissati. *Dīghanikāya,* III, p. 76.

(li) sabbe manussā na kassantā na vaṇijjā arogā....buddhānubhāvena jātaṃ sālibhojanaṃ bhuñjitvā...sukhena jīvissanti. *Dasabodhisattuppattikathā,* p. 121.

(lii) yo pi so, bhikkhave rājā cakkavatti dhammiko dhammarājā so pi na arājakaṃ cakkaṃ vattetī ti. ...ko pana, bhante, rañño cakkavattissa dhammikassa dhammaraññō rājā ti? dhammo, bhikkū, ti bhagavā avoca. idha, bhikkhu, rājā cakkavatti dhammiko dhammarājā dhammaṃ yeva nissāya ...dhammaṃ apacāyamāno dhammaddhajo dhammaketu dhammādhipateyyo dhammikaṃ dhammāvaraṇaguttiṃ saṃvidahitvā...dhammen' eva cakkaṃ vatteti. taṃ hoti appaṭivattiyaṃ kenaci manussabhūtena paccatthikena pāṇinā. *Aṅguttaranikāya,* Vol. I, pp. 109-10.

(liii) Compare: yathā, mahārāja, mahiyā rājāno honti samajaccā, samajaccānaṃ pi tesam eko sabbe abhibhavitvā āṇaṃ pavatteti.... *Milindapañha*, p. 189.

(liv) yasminn eva divase Maitreyaḥ samyaksambuddho 'nuttarajñānam adhigamiṣyati, tasminn eva divase Śaṅkhasya saptaratnāny antardhāsyante. Śaṅkho 'pi rājā... Maitreyaṃ samyaksambuddhaṃ pravrajitam anupravrajiṣyati.

Divyāvadāna, p. 37.

(lv) tato Maitreyaḥ samyaksambuddho 'śitibhikṣukoṭiparivāro yena Gurupādakaḥ parvatas tenopasaṃkramiṣyati, yatra Kāśyapasya bhikṣor asthisaṃghāto 'vikopitas tiṣṭhati. Gurupādakaparvato Maitreyāya... vivaram anupradāsyati. ...Maitreyaḥ samyaksambuddhaḥ Kāśyapasya bhikṣor avikopitam asthisaṃghātaṃ pāṇinā gṛhītvā vāme pāṇau pratisṭhāpya evaṃ śrāvakāṇāṃ dharmaṃ deśayiṣyati:— yo 'sau bhikṣavo varṣaśatāyuṣi prajāyāṃ Śākyamunir nāma śāstā loka utpannas tasyāyaṃ śrāvakaḥ Kāśyapo nāmnā alpecchānāṃ santuṣṭānāṃ dhutaguṇavādinām agro nirdiṣṭaḥ. Śākyamuneḥ parinirvṛtasyānena śāsanasaṅgītiḥ kṛtā iti. *Divyāvadāna*, p. 37.

(lvi) Duṭṭhagāmaṇirājā so rājanāmāraho mahā/
Metteyyassa bhagavato hessati aggasāvako//
rañño pitā pitā tassa, mātā mātā bhavissati,
Saddhātisso kaniṭṭho tu dutiyo hessati sāvako//
Sālirājakumāro yo tassa rañño suto tu, so/
Metteyyassa bhagavato putto yeva bhavissati// *Mahāvaṃsa*, xxxii, 81-83.

(lvii) antime attabhāvamhi Metteyyaṃ munipuṅgavaṃ/
lokaggapuggalaṃ nāthaṃ sabbasattahite rataṃ//
disvāna tassa dhīrassa sutvā saddhammasāsanaṃ/
adhigantvā phalam aggaṃ sobheyyaṃ jinasāsanaṃ// *Visuddhimagga*, p. 614.

(lviii) iminā katapuññena Metteyyaṃ lokanāyakaṃ/
battiṃsalakkhaṇūpetaṃ ketumālāvirājitaṃ//91
disvā sutvāna saddhammaṃ sasaṅghalokanāyakaṃ...
upeto aṭṭhadhammehi byākato tena satthunā/
majjhe devamanussānaṃ buddhatthāya bhaveyya 'haṃ// 94.
G.H. Luce, 'The Shwegugyi Pagoda Inscription, Pagan, 1141, A.D.,' in *The Journal of the Burma Research Society*, Vol.X, 2, 1920, pp. 67-72.

(lix) kecit tatra ekajātipratibaddhā bodhisattvā mahāsattvā yad uta Avalokiteśvara-Mahāsthāmaprāpta-Gandhahasti-Ratnaketu-Dundubhisvara-Durabhisambhava-Mañjuśrīkumārabhūta-Vīrasena-Subāhu-RatnakusumĀmoghadarśi-Maitreya-prabhṛtayaḥ... *Samādhirāja-sūtra* (X Parivarta), p. 119.

(lx) ...ayaṃ deva, ...saṅghī c' eva gaṇī ca gaṇācariyo ca ñāto, yasassī, titthakaro, sādhusammato bahujanassa, rattaññū, cirapabbajito, addhagato, vayo anuppatto. *Dīghanikāya* (Sāmaññaphala-sutta), I, p. 48.

(lxi) addasā kho Upako Ājīvako bhagavantam antarā ca Gayam antarā ca bodhim addhānamaggapaṭipannaṃ, disvāna bhagavantam eted avoca:— ...kaṃ 'si tvaṃ, āvuso, uddissa pabbajito? ko vā te satthā? kassa vā tvaṃ dhammaṃ rocesī ti? *Vinayapiṭaka-Mahāvagga,* I, p. 8.

(lxii) evaṃ vutte bhagavā Upakam Ājīvakaṃ gāthāhi ajjhabhāsi:—
... na me ācariyo atthi sadiso me na vijjati/
sadevakasmiṃ lokasmiṃ n' atthi me paṭipuggalo//
ahaṃ hi arahā loke ahaṃ satthā anuttaro/
eko 'mhi sammāsambuddho sītibhūto 'smi nibbuto// *Ibid.*

(lxiii) yathā kho, tvaṃ, āvuso, paṭijānāsi, arahasi anantajino ti.
mādisā ve jinā honti, ye pattā āsavakkhayaṃ/
jitā me pāpakā dhammā tasmā 'haṃ, Upaka, jino ti// *Ibid.*

(lxiv) kleśakarmavipākāśayair aparāmṛṣṭaḥ puruṣaviśeaṣa īśvaraḥ/ ...sa tu sadaiva muktaḥ sadaiveśvara iti. *Pātañjala-Yogasūtra with Vyāsa-bhāṣya,* I, 24.

(lxv) imīse osappiṇīe dusamasusamāe [samāe] bhuvīkkantāe tīhiṃ vāsehiṃ aḍḍhanavamehi ya māsehiṃ sesehiṃ Pāvāe ...kālagae...parinivvuḍe. *Kalpa-sūtra,* #146.

(lxvi) Ratnaprabhāṃ praviṣṭaḥ san tatphalaṃ madhyamāyuṣā/
bhuktvā nirgatya bhavyāsmin Mahāpadmākhya-tīrthakṛt//
āgamyutsarpiṇīkālasyāditaḥ kṣemakṛt satām/
tasmād āsannabhavyo 'si mā bhaiṣīḥ saṃsṛter iti// *Mahāpurāṇa,* II, ch. 74, vv. 451-52.

(lxvii) accayo maṃ, bhante, accagamā yathābālaṃ yathāmūḷhaṃ yathā-akusalaṃ, yo 'haṃ pitaraṃ dhammikaṃ dhammarājānam issariyakāraṇā jīvitā voropesiṃ.
tassa me, bhante, bhagavā accayam accayato paṭigaṇhātu āyatiṃ saṃvarāyā ti.

Dīghanikāya, I, p. 80.

(lxviii) pitṛpādeṣu nigaḍān bhaṅkṣyāmīti vicintayan/
lohadaṇḍaṃ gṛhītvā so 'bhiŚreṇikam adhāvata// ...
Śreṇikas cintayāmāsa jighāṃsur nūnam eṣa mām/
anyadāgāt kaśāhasto daṇḍahasto 'dhunaiti tu//
na vedmi mama kumāreṇa mārayiṣyati kenacit/
tasmād anāgate 'py asmin maraṇaṃ śaraṇaṃ mama//
iti tālapuṭaviṣaṃ jivhāgre Śreṇiko dadau/
prasthānasthā ivāgre 'pi tatprāṇāś ca drutaṃ yayuḥ//
Triṣaṣṭiśalākāpuruṣacaritra, X, xii, 161-67.

VII

RITUAL TEXTS

CHAPTER 27

Mahādibbamanta: A *Paritta* Manuscript from Cambodia*

Introduction

In 1961, while on a visit to Cambodia, I first came to know of this work from the chief Abbot of Vat Unālom of Phnom Penh. I was informed by the learned Abbot of the existence of a 'Mahāyānist' work known as *Dibbamanta.* The work was not available there but subsequently a palm-leaf MS of this work was found in the National Museum of Bangkok, a microfilm copy of which was made available to me through the courtesy of the curator of that Museum. The MS consists of 48 folios,[1] written in Cambodian characters. It is not dated and does not carry any information regarding the author or the scribe. As it was a common practice in Siam to copy Buddhist texts in Cambodian script, and as the work is not in use at the present day either in Siam or in Cambodia, it is hard to locate the original place of this MS. But on the basis of certain internal evidence which will be noted below I am inclined to believe that it could be of Cambodian origin.

The name of the work, *Dibbamanta,* as it was known to my informant, occurs in the text only once: *yo 'dha saṃgāmaṃ gacchanto bhāsento dibbamantrakaṃ* (91). But in the view of the hybrid form of this title I retain the title *Mahādibbamanta* as given in the colophon.

The language is corrupt and contains several unusual spellings (e.g. Dhaḍḍharaṭṭhaka, Virrupakkha, Virruḷhaka, Pajuṇṇa), a few

*This article was originally published in *BSOAS,* Vol. XXVIII, part 1, pp. 61-80, 1965. Reprinted with kind permission of Oxford University Press.

Sanskrit words (e.g. *mantra, snāna*) and a large number of hybrid forms improvised for the Sanskrit names of *grahas, māsas, rāśis,* and *nakṣatras* unknown to ancient Pali literature.

The text consists of one prose passage and 108 verses all in anuṣṭubh except one in upajāti. The verses are not numbered but they total 108 (together with the prose passage), and this number could not be merely accidental. It is a magic number and is associated with the 108 marks on the feet of the Buddha (cf. *aṭṭhuttarasataṃ yassa maṅgalaṃ caraṇadvaye,* v. 10). The work can be divided into several small sections: (a) vv. 1-4, salutations to the three *maṅgalas*; (b) 5-9, *jaya-gāthās* proclaiming victory to the three *maṅgalas;* (c) 10-13, glorification of the 108 auspicious marks on the feet of the Buddha; (d) 14-17, glorification of the ten *pāramīs* and the victory of the Buddha under the *bodhi*-tree; (e) 18-20, description of a *maṇḍala* consisting of ten Buddhas; (g) 27-33, *Canda-paritta*; (h) 34-7, *Suriya-paritta*; (i) 38-9, *mantra* consisting of the formula *hulu hulu hulu svāhā*; (j) 40-52, enumeration of the nine *grahas* (planets), the twelve Indian *māsas* (months), the twelve animals indicating the Chinese twelve-year cycle (here called *nakṣatras*), the 27 constellations (*nakṣatras*) and twelve signs of the zodiac (*rāśis*) followed by a prayer for protection; (k) 53-5, invocation to eight *devīs* occupying the eight points of the universe; (l)56-62, prayer for the rain of wealth as in the cases of Jotika, Meṇḍaka, Dhanañjaya, Uggata, Jaṭila, Cittaka, and Mandhātu, famous for their wealth and merit; (m) 63-77, enumeration of miscellaneous items; (n) 78-89, *siddhi-gāthās,* invocation to a large number of deities including Hara, Harihara, and Rāma; (o) 90-8, description of the efficacy of the *Dibbamanta* resulting from its recitation, particularly while marching into battle or in counteracting the magical devices of the enemy; (p) 99-108, concluding valedictory verses.

It is evident that the *Mahādibbamanta* has all the ingredients of a short *paritta* work. The two *parittas* included here (the *Canda* and *Suriya-paritta*) form part of the canon (*Saṃyuttanikāya,* i, 50-1) and are found in the list of *paritta-suttas* (nos. 14 and 15) given in the *Catu-bhāṇavāra,* a standard collection of *paritta-suttas.* In addition to these, however, there are six verses (see below) which are also found in a book of non-canonical *paritta* hymns popular even to this day in Ceylon and Burma. The belief of my informant therefore that the work is 'Mahāyānist' is certainly ill-founded.

Nevertheless, there are certain unusual features in this work which are not normally shared even by the popular *paritta* texts, and which could render our text unacceptable to an orthodox Theravādin. First and foremost is the glorification of Hara and Hari appearing immediately after the trio of the Buddha, the arhats, and the *paccekasambuddhas*, and taking precedence over the four *mahārājas* of the Buddhist mythology. At a subsequent place (v. 80) Hara and Harihara head the list of major deities and Rāma takes precedence over various kinds of minor *devas*. The glorification of these purely brahmanical deities in any Pali text is hitherto unknown and reminds us of Tāntric buddhist texts of Balinese origin where Īśvara and Buddha are found placed side by side. We may also note a significant statement (*buddharūpañ ca sabbesaṃ, buddharūpañ ca devatā*, v. 84) indicating the identity of the major and minor deities with the *rūpa* (image or person?) of the Buddha, a major departure from the traditional Theravāda Buddhism.

The reference to the four Brahmanical deities, particularly to Harihara, could point to a Cambodian origin of our text. It is well known that the cult of Harihara[2] flourished there during the Khmer period and was gradually replaced by Buddhism, first by Mahāyāna and finally by Theravāda under the influence of the Thais of Siam. Our text might possibly not go as far back as the Khmer period. But certain of its older portions, particularly those containing a reference to these deities, could have been composed only at a time when their names sounded as familiar to the Buddhists of Cambodia as for instance the names of the four *mahārājas* or of Indra, but without any specific Brahmanical associations.

A reference in our text to a *devī* called Dharaṇi (the Earth goddess) is also significant. As a Buddhist goddess, she enjoys great popularity in Cambodia and Siam, but not, it seems, in India or Ceylon. She is known in Cambodia as Phra Thorni. Her image, a standing figure wringing her long hair, the floods pouring from which drown the hosts of Māra, is carved on the pedestals supporting the statues of the Buddha (in *bhūmi-sparśa-mudrā*) and is also found, in modern times, in the courtyards of temples and in public parks. The legend of Dharaṇi, as pointed out by Coedès,[3] is unknown to the canonical texts and is peculiar to Cambodia and Siam. The earliest image of Dharaṇi is found on a stele at Angkor Vat.[4] It is likely, in view of this iconographical evidence, that the legend of Dharaṇi is of Khmer origin. The reference to her in our text, the only Pali work known to refer to her,[5] together with references to Harihara and such other Khmer deities, could also point to a Cambodian origin of the *Mahādibbamanta.*

The enumeration of twelve animals indicating the Chinese twelve-year cycle with the Indian designation *nakṣatra* could also point to a similar conclusion. The earliest evidence of such a practice is found in a Khmer inscription of Sūryavarman I (A.D. 1039).[6] The Siamese appear to have adopted this practice from the Khmers. The earliest evidence of it from Siam is in a Khmer inscription dated A.D. 1183,[7] followed by the famous inscription of Ram Khamhaeng (A.D. 1292).[8] The practice of using the Chinese year-cycle was prevalent among the Buddhists of northern Siam (Haripuñjaya) as can be seen from the *Jinakālamālī,* a Pali chronicle of A.D. 1516. There is, however, one significant departure here from the old practice. The author of the *Jinakālamālī* has abandoned the use of the designation *nakṣatra*[9] for the twelve years of the Chinese cycle and instead calls them by what must have appeared to him to be the correct designations *vassa, vassika, saṃvacchara,* and also by the newly adopted *sakarāj* of Burmese origin.[10]

Strangely enough none of these four latter terms are known to our text. It is very tempting therefore to assume that the *Mahādibbamanta* was composed at a time when the practice of using the designation *nakṣatra* for the twelve years of the Chinese cycle was still in vogue[11] in the learned Buddhist circles of Cambodia and Siam, i.e. prior to the composition of *Jinakālamālī,* A.D. 1516. Such a date would seem to be in accordance with the other points discussed above, particularly the fact that Harihara is mentioned in our text.

There is, however, a practical difficulty against assuming a date of such antiquity for our text. As pointed out above, it contains six verses (nos. 17, 21-3, 107-8) found also in a book of non-canonical *paritta* hymns popular in Ceylon and Burma. Of these, no. 17 (*jayanto bodhiyā mūle...*) is identical with the second verse of a hymn called *Mahājayamaṅgalagāthā* (consisting of 16 verses and a prose passage). Nos. 21-3 correspond to vv. 2b-5a of *Cūlajinapañjara* (consisting of 14 verses). Nos. 107-8 are identical with two verses appearing at the end of a long prose passage called *Jaya-pirit.* All these works, *Jaya-pirit, Mahājayamaṅgalagāthā,* and *Cūlajinapañjara* in that order although not consecutively, appear in an appendix (*Upagranthaya*) of a work called *Pali-Siṃhala-pirit-pota.*[12] Nothing is known about the date or authorship of these non-canonical *parittas* (or *pirits* as they are called) nor are they listed in the *Dictionary of Pali proper names.* The histories of Pali literature in Ceylon seem to ignore them. Judging by the style and contents of these works they appear to be fairly old and could go back to a period when Buddhist monks are first known to have composed similar incantations in Ceylon. Since *Mahakuveniasna,* a Sinhalese text of magical incantations attributed to a Mahāthera, calls for blessings for King Parākramabāhu VI of Koṭṭe (A.D. 1410-68) it is not impossible that other magical incantations in the guise of *pirits* should have been composed as early as the fifteenth century.[13]

The *pirits* referred to above, particularly the *Jaya-pirit,* appear from their language and style to be works of Ceylonese origin. During the fifteenth century a large number of bhikkhus from Ceylon came over to Siam and there was a constant exchange of monks with these as well as with monks from the neighbours of Siam.[14] It is possible that the *pirits* may have been introduced into Cambodia and Siam through these monks. Portions of these popular hymns might have then been included in our text, possibly at the time of its composition but more probably at a later date since as they stand at least three of the six verses discussed above appear to be later additions. The first of these verses (*jayanto bodhiyā mūle* ...) follows three other verses, nos. 14, 15, and 16 which also appear to be added to our text, and whose origin I have been unable to trace. Verse 14 is in upajāti, the only verse in this text in this metre. This and the following two verses (15-16) seem to belong to some work describing the defeat of Māra. Verses 107 and 108, appearing at the end of the whole work, could easily be treated as an addition since they are preceded by valedictory verses followed by benedictory verses which would normally be expected to mark the end of the work by themselves.

Mahādibbamanta

namo tassa bhagavato arahato sammāsambuddhassa.
buddhaṃ saraṇaṃ gacchāmi. dhammaṃ saraṇaṃ gacchāmi.
saṃghaṃ saraṇaṃ gacchāmi. dutiyam pi. tatiyam pi. 1

buddho maṅgalasambhūto sambuddho dipaduttamo
buddhamaṅgalam āgamma sabbadukkhā pamuñcatu. 2
dhammo maṅgalasambhūto gambhīro duddaso anuṃ[1]
dhammamaṅgalam āgamma sabbabhayā pamuñcatu. 3
saṃgho maṅgalasambhūto dakkhineyyo anuttaro
saṃghamaṅgalam āgamma sabbarogā pamuñcatu. 4
jaya jaya pathavī sabbaṃ[2] *jaya satthā arahantaṃ*
jaya paccekasambuddhaṃ jaya isi mahosuraṃ [3] 5
[4]*jaya Haro Harīdevaṃ* [5]*jaya brahmā Dhaḍḍharaṭṭhakaṃ*[6]
jaya nāgo Virruḷhako[7] *Virrupakkho* [8] *Candimā Ravī.* 6
Indo ca Venatteyyo[9] *ca Kuvero Varuṇo pi ca*
Aggī Vāyu Pajuṇṇo ca kumāro catupālakā.[10] 7
aṭṭhārasa mahādevā[11] *siddhi-tāpasa-ādayo*[12]
asītī sāvakā[13] *sabbe jaya Rāmo bhavantu te.* 8
jaya dhammo ca saṃgho ca dasapālo[14] *ca jayakaṃ*
etena jayasaccena sabbasotthi bhavantu te. 9
aṭṭhuttarasataṃ[15] *yassa maṅgalaṃ caraṇadvaye*
cakkhalakkhaṇasampanne name taṃ lokanāyakaṃ. 10
ime maṅgalatejena sabbasattahitesino
etena maṅgalatejena sabbasiddhi bhavantu te. 11
etena maṅgalatejena taṃ taṃ rakkhantu sabbadā
etena maṅgalatejena taṃ taṃ pālayantu sabbadā. 12
etena maṅgalatejena sabbasiddhi bhavantu te
sabasattū vidhaṃsetu sabbsasotthi bhavantu te. 13
[16]*āyantu bhonto idha dānasīlā nekkhammapaññā saha*
viriyakhantī; sammā[17] *adhiṭṭhānasamett' upekkhā*
yuddhāya vo gaṇhatha āvuddhāni. 14
pāramiyo vijitvāna bodhisattassa cintakam
kesarāri(?)[18] *va āgañchuṃ bodhisatta taṃ abravuṃ:* 15
mayaṃ pāramitā yodhā ciraṃ deva tayā bhattā[19]
ajja dassāma te ciraṃ[20] *jaya bhaddaṃ namatthu te.* 16
jayanto bodhiyā mūle Sakyānaṃ nandivaḍḍhano
evaṃ tvaṃ vijayo hotu[21] *jayassu jaya maṅgalaṃ.* 17
[22]*Buddho ca majjhimo seṭṭho Sāriputto ca dakkhiṇe*
pacchime pi ca Ānando uttare Moggalānako, 18
Koṇḍañño purbbi bhāge ca bāyabbe ca Gavampati
Upāli neharatī ṭhāne āgaṇeyye ca Kassapo
Rāhulo c eva īsāne sabbe te buddhamaṅgalā. 19
yo ñatvā pūjito loke nidukkho nirupaddavo
mahātejo sadā hotu jayasotthi bhavantu te. 20

[23]*Padumuttaro ca pubbāyaṃ*[24] *āgaṇeyye ca* [25]*Revato*
dakkhiṇe Kassapo buddho neharatīye [26] *Sumaṅgalo,* 21
pacchime Buddhasikkhī[27] *ca bāyabbe*[28] *ca Medhaṅkaro*
uttare Sākyamunī[29] *c'eva īsāne Saraṇaṃkaro,*[30] 22
pathavīyaṃ[31] *Kakusandho ākāse ca Dīpaṅkaro*[32]
[33]*ete dasadisā buddhā rājadhammassa*[34]*pūjitā.* 23
natthi rogabhayaṃ sokaṃ khemaṃ sampattidāyakaṃ
dukkharogabhayaṃ natthi sabbasatrū vidhaṃsatu. 24
tesañ ñāṇena sīlena saṃyamena damena ca
te pi taṃ anurakkhantu ārogyena sukhena ca, 25
anāgatassa buddhassa Metteyyassa yasassino
mahādevo mahātejo sabbasotthi bhavantu te. 26
[35]*namo te buddhavīra 'tthu vippamutto 'si sabbadhi*
sambādhapatipanno 'smi tassa me saraṇaṃ bhavā.[36] 27
tathāgataṃ arahantaṃ Candimā saraṇaṃ gato
Rāhu Candaṃ ca muñcassu[37] *buddhā lokānukampakā.* 28
kin nu santaramāno va Rāhu Candaṃ pamuñcasi 29
[38]*dukkharogabhayaṃ nāsti sabbasatrū vidhaṃsetu* 30
tesaṃ ñāṇena ... pi ... bhavantu te (as in verses 24b-26). 31-2
saṃviggarūpo āgamma kin nu bhīto va tiṭṭhasi [39]
sattadhā me phale muddhā jīvanto na sukhaṃ labhe
buddhagāthābhigīto 'mhi no ce muñceyya Candiman ti. 33
[40]*namo te buddhavīra 'tthu vippamutto 'si sabbadhi*
sambādhapatipanno 'smi tassa me saraṇaṃ bhavā.[41] 34
tathāgataṃ arahantaṃ Suriyo saraṇaṃ gato
Rāhu Suriyaṃ pamuñcassu buddhā lokānukampakā. 35
yo andhakāre tamasī pabhaṃkaro
verocano maṇḍali[42] *uggatejo*
mā Rahu gili[43] *caraṃ antalikkhe*
pajaṃ mama Rāhu muñca Suriyan ti. 36
kin nu santaramāno va Rāhu Suriyaṃ pamuñcasi[44]
sattadhā me phale muddhā jīvanto na sukhaṃ labhe
buddhagāthābhigīto 'mhi no ce muñceyya Suriyan ti. 37
namo buddhassa namo dhammassa namo saṃghassa
seyyathīdam: hulu hulu hulu svāhaya heṭṭhimā ca
uparimā ca caviṭṭhārakā[45] *ca tiriyañcā apparimāṇikā* [46]
sabbe sattā sabbe pāṇā sabbe bhūtā sabbe puggalā
sabbe attabhāvapariyāpannā sabbā itthiyo sabbe purisā
sabbe ariyā sabbe anariyā sabbe devā sabbe manussā sabbe
vinipātikā averā hontu abyāpajjhā hontu anīghā hontu

dīghāyukā hontu averā hontu sampatti samijjhatu sukhī
attānaṃ viharantu sabbe taṃ rakkhantu 'paddavā. 38
jalaṭṭhā vā thalaṭṭhā vā ākāse h'antalikkhakā
pabbatā ca samuddā ca rukkhatiṇṇalatāsino
te pi taṃ anurakkhantu ārogyena sukhena ca. 39
[47] *Āditya-Candra-Aṅgāra-Buddha-Brahāsyapatī tathā*
Sukra-Sora-Rāhu-Ketu navagrahā[48] *ca sabbaso.* 40
tesaṃ balena tejena ānubhāvena tena ca
te pi taṃ anurakkhantu ārogyena sukhena ca. 41
[49] *Caitra-Baisākkha-Jeṣṭe ca Āsāde Srāvane tathā*
Bhadrapade ca Āsujje Kṛttike Mṛggasīsake
Phusse Māghe ca Phaguṇe lokam pālenti dhammatā. 42
ete dvādasadhā māsā ānubhāve mahabbhute
te pi taṃ anurakkhantu ārogyena sukhena ca. 43
[50] *Musiko Bṛsabho Byaggho Sassa-Nāgo ca Sappako*
Asso Meṇḍo Kapi c'eva Kukkuro Svāna-Sūkaro. 44
ete dvādasa nakkhattā lokaṃ pālenti dhammatā
te pi taṃ anurakkhantu ārogyena sukhena ca. 45
[51] *Assujjo Bharaṇī c'eva Kṛttikā Rohiṇī pi ca*
Mṛggasirañ ca Adrañ ca Puraṇabbasu Pussā pi ca, 46
Asilesā pi Māghā ca Purabbaphalaguṇī tathā
Uttaraphalaguṇī c'eva Hasta-Cittañ ca Svāti ca, 47
Visākhā 'nuradhā Jeṣṭhā Mūla 'sālha duve siyuṃ
Srāvano ca Dhaniṭṭho ca Satabhisā Purubuttarā, 48
Bhadrapade Revaty api kammato pi sattādhikā,
visā c'evā pi nakkhattā pabbāyanti dine dine, 49
te pi taṃ anurakkhantu ānubhāvena tena ca
te pi taṃ anurakkhantu ārogyena sukhena ca. 50
[52] *Mesa-Bṛsabbha-Methunā Karkāṭaka-Siṃha-Kanyakā*
Tulyā Bṛcchā Dhanū c' eva Maṃkarā Kumbha-Mīnyakā, 51
ete dvādasadhā rāsī ānubhāvena tena ca
te pi taṃ anurakkhantu ārogyena sukhena ca. 52
[53] *Sāvetrīdevī Ruddhāni Dharaṇī Gaṃgā ca deviyā*
Iraggā Naladevīyā Bhiratti(?) mṛcchu Mārikā, 53
aṭṭhadevī bhūmipatī aṭṭhadisesu rakkhitā[54]
tāsaṃ pūjānubhāvena sabbadosaṃ khamantu te. 54
tāsaṃ balena tejena ānubhāvena tena ca
te pi taṃ anurakkhantu ārogyena sukhena ca. 55
mā khayo mā vayo tuyhaṃ mā ca koci upaddavo
ratanāni pavassantu Jotikassa [55] *yathā ghare.* 56

mā khayo mā vayo tuyhaṃ mā ca koci upaddavo
kañcanāni pavassantu Meṇḍakassa [56]*yathā ghare.* 57
mā khāyo...
dhaññadhanā pavassantu Dhanañjayassa[57] *yathā ghare.* 58
mā khayo ...
dhanadhārā pavassantu Uggatassa[58] *yathā ghare.* 59
mā khayo ...
kañcanajālasaṃkāmeso(?) Jaṭilassa[59] *yathā ghare.* 60
mā khayo ...
sabbadhanāni pavassantu Cittakassa[60] *yathā ghare.* 61
mā khayo ...
kahāpaṇāni pavassantu Mandhātusseva[61] *rājino.*[62] 62
Akkharasārinī nāma isī[63] *Himmavante vasī tadā*
siddhi-vijjādharā sabbe devānaṃ pujitā sadā. 63
buddhā paccekabuddhā ca arahantā Indadevatā
Brahmā isī munī c'eva puriso ca mahantako.[64] 64
siddhi-vijjādharā[65] *sabbe dvādasā*[66] *rakkhitā sadā*
ye suddhacittā samādānā manussā[67] *pujitā sadā.* 65
buddhasāvaṃ[68] *guṇaṃ vijjaṃ balaṃ tejañ ca vīriyaṃ*
siddhi kammaṃ dhammaṃ saccaṃ nibbānaṃ mokkhaṃ
tuyhakaṃ. 66
dānaṃ sīlaṃ ca paññā ca nikkhaṃ puññaṃ bhāgyaṃ tapaṃ
yasaṃ sukhaṃ sirī rūpaṃ catuvīsati desanā.[69] 67
evaṃ soḷasadhā dhammā[70] *buddhā devā saranti ca*
paccekā arahantā ca Indā devā sabrahmakā. 68
isī munī ca rājāno puriso[71] *ca vijjādharā*
sabbalokādhipatī devā soḷasā[72] *bhavakammunā.* 69
ahi sarisappā c'eva asso meṇḍo ca kukkuro
go mahiṃsā tathā hatthī tiracchā khāṇu-kaṇṭakā, 70
kūpo papāto aggo[73] *ca ubhaggo*[74] *bhaggo*[75] *pi ca*
ubhaggo visarājā[76] *ca poriko*[77] *aggipotako,* 71
suṃsumāro ca nāgo ca gṛddho surakinnaro
mahāratto[78] *devadevo Kuvero manuso pi ca,* 72
amanussā ca yakkhā ca mahāyakkho ca rakkhaso
mahānāgo pisāco va peto kumbhaṇḍako pi ca, 73
siddhi-vijjādharā sabbe sehmaṃ pittaṃ ca vāyukaṃ
upakkā sannipātañ ca sabbe paññāsapiḷitā.[79] 74
sabbe sattā ca yakkhā ca mettacittā sadā bhave
ekapaññāsa sabbe te sabbe rakkhantu taṃ sadā. 75

akaṃ[80] *lābhī ca lābhānaṃ sakkāro*[81] *pūjito sadā*
sabbe devā manussā ca piyā rakkhantu taṃ sadā. 76
gāmaṃ desañ ca nagaraṃ nadī bhūmi ca pabbataṃ
vannaṃ[82] *samuddaṃ addhānaṃ sabbe rakkhantu taṃ sadā.* 77
siddhi buddhā siddhi dhammā siddhi saṃghā ca uttamā
siddhi paccekasambuddhā siddhi sabbaññusāvakā. 78
siddhi ariyañ ca ariyānaṃ siddhi ca pātihāriyaṃ
siddhi mārabalaṃ yodhaṃ[83] *siddhi nibbānam uttamaṃ.* 79
[84]*siddhi Haro Hariharo siddhi Brahmā ca Dhaḍḍharaṭṭhako*
siddhi nāgo Virūḍḍhako Virupakkho Candimā Ravī, 80
siddhi Indo ca Venatteyyo ca Kuvero Varuṇo pi ca
siddhi Aggī ca Vāyū ca Pajuṇṇo ca kumārako,
siddhi aṭṭhārasā devā catupālañ ca devatā. 81
siddhi Rāmo[85] *siddhi devā siddhi yakkho ca rakkhaso*
siddhi vijjādharā sabbe siddhi isī mahesurā 82
siddhi pabbatadevānaṃ siddhi cetiyadevatā[86]
siddhi pāsādadevānaṃ siddhi cetiyadevatā 83
siddhi bodhirukkhadevānaṃ siddhi ārakkhadhātuyo
buddharūpañ ca sabbesaṃ buddharūpañ ca devatā 84
siddhi tiṇṇā[87] *ca rukkhānaṃ vali*[88] *yā gharadevatā*
siddhi thalā jalaṭṭhā vā siddhi ākāsadevatā 85
siddhi munī ca rājāno siddhi purisalakkhaṇā
siddhi bhummatthadevānaṃ siddhi kammaṃ balaṃ varaṃ. 86
siddhi pādā ca apādā ca dvipādā ca catuppādā ca
bahuppādā ca sattā ca siddhi pakkhā[89] *ca vāyukaṃ.* 87
etena siddhitejena jayasotthi bhavantu te
etena siddhitejena taṃ taṃ rakkhantu sabbadā. 88
etena siddhitejena taṃ taṃ pālayantu sabbadā
etena siddhitejena sabbasiddhi bhavantu te,
sabbasatrū vidhaṃsetu sabbasotthi bhavantu te. 89
yo 'dha saṃgāmaṃ gacchanto bhāsento dibbamantrakaṃ[90]
jayaṃ balaṃ sukhaṃ lābhaṃ sabbasatrū vidhaṃsetu. 90
puttakāmo labhe puttaṃ dhanakāmo labhe dhanaṃ
adhikāraṃ labheyyayuṃ[91] *devānaṃ piyataṃ sadā.* 91
rājā itthī ca seṭṭhī ca puriso maṇḍito pi ca
sīho byaggho varāhā ca asso meṇḍo ca kukkuro. 92
go mahiṃso tathā hatthī tiracchā khāṇu-kaṇṭakā
sabbasattha-ayo lohoṃ tamma-kaṃsañ ca tīpukaṃ. 93
atthi añño ca kurute cakrā nakhā ca visakaṃ
kodanaṃ[92] *dhanunā snānaṃ*[93] *sallaṃ aggī ca vāyukaṃ.* 94

khaggaṃ selañ ca matikaṃ[94] *yantrabhāsānusātrakaṃ*[95]
añño ca kuhakaṃ katvā mantramāyāniyojitaṃ. 95
etena siddhitejena jayasotthi bhavantu te
etena siddhitejena taṃ taṃ rakkhantu sabbadā. 96
etena siddhitejena taṃ taṃ pālayantu sabbadā
etena siddhitejena sabbasiddhi bhavantu te. 97
sabbasatrū vidhaṃsetu sabbasotthi bhavantu te 98
sabbe buddhā arahantā ca paccekānañ ca devatā
koṭisatasahassānaṃ cakkavāḷañ ca devatā,
sabbe te sukham āyantā gacchantu sakaṭṭhānato. 99
siddhanti dibbammantāni yāva kappā ca medinī
sabbe te devā sumanā honti mettacittā samāgatā. 100
sabbe te anumodantu puññaṃ gaṇhantu uddisaṃ
amhe rakkhantu sabbattha antarāyā asesato. 101
siddhi kāyakataṃ kammaṃ siddhi vīraparakkamaṃ
siddhi tejo balaṃ sukhaṃ siddhi lābho nirantaraṃ. 102
siddhi asīti arahantā ca buddhānaṃ catuvīsati[96]
siddhi Cātumahārājikā ca Kāmāvacaradevatā, 103
siddhi soḷasa mahābrahmā[97] *Arupāvacara-catubbidhā.*
etena siddhitejena jayasotthi bhavantu te. 104
etena siddhitejena taṃ taṃ rakkhantu sabbadā
etena siddhitejena taṃ taṃ pālayantu sabbadā. 105
etena siddhitejena sabbasiddhi bhavantu te.
sabbasatrū vidhaṃsetu sabbasotthi bhavantu te.[98] 106
dukkharogabhayā verā sokā santu c'upaddavā[99]
antarāyā anekāni[100] *vinassantu ca tejasā* 107
jayasiddhī[101] *dhanaṃ lābhaṃ sotthī*[102] *bhāgyaṃ sukhaṃ*
balaṃ siri[103] *āyu ca vaṇṇo ca bhogaṃ buddhī*[104] *ca yasavā*
satavassā ca āyu[105] *ca jīvasiddhī*[106] *bhavantu te.* 108
Mahādibbamantraṃ samattaṃ[107] *nitthītaṃ.*[108]
sabbasavassati siddhikāraya.[109]

NOTES

1. The 108 verses in this MS are written in rather an unusual manner. Instead of writing several verses on the same line our scribe has written each verse on a separate line. This could indicate a fairly late date for our MS.
2. On Harihara, see B. P. Groslier, *Indochina* (Art of the World, IX), 76-7. Two images are reproduced here, both from Cambodia, one dating between A.D. 657 and 681, the other belonging to the first half of the twelfth century. See also G. de Coral Rémusat, *L'art khmer*, pl. xxx, 104.

3. View quoted by C. H. Marchal in J. Hackin and others, *Asiatic Mythology,* 206.
4. ibid. For a modern Cambodian image of this goddess, see H. Marchal, *Le décor et la sculpture khmers,* 1951 (illustration no. 251).
5. The word *dharaṇi* is found e.g. in *Buddhavaṃsa* (i. 68) but is not used there as a name of a *devī* : *cavitvā Tusitā kāyā yadā okkami kucchiyaṃ dasahassī lokadhātu kampittha dharaṇī tadā.*
6. *Śaka pañcamī ket caitra bṛhaspatibāra khāl* (tiger) *nakṣatra.* See L. Finot, 'Les inscriptions de Sek Ta Tuy', *BEFEO,* XXVIII, 1928, 50.
7. 1105 *Śaka thoḥ* (here) *nakṣatra.* See G. Coedès, 'Le royaume de Śrīvijaya', *BEFEO,* xviii, 6, 1918, 34.
8. G. Coedès, *BEFEO,* II, 1902, 60.
9. On the use of the term *nakṣatra* in the inscriptions mentioned above, see G. Coedès, 'L'origine du cycle des douze animaux au Cambodge', *T'oung Pao,* XXXI, 1935, 323, where (p. 315) he lists several articles on the Chinese animal-cycle. The animal-cycle is not exclusively used for years and the term *nakṣatra* is already applied to them in Central Asia by the third century A.D. in Niya documents (*Kharoṣṭhī Inscriptions,* ed. Boyer, Rapson, Senart, and Noble, no. 565); Burrow (translation, p. 111) refers also to H. Lüders, 'Zur Ceschichte des Ostasiatischen Tierkreises', *Sb. PAW,* Phil.-hist. Kl., 1933, 998 ff. See also H. W. Bailey, 'Hvatanica', *BSOS,* VIII, 4, 1937, 924-8, where different lists of twelve names of the animal-cycle as found in Khotan Saka, Sogdian, Krorayina Prakrit, Sanskrit, and Kuchean are given. See also his *Khotanese texts,* IV, 11.

   W. Simon in his *Chinese-English Dictionary* (introduction, liii) gives corresponding zodiacal signs for the animal-cycle. According to Needham (*Science and Civilisation in China,* iii, 1959, 258) the Jesuits erroneously equated these two systems during the seventeenth century. For a bibliography on this subject, see *T' oung Pao,* Index gênéral, 71.
10. e.g. *icc evaṃ ... parinibbāṇato ... sata-Sakarāje Mūsikasaññite saṃvacchare ... ayaṃ gantho ... paripuṇṇo ti* (*Jinakālamālī* (PTS), p. 129).
11. Professor Coedés in his article (*T' oung Pao,* xxxi, 1935) states that the term *nakṣatra* is still in use (in Cambodia and Siam) for the twelve-year animal-cycle, but does not refer to the practice adopted in the *Jinakālamālī.*
12. ed. by K. D. Śri Prajñāsāra, Colombo, 1956. This work is based upon a Pali commentary called *Sāratthasamuccaya* (Simon Hevavitarne Bequest, XXVII) on an old *paritta* collection entitled *Catu-bhāṇavāra.* The latter contains 20 suttas used as *paritta* (as against the list of six *parittas* enumerated in the *Milindapañho,* 150-4). But the *Sāratthasamuccaya,* written according to a Ceylonese tradition during the time of Parākramabāhu II, includes seven additional suttas treated separately in an appendix (called *Parisiṭṭhasaṅgaho*). The works included in the appendix (*Upagranthaya*) of the *Pali-Siṃhala-pirit-pota* could be assumed to belong to a period later than the *Sāratthasamuccaya.* Popular *paritta* hymns similar to the one in Ceylon are also found in such works as the *Chauk saung dwé,* Rangoon, 1895, See Bode, *The Pali literature of Burma,* 95.
13. C. E. Godakumbura, *Sinhalese Literature,* 291.
14. The earliest Pali inscription found in Cambodia is dated A.D. 1230 (see Coedès, *BEFEO,* XXXVI, 1936, 14; and Majumdar, *Inscriptions of Kambuja,* no. 188) and the recorded date of the introduction of the sect of Sīhala bhikkhus to Nibbisipura is given as A.D. 1431 (1974 years after the *parinibbāna*). See G. Goedès, 'Documents sur l'histoire politique et religieuse du Laos occidental', *BEFEO,* XXV, 1925, 131.

NOTES

1. *anuṃ* stands for *aṇu* 'subtle'. *Aṇu* is frequently spelt *anu* in Pali.
2. *jaya jaya pathavī sabbaṃ.* This glorification of *pathavī* (Earth) is undoubtedly the most remarkable feature of the *Mahādibbamanta.* Not only is she given precedence over the Buddha (*satthā*) in receiving *jayakāra* (proclamation of glory) but she is also placed almost at the beginning of our text. The practice of glorifying the Mother Earth at the beginning of a text is hardly observed even among the Hindus. The only instance I know occurs in *Pṛthivīstava* (*Oṃ pṛthivīśarīraṃ devī* ...), a short hymn included in *Sanskrit texts from Bali,* ed. S. Lévi, p. 46. I know of no similar instance in the Buddhist literature of Ceylon or Burma. She is recognized as a *devatā* of the Vedic pantheon, where she occupies a prominent place with Dyauḥ (e.g. *Idáṃ dyāvāpṛithivī satyám astu pítar mātar yád ihópabruvé vāṃ,* RV 1.185.11). In the *Atharvaveda* she is called Mother Earth and the poet of this hymn, Atharvan, calls himself 'a son of Pṛthivī' (*mātā́ bhū́miḥ putró ahā́ṃ pṛthivyā́h* ..., AV 12.1.12).

   In the Pali canon the earth (*pathavī*) does not appear as a goddess (*devatā*) but is described on several occasions as shaking violently at the miraculous events in the life of the Buddha (e.g. *ayañ ca kho dasasahassī lokadhātu saṅkampi...,* *Vin.,* 1.11). In the *Jātaka-aṭṭhakathā* the Mahāpathavī is called upon by the Buddha in the course of his victory over Māra, to bear witness to his past good deeds (*ayaṃ acetanāpi ghanamahāpaṭhavī sakkhī ti ...mahāpaṭhavī abhimukhaṃ hatthaṃ pasāresi ...mahāpaṭhavī ...viravasahassena Mārabalaṃ avattharamānā viya unnadi ...,* *J,* I.74). This is the origin of the legend of Dharaṇi and of the *bhūmi-sparśa-mudrā,* noted above, popular in Cambodia and Siam. There is also a belief among the Cambodians that in the beginning of creation man came from the dirt of Prah Thorni (see J. Hackin and others, *Asiatic mythology,* 196). Even assuming that the *pathavī* mentioned in this verse is identical with Phra Thorni or Dharaṇi, it appears extremely unlikely that the Buddhists of Cambodia would give her so prominent a place as to relegate the Buddha to a second position in a Buddhist text.

The alternative suggestion, which I owe to Mr. H. L. Shorto, is that we should join the word *jaya* (the second of the two) to *pathavī*. This gives us a compound *jaya-pathavī*, meaning 'land of victory' a concept well known to the Mons of the sixteenth century. It is connected with a coronation ceremony which included an act called treading the 'soil of victory' (*ti* 'earth', *jamnaḥ* 'victory'). The *Sudhammavatīrājavaṃsa* (*Rājādhirāj*) (Pak Lat edition, 1910, 231) in connection with a story of prince Asaḥ, refers to a 'soil of victory' in Pegu marking the space where the Prince killed an Indian giant and where Rājādhirāj is said to have built a pagoda. In the opinion of Mr. Shorto this *jaya-bhūmi* could be located in the east of Pegu and south of the pagoda.

A Burmese work called *Ayu-daw Min-gala shauk-hton* 'Life and wise sayings of Ayu-daw Min-gala' (a Burmese minister during the reign of Bodawpaya, 1782-1819), by U Aung, also refers to the practice of treading the 'soil of victory'. It is said there (p. 102) that King Bodawpaya made his minister Thado Thiri Maha Uccanā tread the soil of victory (*aung-mye*) on Sunday, the seventh day of the waxing moon of the Tawthalin, and sent him along the Chiengmai route to invade Siam. (I am indebted to Dr. Hla Pe for this reference. See also Harvey, *History of Burma*, 270 ff.)

In view of the close connection between the Mons and Cambodians through the kingdom of Haripuñjaya (*Jinakālamālī*, p. 88 f.; *Cāmadevīvaṃsa*, in *BEFEO*, xxv, 1925, 152 f.) in the sixteenth century, it is possible to assume that the concept of a *jaya-pathavī* was known to the author of our text. Being a *mantra* recommended for recitation while marching into battle (*yo 'dha saṃgāmaṃ gacchanto bhāsento dibbamantrakaṃ*), it is conceivable that our text was used in the coronation ceremony of treading the 'soil of victory'. This could account for a formal glorification (*jaya jaya-pathavī sabbaṃ*) of all 'lands of victory' and for the prominence accorded to *pathavī* in our text.

3. *mahosuraṃ*. We should perhaps read *mahāsura* (i.e. Rāhu who is called Asurinda, *Aṅguttaranikāya*, II. 53). This word, however, occurs again with a different spelling: *mahesurā* (v. 82). The latter appears nearer to the Skt. *maheśvara* meaning Śiva, although here only a general meaning 'great god or lord' seems to be intended. Although *issara* is known, there is no form like *mahissara* in Pali.

4. Verses 6 and 7 are repeated again (vv. 80-1) with a slight difference. The word *jaya* is there replaced by *siddhi*.
5. Instead of *Haro Harīdevaṃ*, v. 80 reads *Haro Hriharo*. By *Harīdeva* (in v. 6), therefore, we should perhaps understand Harihara and not Hari. The latter is known to the *Mahāsamayasutta* (*ath' āgu Harayo devā*), *Dīghanikāya*, II. 260.
6. *jaya brahmā Dhaḍḍharaṭṭhakaṃ*. Dhataraṭṭha, one of the four *mahārājas*, king of the east and lord of the Gandhabbas. He is not called *brahmā* in the canon. Our text appears to be erroneously calling him a *brahmā*.
7. *jaya nāgo Virruḷhako*. Virūḷhaka, called here a *nāga*, is in the canon known as the lord of Kumbhaṇḍas.
8. *Virrupakkho*. Virupakkha, lord of the *nāgas*.
9. *Venatteyyo*. Venateyya, name of a Garuḍa, well known in Hindu mythology. This name, however, occurs only in the *Kuṇālajātaka* (J, v. 428). The inclusion of Venateyya in the list of major Buddhist deities here, is significant. The cult of Garuḍa was very popular in Angkor. His images in a conventionalized form adorn Cambodian art, both ancient and modern. See J. Hackin and others, *Asiatic mythology*, 200.
10. *catupālakā*. The four *mahārājas*, guardians of the four cardinal points.
11. *aṭṭhārasa mahādevā*. The number 18 most probably refers to the 18 *rūpāvacara devas* (see *Vibhaṅga*, p. 570-2).
12. *siddhi-tāpasa-ādayo*. See (65) below on *siddhi-vijjādharā*.
13. *asīti sāvakā*. The figure 80 appears to be only symbolical. See PTS *Pali-English dictionary*, 89. We find a group of 80 *mahātheras* (*dasabalañ ca asīti mahāthere ca vandathā ti*) in the *Dhammapada-aṭṭhakathā*, p. 14, but no list is provided.
14. *dasapālo*. Perhaps refers to the ten Buddhas occupying ten points of the universe. See (23) below.
15. *aṭṭhuttarasataṃ*. The 108 marks on the feet of the Buddha. This also appears to be a symbolical figure based on eight. The *Milindapañho* speaks of the 100 auspicious marks (*satapuññalakkhaṇaṃ*) of the Buddha, but no list is given.
16. These three verses (14-16) appear to have been borrowed from some text describing the Buddha's victory over Māra. Compare, for instance, *Samantakūṭavaṇṇanā*, vv. 345 f., where the ten *pāramitās* are called warriors (*bhaṭas, yodhas*) fighting with the hosts of Māra.

17. *sammā*. This word should be read as *sacca* to complete the number of ten *pāramīs*.
18. *kesarāri*. Reading is doubtful.
19. *bhattā*. Perhaps stands for *bhataka* 'servant'. See *Milinda*., p. 379.
20. *cīraṃ*. Perhaps stands for *vīra*.
21. *evaṃ tvaṃ vijayo hotu*. *evaṃ tuyhaṃ jayo hotu* in *Jayamaṅgalagāthā*. See introduction, above.
22. Verses 18-20. Description of something corresponding to a *maṇḍala* or a magic circle (or even a square) used in sacred rites and well known in the Hindu and Mahāyāna Tāntric works. The Pali scriptures do not contain any such descriptions of the eight chief disciples forming a magic circle. The origin of this practice may be traced to the *Mahāsamayasutta* of the *Dīghanikāya* where the four *mahārājas* are described as occupying and ruling the four cardinal points. (See also *Manusmṛti*, v. 96, where the names of eight *lokapālas* are given.) The earliest allusion to the eight monks sitting in a circle in connection with a *paritta* ceremony is found in the story of Dīghāvukumāra in the *Dhammapada-aṭṭhakathā*. The relevant passage is worth quoting: *sace tvaṃ attano gehadvāre maṇḍapaṃ katvā tassa majjhe pīṭhikaṃ katvā taṃ parikkhipanto aṭṭha vā soḷasa vā āsanāni paññāpetvā tesu mama sāvake nisīdāpetvā sattāhaṃ nirantaraṃ parittaṃ kātuṃ sakkuṇeyyāsi, evaṃ assa antarāyo nāseyyā ti* (xii. 8).

   Maung Htin Aung in his *Folk elements in Burmese Buddhism* (p. 8) states that the Burmese Buddhists cite this passage as an authority for a ceremony entitled the 'Nine Gods'. In this ceremony the Burmese employ a (square) *maṇḍala* occupied by the images of eight chief disciples (the same as in our text with one exception, viz. Kassapa instead of Revata in the south-east) with an image of the Buddha in the centre. The images of eight planets are placed behind the eight *arhats*, Ketu the ninth planet being placed in the centre facing the Buddha. A *maṇḍala* of only the eight planets occupying the eight points is found in *Vedaparikramaḥ*, included in *Sanskrit texts from Bali* (p. 8). It is not possible to determine whether the *maṇḍala* of the *grahas* was a prototype for the 'circle' of the *arhats* or vice versa, but the latter appears to be fairly old. There is a similar set mentioned in the *Sudhammavatīrājavaṃsa*, Pak Lat ed., 1910, 76-7. In this set the Buddha occupies the centre with

Moggallāna in the north, Sāriputta in the south, Kaccāyana in the north-west, and Mahākassapa in the south-west. The west is unoccupied and, while the text is ambiguous, according to Mr. H. L. Shorto to whom I owe this reference, the north-east, east, and south-east are probably to be understood as occupied by Anuruddha, Ānanda, and Gavampati respectively.

It may be noted that in our *maṇḍala* the first four points are clockwise (south, west, north, east) and the remaining four (north-west, south-west, south-east, north-east) anticlockwise. The succeeding *maṇḍala*, however, gives all eight points clockwise.

23. Verses 21-3. Description of another *maṇḍala* consisting of ten Buddhas occupying four cardinal points, four intermediate points, earth, and sky. Ten, like eight, is a magic number in Pali. There may be some connection between this 'circle' and the ten *rājadhammās* (J, II. 367) as indicated by our text (*rājadhammasssa pūjitā*) but I have been unable to trace it to any Buddhist text, Pali or Sanskrit. Dr. Hooykaas in his article 'Buddha brahmins in Bali' (*BSOAS*, XXVI, 3, 1963, 547) gives a Buddhist *mantra* related to ten points of the universe, the last two called *adhaḥ* and *ūrdhvā,* plus the centre (*madhyā*). The *mantra* does not mention the names of the occupants of these points. As pointed out in the introduction, vv. 21-3 correspond to vv. 2b-5a of *Cūlajinapañjara*, a short *paritta* hymn of 14 verses included in the appendix to the *Pali-Siṃhala-pirit-pota.*

The names of the ten Buddhas selected here appear in the traditional list of Buddhas given in the *Buddhavaṃsa.* No reason is given for the choice of these ten out of a total number of 27 Buddhas for forming this *maṇḍala.* It is interesting, however, to note that out of these ten, four Buddhas (Buddhasikhi, Kakusandha, Kassapa, and Sākyamuni) appear in the oldest list of seven Buddhas given in the *Mahāpadānasutta* (*Dīghanikāya,* II. 5 f.) occupying second, fourth, sixth, and seventh place respectively. Four (Dīpaṃkara, Sumangala, Revata, and Padumuttara) appear in the list of 25 Buddhas (nos. 1, 3, 5, and 10) given in the *Buddhavaṃsa.* Medhaṃkara and Saraṇaṃkara appear in the list of three other Buddhas (nos. 2 and 3) mentioned in the twenty-seventh chapter of the *Buddhavaṃsa.* Whether this is a haphazard choice or whether these ten Buddhas were in any way specially connected with *paritta* ceremonies is not known.

24. *puratthimāyaṃ* in *Cūla-jinapañjara.*
25. *aggimhi c' eva,* ibid.
26. *nerutte ca,* ibid.
27. *ca Sikhī buddho,* ibid.
28. *vāyavye,* ibid.
29. *Piyadassī ca,* ibid.
30. *Dīpankaro,* ibid.
31. *pathavyā,* ibid.
32. *Saraṇaṃkaro,* ibid.
33. *evaṃ dasa disā c'eva sabbe buddhā patiṭṭhitā,* ibid.
34. See J, II. 367.
35. Verses 27-37 contain verse portions from the *Candimasutta* and *Suriyasutta* of the *Saṃyuttanikāya,* I. 50-1. These two suttas are also included in the *Catu-bhāṇavāra,* the traditional book of the *paritta-suttas.* The reason for the choice of these two out of a large number of *paritta* texts appears to be their connection with the legends of the eclipse of the moon and the sun by Rāhu, the chieftain of the *asuras.* The prominent place accorded in our text to astrological matters could also explain the selection of these two suttas in particular.
36. *bhavā 'ti, Saṃyuttanikāya,* I. 50.
37. *pamuñcassu,* ibid.
38. Verses 30, 31, and 32 are not required here. They are repetitions of vv. 24b, 25, and 26. Note the changes here: *nāsti* for *natthi, vidhaṃsetu* for *vidhaṃsatu.*
39. *tiṭṭhasī 'ti, Saṃyuttanikāya,* I. 50.
40. *Suriyasutta,* ibid., I. 51.
41. *bhavā 'ti,* ibid.
42. *maṇḍalī,* ibid.
43. *gilī,* ibid.
44. See verse 33. Here we should add: *saṃviggarūpo āgamma kin nu bhīto va tiṭṭhasi.*
45. *caviṭṭhārakā* or *c[h]aviddhārakā?* The reading is doubtful. *Chavi* 'skin', *dhāraka* 'bearer', i.e. a snake?
46. cf. *sabbe sattā sabbe pāṇā sabbe bhūtā ca kevalā ..., Khandhaparitta* (*Aṅguttaranikāya,* II. 72), a *paritta* used against snakes.
47. The following list of *grahas, māsas, nakṣatras,* and *rāśis* is also a

special feature of our text. There are several references in the Pali canon to the festivities celebrated in honour of the *nakṣatras,* but we do not know of any instance where they are propitiated or called upon to protect as in our text. Professor V.S. Agrawala in his *India as known to Pāṇini* (p. 358) shows references in Pāṇini's grammar to a large number of time-denoting words like *māsa* and *saṃvatsara* and to several names of asterisms which were raised to the status of deities (*devatā*). The worship of planets is, as noted above, common among Hindus and Budhists even to this day. Our text, however, appears to indicate the existence of a similar practice extended even to the *māsas* and *nakṣatras* (denoting both the Indian constellations and the years of the Chinese twelve-year cycle).

Although the names of some of these planets, months, constellations, and signs of the zodiac are known to the canon and the *aṭṭhakathās,* a complete list of them is not available in any other Pali text. The *Abhidhānappadīpikā* (Abhp.), a twelfth-century work from Ceylon, enumerates the names of the months and the *nakkhattas* but gives the name of only the first *graha* and the first *rāśi.* The *Jinakālamālī* (*Jkm.*) mentions several of these names in connection with the dates of historical events treated in that work. We note below those references which show different spellings or alternative names for these items.

48. *Sūrādī tu navaggahā; Abhp.*, i.61; *Sūra Canda Aṅgāra Buddha Jīva Sukka Asita Rāhu Ketu iti ete Sūrādayo navaggahā ti Ṭīkā, Abhp.,* p. II (Ahmedabad ed.). *Jkm.* uses the names Guru and Jīva for Jupiter and Soraka, Sorika, Sani, and Sannicara for Saturn.

49. *cf. Citto Vesākha Jeṭṭho cā 'sāḷho dvīsu ca Sāvaṇo*
Poṭṭhapādā 'ssayujjā ca māsā dvādasa Kattiko,
Māgasiro tathā Phusso kamena Māgha Phaggunā. Abhp., i.75—6a. The following names are found in the *Jkm.*: Citra, Visākha, Jeṭṭha, Āsāḷha, Sāvaṇa, Bhadra, Assayuja, Kattika, Māgasira, Phussa, Māgha, Phagguṇa.

50. The Chinese twelve-year cycle is not known to the *Abhp.* The following are mentioned in the *Jkm.*: Mūsika (*vassa-vassika-Sakarāja),* Vyaggha (also called Saddūla—*vassa-saṃvacchara-Sakarāja*), Sasa (*vassa-Sakarāja*), Mahoraga (*vassa-Sakarāja*),

Sappa (*vassa-Sakarāja*), Turaṅga (*vassa*), Aja (*vassa*), Makkaṭa (*vassa-Sakarāja*), Kukkuṭa (*vassa-Sakarāja*), Kukkura (*vassa-Sakarāja*). The *Jkm.* does not use the designation *nakkhatta* for these Chinese years. See introduction above.

51. cf. *Assayujo Bharaṇitthi saKattikā Rohiṇī c'eva*
Maggasira-m-Addā ca Punabbasu Phusso cā 'silesā pi,
Visākhā 'nurādhā Jeṭṭhā Mūlā 'sāḷha duve tathā,
Savano ca Dhaniṭṭhā ca Satabhisajo Puvvottarabhaddapdā
Revaty apī ti kamato sattādhika vīsa nakkhattā. Abhp., i.58—60.

Jkm. mostly follows the *Abhp.*, with the exception of two, viz.. Asvini and Māgasira. Our text has Assujja corresponding to the Assayuja of the *Abhp. Jkm.* appears to have adopted the more familiar word Asvini (Skt. Aśvinī). For the Skt. Mṛgaśirā we have thus three forms: Mṛggasira (our text), Maggasira (*Abhp.*), and Māgasira (*Jkm.*)

kammato in v. 49 should be understood as *kamato*; see *Abhp.*, i.60a.

52. *Rāsi Mesādiko, Abhp.*, i.61. *Jkm.* has the following: Mesa, Usabha, Methuna (also Mithunaka), Kakkaṭaka, Sīha, Kanyā, Tulā, Vicchika, Cāpa, Maṅkara, Kumbha, Mīna.

53. *Sāvetrī.* Pali Sāvittī and Sāvitthī. Known to the Pali canon only as a name of the Vedic verse *Sāvitrī,* but well known in Hindu mythology. This is also a name of the wife of Brahmā and of the river Sarasvatī.

Ruddhāni. Perhaps stands for Rudrāṇī, wife of Rudra. This is also a name of Durgā. Not known in Pali.

Gaṃgā. Known to Pali only as the name of river Ganges, but not as a *devī.*

Iraggā. Not known either in Pali or in Sanskrit. Irā is also a name of Sarasvatī, the goddess of speech. Irāvatī is a name of Durgā. Perhaps this is also a name of a river, like Gaṃgā, raised to the status of a *devī.* Could it possibly refer to the river Irāwaddy (Irāvatī) in Burma?

Naladevī. This *devī* is also not known. In the *Harivaṃśa-purāṇa* one of Rudrāśva's daughters is called Nalā (see Monier-Williams). This word could also be read as *Analā* (*iraggāna-ladevīyā)* in which case it could refer to the Fire goddess. But the name Analā is not known in Sanskrit.

Bhiratti. Not known in Pali or Sanskrit. Should we read *Abhiratti* (i.e. *Abhirati,* i.e. Rati, the wife of Kāma)?

mṛcchu Mārikā. mṛcchu (Pali *maccu,* Skt. *mṛtyuḥ* 'death') qualifies Mārikā. Mārī is a name for smallpox. A deity of that name (identified in popular belief with Kālī) is still worshipped in Indian villages.

As is evident, with the sole exception of Dharaṇi, none of these *devīs* belong to the Buddhist pantheon. Sāvitrī, Rudrāṇī, and Gaṃgā can be traced to the Hindu pantheon. The remaining four could be of purely local origin raised to the status of *devī.*

54. *aṭṭhadisesu rakkhitā* 'placed in (i.e. occupying) the eight directions'.
This could suggest a possibility of a *maṇḍala* of eight *devīs. disesu* is wrong; the text should read *disāsu.*
55. *Jotika.* See *Dhammapada-aṭṭhakathā,* iv.199-213.
56. *Meṇḍaka.* ibid., iii.372 f.; *Vinayapiṭaka,* I. 240 f.
57. *Dhanañjaya. Dhammapada-aṭṭhakathā,* i.384 f., iii. 363; *J.* II. 347.
58. *Uggata.* Most probably refers to Ugga, See (62) below.
59. *Jaṭila. Dhammapada-aṭṭhakathā,* iv.214.
60. *Cittaka.* Probably refers to Citta *gahapati* whose carts were filled with all kinds of valuables by the *devas.* See *Aṅguttara aṭṭhakathā,* I. 210.
61. *Mandhātā. J.* II. 311 f.; *Divyāvadāna,* p. 210 f.
62. Of these seven, three, viz. Jotika, Jaṭila, and Mandhātā are said to possess miraculous powers obtained by merit (*puññavato iddhi*). See *Paṭisambhidāmagga,* II. 213. Meṇḍaka and his son Dhanañjaya are counted in the *Visuddhimagga* (xii.42) among the five *mahāpuññas.* Uggata is the only person unknown. He is perhaps to be identified with Ugga who is described as the best of those who gave agreeable gifts (*manāpadāyakānaṃ aggo, Aṅguttaranikāya,* I. 26). Buddhaghosa quotes a verse where he is listed among the five great persons: *kathaṃ puññamahattato? Jotiko Jaṭilo Uggo Meṇḍako atha Puṇṇako ..., Visuddhimagga,* viii.8.
63. *Akkharasāriṇī nāma isī.* Not known in Pali or Sanskrit.
64. *puriso ca mahantako.* Perhaps stands for *mahāpurisa.*
65. *Siddhi-vijjādharā.* The word *vijjādhara* occurs four times in our text. On three occasions (vv. 63, 65, 74) it is joined in the MS with *siddhi* and in v. 69 it appears alone. Earlier (v. 8) there is a reference to *siddhitāpasa.* We are not sure if we should read these two words together or separately, but have followed the MS. Perhaps in both cases *siddhi* is used as an adjective. Could

it be that our text is referring to two kinds of *vijjādharas*, and also two kinds of *tāpasas*, one with and one without the *siddhis?* Could it refer to a class of beings corresponding to the *siddhas* of the Tāntric texts?

66. *dvādasā.* I have not been able to find any list of *vijjādharas* either in Buddhist or Hindu mythology. It may be noted that none of these words— *siddhi, vijjādhara, and siddha*— are known to the Pali canon. *Vijjā* meaning 'magic' or 'charm' is known to the canon, but *vijjādhara* occurs only in the *Jātaka aṭṭhakathā* (*J*, III. 303, 529) and in the *Milindapañho* (pp.153, 200, 267). On *vijjādharas, siddhas,* and *vidyārājas,* see among others: J. Przyluski, 'Les Vidyārāja', *BEFEO*, XXIII, 1923, 301-18; D.L. Snellgrove, *The Hevajra tantra* (introduction); E. M. Mendelson, 'A messianic Buddhist association in Upper Burma', *BSOAS*, XXIV, 3, 1961, 580.

67. *manussā.* This should be read as *manussehi.*

68. *buddhasāvaṃ. sāvaṃ* (Skt. *srāva* 'juice') makes no sense. We should perhaps read *buddhabhāvaṃ. sāvaṃ* could refer to *sāvaka*, but is unlikely as the latter is a masculine word.

69. *catuvīsati desanā.* The items enumerated in vv. 66-7 give a total of 24 if we include the *desanā* itself. Perhaps this refers to the preaching (*desanā*) of the 24 *paccayas* (*hetu*, etc.) given in the Abhidhamma texts.

70. *evaṃ soḷasadhā dhammā. evaṃ* seems to refer to the items given in vv. 66-7. But the *dhammas* enumerated there are 24 and not 16. There is no known group of 16 *dhammas* in Pali. Assuming that the *catuvīsati desanā* (v. 67) refers to the 24 *paccayas* it is conceivable that the *soḷasa-dhammas* refer to another set, viz. the *paṭiccasamuppāda* (*avijjā*, etc.). The Abhidhamma texts count only 12 *aṅgas* (from *avijjā* to *jarā-maraṇa*) leaving out *soka, parideva, dukkha, domanassa,* and *upāyāsa* as descriptions of *jarā-maraṇa.* If we take *dukkha,* and *domanassa* together then these five *aṅgas* could provide the remaining four items, giving us a total of 16 *dhammas.*

71. *purisa.* Perhaps stands for *mahāpurisa.*

72. The 16 *devas* are most probably the same as the 16 *brahmās* (*Brahmapārisajja*, etc.) of the *rūpāvacara-bhūmi.* See *Vibhaṅga*, 570-2. See below: *Siddhi soḷasa mahābrahmā* (v. 104a). Cf. *rājā sabbe devatāyo soḷasapaṭalabrahmādayo sāretvā ...* (*Cāmadevīvaṃsa*), in *BEFEO*, xxv, 1925, 145. On a group of 16 *vajra-devatās*, see

Sanskrit texts from Bali, xxii.

73. *aggo.* Peak or top of a mountain?
74. *ubhaggo.* Not known in Pali or Sanskrit.
75. *bhaggo. bhagna* 'broken'?
76. *ubhaggo visarājā. ubhagga* could be a name of *visarāja.* The latter word is also not known in Pali or Sanskrit. It could mean a cobra (king of poison).
77. *poriko.* Not known in Pali or Sanskrit. In Marāṭhi *pori* means a young girl.
78. *mahāratto.* Not known in Pali or Sanskrit.
79. *paññāsapiḷitā.* Perhaps we should read *paññāsa piṇḍitā* (a group of 50). The next verse refers to *ekapaññāsa.* It may be noted, however, that only about 42 items are given in vv. 70-4. We should perhaps include eight items from vv. 68-9.
80. *ahaṃ, alaṃ?*
81. *sakkāro.* We should perhaps read *sakkato.*
82. *vannaṃ.* This stands for *vanaṃ*; cf. *tiṇṇā* for *tiṇa* 'grass', v. 85.
83. *siddhi mārabalaṃ yodhaṃ.* Here the *siddhi* must refer to the *yodha* who fights with the army of Māra.
84. Compare vv. 80-1 with vv. 6-8a. See (3) above.
85. *Rāmo.* This name is mentioned twice in our text: *jaya Rāmo* (v. 8) and *siddhi Rāmo* (v. 82). This, I believe, is the only Pali text where Rāma is glorified. He is, however, given a less prominent place than is accorded to Hara and Harihara in our text. See introduction above.
86. *kāraṇadevatā. Kāraṇa* in the sense of an ordeal, a feat or punishment, is known to Pali. But most probably this is an error, and should be read as *kānana.* Cf. *devānaṃ pūjaṃ katvā kānanadevānaṃ rūpañ ca ...pūjetvā ...*(*Cāmadevīvaṃsa*), in *BEFEO*, xxv, 1925, 144.
87. *tiṇṇā.* For *tiṇa* 'grass'.
88. *vali.* As this word follows *tiṇa* and *rukkha* I am inclined to take it for *vallī* 'creeper'. It may also be a misprint for *bali* 'oblation'.
89. *pakkhā* 'birds'.
90. *dibbamantrakaṃ.* This appears to be a reference to the title of our text. The correct Pali form *manta* occurs once (*dibbamantāni,* v. 100) but that could be a scribal improvement. Out text is consistent in retaining the r. Cf. *satrū, yantra, sātrakaṃ, caitra.*
91. *labheyyayuṃ.* Should be *labheyyuṃ.*

92. *kodanaṃ*. Not known in Pali or Sanskrit. Could it be a local word for *kodaṇḍa* 'cross-bow'? The next word also refers to a bow.
93. *dhanunā snānaṃ*. Literally 'a bath with a bow'. This seems to allude to some kind of magic device employed to destroy an enemy. A similar practice, 'drinking the water with which swords were washed', is found mentioned in the *Vinayapiṭaka: tassā evarūpo dohaḷo hoti: icchati suriyassa uggamanakāle caturaṅginiṃ senaṃ sannaddhaṃ ... passituṃ khaggānañ ca dhovanaṃ pātuṃ*, I. 342. Cf. *Mahāvaṃsa*, xxii. 42-5: *yodhānaṃ aggayodhassa sīsachinnāsidhovanaṃ, tasseva sīse ṭhatvāna pātuṃ ceva akāmayi.* Miss I. B. Horner in *The Book of discipline* (IV, p.490, n. 4) notes several non-Pali sources for this belief and particularly for its relation to a pregnant woman.
94. *matikaṃ*. Perhaps stands for *mattikā* 'clay'.
95. *anusātrakaṃ*. Skt. *anuśāstrakaṃ?*
96. *buddhānaṃ catuvīsati*. The *Buddhavaṃsa* enumerates 25 Buddhas. It is possible that here only the Buddhas previous to Gotama are referred to by our text. This number is usually associated with Jainas who enumerate 24 *tīrthaṅkaras*. On the number of Buddhas see (23) above.
97. *soḷasa mahābrahmā*. See (72) above.
98. Our text most probably ended with this verse. The next two verses could have been added at a later time from a Ceylonese work called *Jaya-pirit*. See introduction.
99. *sokā santat 'upaddavā* in *Jaya-pirit*.
100. *anekā antarāyā pi*, ibid.
101. *jayasiddhi*, ibid.
102. *sotthi*, ibid.
103. *sirī*, ibid.
104. *buddhi*, ibid.
105. *āyū*, ibid.
106. *jīvasiddhi*, ibid.
107. *samattaṃ*. For *samāptaṃ*.
108. *nitthītaṃ*. For *niṭṭhitaṃ*.
109. *sabbasavassati siddhikāraya*. Corresponds to *sarvaṃ svasti siddhikārakaṃ* (or *kāryaṃ*).

CHAPTER 28

(Introduction to) *Vasudhārā-Dhāraṇī:* A Buddhist work in use among the Jainas of Gujarat*

The *Vasudhārā-dhāraṇī,* also variously termed *Vasudhārā-stotra* and *Vasudhārā-dhāraṇī-kalpa* is a short (magic formula) text written in Buddhist Sanskrit. The main part of the text consists of various *mantras* to be employed in the ritual, but it is set in the framework of a Buddhist *sūtra* which may be summarised as below:

"Thus have I heard. Once upon a time the Lord while sojourning in the great city of Kośāmbī in a grove called Kaṇṭaka was preaching the Doctrine in an assembly of 500 monks and a large number of *bodhisattvas.* At that time there lived in Kośāmbī a householder by the name of Sucandra. He was a man of tranquil mind, a man of great devotion. He had many sons and daughters and had to support a large number of relatives and servants. He approached the Lord and having saluted him sat in one corner. Seated there he addressed the Lord thus: "May I, Lord, be permitted to ask a question to the Lord who is a Tathāgata, an Arhat, a Samyak-sambuddha?" Thus addressed the Lord said to Sucandra the householder: "You may ask, O householder, whatever you wish. I shall please you by answering your questions".

""Yes, Lord", said Sucandra and asked: "How, O Lord, does a son or a daughter of a good family become rich again once he has become poor, how is he restored to health having become sick?"

---

* This article was originally published in *The Mahāvīra Jaina Vidyālaya Golden Jubilee Volume,* (Bombay, 1968), pp. 30-45. (Text not reprinted.)

Then the Lord said to Sucandra: "Why do you, O householder, ask a question relating to poverty?" To this question the householder replied: "I am poor, O Lord, I am impoverished, O Sugata. I have many sons and daughters, many relatives and servants, many people to feed. May the Lord preach me that Discourse (*dharma-paryāya*) by which the poor may become rich, the sick may become well, endowed with plenty of wealth and corn, gold and silver, pleasing to heart and eyes, may become masters of charity, of great charity. May they become wealthy with pearls and beryls, diamonds and conches, silver and gold, well established with prosperous families, houses, wives, sons and daughters."

"Thus asked, the Lord said to Sucandra: "There, O householder, in the long past, in the incalculable ages bygone, appeared in the world a Lord by the name of Vajradharasāgaranirghoṣa, a Tathāgata, an Arhat, a Samyak-sambuddha, endowed with wisdom and discipline, knower of the universe, supreme charioteer of men, a great teacher of gods and men, a Buddha. From that Tathāgata, O householder, have I heard this *dhāraṇī* called *Vasudhārā* (Shower of Wealth), have learnt and mastered it and have explained it to others. I shall also now teach that *dhāraṇī* to you by the glory of which a son of a good family is not obstructed by human beings or inhuman beings, by *yakṣas* or by *piśācas,* etc. Whosoever, O householder, a son or a daughter of a good family, memorizes this *dhāraṇī,* writes it down in a book, or even listens to it, and one who worships it having first offered elaborate worship to the Tathāgatas, the Arhats and the Samyak-sambuddhas, to him or to her the *devatās* (the goddess Vasudhārā and others), inspired by their devotion to the dispensation (*śāsana*) of the Buddha and the Saṁgha, will approach in person and cause the rains of wealth and corn, of gold and coins."

"Then the Lord uttered the *dhāraṇī* and said: "These, O householder, are the charm-words of this *dhāraṇī.* It should be repeated for six months after worshipping all Tathāgatas. That place where this *mahāvidyā* (powerful charm) is read becomes sacred. Having worshipped the Tathāgatas, Ārya-Avalokiteśvara (a *bodhisattva*) and the *mantra-devatā* (i.e., Vasudhārā) in an auspicious place or in the chamber of treasure a magic circle should be drawn and the *dhāraṇī* should be repeated thrice. One who thus properly propitiates his house is filled with all kinds of wealth and gold and all his obstructions are removed. Therefore, O householder, learn this *Vasudhārā-dhāraṇī,* master it and preach it to others. It will be conducive to your great merit, wealth and well-being."

"Then Sucandra the householder having heard this *dhāraṇī* from the Lord, having become pleased and happy, elated, fell at the feet of the Lord and said: "I have now learnt this *dhāraṇī,* O Lord, and have grasped it well. I shall now explain it in detail to others also."

"Instantaneously, Sucandra the householder's treasury was filled with riches. Then Sucandra departed from the Lord having saluted him and having circumambulated him a hundred-thousand times."

"Then the Lord addressed venerable Ānanda: "Go you, Ānanda go to the residence of Sucandra the householder and see his abode filled with all kinds of wealth."

"Then venerable Ānanda approached the house of Sucandra and returned to the Lord and asked: "What, O Lord, is the cause that Sucandra has suddenly become a man of great wealth?" "Ānanda, Sucandra the householder is devoted, is of great devotion, his intentions are noble. He has learnt this *Vasudhārā-dhāraṇī,* has grasped it and will preach it to others also. Therefore, Ānanda, you too learn this *dhāraṇī,* grasp it, recite it and preach it to others. That will be for the good of many, for the happiness of many, for the well-being of gods and men. I do not see, O Ānanda, anyone in this whole world of gods and demons, of the Māra and Brahma, of the Śramaṇas and Brāhmaṇas who will overcome this powerful charm (*Mahāvidyā*); such a contingency does not exist. Why is it so? Because, O Ānanda, these *mantras* of the *Vasudhārā-dhāraṇī* are unbreakable, they will not even be heard by beings who have lost their roots of good. Why is that? Because it is the word of all Tathāgatas, by all Tathāgatas is this *dhāraṇī* uttered, controlled, and sealed by their own seal, and preached for the well-being of all poor people and for the removal of all fears. obstructions and calamities.

"Then the venerable Ānanda asked the Lord: What is the name of this Discourse, O Lord, and by what title shall I know it? The Lord said: Therefore, O Ānanda, you may call it by the title of *Sucandragṛhapati-paripṛcchā* [1] or the *Vasudhārā-dhāraṇī-kalpa.*"

"The Lord said thus, and the venerable Ānanda and those monks and the *bodhisattvas* and the entire assembly welcomed the preaching of the Lord."

In 1961, while on a visit to Ahmedabad, I first came to know of the *Vasudhārā-dhāraṇī* from Munirāja Śrī Puṇyavijayajī. He knew the Buddhist origin of the work and surprised me by the additional information that the work was being used by the (Śvetāmbara) Jaina community in their *upāśrayas*[2] as a useful text. The Jainas are well known for their liberal attitude towards the use of books originating from their rival schools. Their libraries store them, their *ācāryas* write commentaries on them and even teach them to their disciples in the classical spirit of the *Anekāntavāda*. But we know of no other non-Jaina work than the *Vasudhārā-dhāraṇī* which was employed in their rituals.

Apparently the origins of this work were forgotten. A Buddhist work, like the image of a Buddha, can be very easily confused with a Jaina work. The words like *sarvajña, jina, arhat* and *vītarāga* are a common property of both these schools and could be employed to designate their respective teachers, viz., the Buddha and the Tīrthaṅkaras. The opening words of greeting in our three MSS., viz., (A) *oṃ namaḥ śrī jina-śāsanāya,* (B) *oṃ namaḥ śrī jināya,* and (C) *oṃ namaḥ śrī vītarāgāya* (the only sign of Jainism found in the whole text) were in all probability appended by the Jaina copyists. It is, however, not inconceivable that these, or one of these, might have been an integral part of the original MS. which formed the basis of our MSS. If this conjecture is right then it could be assumed that the Jainas were misled by this into believing it to be a genuine Jaina work. But sooner or later some learned Jaina as he read through the text and found the teacher referred to as the Buddha would have certainly detected the error. The probability thus remains that the work was introduced in the ritual, with the full knowledge of its alien origin, to assist the Jaina layman in propitiating the goddess of wealth on the New-year day. Once introduced to achieve this purely secular end the Jaina layman conveniently ignored its origin. The Jaina *yatis*[3] who must have recited this *stotra* also seem to have apparently participated in the ritual with the same spirit, viz., that of assisting the *upāsaka* in his worldly pursuits, either not suspecting the origin of the text or ignoring it as a matter of little or no consequence.

There are, however, indications in our MSS. that the *dhāraṇī* was recited not in public places (i.e., the Jaina temples) but in private homes and by non-Jaina teachers or priests. It is stated in the colophon of two (B and C) of our three manuscripts that the *stotra* should be recited seated on a magic circle (*maṇḍala*) in the innermost chamber of the house where the treasury is located. The colophon of one MS. (C) further adds that it should be read after offering to the priest (*guru*) milk, clothes and silver coins. It also states that if at the time of its recitation [the *yajamāna*] enters a room to the left of the recitation chamber, and while attentively listening to the *stotra* engages in intercourse, a son will be born to him. It is hard to believe that a Jaina monk could easily be persuaded to render a service of this nature even in a private household of a Jaina layman. It appears more plausible that the term *guru* refers not to a Jaina monk but to a Brahmin priest. It is customary even to this day to find such *pūjārīs* or Brahmin priests employed in the rich Jaina households for the purpose of offering worship of an elaborate nature to the Jaina deities surrounded by *devatās* of Jaina and non-Jaina pantheon. The part played by the *Vasudhārā-dhāraṇī* in the Jaina community thus appears to have been ultimately restricted to private homes of a few Jainas served mainly by Brahmin priests who might have utilized similar other non-Jaina tantric texts like the *Devī-māhātmya* or the *Caṇḍī-stotra* popular among the Hindus of Gujarat.

The peculiar circumstance of coming across this hitherto unpublished Buddhist work enjoying the hospitality of its rival community rendered it a very interesting find, and I decided to collect its manuscripts. Three small MSS. (each of six folios) were made available to me by the courtesy of Munirāja Śrī Puṇyavijayajī and Pandit Dalsukh Malvania, Director of the L.D. Institute of Indology, Ahmedabad.

Upon my arrival in London I learnt that Professor J. Brough, Professor of Sanskrit in the University of London, had also obtained two MSS. of this work from Nepal: (1) *Vasudhārā-dhāraṇī* (No. 41), (2) *Vasudhārā-vrata-kathā* (No. 46a) and one MS. of an allied work called *Sucandrāvadāna* (No. 87). Of these the first and the third are written in Buddhist Sanskrit and the second is in Newārī. One MS. of the *Vasudhārā-dhāraṇī* (No. 1355) agreeing with Professor Brough's No. 41 and one of the *Sucandrāvadāna* (No. 1400) agreeing with Brough's No. 87 were found in the Cambridge University Library.[4] Several MSS. connected with these texts are also listed in the *Catalogue of the Sanskrit MSS. in the Tokyo University Library*, Tokyo, 1965. There are six Tibetan works dealing with *Vasudhārā* in the *Tibetan Tripiṭaka*.[5] There are three Chinese versions dated respectively mid-seventh century, mid-eighth century and late tenth century.[6] Several images and *maṇḍalas* of the goddess Vasudhārā originating in Nepal have also been found.[7] In view of this vast literature connected with the cult of Vasudhārā, it was decided by us to prepare a critical edition of the *Vasudhārā-dhāraṇī* utilizing the various MSS. of its different versions. The work is in progress and may take a longer time than earlier envisaged. As the three MSS. found in Ahmedabad form a distinct group, I have found it desirable to publish them in advance in order to elicit more information about it from the Jaina community and also to emphasize the need of discovering remaining MSS. of this work in their rich *bhaṇḍāras*.

The three Ahmedabad MSS. used here in preparing the text of the *Vasudhārā-dhāraṇī* are referred to as A (No. 3222), B (No. 2848), and C (No. 5730).[8] Despite the different wordings of the initial greetings to the Jina, viz., *jinaśāsanāya* (A), *jināya* (B), and *vītarāgāya* (C) (found only in these three MSS.) all three retain a common error in their first three folios where the sequence of the text has been broken by the misplacement of certain paragraphs as indicated below in the text. This must be the result of following a faulty MS. tradition. It is apparent therefore that all three MSS. have either been copied from a single original MS. yet to be found, or one of them has served as the original for the remaining two.

Of the three again, B and C have many common readings which sometimes appear to be improvements made on the readings in A. B and C have also a long passage at the end of the text of the *stotra* explaining the various blessings obtained by its recitation, a feature totally absent from A. For these reasons we are inclined to believe that A is older than the other two. A is also the only dated MS. and we have chosen it for the basic text. Variant readings in B and C, even when they appear to be better than A, are given in the footnotes. Only a few scribal errors in A have been emended with the help of B and C and are noted in the footnotes as occurring in A. No attempt has otherwise been made to correct the MS. in keeping with the normal practice of editing works in Buddhist Sanskrit.

The colophon of A states that the work was written for the benefit of Sāh Śrī Indrajī Sundarma,[9] son of Pamanīya, in the year Saṁvat 1695, i.e., A.D. 1638. The work has thus been known to the

Jainas of Gujarat for at least three centuries, and it should be possible to find many more MSS. of this work in Gujarat. Great importance attaches to the date of this MS., since the Nepalese MSS. of this work in Professor Brough's collection and in the University Library, Cambridge are based on a different set of MSS. far larger in size than our A, and contain large portions of additional material mainly in the form of *mantras* and details regarding the actual rites. Only one of these, viz. No. 1355 of the Cambridge University Library is dated as Nepali Saṁvat 696 (A.D. 1576). If this be the true date of this MS., it is apparent that the MSS. A, B and C have preserved an earlier redaction, which would render them of great value for a history of the Vasudhārā cult in general and for a critical edition of the *Vasudhārā-dhāraṇī* in particular.

NOTES

1. It would appear from this that this was another title of the *Vasudhārā-stotra.* As a matter of fact, however, this is also a title of a different work, MSS. of which are found in Nepal. See below.
2. A place where the Jaina monks live.
3. A person who is considered lower than the monk but higher than the layman.
4. See C. Bendall's Catalogue of the Buddhist Sanskrit MSS. in the University Library, Cambridge, 1883. The following MSS. may be consulted: (1) *Vasudhārā-dhāraṇī* (No. 1355), (2) *Ārya-śrī Vasudhārā nāmāṣṭottara-śatakaṁ* (No. 1356), (3) *Vasuṁdharā-devī-vrata* (No. 1357), (4) *Sucandrāvadāna* (No. 1400), (5) *Vasudhārā-dhāraṇī-kathā* (No. 1680 and 1690).
5. The following may be consulted: *Ārya-vasudhārā-nāma dhāraṇī* (341-1) *Vasudhārā-sādhana* (4059-80), *Vasudhārā-dhāraṇyupadeśa* (4061-81), *Ārya-vasudhārā-nāma Aṣṭottara-śataka* (4524/81), *Vasudhāriṇīkalpa* (5127/81) and *Vasuśrīkalpa* (5128/87). (Tokyo-Kyoto ed. 1955-61).
6. *Taishō Tripiṭaka,* vol. 20, Nos. 1162, 1163, 1164. I owe these references to Professor J. Brough.
7. See *Art of Nepal* by Stella Kramrisch; Journal of the Indian Society of Oriental Art I, 1933, Calcutta, p. 129, Plates XXXIX, XL.
8. These numbers refer to the Index of the Library of L.D. Institute, Ahmedabad.
9. The name of this patron is not found in any other *praśastis* published recently in the *Catalogue of Sanskrit and Prakrit* MSS. from the L.D. Institute of Indology, Ahmedabad.

CHAPTER 29

(Introduction to and Translation of) *Ākāravattārasutta*: An 'Apocryphal' Sutta from Thailand*

Introduction

With the recent publication of the *Paññāsa-Jātaka*,[1] the term "apocryphal" may have become acceptable when applied to extra-canonical Buddhist narratives claiming the canonical status of *The Jātaka*.[2] This term, however, has never before been used for any piece of Pali literature that can be classified as a "sutta".[3] It is, therefore, an extraordinary find when a Pali manuscript is discovered which purports to contain a hitherto unknown "sermon" of the Buddha and which, moreover, claims to be a part of the *Saṃyutta-Nikāya*. I allude here to a text entitled *Ākāravattārasutta*, found among the Pali manuscripts preserved at the Siam Society, Bangkok. A catalogue of this collection, prepared by Dr. Oskar v. Hinüber, was published in the *Journal of the Siam Society* in 1987.[4] I am grateful to the authorities of the Siam Society for a microfilm which gives me an opportunity to publish this unique manuscript in honour of Professor K.R. Norman.

The catalogue describes this manuscript as "[No.] 47. *Ākārava[ttāra]sutta* (*Vaṇṇanā*) Khmer script; 5 lines 5, 2ī 29,0 cm; gilt edged. Folios: *ka-kaḥ, kha, khā*." The manuscript contains no information on the date or the place of its copying, but the col-

*This article was originally published in *Indo-Iranian Journal* (in Honour of Professor K.R. Norman), Vol. XXXV, pp. 193-223, 1992. Reprinted with kind permission of Kluver Academic Publishers. (Text not reprinted.)

ophon (front cover) gives the name of its donors as [Mr.] Kon Jambhu and [Mrs.] Keev and states that this sutta exists in the *Saṃyutta-Nikāya: "khā. nāy k'on "jam 'bhu nāṅ keev mī saddhā "srāṅ vai nai bra buddha sāss"hnā. bra ākāravattasūtra. mī nai saṃyuttanikāy"*.[5] After consulting all available bibliographical sources, Dr. v. Hinüber has rightly concluded that "this sutta cannot be traced in [the] S[aṃyutta-]N[ikāya] or elsewhere in the Tipiṭaka."[6]

The title *Ākāravattāra* (with or without the word sutta) occurs thirteen times in the body of the text (see #7, #8, #11, #29, #35, #36 twice, #38 five times, #44) and once (see #32) in its shortened form, *Ākāra-sutta.* Strange as it may seem, there is also another title, viz., *Ākāravattāra-suttavaṇṇanā,* which appears only once, almost at the end of the manuscript (see #48). This suggests the possibility of there being two works here, the "Sutta" and its "Vaṇṇanā" (commentary). The end of the "Sutta" portion is probably indicated by the words "*sambuddhena pakāsitaṃ... sattarasavaggehi paṭimaṇḍitaṃ*" (see #35).

These concluding words are followed by two rather corrupt verses [Nos. 18-19] of obscure meaning. The first verse says: "This sutta has been revealed by me (*mayā pakāsitā*) and it should be copied (*likhitabbā*) by a person with faith (*saddhādharā*)." Is it possible that the agent of this sentence is not the Buddha but the composer of the sutta? The second verse seems to allow such a meaning: "By me are tied together (*mayā ganṭhitā*) in this sutta the virtues of the Buddha like clusters of the best flowers." This accords well with the earlier admission that "the *Ākāravattārasutta* was revealed by the Omniscient One after putting together (*sammasitvā*) the Suttanta, Vinaya, and Abhidhamma" (see verse no. 16). A work "derived" from the three Piṭakas can hardly be called a "sutta", but it might be designated a "vaṇṇanā" (commentary). Even this is high honour indeed for this composition, an honour once accorded to the *Visuddhimagga* of Buddhaghosa: "Briefly summing up the three Piṭakas together with the commentary, he wrote the work called *Visuddhimagga.*" (*The Cūlavaṃsa*, I, ch. 37, verse 236).[7]

The remainder of the manuscript (#36 - #46) consists of a motley collection of some 37 verses. The sole function of these repetitious verses is to describe an assortment of fruits that result from the recitation of the *Ākāravattārasutta.* This portion can therefore be termed "vaṇṇanā", forming a sort of appendix to the "sutta", if indeed such a division was intended by the author. The familiar closing formula of a sutta, e.g. "*idaṃ avoca bhagavā... bhagavato bhāsitaṃ abhinandī ti,*" which should have appeared at the end of the "sutta" proper (i.e. at #35), is belatedly introduced at the end of this "vaṇṇanā". In the absence of another manuscript of this work, it is not possible to determine if the stray appearance of the name *Ākāravattāra-suttavaṇṇanā* here is the result of a scribal error or if it truly forms the title of a commentary on the *Ākāravattārasutta.*

The conclusion of the vaṇṇanā (niṭṭhitā, see #48) is followed by what is probably the most intriguing sentence in the entire work: [#49] "Without a doubt, this sutta has been spoken by the Blessed One, in the *Saṃyutta-Nikāya.*" Startling as this is, one would expect this reference — the significance of which will be examined below—to occur within the vaṇṇanā and not outside it. It is not unlikely that this reference to the *Saṃyutta-Nikāya* was appended at a later time by the copyist, the writer of the final words of dedication: [see #50] *iminā puññalikhitena ...nibbānapaccayo hotu.*" But it is also possible that the expression "*iminā puññalikhitena*" might point not to a copyist but to the writer himself, the author of the entire work who, having designated his own composition as a "sutta", must perforce remain nameless. Judging by the language as well as the subject matter of the text (i.e. the consequences of committing pārājika acts and so forth) and the audacity with which this work was put in the mouth of the Buddha, one must conclude that the author was a learned monk of the Theravāda sect of Thailand where the manuscript was found. The work might well have been composed at the request of the donors mentioned above.

One would expect the vaṇṇanā to explain the meaning of the rather strange title like *Ākāravattārasutta.* The word *ākāra* is well known in the sense of manner, condition, state, and so forth, while *vattāra* can mean"a speaker" (cf. *evaṃ vattāro honti, Jātaka,* I, p. 134), but the compound *ākāravattāra* is not attested elsewhere. The two words together can yield the meaning "The sutta which expounds the manner [of]," without however specifying the object of the sermon. A brief look at the contents of the text will show that the meaning of the title is completed if we read it as "A sermon which expounds the manner of [averting rebirth in hells]."

The sutta opens with the appropriate words: [#1] "Thus have

I heard ... when the Blessed One was residing in Sāvatthi at Vultures' Peak." It then introduces the Venerable Sāriputta entertaining the following thought: "These foolish beings may commit all sorts of evil deeds ...the house-holders (*gahatthā*) performing such acts as matricide and so forth, might commit a pārājika offence against the Teaching [#2] and even those who are mendicants (*pabbajitā*), having cut their roots [of good] might commit *pārājika* offences. They, having committed evil deeds, would be reborn in the Avīci hell. Is there any "dhamma," profound and subtle, capable of preventing their suffering?"

Thinking thus he addressed the Buddha: [#3] "A person guilty of a pārājika offence ...suffers for ...aeons in the Avīci hell; ... of a saṃghādisesa ... in the Mahātāpa hell; ... of a thullaccaya ...in the Tāpana hell; ...of a pācittiya...in the Lokantara hell; ...of a pāṭidesaniya ...in the Bherava hell; ...of a dukkaṭa ... in the Kālasutta hell; of a dubbhāsita ...in the Sañjīva hell. [#4] Just as there is cool [water] for extinguishing a hot fire, ... there must be a "dhamma" which could pacify [the effects of] the pārājika and so forth ...[#5] May the Blessed One preach that "dhamma" which is free from (i.e. saves one from) the evil states of rebirth (apāya)."

The Blessed One then spoke: [#6] "O Sāriputta, unabandoned (*avijahitaṃ*) by as many Buddhas as there are grains of sand in the river Ganges ... there is the *Ākāravattārasutta*, capable of preventing beings from suffering [#7] in the eight great and sixteen minor hells ... [#8] Whosoever listens to this sutta and learns it, worships it and remembers it,... such a person, [#10] even if he has committed evil deeds (*dussanakammaṃ*) against his parents, will not be reborn in evil states for ninety thousand aeons ...."

"And which is this *Ākāravattārasutta* of the Tathāgata?" In answer to his own question the Blessed One then uttered the famous formula in praise of the Buddha, known by its beginning words [#11] "*iti pi so bhagavā arahā sammāsambuddho*" and ending with the words "*parisuddhaṃ brahmacariyaṃ pakāseti*".

It is at this juncture that the author of the *Ākāravattārasutta* expands the canonical formula through seventeen sections of varying length called the vaggas. They all begin with the first four words of the original formula: "*iti pi so bhagavā*." The word immediately following these four words, which is different for each section, is used as a marker for a new vagga. Thus, for example, the word *arahaṃ* (see #12) appears at the beginning of the first vagga. It is followed by a string of nine adjectives (e.g. *sugato, lokavidū*) each again preceded by the words "*iti pi so bhagavā.*" The end of the section is marked by "*ti*" and it is then named as "*arahādiguṇavagga.*" This naming pattern continues through the remaining sixteen vaggas. It is possible to surmise that the author was naming the vaggas in imitation of a canonical text like the *Dhammapada,* in which each vagga derives its name from a word occurring in its first verse (e.g. *Appamādavagga, Cittavagga*). The total number of vaggas, seventeen, is probably without any significance.

This first, the *Arahāvagga,* has ten entries, a number that corresponds to the number of adjectives found in the original formula. The subsequent vaggas also conform, by and large, to this arrangement as no less than ten out of the remaining sixteen vaggas have ten entries each of "*iti pi so bhagavā.*"

In the case of the first vagga, the ten words (*arahaṃ* and so forth) are directly taken from the canonical litany. In the subsequent vaggas, however, one becomes aware of a major deviation from the canonical text. This consists of the novel practice of repeating the word *pāramīsampanno,* each time preceded by the name of the particular *pāramī,* and the words *iti pi so bhagavā,* to describe the Buddha. The main body of the *Ākāravattārasutta* thus consists of the phrase "*iti pi so bhagavā*" repeated one hundred seventy-four times and the word "*pāramīsampanno*" only ten less than that number!

The concept of pāramī is, of course, conspicuously absent in the canonical formula of "*iti pi so bhagavā.*" Assuming that the word "sammāsambuddho" in the formula might point to the attainment of the *pāramīs,* the number of perfections should still not exceed the canonical ten (as in the Pāramīvagga, see #17). New Pāramīs must, therefore, be invented to make up the bulk of the sutta. This is accomplished initially by designating some of the chief events in the career of a Bodhisatta, viz., the *abhinīhāra* (resolve to become a buddha), the *gabbhavuṭṭhāna* (emerging from the womb in a purified manner), and *abhisambodhi* (Supreme Awakening), as pāramīs. Beyond this point the author feels free to draw upon the canonical clusters of "dhammas" (*khandha* [consisting of *sīla, samādhi, paññā*], *vijjā, pariññā, ñāṇa, bodhipakkhiya, bala, cariyā, samāpatti, lakkhaṇa* and so forth) to serve as pāramīs. The Blessed One is then described as endowed with these manifold perfections, e.g. "*iti pi so bhagavā cattāro satipaṭṭhānapāramīsampanno*" [#21], "*iti pi so bhagavā thāmabalapāramīsampanno*" [#24].

There is nothing unusual in the idea that the recitation of the "*iti pi so bhagavā*" formula can ward off evil. Indeed, in the *Lokaneyyappakaraṇa,* also an apocryphal text originating in Thailand, not only the entire chant but just the first four syllables "*i-ti pi so*" together with "*bha-ga-vā*" are shown to have magic powers.[8] In this text the Bodhisatta narrates the story of a layman called Soṇa to a yakkha. Soṇa once had climbed a tree in a forest and was bitten by a deadly snake. Foreseeing his imminent death, Soṇa surrendered himself to the protection of the Buddha and, remembering his virtues through the recitation of the "*iti pi so bhagavā*" formula, was saved. The yakkha, having listened to this story, begged the Bodhisatta to reveal to him the function of the "seven syllables" (*sattakkharānaṃ kiccaṃ*)— a usage reminiscent of the Brahmanical *ṣaḍakṣara* (e.g. *oṃ namaḥ śivāya*) or the *aṣṭākṣara* (e.g. *oṃ namo Vāsudevāya*) mantras. The Bodhisatta then composed an acrostic using each syllable of the formula. Several of the items (notably *iddhi, vijjā, ñāṇa,* and *bala*) encountered in the elaboration of the "*iti pi so bhagavā*" formula in the *Ākāravattārasutta* are also found in these seven verses.[9] Whether the *Lokaneyyappakaraṇa* in any way influenced the composition of the *Ākāravattāra* or not is a moot question; but one must note that the former was not presented as a "sutta" but only as a pakaraṇa or a treatise.

Given the prominent place it accords to the canonical formula of "*iti pi so bhagavā,*" the *Ākāravattāra* may be permitted to call itself a "sutta," however the presumption of authority to speak on issues of Vinaya displayed here is quite unprecedented. No extant *Vinaya* text, *Aṭṭhakathā,* or oral tradition of the Theravāda countries is ever on record for punishing Vinaya transgressions with retributions in hells. Sure enough, the five *ānantarika kammas* (matricide and so forth) — evil acts that find retribution without delay —must immediately lead the perpetrator to the Avīci hell. Equally, those who indulge in evil actions are reborn in various states of loss and woe (apāya). But the ingenious manner in which the author of the *Ākāravattārasutta* has arranged retribution for the seven Vinaya offences (*pārājika, saṃghādisesa, thullaccaya, pācittiya, pāṭidesaniya, dukkaṭa,* and *dubbhāsita*) in the seven great hells (Avīci, Mahātāpa, Tāpana, Lokantara, Bherava, Kālasutta, and Sañjīva respectively), is not in keeping with the Vinaya texts of the Theravāda (and probably of any other Buddhist) tradition or even with the law of karmic retribution.

The original source for this innovation can possibly be traced to the *Jātakaṭṭhakathā*, particularly to the Nimijātaka (*Jātaka*, VI, pp. 105-115 [No. 541]). King Nimi is taken to the hellish abodes (nirayas) to witness the retribution for such evil acts as cheating, forgery, hurting the virtuous brahmans and samaṇas, plucking the feathers of birds and killing them, adulteration of food, theft (presented in that order,) and finally the most heinous acts of killing one's mother or father, or an arahanta (varieties of the ānantarika kamma). It is to be noted in this connection that this Jātaka verse uses the Vinaya term "*pārājika*" to describe the [lay] perpetrators of the last category: "*ye mātaraṃ vā pitaraṃ va loke, pārājikā arahante hananti*" (verse 475). The commentator seems to be aware of the rather unusual manner in which the Vinaya term pārājika is used here and adds: "*pārājikā ti jarājiṇṇe mātāpitaro ghātetvā gihibhāve yeva pārājikaṃ pattā.*" Thus it would appear that there was a precedence for the use of this technical term in a less rigid manner, applicable even to those householders who were not qualified to join the Order on account of their evil deeds. The statement in the *Ākāravattārasutta* that the "householders ... would be guilty of pārājika (*tattha gahatthā mātughātādikammaṃ katvā sāsanato pārājikaṃ āpajjeyyuṃ* [#2])" thus establishes a direct link between the Nimijātaka and our sutta. It seems likely that the use of the term pārājikā in this jātaka (coupled with the description of the ussadaniraya) might have given our author the idea to develop this link for the remaining Vinaya offences as well and to further correlate them with the appropriate hells. Although initially used for householders, this karmic retribution plan, elaborated with precise details of duration, was then simply extended to mendicants (pabbajitā) also. This would not be seen as highly objectionable by traditional Buddhists since the "sutta" only helped to demonstrate the ability of the "*iti pi so bhagavā*" formula to destroy the consequences of even ānantarika acts.

Moreover, the assertion that the sutta forms a part of the "*caturāsīti dhammakkhandhasahassa*" [#6], that it was spoken by all of the twenty-eight Buddhas headed by Dīpaṅkara [#31], and also that the "fruit of remembering the Sutta, Vinaya, and Abhidhamma is obtained by reciting this sutta" [see verse 54], removes any doubt concerning its affiliation with the Theravāda tradition. In view of this, a few stray statements like "as many Buddhas as grains of sand on the river Ganges" (#6: *anekāya Gaṅgāya vālokupamehi Buddhehi*), or the promise that "one will obtain living together with the Tathāgata" (#33: "*Tathāgatena so saddhiṃ saṃvāsaṃ paṭilabhati*"), should not be seen as reflecting an unorthodox influence. Indeed, the concluding verse of the sutta "One who sees the Good Law sees me; one who does not see the Good Law, even if he sees me, does not see" (see #45) seems to reaffirm the true nature of the Theravāda faith in the Buddha.

This brings us to the intriguing final sentence (appearing just before the verse of benediction) of the text, claiming that "without a doubt, this (i.e. the *Ākāravattāra*) sutta is spoken by the lord in the *Saṃyutta-Nikāya* ("*Saṃyuttanikāye idaṃ bhagavatā bhāsitaṃ nisaṃsayaṃ,*" #49). This is manifestly incorrect as this sutta cannot be traced to the extant edition of the *Saṃyutta-Nikāya* or to any other parts of the Pali canon. A possible explanation is to take the words "*idaṃ suttaṃ*" to refer not to the *Ākāravattārasutta* itself, but to the "*iti pi so bhagavā*" formula, the central focus of that sutta. This formula is found in the *Saṃyutta-Nikāya* (e.g. v, p. 343) which might indeed have served as the main source for the author of our sutta.[10] What then is the significance of the assuring words "*nisaṃsayaṃ*"? Surely, no one would have questioned the canonical source of so well known a formula as the "*iti pi so bhagavā*"?

A more convincing way of solving this mystery is to take the words "*idaṃ suttaṃ*" to refer not to the entire *Ākāravattārasutta,* but to a single verse in it, namely, verse No. 55: "*yo passati saddhammaṃ so maṃ passati paṇḍito, apassamāno saddhammaṃ maṃ passanto pi na passati.*" This is a versified rendering of the following words uttered by the Buddha to the dying monk Vakkali: "*yo kho, Vakkali, dhammaṃ passati so maṃ passati; yo maṃ passati so dhammaṃ passati. dhammaṃ hi, Vakkali, passanto maṃ passati; maṃ passanto dhammaṃ passati.*" Unlike the "*iti pi so bhagavā*" formula, these words are not of common occurrence. The *Itivuttaka* has a variation: (*dhammaṃ so bhikkhave na passati, dhammaṃ apassanto na maṃ passati*);[11] but the *Ākāravattārasutta* rendition in its entirety is attested only in the *Saṃyutta-Nikāya.*[12] The fact that this verse reads like a quotation, and that it appears at the very end of the work, lends support to the suggestion that the author of the

Ākāravattārasutta (or of its *Vaṇṇanā*, or the copyist) wanted to reassure the reader about the authenticity of these solemn but less known words of the canon.

In addition to its interest in fostering the salvific power of the "*iti pi so bhagavā*" formula, the *Ākāravattārasutta* shares the linguistic peculiarity of irregular geminate consonants with the fourteenth century apocryphal work mentioned above, namely, the *Lokaneyyappakaraṇa*, and hence can be assigned to the same period.

The following signs have been used:

[*] indicates folio No. of MS
(?) indicates doubtful reading or meaning.
<.> indicates irregular geminate consonant.
Additions in []
Emendations in ( )

(A sermon which expounds the manner of [averting rebirth in hells])

[#1] Obeisance. Thus have I heard. Once upon a time, the Blessed One was living in Rājagaha on Mount Gijjhakūṭa. Then the Venerable Sāriputta approached the Blessed One and, having greeted him, sat on one side.

Sitting there and watching the assembly, the following thought occurred to Sāriputta, "Alas, [those among] these beings who have destroyed their roots [of kusala] and who are not happy with the precepts will certainly suffer in the four states of loss and woe after death. There must exist those dhammas leading to Buddhahood and capable of preventing these beings from suffering in this manner. Surely, these alone (i.e. the ones now known) are not the only dhammas which lead to Buddhahood; let me search for others which are profound, which lead to awakening, which have been practised by the former great sages, and [preached] by the Blessed One, the Buddha, in the three Piṭakas.

[#2] Here there are beings of little wisdom who, on account of their foolishness, do not know the dhammas which lead to Buddhahood and may, therefore, commit all forms of evil actions, numbering [as many as] several thousands of crores. Some among them might kill other men, either a king, a minister, a chaplain, or a child. [Some may kill] a bull or a buffalo, or a horse. Some householders might commit acts such as killing their mothers and so forth and will thus be guilty of *pārājika* acts against the Teachings (i.e. will not be ordained in the saṃgha). While those who have renounced the world, having cut off their roots (i.e., having lost their faith) in the words of the Buddha, might commit *pārājika* acts (i.e. those that result in expulsion from the saṃgha). These [beings], having committed evil acts, at the disolution of the body, after their death, will be born in the Avīci hell." He then asked, "Oh Blessed One, is there any dhamma, profound and subtle, which is capable of preventing these beings from suffering [in these hells]?" Having spoken thus, Sāriputta uttered the following verses:

> [#3] How should a person live according to the Law; how does it become his refuge? A person who has committed a *pārājika* trangression is reborn in the Avīci Hell [where he suffers] for thirty thousand crores and ten thousand years. [1]
>
> A person who has committed a *saṃghādisesa* transgression is reborn in the Mahātāpa Hell ... thirty crores and four hundred thousand years. [2]
>
> A person who has committed a *thullaccaya* transgression is reborn in the Tāpana Hell ... one hundred crores and sixty thousand years. [3]
>
> A person who has committed a *pācittiya* transgression is reborn in the Mahāntara (Lokantara?) Hell ... fourteen crores and four hundred thousand years. [4]
>
> A person who has committed a *pāṭidesaniya* transgression is reborn in the Bherava Hell ... for one crore and sixty thousand years. [5]
>
> A person having committed a d*ukkaṭa* transgression is reborn in the Kāl(ḷ)asutta Hell, and experiences great suffering for ninety hundred thousand years. [6]
>
> A person having committed a *dubbhāsita* transgression is reborn in the Sanjīva Hell, and suffers for ninety thousand years. [7]
>
> How does a person abide by the Law? How is he released from the states of woe? How is he protected by the Law? [8]

[#4] Just as in the world there is a thing called happiness, which is opposed to suffering, similarly there must be that which is opposed to the act of *pārājika.* Just as fire is hot, and there is something cold which extinguishes it, similarly there must be that by which the fire, known [by the names] of the acts of *pārājika* and so forth, is extinguished. Just as there is the faultless dhamma, which is opposed to the sinful dhamma, similarly there must be that noble dhamma called Nibbāna, which annihilates all evils and births. He then uttered the [following] verses:

> [#5] Just as where there is suffering, there also is happiness which is meritorious; and just as where there is heat, there also is that which is cool [able to destroy it in the same manner]; what is that dhamma by which a person guilty of a *pārājika* transgression is protected? [9]
>
> Just as a person who has fallen in a pit full of excrement, having seen a full lake, would cleanse himself with that water and would be free from that dirt. [10]
>
> Just as a sick person gets himself cured when there is a physician and thus becomes happy and free from that disease. [11]
>
> Just as a person throws away a disgusting dead body tied around his neck and walks away, alone, happy and free. [12]
>
> Just as a person bitten by a poisonous black viper may be freed from death by the power of medicine and mantras. [13]
>
> Just as a person walking on low ground (*ūnacāri*?), having seen excrement, avoids it and walks away indifferent to it, not wanting it. [14]
>
> In the same manner, how is a person who has committed evil acts protected by the Law? [May the Blessed One] preach that dhamma which is free (i.e. which frees such a person) from the states of woe, [and establishes him] in the immortal state. [15]

[#6] Then the Fully Awakened One, possessed of unobstructed knowledge in all dhammas, in answering his question said, "Oh Sāriputta, there is indeed that subtle and profound dhamma (discourse), found among the eighty-four thousand aggregates of dhammas, preached (lit. not abandoned) by as many Buddhas as there are grains of sand on the banks of the river Ganges. It is the firm support for those who have cut their roots [of good] and for those who are given to evil acts." Having said this, [he then expounded on the career of the Bodhisatta] beginning with his resolution [to become a Buddha] made one hundred and four incalculable aeons previously, consisting of the practice of first, the perfection of giving; second, the perfection of keeping the precepts; third, the perfection of renunciation; fourth, the perfection of wisdom; fifth, the perfection effort; sixth, the perfection of forbearance; seventh, the perfection of truthfulness; eighth, the perfection of resolution; ninth, the perfection of friendliness; and tenth, the perfection of equanimity.

[#7] Oh, Sāriputta, if there are beings who have cut off their [good] roots and have committed evil, even they may be prevented from suffering [rebirth] in the eight great hells and the sixteen prominent hells by the power of this subtle and profound sermon called *Ākāravattārasutta.* [This is because I have preached it] after attaining Full Awakening [through the career of a Bodhisatta] which began with the resolution to become a Buddha, a hundred thousand great aeons and four incalculable aeons ago and was completed through the fulfillment of the thirty perfections, the performance of the five great sacrifices, the completion of the three kinds of proper conduct. Any being who, therefore, listens to this sutta, will not be reborn into these hells.

[#8] Oh, Sāriputta, whosoever, with his mind full of enthusiasm, masters this *Ākāravattārasutta*, or memorizes it, recites, worships or remembers it again and again, such a person will produce excellent merit and will accumulate karma that leads him to auspicious rebirths.

[#9] Oh, Sāriputta, should such a person aspire to the knowledge culminating in the perfection of an Arahā or of a Paccekabuddha, or to that of a Fully Awakened Being, [that wish of his] will be accomplished.

[#10] If such a person has accumulated past evil karma through acts of anger against his mother or father, even that is destroyed. He will not be reborn in evil states for as many as ninety hundred thousand aeons, what to speak of any other [miserable] abodes?

[#11] Oh, Sāriputta, what is this *Ākāravattārasutta* spoken by the Tathāgata? [It begins:]

These auspicious words of fame have risen concerning the Blessed One: The Blessed One is an Arahā, a Fully Awakened One, abounding in wisdom and goodness, happy, who knows all the worlds, unsurpassed as a guide to mortals willing to be led, a teacher of gods and men, a Blessed One, a Buddha. He, by himself, thoroughly knows and sees, as it were, face to face, this universe — including the worlds of the gods, the Brahmas, and the Māras, and the world with its recluses and Brahmans, its princes and peoples, — and having known it, he makes his knowledge known to others. That Blessed One — the possessor of right vision and right knowledge, the most righteous being, the most excellent being, the expounder of good, the bringer of good, the giver of immortality, the master of righteousness, the king of righteousness — proclaims the Dhamma, which is lovely in its origin, lovely in its progress, and lovely in its consummation. He expounds the Dhamma both in the spirit and in the letter, and he makes the higher life known in all its fullness and in all its purity. Meritorious indeed is the sight of the Arahās of that kind.

[#12] The Blessed One is the Arahā. The Blessed One is the Fully Awakened One ... (repeat the words "the Blessed One is") abounding in wisdom and goodness, ...happy... who knows all the worlds .. the unsurpassed ... guide to mortals willing to be led ... the teacher of gods and men, the Buddha ... the Blessed One ... The first section describing the virtues of the Lord as an Arahā and so forth.

[#13] The Blessed One is endowed with the perfection of resolve [to become a Buddha]... the perfection of noble disposition ... the perfection of determination ...the perfection of great compassion ... the perfection of knowledge ... the perfection of means ... the perfection of application ... the perfection of passing away ... the perfection of conception ... the perfection of staying in the womb [unaffected by its impurities]. The second section (beginning with) resolve.

[#14] The Blessed One is endowed with the perfection of emerging from the womb... the perfection of freedom from the dirt of the womb... the perfection of excellent birth ... the perfection of movement (or rebirth)... the perfection of perfect form ... the perfection of golden colour ...the perfection of glory ... the perfection of height ... the perfection of girth ... the perfection of growth. The third section [beginning with] emerging from the womb.

[#15] The Blessed One is endowed with the perfection of Supreme Awakening ... the perfection of the aggregates of morality ... the perfection of the aggregates of meditation ... the perfection of the aggregates of wisdom ... the perfection of the aggregates of freedom ... the perfection of the aggregates of freedom, knowledge, and insight ... the perfection of the thirty-two auspicious marks of a great man ... the perfection of good fortune. The fourth section [beginning with] Supreme Awakening.

[#16] The Blessed One is endowed with the perfection of great wisdom ... the perfection of wide wisdom ... the perfection of quick wisdom ... the perfection of sharp wisdom ... the perfection of wisdom that penetrates (the four Noble Truths) ... the perfection of the eye of wisdom ... the perfection of the five kinds of knowledge ... the perfection of the eighteen dhammas that lead to Buddhahood. The fifth section [beginning with] great wisdom.

[#17] The Blessed One is endowed with the perfection of charity ... the perfection of conduct ... the perfection of renunciation ... the perfection of wisdom ... the perfection of exertion ... the perfection of forbearance ... the perfection of truthfulness ... the perfection of determination ... the perfection of friendliness ... the perfection of equanimity. The sixth section [beginning with] the perfection.

[#18] The Blessed One is endowed with the ten perfections ... the perfection of ten minor perfections ... the perfection of ten supreme perfections ... the perfection of the full thirty perfections ... the perfection of giving of such and such objects ... the perfection of superknowledge ... the perfection of mindfulness ... the perfection of meditation ... the perfection of freedom (from passions)... the perfection of freedom, knowledge, and vision. The seventh section [beginning with] ten perfections.

[#19] The Blessed One is endowed with the perfection of the psychic power of discrimination [of dhammas]... the perfection of the psychic power of mental projection ...the perfection of the psychic powers of various kinds ... the perfection of the psychic power of the "divine ear" ... the perfection of the psychic power of knowing the minds of others ... the perfection of the psychic power of recalling one's past births ... the perfection of the psychic power of the "divine eye" ... the perfection of fifteen kinds of conducts ... the perfection of the dhammas that lead to those conducts(?) ... the perfection of gradually ascending the stages of meditation. The eighth section [beginning with] the psychic powers.

[#20] The Blessed One is endowed with the perfection of comprehension ... the perfection of realization ... the perfection of experiencing ... the perfection of realization and experiencing of the destruction (of passions through) comprehension ... the perfection of the dhammas that constitute the Four Noble Truths ... the perfection of knowledge consisting of the analysis of the meanings ... the perfection of knowledge consisting of the analysis [leading to] definitions ... the perfection of knowledge consisting of the analysis of the causal relations ... the perfection of knowledge consisting of the analysis [leading to] definitions ... the perfection of knowledge consisting of the analysis [leading to] illumination. The ninth section [beginning with] comprehension.

[#21] The Blessed One is endowed with the perfection of the thirty-seven factors contributing to Awakening ... the perfection of the four kinds of mindfulness ... the perfection of the four kinds of right exertion ... the perfection of the four kinds of psychic powers ... the perfection of the five kinds of faculties ... the perfection of the five kinds of powers ... the perfection of the seven factors of wisdom ... the perfection of the dhammas constituting the Noble Eightfold Path ... the perfection of emancipation from all hindrances. The tenth section [beginning with] the factors contributing to Awakening.

[#22] The Blessed One is endowed with the perfection of the knowledge of the ten powers ... the perfection of understanding the possible as possible and impossible as impossible ... the perfection of the knowledge of the result of actions ... the perfection of the knowledge of the path leading to the welfare of all beings ... the perfection of the knowledge of the world with many different elements ... the perfection of the knowledge of the different inclinations of beings ... the perfection of the knowledge of the lower and higher faculties in beings ... the perfection of the knowledge of the extinction of all passions. The eleventh section [beginning with] the ten powers.

[#23] The Blessed One is endowed with the perfection of having the [physical] strength of one hundred crores of untamed (? pakati) elephants. ... the perfection of having the strength of ten thousand crores of men ... the perfection of the knowledge of five eyes (viz., the physical eye, the deva-eye, the wisdom-eye, the Buddha-eye, the eye of all-around knowledge)... the perfection of four self-confidences ... the perfection of the knowledge of the twin miracles ... the perfection of having virtues [appropriate to] the initial [part of the path] ... the perfection of having virtues [appropriate to] the middle [part of the path] ... the perfection of having virtues [appropriate to] the concluding [part of the path]... the perfection of the twenty-four thousand crores of attainments of trances (*samāpatti*). The twelfth section [beginning with] physical strength.

[#24] The Blessed One is endowed with the perfection of the strength of steadfastness ... the perfection of the knowledge which leads to the strength of steadfastness ... the perfection of incomparable [virtues?] ... the perfection of the incomparable knowledge ... the perfection of striving ... the perfection of the knowledge [leading to] the perfection of striving. The thirteenth section [beginning with] the strength of steadfastness.

[#25] The Blessed One is endowed with the perfection of conduct ... the perfection of the knowledge of conduct ... the perfection of the knowledge of conduct for the benefit of the world ... the perfection of the conduct *ñātattha* (for the benefit of kinsmen?) ... the perfection of knowledge [leading to] comprehension ... the perfection of the conduct [leading to the status] of a Buddha ... the perfection of the knowledge of the conduct [leading to the status] of a Buddha ... the perfection of the threefold conduct ... the perfection of the threefold conduct [leading to the ten] minor perfections ... the perfection of the threefold conduct [leading to the ten] supreme perfections. The fourteenth section [beginning with] conduct.

[#26] The Blessed One is endowed with the perfection of seeing the characteristic of impermanence in the five aggregates clinging to existence ... the perfection of seeing the characteristic of suffering in the five aggregates clinging to existence ... the perfection of seeing the characteristic of non-self in the five aggregates of clinging to existence ... the perfection of seeing the characteristic of impermanence in the twelve spheres of perception ... the perfection of seeing the characteristic of suffering in the twelve spheres of perception ... the perfection of seeing the characteristic of non-self in the twelve spheres of perception ... the perfection of seeing the characteristic of impermanence in the eighteen elements ... the perfection of seeing the characteristic of suffering in the eighteen elements ... the perfection of seeing the characteristic of non-self in the eighteen elements ... the perfection of seeing the characteristic of change in those very dharmas. The fifteenth section [beginning with] the characteristics.

[#27] The Blessed One is endowed with the perfection of [knowing] the place where one has gone ... the perfection of the knowledge of the place where one has gone (place of rebirth?) ... perfection of beings (?satta?) ... the perfection of knowledge of the beings [who can be saved?]... the perfection of mastery ... the perfection of the knowledge of mastery ... the perfection of precepts ... the perfection of the knowledge of precepts ... the perfection of restraints ... the perfection of the knowledge of restraints. The sixteenth section [beginning with] the place where one has gone.

[#28] The Blessed One is endowed with the perfection of the lineage of the Buddhas ... the perfection of the knowledge of the lineage of the Buddhas ... the perfection of [performing] the twin miracles ... the perfection of the knowledge leading to the [performing] of the twin miracles ... the perfection of the meditation which cultivates friendliness ... the perfection of the meditation which cultivates compassion ... the perfection of the meditation which cultivates sympathy for others' welfare ... the perfection of meditation which cultivates equanimity ... the perfection of [knowledge] free from obstruction ... the perfection of boundless knowledge ... the perfection of the knowledge of omniscience ... the perfection of the knowledge [leading to] omniscience ... the perfection of the twenty-four thousand crores of the adamantine [meditations]... the perfection of the knowledge of the twenty-four thousand crores of the adamantine [meditations]. End of the seventeenth section [beginning with] lineage.

[#29] Oh Sāriputta, since the night when the Tathāgata attained Supreme Awakening, and the night when he became the refuge, the cave, and the support of the world consisting of gods, Māras, Brahmas, and human beings with the recluses and Brahmans, I recall this *Ākāravattārasutta* to be capable of preventing [rebirth in hells]. This is because, from the time he was wandering in saṃsāra practising the path that leads to the destruction of all suffering, until he enters the Nibbāna which leaves no substratum of life behind, all the physical, vocal, and mental activities of the Tathāgata are preceded by knowledge, are conducted by knowledge. The physical, vocal and mental activities of the Tathāgata, as well as his knowledge and vision, are not obstructed by either the past, present or future [kammas]. [By virtue of which this sutta is capable of removing all evils.]

[#30] Oh Sāriputta, while this sutta is being recited, no opportunity will be available for indulging in evil actions. A person reciting it even once will obtain protection for four months, barring, of course, the fruition of one's past kamma. Whosoever with mindful enthusiasm listens to this sutta or masters it or reads it or recites it or writes it or gets it written or memorizes it or treats it with respect or honours it or holds it in esteem or repeatedly remembers it, whatever he wishes, all that will be accomplished.

[#31] Therefore, this most excellent sutta, not abandoned by the twenty-eight Buddhas beginning with Dīpaṅkara or by me, should be studied according to one's ability and strength. One who is unable to learn it should give ear(?) to it, one who is unable to do it should listen to it ... should at least go to a place where it is recited again and again and should hear it, respectfully folding his hands together. Unable to do even that, he should go to a place where it is preached and listen to it with faith in his heart. Listening [to the sutta] while meditating with the thought "the Blessed One is endowed with such great qualities," his mind is filled with happiness born of his affection for the Buddha [the object of his meditation], and in this way, he will turn back all the evil kamma [he has accumulated which is capable of] producing rebirth in the four abodes of woe. Whatever he wishes, all that will be accomplished.

[#32] If he would remember this *Ākāra[vattāra]sutta* repeatedly, such a person, while he will be reborn, will not gain rebirth among the animals or ghosts or in the hells, namely, Sañjīva, Kāl(ḷ)asutta, Saṃghāta, Rorava, Mahārorava, Tāpana, Mahātāpana, and Avīci.

[#33] Whatever fear, whether from a snake, a dog, a jackal, an ox, a buffalo, a lion, a tiger, a rhino, a panther; or from an elephant, a horse, a king, a thief, fire, or water; or fear of [being beaten by] a stick, fear from one who is mad, fear arising from a yakkha, a kumbhaṇḍa (a spirit), a gandhabba (a demigod), a guardian spirit; or fear arising from Māra, or a sorcerer, or from the ruler of all the worlds, as well as fear of the eye-disease and so forth; or fears arising from hunger and thirst, all these thirty fears will be destroyed.

[#34] Oh Sāriputta, whosoever intentionally takes the life of another person, from the moment he hears this sutta, such a person will not be reborn in states of woe for ninety hundred thousand aeons. His entire house is watched by (divine) guardians, and the six gods of the Kāmāvacara world protect him. Such is the extent, O Sāriputta, of the great magical power, majesty, glory, potency, and merit of this sutta. Having spoken thus, and reaching the summit of his discourse, [the Blessed One] uttered the following verses:

[#35] The Awakened and the Omniscient One, having put together the Sutta, Vinaya, and Abhidhamma Piṭakas into one, has revealed this sutta called *Ākāravattāra* of great magical power and potency, consisting of seventeen sections (vaggas). [16-17]

[#36] I have revealed in this *Ākāravattārasutta* all the various virtues of the Buddha [scattered] in the excellent scriptures (gantha). It should be written down by the hands of a wise person with faith. [18]

I have compiled these collections of the virtues of the Buddha, like excellent flowers, in this *Ākāravattārasutta*. A person desiring his welfare should write this down with faith. [19]

[End of the Sutta and beginning of the Vaṇṇanā ?]

[#37] Attachment, aversion, and illusion do not assault one's mind; one becomes full of faith and respect for the Tathāgata [by the power of this sutta]. His faith and other virtues increase greatly, and he is filled with joy. [20]

He becomes able to bear all fears and miseries, his body strengthened [by remembering] the virtues of the Buddha, [thinking of him as] the foremost, the supreme, the unsurpassed, worthy of worship, a shrine manifest (lit. comparable to a cetiya). [21]

He obtains the state of living together with the Tathāgata. Should a transgression take place, through the happy [meditation on the] face of the Buddha, he is firmly established in the [twin virtues] of shame and scruples. [22]

He who listens to the teaching of the Jina, fearing censure and so forth, stays away from evil actions, as the sky from earth. [23]

He who listens to the teaching of the Jina, fearing censure and so forth, departs from evil actions like the waning moon in the dark fortnight. [24]

He who listens to the teaching of the Jina with contented mind, having destroyed passions, free from influxes, he attains Nibbāna. [25]

A person who holds the Dhamma, the teacher, and the preceptor in great esteem, who is endowed with faith and wisdom, and who is free from wickedness and crookedness, he possesses the Good Law and faces the immortal (i.e. Nibbāna). [26]

[#38] By the majesty of the *Ākāravattārasutta*, beings attain happiness. They become free from diseases and from obstructions. [27]

By the majesty of the *Ākāravattārasutta*, both gods and men look down upon him daily (din<n>e?) with friendliness. [28]

By the majesty of the *Ākāravattārasutta*, various obstructions, both external and internal, are completely destroyed. [29]

By the majesty of the *Ākāravattārasutta*, obstructions arising from kings, thieves, or fire, as well as from [rebirth in] evil abodes, are entirely destroyed. [30]

By the majesty of the *Ākāravattārasutta*, obstructions arising from fire, punishment from the king, fear of nonhuman beings (ghosts, etc.), fear from lions and tigers, and fear from untimely death, are all entirely destroyed. [31]

Elephants, horses, bulls, crocodiles, fish, and tortoises; and beings living in rivers, in oceans, and on land, will never hurt him. [32]

[#39] Such a person, while he moves around in saṃsāra, is endowed with an intelligent mind, a long life, and freedom from disease. He [leads a life] free from fear and passions. [33]

He will, in the future, attain Nibbāna, described by all the Buddhas as the home of tranquillity, the inconquerable, incomparable, and peaceful. [34]

He cleanses [his supernatural power of the knowledge] of the previous births and purifies his "divine eye." He is diligent, possesses a keen intelligence, and becomes a good companion. [35]

[#40] Just as the moon, shining coolly with its rays like [that of a] firefly, brings peace but is overpowered the moment the thousand-rayed (sun) rises, in the same manner is the great majesty of the Buddha, the Tathāgata [36-37]

A person who preserves this profound and perfect dhamma and sutta, his glory will increase like the waxing moon. [38]

[#41] A person who listens to this sutta, [even if] homeless, eats plenty of food, and his enemies do not prevail. [39]

A person who listens to this sutta becomes endowed with a treasure house and so forth, and is decked out in various [ornaments] and becomes possessed of great power and strength. [40]

One who listens to this sutta is reborn with a golden-coloured body, pure sense organs, and is possessed of great speed. [41]

He is endowed with [the supernatural power of divine] eyes and is able to see in all directions. For thirty-six aeons [he reigns as] King of the Gods, and for thirty-six [aeons reigns as] a Universal Monarch. [42]

He possesses golden palaces and is adorned with various jewels. He is endowed with seats made of jewels, ... (?) well established. [43]

A person desirous of the three-fold happiness comes to possess the three-fold treasures. [He becomes] a wise, intelligent, and resolute person by listening to this sutta. [44]

For one who listens, this sutta gives pleasure in the human realm, as well as great happiness in heaven, and then [finally] the bliss of Nibbāna. [45]

Beings who listen to this sutta are not reborn in the hells, in the realm of the ghosts, as animal, or as titans. For ninety thousand aeons, they do not experience great suffering, [because they are not reborn] in the hellish realms of Lohakumbhi, Vetaraṇī, and Avīci. [46]

[#42] Beings who listen to this sutta are not born in the wombs of untouchables (caṇḍāla), nor in those of slaves; nor in [families] who hold wrong views. They are not reborn in the Lokanta[ra] Hells. [47] Beings who listen to this sutta are also not reborn as a female, nor one with organs of both sexes, nor one who is a eunuch, nor as a hermaphrodite, or an abhabbaka (impotent?). [48]

[Such a person] is reborn fully endowed with all major and minor limbs, and with good character, and virtues. [They] call him virtuous, full of faith and charity. [49] He is reborn during the time when the Buddha appears [and has faith] in his teachings. Endowed with great beauty and long life, he lives in happiness and health. [50]

[#43] Let no evils touch him, and may all disease disappear. Possessed with great strength, wisdom, luster, and success [such a person is reborn as] King of Gods among gods, and the Cakravartin King among humans. [51]

Endowed with sharp faculties, mindful, glorious and possessed with magic powers, he attains the four kinds of discriminating knowledges, and becomes a sāvaka (an arahā or a chief disciple) during the time when the next Buddha appears. Such a person, not deluded during the time of death, goes up, straight towards the abode of happiness (i.e. heaven). [52]

Whatever he wishes or prays for [the attainment of the status of] the Buddhas, the Paccekabuddhas or of the Disciples endowed with great magical powers, all that is accomplished for him. [53]

[#44] Whosoever repeatedly remembers this *Ākāravattārasutta* obtains all that is the fruit of [listening to] the Sutta, Vinaya and Abhidhamma [Piṭakas]. [54]

[#45] [For it has been said:]

"One who sees the Good Law, a wise man, he sees me. But one who does not see the Good Law, even if he sees me, does not see." [55]

[#46] At the end of this discourse, eighty thousand crores of beings gained insight into the Law.

[#47] This the Lord said. The Venerable Sāriputta rejoiced in the sermon of the Blessed One.

[#48] The *Ākārasuttavaṇṇanā* (Commentary on the *Ākāravattārasutta*) is completed.

[#49] This sutta, without a doubt, was preached by the Lord in the *Saṃyutta-Nikāya.*

[#50] By the merit of writing this sutta, may I, in the future, until I attain Nibbāna, wherever I am born, be endowed with greater luster, wisdom, success, wealth, and strength. May this result in [the attainment of] Nibbāna.

NOTES

1. *Paññāsa-Jātaka or Zimme Paṇṇāsa* (in the Burmese Recension), 2 volumes, ed. P.S. Jaini, Pali Text Society, London, 1981-83. Translated (by I.B. Horner and P.S. Jaini) as *Apocryphal Birth Stories,* 2 volumes, Pali Text Society, London, 1985-86. For a study of the indigenous Chinese Buddhist scriptures, see *Chinese Buddhist Apocrypha,* ed. Robert E. Buswell, Jr., University of Hawaii Press, 1990.
2. *The Jātaka* (*Jātakatthavaṇṇanā*), 6 volumes, ed. V. Fausböll, Pali Text Society (2nd ed.), London, 1964.
3. A possible exception would be the Buddhāpadāna, the first book of the *Apadāna* (Part I, ed. Mary F. Lilley, Pali Text Society, London, 1925, pp. 1-6) of the Khuddaka-Nikāya. According to Professor Bechert, this section was composed in Sri Lanka by Mahāyānasthaviras and was included in the Pali canon in the first century or in the beginning of the 2nd century A.D. See Heinz Bechert, "Mahāyāna Literature in Sri Lanka: The Early Phase," in *Prajñāpāramitā and Related Systems: Studies in Honour of Edward Conze.* ed. Lancaster and Gomez, Berkeley Buddhist Series, I, 1977.
4. Oskar v. Hinüber, "The Pāli Manuscripts Kept at the Siam Society, Bangkok: A Short Catalogue," *Journal of the Siam Society,* volume 75, pp. 9-74, 1987.
5. Tr.: Mr. Kon Jambhu and Mrs. Keev, having faith, created (i.e. got made) this manuscript of the *Ākāravattasūtra* in the Buddha's Teaching. It exists in the *Saṃyutta-Nikaya.*
6. von Hinüber, op. cit., p.44.
7. *Cūlavaṃsa: Being the more recent part of the Mahāvaṃsa,* Part I., tr. Wilhelm Geiger (and from German into English by C. Mabel Rickmers), Pali Text Society, London,1929.
8. *Lokaneyyappakaraṇaṃ,* ed. P.S. Jaini, Pali Text Society, London, 1986.
9. Ibid., verses 278-84. The following verse, beginning with the second syllable "ti" can be cited as a good example:
   tikāro eva tibhavahitakaro tikam oghapāraṃ,
   tisso vijjānubatto tibhavabhayaharo tikkhañāṇāsiyutto;
   tiṭṭhanto aggamaggaṃ paramasukhadado tiṇṇamohandhakāro,
   tiṇṇaṃ lokānam aggo tibhavasukhadado tiṇṇalokaṃ namāmi. [279]
10. It should be noted, however, that the formula found in our text is not identical with any of its versions attested in the canon. Two parts of this sutta, namely, "*so bhagavā cakkhubhūto ...dhammarājā*", and the last line, "*sādhu kho pana ... dassanaṃ hoti*" are, for example, missing in the *Aṅguttara-Nikāya* (ed.